REAL ESTATE PRINCIPLES
IN CALIFORNIA

**CALIFORNIA REAL ESTATE BOOKS
FROM PRENTICE-HALL**

California Real Estate License Preparation Text, 7th edition
William H. Pivar
1987

Real Estate Principles in California, 5th edition
Homer C. Davey, Ted H. Gordon, and H. Glenn Mercer
1987

The Practice of Real Estate in California
Homer C. Davey and Donald C. Driscoll
1981

Real Estate Law in California, 7th edition
Arthur G. Bowman and W. Denny Milligan
1986

California Real Estate Law: Text and Cases, 2nd edition
Theodore H. Gordon
1985

California Real Estate Finance, 2nd edition
B.E. Tsagris and John P. Wiedemer
1987

California Real Estate Finance, 4th edition
J.W. Pugh and William H. Hippaka
1984

California Real Estate Appraisal: Residential Properties, 3rd edition
George H. Miller, H. Glenn Mercer, and Kenneth W. Gilbeau
1987

REAL ESTATE PRINCIPLES IN CALIFORNIA

FIFTH EDITION

Homer C. Davey

Professor Emeritus, Business Administration and Real Estate
Foothill College

Ted H. Gordon

Attorney at Law
Member, California and Marin Bar Association
Instructor, Golden Gate University, San Francisco

H. Glenn Mercer

Professor Emeritus, Business Administration
City College of San Francisco

Prentice-Hall, Inc., Englewood Cliffs, New Jersey 07632

Library of Congress Cataloging-in-Publication Data

DAVEY, HOMER C.
    Real estate principles in California.

    (Prentice-Hall series in real estate)
    Includes index.
      1. Real property—California. 2. Real estate
business—Law and legislation—California.
I. Gordon, Theodore H. II. Mercer, H. Glenn.
III. Title. IV. Series.
KFC140.D37 1987   346.79404'37   86-25264
ISBN 0-13-765702-1   347.9406437

Forms on pages 61, 63, 64–65, 66–67, 70, 71, 73–74, 75, 76, 80, 81, 119, 120, 131–32, 146, 148, 152, 154, 155, 159, 200, 250, 256–57, 259–60 reprinted by permission, CALIFORNIA ASSOCIATION OF REALTORS®. Endorsement not implied.

Forms on pages 20, 29, 31, 103–04, 106, 111, 112, 162, 163, 189–93 reprinted by permission courtesy of Ticor Title Insurance Company. Ticor Title Insurance makes no representations regarding the legal effect of the forms in any particular transaction.

Forms on pages 182, 183 courtesy of Western Title Insurance Company. Endorsement not implied.

Cover design: Ben Santora
Manufacturing buyer: Carol Bystrom/Margaret Rizzi

© 1987, 1981, 1976, 1972, 1967 by Prentice-Hall, Inc.
A division of Simon & Schuster
Englewood Cliffs, New Jersey 07632

Printed in the United States of America

10 9 8 7 6 5 4 3 2 1

ISBN 0-13-765702-1 01

PRENTICE-HALL INTERNATIONAL (UK) LIMITED, *London*
PRENTICE-HALL OF AUSTRALIA PTY. LIMITED, *Sydney*
PRENTICE-HALL CANADA INC., *Toronto*
PRENTICE-HALL HISPANOAMERICANA, S.A., *Mexico*
PRENTICE-HALL OF INDIA PRIVATE LIMITED, *New Delhi*
PRENTICE-HALL OF JAPAN, INC., *Tokyo*
PRENTICE-HALL OF SOUTHEAST ASIA PTE. LTD., *Singapore*
EDITORA PRENTICE-HALL DO BRASIL, LTDA., *Rio de Janeiro*

CONTENTS

PREFACE   ix

1

INTRODUCTION TO REAL ESTATE PRINCIPLES   1

Career Opportunities in Real Estate   1
History of California Land   3

2

THE NATURE OF REAL ESTATE   5

Real Estate or Real Property   5
Personal Property   6
Methods of Land Description   7
Chapter Questions   11
Multiple-Choice Questions   11

3

OWNERSHIP OF REAL PROPERTY   13

Freehold Estates   13
Less-than-Freehold Estates   14
Absolute and Conditional Estates   14
Methods of Acquiring Real Property   15
Real Property Classified as to Title   18
Forms of Business Entity   21
Recording and Constructive Notice   23
Chapter Questions   24
Multiple-Choice Questions   24

4

LIENS AND ENCUMBRANCES   25

Liens   25
Encumbrances   36
Restrictions   37
Encroachments   38
Homesteads   40
Chapter Questions   43
Multiple-Choice Questions   43

5

THE LAW OF CONTRACTS   44

Valid, Unenforceable, Void, and Voidable Contracts   44
Classification of Contracts   44
Parties Capable of Contracting   45
Mutual Assent or Agreement of the Parties   45
Termination of Offer   47
Genuine Assent   48
A Lawful Object   50
Legally Sufficient Consideration   50
Parol Evidence Rule   51
Conflict between Parts of a Contract   51
Assignment of Contracts   51
Modifying Contracts   52
Performance of Contracts   52
Discharge of Contractual Duties   53
Breach of Contract   54
Chapter Questions   56
Multiple-Choice Questions   57

6

CONTRACTS OF REAL PROPERTY   58

Listing Agreements 59
Expanded Analysis of Exclusive Authorization and Right-to-Sell Listing—California Association of Realtors Standard Form 60
Special Auxiliary Forms Used with Listing Agreements 62
Expanded Analysis of the Real Estate Purchase Contract and Receipt for Deposit 68
Option Agreement 79
Exchange Agreement 83
Broker Responsibilities in Contracts 83
Buying and Selling Your Home 83
Chapter Questions 86
Multiple-Choice Questions 86

7

AGENCIES   88

Definition of Terms 88
Types of Agents 88
Brokers and Salespeople 89
Creation of the Agency Relationship 89
Agency Agreements 89
Agent's Scope of Authority 91
Delegation of Power by an Agent 91
Whose Agent Is the Broker? 92
Duties of the Principal and the Agent 92
Agent's Responsibility to Third Persons 93
Duties of Third Persons 93
Termination of Agency Relationship 93
Broker's Commission 94
Licensing Real Estate Brokers and Salespeople 94
Chapter Questions 94
Multiple-Choice Questions 94

8

FINANCING REAL ESTATE   96

Types of Instruments 96
Deeds of Trust and Mortgages 102
Special Clauses and Rights 105
Alternative Mortgage Instruments 109
Remedies of the Lender in Case of Default 110
Junior Deeds of Trust 114
Agreements of Sale 115
Purchase-Money Trust Deeds 115
Interest 115
Truth in Lending 117
Financing Personal Property 121
Real Estate Settlement Procedures Act 121

Chapter Questions 124
Multiple-Choice Questions 124

9

SOURCES OF REAL ESTATE LOANS   125

Lenders' Procedures and Policies in Loaning 125
Primary Money Market 126
Federal and State Government Participation in Financing 133
Secondary Money Market 140
Creative Financing 141
Chapter Questions 142
Multiple-Choice Questions 142

10

THE LANDLORD-TENANT RELATIONSHIP   143

Types of Leasehold Estates 144
Essential Elements of Leases 144
Recording the Lease 151
Remedies of the Landlord 151
Termination of the Lease Agreement 156
Preventive Law and Precautions for the Landlord at Time of Renting 157
Special Commercial Leases 157
Chapter Questions 160
Multiple-Choice Questions 160

11

DEEDS   161

The Development of Land Transfer 161
The General Nature of Deeds 161
Types of Deeds 165
Acknowledgment and Notary 165
Recording 166
Documentary Stamp Tax 167
Chapter Questions 167
Multiple-Choice Questions 167

12

REAL ESTATE MATHEMATICS   168

Equations 168
Fractions 168
Decimals and Percentages 170
Percentage Problems 170
Calculating Interest 172
Amortization of Loans 173

Typical License Examination Problems   173
Chapter Questions   177
Multiple-Choice Questions   177

13

ESCROW PROCEDURES AND TITLE INSURANCE   180

Escrow Procedures   180
Essential Requisites for a Valid Escrow   181
Escrow Agent   181
Escrow Instructions   181
Termination of Escrow   184
Proration of Charges   185
Title Insurance   187
Title Search   188
Chapter Questions   195
Multiple-Choice Questions   195

14

REAL ESTATE APPRAISAL AND PROPERTY OWNERSHIP   196

Definition of Appraisal   196
Property Value Definitions   196
Essential Elements of Value   197
Forces Influencing Values   197
Factors That Influence Value   197
Application of Values   198
Methods of Appraisal   198
The Appraisal Process   202
Depreciation   204
Depreciation and Income Tax   205
Commercial Property   206
Residential Property   207
Mobile Home   207
Chapter Questions   216
Multiple-Choice Questions   216

15

ZONING, ENVIRONMENTAL REPORTS, AND RESTRICTIONS   217

Authority of County and City Governments to Zone   218
Planning Policies   218
Developing the Master Plan   218
Planning Commission   218
Zoning   218
Relief from Zoning   219
Building Codes and Set-Back Lines   219
Conflict between Zoning and Restrictions   220
Environmental Impact Reports   220

Community Redevelopment Agencies (CRA's)   220
Coastal Control   221
Chapter Questions   221

16

SUBDIVISIONS   222

Subdivision Map Act   222
The Subdivided Lands Act   223
Out-of-State Subdivisions   227
Types of Subdivisions   227
Environmental Impact Reports   228
The Process of Land Development   228
Interstate Land Sales Full Disclosure Act   229
Chapter Questions   233
Multiple-Choice Questions   233

17

LICENSING AND STATE LAWS REGULATING REAL ESTATE BUSINESS   234

Real Estate Advisory Commission   234
The Real Estate Commissioner and the Department of Real Estate   234
Real Estate Licensing—Requirements and Fees   235
Penalties for Being Unlicensed   236
Prerequisites for Licensing   236
Cancellation and Transfer of Salesperson's License   240
Display of License and Business Title   240
Disciplinary Action   240
Real Property Securities Dealer   241
Real Estate Examinations   244
Real Estate Syndications and Investment Trusts   244
Real Estate Education and Research   245
Trust Fund Account   246
Chapter Questions   251
Multiple-Choice Questions   251

18

REAL ESTATE OFFICE ADMINISTRATION AND PRACTICE   252

Organization and Forms of Ownership   252
Problems of Organizing and Opening the Real Estate Office   253
Office Procedures and Relationships   258
Activities of the Real Estate Broker and Salesperson   258
Financing Real Estate Transactions   264
Real Estate Organizations   264
Fair Housing Laws—State and Federal   265

Chapter Questions   266
Multiple-Choice Questions   266

19

PROPERTY INSURANCE   267

Insurance Contract Defined   267
Insurable Interest   267
Types of Insurance Contracts   268
Proof of Loss and Insurer's Liability   270
Assignment   270
Cancellation   270
Coinsurance   270
Liability Insurance   271
Chapter Questions   273

A

ANSWERS TO
CHAPTER-END QUESTIONS   274

Chapter 2   274
Chapter 3   274
Chapter 4   275
Chapter 5   276
Chapter 6   277

Chapter 7   277
Chapter 8   278
Chapter 9   279
Chapter 10   280
Chapter 11   281
Chapter 12   282
Chapter 13   283
Chapter 14   284
Chapter 15   285
Chapter 16   285
Chapter 17   286
Chapter 18   289
Chapter 19   290

B

SAMPLE REAL ESTATE SALESPERSON'S
EXAMINATION   292

Directions   292

C

GLOSSARY   307

INDEX   320

PREFACE

The fifth edition of *Real Estate Principles in California* has been thoroughly revised and updated, while still maintaining the excellent coverage and format that has made this book so popular.

This book covers all the subjects discussed in the Department of Real Estate Principles Instructor's Guide.

The need for updating is obvious. Each year hundreds of new laws and case decisions arise, many of which directly affect real estate. For example, since the last edition, the *Garn–St. Germain Act* controls the rights of lenders to enforce due-on-sale clauses in deeds of trust. The usury limits now depend on the type of lender involved and the purpose for the loan. New mortgage instruments (such as variable rate mortgages, graduated payment mortgages, and reverse annuity mortgages) are popular and require understanding of the concept of reverse amortization. The *Easton* case establishes new liability and requirements for brokers to evaluate and inform others about the condition of property they list. And the Department of Real Estate has enacted new education requirements for licenses. These and many other new laws are covered in this text.

The chapters have been thoroughly revised. Some areas have been expanded, while other sections have been reduced to better meet the needs of students and instructors. The authors enthusiastically welcome suggestions from all users of this book.

The book retains the valuable appendices, including the section of examination questions similar to those used on the real estate salesperson's and broker's examinations. Standardized test questions are available to college professors using this book.

The book's primary use in the college classroom is for

1. The person who wants a working knowledge of real estate that will enable him or her to assume a more effective role as a consumer or an investor.

2. The person who has chosen real estate as a vocation and wishes to pass the real estate salesperson's examination.

3. The licensed real estate salesperson who wishes to review for and pass the real estate broker's examination.

4. The banks, savings and loan associations, mortgage firms, escrow officers, title insurance companies, or property management firms who wish a reference guide to the general practice of real estate.

The authors would like to thank John E. Hempel, George L. Chamberlin, and Cecila Hopkins for their helpful comments and suggestions.

Homer C. Davey
Ted H. Gordon
H. Glenn Mercer

INTRODUCTION TO REAL ESTATE PRINCIPLES

Buying or selling a home is usually the largest single financial transaction in a person's lifetime. For the buyer it involves a large outlay of cash and a very heavy mortgage debt over a number of years. For the seller it involves the sale of the asset in which he or she has invested so much care and money. In addition, the sale or purchase of a home usually involves a real estate broker and sometimes an attorney-at-law. Therefore, the buyer and the seller ought to be familiar with what to expect in a real estate transaction.

At least one-fifth of a person's lifetime earnings will be invested in real estate, even though that person may rent and never own property. Therefore, consumers should know their rights, duties, and obligations in real estate transactions or in landlord-tenant relationships.

Two-thirds of the wealth of this great nation is invested in real estate. Real property represents a major portion of the average individual's personal estate, yet little weight is placed on the study of real estate in most of our educational institutions.

California is at least a decade ahead of other states, not only in its comprehensive real estate law, but in real estate education as well. It was the first state to require professional academic courses for licensing real estate brokers, and approximately ninety community colleges in the state now offer an Associate of Arts degree with a major in real estate. In addition, the community colleges also offer a California Real Estate Certificate requiring twenty-four semester units in real estate.

This book will cover the principles of real estate, with special emphasis on California. It will

1. Survey the entire field of real estate, giving a well-rounded overview of the subject.
2. Serve as an introductory course for those who want to study real estate further.
3. Introduce the field of real estate investments.
4. Show the best way to buy and sell a home. (Checklists are found in Chapter 6.)
5. Explain the rights of landlords and tenants.
6. Update the real estate practitioner in the current law of real estate.
7. Serve as a ready reference guide for people in the business.
8. Teach students all they need to know to pass the California Real Estate Salesperson's Examination. (A sample examination appears in Appendix B.)

CAREER OPPORTUNITIES IN REAL ESTATE

A career in real estate has many rewards for the right people. Real estate salespeople or brokers work with people as well as with property ownership and transfer. They have a great deal of freedom; they schedule their own appointments and, therefore, must be able to organize their time for maximum benefit of both their clients and themselves.

Real estate salespeople or brokers handle a product that everyone needs. They can make a good living in real estate because everyone is a potential customer, but they must be willing to learn and work hard. Most salespeople are not paid a fixed salary but work on a commission based on the actual sale and transfer of property. Talent and hard work can result in a higher income than is possible on a fixed salary.

Agents must learn a great deal about real estate before they can begin to work. To make sure that they are well trained, most states require that they pass a real estate license test before they may act as agents in real property transactions.

The opportunity to counsel and to provide a service to homeowners is important, since six out of ten people own their own homes. The equity in a home and life insurance may represent the entire estate of an individual. It should be pointed out, however, that not all people have salesmanship abilities. To serve the needs of these homeowners, real estate agents should possess the following characteristics:

1. They must be energetic and hard-working.
2. They must not be interested in sitting at a desk all day.
3. They must be interested in gaining knowledge of the community.
4. They must be enthusiastic.
5. They must have a knowledge of contracts, financing, and appraisal; and they must avail themselves of every opportunity to know the product.
6. They must like people and enjoy helping them solve their problems.

No other field offers the rewards of personal satisfaction and income potential that real estate does. The objective of education and training in real estate is not limited to making property sales; many areas of specialization exist in this complex industry, and it is steadily being upgraded as a profession. As mentioned earlier, degree programs with majors in real estate have been introduced by some universities and colleges, and others include real estate courses as a part of the business administration program.

Areas of specialization

Areas of specialization within the field include real estate brokerage, property management, appraisal, land development, industrial brokerage, mortgage lending, farm brokerage, investment counseling, and research.

Brokerage   The real estate brokerage business is concerned with the selling and leasing of property. Brokers or salespeople work on a commission basis. Their activities include

1. Selling or offering to sell.
2. Buying or offering to buy.
3. Listing or soliciting prospective purchasers.

4. Negotiating the purchase, sale, or exchange of real property.
5. Negotiating loans or soliciting borrowers for lenders.
6. Leasing or offering to lease real property.
7. Negotiating the sale, purchase, or exchange of a lease.
8. Renting, placing for rent, or collecting rents.
9. Selling, buying, and negotiating promissory notes and mortgages.
10. Assisting persons wishing to file and purchase, lease, or locate state or federal land.

A large number of brokerage firms deal in residential housing. Although their activities may be principally concerned with soliciting listings and selling homes, brokers should have a knowledge of available real estate financing, local zoning laws, and the most practical and profitable use of property. They should also take every opportunity to serve the needs of their communities.

Property management   Professional managers are custodians of the property of others and normally earn 5 to 6 percent of a property's gross income. Property managers (1) act for the property owner in the management and maintenance of the property, whether it be single or multiple units, office buildings, industrial buildings, or commercial shopping centers; and (2) serve as interpreters of financial statements.

Professional property managers devote their entire time to the management of properties. They must be aware of current real estate trends in the community and economic conditions in the state and the nation. They should be expert in the preparation of rental schedules, income, and expense analyses for the buildings that they manage. They know what the average expenses are for similar buildings in the community in which the property is located. Frequently, new real estate brokerage firms will have a property management department separate from their sales department.

Appraisal   Professional real estate appraisers are valued for their opinions and judgments as to the value of property. They should be expert in the appraisal of residential, commercial, industrial, and special-purpose property. Members of the American Institute of Real Estate Appraisers are privileged to use the designation MAI are perhaps the most respected members of the real estate industry. Appraisers are consulted as experts in condemnation proceedings. They may work on an hourly or fee basis.

Opportunities for employment in the appraisal field exist through savings and loan institutions, commercial banks, an apprenticeship with full-time appraisers, and many government agencies.

Land development Land development is a highly specialized field. Developers create residential subdivisions, industrial parks, commercial shopping centers, and office complexes, among others.

Land developers must keep abreast of local, state, and national economic trends and conditions. They will build and hold inventories of land for as long as six months in advance of large land developments. Developers understand trends of community growth and zoning. A residential subdivision located in the wrong area within a community might mean disaster to a developer, in addition to creating a blight on the community itself.

Industrial brokerage Industrial brokerage deals with the sale and lease of properties used by companies that manufacture goods for industry and consumers.

Industrial brokers are alert to community needs and objectives and assist industry in locating in their communities. They know the assets of their communities and have firsthand knowledge of transportation facilities, schools, churches, tax bases of their communities and so forth. Industrial developers may be creators of industrial parks, a growing trend in many communities. They know how to merchandise industrial property and present it attractively to the industrialist. They understand industrial financing and know what money is available for smaller industries wishing to locate in their communities.

Commercial brokerage Commercial brokerage deals with the sale and lease of properties used by companies that sell goods and services to other businesses or to the consumer. Like industrial brokers, commercial brokers must have special knowledge about community resources, trends, development potential, and land values. Most brokerage companies require new commercial brokers to begin by leasing office buildings, shopping centers, and freestanding buildings. Only after a broker has gained awareness of the market and commercial transactions does the broker branch out to sales.

Mortgage lending The mortgage lending phase of the industry offers opportunities for the young college student and for others wishing to enter real estate. Opportunities exist as loan officers in savings and loan institutions, commercial banks, insurance companies, mutual banking institutions, and so forth.

Loan officers must be familiar with current money market conditions in the community, the state, and the nation. They should have a thorough knowledge of FHA-insured loans, Veterans Administration guaranteed loans, and conventional loans. They should be familiar with the mortgage-money market and understand its relationship to such types of investment as stocks, bonds, and mutual funds.

Farm brokerage Farm brokerage is a specialized field. Successful farm brokers are familiar with crops and soil conditions in the areas in which they operate. They have a knowledge of farming methods and are familiar with farm equipment and other chattels that may be transferred with the sale of real property. They are aware of community growth trends and are alert to changes in the highest and best use for the property of owners whom they represent.

Investment counseling Real estate investment counselors should have wide experience in the investment field, and they should have bachelor's or even master's degrees. They should divorce themselves from real estate activities to provide the best possible impartial advice. Investment counselors usually work on a fee basis. Counselors are employed by buyers, sellers, investors, and developers in the field. Counselors may solve the problems of investors by providing advice as to the most opportune time to sell, buy, or lease property. Counselors' success will naturally depend on the success of the follow-through on their suggestions to their clientele. A counselor may make a feasibility study for the purpose of advising a developer as to whether land is suitable for development and may perform a service as adviser to industry wishing to locate in the community.

Business opportunities Real estate brokers can also specialize in the sale of businesses, such as furniture stores, barbershops, restaurants, and other enterprises. The business is personal property. Such sales may include inventory, fixtures, good will, accounts receivable, liquor licenses, permits, and contract assignments. The broker must be knowledgeable about general business, taxes, license transfers, and the California Commercial Code.

Research Many private concerns, as well as universities and colleges, provide research facilities. The University of California, for example, institutes many helpful real estate projects each year.

Many graduate students at California state universities supply the local real estate industry with research data on local problems.

HISTORY OF CALIFORNIA LAND

Early history

The Spanish discovered California in 1513, although they did not begin colonizing the land until 1769. Spanish settlers ultimately established 21 missions (church settlements), 4 presidios (military forts), 3 pueblos (towns), and nearly 25 ranches (large private land grants for farming and grazing).

When Mexico won its independence from Spain in 1822, California became part of Mexico. In 1848, California became a territory of the United States. The Peace Treaty of Guadalupe required the United States to recognize existing property rights of Mexican citizens. The concept of community property came from Mexican law.

The United States also recognized existing Mexican land grants, and those that proved valid were issued a patent (deed) to that property. In 1850 California became the 31st state in the nation.

Government ownership

The federal government owns approximately 45 percent of all land in California. In 1980, it was estimated that California owned approximately 3 percent, and local governments owned another 2 percent. The other 50 percent of the state is privately owned.

2 THE NATURE OF REAL ESTATE

Since medieval times, the meaning of property and its method of transfer have basically remained the same. *Property* refers to the rights or interests the owner has in what is owned and to his or her power to dispose, use, and encumber it to the exclusion of others.

Property may be either *personal* or *real*. Personal property consists of every kind of property that is not real. It includes movable goods, chattels, evidence of debt, money, and the right to bring legal action when necessary to protect one's interest. Fixtures, on the other hand, are items of personal property that are attached to the real property (land) in such a manner as to be considered as part of the land itself.

The California Civil Code states that "the thing of which there may be ownership is called property." It is often difficult to distinguish between the two kinds of property; however, it is the purpose of this chapter to do so.

REAL ESTATE OR REAL PROPERTY

Real estate or real property consists of the following: land; anything affixed to the land; that which is appurtenant to the land; and that which is immovable by law.

Land

The California Civil Code defines land as "solid material of the earth . . . whether soil, rock, or other substance." The common law broadens this concept to include not only the surface of the earth but also the space beneath it to the center of the earth and the air space above to infinity.

Minerals

Minerals are classified as solids or as liquids. Solids are called *minerals-in-place* and include gold, silver, coal, and other ores. The owner of the land owns all solid minerals located under the property. Liquid minerals include gas, oil, and other nonsolid minerals. A property owner does not own the liquid minerals below his or her property. The owner only has the right to drill and recover those minerals.

Minerals such as oil and gas are incapable of absolute ownership until reduced to personal possession because of their moving nature beneath the surface of the land. An owner of real property is entitled to drill on his or her land for oil and gas providing he or she has not previously conveyed these rights to another person. The owner must, however, drill straight down on his or her property and not slant-drill into the land of a neighbor.

Water

While minerals may represent great wealth, water is probably of greater importance to Californians. A large body of law exists dealing with surface and underground water, and decisions recently rendered by the United States Supreme Court will have far-reaching effects on Californians for years to come.

Percolating water, underground water not confined to any well-known channel or bed beneath the surface of the earth, is governed by the *doctrine of correlative user*. The owner of land has a right in common with other adjoining landowners to use his or her fair share, but he or she must not waste the water.

Water beneath the surface of the earth confined to a well-known channel or stream is governed by substantially the same rules of law that are applied to surface streams and lakes. The owner of property whose land adjoins a lake or outer courses on the surface of the land enjoys what are known as *riparian rights* to the use of the water. Riparian rights mean that he or she has no absolute ownership of the waters but has a right in common with adjoining landowners to a fair share of the water. Owners of property on a navigable stream own to the low-water mark of the stream. An owner whose property adjoins a nonnavigable stream owns to the center of the stream. The boundary of an owner's land on a seacoast is the high-water mark.

Floodwaters are considered a common enemy. The owner may use any reasonable means to keep them off his or her land.

Property owners who own land not abutting on a water course or stream may arrange to bring water to their property by applying to the State Water Commission.

Fixtures

Fixtures   Fixtures are items of personal property which have become so permanently affixed to the real estate so as to become part of it.

Anything attached or affixed to the land may be regarded as a part of the land itself. A legal description may describe a ten-acre parcel of land only, yet it will convey all buildings, fences, and other pieces of permanently attached property on the land. For example, a building on a foundation is real property. If rollers are placed beneath the building and it is moved off the foundation, it becomes personal property. Fence posts and fences may be considered personal property. Once the fence posts are placed in the ground, and fencing on the posts, they become real property.

The California legislature has declared that a thing is affixed to land when it is attached by roots, as in the case of trees, vines, or shrubs; embedded in it, as in the case of walls; permanently resting upon it, as in the case of buildings; or permanently attached to what is thus permanent by means of cement, plaster, nails, bolts, or screws.

The courts have used five general tests to determine whether a piece of property is a fixture and should be considered real property.

These five tests are easily remembered by the mnemonic word MARIA for: method of attachment, adaptability, relationship of the parties, intent, and agreement between the parties.

1. Attachment.   The courts consider how an item is attached to the realty. Items permanently attached by bolts, cement or other methods so that removal would cause injury to the property are fixtures. Conversely, items that are attached by screws and other methods of attachment which makes their removal easy, remain personal property.

2. Adaptability.   Items which are only suited for one property, such as front door keys, are considered fixtures.

3. Relationship.   The courts favor certain relationships. Tenants are favored over landlords, buyers have priority over sellers, and borrowers receive consideration over lenders. In close cases, the relationship can make the difference.

4. Intent.   The intention of the party attaching the item is the most important test. If the item is bolted and cemented to the wall, the courts consider that the owner intended the item to be a fixture.

5. Agreement.   Between the parties, they can agree to anything. The parties can agree a building will be personal property, and it will be between the parties. However, the agreement will not bind third parties without notice.

Trade fixtures   Trade fixtures, those fixtures used in conducting a business, are considered an exception to the rule. If a tenant installs trade fixtures for use in his or her business, the tenant may remove them from the premises providing the property is returned to the same condition in which he or she found it.

Appurtenances   *That which is incidental or appurtenant to the land may be considered real property.* Appurtenant means belonging to. Appurtenances include anything that is by right used with the land for its benefit.

Crops   *All property immovable by law is considered real property.* Exceptions to this rule would include industrial growing crops and things attached to or forming a part of the land, which are agreed to be severed before the sale or under the contract of sale. Industrial crops refer to the vegetable production of the soil produced annually by labor known as an emblement—not spontaneously. The disposal of such goods will be governed by the provisions of the California Civil Code relating to the sale of goods. The Civil Code provides that all industrial growing crops and other crops agreed to be severed before the sale or under contract of the sale should be treated as personal property and are thus governed by laws of sales.

PERSONAL PROPERTY

Anything that is not real property is considered personal property. Personal property is movable. Items of tangible property (called *choses* [things] *in possession,* or *chattels*) include clothing, furniture, and automobiles. Items of intangible personal property (called *choses in action*) include stocks, bonds, contracts, and trust deeds; that is, those things that represent a right to something of value but in and of themselves are not valuable.

Contracts are personal property. A lease is a contract to use the land of another and is a personal interest therein. In real estate a lease is called a *chattel real*.

Other distinctions should be made between real and personal property. All contracts dealing with sales of real property must normally be in writing and signed by the party whose title is charged to be enforceable. Sales of personal property, however, need not be in writing if the price is less than five hundred dollars, though they should be. The acquisition and transfer of land is governed exclusively by the laws of the state in which the property is located. Thus, real estate located in New York is always governed by New York law, regardless of where the owner lives. Conversely, personal property is governed by the laws of the owner's personal residence, regardless of the state in which the property physically resides.

Neither the federal government (except with reference to federal lands and bankruptcy proceedings) nor any of the other forty-nine states has authority over real property in California; real property in California is solely California's domain. Instruments affecting the title or interest in real property may be recorded in the county recorder's office in the county or counties in which the real property is located. Some personal property contracts may also be recorded.

Tax laws between real and personal property also have significant differences. The real estate broker and investor should consult an accountant concerning tax regula-

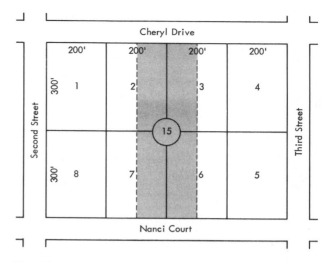

Figure 2–1

tions and laws. Personal property when sold is usually transferred by using a bill of sale. Real property is transferred by delivery of a written conveyance called a *deed*.

METHODS OF LAND DESCRIPTION

Every parcel of land sold, mortgaged, or leased must be properly described or identified. Legal descriptions are usually based upon the field notes of a civil engineer or a surveyor. When dealing with property, such descriptions can usually be obtained from tax receipts, title insurance policies, deeds, or mortgages. The real estate

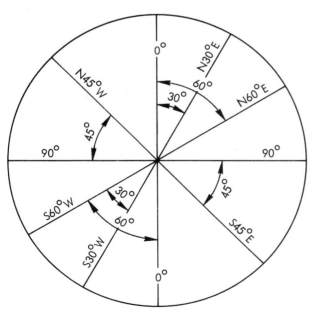

Figure 2–2 Circle illustrating metes and bounds descriptions.

There are 360° in a circle.

There are 180° in a half-circle.

There are 90° in a quarter-circle.

Each degree is divided into 60 minutes.

Each minute is divided into 60 seconds.

The point of beginning is at the intersection (center of the circle).

The "bearing" of a course is described by measuring easterly or westerly from north and south lines.

MAP SHOWING TOWNSHIP AND RANGE SURVEY SYSTEM IN CALIFORNIA

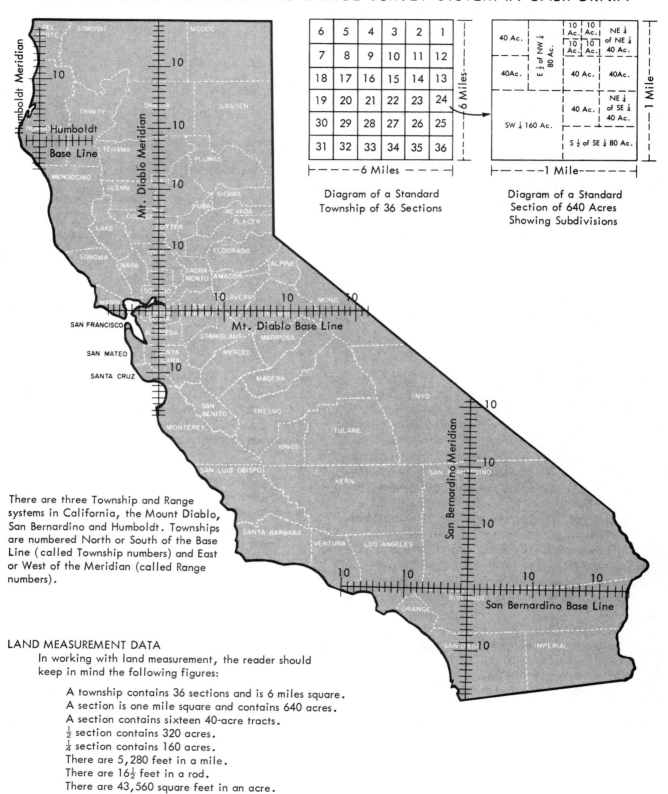

Diagram of a Standard
Township of 36 Sections

Diagram of a Standard
Section of 640 Acres
Showing Subdivisions

There are three Township and Range systems in California, the Mount Diablo, San Bernardino and Humboldt. Townships are numbered North or South of the Base Line (called Township numbers) and East or West of the Meridian (called Range numbers).

LAND MEASUREMENT DATA

In working with land measurement, the reader should keep in mind the following figures:

A township contains 36 sections and is 6 miles square.
A section is one mile square and contains 640 acres.
A section contains sixteen 40-acre tracts.
$\frac{1}{2}$ section contains 320 acres.
$\frac{1}{4}$ section contains 160 acres.
There are 5,280 feet in a mile.
There are $16\frac{1}{2}$ feet in a rod.
There are 43,560 square feet in an acre.

Figure 2–3

broker or salesperson should exercise care when writing such a description.

Real estate in California is described by three principal methods: metes and bounds; U.S. government section and township system; and recorded tract, map, or lot and block system. A combination of these three is used in some descriptions.

Metes and bounds description

Metes and bounds means outside measurements and boundaries. Metes are measures of length, such as inches, feet, yards, or rods. Bounds are measures of both natural and artificial boundaries, including rivers, roads, and monuments (markers).

Older descriptions included references to objects such as sycamore trees, stones, rivers, farms, and other markers that over the years might have been erased. Such an older description might have referred to the southerly line of the "White Farm."

Metes and bounds descriptions are further complicated in that they include angles and measured distance from stakes or other objects that are not always permanent. They further include language not common to most students of real estate and can be understood only by a civil engineer or a surveyor.

Figure 2–1 illustrates a metes and bounds description in which portions of four lots are defined as follows:

> *Beginning at a point on the southerly line of Cheryl Drive, 300 feet westerly of the SW corner of the intersection of Cheryl Drive and Third Streets; running thence due south 600 feet to the northerly line of Nanci Court; thence westerly along the northerly line of Nanci Court, 200 feet, thence northerly and parallel to the first course, 600 feet, to the southerly line of Cheryl Drive; thence easterly along the southerly line of Cheryl Drive, 200 feet, to the point or place of beginning.*

Figure 2–2 illustrates how the more complicated metes and bounds description is constructed. This type of description should be used only as a last resort because of its many disadvantages. Most are long, sometimes running several pages, and are not understood by anyone except a civil engineer or a surveyor. A portion of such a description follows.

> *Beginning at the Northeastern corner of Section 36, Township 9 South Range 4 East, M.D.B. & M., a 1 inch galvanized pipe set in the original mound of stone at said section corner and from which the original witness trees, as described by Healy in 1869, bears the following, a White Oak, now 30" in diameter, bears South 40° 05' West 51.42 feet and a Live Oak, now 15" in diameter bears South 0° 23' East 74.17 feet distant; thence from said point of beginning along the Northern boundary of said Section 36 South 89° 37' West 2272.79 feet to a 1"*

> *pipe set in a mound of stone approximately 130 feet West of center of Coyote Creek, from said 1" pipe a 20" Live Oak bears South 51° 23' to the place of beginning and containing approximately 158.07 acres of land.*

U.S. government section and township system

California became a part of the United States in 1848, and all public lands not within the boundaries of pueblos and valid Mexican or Spanish grants came under the jurisdiction of the United States Surveyor General. In order to locate and describe lands in California, certain *base lines* and *meridians* were established. From these base lines and meridians, the location of land may be accurately described. California has three base lines and meridians. As shown in Figure 2–3, the Humboldt Base Line and Meridian is located in the northwestern part of the state, the Mt. Diablo Base Line and Meridian is located in the central part of the state, and the San Bernardino Base Line and Meridian is located in the southern part of the state.

The intersection of the base line and the meridian is the starting point for all calculations. Each of the principal base lines is divided by lines running north and south, spaced six miles apart, called *range lines*. The area between two range lines is called a *range of townships* (see Figure 2–4). The three principal meridian lines are divided by lines running east and west, also spaced six miles apart, called *township lines*. The area between two township lines is called a *tier of townships* (see Figure 2–4). Township (T2N, R3E) two north, range three east, is a standard six-mile-square township containing thirty-

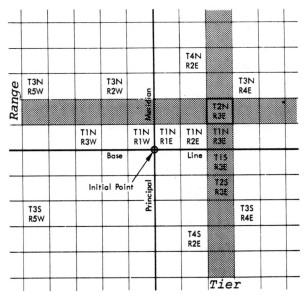

Figure 2–4

six square miles. A "legal" description of this township might thus read, T2N, R3E, San Bernardino Base Line and Meridian (see Figure 2–4).

Townships are divided into sections. Each township contains thirty-six sections, and each section is one square mile. In each township, sections are numbered from right to left and from left to right, as shown in Figure 2–5. Figure 2–6 illustrates how a section is broken down into smaller parcels and the various measurements that may be used to describe each.

The following are examples of land descriptions by the United States Government section and township system illustrated by Figure 2–7.

1. The NW¼ of section 4. Since this is ¼ of a section that contains 640 acres, this description contains 160 acres.

2. Starting at the NW corner of section 17; thence in a southeasterly direction to the southeast corner of the NE¼; thence in a southeasterly direction to the southeast corner of the SW¼ of the SW¼ of section 16; thence due west to the SW corner of section 17; thence back to the point of beginning (520 acres).

3. The E½ of the NE¼ and the N½ of the SE¼ of section 15; the W½ of the W½, the SE¼ of the NW¼, the SW¼ of the NE¼, the NW¼ of the SE¼, and the NE¼ of the SW¼ of section 14 (480 acres).

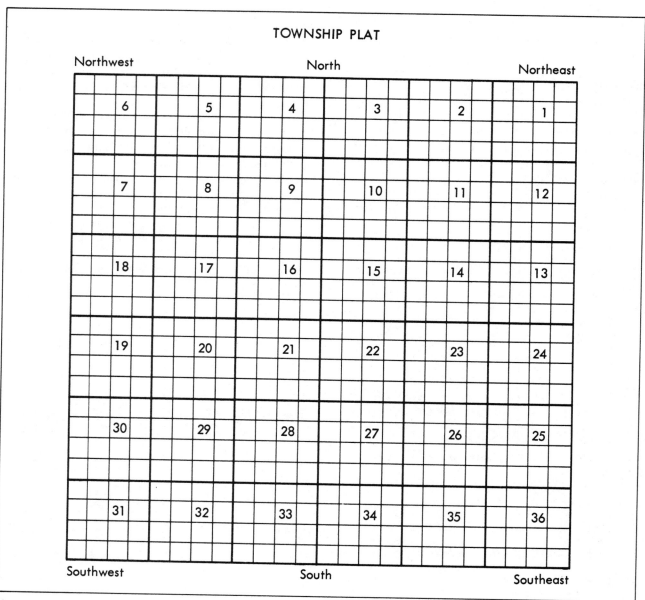

Figure 2–5

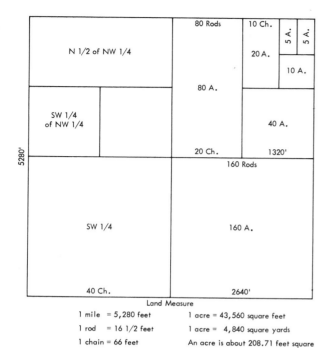

Land Measure

1 mile = 5,280 feet	1 acre = 43,560 square feet
1 rod = 16 1/2 feet	1 acre = 4,840 square yards
1 chain = 66 feet	An acre is about 208.71 feet square

Figure 2–6 Map of a section

4. The NW¼ excepting therefrom the NW¼; the NE¼, and the SE¼ excepting therefrom the SW¼ of section 29 (400 acres).

A land description is read backwards. In the first entry of the preceding land description, note that we first find the section and then go to the NW¼ of that section.

In the second entry, we start with the first semicolon, or section 17, locating the northwest corner. Starting with the next semicolon we find the NE¼ and take the SE corner of the portion of the section and draw a line connecting the two points. The next semicolon starts with section 16 in which we locate the SW¼ and again the SW¼ of the portion and put a dot in the SE corner. In the next portion of the description, we again locate section 17 and place a dot at the SW corner and draw a line between the two points. Now proceed to the point of beginning.

In practice, however, such description would include the township and range numbers such as:

> *The E½ of the NE¼ of the SW¼ of section 36 T1N R2E Mt. Diablo Base Line and Meridian.*

Lot, block, and tract description

Subdivisions are discussed in Chapter 16. When a developer subdivides property, a subdivision map must be filed with the appropriate government agency. Once this map is recorded, all future conveyances of lots may refer

to it. Such a description might state: Lot 4, Block 10, tract 1236 as per maps recorded October 20, 1964, page 72, Book 107, Official Records, County of Santa Clara, City of Los Altos, State of California.

The assessor's parcel number

For convenience, the county assessor makes maps of the county showing each tract of land under separate ownership. In real estate purchase contracts, a parcel of land is frequently referred to by stating the assessor's parcel number. This type of description is sufficient for many contracts but is not sufficient for a deed or other instrument that must be recorded.

CHAPTER QUESTIONS

1. Distinguish between *real* and *personal* property.
2. What is meant by *riparian rights*?
3. In the transfer of real property, define the term *appurtenant to the land*.
4. Real estate in California may be described by three principal methods. Name and briefly describe each.
5. Name each of the township and range systems in California.

MULTIPLE-CHOICE QUESTIONS

1. Personal property is (a) immovable; (b) appurtenant; (c) trees; (d) land; (e) other than real property.
2. Tests used to determine whether a piece of property is a fixture and should be considered real property include: (a) length of time the personal property has been on the land; (b) manner in which title to the land is held; (c) marital status of the property owner; (d) the intention of the person affixing the personal property to the land; (e) none of the foregoing is correct.
3. Real estate or real property would *not* include which of the following: (a) minerals in place; (b) land; (c) that which is appurtenant to the land; (d) growing trees; (e) chattels.
4. A right which goes with the land and cannot be separated from it is known as: (a) an encroachment; (b) an appurtenance; (c) a fixture; (d) a chattel; (e) a chose.
5. Property owners who own land not abutting on a water course or stream may arrange to bring water to their property by applying to the: (a) senator of their district; (b) city council or board of supervisors; (c) State Water Commission; (d) secretary of state; (e) California Department of Real Estate.
6. In California, oil and gas are: (a) considered to be real property; (b) owned by the surface owner; (c) considered to be personal property before mined; (d) not

TOWNSHIP PLAT

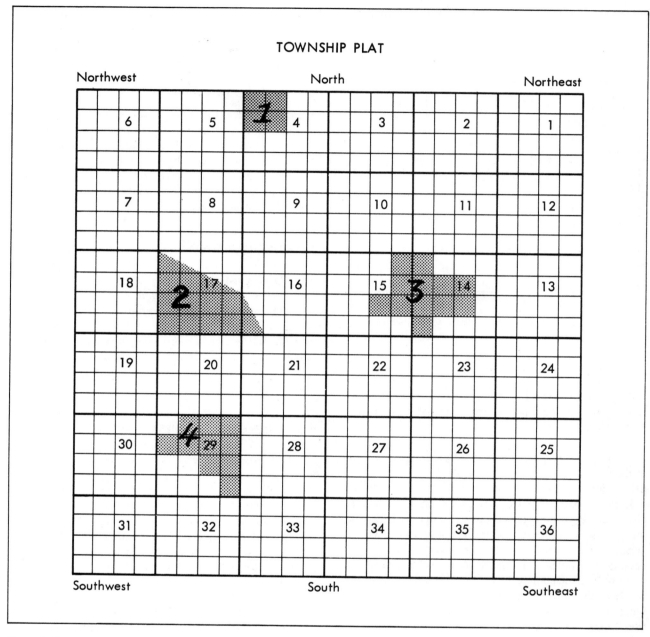

Figure 2–7

subject to ownership as such until reduced to possession; (e) all of the foregoing are correct answers.

7. Base lines run (a) east and west; (b) north and south; (c) south and west; (d) north and east; (e) north and west.

8. A survey that refers to fractional sections, townships, and ranges is a legal description by: (a) recorded map; (b) U.S. Government Survey; (c) metes and bounds; (d) lot, block, tract description; (e) measurements and boundaries.

9. One fourth of a section of land contains: (a) 40 acres; (b) 640 acres; (c) 160 acres; (d) 320 acres; (e) 180 acres.

10. A parcel of land that is 330 feet by 660 feet contains how many acres? (a) 10; (b) 20; (c) 50; (d) 5; (e) 30.

Answers to all questions at the end of each chapter are located in Appendix A.

OWNERSHIP OF REAL PROPERTY

All land in California has an owner, whether it be an individual, the state, or the federal government. About 50-percent of all the land in California is owned by the federal, state, and local governments. This is a surprising figure until we think about the tremendous number of acres of land in state and national forests and parks, approximately 101,000,000 acres.

The average person thinks of *property* as a physical thing, such as land or a building. The law conceives of property as a *bundle of rights*. These rights are commonly stated as the rights of possession, use, encumbrancing, disposition and exclusion. You can possess, use and exclude others from your property. You can also encumber and dispose of it as desired. Property exists only because the law allows an owner to use the property to the exclusion of all others and to dispose of it by sale, gift, or inheritance as that owner desires. Take away some of the legal protections and the *value* of property may be reduced, but its *existence* remains unchanged.

For example, the law no longer gives shopping-center owners the right to prohibit peaceful demonstrators from entering the property. Despite this loss of a right from the full bundle of rights, the shopping-center owner still owns the property. In fact, in a democracy, no rights in the owner's bundle of rights are absolute. Property is affected by zoning laws, building codes, condemnation rights, and numerous other rights held by the government and its inhabitants.

In this chapter, we will discuss the various types of ownership interests a person may have in real property. These interests are called *estates*.

You may own the whole bundle of these rights, which gives you the highest possible estate in the land. Or, you may own only some of the rights, or you may possess them only temporarily. That gives you a lesser estate.

The two major classes of estates are (1) freehold estates and (2) less-than-freehold estates, which are also called *chattels real*. The unusual names given the estates came from old English feudal law. If you were "free" you owned a freehold estate. Otherwise you were a surf, who could own property only as long as your lord allowed. This nonfree person held nonfree estates, known today as leases.

FREEHOLD ESTATES

In California today, there are two types of freehold estates. They are called *fee simple* estates and *life estates*.

Fee simple

A fee simple estate—often called a "fee"—is the largest estate you can own in land. It is the estate most owners possess. It gives you the entire bundle of ownership rights, and has no time limits on those rights—they continue indefinitely. You may own them or you have the right to convey them to someone else.

When a deed is given to real property, it is presumed to convey a fee simple estate unless it states otherwise. The fact that there is a mortgage, a deed of trust, or other encumbrance on the property does not change the fact that the owner's estate is a fee simple.

Life estate

Suppose Mr. Gavilan who has fee simple title wants to give his property to his daughter Lola during his lifetime.

Yet he would like to keep the right to live on the property until he dies. He can give the property to Lola but keep a life estate in it for himself. The life estate gives him the right to use the property for his lifetime.

What he has done is divide the fee simple estate into two parts: The life estate continues as long as Mr. Gavilan lives. He can enjoy the property during that time. At his death, his life estate ends and Lola then owns the entire property in fee simple.

Life estates are sometimes called the "poor persons trust" since they avoid probate and cost almost nothing to create. However, such an estate should be used only after consulting an accountant or an attorney, because of potential federal gift tax consequences.

LESS-THAN-FREEHOLD ESTATES

Nonfreehold estates are often called *leasehold estates* because they are simply a lease of property. There are four types of leasehold estates:

1. Estate for years The name "estate for years" is misleading. This estate is any *lease* that has a *definite term,* fixed in advance. It may be for years (as it originally was in feudal England), but it may be for only months or days—or even hours, as when an auditorium is leased for one evening. But as long as it is a lease with a definite term, it is called an "estate for years." Such leases are common in renting houses, apartments, and all kinds of property.

2. Periodic tenancy A periodic tenancy is also quite common in renting apartments and houses. It is a type of lease that has *no* definite term. It runs from period to period—usually from month to month—until either the landlord or the tenant gives the other legal notice that he or she is ending it, usually 30 days notice.

3. Tenancy at will This is a rare estate. It gives the tenant the right to possession for an indefinite period. It may be ended at the will of either the landlord or the tenant by giving the other thirty days' notice that he or she is ending it.

4. Tenancy at sufferance This is the lowest estate you can have in land. It is one in which the tenant stays on after the expiration of the lease. He or she is there, as the name implies, at the sufferance of the landlord. The landlord can file suit to evict him or her at any time by filing a court action called an unlawful detainer and then eviction by the sheriff. This procedure is discussed in Chapter 10. The tenant is not a trespasser, so the landlord cannot bar him or her from the property or evict him or her without going to court.

ABSOLUTE AND CONDITIONAL ESTATES

The estates we have described so far have been classified according to their duration. There are other ways of classifying estates, and one is according to whether they are *absolute* or *conditional.*

Most estates are subject to no conditions. They are *absolute estates.* An example is a *fee simple absolute,* which is the most complete estate in land our law allows.

A *conditional estate* is one that is subject to a condition. It is also called *defeasible estate.*

First, let us define a "condition." It is a fact or an event that creates or ends an estate or other right. *Example:* I convey a house to my 18-year-old daughter in fee simple, but I provide in the deed that the title will come back to me if she marries before the age of 25. Her marriage before the age of 25 is a condition; if it happens, it terminates her estate in the property. I could instead provide that the title will come back to me if she does *not* marry by age 40. Then her *not* marrying by age 40 is a condition that terminates her estate.

An example of a conditional estate is an estate in *fee simple defeasible,* also called a *qualified fee.*

Conditional estates are classified by what happens when the condition occurs. The estate is subject to either a condition precedent or a condition subsequent. A condition precedent creates an estate where none existed before. A condition subsequent causes a forfeiture of an existing estate.

Estate on a condition precedent

This unusual estate does not begin until a particular event has first occurred. For example, I deed five acres of land to the city of Los Angeles for a park, but I provide that the title of the city shall not commence unless the city appropriates $25,000 to develop the park within twelve months. Before the city will get an estate in the land, the condition—the appropriation of $25,000 within twelve months—must occur.

Estate on a condition subsequent

Much more common, this estate will terminate upon the occurrence or nonoccurrence of a certain event. *Example:* I deed you a vacant lot next to my home but provide in the deed that the title will come back to me if you ever use it for any purpose other than for a one-family residence.

Almost every lease contains a condition subsequent, providing that the landlord may terminate the tenant's leasehold estate if the tenant does not pay the rent.

When a condition subsequent occurs, the owner does not lose his or her estate automatically. The person entitled to take back the estate must take action to do so, such as filing a suit to get title. Until he or she does, the estate continues. If the person does nothing for an unreasonable length of time after the breach of the condition, the person entitled to the estate waives the right to terminate the estate.

Future interests

So far we have discussed estates in land that can be enjoyed in the present. But some estates can be enjoyed only in the future. The most common are a *reversion* and a *remainder*.

Reversion

Suppose an owner of land in fee simple leases it to a tenant. By doing this, the owner has divided up his or her bundle of rights so that most of those rights, such as the right to use the land and the right to exclude others, have been granted to the tenant for the period of the lease. At the end of the lease, these rights revert to the owner. The estate that the owner has left after granting the leasehold estate or some other temporary estate is called a *reversion*.

Example: John Vogel may grant his father a life estate in a house he owns. After the father dies and the life estate ends, the property will revert to Vogel. Vogel's interest is a reversion.

Remainder

Suppose Vogel were to grant his father a life estate as in the example above. But in the deed he provides that when his father dies, the property will not revert to Vogel but will go to Vogel's son Benjamin. This interest does not go back—that is, it does not revert—to Vogel, so it is not called a reversion. Instead it is called a *remainder*. (This word is easy to remember because it "remains away" from the person who created the life estate.)

Condominiums

In California, a condominium is an estate consisting of a separate ownership in some particular space in a parcel of real estate, together with an interest in common with others on other parts of the parcel. An individual unit actually lies in airspace above the ground, with only the common areas resting on the land. The occupied airspace is real property described in the deed.

A condominium estate may be created in residential, industrial, or commercial buildings on the property such as an apartment, office, or store. The owner owns the apartment, office, or store separately. He or she owns certain other areas, such as parking lots, walkways, lawns, and lobbies, in common with other condominium owners in the same tract.

A condominium may, with respect to the duration of its enjoyment, be a fee simple estate, a life estate, or an estate for years.

Stock cooperatives A stock cooperative, often called a "co-op," has a corporation owning the title to all the property. Each owner buys shares in the corporation, which includes the right to exclusive possession of his or her individual unit. Before 1977, the corporation obtained a blanket deed of trust against the project, making each shareowner in default if any one shareowner failed to pay his or her monthly percentage of the deed of trust. Now, lending institutions are allowed to make individual loans, secured by an owner's shares in the cooperative, so co-ops are almost the equivalent of condominiums.

Planned development project

A *planned development project* is similar to an ordinary subdivision with privately owned lots and homes. But in addition there are common areas such as lawns, a pool, or a clubhouse that are reserved for use by some or all the private owners. Usually an owners' association is set up to provide management and maintenance of the common areas. The private owners are members. The association can enforce the members' obligations by levying assessments that become liens on the private owners' property.

METHODS OF ACQUIRING REAL PROPERTY

The California statutes declare that there are five ways to acquire title to real property: transfer, will, succession, accession, and occupancy.

Property acquired by transfer

Transfer is the *usual* method of acquiring title. One person, called the *grantor*, conveys the property to another, called the *grantee*. This is usually done by sale. Occasionally, it is done by gift.

Wills and succession

A will is a document in which you direct who will get your property when you die. It does not take effect until death.

If you leave no will, the *law of succession* states which relatives will succeed to, or get, your property. Community property (property accumulated by a husband and wife during marriage) goes to the spouse who survives; however, either spouse may will his or her half of the community property. Separate property (everything except community property) is divided between your spouse and your children: If you leave one child, your spouse and child each get half. If you leave more than one child, your spouse gets one-third and your children, two-thirds. If you leave no spouse, your children divide all property equally.

There are three common types of wills in California:

1. A *formal will,* also called a *witnessed will* (Figure 3–1), is the type we are most familiar with. It is usually drawn up by an attorney. Two witnesses are required.

2. A *holographic will* is not common. It must be written, dated, and signed entirely in your own handwriting. It is best avoided because will provisions are technical and should be prepared by an attorney. After all, you won't be around to explain any unclear provisions.

3. A *statutory will* is a preprinted will following a specified statutory form, in which you fill in the names

Some quick definitions

Decedent (''Dee-SEED-ent'') a person who is deceased.

Estate (as the word is used in a will) The real estate and personal property left by a deceased person.

Testament This is another name for a will.

Testator (''Test-ATE-or'') A person who makes a will.

Testate (''TEST-ate'') Having left a will; as ''a person dying testate.''

Intestate (''In-TEST-ate'') Leaving no will.

Executor (''Ex-ECK-you-tor'',) A person, or an organization such as a bank, that is named in a will to administer (take charge of) the estate and to carry out the provisions of the will.

Administrator A person named by the court to administer an estate when there is no executor.

Codicil (''COD-i-sill'') An amendment that changes a will. It is a separate document that is executed and witnessed like a will.

LAST WILL AND TESTAMENT OF
KENNETH L. JONES

I, KENNETH L. JONES, a resident of the City of San Diego, California, declare that this is my will.

FIRST: I revoke any former Wills and Codicils I may have made.

SECOND: I am married to EDITH JONES. I have two children now living named DONALD JONES and SUSAN JONES. I have no deceased children.

THIRD: I give my entire estate to my wife EDITH if she survives me and if she does not then in equal shares to those of my children who survive me, provided however, if any child of mine predeceases me leaving children who survive me, then those grandchildren shall take, by right of representation, the share that such deceased child of mine would have taken had he or she survived me.

FOURTH: I direct that all estate or other death taxes that may be imposed because of my death be paid by my executrix out of the residue of my estate and not charged to or collected from any beneficiary of my probate estate.

FIFTH: I appoint my wife EDITH as executrix of this Will, to serve without bond. If she dies before me or fails or declines to serve, I appoint my daughter SUSAN as executrix, to serve without bond.
This Will is signed by me on the second day of January, 1987, at San Diego, California.

_____
KENNETH L. JONES

The foregoing Will, consisting of one page, was signed by the testator, KENNETH L. JONES, in our joint presence and, at the same time, he declared it to be his Will. At his request, we sign as witnesses in the presence of the testator and in the presence of each other.

Each of us is now more than 18 years of age and a competent witness and resides at the address set forth after his or her name. We are acquainted with the testator, KENNETH L. JONES. At this time, he is over the age of 18 years and, to the best of our knowledge, is of sound mind and is not acting under duress, menace, fraud, misrepresentation, or undue influence.

Executed on January 2, 1987, at San Diego, California.

We declare under penalty of perjury that the foregoing is true and correct.

_____ residing at _____

_____ residing at _____

_____ residing at _____

Figure 3–1 A will (*Caution:* Only an attorney should write a will. Do not write your own.)

and amounts in the blank spaces provided. It is a good will *if* your desires exactly fit the will form. Most attorneys advise that they review your estate objectives and tax planning options before using these forms.

Should you make a will? The answer is yes if you expect to leave property. Here are a few of the reasons:

1. The laws of succession seldom pass your property on in exactly the way you wish.

2. If you have no will, your property will go to your children when they reach age 18. Many children can handle property at that age. But some cannot and would actually be hurt by having it. Perhaps your son, upon receiving $10,000 at age 18, would feel he has all the money he will ever need. He may drop out of school, buy a sports car, and join a commune. In a will, you may provide that a trustee will hold the property until the child reaches age 30 or some other age you choose. Meanwhile, the trustee will take care of the child's needs for support, health, education, and so forth.

3. A knowledgeable attorney can point out many ways to plan your estate and avoid excess estate taxes.

4. If you have minor children you can name a guardian for them and decide what type of powers you wish to give that guardian.

5. In most cases, you will want to dispense with the requirement that any executor, guardian, or trustee post a bond to insure that he or she does not misappropriate estate assets. The cost of the bond comes from the estate, which leaves less for your heirs.

When a person makes a will, he or she may name an executor to administer the estate, under the supervision of the superior court, and to carry out the provisions of the will. If a person dies intestate (without leaving a will), the superior court of the county where that person resided names an administrator to determine the decedent's assets, pay his or her debts, pay the inheritance and estate taxes, and distribute the property to the people entitled to it. This process is usually referred to by laymen as *probating the estate*. The executor and the administrator perform substantially the same duties.

Accession

Accession is any process that adds to your real property without any action on your part. There are three processes that can do this: annexation, accretion, and reliction.

Annexation This occurs when someone other than yourself adds fixtures or improvements to your property in such a way that they become part of your property.

Suppose Hansen attaches her personal property to your real property; for instance, she builds a partition in a building she rents from you. Her personal property, that is, the building materials, becomes a part of your real property if (1) she had no agreement with you allowing her to remove it, and (2) she cannot remove it without materially damaging your real property.

Sometimes a person innocently improves the wrong property. For example, Smith builds a house on your lot thinking it is his lot. In California, he may remove his improvements, paying for any damage; or a court may work out some other fair settlement of the matter.

Accretion and reliction These processes occur when property borders on water, such as a stream, a lake, or an ocean. The water may gradually wash soil onto the boundary line, building up the land. This new land is called *alluvion.* It belongs to the owner of the old land. The process is called *accretion.*

Sometimes alluvion is added to a person's land by a gradual uncovering of the land because the land rises or the water level falls. This process is called *reliction.*

Accretion and reliction take place so slowly that the eye cannot detect the changes from day to day. But if part of the real property is carried away by water or by sudden violence, the process is called *avulsion*, and the owner has one year to reclaim it.

Occupancy

Adverse possession

Suppose someone takes possession of your real estate, claiming he or she is the owner and has paid the taxes on it. In California, you have five years to file suit to evict that person. If you wait over five years, you may have lost your right to evict the person and he or she may get title to the property. This process of gaining ownership is called *adverse possession.* There are five requirements that must be met before a person can acquire title by this process:

1. The possession must be open so that it can be seen.

2. It must be adverse to the true owner's title. That is, the possessor does not claim he or she is occupying by permission of the true owner.

3. The possessor must claim he or she is the owner. Possession without such a claim is insufficient.

4. The possession must be continuous for five full years.

5. The possessor must pay all real property taxes assessed on the property for the full five years.

The person claiming title by adverse possession may acquire the rights of an earlier possessor of the land and *tack on* (add on) the period of the earlier possession to his or her own period to make up the full five years.

In California, you cannot acquire title by adverse possession to land owned by the government or land dedicated to a public use by a public utility.

Prescription

Adverse possession is a rare process in California because of the requirement that five years' taxes must be paid. But there is another process that is much more common. It is called *prescription,* and in it the claimant acquires a right, called an *easement,* upon the land of another. An easement is described in the next chapter. It is the right to use another's land for a special purpose. For example, you might have an easement for a driveway or for water pipes across a neighbor's land.

The requirements for obtaining an easement by prescription are the same as those for adverse possession, with two exceptions:

1. In prescription, *use* rather than *possession* is involved. The claimant does not possess the other person's land but merely *uses* the easement he or she claims for the five-year period. He or she must claim the right to use the easement (similar to the adverse possessor claiming ownership).

2. There is no requirement to pay any taxes on the easement.

You can prevent someone from obtaining an easement for a right-of-way over your land by posting a sign at the entrance to the property or every two hundred feet around the perimeter. These signs state, ''Right to pass by permission, and subject to control, of owner. Section 1008, Civil Code.'' You may have seen such a sign. Also, you can prevent an easement by prescription by recording a special notice stating that you give permission for the public to use your land.

REAL PROPERTY CLASSIFIED AS TO TITLE

There are five ways you may hold title to real or personal property in California: severalty ownership, tenancy in common, joint tenancy, community property, and tenancy in partnership.

Severalty ownership

Severalty ownership means sole ownership rather than ownership shared with someone else; for instance, when Alice Hansen, an unmarried woman, buys a lot in her own name.

Co-ownership

Two or more people may share the ownership of a piece of property. This is called *co-ownership, concurrent ownership*, or *joint ownership*. Each owner has an equal right to possession of the property; no one owner can exclude another. It is similar to the way a husband and wife occupy the same home. In California, the types of co-ownership are tenancy in common, joint tenancy, community property, and tenancy in partnership. (See Table 3–1.)

Tenancy in common

Tenancy in common is a way of owning property with one or more people. You each have an equal right to possession, even though you may own unequal interests. When you die, your interest in the property goes to your heirs by your will (or by intestacy if you do not have a will).

In California, whenever two or more people who are not husband and wife acquire title to property, they are presumed to hold title as tenants in common, unless the deed specifies a different form of ownership.

Suppose you, Ted Gordon, and Homer Davey decide to buy a $100,000 parcel of property together. You and Homer each pay $25,000, and Ted contributes $50,000. The deed would read:

> *YOU as to a 25-percent interest, HOMER DAVEY as to a 25-percent interest, and TED GORDON as to a 50-percent interest.*

Since you are obviously not married, and since no specific form of ownership was designated in the deed, you would hold title as tenants in common. You and Homer would each receive 25-percent of the rent proceeds, and Ted Gordon would be credited with 50-percent of the property's income.

Joint tenancy

Joint tenancy is similar to tenancy in common, but it has some very vital differences:

1. If one joint tenant dies, his or her title immediately passes to the surviving joint tenant or joint tenants. It does not go to the heirs or become part of the estate. This ''right of survivorship'' is the most important feature of joint tenancy. Thus, if Jim and Mary are joint tenants and Jim dies, Mary becomes the sole owner of the property.

2. The interests of all joint tenants must be equal: If there are two, each must own one-half; if there are three, each must own one-third. All their interests must be created at the same time by the same document.

3. Because of the right of survivorship, the property is not subject to probate. Since it is not part of a probate estate, the property is not subject to a decedent's debts. Suppose that you and Ted Gordon held property as joint tenants, and Ted's one-half interest was worth $100,000,

Table 3–1 Methods of Owning Property

	Joint Tenancy	Tenancy in Common	Community Property
Definition:	Ownership by two or more people with right of survivorship	Ownership by two or more people without right of survivorship	Ownership by husband and wife as a kind of marital partnership
Deed Reads:	To A and B, as joint tenants	To A and B; also to A and B as tenants in common	To H and W; also to H and W as community property
Presumed:	Never presumed; must be created by express language in deed	Whenever two people not husband and wife acquire title	Whenever husband and wife acquire property
On Death:	Automatically goes to surviving joint tenants; will has no effect	Passes by will or by intestacy if no will	Spouse's one half passes by will or by intestacy if no will
% Ownership:	Can be any percentage; need not be equal	Must be equal between joint tenants	Is equal between spouses
Transfer:	Any tenant can transfer interest at any time without other's consent	Any tenant can transfer interest at any time without other's consent	Can only be transferred with consent of both spouses
Transferee:	Is tenant in common with remaining joint tenants who hold as joint tenants between themselves	Is tenant in common with remaining tenants in common	N.A.

and on his death Ted's only asset is the joint tenancy property. Further suppose that when Ted dies he owes his creditors $100,000. You would receive Ted's interest in the property, and Ted's creditors would get nothing.

To create a joint tenancy required four unities: unity of time, title, interest and possession. Unity of time requires all owners to acquire their interest at the same time. Unity of title requires the owners' rights come from the same document. Unity of interest requires each owner to have same equal interest as all other owners. Unity of possession requires that all owners have rights to possess the property.

Husbands and wives frequently take title to their homes in joint tenancy, although, as the book will later explain, community property may have specific tax advantages over joint tenancy.

No probate is required. On the death of a joint tenant, the surviving joint tenant only needs to record a certified copy of the death certificate and an affidavit of death of joint tenant. See Figure 3–2. No other procedures are required, which is one of the main reasons people favor joint tenancy.

Often, two unrelated people will take title in joint tenancy, so that the survivor will receive the property on the death of one of them. Two women rooming together may buy a house together in joint tenancy. Suppose that the women are named Alice and Rayna and that Alice by will has left her half interest in the property to her brother. If Alice dies, her half of the property will automatically, and without probate, go to Rayna.

Because joint tenancy prevents a person from leaving property by a will, the law allows joint tenancy to be easily changed to tenancy in common. Thus, in the above example, if Alice, without telling Rayna, deeded the property from herself as joint tenant to herself as a tenant in common, the joint tenancy would be severed. Now, Alice would own the property as a tenant in common, and on her death, Alice's one-half interest would pass to her brother by her will. Rayna would receive nothing.

To protect themselves, the women could have gone to an attorney to draft an agreement making the joint tenancy irrevocable without the consent of both of them. You should consider such a document if you ever buy property in joint tenancy with someone other than your spouse.

RECORDING REQUESTED BY

TED H. GORDON, ESQ.
GORDON, MC FARLAN, STEWART AND
BLECHER
HOLIDAY PLAZA, SUITE 475
1050 NORTH GATE DRIVE
SAN RAFAEL, CA 94903

AND WHEN RECORDED MAIL TO

Name JOHN SMITH
Street Address 1234 BROWN STREET
City & State SAN FRANCISCO, CA 98765

SPACE ABOVE THIS LINE FOR RECORDER'S USE

CAT. NO. NN00110
TO 426 CA (1–84)

Affidavit—Death of Joint Tenant

THIS FORM FURNISHED BY TICOR TITLE INSURANCE

ALL | PTN.

STATE OF CALIFORNIA,
County of SAN FRANCISCO } SS.

JOHN SMITH, of legal age, being first duly sworn, deposes and says:
That MARY SMITH, the decedent mentioned in the attached certified copy of Certificate of Death, is the same person as named as one of the parties in that certain DEED dated 1-1-42, executed by JOHN DOE to JOHN SMITH AND MARY SMITH, HUSBAND AND WIFE, as joint tenants, recorded as Instrument No. D302302, on 2-1-42, in Book/Reel 3202, Page/Image 202, of Official Records of SAN FRANCISCO County, California, covering the following described property situated in the CITY AND, County of SAN FRANCISCO, State of California:

Lot 1, Block 10 as shown on that certain map entitled "Gift Map No. 1" and filed for record on January 1, 1908 in the City and County of San Francisco, State of California

That the value of all real and personal property owned by said decedent at date of death, including the property above described, did not then exceed the sum of $ ______

Dated ______

JOHN SMITH

SUBSCRIBED AND SWORN TO before me

this ______ day of ______

Signature ______

(This area for official notarial seal)

Title Order No. ______ Escrow or Loan No. ______

Figure 3–2 (Affidavit–Death of Joint Tenant)

Community property

Community property is a special form of shared ownership *between husband and wife*. It comes down to us from Spanish and Mexican law and exists in only eight states, including California.

In California, all property acquired while a person is married and living with his or her spouse is presumed to be community property. Thus, a spouse's salary would be community property. A spouse's winnings from a television game show would also be community property. Interest and dividends received from community bank accounts and stock brokerage accounts would be community property.

There are several exceptions to the general rule that all property acquired by a married person in community property. The important special exceptions, that is, the important items that are separate property, are

1. Any property or money a person had before marriage.
2. Property or money acquired by gift or inheritance during marriage.
3. Earnings of married people who have separated and are living apart from each other.
4. Any property exchanged for separate property or bought with money that was separate property.
5. Income from separate property.

If any separate property becomes so *commingled* with community property so as to become indistinguishable from the community property, then it changes its character to community property.

California has attempted to equalize the rights of husband and wife in community property. The husband and wife have equal rights to control and manage the community property. However, if a business is run by one spouse, he or she has the control and management of the business.

Liability Community property is fully liable for the debts of either spouse run up before or after marriage. However, a spouse's earnings are not liable for another spouse's debts incurred before marriage. One spouse's separate property is liable for his or her debts whenever incurred. That party's separate property is generally not liable for the other spouse's debts incurred before or after marriage. However, separate property is generally liable for necessities of life furnished to either spouse. Finally, a spouse's separate property is only liable for a deed of trust or other encumbrance on community real property if that spouse consented in writing to binding his or her separate property.

Any sale, lien, or lease of community real property requires both spouses' signatures to be valid and binding.

Thus, in one famous case, the husband agreed to sell the family home, and he signed the deposit receipt. The wife never signed the deposit receipt and refused to sell. The court held that because both signatures were required for a valid sale, there never was a binding contract. Therefore, there was no sale, and the husband and wife had no obligation to honor the contract signed by only one spouse.

Joint tenancy versus community property

There is a widespread belief in the real estate business that married people should take title to real estate "as joint tenants." Then, so the story goes, when one spouse dies, the property will go directly to the surviving spouse without the expense of having to go through probate. Brokers, salesmen, and escrow officers frequently give this advice.

This advice is usually *wrong*! When property is rapidly increasing in value, as most California real estate has been, it is often best to hold title as community property. Because of tax technicalities, there may be a great savings in income tax when the survivor sells the property if the property is held as community property.

Additionally, the new California probate laws allow community property to pass to the surviving spouse by an inexpensive summary probate. Only a simple petition and order signed by the judge is needed in most cases. The surviving spouse usually does not even appear in court.

Still, this does not mean that a couple should necessarily take title "as community property." Only a knowledgeable attorney can advise which is the best way to take title. Only he or she can properly draw such an agreement between the spouses. But not all attorneys specialize in this area, so you must ask the attorney you consult with if this is a subject on which he or she has any special expertise.

How can a person find an attorney knowledgeable about such matters? A broker, escrow officer, or even another attorney can probably give you the name of someone. If not, in most urban areas the local bar association has a Lawyers Reference Service advertised in the yellow pages of the phone book under Attorneys. This service will refer you to a knowledgeable attorney who will, for $15 to $25, give a half hour of consultation and advice. This is usually all the time necessary to determine which form of ownership is best.

FORMS OF BUSINESS ENTITY

People may do business or own property as individuals, or they may band together into some sort of group, such as a partnership or a corporation. Such an individual or group is called a *business entity*. A person interested in real estate should have some knowledge of the more common forms of business entities.

Sole proprietorship

A sole proprietorship is a business owned by one individual. It is the usual way that the owner of a small business operates. The income from the business is his or hers, and he or she pays income tax on it as on any other earned income. The owner is liable for all its debts. He or she may or may not have employees.

Partnership

A partnership, as we said previously, is a group of two or more people who join together to conduct a business for profit. The partners run the business together. Partnership business should be done in the name of the partnership. Title to partnership property should be taken in the partnership name.

Under the law, each partner has the right to make contracts or execute documents that bind the whole partnership. This is true even if the partners have an agreement among themselves that a partner will not do these things by himself or herself. The agreement is binding between the partners and one can sue another for violating it. But third parties who do not know about it are not affected, which is a great disadvantage to the partnership as a form of business entity.

The other great disadvantage to the partnership form of doing business is that each partner has *unlimited liability* for partnership debts. That is, if the partnership owes money, a creditor has the right to collect all of it from any one partner. Suppose Abel and Baker are partners and the partnership goes broke, owing $100,000. The creditors have the right to collect their debts from Abel and Baker together, or from either one alone. They might choose to collect the full $100,000 from Abel. Abel would have the right to recover half from Baker—but this right would be worthless if Baker had no money or had disappeared.

No one should form a partnership or go into business with another person without the advice of an attorney. There are too many problems and pitfalls.

Joint venture

A joint venture might be called a "one-shot partnership." It is a group of two or more people joined together for profit on a *single project*. For example, a group of people may buy a lot together hoping to sell it later at a profit.

A joint venture is governed by almost all the same rules as a partnership. Each member has the same unlimited liability for debts as in a partnership.

Corporation

A corporation is an organization in which people own shares. These people, called, "shareholders" or "stockholders," elect a board of directors to guide and oversee the corporation. The board elects officers, such as president, vice president, and secretary, to manage the business. A corporation must obtain a charter from the state in which it incorporates. It may be small with few shareholders or assets, or it may be a multibillion-dollar company like General Motors Corporation.

The most important feature of a corporation is that for many purposes it is treated as a person by law. Therefore, it can sue and be sued in its own name, and if it has debts and liabilities, the corporation—not the shareholders—is liable. If there are not enough corporation assets to pay the debts, the creditors cannot collect from the shareholders. This *limited liability* of shareholders is a great advantage.

Limited partnerships

To enable partnerships to overcome the disadvantage of unlimited liability, most states, including California, allow the formation of *limited partnerships*. In a limited partnership there are one or more *general partners*. They run the business and have unlimited liability for all debts of the partnership.

In addition, other people are allowed to become *limited partners*. They have *no* liability; they can lose the money they invested, but they cannot be held for the debts or liabilities of the partnership. Limited partners may have only a very nominal part in managing the partnership; if they do more, they may become general partners and are liable for all partnership debts.

The limited partnership is a popular method of allowing a group of people to invest in real estate. Limited partners invest money and get the tax advantage of a partnership and the limited liability of corporation shareholders. "Passive" income, such as rents and interest, is taxed somewhat different from other income.

Most *syndications* formed in California to invest in real estate are limited partnerships. Often the general partner in a syndicate is a corporation.

Trusts

In a trust one person, called the *trustor*, gives money or conveys property to a second party, called the *trustee*, to hold and use for the benefit of a third person called the *beneficiary*. The powers of the trustee are set out in the document that appoints the trustee or by the state statutes. People set up trusts for various reasons—sometimes for tax advantages, sometimes to make sure that property is preserved and managed for a beneficiary. The law regarding taxation of a trust is too involved to discuss here. Because each trust is different, you will have to determine in each case whether the trustee may acquire or convey real estate and whether a court must approve the conveyance. Very often the trustee is a corporation, such as a bank or a trust company.

Real Estate Investment Trust A special form of trust is the Real Estate Investment Trust, often called a "REIT," in which investors buy shares. The trustee then invests the money in real estate or mortgages. The income and gains are distributed to the investors. There are *equity trusts* that invest in real estate, *mortgage trusts* that invest in mortgages, and *combination trusts* that invest in both.

REIT investors get special tax advantages under the Internal Revenue Code. REITs are fairly popular nationally. But in California the syndicate, in the form of a limited partnership, has been much more popular under the pre 1987 tax laws.

RECORDING AND CONSTRUCTIVE NOTICE

Under the Mexican and Spanish governments, there was no system for registering or recording documents affecting the conveyance of real property. After California became part of the United States, the legislature, as one of its first acts, adopted a recording system that would more fully inform those purchasing or investing in real property as to the ownerships and conditions of title. California adopted a recording system modeled after that of the earlier American states.

The basic purpose of the recording system is to protect against secret conveyances of land and provide a system that informs parties as to the conditions of title by inspection of the records. Under this system, recording is allowed but not usually required.

In California, an instrument may be recorded after it has been properly acknowledged or verified. An instrument affecting title to real property is recorded in the county where the property is located. When property lies in more than one county, it should be recorded in both counties. When an instrument is properly recorded, it gives *constructive notice* to all purchases or encumbrances of the conveyance of the property. This means that all persons are deemed to have knowledge of everything existing on the county records. Therefore, anyone dealing with property for which a instrument has been recorded would have notice. This would be true even if the person had not availed himself or herself of the opportunity to inspect the records and had no actual notice of the conveyance.

A distinction should be made at this time between constructive notice, which is imputed by law, and actual notice, which consists of actual knowledge of a fact. Thus, if a person records a valid instrument or document with the county recorder, constructive notice is given. For actual notice, he or she must go to the individual concerned and give such notice.

Recording an instrument does not necessarily make it valid. It may be void or ineffective before such recording. Examples of such instruments would be undelivered deeds or forged instruments or documents.

Let us now examine the effect of recording with an example. Adam, the owner of a vacant piece of land, conveys it to Brown by a grant deed. Brown, trusting Adam and not wishing to go to a great deal of work, accepts the grant deed but fails to record it with the county recorder. Adam, an unscrupulous individual, resells the same parcel of land to Cole. Cole has no knowledge of the prior conveyance and records the deed. Cole's deed will prevail over the deed of Brown. Brown will have to look to Adam for damages suffered.

However, if Cole had knowledge of the earlier conveyance, then Brown's deed would prevail, because if the person receiving the second conveyance has knowledge of a prior conveyance, his or her title will not stand, even though recorded. The recording statutes are designed to protect bona fide (good-faith) purchasers for value, and not the unscrupulous who attempt to perpetrate fraud.

A person has constructive notice not only of all recorded instruments but also of anything that person would have learned if he or she had asked the people in possession of the property. Suppose, in the above example, Adam's property had a house on it. And suppose Brown, while not recording his deed, went into possession or put a tenant in possession of the house. In this case, Brown's deed will prevail over Cole's. Why? Because if Cole by questioning the party in possession, Cole would have learned of Brown's deed; therefore, Cole has constructive notice of Brown's deed. So before you complete the purchase of property, you should get a written statement from the people in possession stating what their rights are, if you don't want unpleasant surprises later.

When an instrument has been deposited with the county recorder and properly acknowledged or verified, it is marked "filed for record" and at this time the deed is considered recorded. When a grant deed is filed, it is cross-indexed under the names of both grantor and grantee. Therefore anyone who knows one of these names may learn the other by inspecting the records.

It is seldom practical for an inexperienced person to determine the condition of a title by examining the records of the county recorder. It is much faster, safer, and more accurate to pay a title insurance company to prepare a report on the title called a *Preliminary Title Report*.

What instruments are entitled to be recorded? Any

instrument or judgment affecting the title or possession of real estate may be recorded. This includes deeds, mortgages, deeds of trust, contracts of sale, leases, agreements between property owners, and so forth.

If an instrument is not authorized by law to be recorded, and it is recorded by mistake, no constructive notice to third parties is given.

Certain instruments are not effective unless they are recorded. These include a power of attorney where it is needed to execute instruments that affect real property, declarations of homestead, declarations of abandonment of homestead, and the mechanics' liens. All of these will be discussed in later chapters.

CHAPTER QUESTIONS

1. Distinguish between ownership and tenancy interests as classified under estates and freehold estates.

2. List and explain the five principal ways in which a person may acquire title to property.

3. Name and discuss the three common types of wills.

4. Name and discuss five of the more common ways in which a person may take title to property.

5. State the basic purpose of a recording system, and distinguish between actual and constructive notice.

MULTIPLE-CHOICE QUESTIONS

1. A will entirely written, dated, and signed in the testator's own handwriting is called a: (1) statutory will; (b) holographic will; (c) intestate will; (d) witnessed will; (e) formal will.

2. Upon the death of a married woman intestate, her interest in *community property:* (a) is divided equally between her spouse and children; (b) all goes to the surviving spouse; (c) goes two-thirds to the surviving spouse and one-third to the children; (d) escheats to the state of California; (e) goes to her parents.

3. Which one of the following would be considered constructive notice? (a) Filed with a notary public; (b) notified in person; (c) notified by registered mail; (d) recorded in the county recorder's office; (e) filed with an attorney-at-law.

4. An interest acquired in real property by adverse possession differs from prescription in which of the following ways? (a) Five years' continuous use; (b) open and notorious; (c) against the will of the true owner; (d) title; (e) claim of right.

5. Property owned by a husband or wife is separate property if acquired: (a) before marriage; (b) after marriage with community property funds; (c) there can be no separate property after marriage; (d) in any of the foregoing cases; (e) in none of the foregoing cases.

6. A formal or a witnessed will in California requires: (a) two witnesses; (b) three witnesses; (c) no witnesses; (d) one witness; (e) five witnesses.

7. A grants an estate to B for the life of X. B dies. The estate: (a) goes to the heirs or devisees of B until X dies; (b) vests in X in trust until A's death; (c) reverts to the original owner; (d) ceases to exist; (e) goes to B's church.

8. A broker leases property from Mrs. Smith for five years. Mrs. Smith dies before the lease expires. It is learned after her death that she had only a life estate. The property reverts to heirs, and the heirs tell the broker to vacate. The lease was: (a) valid until the end of the lease; (b) valid only during the life of Mrs. Smith; (c) never valid because it extended over a period of more than one year; (d) valid and may be enforced by the heirs; (e) valid only if recorded in the county recorder's office.

9. A married couple may hold title: (a) as community property; (b) as tenants in common; (c) as joint tenants; (d) in any of the foregoing; (e) in none of the foregoing.

10. Mr. Baker was given real property for the term of his natural life. State which of the following statements is *incorrect:* (a) Baker has a freehold estate; (b) Baker has a fee simple estate; (c) a life estate can be a freehold estate; (d) a person holding a life estate does not have fee title; (e) Baker may not will his life estate.

LIENS
AND
ENCUMBRANCES

An *encumbrance,* broadly defined, is any claim, interest, or right in property possessed by another that may diminish the true owner's rights or value in the estate. It does not necessarily prevent the owner from transferring the fee or an interest therein, however. Encumbrances may be divided into two categories: liens (encumbrances or debts that affect title) and encumbrances that restrict the use or affect the physical condition of the property. These will be discussed separately.

LIENS

A lien makes the debtor's property security for the payment of a debt or discharge of an obligation. Typical examples of liens are trust deeds, mortgages, mechanic's liens, taxes, special assessments, attachments, and judgments. Trust deeds and mortgages are considered in Chapter 8.

Real property liens may be classified as *specific liens* and *general liens.* The specific lien affects a specified parcel of real property, whereas the general lien affects all parcels of the debtor's property. Examples of specific liens would include mechanic's liens, property taxes and assessments, trust deeds and mortgages, agreement of sale, and attachments. An example of a general lien would be a general judgment rendered by a court of proper jurisdiction.

Liens may further be classified as *statutory liens* and *equitable liens.* A statutory lien is one created by statute, such as the mechanic's lien. Equitable liens are liens that the court of equity will enforce mainly because of the circumstance; right and justice would seem to require such action. For example: A orally agrees to sell land to

B. The statute of frauds requires that this contract be in writing. Under the oral agreement, B enters upon the property and constructs valuable improvements thereon. A refuses to follow through with the conveyance. B sues A after A refuses to convey property to B. In most states the court would require a conveyance by A. To do otherwise would permit an unjust enrichment at the expense of B.

An equitable lien would also arise if the owner entered into a written contract or agreement to borrow money on his land.

Mechanic's liens

The law in California expressly provides that all persons who perform their labor or furnish materials for the improvement of real property will be paid. This is true even if the property upon which these persons worked or furnished materials must be sold. It matters not that the owner of the property has paid the contractor in full; if the contractor has not paid his employees, those employees may file a lien upon the property in question for the amount due them. Thus if Jones, a homeowner, employs Smith, a carpenter, to put a new roof on his house and Smith performs under the contract, Smith is entitled to file a lien upon Jones's property if Jones does not pay him as stated in the contract. Let us assume that Jones pays Smith but Smith fails to pay his employees. These workers have performed their work and have the right to be paid. They, too, may file a lien against Jones's property. In this case, if Jones has already paid Smith, Jones would have to file for money damages against Smith, the contractor. This same right extends to material suppliers, architects, contractors, builders, and all persons of every category who provide labor or other services, or furnish materials or equipment that contributes to the improvements of the real property. The California Civil Code list of persons entitled to mechanic's liens is limited to the materials furnished and to the persons who perform labor. In order for the mechanic's lien to be valid, it must be based upon a valid contract with the contractor or vendor.

A preliminary notice, in writing, must be given by the prospective claimant to the owner, his agent, general contractor, and lender within *twenty days* of the first furnishing of labor, equipment, or materials. Such notice may be hand-delivered or mailed (first class, registered, or certified). The notice must contain (1) a description of labor furnished; (2) a description of equipment or materials furnished; (3) the name and address of the person who contracted for the purchase of the labor; (4) a description of the job site; and (5) a statement that if bills are not paid in full for the labor, material, and equipment furnished, the improved property may be subject to a mechanic's lien. The lender's copy must contain an estimate of the total cost of labor, equipment, and materials furnished. Where notice is not given within the twenty-day period, it may be given later, but claim rights may be subordinated.

The mechanic's lien dates back to the start of the project involved; therefore, it is crucial to determine exactly when work commenced on the improvement. Courts are sometimes asked to determine the priority of a mechanic's lien or a deed of trust. In defining commencement time, a California appellate court has stated:

> Some work and labor on the ground, the effects of which are apparent—easily seen by everybody; such as beginning to dig the foundation or work of like description, which everyone can readily see and recognize as the commencement of a building.*

After it has been filed with the county recorder, the mechanic's lien has priority over all other liens, including mortgages, deeds of trust, or other encumbrances attached after the building was commenced or the first materials were furnished. Real property taxes and assessments do have priority over the mechanic's lien. If the worker or contractor had no notice of another lien, and no lien was recorded when the work on the improvement first began, such a lien has priority over any other lien. (See Figure 4–1.)

Notice of completion   It is crucial that the owner establish the exact time to the day when the improvement is completed. The owner may do so by filing a *Notice*

*Simons Brick Co. v. Hetzel, 72 C.A. 1.

of Completion with the county recorder in the county in which the property is located. Such notice must be verified rather than acknowledged by the owner or the owner's agent. The property owner or the agent has ten days in which to file the Notice of Completion from the date of the completion of work on the improvement. (See Figure 4–2.)

What constitutes the completion of a building or structure? The completion of an improvement would be any of the following:

1. The formal acceptance by the owner or the owner's agent of the work of improvement

2. The occupation of the improvement or its use by the property owner or the owner's agent and cessation of labor

3. Cessation of labor for a period of thirty days or more; the owner files a *Notice of Cessation* with the county recorder

4. Cessation of labor for a period of sixty days

Time limit to file lien   The owner usually protects himself or herself against mechanic's liens by making contract payments in stages, withholding payments until receipt of copies of bills for previous work marked paid, and withholding the last payment until the time for filing a lien has expired. It is very important to promptly record the Notice of Completion (or cessation of labor) to begin the time for which all mechanic's liens must be filed. If a mechanic does not file within the specified time period, he or she cannot obtain payment through the procedure of a mechanic's lien.

An *original contractor*—one who deals and contracts directly with the owner or the owner's agent—must file a lien within sixty days after a Notice of Completion has been filed by the owner or the agent. All persons claiming moneys due, other than the original contractor, have thirty days after the recording of the Notice of Completion in which to file their liens. If no Notice of Completion has been filed by the owner or the agent, both the original contractor and all others have ninety days from the completion of the project in which to file their liens. The original contractor and other claimants must move to enforce their liens within ninety days after the filing of such liens if they are to use the services of the court.

Assume Ted Gordon hires a contractor to build a new room on his house. Ted could pay the general contractor in stages, such as 20 percent when the foundation is poured and the subfloor is installed, 20 percent when the walls are framed and the roof is on, 20 percent when the walls are finished and painted, and 20 percent when the room is finished. Ted could then pay the final 20 percent thirty-one days after the Notice of Completion is recorded. Since all subcontractors, material suppliers, and

RECORDING REQUESTED BY

Henry C. Doe

AND WHEN RECORDED MAIL TO

Name   Henry C. Doe
Street   9898 April Way
Address Sunnyvale, California
City &
State

——— SPACE ABOVE THIS LINE FOR RECORDER'S USE ———

Mechanic's Lien

The undersigned .... Henry C. Doe ....
(Name of person or firm claiming mechanic's lien. Contractors use name exactly as it appears on contractor's license.)

Claimant, claims a mechanic's lien upon the following described real property: in the

City of ...... Cupertino ...., County of .... Santa Clara .... California,

20653 Ronald Drive, Cupertino, CA. Lot 4, Block 10, Tract 1234. Recorded 1973
General description of property where the work or materials were furnished.
A street address is sufficient, but if possible, use both street address and legal description.

in Book 112 at page 73, Official Records of Santa Clara County, California ....

The sum of $95.00 (Ninety-five and no/100 dollars.)~~~~~~~ together with interest thereon
(Amount of claim due and unpaid)

at the rate of ....7.. percent per annum from .... May 6 .... , 19 82
(Date when balance became due)

is due claimant (after deducting all just credits and offsets) for the following work and materials furn-

ished by claimant ..Labor on painting the above described property improvements,..........
(Insert general description of work or materials furnished)

///
....

Claimant furnished the work and materials at the request of, or under contract with ....
....
Henry C. Doe
(Name of person or firm who ordered or contracted for the work or materials)

The owners and reputed owners of the property are .... Robert Jones and May Jones ....
//
(Insert name of owner of real property. This can be obtained from the County Recorder
or by checking the building permit application at the Building Department)

SEE REVERSE SIDE FOR   Firm Name   Henry C. Doe
COMPLETE INSTRUCTIONS   By: ....
                                          (Signature of claimant or authorized agent)

VERIFICATION

I, the undersigned, say I am the .... owner of ....
"President of," "Manager of," "A partner of," "Owner of," etc.

the claimant of the foregoing mechanic's lien. I have read said claim of mechanic's lien and know the

contents thereof; the same is true of my own knowledge.

I declare under penalty of perjury that the foregoing is true and correct.

Executed on   May 6, 1982   at ..... San Jose ...., California
                                          (City where signed)

....
Personal signature of the individual who is swearing that the
contents of the claim of mechanic's lien are true.

Crowley's Form No. 379 - MECHANIC'S LIEN   Printed 5/71

Figure 4–1

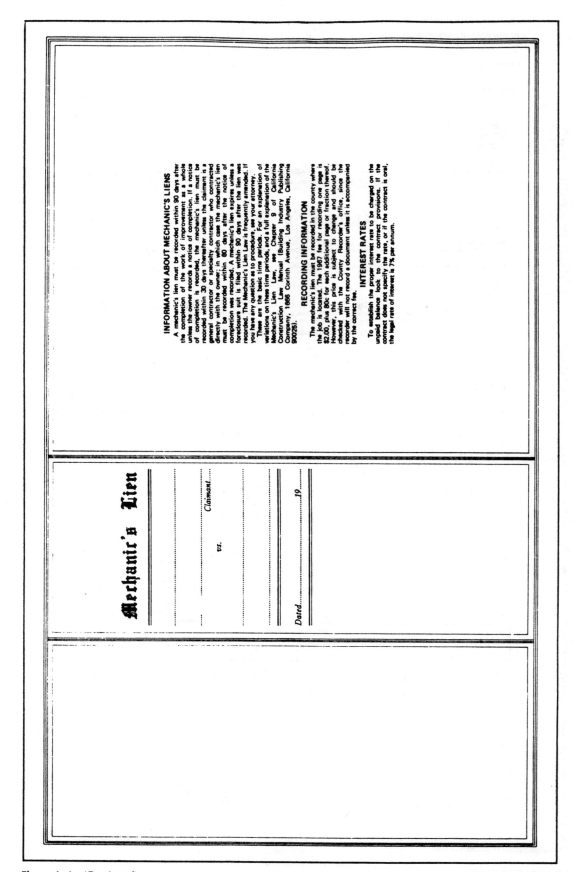

Figure 4–1 (Continued)

28

RECORDING REQUESTED BY

TED H. GORDON, ESQ.
GORDON, MC FARLAN, STEWART AND BLECHER
HOLIDAY PLAZA, SUITE 475

AND WHEN RECORDED MAIL TO

1050 NORTH GATE DRIVE
SAN RAFAEL, CA 94903

Name: Ted H. Gordon, Esq.
Gordon, McFarlan, Stewart and Blecher
Street Address: Holiday Plaza, Suite 475
1050 North Gate Drive
City & State: San Rafael, CA 94903

SPACE ABOVE THIS LINE FOR RECORDER'S USE

INDIVIDUAL FORM

Notice of Completion

TO 1927 CA (3-75)

Before execution, refer to title company requirements stated on reverse side. A. P. N.

Notice is hereby given that:

1. The undersigned is owner of the interest or estate stated below in the property hereinafter described.
2. The full name of the undersigned is John Adam Buyer
3. The full address of the undersigned is 123 Pine Street, San Francisco, CA 94111
4. The nature of the title of the undersigned is: In fee.
   (If other than fee, strike "In fee" and insert, for example, "purchaser under contract of purchase," or "lessee".)
5. The full names and full addresses of all persons, if any, who hold title with the undersigned as joint tenants or as tenants in common are:

NAMES	ADDRESSES
Jane Louise Buyer	123 Pine Street, San Francisco, CA 94111

6. The names of the predecessors in interest of the undersigned, if the property was transferred subsequent to the commencement of the work of improvement herein referred to:

NAMES	ADDRESSES
N/A	

(If no transfer made, insert "none".)

7. A work of improvement on the property hereinafter described was completed on July 1, 1985
8. The name of the contractor, if any, for such work of improvement was ABC Construction Company, General Contractor
   (If no contractor for work of improvement as a whole, insert "none".)
9. The property on which said work of improvement was completed is in the City of San Francisco, County of San Francisco, State of California, and is described as follows: Lots 5 and 6, in Block 5, in the City of San Francisco, County of San Francisco, State of California, as per Map recorded in Book 11 Page 68 of Miscellaneous Records in the office of the County Recorder of said County.
10. The street address of said property is NONE
    (If no street address has been officially assigned, insert "none".)

Dated: July 15, 1985

Signature of owner named in paragraph 2
(Also sign verification below at X)

STATE OF CALIFORNIA,
COUNTY OF } SS.

John Adam Buyer
John Adam Buyer

The undersigned, being duly sworn, says: That __he is the owner of the aforesaid interest or estate in the property described in the foregoing notice; that __he has read the same, and knows the contents thereof, and that the facts stated therein are true.

SUBSCRIBED AND SWORN TO before me

Signature of owner named in paragraph 2 X John Adam Buyer

on

Signature

Notary Public in and for said State

Title Order No.
Escrow or Loan No.

SEE REVERSE SIDE FOR TITLE COMPANY REQUIREMENTS AS TO NOTICE OF COMPLETION

(This area for official notarial seal)

Figure 4–2

laborers have only thirty days after recordation to record a mechanic's lien, on the thirty-first day Ted would be sure no one but the general contractor could file a lien. Ted would then be safe paying the remaining 20 percent. Of course, these stages are only an example, and the contractor and owner usually establish their own percentages and stages.

Release of mechanic's liens   Mechanic's liens may be released by a document entitled Release of Mechanic's Lien, shown in Figure 4–3.

Notice of non-responsibility   A property owner may give notice to all persons concerned that he or she may not be held responsible for the work being done by tenants or other persons occupying the property. This is accomplished by filing a verified copy of a Notice of Non-Responsibility (Figure 4–4) with the county recorder in the county in which the property is located and by posting a copy of it in a conspicuous place on the property within ten days of having actual or constructive notice of the work. Let us assume that Alice, the owner of a duplex, notices that one of her tenants is having painting done by a contractor on the interior of his apartment. Alice, not wanting to be responsible, immediately files a verified copy of a Notice of Non-Responsibility with the county recorder, and another is posted on a conspicuous part of the property. This gives constructive notice that Alice, owner of the property, will not be responsible for improvements being done, and the contractor or material suppliers must look to the tenants for their compensation. Legal advice should be sought by the property owners to verify that all code requirements are met.

Filing contract and recording bond   A mechanic's lien must be founded upon a valid contract either expressed or implied. The valid contract may be executed by the owner or the owner's agent.

If the original contract and a *statutory labor and material bond* are filed before work is commenced, the liability of the owner is limited to the amount equal to what he or she owes the contractor at the time the liens are claimed. The amount of the bond must be not less than 75 percent of the contract price and conditioned for payment in full of all lien claimants. In the event liens are filed, judgment is rendered against the contractor. The owner or the owner's agent may deposit with the court any sum of money owed to the contractor, and the court will issue an order freeing the property from the mechanic's liens recorded.

Progress payments   Construction lenders who lend money to an owner to finance the project or improvement will withhold certain funds to ensure that the moneys will be used for construction purposes. Under an agreed pay-out plan, certain of these moneys will be advanced to the contractor when certain phases of the project have been completed.

Stop notice   An unpaid subcontractor, material supplier, or laborer can serve a *stop notice* on a lender, an owner, or anyone else who holds funds for the project. A stop notice directs the person not to pay the general contractor sums due the unpaid mechanic. In effect, it is almost like ''attaching'' the unpaid funds.

The notice may be filed at any time prior to the lien expiration period. A bond must accompany the stop notice in an amount equal to one and one-quarter times the claim. Furthermore, a preliminary notice must be given to the lender within twenty days after the first furnishing of such materials and labor.

Federal tax liens

Federal income tax

The Internal Revenue Code provides that any internal revenue taxes unpaid after demand is made become a lien on all property and property rights of the person who is liable. This lien exists from the time the assessment list is received by the collector. The lien is valid against any mortgagee, purchaser, or judgment creditor only when constructive notice is given by filing *notice* of the lien in the county where the land is located.

Federal gift and estate taxes

The federal government imposes a tax on gifts made during lifetime and estates left at death. At one time federal gift and estate taxes were separate, but the Tax Reform Act of 1976 combined them into one tax system. The gifts a person makes during lifetime are added to the transfers by will or inheritance at his or her death.

You can give $10,000 ($20,000 for a husband and wife together) per year to any one person without paying any gift taxes. Any sum over that amount either is taxed or is deducted from the lifetime estate tax credit. The tax credit increases to a maximum of $600,000 in 1987. Generally, you can pass by will or by intestacy up to $600,000 in property (if you have not used any of the amount by lifetime gifts).

The rules governing gift and estate taxes are fantastically complicated. But a taxpayer may avoid part of these taxes by careful estate planning through legal counsel, especially when done before a person has accumulated a large estate.

Unemployment tax

Both the federal and the state governments have acts covering unemployment compensation. The tax is levied against the employer only, and tax forms may be obtained

Ted Gordon, Esq.
Gordon, McFarlan, Stewart and Blecher
Holiday Plaza, Suite 475
1050 North Gate Drive
AND WHEN RECORDED MAIL TO
San Rafael, CA 94903

Name	Ted Gordon, Esq.
	Gordon, McFarlan, Stewart & Blecher
Street Address	Holiday Plaza, Suite 475
	1050 North Gate Drive
City & State	San Rafael, CA 94903

——— SPACE ABOVE THIS LINE FOR RECORDER'S USE ———

Release of Mechanic's Lien

THIS FORM FURNISHED BY TICOR TITLE INSURERS

TO 429 CA (3-76)

Know All Men by These Presents:

THAT the Mechanic's Lien claimed by _Great Construction Company, a California corporation_

against * _John Buyer and Jane Buyer_

upon the following described real property in the _City and_
County of _San Francisco_, State of California:

Lots 5 and 6, in Block 5, in the City of San Francisco, County of San Francisco, State of California, as per Map recorded in Book 11 Page 68 of Miscellaneous Records in the office of the County Recorder of said County.

is hereby released, the claim thereunder having been fully paid and satisfied, and that certain Notice of Mechanic's Lien recorded as Instrument No. _D216504_ on _July 10, 1985_, in Book/Reel _D102699_, Page/Image _951_, Official Records of _San Francisco_ County, California, is hereby satisfied and discharged.

Dated _July 1, 1985_

STATE OF CALIFORNIA
COUNTY OF_____ } SS.
On_____ before me, the undersigned, a Notary Public in and for said State, personally appeared

_____
_____
_____, known to me
to be the person___ whose name_____subscribed to the within
instrument and acknowledged that_____executed the same.
WITNESS my hand and official seal.

Signature_____

Great Construction Company, a California

Corporation

By: _____
        Vice President

Title Order No._____

Escrow or Loan No._____

(This area for official notarial seal)

*_Owner or purported Owner and Contractor as named in Notice of Mechanic's Lien._

Figure 4–3

RECORDING REQUESTED BY

James C. Propertyowner

AND WHEN RECORDED MAIL TO

Name James C. Propertyowner
Street Address 12345 Sunnyland Court
City & State Los Altos, CA. 94022

SPACE ABOVE THIS LINE FOR RECORDER'S USE

Notice of Non-Responsibility

NOTICE is hereby given that my name is James C. Propertyowner *(print name)* *and that I am* owner in fee *(*nature of estate or interest)* *in the following described site:*

2972-76 December Court, San Jose, California.
(street address and legal description sufficient for identification of real property)
Lots 4, 5, and 6; Block 10, Tract 10245 as shown by Map. Recorded May 4, 1979 in Book 203 of Map at page 75, Official Records of Santa Clara County, California.

*That ***No one** *purchaser....... under contract of said property;*

*That **** Eriz J. Tenant-- is the *Lessee........ of said property* Apartment No. 13

That within 10 days I have obtained knowledge that a work of improvement is being constructed on the described real property (site).

That I will not be responsible for any claims rising from the work of improvement.

James C. Propertyowner
(signature)

*I, the undersigned state: That I am ** the owner in fee *of the property described in the foregoing notice; that I have read the foregoing notice, and know the contents thereof, and that the facts therein stated are true of my own knowledge; and that the foregoing notice is a full, true, and correct copy of a notice in writing posted in a conspicuous place on said property on* August 9 *, 19* 82

I declare under penalty of perjury that the foregoing is true and correct.

Executed at San Jose *, California, on* August 9, *, 19*82

James C. Propertyowner
(signature)

This document is only a general form which may be proper for use in simple transactions and in no way acts, or is intended to act, as a substitute for the advice of an attorney. The publisher does not make any warranty, either express or implied as to the legal validity of any provision or the suitability of these forms in any specific transaction.

Cowdery's Form No. 807—Notice of Non-Responsibility (C.C. Sec. 3094)

Figure 4–4

Notice of Non-Responsibility

Dated...................., 19........

DO NOT RECORD

* Insert "owner in fee" or "a lessee" or "A joint tenancy" or nature of interest in the real property (site).

** If the real property is being purchased under a contract of sale, insert purchaser's name; otherwise insert "no one."

*** If the property is under lease, insert lessee's name if known or "unknown" if not known; if property is not under lease insert "no one."

SECTION 3094 Civil Code of CALIFORNIA

"Notice of non-responsibility" means a written notice, signed and verified by a person owning or claiming an interest in the site who has not caused the work of improvement to be performed, or his agent, containing all of the following:

(a) A description of the site sufficient for identification.
(b) The name and nature of the title or interest of the person giving the notice.
(c) The name of the purchaser under contract, if any, or lessee, if known.
(d) A statement that the person giving the notice will not be responsible for any claims arising from the work of improvement.

Within 10 days after the person claiming the benefits of nonresponsibility has obtained knowledge of the work of improvement, the notice provided for in this section shall be posed in some conspicuous place on the site. Within the same 10 day period provided for the posting of the notice, the notice shall be recorded in the office of the county recorder of the county in which the site or some part thereof is located.

Figure 4–4 (Continued)

from the district director of Internal Revenue. The tax is due from the employer once a year, within one month of the end of the tax year. The employer is allowed a credit up to 90-percent for state unemployment taxes paid, and this credit is limited to 90-percent of the federal taxable payroll.

State taxes liens

State income tax

In many respects, California income tax laws are patterned after the federal. There are many differences, however, that are beyond the scope of discussion in this text.

Penalties may be imposed for failure to file a return and also for underpayment of the tax by the original or extended due date. Interest must be added to any tax due when it is not paid by the due date, even though an extension of time to file the return has been granted. State income taxes become a lien on an individual's real and personal property when notice is filed with the clerk of the court of proper jurisdiction.

Gift and inheritance tax

California abolished its gift and inheritance taxes, beginning January 1, 1981.

Technically, California retained a limited inheritance tax, called a ''pick-up'' tax, which is really a revenue-sharing measure. It allows California to receive part of the federal estate tax. However, it imposes no new taxes and does not cost the taxpayer any additional tax. So, for all practical purposes, California has no inheritance or gift taxes.

Real and personal property taxes

Both counties and cities collect taxes to provide funds for local government expenses. The board of supervisors sets the tax rate for the county. Some cities make their own assessed valuations, in which case the city council performs the same function as the county board of supervisors. The county may arrange with the city to handle all tax assessments and collections for them. If the person owns both personal and real property, the personal property tax is a lien on the real property. This is true of both city and county property taxes.

Taxes become a lien on the real property at 12:01 A.M. on the first day of March preceding the tax year, which in California is July 1 through June 30. Therefore, property taxes for the year 1986–87 became a lien on real property the first day of March 1986. When a person owns no real property and owns only taxable personal property, these taxes must be paid by 5:00 P.M. August 31 of the tax year. Taxes may be paid in two installments. The first installment of taxes is due November 1. This installment of taxes becomes delinquent if not paid in full by 5:00 P.M. December 10. The second installment of taxes on the real property is due February 1 and is delinquent if not paid in full by 5:00 P.M. April 10. If an installment of taxes is not paid by the delinquent deadline, a penalty is added to it. If the due date should fall on a Saturday, Sunday, or holiday, the taxes will be due on the next business day. Therefore, a tax statement might give as a due date December 12 instead of December 10.

If taxes are not paid at the end of the taxable year, the tax collector will publish the delinquent list on or before June 8, listing the properties and the owner's name in a newspaper of general circulation. The property is *sold to the state*—a ''stamped'' sale—approximately thirty days after the first publication of the delinquent list. This sale merely starts a five-year redemption period running, and at anytime during the five years the property owner or a *successor in interest* may redeem the property by paying the taxes plus all penalties. A successor in interest, for example, may be a relative or a creditor.

If the property is not redeemed, it is deeded to the state, and it may be sold at a public auction for cash. Such a sale is usually initiated by a prospective purchaser or the county tax collector.

Real property taxes are an *ad valorem tax* (Latin for ''according to value'') based on the assessed valuation of the property; that is, each property has a tax proportionate to its value. Since the passage of *Proposition XIII* in 1979, all property is taxed at its *full cash value*. The basic tax value is the property's full cash value for the 1975–76 tax year. Every year after 1975 tax year, the value can increase by only 2 percent per year. The taxes are one percent of the full cash value.

Thus, if you owned a home worth $100,000 in 1975, your taxes would be one percent of that amount, or $1,000. Next year your full cash value could only increase by two percent ($2,000), so that your value would be $102,000 and your taxes would be $1,020. The next year two percent of $102,000 would be $2,040, so the full cash value would be $104,040 and real estate taxes would be $1,040.

Any time the property is sold, the full cash value is readjusted to an assessor's determination of its approximate fair market value. Assuming that a homeowner paid taxes of $1,900 per year and that you bought the home for $400,000, your taxes would be one percent of the full cash value, which would be $4,000. The next year your value would rise to $408,000 and your taxes would be $4,080.

Any time the property has new construction, that new construction is taxed at its then full cash value. Assume that in 1986 you added a new room to a home you have owned since 1981. The full cash value of the new room would be based on its 1986 value and would increase two percent per year thereafter. However, the rest of your home would have its 1981 full cash value, which kept increasing at two percent per year. Thus, different parts of your home would have different base years.

Homeowner's exemption   If a homeowner owned a home prior to March 1 preceding the taxable year, he is eligible for a homeowner's exemption, which amounts to $7,000 of the *full cash value* of a property. Under a 1974 law, the government renews the exemption each year without the homeowner's having to file a new claim, if the homeowner remains eligible. The government mails these claims, which must be filed by April 15 preceding the tax year, to new homeowners.

Any homeowner who has received the exemption and later becomes ineligible should notify the assessor either by returning the "Notice of Circumstances of Eligibility," which the assessor's office mails each March, or by giving written notice. If the homeowner fails to do either by June 30, he or she must pay a penalty assessment required by law. If a homeowner moved before March 1 and sold his or her dwelling shortly after this date, the homeowner still must notify the assessor that he or she is not eligible for the exemption. If a homeowner believes he or she was eligible for the exemption on March 1 and it does not appear on the tax bill, the homeowner has until December 1 to make a late filing for 80 percent of the exemption.

Veterans' exemption   The veterans' exemption excludes from property taxation $4,000 of the *assessed* value of taxable property owned by a veteran of the armed services, the unmarried spouse of a deceased veteran, or the parent of a deceased veteran. Eligible persons must own property valued at less than $20,000 for single persons and $40,000 for married persons to qualify for the exemption. Because of the low values required to qualify, the exemption is rarely used.

Senior citizens and totally disabled persons   The Gonsalves-Deukmejiam-Petris Senior Citizens Property Tax Assistance Law provides cash reimbursement for part of the property taxes to qualified senior citizens who will be 62 or older on December 31 or totally disabled persons of any age. The filing period for claims based on 1986–87 taxes would run from May 16 to August 31, 1987.

The Senior Citizens Property Tax Postponement Law gives eligible senior citizens the option of having the state pay all or part of the taxes on their homes. In return, a lien is placed on the property for the amount the state pays. The lien is payable when the taxpayer moves or dies. The filing period for claims for postponement of 1986–87 taxes runs from May 16 to December 31, 1987.

Eligibility requirements are similar for the assistance program and the postponement program. A claimant may qualify for one program or for both. Additional information may be obtained by writing to: Senior Citizens Programs, Post Office Box 1588, Sacramento, California 95807.

Special assessments   Special assessments differ from property taxes in that they are in support of the local government function. If approved by the voters, special assessments may be levied (for the cost of certain local improvements such as the construction and maintenance of schools, sewers, irrigation, and drainage). The assessments may be paid by the property owner over a period of years or, in some cases, the property owner may pay cash in one payment. In any event, these assessments are specific liens against real property, and when created they are usually on a parity with general tax liens.

The district generally issues its own bonds to finance the improvements and then through their power of assessment will assess all lands in the district on an *ad valorem* basis. Such liens can be foreclosed by sale, and their rights are prior to private property interests.

Sales and use tax   California imposes a sales tax on retailers who sell personal property. The retailer is responsible for the tax even though it is not collected. A use tax is imposed upon storage, use, or other consumption if the retailer purchases or leases personal property. This use tax is the liability of the purchaser and continues to be so until paid to the state unless the state authorizes the retailer to collect the tax from the purchaser. The State Board of Equalization administers the sales and use tax. This Board has offices throughout California and questions should be referred to them. Licensees involved in the sales of mobile homes and business opportunities are well advised to make such contact.

Worker's compensation law   An employer has a legal responsibility for an employee injured on the job and must be covered by worker's compensation insurance. This insurance provides for weekly benefit payments to employees unable to work because of an industrial injury or job-related illness. Real estate brokers, in signing a salesman's application, state that they are aware of the workman's compensation laws. Problems may arise in areas of independent contractors versus employee relationship. Brokers should refer to Sections 3351–3700 of the California Labor Code and, if in doubt, carry workman's compensation insurance.

Attachment liens

Because of the need to post a bond in order to obtain a prejudgment attachment, and the restrictions on the types of cases in which these attachments are allowed, such attachments are not very common on California real estate.

Such a lien is obtained prior to the entry of a judgment so that assurances will be given to the plaintiff that the property will be available to sustain his or her judgment, assuming that judgment will be in favor of the plaintiff.

Judgment liens

A *judgment* is the final decree or determination by a court of competent jurisdiction as to the rights of the parties involved. The final decree or determination is always subject to appeal to a higher court which, of course, may reverse, amend, or affirm the decision of the lower court. After the time period for such appeals has passed, the judgment becomes final. Once the decree of any court is recorded with the county recorder in the county or counties where the nonexempt property of the judgment debtor is located, the judgment becomes a lien.

Judgment liens are very common and are an excellent way to collect a judgment. You normally record a one-page summary of the judgment, called an *abstract of judgment*. (See Figure 4–5.) For ten years from the date of the judgment, the judgment lien exists against all non-exempt real property owned by the judgment debtor. After ten years, you can return to court and have the unsatisfied judgment renewed for another ten years.

Assume you have a judgment against Ted Gordon. If you record an abstract in Marin County and in San Francisco County, it becomes a lien against Ted Gordon's property. If Ted now has or later acquires any property within those two counties within the ten-year period of the judgment, you automatically have a lien against that property. You can foreclose to satisfy your lien, or you can wait until Ted's property is ultimately sold. Upon sale, you would automatically collect the amount of your judgment if there were adequate proceeds from the sale.

ENCUMBRANCES

Encumbrance is a generic term that includes liens. A lien is a particular type of encumbrance. An encumbrance affects the title or use of property, or affects the physical condition of the property. A lien arises from a debt.

Easements.

An *easement* is an interest that one has in the land of another that entitles him to a limited use or enjoyment of the land. Easements are of two classes: easements appurtenant and easements in gross.

Easements appurtenant   An easement appurtenant is said to "run with the land." Such an easement is created for the benefit of and belongs to a particular tract of land; therefore, two tenements exist as illustrated in Figure 4–5: the *dominant tenement* and the *servient tenement*. The dominant tenement has the benefit of the easement and the servient tenement is burdened with the easement. For example, Adam is the owner of Green Acre, Brown the owner of Black Acre. Brown grants Adam an easement over the east twenty feet of his lot for road purposes. Brown has what is called the servient tenement, and Adam the dominant tenement.

Adam now transfers his property to Smith. The easement that Adam acquired is transferred to Smith and is said "to run with the land." It does not matter that the easement is not mentioned in the grant that Adam gives. The fact that Adam gives a grant deed to Smith means that Smith automatically gains the easement, or the right that Adam has in the property.

Easements in gross   An easement in gross is a personal right in the land of another with no dominant tenement. Such a right does not attach to the land owned by the easement holder; therefore, easements in gross must be expressly transferred. Examples of easements in gross would include easements held by utility and telephone companies.

The easement is called *in gross* because a person or, in this case, a corporation owns the easement, instead of its belonging to a specific, neighborhood parcel of property.

Creation of easements

Although easements may be created in a number of different ways, they are usually created by express grant, express reservation, operation of law, prescription, dedication, and condemnation. We shall concern ourselves in the text only with easements created by express grant, express reservation, operation of law, or prescription. Easements may also be created by agreement between adjoining landowners, but they are usually created by deeds.

Deed grant or reservation   Because easements by express grant or express reservation are usually created by deeds, all of the necessary essentials of a deed must be present. Such essential elements include

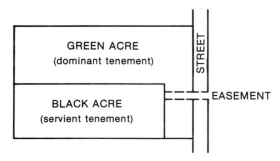

Figure 4–5

1. Proper description of the parties.
2. Granting clause or operative words of a conveyance.
3. Sufficient description of the easement so that it can be easily located.
4. Execution of the instrument by the grantor.
5. Proper delivery.

A deed conveying fee simple title to a parcel of land may be void where the description is indefinite, but a deed to an unlocated easement might be valid. For example, a twenty-foot easement "over lot 23" would be valid, although the exact location might not be specified. Such location could be determined by agreement of the parties or subsequently by use.

An easement created by reservation might be made when a landowner sells a portion of his or her land and desires to reserve for himself or herself an easement over a portion of the property. Such a description might read as follows:

> *The North ½ of the Northeast ¼ of section 17, Township 1 South, Range 2 East, Mt. Diablo Base Line and Meridian. Grantors reserve for themselves, their heirs, and assigns an easement appurtenant over the west thirty feet of said parcel of land for ingress and egress.*

Implied easements Assume that Ted Gordon has two adjoining parcels of property or that he has one parcel of land, and that Ted will be selling off part of the land. Also assume that you are buying the part called parcel "B" and that the part Ted retains is called parcel "T".

If there is no mention in your deed about any easements, the law will allow you to obtain an *implied easement* over any preexisting use that was obvious and that was permanently used by Ted. For example, if Ted used a dirt roadway across parcel T to get to parcel B, then when you buy parcel B you are entitled by implication to retain use of that roadway as an easement.

If Ted sold parcel B and found that his parcel T was landlocked, with no means of ingress or egress, Ted could force an *easement by necessity* across your parcel B. Ted must show a strict necessity, with no other way to the street, to obtain this easement.

Easement by prescription In California, an easement by prescription may be acquired by adverse use. If you walk through a path across your neighbor's land continuously for five years on your way to work, you could have an easement by prescription. You must go to court to prove your use. The neighbor cannot now interfere with your use, nor can the owner build on or fence across your easement.

Certain essential elements are necessary, however, to establish such an easement:

1. There must be open and notorious use of the easement.
2. Its use must be continuous and uninterrupted for a period of five years.
3. It must be hostile to the true owner's wishes.
4. The person so claiming must claim some right of use.

In order to prevent easements by prescription from being created, the owner can post a special sign at the entrance to the property or along its boundaries every two-hundred-feet. The sign must state "Right to pass by permission, and subject to control, of owner. Section 1008, Civil Code." Alternatively, the owner could record a special notice of consent, which grants permission for others to use the property.

Title insurance companies will not insure an easement obtained by prescription unless the claimant establishes his right through a quiet title action or a deed from the landowner.

Termination of easements

Easements may be terminated in a number of ways, the most important of which include

1. Express release, usually by a quitclaim deed form the holder of the dominant tenement to the holder of the servient tenement.
2. Merger of the estates, whereby the holder of the dominant tenement becomes the owner of the servient tenement, or vice versa.
3. Prescription, whereby the easement is destroyed by the use of a servient tenement in an adverse manner for a period of five years continuously.

RESTRICTIONS

Restrictions are usually of two kinds, private deed and zoning. *Private deed restrictions* are placed on property for the protection of all lots in the tract by subdividers or developers. These restrictions are called "covenants, conditions and restrictions," or "CC&R's" for short.

Zoning restrictions, on the other hand, are created by governmental agencies such as cities and counties in their adoption of zoning ordinances (discussed in Chapter 15).

Private deed restrictions are usually recorded in a separate document; thus, all deeds to parcels of land or lots within a given tract will contain a reference to the recorded Declaration of Restrictions. The recording of the Declaration of Restrictions gives constructive notice to all of their existence.

Today modern subdividers and developers usually draft their general plan restrictions in the form of covenants and conditions, which are enforceable by the grantor and also by the purchasers of lots in the subdivision between themselves.

Single plan restrictions

A distinction should be made between *general plan restrictions* and *single plan restrictions*. Single plan restrictions are in favor of the grantor alone, his or her successors, or his or her assignee and are not necessarily for the benefit of other lot owners.

General plan restrictions

If a subdivider or a developer intends the general plan restrictions to be for the benefit of all the lots in a designated area, the restrictions must so state. Otherwise, difficulties may be encountered in enforcing such restrictions.

A set of valid building restrictions within any given subdividion are enforceable between the landowners if they act in time to enforce such restrictions. Restrictions must be uniformly enforced against all lot owners without discrimination. Thus if Adam, the owner of lot 10, does not comply with the restrictions and later Cole fails to comply, the other lot owners may be prevented from enforcing the restrictions, claiming they have been waived.

If restrictions state ''for residential purposes only,'' this will include all types of family residences, including single-family dwellings, duplexes, triplexes, apartment units, and so forth.

Restrictions will usually not prohibit the owner from building a private garage on the property, even though it is not attached to the main residence. Also, where restrictions state that outbuildings must be a certain distance from the rear portion of the property, this does not prevent the lot owner from building an attached garage to his house, if it is constructed as an integral part of the residence.

Restrictions in a modern subdivision will sometimes provide that all plans and architectural designs shall be approved by a planning committee composed of property owners within said subdivision. Such restrictions will be valid as long as refusals are made in good faith by such committee. When such provisions prevail and the planning committee no longer functions, the approval of plans will probably not violate the building restrictions so long as the improvements remain in harmony with the rest of the subdivision.

Termination of deed restrictions

Restrictions may be terminated in several ways:

1. Termination of the prescribed period of restrictions
2. Agreement of the grantor and the owners of lots within the subdivision

3. Merging of ownership
4. Operation of law

Usually the person creating the deed restrictions will provide for a date of termination, but a date is not essential to the validity of such restriction. When no date is given, restrictions will remain in effect for a reasonable period of time. Two rights exist in the enforcement of restrictions. First is the *right of the grantor* to enforce the restrictions against all grantees in the tract. The second right is the *mutual right of various lot owners* within the tracts to enforce the restrictions in favor of themselves. Individual lot owners may ask for an injunction or may sue for money damages suffered.

A restriction, whether in the form of a covenant or a condition, may be changed, waived, or released by agreement of the parties. This may be done by having the party entitled to enforce the restriction execute a quitclaim deed. The same purpose may be accomplished by an agreement signed by the proper parties.

When ownership of property is merged into a single fee simple estate, the restrictions will be terminated. Should certain portions of the property be sold later, new restrictions must then be created if it is the wish of the grantor.

If restrictions prove to be inequitable to the property owners involved, courts will sometimes deny the enforcement of these restrictions, as in a case where hardships would result to the owners. CC&R's will also not be enforced when their original purpose cannot be realized.

Zoning

Zoning may be defined as the right of governmental agencies to regulate the use of buildings and land. The constitution of the state of California provides that any county, city, town, or township may make and enforce (within its scope) zoning regulations pertaining to the use of land (Article XI, Section 11, of the state constitution). The planning commission, whether city or county, is charged with the responsibility of zoning. Its power, however, is limited to recommendations. Final approval of its action rests with the city council or county board of supervisors, whichever applies. Zoning will be discussed more fully in Chapter 15.

ENCROACHMENTS

An *encroachment* may be defined as the wrongful projection of a building, wall, or fence of one property onto that of another. Such encroachment may be from the air as well as from the ground. If the encroachment rests on the land of another, it constitutes a *trespass*, but if it encroaches from the air, it constitutes a *nuisance*.

Encumbrances (Burdens)

Money-Wise	*Non Money-Wise (Affects physical condition)*	

Liens (To collect money)
1. Mechanic's
2. Taxes and Assessments
3. Mortgage, Trust Deed, Agreement of Sale
4. Attachment
5. Judgment

Can Be

Voluntary	**Involuntary**
(we create)	(created by others)
Mortgage	Mechanic
Trust Deed	Taxes and
Agreement of Sale	Assessments
	Attachment
	Judgment

General	**Specific**
(Against person)	(Against property)
Judgment	Mechanic
	Taxes and
	Assessments
	Mortgage,
	Trust Deed,
	Agreement of Sale
	Attachment

Secured	**Unsecured**
(Title at Stake)	(Title not at Stake)
Mechanics	Attachment
Taxes	Judgment
Mortgage,	
Trust Deed,	
Agreement of Sale	
Attachment	
Judgment	

Easements (Right to use)
1. Appurtenant
2. In Gross

Ways to Acquire
1. Writing (deed or agreement)
2. Necessity
3. Long use (prescription)
4. Dedication

Ways to Abandon
1. Quitclaim
2. Merger
3. Quiet Title Action
4. Non-use
5. Destruction
6. Abandonment

Restrictions (Limits use)
1. Private
2. Public

Ways to Establish

a. Covenant
b. Condition
2. By law
  a. Zoning
  b. Set-back
  c. Building line

Voluntary Liens Consist of Two Security Devices, Evidence and Security

		"Security"			
Voluntary Liens	*"Evidence"*	*Title*	*Possession*	*Promise*	*Instrument*
Personal Property				**Completed** **Breached**	
(1) Pledge or Pawn	Promissory note	Borrower retains	Borrower relinquishes (surrenders)	Lender to return pawn / Title to lender	Pawn ticket
Real Property					
(2) Sales contract	Promissory note	Vendor retains	Vendee receives	Vendor to give title cancel note / Vendor evict vendee; loss of equity	Contract
(3) Mortgage*	Mortgage note	Borrower receives	Borrower receives	Mortgage satisfied / Title given for foreclosure	Mortgage contract
(4) Trust deed*	Trust note	Borrower receives but puts in trust with trustee	Borrower receives	Lender tells trustee to reconvey title to borrower / Lender tells trustee to sell title for money owed	Deed of trust

*Hypothecation means title at stake but the borrower retains possession of the property; it is the opposite of pledging, as with personal property.

If the encroachment (in the case of a building) is resting upon the land of another, it is a permanent trespass. Actions against trespass on this type of encroachment must be brought before the court within three years. Usually the action requested is for the removal of the encroachment and for damages suffered.

Encroachments from the air constitute a nuisance rather than a trespass, and actions against these have no time limit. Where such encroachments remain, they are considered a continuing trespass and are actionable until the nuisance is abated.

Where the encroachment is intentional, an injunction can be granted by the court, and even though the damage may appear slight and the cost of removal of the encroachment great, the court will usually require that the nuisance be abated.

HOMESTEADS

Most constitutions or statutes of the various states provide for a *homestead*. The purpose of such a homestead is to provide a roof over the debtor's head, should a financial crisis develop. At any given time the debtor may have only one valid homestead that protects him against creditors.

A homestead, as provided for in California law, consists of a family dwelling, together with all outbuildings and the land upon which they rest. When a valid Declaration of Homestead (Figure 4–6) is executed by the claimant, acknowledged, and recorded with the county recorder, the owner's equity from creditors is exempt up to certain statutory amounts. It is essential that the claimant actually reside in the homestead as a residence.

The debtor of a *family unit*, or his or her spouse, who files a homestead is protected from creditors to $45,000 of the actual cash value, excluding all liens and encumbrances on the property. A homestead will not defeat mortgages placed on the property by the claimant.

Persons age 65 or older, or persons who are mentally or physically disabled, are allowed an exemption up to $55,000. All other persons not entitled to the $45,000 or $55,000 homestead, have an exemption of $30,000.

Homestead amounts

Regular	$30,000
Family Unit	$45,000
Age 65 or Disabled	$55,000

The homestead protects equity only, and the value of the dwelling is immaterial. If you and your spouse lived in a house worth $200,000, encumbered by a $155,000 deed of trust, a family unit homestead would shelter all the equity in your home. Since you have no equity over

and above your homestead amount, a creditor could not force a sale of your home.

The Code of Civil Procedure describes the *family unit* as

1. The debtor property owner or, when the claimant is married, his or her spouse.

2. The debtor property owner, and at least one of the following persons who has resided on the premises with him or her and under his or her care or maintenance:

    a. his or her minor child, or minor grandchild, or the minor child of his or her deceased wife or husband

    b. a minor brother or sister or a minor child of a deceased brother or sister

    c. a father, mother, grandfather, or grandmother either of himself or of a deceased husband or wife

    d. any other relatives above mentioned who have reached majority and are unable to take care of or support themselves.

For a valid homestead to exist, it must meet certain essential requirements. These include

1. A statement showing the status of the person or persons filing, establishing such person(s) qualify for the amount of the homestead selected. If both spouses are the declarants, they must both own the property.

2. Notarized signatures of all declarants, with the document being recorded.

3. Certification that the claimant resides on the premises and that he or she claims such premises as his or her homestead.

4. A proper description of the premises.

When a valid declaration has been filed meeting all statutory requirements but it is found that false statements are contained therein, such a homestead may be defeated. Where attachments are sought or judgment creditors are involved, it may be necessary to have a judicial determination concerning th truth of statements made in the declaration. Where statements made in the Declaration of Homestead are found to be untrue, the declaration is voidable.

A homestead, even though it is a valid one, will not defeat certain liens. Such liens include taxes; mechanic's liens; mortgage and trust deed instruments; and all mortgage instruments recorded before the Declaration of Homestead was filed.

When a valid Declaration of Homestead has been executed, acknowledged, and recorded before a petition of bankruptcy is filed, it affords the homeowner protection.

A declaration of homestead may be recorded any time prior to the levy (enforcement) of a judgment lien, under

---

HOMESTEAD

(Jointly Declared by Husband and Wife)

We, John-Husband and Jane-Wife, residents of the City of San Rafael, County of Marin, State of California, hereby certify and declare:

I.

We, John-Husband and Jane-Wife, are married, and declare this homestead in both of our names on our jointly owned property.

II.

The property we are homesteading is a single-family residence, commonly known as 123 Jones Street, in the City of San Rafael, County of Marin, State of California, and more fully described as [legal description].

III.

The property which we are hereby homesteading is our principal dwelling, and we actually reside in this property on the date this declaration of homestead is recorded.

IV.

This declaration of homestead is executed on this _____ day of _____, 19___.

_____   _____
[Husband's Signature Line]   [Wife's Signature Line]

We, John-Husband and Jane-Wife, certify and declare that we are the declarants herein, and that the above facts are true and correct and known to be so from our own personal knowledge. We declare under penalty of perjury the foregoing is true and correct, and therefore we execute this homestead on this _____ day of _____, 19___.

STATE OF CALIFORNIA)
) ss.
COUNTY OF _____)

On this day of ___, 19_____, before me, ____[name of notary]____, a Notary Public, personally appeared [John-Husband and Jane-Wife], personally known to me (or proved to me on the basis of satisfactory evidence) persons whose names are subscribed to the above homestead, and acknowledged that they executed the same.

[Notary Seal]

_____
NAME OF NOTARY

Figure 4–6

the *dwelling house* homestead exemption. Assume that Ted Gordon obtains a judgment lien against you in 1976 and you record a homestead in 1986 before Ted actually levies on the property (tries to have the property seized and sold). Your homestead would have priority over Ted's judgment lien.

Termination of homesteads

Homesteads do not automatically terminate when the claimant moves from the property where he resides. Once a valid Declaration of Homestead is filed it may be terminated in only two ways: by the claimant's filing a new homestead on another property or by the claimant's filing a notice of Abandonment of Homestead with the county recorder in the county where the property is situated. (Figure 4–7). Such a Notice of Abandonment takes effect from the date of its recording.

Of course, a homestead can be invalid if it fails to meet the requirements for a valid homestead. For example, if you cease to live on homesteaded property, you lose your exemption. One of the elements for a homestead is that you live on the property as your primary residence. If you qualified for and claimed a family unit homestead, and if by divorce you ended up living alone on the property, your homestead would drop to $30,000 protection.

Is a homestead desirable?

Should the average person file a declaration of homestead? The answer is *No*. Some credit bureaus include in their reports the fact that you homesteaded your home, which makes some creditors suspect that you may have debt problems.

You do not need a homestead unless a judgment against you is imminent. If you are sued, then consider it—but not before.

RECORDING REQUESTED BY

AND WHEN RECORDED MAIL TO

Name

Street Address

City & State

SPACE ABOVE THIS LINE FOR RECORDER'S USE

KNOW ALL MEN BY THESE PRESENTS:

That the homestead heretofore declared and created by that certain declaration of homestead dated April 15, *, 19* 82*, made and executed by* Henry C. Homesteader *and recorded* April 16 *, 19* 82*, in Volume* 1166 *of Official Records at page* 92*, in the office of the County Recorder of the* town of Cucamonga *County of* San Bernardino*, State of California, be and the same is hereby abandoned, and the property in said declaration of homestead described is hereby released from all claim by* Henry C. Homesteader *as a homestead.*

IN WITNESS WHEREOF I *have hereunto set* my *hand this* 20th *day of* January *, 19* 83.

Henry C. Homesteader

____

STATE OF CALIFORNIA

County of ______________ } ***ss.***

On this ______ ***day of*** ______________ ***in the year one thousand nine hundred and*** ______________***, before me,*** ______________ ***a Notary Public, State of California, duly commissioned and sworn, personally appeared*** ______________ ***known to me to be the person*** ___ ***described in and whose name*** ______ ***subscribed to the foregoing instrument, and acknowledged to me that*** ______ ***executed the same.***

IN WITNESS WHEREOF I have hereunto set my hand and affixed my official seal in the ______ ***County of*** ______ ***the day and year in this certificate first above written.***

____

Notary Public, State of ______________

My Commission expires

This document is only a general form which may be proper for use in simple transactions and in no way acts, or is intended to act, as a substitute for the advice of an attorney. The publisher does not make any warranty, either express or implied, as to the legal validity of any provision or the suitability of these forms in any specific transaction.

Cowdery's Form No. 4—ABANDONMENT OF HOMESTEAD. (C. C. Secs. 1243-1244)

Figure 4–7

CHAPTER QUESTIONS

1. Define the two categories of encumbrances that affect a title.

2. Distinguish between the specific lien and the general lien.

3. Discuss the full implication of the mechanic's lien and its effect on the owner's title to real property.

4. What constitutes the completion of a building or structure, and how can an owner protect himself against mechanic's liens after the final construction contract payment?

5. What is meant by deed restrictions, and how may they be removed?

MULTIPLE-CHOICE QUESTIONS

1. John Smith files a Notice of Completion. The original contractor may file an effective mechanic's lien within: (a) 60 days; (b) 30 days; (c) 90 days; (d) 120 days; (e) six months.

2. Before being recorded, a mechanic's lien must be: (a) witnessed; (b) verified; (c) acknowledged; (d) approved by the court; (e) approved by the Assessor's office.

3. Real property taxes (both local and state assessed) become a lien on real property: (a) the first Monday in March preceding the tax year at 12:00 noon; (b) the first of February preceding the tax year; (c) the first day of March at 12:01 A.M. preceding the tax year; (d) are never a lien on real property; (e) on April 15 at midnight.

4. The tax assessor, according to law, must assess property at: (a) loan value; (b) market value; (c) leasehold value; (d) liberal loan value; (e) full cash value.

5. When property is legally seized as security for a judgment in a pending lawsuit, the act is referred to as: (a) a *lis pendens;* (b) a writ of attachment; (c) a writ of execution; (d) a judgment; (e) a sale.

6. Mr. Smith sold a home with a grant deed that had been homesteaded but did not file a declaration of abandonment. He then bought a new home and filed a homestead on it. This new homestead was: (a) legal, because recording a new homestead terminates the old homestead; (b) ineffective, because he did not file an abandonment; (c) legal, because he could file two or more homesteads as the head of the household; (d) void; (e) invalid.

7. Easements created by a deed may be terminated by: (a) death of the property owner; (b) mortgaging of the property; (c) quitclaim deed; (d) transfer of the property; (e) non-use of the easement for five years.

8. Prescription means gaining an easement by: (a) grant deed; (b) duress; (c) open and notorious use for five years; (d) death of a relative; (e) written agreement.

9. Zoning regulations permit certain construction on a parcel of land; however, the private deed restrictions prohibit the construction. In this case, which of the following will prevail? (a) Private deed restrictions; (b) zoning regulations; (c) city building code; (d) city master plan; (e) a court of law will make the decision.

10. Of the following, which may be homesteaded? (a) A duplex, one-half of which is owner occupied; (b) a home, including several acres of farmland; (c) a home in a city, including adjoining plot for gardening; (d) all of the foregoing may be homesteaded; (e) none of the foregoing may be homesteaded.

# THE LAW OF CONTRACTS

Every day, each of us enters into some contract, even if it is only buying a cup of coffee at a cafe. Probably nothing is more important to the student of real estate than an understanding of the law of contracts. In this chapter we will discuss the law of contracts generally, but emphasizing the field of real estate. In Chapter 6 we will cover contracts for the sale and exchange of real property.

Definition of contract A contract may be defined as an agreement to do or not do a certain thing, for the breach of which the law will give a remedy.

VALID, UNENFORCEABLE, VOID, AND VOIDABLE CONTRACTS

A *valid* contract is one that is binding and enforceable on all parties and contains all the essential elements of a contract.

An *unenforceable* contract is one that for some reason cannot be enforced through court. For example, an oral contract to sell a piece of real property may be valid; nevertheless, it would be unenforceable because the law will not enforce a contract to sell real estate unless it is in writing.

A *void* contract lacks legal effect. Legally it does not exist. Examples include contracts to commit crimes and agreements interfering with justice.

A *voidable* contract appears valid on its face, but for some reason it may be rejected and canceled by one of the parties. Sometimes legal action is required to cancel such a contract, and sometimes not. However, until re-jected or canceled, it is valid and enforceable. Examples are contracts by a minor and contracts obtained by fraud.

If a contract is voidable, ordinarily only one side can reject it; the other side remains bound. A person who has the right to reject a voidable transaction may lose his or her right if the property involved gets into the hands of an innocent purchaser. Suppose Alice, by fraud, induces Rayna to sell her goods. Rayna, in turn, sells the goods to Susan, an innocent purchaser. Alice cannot then reject the sale and get back the goods.

Void and voidable

Here is a way to remember the difference between "void" and "voidable":

A void contract has no legal effect.

A void*able* contract is one that a party is *able* to have declared void.

CLASSIFICATION OF CONTRACTS

Express or implied Contracts may be express or implied. An *express* contract is one in which the parties express (state) the terms in words—orally or in writing. An *implied* contract, on the other hand, is one that is shown by the acts and conduct of the parties. For example, suppose you go to an attorney and ask for legal advice and say nothing at the time about paying him or her. You would be bound by an implied contract to pay the attorney's fee.

Executed or executory Contracts may also be classified as to performance. An *executed* contract is one where both parties have performed. A contract is *executory* where something remains to be done by one or both of the parties.

Four essential elements of a contract

There are four essential elements to every contract:

1. Parties capable of contracting
2. Mutual assent or agreement of the parties
3. A lawful purpose or object
4. Legally sufficient consideration

PARTIES CAPABLE OF CONTRACTING

Most people are competent and capable of contracting. Those who cannot include

1. Minors.
2. Mental incompetents.
3. Drugged or drunken persons.
4. Convicts.

Minors In California, a minor is a person under 18 years of age. Persons over 18 have all adult rights, although they must be 21 to purchase alcoholic beverages.

There is an important exception. Any person under the age of 18 is said to be an emancipated minor if that person has entered into a valid marriage, is on active duty with any of the armed forces, or willingly lives apart from his or her parents or legal guardian with their consent, managing his or her own finances regardless of their source. A minor may petition the superior court for a declaration of emancipation that is deemed conclusive evidence that the minor is emancipated.

Mental incompetents A person of any age is considered mentally incompetent to make a contract when his or her mental processes are so deficient that he or she lacks understanding of the nature, purpose, and effect of the transaction.

Drugged or drunken persons are people with temporary incapacity. If the person was so intoxicated that he or she could not understand the nature, purpose, and effect of the transaction, he or she is considered to have been temporarily incapacitated, and the contract is voidable.

If a minor or a mental incompetent makes a contract, it may be void or voidable depending upon the facts and the type of contract.

Contracts that are absolutely *void* are

1. Appointment of an agent or any delegation of authority by a minor. Therefore, a broker cannot act as an agent for a minor to buy or sell.

2. A deed to real property by a minor.

3. A contract or deed by a person who has been previously adjudged a mental incompetent by a court.

4. A contract or deed by a person *entirely* without understanding.

Except for the above, a contract by a minor or an incompetent is *voidable*, not void. The guardian of the minor and the guardian or conservator of the incompetent may have a court cancel it. Also, the minor or incompetent may disaffirm the contract—that is, notify the other side he or she will not be bound—while he is still under age or still incompetent, and for a reasonable time after he or she becomes of age or becomes competent. However, unless the minor or incompetent or someone on his or her behalf disaffirms the contract or has a court declare it canceled, either party may enforce it against the other side.

A minor or an incompetent is always liable for the reasonable value of *necessaries*. There are things necessary for his living, such as food, clothing, shelter, health care, and even education. Whether a thing is a necessary depends upon the person's age, condition, and station in life. This varies from person to person. Also, a minor may maintain a commercial bank account in his or her own name in the same way as an adult.

The proper method of contracting with a minor or a mental incompetent is through a court-appointed guardian or conservator. The court must approve the more important contracts of a guardian or conservator.

You should note that minors and mental incompetents can *acquire* title to real property by gift or inheritance, and that no guardian or conservator is required for this.

Convicts A person convicted of a felony, that is, a crime for which he or she is sentenced to state prison rather than county jail, loses his or her civil rights while imprisoned and while on parole. If sentenced to death or life imprisonment, the loss is permanent and is restored only if there is a later pardon.

A prison inmate or prison parolee may enter into an enforceable contract, provided it is ratified by the California Adult Authority.

MUTUAL ASSENT OR AGREEMENT OF THE PARTIES

The second requirement for a valid contract is that the parties mutually consent to contract. This requires an *offer* by one party and an *acceptance* of the offer by the other. When the offer is accepted, the law says the contract is made and the parties are bound. After that, neither party can back out without the consent of the other.

Offer

An offer is a proposal by one party, called the *offeror*, to the other, called the *offeree*, expressing an intention to enter into a contract if the offeree accepts the proposal. There are three requirements for an effective offer:

1. *Requirement that offer must show present contractual intent* The offer must be stated so that a reasonable man or woman in the shoes of the offeree would feel that, if he or she accepted the proposal, a legal contract would be fully made with all the terms complete. Words such as "Would you be interested in purchasing this house?" or "I'd like to buy a $60,000 home" are not offers because they do not show present contractual intent. Likewise, the usual advertisement of real estate for sale is not an offer but merely an invitation to deal.

2. *Requirement that the terms must be definite and certain* The terms must be sufficiently clear and complete that a court could determine what the parties were intending and could fix damages if one party does not perform. There are four essential terms:

1. Parties to the contract
2. Subject matter
3. Time for performance
4. Price

Sometimes the parties do not express one or more of the terms, yet a court will decide that a "reasonable" term was intended by the parties. For example, if the time for performance is not stated, the court may find that performance is to be within "a reasonable time."

Whether or not the court will find that reasonable terms were implied depends upon the facts in each case. Suppose Adam offers to repair Brown's roof, but no price is mentioned, and Brown accepts. The courts will imply that the repairs were to be performed for a reasonable price.

But if Adam offers to buy Brown's house, no price is mentioned, and Brown accepts, the courts will not imply a reasonable price, because in this instance price is too crucial a term to be considered implied.

Agreement to agree

One type of contract that can never be binding is an "agreement to agree." For example, a seller contracts to sell his house to a buyer and take back a mortgage as part of the selling price "for an amount to be agreed upon." Since the courts can never force the parties to agree, and the amount is an essential term, this is not a valid contract.

3. *Requirement of communication* Before a proposal can become a valid offer, it must be communicated to the other party. For example, Alice advertises a $100 reward for the return of her lost dog. Rayna finds the dog and returns it without knowledge of the reward. Since Alice's offer was not communicated to Rayna, Rayna did not accept it and there is no contract. Rayna cannot collect the reward.

Suppose you prepare an offer to buy Smith's bicycle but decide to wait before submitting it. Smith learns of the offer you have prepared and says he accepts. There is no contract because you never communicated your offer to Smith.

Acceptance

An acceptance is a voluntary act by the person to whom the offer is directed, showing his assent to the offer. It must be communicated to the offeror.

Only the offeree can accept An offer can be accepted only by the person to whom it is made. If you offer your car for sale to Alice, Rayna cannot accept. However, if an offer is made to the public, anyone can accept, provided the offer is actually communicated to the person accepting; that is, he or she knows of it.

Silence is not acceptance Silence cannot be acceptance, except in special circumstances. An offeror cannot force you to reply by saying in his offer, "Your silence will be an acceptance of this offer."

The exceptions to the rule about silence usually arise when the parties have had previous dealings together. *Example:* Every spring, Jones writes to you, "I will disc the weeds on your vacant lot this spring as I have in past years for $50, unless you tell me you don't want it done." Each year, you say nothing, he discs the lot, and you pay him $50. One year you remain silent and he discs your lot. You may not then claim your silence did not give consent in view of your previous dealings with him.

An acceptance must be unequivocal and unqualified The offeree must accept the exact terms of the offer without changing or adding to them. If the offeree adds some new condition or varies even one term of the offer in the slightest, that is a *rejection* of the offer and amounts to a *counteroffer*. A counteroffer is a new and different offer given back to the other party. The original offeror can accept the counteroffer or not, as he or she chooses. The rejection terminates the original offer, and the original offeree can no longer accept it.

Example: A makes a written offer to sell her house to B for $50,000, payable in cash in sixty days. B accepts "provided you give me sixty-one days to pay." B has rejected A's offer. B's attempted acceptance is a counteroffer. If A says no to the counteroffer, B cannot then go back and accept A's original sixty-day offer, because it died when it was rejected. Of course, A could renew her sixty-day offer if she wishes.

Unilateral and bilateral contracts

The act of acceptance called for by the offer may be either (1) an act by the offeree or (2) a promise by the offeree to do something. The first type of acceptance gives rise to a *unilateral* contract. The second type gives rise to a *bilateral* contract.

Unilateral contract In this type of contract, the offeror promises to do something if the offeree will accept by performing an act. A promise is given for an act.

Green says to Smith, "If you will mow my lawn Saturday morning, I will pay you $10." If Smith says, "I accept," that is not a proper acceptance. This offer can be accepted only by performing the act of mowing the lawn on Saturday morning.

Bilateral contract In a bilateral contract, a promise is given for a promise. Green says to Smith, "If you will promise to mow my lawn on Saturday morning, I promise to pay you $10." Smith says, "I promise to do so." A bilateral contract has been formed.

There is an important difference between unilateral and bilateral contracts: Once a unilateral contract is accepted, the contract is fully executed on the side of the person who is accepting; it is executory only by the offeror. But a bilateral contract is executory on both sides at the time it is accepted.

Memory aid: "Uni" means "one;"
"Lateral" means "side."

In a *uni*lateral contract, there is a promise on only *one* side.
In a *bi*lateral contract, there is a promise on *two* sides.

Manner of accepting a bilateral contract

An offer can be accepted only in the manner specified or authorized by the offeror. Suppose the offeror says, "If you accept, mail me your answer." Sending a telegram or hand-carrying a letter of acceptance would not be a valid acceptance. The acceptance must be mailed.

Ordinarily, an acceptance is not effective until it is communicated to the offeror; that is, until he or she receives it. But there is an important exception that says an acceptance is effective as soon as it is dispatched in a manner specified or authorized by the offeror. Thus, if the offeror had mailed the offer to you, and he or she says nothing about how you should answer, answering by mail is authorized. Therefore, your acceptance is effective as soon as it is properly mailed, even though the letter never reaches the offeror.

The above exception can pose a problem for the offeror if the acceptance does not reach him or her. To avoid this, the offeror may specify, "If you accept, I must receive your reply in my office by next Tuesday." Then the acceptance is not effective unless received in the office by Tuesday.

TERMINATION OF OFFER

When an offer is terminated, it is at an end and cannot be accepted. Here are some of the more important ways an offer can be terminated:

1. *By lapse of time.* An offer may state how long it may remain open. If it does not, it expires at the end of a "reasonable" period of time. What is reasonable depends upon the facts of each case.

2. *By destruction of the subject matter.* Henderson offers to sell his house, but it burns down before the offer is accepted. The offer is automatically terminated.

3. *By death or insanity of the offeror or offeree.* Offers are personal. When either party no longer has the capacity to contract, the offer is automatically terminated.

4. *By rejection by offeree.* If the offeree once rejects the offer, it is terminated. He or she cannot later accept. A rejection is effective when it is received by the offeror.

5. *Revocation by offeror.* Ordinarily an offeror may revoke his or her offer at any time before it is accepted. The revocation must be communicated to the offeree before it is effective.

Almost all offers for the purchase of property contain a clause that states, "This offer is void if not accepted within [e.g., 2] days." The offeror can change his or her mind and revoke the offer at any time before it is accepted. Suppose a seller submits a counteroffer to the buyer, giving the buyer five days to accept. If the seller receives a better offer on the property before the buyer accepts, the seller can revoke the offer and accept the higher bid.

There are two important exceptions to the rule that an offeror can revoke his or her offer before acceptance. One is that courts do not allow the offeror to revoke his or her offer to a unilateral contract after the offeree has started performance of the act that will be the acceptance. The other exception is an option, which is described below.

Option

An option is a contract to keep an offer open. For example, Smith is considering buying Green's office building, which Green is offering for $1 million. Smith wants ninety days to see whether he can raise the money for the purchase price. To be sure that the offer is still open at the end of ninety days, he pays Green $100 as consideration for Green's contracting with him to allow him, if he chooses, to buy the building for $1 million at any time within the next ninety days.

Unlike other offers, an option is *assignable* by the offeree unless the option contract states otherwise. This means that the person who holds the right to buy (the optionee) may assign his or her right to someone else, who then stands in the shoes of the optionee. An option is also an exception to the rule that death or insanity of one of the parties terminates the offer. It is binding on the optionor's estate or guardian.

Since an option is an interest in the land, it should be recorded in the county recorder's office. This gives notice of the option to the world. After that, anyone buying the property from the owner during the option period takes it subject to the optionee's right to purchase it for the option price during the option period. In the example above, if Smith recorded his option to purchase the office building and Green sold it to Zimmerman during the ninety-day period, Smith would still have the right to purchase it from Zimmerman for $1 million during the ninety-day period.

GENUINE ASSENT

Even when there is an offer and acceptance, one of the parties may claim that the contract is voidable because his or her assent was not real or genuine. Such a claim may be based on one of the following:

Fraud
Ambiguity
Mistake
Duress and Menace
Undue Influence

Fraud

Fraud is also called "deceit" or "misrepresentation." It consists of five elements, and unless every one is present, the law does not consider the transaction fraudulent.

1. *Material misrepresentation or concealment-* There must be a *false representation* or a *concealment* about a *material fact*. A material fact is one that would have influenced the other person to enter into or stay out of the transaction.

California has an additional "full disclosure rule" that requires a seller of real property to disclose important material facts about the property known to the seller but not known to the buyer. Failure to do so is fraud. Some things that the courts have held must be disclosed are that

The roof leaked badly when it rained.
The property had been condemned.
The building was infested with termites.
The land was filled.
The building encroached on a state right-of-way.
The improvements were constructed in violation of local
    zoning, health, and building ordinances.

Also, a misrepresentation about a person's state of mind can be material. Therefore, a promise made with *no intention* of performing it is fraudulent because it is a misrepresentation of intention to perform.

Real property is frequently offered for sale "as is." This is intended to mean that the buyer takes the property in the condition visible or observable to him or her. To what extent this should alert the buyer that there may be something wrong with the property depends upon the facts of each case. However, it will not relieve the seller if he or she misrepresents or fails to disclose facts not within the buyer's reach.

2. *Knowledge of the falsity, or negligence* The person accused of fraud must (1) have known that the representation was false or (2) have intentionally or negligently represented the statement as true without knowing whether it was true or not.

3. *Intent to induce reliance* The person making the statement must have intended that there would be reliance upon it.

4. *Justifiable reliance* The person deceived must have relied upon the representation. If he or she did not rely upon it, for example, where he or she made an independent investigation, that person cannot claim deceit. However, a person is under no duty to investigate.

If a person's reliance was unjustified, he or she has no remedy. Ordinarily, a person is not justified in relying upon a representation of opinion, value, or quality unless either

a. The speaker has superior knowledge not available to the listener. For instance, the speaker is an art dealer or a real estate broker; or
b. The speaker occupies some position of confidence,

such as a financial advisor or an apparently disinterested banker.

Usually, a person is not considered justified if he or she relies upon a statement such as, ''This is a colossal bargain'' or ''This is a wonderful opportunity.''

5. *Damage* The misrepresentation must cause the person damage. For example, the person may have a financial loss, or the thing the person buys may be less useful to him or her than it would have been had the representation been true.

Remedies for fraud

The remedies of the defrauded person depend upon the type of fraud committed. If a person is deceived so that he or she did not know what transactions he or she was getting into—for example, the person signs a contract thinking it is an autograph book—this is called *fraud in the inception or execution.* The contract is void. The defrauded person can sue for any damages the misrepresentation caused him or her, but he or she need not take any steps to rescind (cancel) the contract, because a void contract has no legal effect.

However, if the person knew that he or she was entering into a contract, but was induced to enter into it by fraud, it is *fraud in the inducement* and the contract is merely voidable. He or she has a choice of three remedies:

1. *Rescind the contract.* He or she may declare the contract canceled, offer to give back what he or she has received under the contract, and demand what he or she gave the other party. If the other party will not rescind voluntarily, the defrauded party can bring legal action to force rescission (cancellation). But until he or she does so, the contract is binding.
2. *Sue for damages.* He or she may give up the right to rescind and sue for damages.
3. *Enforce the contract.* He or she may give up the right to rescission or damages and hold the other party to the contract as though there were no fraud.

A person may act through an agent. Therefore, he or she is responsible for misrepresentations made by that agent unless the contract expressly states that the agent has no authority to make representations. Even when the contract states this, the person deceived by the agent may rescind, and he or she can recover damages from the agent. However, he or she cannot recover damages from the person the agent represented if the latter was innocent.

An exculpatory clause is frequently put into contracts. This relieves a party from liability for his or her own wrongful act or conduct. A court will refuse to enforce such a clause when it attempts to relieve a person from his or her own fraud, willful misconduct, or violation of the law. But a clause that merely prevents or limits liability for a party's mistakes or negligence is usually enforceable.

Ambiguity

Ambiguity arises when a term of the contract can have more than one meaning, and it can render a contract void.

Suppose there is a contract to sell ''Sutton Rest Home, on Phillips Avenue, Indio, California.'' Unknown to the parties, there are two Sutton Rest Homes on Phillips Avenue in Indio. The buyer had one in mind and the seller the other. If neither party knew of the other rest home, the contract is void. There was no genuine assent or meeting of the minds on the same subject matter.

But suppose one party knew the wording of the contract was ambiguous because he or she knew of both rest homes, and suppose the second party knew of only one rest home. There is a binding contract based upon what the second party—the innocent party—actually intended.

Mistake

Mistake can render a contract voidable.

Mutual mistake If both parties are mistaken about the same material fact, neither can enforce the contract, and either may rescind it. *Example:* Jones and Smith contract for the purchase of a home. Neither knows that the home has burned down. The contract may be rescinded by either party.

Unilateral mistake If only one party is mistaken, and the other neither knew of nor was chargeable with knowledge of the mistake, there is a binding contract. The mistake is no defense—whether a mistake about a fact or about the law.

Example: Zimmerman makes a mistake in computing the net income of a piece of investment property. Based on her error, she offers to buy it for $500,000. If she had done her arithmetic correctly, she would have offered only $450,000. There is a binding contract unless the seller knew or was chargeable with knowledge of the error. If the offer was so high, for example $1.5 million, that it would charge the seller with knowledge that there was very likely a mistake, he cannot ''snap up'' the offer and bind the other party.

Another example: Jones contracts to buy a vacant lot, thinking it is zoned for a four-family dwelling. In fact, it is zoned for only a one-family dwelling and is therefore worth much less. This is a mistake of law, but the contract is binding unless the other party knew or was chargeable with knowledge of the mistake.

Duress or menace

Suppose one party uses physical force (duress) or the threat of it (menace) against the other party or the other party's family or property. If the consent was compelled this way, the contract is voidable and may be rescinded.

But *economic duress* is usually not grounds for rescission. If an owner is in such desperate economic need that he or she contracts to sell his or her property far below its true value, the contract is still binding.

However, economic duress may be a defense when one party is responsible for putting the other party in desperate economic need. In one case, an attorney was hired to resist a large tax assessment. He waited until just before the deadline for filing the necessary papers and then threatened not to file unless the taxpayer signed a contract with a very high fee. The court held the contract was unenforceable.

Undue Influence

Undue influence is found when one person has the confidence of another or holds real or apparent authority over another, and uses this confidence or authority to obtain an unfair advantage. It may involve taking an unfair advantage of another's weakness of mind or taking a grossly oppressive and unfair advantage of another's necessities or distress.

Suppose Alice is very sick and her nephew, living in her home, hounds her to sign a contract. If Alice signs so that she may have peace, this would be undue influence.

Undue influence is most frequently encountered where people are in a confidential relationship, such as principal and broker, attorney and client, principal and agent, parent and child, or husband and wife.

A LAWFUL OBJECT

The third of the four essential elements of a contract is that it must have a *lawful object*. Under California law, any contract that is contrary to statute, public policy, or good morals does not have such an object. Examples are gambling contracts and contracts to commit a crime.

California statutes forbid a person from engaging in certain occupations or businesses without a license; for example, a real estate broker, an attorney, or a contractor. When a person sues to collect for services he or she has rendered in these fields, that person must prove that he or she was licensed before the court will give him or her a judgment.

LEGALLY SUFFICIENT CONSIDERATION

The last of the four essential elements of a contract is that there must be *legally sufficient consideration*. Such consideration may be

1. *Performing* an act that a person is not legally bound to, such as paying $100 or painting a house.
2. *Forbearing* to perform an act a person has a legal right to do, such as refraining from marrying before the age of twenty-five or from foreclosing on a past-due mortgage.
3. A *promise* to act or forbear as described above.

The act, forbearance, or promise must be given by one side *in exchange* for an act, forbearance, or promise by the other side. *Each* side must give consideration to the other, or there is no contract.

Adequacy of consideration

As a rule, courts will not inquire into whether the consideration is fair or adequate. In one case, 25 cents was considered legally sufficient consideration for a four-month option to purchase real estate at a price of $100,000.

The act, forbearance, or promise need not have economic value or even be of benefit to the other side. For example, Hogan promises $1,000 to Alexander if Alexander will give up his drinking habits. Giving up drinking habits is legally sufficient consideration.

Mutuality of obligation

Courts have a rule that there is no contract unless *both* sides are bound by it. This is called "mutuality of obligation."

A contract that tries to bind one side but not the other is called an *illusory contract;* it is not a contract at all, merely illusion of one.

Suppose a paint-store owner says to an apartment-house owner, "I offer to supply you with as much latex paint as you want to order for the next twelve months for $8 a gallon." The apartment-house owner says, "I accept." This agreement does not bind the apartment-house owner, because she may never "want to order" any paint. Since she is not bound, neither is the other side.

Similarly, a contract that gives one party "the right to cancel this contract at any time" leaves that party unbound and is illusory.

But there is a binding contract when a landlord and Jones agree that Jones will rent "the first apartment in the Laguna Cove Apartment House that becomes vacant in 1977." True, no apartment may become vacant in 1977. But, if one does become vacant in that year, the landlord is bound to rent it to Jones. Jones is bound to take it. This is simply a *conditional promise* to rent: The condition is that there will be a vacancy in 1977. A conditional promise is good consideration.

In a few cases, the rule of mutuality of obligation does not apply. A notable exception is a contract that is voidable by one side because of fraud, mental incompetency, or the like, as described earlier. One party has the power to rescind it, but the other party is bound.

Statute of frauds

The statute of frauds was made part of English law in 1677. It is a statute to *prevent* frauds and perjury by providing that some kinds of contracts are not enforceable unless they are in writing. All fifty states have similar statutes.

The most common real estate contracts that the statute of frauds requires to be in writing to be enforceable are

1. A contract for the sale of real property or any interest in real property such as deposit receipts, options, and grants of easements.

2. A debt obligation secured by an interest in real property, such as deeds of trust and mortgages.

3. A lease of real property for more than one year.

4. An employment contract between a broker and his or her salesperson, such as listing agreements.

When the statute of frauds says a contract must be in writing, another rule called the *Equal Dignities Rule* says that an agent's authority to make such a contract must also be in writing. Thus, a contract to buy real estate must be in writing; therefore, authorization for an agent to buy real estate must also be in writing.

The writing required by the statute of frauds need not be a formal contract. It may be an informal memorandum or even a series of letters or telegrams, as long as the writing contains the terms the law considers essential. These are

1. Identity of the parties to the contract.

2. Description of the subject matter of the contract.

3. Terms and conditions of the contract.

4. Statement of the consideration.

The writing or writings must be signed by the person sought to be held liable, or by that person's agent; but it need not be signed by the party who seeks to enforce the contract.

Sometimes a court will enforce an oral contract despite the statute of frauds to avoid "unjust enrichment" to one party or "unconscionable injury" to the other. Courts will also enforce an oral contract where the person now claiming the statute as a defense had misled the other into thinking he or she would not make such a claim or that he or she would put the agreement into writing. In addition, even when courts allow the statute as a defense, they say that a person who received benefits under an oral contract must pay the reasonable value of them to the other party.

PAROL EVIDENCE RULE

The parol evidence rule applies when parties draw up a written document intended to cover their entire agreement—whether the law requires the agreement to be in writing or not. Under this rule, such a writing takes the place of all earlier agreements and negotiations. Other evidence cannot be considered that would add to, change, or contradict the terms of the writing.

Example: Simms and Costello negotiate the terms of a lease on a store near a college. They sign a formal written lease providing that the rent is $2,000 per month. Later, Simms cannot show that they had an oral understanding at the time of the lease that the rent was to be reduced to $1,000 per month during the period the college was on summer vacation.

Of course, if a term of the writing is ambiguous or a nonessential term is incomplete, outside evidence may be used to explain the ambiguity or supply the missing terms.

CONFLICT BETWEEN PARTS OF A CONTRACT

When there is a conflict between parts of a contract, the rule is that typewritten terms will prevail over printed matter, and handwritten terms will prevail over both. One overriding rule is that courts try to interpret a contract according to what the parties intended.

ASSIGNMENT OF CONTRACTS

Assignment of rights

A party may assign, that is transfer, all or part of his or her rights under a contract to a third person unless

1. The terms of the contract forbid assignment—a common provision in real estate contracts.

2. The assignment would materially change the duties or risks of the other party to the contract.

Such a material change may occur if there is an assignment of a personal service contract. Suppose Hansen, an attorney, contracts to render legal services to Allen for one year. Allen may not assign the contract to Holmes because this would require attorney Hansen to render services to a different person, Holmes, which may be more difficult. This is true whenever the personal services require special skill, talent, or knowledge.

However, if the personal services do not call for such qualities, the right to receive them may be assigned—for instance, the services of a repair contractor or a swimming-pool maintenance person.

Where personal credit will be given under a contract, the person who will be the debtor cannot substitute another person in his or her place because this would materially change the risk to the party granting credit. Similarly, an insured person cannot substitute another person as the insured unless the insurance company consents.

Delegation of duties

A person may delegate, that is transfer, all or part of his or her *duties* under a contract to someone else, unless the contract forbids delegation or the duties call for personal services needing special skill, talent, or knowledge as described above. For example, an attorney who contracted to do legal work could not delegate this duty to another attorney unless the client consents. Even when delegation of duties is permitted, the person making the delegation remains liable if the party to whom they are delegated performs improperly.

MODIFYING CONTRACTS

The parties to a contract may change its terms by agreement between themselves. Also, they may make a new contract that revokes the original or is a substitute for it, or they may substitute a new party for one of the original parties.

Example: Abel contracts to sell his house to Baker for $50,000. Later Abel, Baker, and Cole make a new contract that transfers all of Baker's rights and obligations to Cole.

A written contract can be modified by three methods:

1. By a new written contract The new contract must meet all of the requirements of a contract, including consideration.

2. By an executed oral agreement No consideration is required, since the agreement is fully performed on both sides.

3. By a new oral contract The original contract did not have to be in writing. The new contract requires consideration. Since the Statute of Frauds requires most real estate contracts to be in writing, this method of modifying a contract is rarely used in property transactions.

PERFORMANCE OF CONTRACTS

Covenants and conditions

Before we discuss a party's duty to perform a contract, we must distinguish between two types of provisions that appear in contracts—*covenants* and *conditions*.

A covenant is a promise, the breach of which gives rise to damages, an injunction, or other remedy not creating or defeating the basic contract. A condition is a promise, the breach of which creates or defeats a party's duty to perform when it does not happen. The main difference between a condition and a covenant is the remedy.

If a lease provides a landlord must paint a room, and a landlord fails to do so, the tenant is normally allowed to collect damages. The tenant cannot normally terminate the lease. Conversely, a tenant's obligation to pay rent is a covenant. If a tenant fails to pay the rent, the landlord can terminate the lease.

Example: "I promise to pay you $500 if you will find me a tenant for my building." Your finding me a tenant for my building is a condition. If this condition occurs, it creates a duty for me to pay you $500.

Another example: "I promise to buy your house provided, however, that I won't have to buy it if the bank turns down the loan application I have made for $40,000." My duty to buy is ended if the bank turns down the loan application.

There are three types of conditions:

1. *Condition precedent* This is a condition that must occur first, that is, it must precede, before the duty is created. *Illustration:* For sufficient consideration I promise to loan you $100,000 on August 1 if you have completed the office building you are constructing on your property by that date. My duty to lend you $100,000 will never arise unless your building is completed by August 1.

2. *Conditions concurrent* These are conditions that are dependent upon each other and are to be performed concurrently, that is at the same time. You and I contract in writing that I will sell you my vacant lot for $20,000. The deed from me and the purchase price from you are to be exchanged on December 15. As can be seen, each of us must perform before the duty by the other person is created, so we must both perform at the same time.

3. *Condition subsequent* This is a condition that happens after a duty has been created. It extinguishes the duty. This type of condition is rather rare in contracts. An example is a sale of an automobile to you for $1,000 to be paid in one week, but subject to your right to return the automobile within the week and cancel your obligation to pay.

Faulty conditions

Real estate people often refer to conditions precedent as *contingencies*. For example, the contract a buyer and a seller sign for the purchase of property, called a *Real Estate Purchase Contract and Receipt for Deposit*, may state, "This contract is contingent upon the buyer's completing within thirty days the sale of his home at 91299 Terasita Street, Los Angeles, to James Joyce, which sale has already been contracted for."

Now consider a shocking fact: *Many contracts drawn by real estate licensees with contingencies in them are void*. Why? Because, when they insert a condition, (1) they fail to state it properly, and (2) they fail to put in a proper covenant to go with it.

Suppose, for example, a real estate licensee writes up a contract and inserts: "This contract is contingent upon the buyer's obtaining within thirty days a loan of $25,000 secured by a first deed of trust on the property." Such a clause may be fatal to the contract for two reasons:

1. It does not spell out completely the terms of the loan. It does not specify the interest rate or the loan period. If the buyer wants to get out of the contract, he or she may be able to insist that the only acceptable loan is a 2 percent interest payable over 90 years. Such terms are considered too crucial for a court to say that they were implied.

2. Even if all the terms of the loan were spelled out, such a condition might perhaps render the contract illusory and void. A court might hold it does not bind the buyer to seek or even apply for a loan. It is completely in his or her power to perform or not to perform. Alternatively, a court could hold that the implied covenant of good faith and fair dealing is sufficient to require the buyer to diligently apply for the loan.

Because the buyer is not bound, the seller is not bound, either. There is lack of "mutuality of obligation," so no contract exists.*

How can this problem be solved? First, by fully stating all the terms of the condition and, second, by adding a covenant to go with the condition. For example, "The buyer will use his best efforts to obtain such a loan."

Caution: Most books that purport to provide real estate salespeople and brokers with contingency clauses state only the condition and fail to state the covenant. If you use such clauses by themselves, you may perhaps render the contract illusory and void.

*Real Estate Reference Book, 1970–80 Edition (Sacramento, California: California Department of Real Estate, 1980).

Excuse of conditions and counterperformance

Sometimes the law excuses conditions; that is, the law makes one party's duty absolute without the condition occurring. Acts or events that excuse conditions include:

1. *Preventing a party from fulfilling the condition*

Example Yamamoto has an option to purchase real estate from Chase. The option has a condition that Yamamoto must pay the purchase price to Chase at her office on July 1. On June 30, Chase locks her office and leaves town for a week. The condition is excused.

2. *Breach of the contract by the other side*

Ordinarily, when one party is performing, the other party has the duty of counterperformance—that is, the duty to continue to perform any duties still owing from him or her. Frequently, performance on each side is conditioned upon counterperformance by the other side.

Consider a one-year employment contract. Jones is the employer. Smith is the employee, at $200 per week. If Jones stops paying at the end of five months, he is breaching the contract. This relieves Smith of his duty of counterperformance (the duty to go on working). He can sue Jones for the $200 per week for the remaining term of the contract without continuing to work for him.

3. *Waiver of a condition*

Waiving a condition is giving up the right to insist on it. This can be done by words or by conduct. Suppose installment payments under a contract are habitually paid late and accepted without protest. This may be a waiver of prompt payment—at least until the receiving party gives notice that future payments must be made on time.

DISCHARGE OF CONTRACTUAL DUTIES

Once a party's duties become absolute, they may be discharged in the following ways:

1. *Performance*

Full and complete performance is the usual way of discharging duties.

2. *Tender of performance*

A *tender* is a good-faith offer to perform fully, with a demonstration of the ability to perform immediately. If the other side will not accept your tender, there is nothing more you can do—so in many cases your duty to perform is discharged.

Sometimes a tender will not discharge the duty. If the duty is to pay money, a tender of payment would be to offer cash at the time and place required for payment. In fact, if you will look at the paper money in your pocketbook, you will see printed on it, ''This note is legal tender for all debts, public and private.'' Suppose you tender the amount of a debt in cash, at the time and place called for in your contract, but it is not accepted. Then further interest on the debt stops. But your duty to pay is not discharged. You will still owe the debt itself.

3. Impossibility

After a contract has been made, a duty under it will be discharged if, without the promisor's fault, it becomes impossible to perform. *Example:* After contracting, the subject matter of the contract is destroyed; for instance, you contract to paint my house and it burns down before you can start, or a change in zoning ordinances makes the building contracted for illegal.

4. Impracticability

Sometimes a court will allow a contract to be discharged when performance is turning out to be something vastly different from what the parties expected, and there is extreme difficulty and expense. A California court excused performance in a case where the cost was ten times what had been expected. But even courts that consider this a ground for discharge do so quite hesitantly.

5. Occurrence of condition subsequent

As discussed under Covenants and Conditions, a contract may contain a condition subsequent that will end the promisor's duty. For example, one party may have been given the right to return the goods and end the duty to pay for them.

6. Rescission

Cancellation of a contract is called *rescission*. It is mutual when both parties agree. However, one party may exercise the right to rescind for reasons of fraud, minority, mental incompetency, or other grounds described earlier in this chapter.

7. Release

Duties under a contract may be discharged by a release, which is a statement made by one party that he or she gives up those contract rights in his or her favor. In California, consideration is required for an oral release, but not for one in writing. But when the statute of frauds requires the original contract to be in writing, the release must be in writing.

8. Accord and satisfaction

An ''accord'' is an *executory* contract to discharge a contract. It requires consideration. A ''satisfaction'' is the *performance* of the accord contract.

Suppose Bostic contracts with you to build you a house for $40,000. Later she wants to get out of the contract. So on April 1, you and she agree that she may be released in consideration of her promise to pay you $5,000 on June 1. This agreement is an accord. Once it is made, it suspends your right to enforce the original building contract until June 1. If she pays you on June 1, that is a satisfaction and discharges the original contract. If Bostic does not pay $5,000 on June 1, you may sue her either on the original contract or on the new contract that required her to pay $5,000.

Sometimes a person will send a creditor a check for a smaller sum than is owed, writing on it that it is ''payment in full'' of the debt. If there is a good-faith dispute over whether a debt is owed or over the amount, cashing this check will usually discharge the debt on the basis that it is an accord and a satisfaction. California courts have gone further and held that there is a discharge even when the debt and amount were not disputed.

9. Running of statute of limitations

A statute of limitations is a statute that provides that you have only a certain period of time to sue on a claim. The period starts as soon as you have a legal right to sue, usually on the date the contract is breached. When the period has run, your right to sue is barred.

The California statute of limitations for breach of contracts is

Four years on a written contract.
Two years on an oral contract.

If a part payment is made *before* the period has run out, the full period starts running all over again from the date of payment. However, if the payment is made after the period has expired, the debt is not revived and remains barred.

BREACH OF CONTRACT

Breach of contract is the failure by one party to perform a duty required by a *covenant* in a contract at the time and place provided.

There are two types of breaches with different legal consequences:

1. Minor breach

A minor breach is something small, usually something that does not substantially deprive the other party of what he or she contracted for. *Example:* Anson contracts with Builders, Inc. He promises to pay them $50,000, and they promise to build him a house according to his plans and specifications by May 1. If the house is completed on May 3, or if Builders, Inc., unintentionally leaves out two light fixtures, these are minor breaches.

A minor breach *temporarily suspends* the other party's duty of counterperformance. Therefore, Anson could delay paying for the house from May 1 until it is completed. A minor breach also allows the injured party to sue for any damages caused by the breach. Anson could sue Builders, Inc., for the loss caused by the two-day delay and for the materials and labor needed to put in the light fixtures. Or, what is more likely, he could simply deduct these amounts from what he owes Builders, Inc.

2. Major breach

A major breach is substantial. In the example above, it would be a major breach to complete the house four months late or use lumber that was definitely inferior to what the contract called for.

A major breach *immediately and permanently ends* the duty of counterperformance by the injured party. It also gives the injured party the right to sue at once for damages or for the other remedies described later in this chapter.

Voluntary disablement or anticipatory breach by the other party

Suppose Singer and Zuckoff have a contract stating that Singer will sell Brookside Farm to Zuckoff, and that they will exchange the deed and the purchase price on July 1. On June 25, Singer deeds the property to O'Grady without any provision for getting it back. This is a voluntary disablement by Singer. She has disabled him from being able to perform her part of the contract. This excuses Zuckoff from the need to tender the purchase price on July 1 as a condition to requiring Singer to convey. Singer's failure to convey on July 1 is a breach of the contract.

Suppose instead that on June 25 Singer tells Zuckoff that she does not intend to perform. This is an anticipatory repudiation or anticipatory breach of the contract; it is a repudiation or breach in advance. Zuckoff does not have to tender the purchase price and may sue Singer just as though Singer had breached the contract.

Damages

Damages are a money award by a court designed to compensate the injured party by giving him or her, in most cases, the benefit of his or her bargain as far as practical. Damages are the remedy usually sought by the injured party.

The formulas for determining damages vary with the type of contract that is breached. Noncontract-related damages, such as those arising from an automobile accident, have their own formulas for determining the amount of damages. Such formulas are beyond the scope of this book.

In most breach of contract cases, the measure of damages is the amount needed to make the nonbreaching party whole. These damages cover all losses proximately caused by the breach or likely in the ordinary course of events to arise from that breach.

Breach of real estate sales contract However, if a party breaches a contract to buy or to sell real estate, almost all attorneys admit the measure of damages is inadequate. One of the leading law books for real estate attorneys begins by stating that "no existing legal remedy satisfactorily meets the needs of an aggrieved party when the other party has breached a contract for the sale or purchase of land."

If you enter into a contract to sell your house, and the buyer simply refuses to complete the contract, your *general* damages are limited. The law gives you only the difference between the contract price and the market value of the property at the time of the breach. You can also recover *special* damages, equal to interest payments on your deed(s) of trust, taxes and insurance until you resell your home.

If your home is worth $150,000 and the buyer agrees to purchase it for $150,000, then defaults on the contract, you have no general damages. Homes in California in the short run usually stay at the same value or go up in value; they rarely decline. In other words, for all the inconvenience, lost time, and possible inability to move into a new home, you could only recover carrying costs.

Limit on special damages The law draws a limit on the amount of special damages you can claim on breach of a contract. Damages that a reasonable person could *not* have foreseen *at the time the contract was made* are not allowed or compensated.

Example: Swift contracts to complete a building for Lacroix before May 1. But Swift does not finish until June 15. Lacroix can recover the standard damages described above. But, suppose Lacroix had a lease on premises she had been occupying when the contract was made, and that lease required her to pay double rent for each day she stayed over beyond May 1. Therefore, Lacroix needed to move into the new building on May 1 to avoid the double rent. *Question:* Will Lacroix be awarded damages for the double rent she was forced to pay from May 1 to June 15?

Yes, if Swift knew of the double rent provision at the time she made the contract. Then she is liable for Lacroix's loss.

No, if Swift did not know of this provision when she contracted, because she is liable for only the losses a reasonable person could have foreseen based upon the facts he or she had notice of at the time he or she made the contract.

Why does the law limit special damages to losses a reasonable person could foresee at the time the contract *was made*? Because a person should know what he or she will be liable for when that person makes a contract. Otherwise, someone might make a $500 contract and find himself or herself liable for $1 million in damages he or she could not foresee. Had the person known of such high potential damages, he or she might have chosen not to contract or might have demanded a higher price.

Duty to reduce damages

The injured party has a duty to avoid and cut down damages where practical. *Example:* Under a construction contract, the building contractor should not add to his or her damages by going on with the work after the other party breaches. When an employer breaches an employment contract, the employee should seek other, similar work to keep down the damages from the loss of wages.

Liquidated damages

At the time a contract is made, it may be very difficult to estimate what the damages will be if the contract is later breached. If so, the parties may state in the contract that a particular amount will be awarded if a breach occurs. This amount is called *liquidated damages.* It is a common provision to make an allowance for liquidated damages in a contract for the sale of real property.

At the time the contract is made the amount stated as liquidated damages must be a reasonable forecast of those damages. If it is excessive, based on such a reasonable forecast, it is considered a penalty. Courts will not enforce a provision for a penalty. For instance, a requirement that a builder pay $500 per day for failure to complete an office building on time would be a penalty if the rental from the building would be only $100 per day.

Residential purchase contracts Most deposit receipts (contracts for the sale of real property) provide that the amount of the buyer's deposit is the amount of liquidated damages. In contracts for the purchase of a one- to four-family residence, the law has special rules. The overriding rule is that the amount of liquidated damages must be reasonable.

If the amount is over 3 percent of the purchase, it is presumed to be unreasonable. Anything less is presumed to be reasonable. Further, liquidated damage clauses are

valid only if they are in boldface type and are specifically initialed or signed by all parties.

Other remedies

In addition to damages, the injured party has other remedies through the court that include:

1. *Specific performance.* This is the right to have the court order the breaching party to perform. In most cases, where the price is adequate and the contract is just and reasonable, the court will order a party to buy, sell, or convey real property as agreed. But in some types of cases the court will not order performance; for example, a person will not be made to render personal services, because this acts as slavery. A seller will not be ordered to deed real property when the purchase price is not adequate or the contract is not just and reasonable.

2. *Rescission.* A court can order rescission (cancellation) of a contract where proper. Each party must then give back what he or she received from the other.

Provision for attorney's fees

When one person sues another, the party who wins ordinarily cannot recover the attorney's fees he or she was forced to spend. They are not considered part of the court costs. However, the parties may agree in a written contract that if suit is brought on the contract, the winning party will be awarded a reasonable attorney's fee. This fee is set by the court and added to the amount of the judgment. An attorney's fee clause is very common in contracts such as leases, notes, mortgages, and deeds of trust. However, you should be warned that in most cases the attorney's fee awarded by the court is less than the attorney will actually charge the winning party.

Often the contract will provide for awarding the attorney's fees to only one of the parties if he or she wins. It makes no mention of attorney's fees for the other party. But the California statutes say that when the contract allows attorney's fees to one party, the other party has the same right to such fees if he or she wins.

CHAPTER QUESTIONS

1. Review the definition of a contract. Distinguish between an *express contract* and an *implied contract.*

2. How does an option differ from a regular contract? Give one illustration of the option contract.

3. What is meant by *parol evidence rule*? When will the court admit its use for evidence to a contract?

4. What remedies are available to one party to a contract if the other party does not perform and a breach of contract occurs?

5. Who may use specific performance to enforce a contract, and what are the limitations of its use?

MULTIPLE-CHOICE QUESTIONS _____

1. All of the following are essentials of a *simple* contract *except:* (a) parties capable of contracting; (b) legal object; (c) proper writing; (d) mutual agreement or consent; (e) a consideration.

2. A purchaser has the *legal* right to withdraw his or her offer: (a) anytime before escrow closes; (b) only if the amount of the deposit is equal to 10 percent of the offered price; (c) only after the time limit for acceptance by the seller has expired; (d) any time before the seller signs the acceptance and the buyer is so notified; (e) in none of the foregoing cases.

3. If an existing contract is replaced with an entirely new contract, this amounts to an act of: (a) rescission; (b) novation; (c) subrogation; (d) assignment; (e) misrepresentation.

4. Consideration is: (a) work; (b) money; (c) giving up some legal right; (d) taking on a legal burden you were not obligated to; (e) all of the foregoing.

5. A contract, supported by a consideration, in which one party promises to keep an offer open for a stated period of time is: (a) an exchange agreement; (b) a counteroffer; (c) an open listing; (d) an option contract; (e) none of the foregoing.

6. A bilateral contract is one in which: (a) something is to be done by one party only; (b) only one of the parties is bound to act; (c) the promise of one party is given in exchange for the promise of the other party; (d) a restriction is placed by one party to limit the actual performance by the other party; (e) something has been fully performed by both parties.

7. The statute of frauds requires that all of the following contracts must be in writing to be enforceable *except:* (a) an agreement allowing a broker to sell real estate for compensation; (b) a lease agreement of one year to commence one month after date of execution; (c) an agreement to sell land; (d) an agreement between two brokers to split a commission.

8. A single man or woman who is eighteen years old is considered an adult: (a) if he or she is a college student; (b) if he or she is earning his or her own living; (c) if he or she is buying a home; (d) if he or she is buying an automobile; (e) in any of the foregoing cases.

9. A contract based on an illegal consideration is: (a) valid; (b) void; (c) legal; (d) enforceable; (e) all of the foregoing.

10. An executory contract is: (a) a contract to be rewritten; (b) a contract fully performed by both parties; (c) a contract not fully performed; (d) an executed contract; (e) none of the foregoing.

6 CONTRACTS OF REAL PROPERTY

In the previous chapter we examined the general law of contracts. This chapter will deal exclusively with contracts for the sale or exchange of real property and will provide a checklist for buying and selling your home. The completed forms in this chapter are provided merely as examples. They should not be used or copied without first being thoroughly reviewed by an attorney and, where applicable, an accountant.

Although real estate transactions differ, the sequence of steps is generally the same. The listing of a property with a real estate broker is the first step in a real estate transaction. The property owner should use care in the selection of the broker. The selection may be based upon the recommendation of a friend or upon previous service of the brokerage firm for the property owner.

The broker, having a valid listing agreement, is now expected to perform under his or her agency contract. The broker advertises the property and shows it to prospective buyers. These prospective buyers may not be in a position to pay cash, so it may be necessary for the broker to arrange adequate financing on the property. He or she may do this by going to various lenders and securing conditional loan commitments from them for amounts they would be willing to lend on the property should a sale occur.

Once a buyer is found ready, willing, and able to purchase the property on the terms and conditions of the listing agreement, the broker will fill out a real estate purchase contract and receipt for deposit incorporating the terms under which the buyer offers to purchase the property. The broker has a responsibility to make certain that all terms and conditions under which the buyer is willing to buy the property are set forth clearly and concisely in this instrument.

The offer to purchase is now presented to the seller for acceptance or rejection. The broker is required by law to present all offers to the seller. The only exception exists for frivolous offers. Since it is sometimes difficult to tell a frivolous offer from a very low offer, the licensee is well advised to present all offers. If the seller accepts all the terms and conditions as set forth in the offer to purchase, it will constitute a binding agreement between the buyer and the seller. If either party withdraws, he or she may be liable to the other for breach of contract. If the seller does not accept all the terms and conditions of the agreement, he or she may counter-offer to the buyer on those conditions that are not acceptable to him or her. In this case, it becomes necessary for the broker to return to the buyer for his or her authorization or approval of the new terms in the contract. In the sale of large parcels of property, it is not uncommon for several counteroffers to be made before a binding agreement is in effect.

Once the agreement has been accepted and signed by both the buyer and the seller, and the acceptance has been transmitted to all parties, they are ready to go to escrow. The escrow agent is a stakeholder for the buyer and the seller. The agent takes the seller's escrow instructions and obtains from him or her a grant deed to transfer title to the property. Instructions are also taken from the buyer, as well as cash or other assets that the buyer is depositing on the purchase. The escrow agency may also complete for the buyer's signature a promissory note and deed of trust if a bank or other institution is lending the buyer money for the property purchase.

The title insurance company immediately searches the title to the property and issues a preliminary report giving a legal description of the property and showing all liens and encumbrances of record. Upon the closing of the transaction, the company issues a policy of title insurance, guaranteeing title to the buyer. The county in which the property is located normally determines who pays the title insurance fee; whatever the county's policy, though, it can be waived if all concerned parties agree to do so.

LISTING AGREEMENTS

A listing agreement creates an agency; therefore, a broker holding a listing agreement is the agent of his or her principal.

Brokers may collect a commission on the sale of real property only if the listing agreement is in writing. Contracts for the conveyance of real property are required to be in writing; thus, the listing contracts creating the authorization to sell must also be in writing. A listing agreement need not be in any particular form, but many standard forms are available today.

To assure that his or her commission is paid, the broker should have the listing agreement signed by all owners of the property. This would include all signatures of parties where real property is owned in joint tenancy, in tenancy in common, or as community property. If only two of three joint tenants signed the listing, then those two owners would be bound by the listing. The law requires that both spouses selling community real property agree to the sale. Therefore, both spouses must sign a listing involving the sale of community property.

The broker is entitled to a commission—even though a valid listing agreement was not in effect—if signed escrow instructions provide for it in a certain sum in dollars to be paid to the real estate broker. Further, where the real estate purchase contract and receipt for deposit provides for a commission, and it is properly signed by the sellers, the broker may enforce a commission.

Types of listing agreements

Open listing   An open listing gives several brokers an opportunity to procure customers for a property. If the property is sold by a broker, the owners need not give formal notice of the sale to the other brokers. The open listing says in effect that if any broker furnishes a buyer ready, willing, and able to purchase the property under the agreed terms and conditions, that broker will be paid a commission as provided for in the agreement. However, if the owner sells his or her own property, the owner does not have to pay a commission to the brokers. Contractors or builders will use this type of listing on occasion.

The broker, under the terms of an open listing agreement, cannot normally afford to spend a great deal of time or money on the sale of the property. Also, if the property owner quotes a price different from that being quoted by the broker, difficulties may sometimes arise

Net listing   In a net listing, the broker retains anything received above a sale amount set by the property owner. For example, A, a property owner, lists his property with B, a broker, for $120,000 net to the owner. If B sells the property for $130,000, he may retain the difference of $10,000, excluding any expenses in connection with the sale. The real estate law requires the broker to notify both the buyer and the seller of the amount of the sale price within one month of the closing of the transaction. The agent must disclose the amount of his or her compensation prior to or at the time the principal binds himself or herself to the transaction. The broker as a *fiduciary* agent must act in good faith toward his or her principal. The question may arise, "Did the broker advise his or her principal as to the true value of the property?" In the example given, assume that the broker sold the property for $140,000. The burden of proof is upon the broker to show that he did act in good faith; otherwise, his license might be in jeopardy.

Exclusive agency listing   Under an exclusive agreement, the property owner appoints one agent as his or her exclusive agent to sell the property. Since the owner is not the agent, the owner reserves the right to sell his or her own property. If anyone other than the exclusive agent sells the property, a commission must be paid to the exclusive agency broker. Under California law, such agreements must have a definite date of termination. If they do not, the broker's license can be suspended or revoked in the event he or she attempts to collect a commission. Assume that B, a broker, secures an exclusive agency agreement to sell A's house. The listing agreement is dated and signed by the property owner and provides that the listing agreement shall remain in effect until canceled by her. This is in violation of the Real Estate Law because the agreement does not have a definite termination date.

Exclusive-right-to-sell listing   The exclusive-right-to-sell agreement gives only the listing broker the exclusive and irrevocable right to sell property. If anyone else makes the sale, whether another agent or the property owner, during the time the agreement is in effect, the listing broker is entitled to his or her commission. Like the exclusive agency agreement, the exclusive authorization and right-to-sell agreement must have a definite date of termination. Any deviation is in direct violation of the Real Estate Law, and, again, the broker's or salesperson's license may be suspended or revoked.

Under the exclusive-right-to-sell listing agreement, the broker, as in all agency relationships, owes a high duty to his or her principal. The broker must advertise and use due diligence in procuring a purchaser for the property. The broker must keep his or her principal informed at all times as to the progress being made and inform him or her of all material facts. The Real Estate Commissioner receives complaints from time to time stating that some broker has not used diligence in procuring a purchaser for someone's property, with the result that the property has been tied up for a long period of time. All such written complaints must be investigated by the Real Estate Commissioner or one of his or her deputies. In some cases, the broker may have expended time and effort in procuring a purchaser for the property and yet failed to inform the property owner as to the progress he or she was making throughout the listing period. If he or she had serviced the listing properly and kept the principal informed, but was not successful in selling the property, it might be possible for him or her to get such a listing renewed. It is usually considered inadvisable for a broker to take in large numbers of listings unless the broker feels that he or she can expend a reasonable sum for advertising and believes in good faith that the properties can be sold.

Multiple listing   Multiple-listing associations are conducted by a group of real estate brokers organized to present a service to property owners. Multiple-listing associations are usually a part of the board of Realtors within a given community. Multiple-listing agreements are usually drawn up using the exclusive-right-to-sell form. These agreements are sent to a central multiple-listing office and copies are distributed to all members of the association. Commissions are split between the listing office and the selling broker's office, with a small percentage going to the multiple-listing association to cover costs of operation. Where the listing office also sells its own listing, it may retain the entire commission by paying the association its fee. Such listing agreements and associations have the advantage of exposing the property to a wide group of buyers, thus increasing the probability of the property sale in the shortest time possible.

EXPANDED ANALYSIS OF EXCLUSIVE AUTHORIZATION AND RIGHT-TO-SELL LISTING—CALIFORNIA ASSOCIATION OF REALTORS STANDARD FORM (Figure 6–1)

1. *Right to sell*   The words "exclusive and irrevocable" mean that the property is listed exclusively with *one* brokerage firm and the listing cannot be prematurely terminated without the broker's consent. If any other agent, any other person, or the owner sells the property during the term of the listing agreement, a commission based on the listed price will be paid to the exclusive agent.

The Exclusive Authorization and Right to Sell and the Exclusive Agency Listing Agreements must contain a *definite date of termination*; otherwise, the Real Estate Law has been violated and the licensee may be subject to disciplinary action by the Commissioner.

The description of the property should include the *legal description*; however, the street address is acceptable if it describes a unique piece of real property. Since unimproved real property is often not describable by street address, a full legal description is usually used.

2. *Terms of sale*   The broker or the salesperson should take sufficient time with the property owner to secure all terms and details of the transaction, including the total consideration or purchase price of the property and how it will be paid. *Example:* Can the buyer assume the deeds of trust existing on the property, or must the buyer secure his or her own loan? Is the seller willing to accept a promissory note and deed of trust as a part of the purchase price? Will the existing assessment bonds on the property be paid by the seller, or must the buyer assume them?

a. The items of personal property that the owner will agree to transfer to the buyer should be set forth in the listing agreement. If there are other items within the household that might be considered real property or items of real property that the owner wishes to reserve, they also should be set forth in the listing agreement.

b. A listing agreement must authorize the broker to collect a deposit for his or her principal; otherwise, he or she is authorized only to find a buyer ready, willing, and able to purchase the property. If a deposit is collected without authorization the broker holds it as agent of the buyer and not of the seller. Today, most listing agreements do provide for the collection of a deposit.

c. Customs differ in California as to who pays for the standard coverage policy of title insurance. In some counties the seller pays for it, and in others the buyer pays for it. The student should check the custom of the county in which he or she resides.

d. All owners of the real property should sign the listing agreement, whether they hold title as tenants in common, joint tenancy, or community property. A real estate commission may be enforced, however, where only two of the three joint tenants sign. In the case of community property, both the husband and the wife must sign the agreement. The person or persons so signing obligate their portion of ownership for the commission.

The agent should be given authorization before placing a "For Sale" sign on the property.

3. *Compensation to agent*   The real estate commission is not fixed by law, and trade associations may not

EXCLUSIVE AUTHORIZATION AND RIGHT TO SELL

THIS IS INTENDED TO BE A LEGALLY BINDING AGREEMENT—READ IT CAREFULLY.

CALIFORNIA ASSOCIATION OF REALTORS® STANDARD FORM

1. **Right to Sell.** I hereby employ and grant ___Executive Brokerage Company___ hereinafter called "Agent," the exclusive and irrevocable right commencing on ___May 16___, 19 __85__, and expiring at midnight on ___August 4___, 19 __85__, to sell or exchange the real property situated in ___the City of Ontario___ County of ___San Bernadino___, California described as follows: ___Lot 12, Block 6, Tract 1345, Beverly Estates, recorded 1979 in the San Bernadino County Records, Book 72 at Page 128. Also known as 67245 Linda Sue Court, Ontario, California.___

2. **Terms of Sale.** The purchase price shall be $___145,000.00___, to be paid in the following terms: ___$45,400 cash including a deposit. Buyers to assume existing loan of approximately $99,600, 11 1/4 percent interest, beneficiary, Bank of America, Loan #78901.___

   (a) The following items of personal property are to be included in the above-stated price:

   (b) Agent is hereby authorized to accept and hold on my behalf a deposit upon the purchase price.

   (c) Evidence of title to the property shall be in the form of a California Land Title Association Standard Coverage Policy of Title Insurance in the amount of the selling price to be paid for by ___the sellers___-------------------------------

   (d) I warrant that I am the owner of the property or have the authority to execute this agreement. I hereby authorize a FOR SALE sign to be placed on my property by Agent. I authorize the Agent named herein to cooperate with sub-agents.

3. **Notice: The amount or rate of real estate commissions is not fixed by law. They are set by each broker individually and may be negotiable between the seller and broker.**

   Compensation to Agent. I hereby agree to compensate Agent as follows:

   (a) ___Six percent___ __6__ % of the selling price if the property is sold during the term hereof, or any extension thereof, by Agent, on the terms herein set forth or any other price and terms I may accept, or through any other person, or by me, or ___six percent 6__ % of the price shown in 2, if said property is withdrawn from sale, transferred, conveyed, leased without the consent of Agent, or made unmarketable by any voluntary act during the term hereof or any extension thereof.

   (b) the compensation provided for in subparagraph (a) above if property is sold, conveyed or otherwise transferred within ___ninety (90)___ days after the termination of this authority or any extension thereof to anyone with whom Agent has had negotiations prior to final termination, provided I have received notice in writing, including the names of the prospective purchasers, before or upon termination of this agreement or any extension hereof. However. I shall not be obligated to pay the compensation provided for in subparagraph (a) if a valid listing agreement is entered into during the term of said protection period with another licensed real estate broker and a sale, lease or exchange of the property is made during the term of said valid listing agreement.

4. If action be instituted to enforce this agreement, the prevailing party shall receive reasonable attorney's fees and costs as fixed by the Court.

5. In the event of an exchange, permission is hereby given Agent to represent all parties and collect compensation or commissions from them, provided there is full disclosure to all principals of such agency. Agent is authorized to divide with other agents such compensation or commissions in any manner acceptable to them.

6. I agree to save and hold Agent harmless from all claims, disputes, litigation, and/or judgments arising from any incorrect information supplied by me, or from any material fact known by me concerning the property which I fail to disclose.

7. This property is offered in compliance with state and federal anti-discrimination laws.

8. **Other provisions:** ___Sellers may, depending upon qualifications of the buyers, carry back a note secured by a TD of $10,000, 12% interest, payable at 1% or more per month including principal and interest. Said note due in 3 years.___

9. I acknowledge that I have read and understand this Agreement, and that I have received a copy hereof.

Dated ___May 16___, 19 __85__ ___Ontario___, California

Owner ___Homer C. Principal___ Address ___67234 Linda Sue Court___

Owner ___Laura M. Principal___ City, State, Phone ___Ontario, California (714) 986-4444___

10. In consideration of the above, Agent agrees to use diligence in procuring a purchaser.

Agent ___Executive Brokerage Company___ Address ___2000 Euclid Avenue___ City ___Ontario, CA___

By ___William T Jones___ Phone ___(714) 986-0000___ Date ___5/16/85___

NO REPRESENTATION IS MADE AS TO THE LEGAL VALIDITY OF ANY PROVISION OR THE ADEQUACY OF ANY PROVISION IN ANY SPECIFIC TRANSACTION. IF YOU DESIRE LEGAL ADVICE, CONSULT YOUR ATTORNEY.

To order, contact—California Association of Realtors®
525 South Virgil Avenue, Los Angeles, California 90020
Copyright © 1978 by California Association of Realtors® (Revised, 1980 Reviewed, 1984)

FORM A-11

BROKER'S COPY

Figure 6–1

establish commission schedules. The commission is a matter of agreement between the parties. The amount need not be given in dollars, since the sales price of the property may be different from the listing price.

On one-to-four-family residences occupied by the owner, it is illegal to preprint the amount of the commission preprinted on the listing form. The agent must write in the amount of the commission by hand at the time of the listing is signed. The broker should also tell the seller that the amount of commission is not set by law or custom, and is subject to negotiation.

> *a. The owner promises to pay the commission if he or she—without consent of agent—withdraws the property from the market, sells it, leases it, or otherwise makes it unmarketable by his or her own act. The same would apply if the term of the agreement were extended. This agreement is an "exclusive and irrevocable right to sell."*
>
> *b. This paragraph is often referred to as a "safety clause." Prior to or on the expiration date of the listing, the broker should provide the owner, in writing, with a list of all prospective buyers for the property with whom the broker has had negotiations. If the broker fails to do this and the owner should sell to one of these prospective buyers, the broker is not entitled to a commission. Each listing contract should be checked, because all do not read the same.*

4. *Attorney's fees*   Attorney's fees were discussed in Chapter 5. This is a common clause in most contracts. Attorney's fees are awarded to the winning party. The fees awarded by the court, however, may be less than the attorney will actually charge the winning party.

5. *Subagent cooperation*   A subagent cooperates in the sale of property with the listing agent. The subagent also represents the property owner, since he or she does cooperate with the listing broker.

6. *Discrimination*   Fair-housing laws, both federal and state, do not permit discrimination with respect to race, creed, color, marital status, sex, or national origin.

7. *Full disclosure*   An agent may not represent and receive compensation from more than one party to a transaction without the knowledge and consent of all parties. There must be a *full disclosure* to all principals. If there is not, the licensee is subject to disciplinary action by the Real Estate Commissioner.

8. *"Hold harmless clause"*   The fact that an agent repeats what his or her principal has said without verification can constitute misrepresentation. The agent is advised to qualify facts of which he or she does not have firsthand knowledge. This is a "hold harmless clause," but the agent could still be sued even though he or she may later have a right of action against the principal.

9. *Other provisions*   Any provision of the contract

not stated elsewhere should be inserted in this blank space.

10. *Receipt of copy*   When the prospective seller signs the listing agreement, he or she is entitled to a copy. Should the broker or salesperson fail to give the seller a copy, the broker's or salesperson's license may be suspended or revoked. The burden of proof is always upon the agent. The fact that the seller acknowledges receipt of a copy of the listing contract does not matter. The agent would be required to submit proof in litigation that he or she did give a copy of the agreement to the seller. Further, the signatures of all owners of the property should be obtained. See item 2d in this section.

11. *Bilateral contract*   This sentence makes the contract or listing agreement bilateral. The property owner promises to sell his or her property under the terms and conditions of the agreement, and the broker agrees to use diligence in procuring a purchaser. The courts in California tend not to enforce unilateral listing agreements.

SPECIAL AUXILIARY FORMS USED WITH LISTING AGREEMENTS

At the time a listing agreement is executed, two other documents need to be executed, if the broker is being professional. Neither of these forms is as yet required by law to be signed. However, if they are not signed, the broker is inviting litigation if problems arise. The two forms are the seller's affidavit of nonforeign status and the listing information disclosure statement.

Nonforeign status

Recent amendments to the Internal Revenue Code now require a buyer to withhold 10 percent of the gross sales price of property if the seller is not a U.S. citizen or a U.S. resident alien. If the seller is a foreigner and the buyer does not withhold the required 10 percent, and if the seller does not pay the appropriate taxes on the sale, the buyer is personally liable for the full amount of the seller's tax, plus significant penalties.

There is an exemption if the buyer is purchasing a home for his or her residential use and the home costs under $300,000. However, you never know if the buyer is purchasing the home for his or her use or for investment property until the buyer is found.

Many brokers delay taking information about the seller's citizenship status until a buyer is found. However, it is recommended that the information be ascertained at the time the listing is sold. If the seller is a foreigner, offers will have to be structured so that there is 10 percent in cash, over and above commissions and selling costs, to give the IRS. Figure 6–2 can be used to meet the

SELLER'S AFFIDAVIT
OF NONFOREIGN STATUS
CALIFORNIA ASSOCIATION OF REALTORS® STANDARD FORM

(FOREIGN INVESTMENT IN REAL PROPERTY TAX ACT)

Section 1445 of the Internal Revenue Code provides that a transferee of a U.S. real property interest must withhold tax if the transferor is a foreign person. To inform the transferee that withholding of tax is not required upon the disposition of a U.S. real property interest located at ___67245 Linda Sue Court, Ontario, California___

by ___Lona M. Principal___ [name of transferor], I hereby certify the following (if an entity transferor, on behalf of the transferor):

THIS SECTION FOR INDIVIDUAL TRANSFEROR(S):

1. I am not a nonresident alien for purposes of U.S. income taxation;

2. My U.S. taxpayer identifying number (Social Security number) is ___547-00-0000___ ; and

3. My home address is ___67245 Linda Sue Court, Ontario, California___

___ .

THIS SECTION FOR CORPORATION, PARTNERSHIP, TRUST, OR ESTATE TRANSFEROR(S):

1. ___ [name of transferor] is not a foreign corporation, foreign partnership, foreign trust, or foreign estate (as those terms are defined in the Internal Revenue Code and Income Tax Regulations);

2. ___ [name of transferor]'s U.S. employer identification number is ___ ;

3. ___ [name of transferor]'s office address is ___ ; and

4. I, the undersigned individual, declare that I have authority to sign this document on behalf of ___ [name of transferor].

THIS SECTION FOR ALL TRANSFEROR(S):

___Lona M. Principal___ [name of transferor] understands that this certification may be disclosed to the Internal Revenue Service by transferee and that any false statement I have made here (or, for entity transferor, contained herein) could be punished by fine, imprisonment, or both.

Under penalties of perjury I declare that I have examined this certification and to the best of my knowledge and belief it is true, correct and complete.

Date ___5/16/85___   Signature ___*Lona M Principal*___

Typed or Printed Name ___Lona M. Principal___

Title [if signed on behalf of an entity transferor] ___

IMPORTANT NOTICE:

An affidavit should be signed by each individual or entity transferor to whom or to which it applies. Before you sign, any questions relating to the legal sufficiency of this form, or to whether it applies to a particular transaction, or to the definition of any of the terms used, should be referred to an attorney, a certified public accountant, or other professional tax advisor, or to the Internal Revenue Service.

To order, contact—California Association of Realtors®
525 S. Virgil Avenue, Los Angeles, California
Copyright© 1985, California Association of Realtors®   FORM AS-11

Figure 6–2

LISTING INFORMATION DISCLOSURE STATEMENT
CALIFORNIA ASSOCIATION OF REALTORS® STANDARD FORM

BUYER: On __May 16__, 19 _85_, the undersigned Agent, in conjunction with an inquiry of the Seller(s), conducted a reasonable visual inspection of the property commonly known as ___67245 Linda Sue Court, Ontario, California___ _____, ☒ Residential 1-4 ☐ other_____, in the (city) (county) of ___San Bernardino___. The information contained herein is the result of that inquiry and inspection.

THIS INFORMATION IS A DISCLOSURE OF THE CONDITION OF THE PROPERTY AS OF THE ABOVE DATE. IT IS NOT A WARRANTY OF ANY KIND BY THE SELLER(S) OR THE AGENT(S) AND IS NOT A SUBSTITUTE FOR ANY INSPECTIONS THE BUYER MAY WISH TO OBTAIN.

I.
SELLER'S INFORMATION

The Seller discloses the following information with the knowledge that even though this is not a warranty, prospective Buyers may rely on such information in deciding whether and on what terms to purchase the subject property. Seller hereby authorizes the undersigned agent to provide a copy of this statement to any person or entity in connection with any actual or anticipated sale of the property.

THE FOLLOWING ARE REPRESENTATIONS MADE BY THE SELLER(S) AND ARE *NOT* THE REPRESENTATIONS OF THE AGENT(S). THIS INFORMATION IS A DISCLOSURE ONLY AND IS *NOT* INTENDED TO BE A PART OF ANY CONTRACT BETWEEN BUYER AND SELLER.

Seller ☒ is ☐ is not occupying the property.

A. The subject property has the items checked below (read across):

☒ Range	☒ Oven	☒ Microwave
☒ Dishwasher	☐ Trash Compactor	☒ Garbage Disposal
☒ Washer/Dryer Hookups	☒ Window Screens	☒ Rain Gutters
☐ Burglar Alarms	☒ Smoke Detector(s)	☐ Fire Alarm
☒ T.V. Antenna	☐ Satellite Dish	☐ Intercom
☒ Central Heating	☐ Central Air Conditioning	☐ Evaporator Cooler(s)
☐ Wall/Window Air Conditioning	☒ Sprinklers	☒ Public Sewer System
☐ Septic Tank	☐ Sump Pump	☐ Water Softener
☒ Patio/Decking	☐ Built-in Barbeque	☐ Gazebo
☐ Sauna	☐ Pool	☐ Spa ☐ Hot Tub
☐ Security Gate(s)	☒ Garage Door Opener(s)	☒ Number of Remote Controls ___2___
Garage: ☒ Attached	☐ Not Attached	☐ Carport
Pool/Spa Heater: ☐ Gas	☐ Solar	☐ Electric
Water Heater: ☒ Gas	☐ Solar	☐ Electric
Water Supply: ☒ City	☐ Well	☐ Private Utility ☐ Other_____

Exhaust Fan(s) in ___Kitchen___   220 Volt Wiring in ___Kitchen & Garage___

Fireplace(s) in ___Den___   ☐ Gas Hookup   Insulation in _____

☒ Roof: Type: ___Shake___   Age: ___2 years___ (approx.)

☐ Other: _____

Are there, to the best of your (Seller's) knowledge, any of the above that are not in operating condition? ☐ Yes ☒ No   If yes, then describe. (Attach additional sheets if necessary.):

_____
_____
_____

B. Are you (Seller) aware of any defects/malfunctions in any of the following that could affect the value or desirability of the property? ☐ Yes ☒ No   If yes, check appropriate box(es) below.

☐ Interior Walls ☐ Ceilings ☐ Floors ☐ Exterior Walls   ☐ Roof ☐ Windows ☐ Doors ☐ Foundation ☐ Slab(s)   ☐ Driveways ☐ Sidewalks ☐ Walls/Fences   ☐ Electrical Systems ☐ Plumbing/Sewers/Septic   ☐ Other Structural Components (Describe: _____)

If any of the above is checked, explain. (Attach additional sheets if necessary.): _____

_____
_____

To order, contact—California Association of Realtors®
525 S. Virgil Avenue, Los Angeles, California 90020
Copyright © 1985, California Association of Realtors®

FORM LID-11-1

Page 1 of 2

Figure 6–3

LISTING INFORMATION DISCLOSURE STATEMENT (Page 2)

C. Are you (Seller) aware of any conditions that could affect the value or desirabilty of the property?

1. Common walls, fences and driveways that may have an effect on the subject property. . . . . □ Yes ☒ No
2. Any encroachments, easements or similar matters that may affect your interest in the subject property. . . . . □ Yes ☒ No
3. Room additions, structural modifications, or other alterations or repairs made without necessary permits. . . . . □ Yes ☒ No
4. Room additions, structural modifications, or other alterations or repairs not in compliance with building codes. . . . . □ Yes ☒ No
5. Landfill (compacted or otherwise) on the property or any portion thereof. . . . . □ Yes ☒ No
6. Settling, slippage, sliding or other soil problems. . . . . □ Yes ☒ No
7. Flooding, drainage or grading problems. . . . . □ Yes ☒ No
8. Major damage to the property or any of the structures from fire, earthquake, floods, slides, etc. . . . . □ Yes ☒ No
9. Any zoning violations, non-conforming units, violations of "setback" requirements, etc. . . . . □ Yes ☒ No
10. Neighborhood noise problems or other nuisances. . . . . □ Yes ☒ No
11. Homeowner's Association obligations (dues, lawsuits, etc.), CC & R's or other deed restrictions or obligations. . . . . □ Yes ☒ No
12. Any "common area" problems. . . . . □ Yes ☒ No
13. Any notices of abatement or citations against the property. . . . . □ Yes ☒ No
14. Other _____

If the answer to any of these is yes, explain. (Attach additional sheets if necessary.):

_____
_____
_____
_____
_____

Seller certifies that the information herein is true and correct to the best of the Seller's knowledge as of the date signed by Seller.

Seller _____ *Lora M Princeton* _____ Date ___ May 16, 1985 ____

Seller _____ Date _____

II.

AGENT'S INSPECTION DISCLOSURE

BASED ON THE ABOVE INQUIRY OF THE SELLER(S) AS TO THE CONDITION OF THE PROPERTY AND BASED ON A REASONABLE VISUAL INSPECTION OF THE PROPERTY BY THE UNDERSIGNED AGENT IN CONJUNCTION WITH THAT INQUIRY, AGENT STATES THE FOLLOWING (This Section to be used by Agent to make Buyer(s) aware of the results, if any, of the Agent's visual inspection. Attach additional sheets if necessary.):

_____
_____ As stated above, by seller _____
_____
_____
_____

BUYER(S) AND SELLER(S) MAY WISH TO OBTAIN PROFESSIONAL ADVICE AND/OR INSPECTIONS OF THE PROPERTY AND TO PROVIDE FOR APPROPRIATE PROVISIONS IN A CONTRACT BETWEEN BUYER(S) AND SELLER(S) WITH RESPECT TO ANY ADVICE/INSPECTIONS/DEFECTS.

Real Estate Broker __Executive Brokerage Co.__   By __*William J Jones*__   Date __5/16/85__
                     Please Print   *Agent's Signature*

I/WE ACKNOWLEDGE RECEIPT OF A COPY OF THIS STATEMENT.

Seller _____ Date _____   Buyer _____ Date _____

Seller _____ Date _____   Buyer _____ Date _____

                                   Selling Agent _____ Date _____

A REAL ESTATE BROKER IS THE PERSON QUALIFIED TO ADVISE ON REAL ESTATE. IF YOU DESIRE LEGAL ADVICE CONSULT YOUR ATTORNEY.

To order, contact—California Association of Realtors®
525 S. Virgil Avenue, Los Angeles, California 90020
Copyright © 1985, California Association of Realtors®   FORM LID-11-2   Page 2 of 2

Figure 6–3   (Continued)

REAL ESTATE PURCHASE CONTRACT AND RECEIPT FOR DEPOSIT

THIS IS MORE THAN A RECEIPT FOR MONEY. IT IS INTENDED TO BE A LEGALLY BINDING CONTRACT. READ IT CAREFULLY.

CALIFORNIA ASSOCIATION OF REALTORS' STANDARD FORM

Los Angeles   , California. February 24   , 19 85

Received from William T. Fischer and Barbara Jean Fischer, his wife

herein called Buyer, the sum of Eight Hundred and No/100------------------------ Dollars $ 800.00

evidenced by cash ☐, cashier's check ☐, or ///////////////////////////// personal check ☒ payable to Security Title Insurance Company------, to be held uncashed until acceptance of this offer, as deposit on account of purchase price of

---One Hundred Ten Thousand and No/100------------------------- Dollars $ 110,000.00

for the purchase of property, situated in the City of Los Angeles, County of   Los Angeles   , California,

described as follows: 10234 Laguna Avenue, a three-unit apartment complex

1.   Buyer will deposit in escrow with Security Title Insurance Company the balance of purchase price as follows: $110,000, payable as follows:

$12,000 cash down payment, of which the above $800 deposit is a part.

$88,000 cash from buyers obtaining a new fixed rate loan, secured by the property, with equal monthly payments of not more than $1007.97 per month, including interest not to exceed 13.5% per annum, amortized in not less than 30 years.

This offer subject to and conditioned upon buyers obtaining the above loan commitment within 15 business days of acceptance hereof, or by waiving this condition in writing.

$10,000 promissory note executed by buyers in favor of sellers, and secured by a second deed of trust on the property. The note to be payable in equal monthly installments of not more than $158.29 per month, including interest not to exceed 14.5% per annum, amortized in not less than 5 years, or upon sale or transfer of the property, whichever occurs first.

Included as a part of this sale are all refrigerators, washers, dryers and draperies now located on the property. Sellers will deliver the above items in good working order, free and clear of any liens or encumbrances, and evidenced by a bill of sale.

Set forth above any terms and conditions of a factual nature applicable to this sale, such as financing, prior sale of other property, the matter of structural pest control inspection, repairs and personal property to be included in the sale.

2.   Deposit will ☒ will not ☐ be increased by $ 2,500.00---- to $ 3,300.00----- within ten (10) ----days of acceptance of this offer.

3.   Buyer does ☒ does not ☐ intend to occupy subject property as his residence.

4.   The following supplements are incorporated as part of this agreement:

		Other
☒ Structural Pest Control Certification Agreement	☒ Occupancy Agreement	☒ Res. Lease Agreement After Sale
☒ Special Studies Zone Disclosure	☐ VA Amendment	☐
☐ Flood Insurance Disclosure	☐ FHA Amendment	☐

5.   Buyer and Seller shall deliver signed instructions to the escrow holder within _____days from Seller's acceptance which shall provide for closing within _____days from Seller's acceptance. Escrow fees to be paid as follows:

6.   Buyer and Seller acknowledge receipt of a copy of this page, which constitutes Page 1 of _2_ Pages.

Buyer *William T Fisher*   Seller _____

Buyer *Barbara Jean Fisher*   Seller _____

A REAL ESTATE BROKER IS THE PERSON QUALIFIED TO ADVISE ON REAL ESTATE. IF YOU DESIRE LEGAL ADVICE CONSULT YOUR ATTORNEY.

Figure 6–4

REAL ESTATE PURCHASE CONTRACT AND RECEIPT FOR DEPOSIT
The following terms and conditions are hereby incorporated in and made a part of Buyer's Offer

7.   Title is to be free of liens, encumbrances, easements, restrictions, rights and conditions of record or known to Seller, other than the following: (a) Current property taxes, (b) covenants, conditions, restrictions, and public utility easements of record, if any, provided the same do not adversely affect the continued use of the property for the purposes for which it is presently being used, unless reasonably disapproved by Buyer in writing within __five__ days of receipt of a current preliminary title report furnished at __Buyer's__ expense, and (c) _____

Seller shall furnish Buyer at __Buyer's__ expense a standard California Land Title Association policy issued by __Security Title Insurance__ Company, showing title vested in Buyer subject only to the above. If Seller is unwilling or unable to eliminate any title matter disapproved by Buyer as above, Seller may terminate this agreement. If Seller fails to deliver title as above, Buyer may terminate this agreement; in either case, the deposit shall be returned to Buyer.

8.   Property taxes, premiums on insurance acceptable to Buyer, rents, interest, and ////////////////////////////// shall be pro-rated as of (a) the date of recordation of deed; or (b) // Any bond or assessment which is a lien shall be //paid// _assumed_ // by __buyers__. Transfer taxes, if any, shall be paid by __Sellers__.

9.   Possession shall be delivered to Buyer (a) on close of escrow, or (b) not later than ////////////////////////// days after close of escrow, or (c) /////////////////////////////

10.   Unless otherwise designated in the escrow instructions of Buyer, title shall vest as follows: _____ __Instructions to be delivered to the escrowholder_____

(The manner of taking title may have significant legal and tax consequences. Therefore, give this matter serious consideration.)

11.   If Broker is a participant of a Board multiple listing service ("MLS") the Broker is authorized to report the sale, its price, terms, and financing for the information, publication, dissemination, and use of the authorized Board members.

12.   If Buyer fails to complete said purchase as herein provided by reason of any default of Buyer, Seller shall be released from his obligation to sell the property to Buyer and may proceed against Buyer upon any claim or remedy which he may have in law or equity, provided, however, that by placing their initials here Buyer: ( ) Seller: ( ) agree that Seller shall retain the deposit as his liquidated damages. If the described property is a dwelling with no more than four units, one of which the Buyer intends to occupy as his residence, Seller shall retain as liquidated damages the deposit actually paid, or an amount therefrom, not more than 3% of the purchase price and promptly return any excess to Buyer.

13.   If the only controversy or claim between the parties arises out of or relates to the disposition of the Buyer's deposit, such controversy or claim shall at the election of the parties be decided by arbitration. Such arbitration shall be determined in accordance with the Rules of the American Arbitration Association, and judgment upon the award rendered by the Arbitrator(s) may be entered in any court having jurisdiction thereof. The provisions of Code of Civil Procedure Section 1283.05 shall be applicable to such arbitration.

14.   In any action or proceeding arising out of this agreement, the prevailing party shall be entitled to reasonable attorney's fees and costs.

15.   Time is of the essence. All modification or extensions shall be in writing signed by the parties.

16.   This constitutes an offer to purchase the described property. Unless acceptance is signed by Seller and the signed copy delivered to Buyer, in person or by mail to the address below, within __two (2)__ days, this offer shall be deemed revoked and the deposit shall be returned. Buyer acknowledges receipt of a copy hereof.

Real Estate Broker __HOMER & DAVEY ASSOCIATES__

By __/s/ Homer C. Davey__

Address __10045 Euclid Boulevard__

Telephone __(213) 476-0000__

Buyer: __William J Fisher__

Buyer: __Barbara Jean Fisher__

Address __1232 Lonesome Rd., San Clements, CA.__

Telephone __(213) 592-9999__

ACCEPTANCE

The undersigned Seller accepts and agrees to sell the property on the above terms and conditions. Seller has employed __Homer C. Davey & Associates__

as Broker(s) and agrees to pay for services the sum of __Six Thousand Six Hundred and No/100_____ Dollars ($__6,600.00__), payable as follows: (a) On recordation of the deed or other evidence of title, or (b) if completion of sale is prevented by default of Seller, upon Seller's default or (c) if completion of sale is prevented by default of Buyer, only if and when Seller collects damages from Buyer, by suit or otherwise and then in an amount not less than one-half of the damages recovered, but not to exceed the above fee, after first deducting title and escrow expenses and the expenses of collection, if any. In any action between Broker and Seller arising out of this agreement, the prevailing party shall be entitled to reasonable attorney's fees and costs. The undersigned acknowledges receipt of a copy and authorizes Broker(s) to deliver a signed copy to Buyer.

Dated __2/25/85__ Telephone __(213) 597-2222__

Address __10234 Laguna Avenue__

Seller _____

Seller _____

Broker(s) agree to the foregoing. Broker __Homer C. Davey & Associates__

Broker _____

Dated __2/25/85__ By __/s/ Homer C. Davey__

Dated _____ By _____

    FORM D-11-2

Page ____ of ____ Pages

Figure 6–4   (Continued)

Internal Revenue Service's requirements. An attorney or a CPA should be consulted on any sale involving a foreigner.

Property disclosure statement

In 1984 the California Court of Appeals handed down its now-famous *Easton* decision. (The full case name is *Easton* v. *Strassburger*, 1984, 152 C.A.3d 90.) The court held that a listing broker selling residential property was liable to the buyer for failing to point out not only known defects in the property but also defects that *should have been known* after a reasonable inspection of the property.

Easton held that the mere fact that the seller had lied and told the broker there was "nothing wrong" with the property was insufficient. The broker should have observed that certain "red flags," such as water stains on the ceiling and netting over a dirt slide area, indicated that there might be serious problems with the property. Noting these facts, the broker had a duty to investigate. This error cost the listing broker over $200,000.

To protect themselves, brokers should obtain detailed statements from sellers about the condition of the property. Figure 6–3, the California Association of Realtors (CAR) form, elicits this information. Additionally, the broker must still inspect the property independently.

All brokers who list residential property must complete a Listing Information Disclosure Statement (See Figure 6–3). Both the seller and the broker must state all observable and known defects in the property's condition. A copy of this form must be given to the buyer. These mandatory requirements are now required by the California Civil Code for all residential transactions.

EXPANDED ANALYSIS OF THE REAL ESTATE PURCHASE CONTRACT AND RECEIPT FOR DEPOSIT (Figure 6–4)

The form is in two separate contracts. The first is the buyer's unilateral offer to purchase the described property, which if countersigned by the seller becomes a bilateral agreement to purchase and sell. The second is the broker's employment contract with the seller, which may supersede the broker's listing agreement unless the acceptance clause by the appropriate reference incorporates the terms of the listing agreement.

Figure 6–4 shows the completed contract. The following text in this section breaks the contract into parts. First it examines the introductory part of the contract. This part includes the (1) date and location of entering into the contract, (2) name of the persons putting up the deposit, (3) size of the deposit, (4) type of deposit, (5) purchase price, and (6) description of the property.

In filling in this portion of the contract, the place where the signing occurs should be inserted. The full names of the buyers must be spelled correctly, and the marital status of the buyers should be designated, such as "husband and wife," "a single woman," "an unmarried man." The amount of deposit as well as the purchase price should be identified in both letters and figures. A deposit may take the form of cash, a personal check, a cashier's check, a promissory note, or an item of personal property, such as an automobile. It is important for the seller to understand the agent's form of deposit. Note that this contract provides that a personal check is "to be held uncashed until acceptance of this offer." If this is not the case, the contract should be amended to establish the conditions under which the check may be cashed. A postdated check should be so indicated and should be presented to the sellers. Normally, deposit monies must be placed in the broker's trustee account or in a neutral depository by the end of the next working day after the broker receives them and in accordance with the provisions of the contract.

The broker, by specific instructions from the buyer, can hold the check uncashed until acceptance. Then the broker must within the next working day deposit the check into a trustee or escrow account.

The deposit belongs to the buyer until the seller accepts the contract, at which time the seller has the right to control its disposition. Once the contract has been accepted by the seller it can be returned to the buyer only with the seller's permission.

In most contracts for the sale of real property it is sufficient if the street address is given. The legal description, however, may be necessary on unimproved land. The legal description on unimproved land may be two or three pages or even longer; therefore it is not uncommon to have this description attached to the contract as "Exhibit A."

Paragraph 1 of the contract deals with the escrowing of the transaction and the terms and conditions of the sale. The seller may specify in the listing agreement where he or she wishes the transaction to be escrowed. The transaction may be escrowed at any place authorized by law to handle escrows. Whether the seller selects an escrow agent or not, the buyer may specify the escrow agent in the offer to purchase. If the seller does specify an escrow agent in the listing agreement and the broker brings in an offer to purchase the property under the terms and conditions of the listing, *except* for the escrow agent, the broker has not earned his or her commission.

The terms of the purchase and sale should be stated clearly for the protection of all parties in the contract. *Remember*, this is more than a receipt for money: it is a legally binding contract. Make sure these terms and conditions protect you as a buyer and as a seller.

Remember that most "conditions" are explicitly des-

REAL ESTATE PURCHASE CONTRACT AND RECEIPT FOR DEPOSIT

THIS IS MORE THAN A RECEIPT FOR MONEY. IT IS INTENDED TO BE A LEGALLY BINDING CONTRACT. READ IT CAREFULLY.

CALIFORNIA ASSOCIATION OF REALTORS' STANDARD FORM

<u>Los Angeles</u>, California. <u>February 24</u>, 19 <u>85</u>

Received from <u>William T. Fischer and Barbara Jean Fischer, his wife</u>

herein called Buyer, the sum of <u>Eight Hundred and No/100———————————</u> Dollars $ <u>800.00</u>

evidenced by cash ☐, cashier's check ☐, or ///////////////////////personal check ☒ payable to <u>Security Title</u> <u>Insurance Company———————</u>. to be held uncashed until acceptance of this offer, as deposit on account of purchase price of

<u>———One Hundred Ten Thousand and No/100——————————————</u> Dollars $ <u>110,000.00</u>

for the purchase of property, situated in <u>the City of Los Angeles</u>. County of <u>Los Angeles</u>, California,

described as follows: <u>10234 Laguna Avenue, a three-unit apartment complex</u>

1.   Buyer will deposit in escrow with <u>Security Title Insurance Company</u> the balance of purchase price as follows: $110,000, payable as follows:

    $12,000 cash down payment, of which the above $800 deposit is a part.

    $88,000 cash from buyers obtaining a new fixed rate loan, secured by the property, with equal monthly payments of not more than $1007.97 per month, including interest not to exceed 13.5% per annum, amortized in not less than 30 years.

    This offer subject to and conditioned upon buyers obtaining the above loan commitment within 15 business days of acceptance hereof, or by waiving this condition in writing.

    $10,000 promissory note executed by buyers in favor of sellers, and secured by a second deed of trust on the property. The note to be payable in equal monthly installments of not more than $158.29 per month, including interest not to exceed 14.5% per annum, amortized in not less than 5 years, or upon sale or transfer of the property, whichever occurs first.

    Included as a part of this sale are all refrigerators, washers, dryers and draperies now located on the property. Sellers will deliver the above items in good working order, free and clear of any liens or encumbrances, and evidenced by a bill of sale.

Set forth above any terms and conditions of a factual nature applicable to this sale, such as financing, prior sale of other property, the matter of structural pest control inspection, repairs and personal property to be included in the sale.

ignated by brokers as true conditions. The conditions should be preceded by wording such as, "This contract subject to and conditioned upon . . . and if the above conditions are not met, this contract shall be null and void."

The common problem of the pest control inspections and certifications are often included here. Usually the problem is dealt with by incorporating by reference a form such as the one in Figure 6–5, published by the California Association of Realtors.

2.   Deposit will ☒ will not ☐ be increased by $ <u>2,500.00————</u> to $ <u>3,300.00—————</u> within <u>ten (10) ————</u> days of acceptance of this offer.

Paragraph 2 deals with the buyer's willingness to increase the deposit if the seller accepts the buyer's offer. Figure 6–6, Receipt for Increased Deposit and Supplement to Real Estate Purchase Contract, should be used

as a supplement to paragraph 2. The seller may have provided for an increased deposit in the listing contract. (See also paragraph 12—liquidating damages.)

3.   Buyer does ☒ does not ☐ intend to occupy subject property as his residence.

Paragraph 3 is important because the Liquidated Damages Law makes a distinction between residential property (four units or fewer, one of which the buyer intends to occupy as his or her residence) and nonresidential

property. In the sale of residential property, the seller may retain the deposit actually paid or an amount from the sellers actual damages, which is presumed to be the amount of the deposit if that deposit is equal or less than

STRUCTURAL PEST CONTROL CERTIFICATION AGREEMENT
CALIFORNIA ASSOCIATION OF REALTORS' STANDARD FORM

This agreement is part of and is hereby incorporated in that "Real Estate Purchase Contract and Receipt for Deposit" between the parties hereof dated_February 24____ 19_85_, pertaining to the property described as follows:__-------------_
10234 Laguna Avenue, a three unit apartment complex-----------------------
_--_

1_William T. Fischer and Barbara Jean Fischer (buyers)--_agrees at his expense to furnish
Seller/Buyer

_Max J. Homeseller and Marie M. Homeseller (sellers)--------_within__10_days from date
Buyer/Seller

of SELLER'S approval of this agreement with a current written report of an inspection by a licensed Structural Pest Control Operator of the main building and all attached structures.
Inspection to include swimming pool, cabana and detached garages-----------
_--_
(specify any additions or exceptions)

2. If no infestation or infection of wood destroying pests or organisms is found, the report shall include either in the form of an endorsement or as a separate written statement by the inspecting licensed Structural Pest Control Operator a CERTIFICATION to provide in accordance with B & P Code 8519(a): "This is to certify that the above property was inspected on_February 28, 1985____(date) in accordance with the Structural Pest Control Act and rules and regulations adopted pursuant thereto, and that no evidence of active infestation or infection was found."

3. All work recommended in said report to repair damage caused by infestation or infection of wood-destroying pests or organisms found and all work to correct conditions that caused such infestation or infection shall be done at the expense of SELLER.
Regardless of the amount quoted by the Pest Control Operator for the work set forth above and more (specify any additions or exceptions)_particularly as described in the inspection report, SELLER'S liability for such work shall not exceed the sum of $1,200._
Funds for work to be performed shall be held in escrow and disbursed upon receipt of a CERTIFICATION on the "Notice of Work Completed" to provide, in accordance with B & P Code 8519(b): "This is to certify that the property described herein is now free of evidence of active infestation or infection."

4 With the additions or exceptions, if any, noted below, BUYER agrees that any work to correct conditions usually deemed likely to lead to infestation or infection of wood-destroying pests or organisms, but where no evidence of existing infestation or infection is found with respect to such conditions, is NOT the responsibility of the SELLER, and that such work shall be done only if requested by BUYER and then at the expense of BUYER.
----No additions or exceptions--
_--_
(specify any additions or exceptions)

5. If inspection of inaccessible areas is recommended in the report, BUYER has the option of accepting and approving the report or requesting further inspection be made at the BUYER's expense. If further inspection is made and infestation, infection, or damage is found, repair of such damage and all work to correct conditions that caused such infestation or infection and the cost of entry and closing of the inaccessible areas shall be at the expense of SELLER. If no infestation, infection, or damage is found, the cost of entry and closing of the inaccessible areas shall be at the expense of BUYER.

6_Buyers (William T. Fischer & Barbara Jean Fischer)____hereby selects the following named
Seller/Buyer

licensed Structural Pest Control Operator:_Ace Termite Control Company-----------------------_
SELLER consents to such inspection.

COPY OF REPORT TO BUYER

SELLER acknowledges his responsibility under Civil Code Section 1099 to deliver to BUYER as soon as practical before transfer of title or the execution of a real property sales contract as defined in Civil Code Section 2985 a copy of the inspection report, a "NOTICE OF WORK COMPLETED" OR A "CERTIFICATION pursuant to B & P Code 8519" as may be required.
SELLER directs_Homer C. Davey & Associates------------------------------------_
name of Broker

to deliver such copies of the above documents as may be required.
BUYER AND SELLER ACKNOWLEDGE RECEIPT OF A COPY OF THIS AGREEMENT WHICH INCORPORATES THE EXCERPTS FROM THE BUSINESS AND PROFESSIONS CODE AND THE CIVIL CODE PRINTED ON THE REVERSE HEREOF.

APPROVED AND ACCEPTED:

Dated_February 26____, 19_85_   Dated_February 26____, 19_85_

Buyer_____   Seller_____

Buyer_____   Seller_____

NO REPRESENTATION IS MADE AS TO THE LEGAL VALIDITY OF ANY PROVISION OR THE ADEQUACY OF ANY PROVISION IN ANY SPECIFIC TRANSACTION A REAL ESTATE BROKER IS THE PERSON QUALIFIED TO ADVISE ON REAL ESTATE. IF YOU DESIRE LEGAL ADVICE CONSULT YOUR ATTORNEY.

To order, contact—California Association of Realtors®
525 S. Virgil Avenue, Los Angeles, California 90020
California Association of Realtors® (Revised 1980)   FORM SPC-1

Figure 6–5

RECEIPT FOR INCREASED DEPOSIT AND
SUPPLEMENT TO REAL ESTATE PURCHASE CONTRACT
CALIFORNIA ASSOCIATION OF REALTORS® STANDARD FORM

THIS IS INTENDED TO BE A LEGALLY BINDING CONTRACT. READ IT CAREFULLY.

Received from WILLIAM T. FISCHER and BARBARA JEAN FISCHER herein

called BUYER, the sum of TWO THOUSAND FIVE HUNDRED DOLLARS

Dollars ($ 2,500.00) evidenced by cash ☐, personal check ☒, cashier's check ☐ as

additional deposit payable to SECURITY TITLE INSURANCE COMPANY

for the purchase of the property described in the Real Estate Purchase Contract and Receipt for Deposit dated

FEBRUARY 24, 1985 , executed by WILLIAM G. FISCHER and BARBARA JEAN FISCHER

as BUYER and accepted by SELLER on FEBRUARY 25, , 1985 .

Dated FEBRUARY 25, 1985

Real Estate Broker HOMER C. DAVEY & ASSOC.   By *Homer C. Davey*

The following is hereby incorporated in and made a part of said Real Estate Purchase Contract and Receipt for

Deposit, which remains in full force and effect:

    Buyer hereby increases the total deposit to $ 3,300 and Buyer and Seller Agree

that should Buyer fail to complete the purchase by reason of any default of Buyer, Seller shall

retain the total deposit as liquidated damages. If the described property is a dwelling with no more

than four units, one of which the Buyer intends to occupy as his residence, Seller shall retain as

liquidated damages the deposit actually paid, or an amount therefrom, not more than 3% of the

purchase price, and promptly return any excess to Buyer.

The undersigned agree to the above and acknowledge receipt of a copy hereof.

Dated February 25, 1985   Dated February 25, 1985

BUYER *William T. Fischer*   SELLER *Max T. Homeseller*

BUYER *Barbara Jean Fischer*   SELLER *Marie W. Homeseller*

To order, contact California Association of Realtors®
525 S. Virgil Avenue, Los Angeles, CA 90020
Copyright© (1984), California Association of Realtors® Reviewed 1984 FORM RID-11

Figure 6–6

3 percent of the purchase price. If the deposit is more than 3 percent of the purchase price, then the amount is presumed unreasonable. Of course, the parties must have initialed paragraph 12 in the contract for liquidating damages to apply.

---

4.   The following supplements are incorporated as part of this agreement:

		Other
☒ Structural Pest Control Certification Agreement	☒ Occupancy Agreement	☒ Res. Lease Agreement After Sale
☒ Special Studies Zone Disclosure	☐ VA Amendment	☐ _____
☐ Flood Insurance Disclosure	☐ FHA Amendment	☐ _____

Paragraph 4 deals in part with certain disclosure laws and occupancy agreements between the buyer and the seller. FHA or VA amendments, in the case of new federally insured and guaranteed loans, are required that provide that the borrower has the right of cancellation if the contract price exceeds the appraisal made by the Federal Housing Administration or the Veterans Administration. This clause also provides for the incorporation of the California Association of Realtors Structural Pest Control Certification Agreement mentioned in paragraph 1 (see Figure 6–5). The Occupancy Agreement mentioned in this paragraph is important if the buyer is to occupy the property prior to the transfer of title or if the seller is to do so after its transfer. CAR publishes two forms to cover these two common situations: the Interim Occupancy Agreement, used when the buyer is placed in possession prior to the close of the sale, and the Residential Lease Agreement After Sale, used when the seller remains in possession after the sale (see Figures 6–7 and 6–8). In either situation, the buyer or the seller should make provisions for it in the contract. If, for example, the buyer takes possession prior to the close of escrow and the property is destroyed by fire or materially damaged and no provision is made for the payment of rent, the buyer may become obligated to complete the transaction. The buyer further has an insurable interest in the property because the buyer's fire insurance would be good, not the seller's. Remember "possession is 9/10ths of the law." Space is also provided for other disclosure statements, supplementary agreements, and personal property inventories (see Figures 6–7, 6–8, 6–9, VA Amendment, and FHA Amendment). Where all such documents are used, it is necessary to indicate the total pages to the contract. In this example, four supplemental forms are incorporated by reference into the deposit receipt.

---

5.   Buyer and Seller shall deliver signed instructions to the escrow holder within _____ days from Seller's acceptance which shall provide for closing within _____ days from Seller's acceptance. Escrow fees to be paid as follows:

Paragraph 5 is the acknowledgment that both the buyer and the seller have received a copy of page 1 of the agreement. The buyers sign when the offer to purchase is prepared, and the sellers sign when the acceptance of page 2 of the printed form contract is signed. Section 2902 of the Regulations of the Real Estate Commissioner requires that a licensee give *immediately* a copy of the original or corrected contract, writing, or other document to the person signing or altering it at the time of signing or initialing this original or correction. The burden of proof is on the licensee. Even when the buyer signs the contract, if the licensee fails to give the buyer a copy, his or her license may be in jeopardy and may be suspended or revoked. It is important that both parties sign when community funds are being expended to purchase the property.

---

6.   Buyer and Seller acknowledge receipt of a copy of this page, which constitutes Page 1 of __2__ Pages.

Buyer _____*William J Fisher*_____   Seller _____

Buyer _____*Barbara Jean Fisher*_____   Seller _____

A REAL ESTATE BROKER IS THE PERSON QUALIFIED TO ADVISE ON REAL ESTATE. IF YOU DESIRE LEGAL ADVICE CONSULT YOUR ATTORNEY.

Paragraph 6 (page 2 of the Form Contract) provides for space to determine who is to pay for escrow fees. *Paragraph 1* allowed for the name of the escrow agent designated by the buyer to receive the deposit of the balance of the purchase price. There is some variation in escrow practices in California. Institutions exempt from

INTERIM OCCUPANCY AGREEMENT
THIS IS INTENDED TO BE A LEGALLY BINDING AGREEMENT—READ IT CAREFULLY.
CALIFORNIA ASSOCIATION OF REALTORS® STANDARD FORM

(Buyer in Possession)

Los Angeles _____, California _____ February 25 _____, 19 85 .

Max J. Homeseller and Marie M. Homeseller, his wife _____, "LESSOR" and

William T. Fischer and Barbara Jean Fischer, his wife _____, "LESSEE" agree:

1. On ___February 25___, 19 85 LESSOR as SELLER and LESSEE as BUYER entered into an agreement for the sale and purchase of the real property commonly known as 10234 Laguna Avenue, 3-unit apartment, Los Angeles, California ("Premises") and the escrow thereof is scheduled to close on or before_____;
___April 26___, 19 85 .

2. Pending completion of sale and close of escrow, LESSEE is to be given immediate occupancy of the premises in accordance with the terms of this agreement.

3. LESSEE acknowledges an inspection of, and has found the premises in satisfactory condition and ready for occupancy, except as follows: Property inspection by a licensed pest control operator as provided for in paragraph #1 of the Real Estate Purchase Contract and Receipt for Deposit.

4. LESSEE shall pay to LESSOR for the occupancy of said premises the sum of $ _____ per _____
day/week/month
commencing ___March 15___, 19 85 to and including the date of recordation of the deed.
specific date/other

_____: Said sum shall be paid weekly (Monday of each week) in advance.
weekly/monthly

Prorations, if any, shall be predicated upon a 30 day month. As additional consideration, LESSEE shall pay for all utilities and services based upon occupancy of the premises and the following charges: //
except ___the water bill___ which shall be paid by LESSOR.

5. If the purchase and sale agreement between LESSOR and LESSEE is not completed within its designated term, or any written extension thereof through no fault of LESSOR, LESSEE agrees to vacate the premises upon service of a written notice in the form and manner provided by law. Any holding over thereafter shall create a day-to-day tenancy with a fair rental value of $ 20.00_____ per day. Except as to daily rent and tenancy, all other covenants and conditions herein contained shall remain in full force and effect.

6. Except as provided by law LESSEE shall keep the premises and yards clean, sanitary, and in good order and repair during the term hereof and shall surrender the same in like condition if the said sale is not completed, reasonable wear and tear excepted. Additionally, LESSEE shall save and hold LESSOR harmless from any and all claims, demands, damages or liabilities arising out of LESSEE'S occupancy of the premises caused or permitted by LESSEE, LESSEE'S family, agents, servants, employees, guests and invitees.

7. As additional consideration passing from LESSEE to LESSOR, LESSEE shall obtain and maintain during the term of this agreement public liability insurance naming both LESSOR and LESSEE as co-insureds in the amount of not less than $ 25,000.00 for injury to one person; $ 75,000.00 for injury to a group; and $ 50,000.00 for property damage. If permitted, LESSOR agrees to retain his fire insurance on the premises until close of escrow. Otherwise, LESSEE shall obtain fire insurance on the premises in a sum of not less than that designated as the sales price of the subject property.

8 The premises are to be used as a residence only by LESSEE and his immediate family and no animal, bird or pet except __one__ English Bulldog shall be kept on or about the premises without LESSOR'S prior written consent. LESSEE shall not violate any law or ordinance in the use of the premises, nor permit waste or nuisance upon or about the premises and, except as provided by law, LESSEE shall not make any additions, alterations, or repairs to the premises without the prior written consent of LESSOR.

9. $_____ as security has been deposited. LESSOR may use therefrom such amounts as are reasonably necessary to remedy LESSEE defaults in the payment of rent, to repair damages caused by LESSEE, or to clean the premises if necessary upon the termination of tenancy. If used toward rent or damages during the term of this agreement, LESSEE agrees to reinstate said total security deposit upon 5 days written notice delivered to LESSEE in person or by mail. The balance of the security deposit, if any, shall be mailed to LESSEE'S last known address within 14 days of surrender of premises. Alternatively, and upon completion of sale, said security deposit shall be mailed to LESSEE at the subject premises within 10 days of close of escrow.

10. In the event of any action or proceeding between LESSOR and LESSEE under this agreement, the prevailing party shall be entitled to recover reasonable attorney's fees and costs.

To order, contact—California Association of Realtors®
525 S. Virgil Avenue, Los Angeles, California 90020
Copyright©1977, California Association of Realtors®

FORM IOA-11

Figure 6–7

11. The right to occupy the premises as granted LESSEE herein is personal to LESSEE and any attempt to assign, transfer, or hypotecate the same shall be null and void.

12. The undersigned LESSEE acknowledges having read the foregoing and receipt of a copy.

LESSOR and LESSEE have executed this agreement on the day and year above written.

_____ LESSOR   _____ LESSEE

_____ LESSOR   _____ LESSEE

FORM 10A-11

Figure 6–7   (Continued)

RESIDENTIAL LEASE AGREEMENT AFTER SALE
THIS IS INTENDED TO BE A LEGALLY BINDING AGREEMENT— READ IT CAREFULLY.
CALIFORNIA ASSOCIATION OF REALTORS® STANDARD FORM
(Possession Retained by Realtor)

Los Angeles _____ , California, _____ February 25 _____ , 19 85 .
William T. Fischer and Barbara Jean Fischer, his wife _____ , "LESSOR" and
Max J. Homeseller and Marie M. Homeseller, his wife _____ , "LESSEE"
agree:

1. On February 25 _____ , 19 85 , LESSOR as Buyer and LESSEE as Seller entered into an agreement for the sale and purchase of the real property commonly known as 10234 Laguna Avenue, 3-unit apartment complex------------ , _____ Los Angeles _____ , California ("Premises"), wherein escrow is designated to close on or about April 26 _____ , 19 85 .

2. LESSOR leases to LESSEE the premises as LESSEE'S personal residence in accordance with the terms of this lease.

3. Occupancy shall commence on the day following close of escrow and terminate not later than 5/15/85 _____ thereafter
days/weeks/months
at which time the premises shall be vacated and possession surrendered to LESSOR.

4. LESSEE shall pay to LESSOR as rent for the said premises the sum of $ 20.00---- per day------------------ commencing April 26 _____ , 19 85 to and including May 15, 1985 _____ . Said
specific date/other
sum shall be paid weekly (each Monday) in advance. Prorations, if any, shall be predicated upon a 30 day month. Additionally,
weekly/monthly
LESSEE shall pay for all utilities and services based upon occupancy of the premises and the following charges/ ////////////////// except, the water bill _____ which shall be paid by LESSOR. Any holding over without the express written consent of LESSOR shall create a day-to-day tenancy with a fair rental value of $ 25.00---- per day. Except as to daily rent and tenancy, all other covenants and conditions herein contained shall remain in full force and effect.

5. As part of the consideration passing from LESSEE to LESSOR, but for which LESSOR would not have entered into this agreement, except as provided by law, LESSEE shall maintain the premises and yards and all real and personal property as conveyed by LESSEE to LESSOR in clean, sanitary, operable condition and repair, reasonable wear and tear excluded, at LESSEE'S sole cost and expense. LESSEE further agrees upon surrendering possession that said premises shall otherwise be in the same condition as required of LESSEE to have delivered them to LESSOR at close of escrow.

6. $ 100.00--- as security has been deposited. LESSOR may use therefrom such amounts as are reasonably necessary to remedy LESSEE'S defaults in the payment of rent, to repair damages caused by LESSEE, or clean the premises if necessary upon the termination of tenancy. If used toward rent or damages during the term of this agreement, LESSEE agrees to reinstate said total security deposit upon 5 days written notice delivered to LESSEE in person or by mail. The balance of the security deposit, if any, shall be mailed to LESSEE's last known address within 14 days of surrender of the premises.

7. As additional consideration passing from LESSEE to LESSOR, LESSEE shall obtain and maintain during the term of this lease, public liability insurance naming both LESSOR and LESSEE as co-insureds in the amount of not less than $ 25,000.00 for injury to one person; $ 75,000.00 for any injury to a group; and $ 50,000.00 for property damage. If permitted, LESSEE agrees to retain his fire insurance on the premises in a sum of not less than designated as the sales price of the subject property.

8. In the event of any action or proceeding between LESSOR and LESSEE under this agreement, the prevailing party shall be entitled to recover reasonable attorney's fees and costs.

9. The undersigned LESSEE acknowledges having read the foregoing and receipt of a copy.

LESSOR and LESSEE have executed this lease on the day and year above written.

LESSOR _William F Fischer_____ LESSEE _Max J. Homeseller_____

LESSOR _Barbara Jean Fischer_____ LESSEE _Marie Homeseller_____

NO REPRESENTATION IS MADE AS TO THE LEGAL VALIDITY OF ANY PROVISION OR THE ADEQUACY OF ANY PROVISION IN ANY SPECIFIC TRANSACTION. A REAL ESTATE BROKER IS THE PERSON QUALIFIED TO ADVISE ON REAL ESTATE. IF YOU DESIRE LEGAL ADVICE CONSULT YOUR ATTORNEY.

To order, contact—California Association of Realtors®
525 S. Virgil Avenue, Los Angeles, California 90020   FORM RLAS-11
Copyright © 1977 California Association of Realtors® (Revised 1977)

Figure 6–8

SPECIAL STUDIES ZONE AND FLOOD HAZARD DISCLOSURE
CALIFORNIA ASSOCIATION OF REALTORS® STANDARD FORM

This Addendum is attached as Page _____ of _____ Pages to the Real Estate Purchase Contract and Receipt for Deposit dated <u>February 24</u> 19<u>85</u> in which <u>William T. Fischer and Barbara Jean Fischer</u>
----
is referred to as Buyer and <u>Max T. Homeseller and Marie M. Homeseller----------------</u>
-- is referred to as **Seller.**

SPECIAL STUDIES ZONE DISCLOSURE

The property which is the subject of the contract is situated in a Special Study Zone as designated under Sections 2621-2625, inclusive, of the California Public Resources Code; and, as such, the construction or development on this property of any structure for human occupancy may be subject to the findings of a geologic report prepared by a geologist registered in the State of California, unless such report is waived by the city or county under the terms of that act. No representations on the subject are made by Seller or Agent, and the Buyer should make his/her own inquiry or investigation.
Note: California Public Resources Code #2621.5 excludes structures in existence prior to May 4, 1975;
California Public Resources Code #2621.6 excludes wood frame dwellings not exceeding two (2) stories in height and mobilhomes over eight (8) feet in width;
California Public Resources Code #2621.7 excludes conversion of existing apartment houses into condominiums;
California Public Resources Code #2621.8 excludes alterations and additions under 50% of value of structure from the Special Studies Zone Act.

Buyer is allowed _____ *2* _____ days from date of Seller's acceptance to make further inquiries at appropriate governmental agencies concerning the use of the subject property under the terms of the Special Study Zone Act and local building, zoning, fire, health and safety codes. When such inquiries disclose conditions or information unsatisfactory to the Buyer, Buyer may cancel this agreement. If notice in writing has not been delivered within such time, this condition shall be deemed waived.

Receipt of a copy is hereby acknowledged.

DATED: <u>February 24</u>, 19<u>85</u>   BUYER: <u>William T. Fischer</u>
                                                     <u>Barbara F Fischer</u>
Receipt of a copy is hereby acknowledged

DATED: <u>February 28</u>, 19<u>85</u>   SELLER: <u>Max T. Homeseller</u>
                                                      <u>Marie Homeseller</u>

FLOOD HAZARD ZONE DISCLOSURE

The property which is the subject of the contract is situated in a "Flood Zone" as set forth on H.U.D. "Special Flood Zone Area Map". The law requires that as a condition of obtaining financing on most properties located in a "Flood Zone", Banks, Savings and Loan Associations, and some insurance lenders will require that H.U.D. flood insurance be carried where the property or its attachments are security for the loan.

This requirement is mandated by the H.U.D. National Insurance Program, which requirement became effective March 1, 1976. The purpose of the program is to provide flood insurance to property at a reasonable cost.

The extent of coverage available in your area and the cost of this coverage may vary, and for further information you should consult your lender or insurance carrier. No representation or recommendation is made by the Seller and the Brokers in this transaction or their agents or employees, as to the legal effect, interpretation, or economic consequences of the National Flood Insurance Program and related legislation.

Receipt of a copy is hereby acknowledged.

DATED: _____, 19_____   BUYER: _____

Receipt of a copy is hereby acknowledged

DATED: _____, 19_____   SELLER: _____

NO REPRESENTATION IS MADE AS TO THE LEGAL VALIDITY OF ANY PROVISION OR THE ADEQUACY OF ANY PROVISION IN ANY SPECIFIC TRANSACTION. A REAL ESTATE BROKER IS THE PERSON QUALIFIED TO ADVISE ON REAL ESTATE. IF YOU DESIRE LEGAL ADVICE CONSULT YOUR ATTORNEY.

To order, contact—California Association of Realtors®
525 S. Virgil Ave., Los Angeles, California 90020
Copyright © 1977, California Association of Realtors® (Revised 1978)   FORM SSD-FHD-11

Figure 6–9

the escrow laws in the Financial Code—such as title insurance companies, banks, and savings and loan associations—perform a majority of escrows in Northern California. In the southern part of the state, private es-crow corporations, banks, and savings and loan associations handle escrows. For a more detailed discussion of escrows, see Chapter 13.

7.   Title is to be free of liens, encumbrances, easements, restrictions, rights and conditions of record or known to Seller, other than the following: (a) Current property taxes, (b) covenants, conditions, restrictions, and public utility easements of record, if any, provided the same do not adversely affect the continued use of the property for the purposes for which it is presently being used, unless reasonably disapproved by Buyer in writing within __five__ days of receipt of a current preliminary title report furnished at __Buyer's__ expense, and (c) _____
Seller shall furnish Buyer at _____Buyer's_____ expense a standard California Land Title Association policy issued by __Security Title Insurance__ Company, showing title vested in Buyer subject only to the above. If Seller is unwilling or unable to eliminate any title matter disapproved by Buyer as above, Seller may terminate this agreement. If Seller fails to deliver title as above, Buyer may terminate this agreement; in either case, the deposit shall be returned to Buyer.

Paragraph 7 allows an ''out'' for the buyer, providing he or she finds things in the preliminary title report of which he or she disapproves and providing this disapproval is not unreasonable. In many so-called standard form contracts the buyer obligates himself to purchase certain real property and finds out later he or she disapproves of certain items. The seller is required to furnish a standard California Land Title Association (CLTA) policy, but the parties may agree to shift the expense.

Again, customs differ in Northern and Southern California. If a new loan is to be placed on the property, most lenders, as a condition of granting a loan, will require the more comprehensive ALTA (American Land Title Association) policy in addition to the buyer's CLTA title policy.

For a fuller definition and discussion of these two policies, see Chapter 13.

8.   Property taxes, premiums on insurance acceptable to Buyer, rents, interest, and ///////////////////////////////// shall be pro-rated as of (a) the date of recordation of deed; or (b) ///////////////////////////////. Any bond or assessment which is a lien shall be //paid///assumed// by __buyers__. Transfer taxes, if any, shall be paid by __Sellers__.

Paragraph 8. The seller is responsible for property taxes, insurance premiums, and other expenses *up to and including* the date of transfer. Therefore, the seller is entitled to the rents and profits from the property for the same period. The buyer is entitled to the security and cleaning deposits, because they are held in trust for the tenants. The date of proration for rents and expenses is usually the date on which the deed is recorded, trans-ferring legal title to the new owner. The transfer tax mentioned in this paragraph refers to the documentary stamps discussed in Chapters 11 and 14. These stamps should not be confused with another form of transfer tax charged by some cities and counties in California, such as 1 percent of the sales price. The licensee and the consumer should investigate this tax in the city where they live.

9.   Possession shall be delivered to Buyer (a) on close of escrow, or (b) not later than ////////////////// days after close of escrow, or (c) ///

10.   Unless otherwise designated in the escrow instructions of Buyer, title shall vest as follows: _____ __Instructions to be delivered to the escrowholder.__ _____
(The manner of taking title may have significant legal and tax consequences. Therefore, give this matter serious consideration.)

Paragraphs 9 and *10* explain when the buyer will take possession of the property. Possession of the property passes to the buyers at the close of escrow and upon recordation of the deed. If the buyer wishes to obtain possession prior to the close of escrow, he or she must provide for this in the contract. The buyer may become obligated to complete the transaction if the property is destroyed by fire or materially damaged, he or she takes possession prior to the close of escrow, and he or she makes no provision for the payment of rent. See paragraph 4 and occupancy agreements, Figures 6–7 and 6–8.

11.   If Broker is a participant of a Board multiple listing service (''MLS'') the Broker is authorized to report the sale, its price, terms, and financing for the information, publication, dissemination, and use of the authorized Board members.

Paragraph 11 provides authorization to the broker who is a member of a multiple-listing service to report the sale, price, terms and financing of the transaction to authorized members of the multiple-listing service.

12. If Buyer fails to complete said purchase as herein provided by reason of any default of Buyer, Seller shall be released from his obligation to sell the property to Buyer and may proceed against Buyer upon any claim or remedy which he may have in law or equity; provided, however, that by placing their initials here Buyer: (　　) Seller: (　　) agree that Seller shall retain the deposit as his liquidated damages. If the described property is a dwelling with no more than four units, one of which the Buyer intends to occupy as his residence, Seller shall retain as liquidated damages the deposit actually paid, or an amount therefrom, not more than 3% of the purchase price and promptly return any excess to Buyer.

Paragraph 12, if initialed by both buyers and sellers, limits the amount of liquidated damages to 3 percent of the purchase price in the event the buyers fail to complete the purchase as set forth in the contract. If the parties leave open the blank in this clause, they are, in fact, choosing to abolish liquidating damages. In either case, the seller would have the option to sue for specific performance or to prove actual damages. By initialing the paragraph, the deposit becomes a substitute for actual damages. The Liquidated Damages Law makes a distinction between *residential and nonresidential property*. The law provides that 3 percent of the purchase price of residential property, to the extent of the deposit, is *valid* as liquidating damages. The California Civil Code defines residential property as a place being used as a dwelling and containing no more than four units when the contract is made. Paragraph 3 of this form contract covered the matter of occupancy. If an increased deposit is required by the contract (paragraph 2), the total deposit shall constitute liquidating damages to 3 percent of the purchase price, and each party must sign another form to the contract for each subsequent payment (see Figure 6–6). By limiting the seller to 3 percent of the purchase price for damages, the burden of proving unreasonableness is on the buyer. If the contract allowed for the retention of more than 3 percent, the seller would have to prove that the excess paid was reasonable. If the amount paid to increase the deposit (paragraph 2) and the original deposit in a total amount is to be liquidated damages, an additional sentence should be added to paragraph 2, such as: "Total deposit to be subject to provisions of paragraph 12." In nonresidential property the provision to permit retention of the deposit as liquidated damages is valid unless the party seeking to invalidate it establishes that the provision was unreasonable under the circumstances when the contract was made.

To summarize, in residential contracts, the seller may never recover more than his or her actual damages. If the deposit is 3 percent or less than the purchase price the damages are presumed to equal the deposit. If the deposit is more than 3 percent of the purchase price, the amount is presumed unreasonable, and the burden is on the seller to justify the amount.

13. If the only controversy or claim between the parties arises out of or relates to the disposition of the Buyer's deposit, such controversy or claim shall at the election of the parties be decided by arbitration. Such arbitration shall be determined in accordance with the Rules of the American Arbitration Association, and judgment upon the award rendered by the Arbitrator(s) may be entered in any court having jurisdiction thereof. The provisions of Code of Civil Procedure Section 1283.05 shall be applicable to such arbitration.

14. In any action or proceeding arising out of this agreement, the prevailing party shall be entitled to reasonable attorney's fees and costs.

Paragraph 13 covers arbitration in the event a controversy or claim concerning the buyer's deposit should arise. If the parties elect to arbitrate their dispute, which they may do at their option, then the decision of such arbitration shall be binding on all parties.

Paragraph 14 provides that attorney's fees and costs be awarded to the prevailing party. The *reasonable* attorney's fees awarded by the court, however, may be less than the attorney actually charged the prevailing party. For example, if you promise to pay your attorney $1,000 to handle the case and the court awards only $800, you must pay your attorney the extra $200 because that was your contract with him or her.

15. Time is of the essence. All modification or extensions shall be in writing signed by the parties.

In *Paragraph 15* the statement "Time is of the essence" means that the parties to the contract will perform their obligations and adhere to all provisions of the contract within the period specified. It further emphasizes that all modifications or extensions shall be in writing and signed by the parties. A real estate agent may not extend the time in the contract for any act to be performed, because the agent is not a party to it. The agent is a third-party beneficiary only for his or her real estate commission.

16. This constitutes an offer to purchase the described property. Unless acceptance is signed by Seller and the signed copy delivered to Buyer, in person or by mail to the address below, within ___two (2)___ days, this offer shall be deemed revoked and the deposit shall be returned. Buyer acknowledges receipt of a copy hereof.

Real Estate Broker __HOMER & DAVEY ASSOCIATES__   Buyer __William J Fisher__
By __Homer C Davey__   Buyer __Barbara Jean Fischer__
Address __10045 Euclid Boulevard__   Address __1232 Lonesome Rd., San Clements, CA.__
(213) 476-0000   (213) 592-9999
Telephone _____   Telephone _____

ACCEPTANCE

The undersigned Seller accepts and agrees to sell the property on the above terms and conditions. Seller has employed __Homer C. Davey & Associates__ as Broker(s) and agrees to pay for services the sum of __Six Thousand Six Hundred and No/100__ Dollars ($ __6,600.00__), payable as follows: (a) On recordation of the deed or other evidence of title, or (b) if completion of sale is prevented by default of Seller, upon Seller's default or (c) if completion of sale is prevented by default of Buyer, only if and when Seller collects damages from Buyer, by suit or otherwise and then in an amount not less than one-half of the damages recovered, but not to exceed the above fee, after first deducting title and escrow expenses and the expenses of collection, if any. In any action between Broker and Seller arising out of this agreement, the prevailing party shall be entitled to reasonable attorney's fees and costs. The undersigned acknowledges receipt of a copy and authorizes Broker(s) to deliver a signed copy to Buyer.

Dated __2/25/85__ Telephone __(213) 597-2222__   Seller _____
Address __10234 Laguna Avenue__   Seller _____

Broker(s) agree to the foregoing. Broker __Homer C. Davey & Associates__   Broker _____
Dated __2/25/85__ By __/s/ Homer C. Davey__   Dated _____ By _____

To order, contact—California Association of Realtors®
525 S. Virgil Ave., Los Angeles, California 90020
Copyright© California Association of Realtors® (Revised 1984)   FORM D-11-2   Page ___ of ___ Pages

Paragraph 16 establishes the buyer's offer to purchase under the terms in the contract and that a *signed copy* must be delivered to the buyer, *in person* or *by mail*, to his or her *address* within *two days*. Remember the general law of contracts: Any offer may be withdrawn before its acceptance. The period for acceptance binds the seller (offeree) but does not bind the buyer (offeror), because the buyer did not receive a consideration for keeping his or her offer open. The person to whom an offer is made must accept it within this designated period. The paragraph further states that the "Buyer acknowledges receipt of a copy hereof." Please see the explanation given in paragraph 5 of page 1 to the contract.

The *acceptance clause* provides for the real estate broker's commission. The amount of commission may be given as a percentage of the sales price or as an actual dollar amount. It may be more practical to use a percentage of the total sales price where counteroffers are expected. While minor changes or modifications may be made in the contract and initialed by the respective parties, it is preferable to use a separate counteroffer form (see Figure 6–10). The amount of real estate commission is a matter of agreement between the parties. The division of the split of commission between real estate brokers is also by agreement.

Once the respective parties have signed the contract, it is a legally binding agreement. If the parties mutually desire to rescind the contract, it must be done in writing. It would also require the real estate agent's approval since

the agent is a third-party beneficiary to the contract. It is best to use a separate form for this (see Figure 6–11).

OPTION AGREEMENT

An option is a contract to make a contract in the future. It gives the person acquiring the right to purchase (*optionee*) a right to acquire a property interest within a limited time. The option agreement binds the property owner (*optionor*) but does not bind the purchaser; it merely gives the purchaser an election to exercise his or her right if he or she desires. If the option is exercised in the manner provided for in the agreement, a binding contract of sale is created that relates back to the date of the option agreement. For long-term capital gains, however, it does not relate back, and the holding period will be taken from the date the option is exercised.

Option agreements may be used by real estate agents, developers, syndicators, speculators, or individuals wishing time to arrange a special type of financing. The option may also be part of a lease agreement referred to as a *lease/option agreement* (Figure 6–12). In the latter case the individual may wish to lease the property for a year before he or she decides to buy it. Attorneys representing purchasers may recommend options when the purchaser must make investigations into such things as records of survey or engineering studies to see if it is feasible to develop the subject property.

COUNTER OFFER
THIS IS INTENDED TO BE A LEGALLY BINDING AGREEMENT. READ IT CAREFULLY.
CALIFORNIA ASSOCIATION OF REALTORS® STANDARD FORM

This is a counter offer to: ☒ the Real Estate Purchase Contract and Receipt for Deposit, ☐ Mobile Home Purchase Contract and Receipt for Deposit, ☐ Business Purchase Contract and Receipt for Deposit, ☐ other _____
dated __February 24__, 19 85, on property known as: _____
in which __William T. Fischer and Barbara Jean Fischer, his wife---__ is referred to as buyer
and __Max T. Homeseller and Marie M. Homeseller, his wife-------__ is referred to as seller.

Seller accepts all of the terms and conditions set forth in the above designated agreement with the following changes or amendments:

__$110,000 all cash to sellers. Sellers do not wish to carry back a purchase__
__money deed of trust and a promissory note signed by buyers.__
__Buyers have until May 15, 1985 as per said agreement to obtain__
__and qualify for a new loan provided that said buyers agree to__
__use due diligence and good faith in obtaining such loan.__

The seller reserves the right to continue to offer the herein described property for sale and accept any offer acceptable to seller at anytime prior to personal receipt by seller or __Homer C. Davey & Associates__ , seller's authorized agent, of a copy of this counter-offer, duly accepted and signed by buyer. Unless this counter offer is accepted in this manner on or before __February 28__ , 19 85 at __10:00__ a.m./p.m. it shall be deemed revoked and the deposit shall be returned to the buyer. Seller's acceptance of another offer shall revoke this counter offer.

Receipt of a copy hereof is hereby acknowledged.

Dated __February 26__ 19 85   Seller *Max T. Homeseller*

Time __8:00 p.m.__   Seller *Marie M. Homeseller*

The undersigned buyer hereby accepts the above counter offer.
__Without exceptions.__

Receipt of a copy hereof is hereby acknowledged.

Dated __February 27__ 19 85   Buyer *William T. Fischer*

Time __1:00 p.m.__   Buyer *Barbara J. Fischer*

Receipt of buyer's acceptance is hereby acknowledged and seller agrees to sell on the terms and conditions set forth above.

Dated __February 28__ 19 85   Seller *Max T. Homeseller*

Time __9:00 a.m.__   Seller *Marie M. Homeseller*

NO REPRESENTATION IS MADE AS TO THE LEGAL VALIDITY OF ANY PROVISION OR THE ADEQUACY OF ANY PROVISION IN ANY SPECIFIC TRANSACTION. A REAL ESTATE BROKER IS THE PERSON QUALIFIED TO ADVISE ON REAL ESTATE AND ON BUSINESS TRANSACTIONS. IF YOU DESIRE LEGAL ADVICE, CONSULT YOUR ATTORNEY.

To order, contact—California Association of Realtors®
525 S. Virgil Ave., Los Angeles, California 90020
Copyright © 1978, California Association of Realtors® (Revised 1983)   FORM CO-11

Figure 6–10

RELEASE OF CONTRACT
THIS IS INTENDED TO BE A LEGALLY BINDING CONTRACT. READ IT CAREFULLY.
CALIFORNIA ASSOCIATION OF REALTORS® STANDARD FORM

The undersigned Buyer and Seller, the parties to that certain: ☒ Real Estate Purchase Contract and Receipt for Deposit,

☐ Mobile Home Purchase Contract and Receipt for Deposit, ☐ Business Purchase Contract and Receipt for Deposit, ☐ other

dated February 24 , 19 85 , covering the following described property:

Home at 10234 Laguna Avenue, in the City and County of Los Angeles, CA.

All parties hereby waive any rights under Cal. Civil Code §1542, providing:

A GENERAL RELEASE DOES NOT EXTEND TO CLAIMS WHICH THE CREDITOR DOES NOT KNOW OR SUSPECT THAT EXIST IN HIS FAVOR AT THE TIME OF EXECUTING THE RELEASE, WHICH IF KNOWN BY HIM MUST HAVE MATERIALLY AFFECTED HIS SETTLEMENT WITH THE DEBTOR.

All parties to this contract release

hereby mutually release each other from any and all claims, actions or demands which each may have up to the date of this Agreement

against the other by reason of said Contract.

It is the intent of this Agreement that all rights and obligations arising out of said Contract are declared null and void.

Security Title Insurance Company _____ holding
(Name of Broker or Escrow Holder)

the deposit under the terms of said Contract is hereby directed and instructed to disburse said deposit in the following manner:

$ 100.00 TO Security Title Insurance Company

$ 1,000.00 TO Homer C. Davey & Associates

$ 1,100.00 TO Max and Marie Homeseller

$ 1,100.00 TO William and Barbara Fischer

Dated June 20, 1985   Dated June 20, 1985

Buyer _____   Seller _____

Buyer _____   Seller _____

Dated June 20, 1985   Dated _____

Broker Homer C. Davey & Associates   Broker _____

By _____   By _____

NO REPRESENTATION IS MADE AS TO THE LEGAL VALIDITY OF ANY PROVISION OR THE ADEQUACY OF ANY PROVISION IN ANY SPECIFIC TRANSACTION. A REAL ESTATE BROKER IS THE PERSON QUALIFIED TO ADVISE ON REAL ESTATE OR BUSINESS TRANSACTIONS. IF YOU DESIRE LEGAL ADVICE CONSULT YOUR ATTORNEY.

To order, contact California Association of Realtors®
525 S. Virgil Avenue, Los Angeles, California 90020
Copyright© 1974, 1978, California Association of Realtors® (Revised 1984)   FORM RC-11

Figure 6–11

Option

THIS AGREEMENT, made this 15th day of February 1982 between Earl S. Brown called OPTIONOR, and John H. Adam called OPTIONEE.

WITNESSETH

IN CONSIDERATION OF THE SUM OF $1,000.00, paid by OPTIONEE, the receipt whereof is hereby acknowledged, OPTIONOR gives and grants to OPTIONEE, and to its assigns, the exclusive right and option to purchase at any time before 5:00 o'clock P.M. on the 16th day of April 1982, the following described property situated in the County of Santa Clara, State of California

Lot 4, Block 10, tract 1236 as per maps recorded
October 20, 1964, page 72, Book 107, Official Records,
County of Santa Clara, City of Los Altos, California.

SUBJECT to covenants conditions, restrictions, reservations and easements of record.

ALSO SUBJECT TO:

This option may be exercised only by written instrument signed by OPTIONOR personally or deposited in the mail by registered letter, postage prepaid, addressed to the OPTIONOR at 20653 Cheryl Drive, Cupertino, California 95014, within the time above specified, whereupon this option shall be deemed to have been exercised.

The purchase price, if this option is exercised, shall be Fifty Thousand Dollars payable as follows:

$10,000.00	Cash including the above consideration on this option agreement.
40,000.00	Purchaser/optionee obtaining and qualifying for a new loan in such minimum amount for a minimum period of 25 years with an interest rate not to exceed 10 percent per annum. Purchasers herein agree to pay a maximum of 2 points for said loan.
$50,000.00	Total Purchase Price.

OPTIONOR shall deliver to OPTIONEE a grant deed conveying said property to OPTIONEE, or its NOMINEE, together with a Policy of Title Insurance issued by any responsible Title Insurance Company, showing record title to said property in OPTIONEE, free and clear of all encumbrances except as above stated, should OPTIONEE elect to exercise this agreement.

If OPTIONEE does not exercise this option in the time and manner above provided, this option shall be thereafter null and void and OPTIONOR no longer bound hereby.

THIS AGREEMENT shall be binding upon and inure to the benefit of the heirs, executors, administrators and assigns of OPTIONOR and the successors and assigns of OPTIONEE.

_____   _____
OPTIONOR   OPTIONEE

_____   _____
OPTIONOR   OPTIONEE

OPTIONOR agrees to pay the undersigned Real Estate Broker as commission 6 percent of the above purchase price, or one-half the amount paid by OPTIONEE, provided same shall not exceed the full amount of the commission.

_____   _____
Real Estate Broker   OPTIONOR

_____
OPTIONOR

STATE OF CALIFORNIA   On _____ before me, a Notary Public, in and for said County and State,
COUNTY OF _____ SS.   personally appeared

_____   known to me or proved to me on the basis of satisfactory evidence to be the person
whose name _____ subscribed to the within instrument and acknowledged
to me that _____ he _____ executed the same.
IN WITNESS WHEREOF I have hereunto set my hand and affixed my official seal in the
_____ County of _____
the day and year in this certificate first above written.

My Commission Expires _____   _____
Notary Public in and for Said County and State

Figure 6–12

The option agreement must be supported by a valid consideration, and the consideration must be delivered to the property owner/optionor. It is not necessary that the consideration paid be cash. It may be in the form of services rendered, such as records of survey, special zoning, architect fees, engineering costs, and so on. Unless the agreement provides otherwise, however, the consideration is earned by the property owner/optionor when he or she signs the option contract.

The option should clearly state the termination date. The manner in which the option agreement is to be exercised should be adhered to closely by the purchaser/optionee. If it is exercised in a manner other than that provided for in the agreement, the option may become null and void.

The terms and conditions of purchase should be set forth in clear and concise terms, or else the purchaser may be expected to pay cash.

The option agreement may be recorded in the county or counties in which the real property is located, thus giving constructive notice to all persons of the rights of the purchaser/optionee. It is especially for the benefit of the purchaser/optionee that such agreements be recorded.

EXCHANGE AGREEMENT

The trained broker or salesperson will invariably come upon many opportunities to trade or exchange equities in property. If licensees are prepared to recognize opportunities for trading real estate, they may increase their efficiency in the business as much as 10 to 30 percent. The majority of brokers and salespeople, however, depend upon straight cash sales for their commissions.

An exchange of properties may qualify as a tax-free exchange or, more properly, as a tax-deferred exchange. In order to qualify as a tax-free exchange, the real property must be held for productive use in trade or business or for investment. It is rare to find a case where both properties involved are clear of encumbrances or are of equal value. Where "boot" (cash given in addition to the exchange of properties) accompanies the exchange, the amount of boot must be recognized as taxable income.

The rules to qualify for a tax-free exchange are technical and, in delayed exchanges, very complex. You should not complete such a transaction without the advice of an attorney or an accountant or both.

BROKER RESPONSIBILITIES IN CONTRACTS

Article 4, Section 2725(a) of the Real Estate Commissioner's *Outline of License Law Regulations* states: "Every instrument prepared or signed by a real estate salesperson in connection with any transaction for which a real estate license is required, which may have a material effect upon the rights or obligations of a party to the transaction shall be reviewed, initialed and dated by the broker of the salesperson within five working days after preparation or signing by the salesperson or before the close of escrow, whichever occurs first."

The broker, however, may delegate the above authority so long as he or she does not relinquish his or her overall responsibility for supervision of the acts of salespersons licensed to him or her.

In addition, Section 2726 of Article 4 provides that every real estate broker shall have a written agreement with each of his or her salespeople, whether licensed as salespeople or as brokers under a broker-salesperson arrangement; this agreement shall be dated and signed by the parties, and it shall cover material aspects of the relationship between the parties, including supervision of licensed activities, duties, and compensation. Signed copies of these agreements must be retained by the parties for three years from the date of termination of the agreement. These agreements must be available for inspection by the department of real estate.

BUYING AND SELLING YOUR HOME

III. Financing a Home

First, decide what you can pay. Read the want ads, but remember that most ads carry "puffed-up" information.

A. How much cash can you put in? Your broker or salesperson will leave the matter of how much cash you should put into your purchase up to you, but you should always have enough cash in reserve. "If you buy in inspiration, you pay in perspiration, and sell in desperation."

B. What monthly payments can you soundly afford? Schedule-of-payment books are available at the bank and are useful in telling you what your principal and interest payments will be on a loan amount for any given time.

C. Consult the mortgage loan manager or officer of your nearest financial institution. People who will tell you about loans that can be obtained are available in every institution. You should always inquire about taxes in each area before you decide to look there. The timing of buying your home is important. You may not have a choice, but money is a commodity on the open market, and interest rates will vary according to the season of the year. Almost all financial institutions have more money in the first two quarters of the year. Your payments are governed by *length of the loan, interest*, and *down payment*. Home loans are usually for twenty-five to thirty years. In applying for a loan, you should consider your age, your present and potential income, and your monthly expenses. According to the FHA, if your monthly income is four to five times your monthly payment on the home selected, you are generally in a good financial position to buy.

II. Choosing a Neighborhood

A. Does the neighborhood appeal to you and your family? Is it apt to maintain its present desirability, or is it apt to deteriorate?

In the selection of the neighborhood, you should consider all amenities and things that concern the family, such as schools, shopping centers, churches, theaters, playgrounds, and parks. The breadwinner, of course, should have the final decision in making a selection because his or her transportation is most important financially. Adequate fire protection is essential, or fire insurance rates will be higher. Also essential is the availability of utilities. The rights of ingress and egress are the property owner's responsibility. When buying subdivided property, the restrictions should be read. Easements, rights of entry, dominant easements, servient easements, and so forth, should all be checked.

B. Distance of home from essential services, business, and other important considerations.

Traffic and noise affect the value of property. You should not pay top price for property that has undesirable features. Neighborhood maintenance should be evaluated. The age of property is not as important as the way in which people maintain their property in the neighborhood.

III. Selecting a Location for Your Site or Lot

A. Value of the lot
The price of the lot should be discussed with a broker who is fully aware of land values.

B. Soil
The soil must be compacted properly and the house must be built on a pad. The way the soil will compact depends upon the way the pad is prepared.

C. Filled ground or a natural site
A soils engineer is the only person who should be relied upon for information as to how the land is filled and compacted.

D. Drainage
Be sure to investigate the drainage of water. You may be liable for a suit if you divert the course of water from your property to someone else's.

E. Size of the lot
A lot should be large enough for expansion, privacy, air, and setback restrictions.

F. Orientation of the lot
Some open exposure for the house, with a good balance of heat and light, is desirable.

IV. Selecting a Home

A. Size and arrangement
American people tend to want ever-larger homes, and your selection of a house should be one that has adequate space for the present and the future. There should be closets available for everything—linens, clothes, coats, bath necessities.

B. Type of house
1. Most modern houses have both a formal living area and an informal living area, but this, naturally, depends on the owner's financial category. The functional utility of the house must be considered, especially in the kitchen. Most of the electric gadgets and equipment in today's kitchen can be financed by the FHA, if they are attached to the house.
2. The house should have eye appeal as well as functional appeal. The colonial house has been accepted for over 150 years and is still popular. Don't forget to consider the furniture and its placement—reasonable wall space should be left after all the furniture is arranged.

C. Equipment
1. Plumbing should be inspected by a licensed plumber to inform the buyer if it is in good condition.
2. Heating should have an inspection if it seems advisable, since an efficient heating system is very important to the home.
3. The type of wiring in the home should be investigated, and the buyer should check to see that circuits are adequate to carry the load required for electrical fixtures. In almost every old house, the circuits are inadequate.

D. Construction
1. The foundation should be investigated if it is cracked and slippage has started on the house. Termites will build a stack right up through the cracks to the wood structure, so be certain that all soil is removed from wood contact. Good ventilation of the foundation makes it dry, and poor ventilation makes it damp; so don't overlook the ventilation of the house.
2. The roof is designed according to the style of architecture. Don't hesitate to contact someone familiar with roofing if it looks as if it may leak. Light spaces between the shingles do not mean that the roof is no good—this is normal air ventilation. Roofs are usually good for fifteen to twenty years.
3. How can you tell the age of a house? The meter box usually has a date stamped on it and the toilet usually has a date stamped on the water bowl. However, chronological age doesn't always make a big difference. It is the maintenance of the house that counts.

4. FHA requires hardwood floors, and it is generally a good idea to have them anyway. This is an individual choice in building, however. Check all fireplaces—when you burn wood in a fireplace, it may smoke up the entire room if it is poorly ventilated. A properly insulated house keeps heat in when it is cold outside and keeps heat out when it is warm outside. Proper insulation makes for heating and cooling economy.

Whether you hope to build, buy, or improve your present home—immediately or in the future—it's a good idea to start discussing your plans with your broker, loan agent, and builder.

Points to check before you buy

1. Shopping
2. Churches
3. Community pride
4. Neighbors
5. Police and fire protection
6. Schools
7. Playgrounds and amusements
8. Trash and garbage disposal
9. Street layout
10. Transportation
11. Growth trend
12. Lay of the land
13. Trees
14. Water
15. Sewerage
16. Protection against encroachment
17. Traffic
18. Hazards
19. Privacy
20. Nuisances

The preceding twenty points are to be considered about any neighborhood. To compare houses, rate them on these points as good, fair, or poor.

The dollar value of real estate is going up almost constantly. Real estate is something you buy, use, and, when you no longer need it, sell.

In many areas the average homeowner sells his or her property after six or seven years. At that time, he or she should have the assistance of a realtor. The realtor not only has the legal ability to deal in property but also has the moral obligation to support the Real Estate Code of Ethics. The homeowner can usually rely on a Realtor, because the code must be followed or the Realtor's membership will be subject to revocation.

To get the highest price possible for a home, the owner should do the following:

1. Avoid rushing into a sale
2. Allow enough time to contact as many potential buyers as possible
3. Be sure the price is right
4. Prepare for the sale—put the home on the market only when it looks its best
5. Have a planned sales program, including financing

If a new loan is to be obtained, the purchaser should protect himself or herself by a proper stipulation in the contract. For example:

> *Purchasers to obtain new loan in the minimum amount of $25,000 for a minimum period of 25 years with interest not to exceed 8½ percent per annum.*

The purchaser may also wish to specify the lender, the type of loan, and the real estate points he or she is willing to pay for the loan.

Some people sell their homes without professional help. However, most homes are sold with the help of professional real estate people. The help of a licensed real estate broker is desirable when a home is to be sold because

1. The broker has a great deal more knowledge about fair prices, possible buyers, and legal requirements than do most homeowners.
2. The broker is licensed and examined by a state real estate commission.
3. If permitted to use the title "Realtor," the broker belongs to an organization that maintains a strict code of ethics. The broker must live up to this code in order to use the title.

Real estate brokers charge a fee based on the selling price of the property. The real estate agent will usually secure a better selling price, including his or her commission, than the owner—this has been proven by surveys of sales records. The Realtor must do everything necessary to sell the property. A reasonable amount of property showing is essential. If the realtor fails to do this, you may wish to go to the Board and report the matter. Your property will sell faster and at a better price if you follow these suggestions:

1. Have your property looking its best at all times.
2. Keep the yard neat and clean. Have the shrubs trimmed and the lawn cut. Make the prospect want to come inside. The first impression is extremely important.
3. Dress up the windows. They are the "eyes" of the house.
4. Keep the house tidy—not as a furniture store display window, but as a comfortable home in which to live.

5. Have the garage clean and neat. Broken window-panes or loose doorknobs make an unfavorable impression.

6. Make all minor repairs on such things as sticking doors, leaky plumbing, and broken light switches. These things make a house hard to show and often kill a sale.

7. If you have a dog, keep him out of the house and under control. Many buyers are afraid of dogs.

8. Shut off or tune down the radio or television set. They are distracting.

9. Let plenty of light into the rooms. Nothing more effectively adds to a cheerful atmosphere than light.

10. A moderate amount of heat adds a feeling of coziness in cold weather. Fresh air is equally desirable on hot days.

11. Never apologize for the appearance of the house. It only emphasizes the faults.

12. If redecorating is needed, do it if possible. Properly done, it creates appeal. Some decorators will do a limited amount of work and take their fee out of the sale.

13. Be prepared at all times to show your property. The prospect you turn away might be the logical buyer.

14. If the prospect asks questions about the house and the neighborhood, answer directly and honestly. Questions about the transaction should be referred to the agent.

15. Leave the showing of the house to the salesperson. Interrupting the sales presentation may lose the sale.

16. Discuss frankly any problems that may arise relative to the marketing of your property with your realtor.

The selling of property, especially a home, involves a certain amount of inconvenience to the occupant. All real estate salespeople are aware of this and will be as considerate as possible. With your cooperation, they will work energetically to find a buyer—and the possibilities of a sale will be greatly enhanced if your property bears a marketable price tag.

CHAPTER QUESTIONS _____

1. List the types of listing agreements and describe each.

2. How does multiple listing differ from the ordinary type of listing of property for sale?

3. Explain the meaning of the following clause found in most real estate contracts: "Time is of the essence."

4. Define a "tax-free" or a "tax-deferred" exchange. What is meant by the term "boot"?

5. When may a real estate broker sue for a commission, assuming that he or she has no signed listing agreement?

MULTIPLE-CHOICE QUESTIONS _____

1. Broker Jones takes a listing on Smith's property. Jones finds a buyer who is ready, willing, and able to purchase the property. Jones may: (a) accept a deposit from the buyer only if the agency agreement permits him to do so; (b) accept a deposit from the buyer as the buyer's agent; (c) not accept a deposit; (d) accept a deposit and put it in his commercial account; (e) cash the check and keep it as his commission.

2. The printed portion of the CAR Real Estate Purchase Contract and Receipt for Deposit has no provisions for the following: (a) proration of property taxes; (b) bond or assessment liens; (c) restrictions, rights, and conditions of record; (d) discount points; (e) a deposit on the purchase price.

3. A description by street address only on the Real Estate Purchase Contract and Receipt for Deposit is: (a) valid, but always invalid in a deed; (b) valid, but would likely cause a title company to refuse to insure title; (c) always invalid in the deposit receipt but can be corrected by a later deed; (d) always invalid in the deposit receipt but can be corrected by a quiet title action.

4. A net listing: (a) places upon the broker the obligation to disclose to the seller the full amount of compensation he will receive from the sale, prior to seller's acceptance of the offer; (b) is illegal in California; (c) gives the broker an exclusive right to sell the property for an amount not to exceed the net sum plus a 10 percent commission; (d) is considered merely an option agreement; (e) any of the foregoing is a correct answer.

5. Broker Jones secured a listing, and the seller signed only one copy. Broker Jones then took the signed copy to his office to have duplicates made for the sales force: (a) Jones has not violated the real estate law; (b) the law requires only that the seller be given a copy of the deposit receipt offer if and when the seller accepts it; (c) the seller's signature below a statement that he or she had received a copy of the listing is sufficient protection for Broker Jones; (d) Broker Jones could be disciplined by the Real Estate Commissioner for breaking a provision of the Real Estate Law; (e) the seller is not entitled to a copy of any signed agreement.

6. An owner signed a listing with a broker in which it was understood that if the property were sold through the efforts of any other broker or the owner, the listing broker would not be entitled to a commission. This kind of contract is called: (a) an open listing; (b) an exclusive right listing; (c) an exclusive agency listing; (d) a listing option; (e) all of the foregoing.

7. A real estate salesperson working for Broker Smith took a listing on a piece of real property. One month after taking the listing, the salesperson transferred to another broker's office: (a) the listing is the property of the salesperson and she may take it with her to her new broker; (b) the listing is void; (c) the listing is voidable; (d) the listing is the property of Broker Smith; (e) the listing is the property of the new employing broker.

8. A broker receives a written offer and deposit with a ten-day acceptance clause. On the fifth day, prior to acceptance by the seller, the buyer notifies the broker he is withdrawing his offer and demands the return of the deposit: (a) the broker may declare the deposit forfeited and retain it for his services and commission; (b) the broker should notify seller that the buyer is withdrawing the offer and broker and seller each may retain one-half of the deposit; (c) the buyer has the right to revoke his offer at any time before he is notified of the seller's acceptance and secure return of deposit; (d) the buyer cannot withdraw the offer—it *must* be held open for the full ten-day period.

9. If a seller agreed to pay a broker a 20-percent commission on a sale: (a) it is in violation of the Real Estate Law; (b) it is in violation of the usury law; (c) it is in violation of the corporations code; (d) it is in violation of the federal constitution; (e) it is permissible.

10. A valid listing agreement provides for a minimum deposit of $1,000 and certain other terms and conditions. The listing broker presents an offer from a buyer with a $700 deposit that meets all other terms and conditions of the listing agreement. The sellers refuse to accept this offer: (a) the sellers cannot refuse to accept the offer; (b) the broker can maintain a suit for her commission in a court; (c) the buyer can maintain a suit to force the seller to sell, since the sellers had signed the listing agreement; (d) the broker cannot maintain a suit for her commission in court because she has not fulfilled his contract; (e) the broker should sue the buyers for her commission.

AGENCIES

In the early history of our country, almost all persons were able to represent themselves in business transactions. Today, our society, economy, and business have become so complex that it is impossible for us to make all of our own transactions. Thus, the *agent* has come into existence.

Distinctions should be made among agent, principal, employer-employee, and independent contractor.

DEFINITION OF TERMS

Agent An agent is defined by the California Civil Code as one who represents another (called a principal) in dealings with third persons. These representations are referred to as an agency. A majority of businesspeople in our society today are agents for someone else. The agent may be employed to sell, give advice, purchase, and perform a variety of other transactions related to modern business. In every agency three parties are involved: the person represented, or the *principal*; the *agent* who represents the principal; and the *third party* with whom the agent deals on behalf of his or her principal.

Principal Any person capable of conducting his or her own business transactions may appoint an agent, except in voting, executing a will, and taking an oath. The principal must be not only mentally competent but also of legal age. A minor is incapable of appointing an agent; however, the agent may be a minor.

Employer-Employee An employer-employee relationship exists when, by expressed or implied agreement, one person, called the employee, undertakes personal services for another, called the employer, under the employer's supervision and control. A person may be both an agent and an employee, depending upon the scope of his or her authority. For example, a secretary may be an employee of a business firm, but when he or she delivers documents to another firm, the secretary may in fact become an agent. This distinction may be important, particularly in the area of tort liability. (A *tort* is any civil wrong.)

Independent contractor The independent contractor is one who is responsible to his or her employer only for the final results of his or her work. He or she is independent in employment or occupation, exercises his or her own judgment on the job being done, and is responsible for all his or her own acts. Because an independent-contractor relationship exists, the employer has no right of control as to the method of doing the work under contract. Adam contracts with Brown, an independent contractor, to build a house. Adam is interested in only the final product. He does not tell Brown whom she must hire, where she must buy the materials, and so forth. He is concerned only that the house meet the plans and specifications set forth under the contract. As a general rule, Brown, as an independent contractor, is responsible for all of her own acts or torts.

TYPES OF AGENTS

An agent may be classified according to his or her scope of authority. A *special agent* is one who is employed to perform a particular act or business transaction. Adam, a property owner, employs Brown, a real estate broker, to sell his home. Brown is a special agent hired for the sole purpose of selling Adam's home. A valid listing agreement is signed. Later, Brown, the real estate broker, sells Adam's home. Her particular function has been completed and the agency agreement is executed. A *general agent* includes all others. The general agent is authorized to do anything and everything that his or her principal can do. The contracts performed may be of both a personal and a business nature. Adam employs Brown as his agent to conduct all of his business and personal affairs. In such cases, Adam, as the principal, is responsible for all acts of the general agent.

BROKERS AND SALESPEOPLE

Under the law of agency, *brokers* are usually classified as agents or special agents. They have no custody and control over the subject matter of the agency and, further, operate in the names of their principals. The independent contractor operates under his or her own name. *Salespeople* are classified as employees of a broker. Real estate law requires that the broker exercise reasonable supervision over the salespeople's activities.

Brokers and salespeople have a close relationship with their principals or customers, much the same as that of the lawyer with a client. Such association is termed a *fiduciary*, or *faithful*, *relationship*.

The law demands that the agent maintain this relationship with his or her principal and that he or she act only in the best interest of that principal. Further, the licensed real estate broker must, by law, have a written employment agreement with each salesperson, broker, or sales manager working under his or her employment.

CREATION OF THE AGENCY RELATIONSHIP

The agency relationship is created in four principal ways: authorization or express appointment, subsequent ratification, ostensible acts and necessity.

An actual agency is created by authorization or by subsequent ratification. Most agency agreements are voluntary and are formed by prior authorization, either oral or written, expressed or implied. A listing agreement signed by both principal and agent prior to the agent's fulfilling his or her function as a special agent would be an example of an agency formed by *authorization* or by *express appointment*.

When a person attempts to act for another without his or her permission, expressed or implied, and said person's acts are approved by the principal, the principal is bound, and an agency by *subsequent ratification* has been formed. When a principal learns of unauthorized representations made by another proposing to be his or her agent, the principal may repudiate the acts, ratify them, or imply approval by his or her conduct.

In either of these cases an actual agency is said to exist—that is, it has been formed by authorization or by subsequent ratification.

An *ostensible* agency is created when the principal causes a third person to believe another to be his or her agent who is not in fact employed by him or her. This may have been intentional on the part of the principal or simply due to carelessness. This is an involuntary agency relationship created by law to prevent an injustice. The elements necessary to create an ostensible agency are (1) conduct on the part of the principal that indicates the agent's apparent authority and (2) the third party's reliance upon such apparent authority.

Necessity is another type of involuntary agency that may be created by law without the actual consent of the principal, on the grounds of public policy. A wife, for example, has the authority to pledge her husband's credit for the necessities of life. The law may confer certain authority upon the employee or agent who must act in the best interests of the employer and yet is unable to consult his or her principal or employer. In an emergency, a store employee may call a physician to attend to a customer who has received an injury in the store.

An attorney-in-fact is a person who has been appointed an agent under an instrument called a *power of attorney*. (Figure 7–1). Such a person should not be confused with an attorney-at-law. Adam, through a power of attorney, appoints Brown to act for him. Brown would be an attorney-in-fact.

A *dual* agency exists where the same person represents more than one principal. Under California Real Estate Law, the broker may not represent two parties unless he or she so informs them and has their consent. The broker may collect a commission from both as long as each party understands that the broker is collecting a commission from the other. In the exchange of properties, a broker will frequently represent both parties. Assume that Adam, a real estate broker, arranges an exchange of properties between Brown and Cole. Two sales have actually taken place. Adam, the broker, may collect a commission from both Brown and Cole as long as both consent. Failure to make this fact known to both parties may mean suspension or revocation of the broker's license.

AGENCY AGREEMENTS

An *agency agreement* is a contract between the principal and the agent. Because it is a contract, the agreement must contain all the essential elements of a contract.

When Recorded Mail To:

    Mr. John Property Owner
    123 Jones Street
    San Rafael, California 94903

)
)
)
)
)
)
)
)

S P E C I A L   P O W E R   O F   A T T O R N E Y

I, JOHN PROPERTY OWNER, the Principal, a resident of Marin County, State of California, hereby appoint JOE AGENT, of 321 Smith Street, San Rafael, California, the agent, as attorney-in-fact to act for me and in my name as authorized in this document.

Special Grant of Powers. My attorney-in-fact is authorized and empowered to sell and convey my real property, commonly known as 123 Jones Street, San Rafael, California, and more particularly described as:

> *Lot 5, of Block B, of the Freitas Subdivision #4, filed on May 2, 1946, in Book 123, Page 456, in the Official Records of Marin County Recorder's Office, State of California.*

Such authorization includes the power to sell on such terms and conditions as authorized herein, and, in accordance therewith, to execute such contract, promissory notes, deeds of trust, grant deeds, escrow instructions, and to perform those acts and any other acts necessary or incidental to the exercise of such powers.

Limitations. Any sale of the above property must be for a sum of not less than $250,000, with not less than twenty percent (20%) down. The sale may include the carrying back of a promissory note for part of the purchase price, provided that note is fully amortized, bearing interest at a rate not less than twelve percent (12%) per annum, for a period of not more than three (3) years, and secured by a second (purchase money) deed of trust on the aforesaid property, and containing an acceleration clause in the event of late payment, and a due on sale clause.

Duration. This instrument shall be valid for a period of ninety (90) days from the date hereof.

SIGNED on this _____ day of May, 1986, in the City of San Rafael, County of Marin, State of California.

JOHN PROPERTY OWNER

[ACKNOWLEDGMENT]

Figure 7–1

There must be mutual assent, the parties must be capable of contracting, and the agreement must be for a lawful object. The one exception is consideration. To be enforceable, an agency agreement for the sale of real property must be in writing.

As stated above, consideration is not essential to the creation of an agency agreement; that is, the agent may act gratuitously. Adam is the owner of a retail store. Brown, his friend, enters the store. Adam wishes to go to the corner drugstore for a cup of coffee, and Brown agrees to watch the store while he is out. While Adam is out, Brown commits a tort. She cannot deny that she was in fact Adam's agent even though she acted without compensation. Adam, her principal, may be as liable for Brown's acts or torts as Brown herself is.

Agency agreements may take the form of *unilateral* contracts. Listing agreements of this nature are generally nonenforceable in California. Most listing agreements provide that the broker will use diligence in procuring a purchaser for the property in question. This will make the contract a *bilateral* one in which there is a promise for a promise. The property owner promises to sell under the terms and conditions of the listing agreement, and the broker promises to use due diligence in finding a purchaser for the property.

If the agent is to enter into a contract that is required by law to be in writing, the agency agreement must be in writing. This is known as the *Equal Dignities Rule*.

When an agent or a broker enters into a contract for compensation or a commission in the sale of real property, some note or memorandum thereof must be written and subscribed to by the party to be charged if the agreement is to be valid. Adam verbally employs Brown to sell his property under certain terms and conditions and states that he will pay Brown a 6-percent commission if he should sell said property. Brown finds a buyer ready, willing, and able to purchase the property. Adam sells the property to Brown's buyer, then refuses to pay Brown a commission; Brown may not enforce the contract because there was no written note or memorandum relating to her employment. (*Note:* Exceptions to this rule exist where the agent or the broker acts in the immediate presence of his or her principal and executes instruments under the direction of his or her principal.)

AGENT'S SCOPE OF AUTHORITY

A real estate broker's authority is governed by the terms of his or her agency contract. Generally, we may classify such authority as: (1) express, (2) incidental, and (3) customary.

An agreement to sell or to purchase real property will set forth the terms of the agency agreement. *Express* authority may also be by conduct of the parties, or it may be *implied* authority when the agent informs the principal of his or her intentions and the principal says or does nothing.

Incidental authority is authority that is reasonably necessary to execute the agreement. For example, the advertising of the principal's real property would be incidental to the authority granted in the agreement.

Customary authority may be used by the professional property manager in the collection of rents from tenants or in the eviction of said tenants in the event that such rents are not paid as provided in the lease agreement.

In most cases, a contract merely authorizes the broker or his or her salesperson to find a purchaser for the real property. Unless the agreement provides for accepting a deposit, the broker or the salesperson is not authorized to collect same. If he or she does so, it will be as agent of the buyer rather than as agent of the principal. However, most form listing agreements do authorize the agent to accept a deposit.

DELEGATION OF POWER BY AN AGENT

Agents may delegate certain powers to other persons unless the agency agreement specifically forbids the agency to do so. The general rule is that an agent may not delegate authority granted to him or her in the agency agreement except where (1) the act is purely mechanical in nature, (2) it is customary to do so, (3) a necessity or sudden emergency exists, or (4) subagents are contemplated.

An artist is employed to paint a portrait because of her skill in painting; therefore, she may not delegate another to do her work. A secretary, however, may do the typing on a form agreement for his employer because it is purely mechanical.

A real estate agent may fill in a form contract, but he or she may not draw or create a new contract. The actual drawing of a contract must be done by an attorney licensed to practice law. It is also customary to delegate certain authority to the escrow officer in closing a transaction.

In an emergency, it may be necessary for the agent to delegate authority to protect his or her principal's interest. Thus, the agent may delegate to another the call for a medical doctor in case of injury to someone on the principal's property.

When a home is listed by the broker and said agreement provides that the property will be placed on the multiple-listing interchange, subagents are approved by such listing.

WHOSE AGENT IS THE BROKER?

Legal questions often arise as to whom the broker represents. The general rule is that the broker is the agent of the party who first employs him or her; usually, that is the seller. Buyers are often unpleasantly surprised to find that by law "their" broker is really representing the other party.

Listing broker

When a broker lists property, the listing agreement acts as an employment contract appointing the broker as the seller's agent. This broker is commonly called the "listing broker."

Sometimes the listing broker is the only broker in the transaction. This broker acts for the owner to obtain the highest possible price and also works with the buyer to purchase the property at the lowest price. Even with the broker negotiating for both parties, most courts hold that this broker still remains the sole agent of the seller. The rationale is that the broker was first employed by the seller, and the buyer is not paying the broker's commission.

There is a trend suggesting that some trial courts may be recognizing the broker as an agent of both the seller and the buyer. However, such law is only slowly emerging. Most courts still follow the traditional view that the broker functions exclusively as the seller's agent.

Two brokers, using MLS

Generally, the listing broker places the property with the multiple-listing service (MLS). The broker then invites other brokers to find a buyer and become a "subagent." As a subagent of the listing broker, this "cooperating" broker remains an agent of the seller.

Even though the buyer first contacted the broker and the seller may never have met the cooperating broker, almost all courts hold this broker to be the seller's exclusive agent. One of the greatest misconceptions among buyers is that "their agent" is representing "their" interest.

The Federal Trade Commission is looking into this problem. One of their recent studies found that, nationwide, two-thirds of surveyed sellers knew the buyer's confidential "top" purchase price. Obviously, the buyer's bluffing and purchasing strategy is severely weakened when the seller knows the buyer's "secret" intentions.

There has been considerable discussion at the federal and state levels of the need to amend the law and have the cooperating broker represent the buyer. Perhaps future consumer legislation will remedy this inequity.

A new California law, to become effective in 1987 will require brokers to provide both buyers and sellers in residential transactions a written disclosure of the broker's agency relationship and representation. Further, it will prevent the broker from revealing the buyer's secret information about their maximum purchase price to the seller. This law is a first step in controlling an agent's dual representation.

DUTIES OF THE PRINCIPAL AND THE AGENT

Certain duties and responsibilities rest with both the principal and the agent:

1. Both the principal and the agent must act in good faith and in fairness to each other. The agent may have no personal interest in conflict with that of his or her principal.
2. An agent may act for two parties only when he or she has the consent of both.
3. The agent may make no secret profit at the expense of his or her principal. If the agent does so, he or she is liable to the principal. The same relationship exists between principal and agent as between a trustee and the beneficiary of an estate.
4. The agent must inform the principal of all material facts in a transaction.
5. The agent must be both obedient and responsible to his or her principal. The agent must obey lawful instructions, and if he or she does not, he or she is liable for damages to the principal.
6. The principal must compensate the agent for his or her services as well as for expenses incurred in the line of duty.
7. An agent, for the purpose of effecting the agency agreement, must do everything necessary or usual in the ordinary course of business.
8. An agent may make actual representations to fulfill the agency agreement as long as he or she knows they are true. The agent must act in the name of his or her principal and not in his or her own, unless it is the usual course of business to do so.
9. In an emergency, the agent's power is broadened and he or she may disobey instructions if it should be in the best interest of his or her principal.
10. An agent is liable for his or her own torts. However, since the principal reaps the benefits of those acts performed by his or her agent, the principal may be responsible for torts caused by the agent to third persons, if such torts are caused within the scope of the agency.

The most common violations by real estate licensees are for misrepresentations, false promises, commingling, and secret profits.

1. Misrepresentations. A misrepresentation is a false statement of fact, which the licensee knowingly makes, with the intent of inducing another party to act.

2. False Promises. A false promise is a promise about a future event, which the licensee knows is false. A typical example would be a broker promising to fix a light fixture, when that broker has no intent of doing so.

3. Commingling. Whenever a broker mixes a client's fund with his or her funds, commingling has occurred. It does not matter that the client does not suffer any loss.

4. Secret Profits. A secret profit occurs whenever the licensee directly or indirectly makes a profit at the expense of his or her client, without the client's knowledge.

AGENT'S RESPONSIBILITY TO THIRD PERSONS

An agent is responsible for his or her own torts, negligence, or fraudulent acts against third persons. It matters not that these were ordered by his or her principal. Adam employs Brown, his agent, to sell his home. Adam knows of termites in the home and conveys this information to Brown but tells him not to give this information to a customer. Brown, in showing the property to Cole, represents that the property does not have termites. Cole later finds out that the property does have termites and, having relied upon Brown's information, suffers damages. In such cases, the agents, as well as their principals, may be held responsible.

The broker remains liable for fraud, misrepresentation, concealment, or other wrongful acts. However, except for such torts, the broker owes almost no other duty to third persons.

Further, brokers rarely have contracts with buyers or other third persons. Therefore, there is no contractual obligation to that third person.

Easton liability—residential property

In 1974 the California Supreme Court handed down a landmark decision, *Easton* v. *Strassburger*. This case holds that residential brokers owe a duty of reasonable investigation and disclosure to buyers.

In *Easton* the listing brokers observed certain indications of potential trouble (called "red flags" by the court). The agents knew the property was on filled land, and they noticed a rope netting suggesting potential slide problems. The listing brokers did not investigate these red flags, nor did they advise the buyer of their findings.

The *Easton* Court found the listing brokers owed a duty to the buyer (1) to conduct a reasonably competent visual inspection and (2) to disclose any observable problem areas.

The legislature codified the decision of *Easton* and

now requires that brokers use a property disclosure form in all residential transactions. The contents of the form are specified by statute and require the broker to list any known or reasonably discoverable problems. A copy of the statutory form is provided in Chapter 6.

It appears that disclosure and investigation requirements of *Easton* are inapplicable to commercial brokers.

DUTIES OF THIRD PERSONS

Third persons have certain responsibilities to protect themselves. Basically, third persons have the following obligations and protections:

1. Third persons should take reasonable steps to determine the extent of the agent's authority. As a general rule, a third party cannot rely upon the agent's statements alone, and if he or she has reason to doubt the agent's authority, he or she should check with the principal.

2. Where the third person has reason to believe that the agent may be dealing adversely with his or her principal, such third person may deal at his or her own peril.

3. A third person cannot generally rely upon the agent's statement as to the happening of a future event.

4. As a general rule, the third person may hold a disclosed principal liable on a contract when the agent is acting within the scope of his or her authority or apparent authority. When there is neither apparent authority nor actual authority, the principal may not be bound.

5. When the agent acts for an undisclosed principal and the third party enters into such contract, the third party may generally enforce a contract against the agent. When the third party learns of the undisclosed principal, he or she may hold either the agent or the principal liable. Until relief is obtained from one, it does not bar a right of action against the other. Therefore, if the agent wishes to avoid liability, he or she should disclose his or her principal.

TERMINATION OF AGENCY RELATIONSHIP

The agency relationship may be terminated in any one of the following ways: (1) mutual agreement, (2) expiration of the term, (3) destruction or extinction of the subject matter, (4) death of either principal or agent, and (5) operation of law.

The parties to an agency agreement may terminate it by mutual agreement. Thus, when the real estate agent and the property owner agree to cancel the listing agreement, they may do so.

The expiration of time stated on the agreement will cancel the contract of agency. Thus, a listing agreement expiring at midnight on March 31 will be terminated.

If the subject matter of the agency agreement becomes extinct, the agreement is terminated. To illustrate: Adam, a broker, has an exclusive listing on a piece of property. The property is destroyed by fire. Since the subject matter is now destroyed, the agency agreement is terminated.

The death of either the principal or the agent will terminate the agency agreement. Adam, a broker, has a file of listings of numerous properties in the city of Sunnyvale. When he dies, his son Bill takes over the business. Adam's death terminates the agency agreements. Bill must now secure new agency agreements from each of the property owners.

The general rule is that an agency agreement will be terminated by operation of law, as in the case of bankruptcy. When bankruptcy takes place, all assets are placed in the hands of a receiver appointed by the court that has jurisdiction.

BROKER'S COMMISSION

The real estate broker's commission is fixed by custom rather than by law. It is a matter of agreement between the principal and the agent.

When has the broker earned his or her real estate commission? He or she has earned it when he or she has found a buyer ready, willing, and able to purchase the property at the listed price, on the exact terms, and within the life of the listing agreement or any extension thereof. It matters not how little or how much effort has been expended by the broker. The broker is entitled to his or her commission if he or she gets the desired results. In general practice, real estate commissions are normally paid directly out of escrow.

When brokers cooperate in the sale of land or other properties, they may decide how fees or commissions will be divided. Binding agreements between brokers are effective. Such agreements may be made orally and may be enforced the same as any other contract not required to be in writing. As a matter of practice, however, to save disagreement at a later date, brokers normally exchange letters as to the division of commissions. For example, Adam has a customer in Los Altos looking for land in Red Bluff. He calls Brown, a real estate broker in Red Bluff, and they agree to share commissions equally. Should Brown have property of interest to the customer, an exchange of letters concerning the division of commissions is in order because such a letter is proof in a court of law of such an agreement.

In common practice, the client or the principal is the one who employs the broker to sell his or her property; however, it is not unusual for a buyer to employ a broker to find property for him or her, in which case the buyer may agree to pay the broker a commission or a finder's fee. The broker could, under these circumstances, collect a commission from both the customer and the principal, but he or she must inform both that he or she is collecting a commission from each.

LICENSING REAL ESTATE BROKERS AND SALESPEOPLE

A majority of the states today have statutes regulating the licensing and activities of real estate brokers and salespeople. The purpose of these statutes is to protect the land-buying public from fraudulent acts on the part of a few unscrupulous or incompetent individuals. Basically there are two parts to most state laws governing real estate: (1) the statutes enacted by the state legislatures and (2) the Rules and Regulations of the Real Estate Commissioner, administrator, or executive secretary who is charged with the enforcement of the statute. The latter, called *administrative law*, once made in accordance with the statutes of a state have the same force as the law itself. Chapter 17 discusses these laws in more detail.

CHAPTER QUESTIONS _____

1. Define an *agent* and relate your definition to the real estate broker.
2. Contrast the employer-employee relationship and the status of an independent contractor.
3. In what four ways can an agency relationship be created?
4. In what ways may an agency relationship be terminated?
5. When has a broker earned his or her commission on a sale?

MULTIPLE-CHOICE QUESTIONS _____

1. Broker Stanton had a listing, and Broker Johnson sold the property. They had orally agreed to split the commission, but Stanton refused to pay Johnson anything: (a) Johnson has grounds for a civil action in court; (b) Johnson could do nothing because the agreement was not in writing; (c) Stanton is subject to discipline by the Real Estate Commissioner; (d) Johnson should request the city council to take action; (e) Johnson should request the county board of supervisors to take action.
2. "Fiduciary relationship," under the law of agency, refers to: (a) the relationship between a broker and his or her salespeople; (b) the position of trust between a broker and his or her principal; (c) the relationship created between plaintiff and defendant; (d) all of the foregoing; (e) none of the foregoing.

3. To create an agency for the purpose of selling real estate, a broker must have: (a) a general power of attorney; (b) a quitclaim deed; (c) a written contract; (d) a license to practice law in California; (e) a college degree.

4. One who signs a listing authorizing the sale of his or her property is known as: (a) an agent; (b) a subagent; (c) an attorney-in-fact; (d) a principal; (e) a defendant.

5. Through negligence, Adam led Brown to believe that Jones was his agent when Jones was not really employed by Adam. This agency is referred to as: (a) actual; (b) ratified; (c) specific; (d) ostensible; (e) special.

6. State which of the following is free to accomplish a result as he or she sees fit: (a) agent; (b) independent contractor; (c) employee; (d) subagent; (e) all of the foregoing.

7. Broker Jones, knowing that Smith wants a certain parcel of land, contacts the owner to purchase it and does so without authority from Smith. Smith ratifies Broker Jones's action. This agency was formed by: (a) prior agreement; (b) ratification; (c) estoppel; (d) none of the foregoing.

8. A real estate salesperson is an agent: (a) for the principal directly; (b) for his or her employing broker; (c) for the third party; (d) for the principal's attorney; (e) the principal's wife.

9. An agent is one who: (a) represents another to third persons; (b) always acts as an independent contractor; (c) must always be an ostensible agent; (d) operates only under a power of attorney; (e) always represents the buyer.

10. The agency relationship may be terminated by: (a) mutual agreement; (b) expiration of the term; (c) destruction or extinction of the subject matter; (d) death of either the principal or the agent; (e) any of the foregoing.

8 FINANCING REAL ESTATE

Financing is the lifeblood of the real estate business. Why? Because few people can afford to pay all cash when they buy real estate or build on it.

If financing were cut off, real estate activity would collapse. In this chapter, you will read about the general field of real estate finance and the laws and documents involved. In Chapter 9, you will cover the sources of funds for real estate financing.

TYPES OF INSTRUMENTS

A number of instruments are used in real estate financing. The two most important are

1. The *promissory note*. This is the written promise to pay given by the person who owes the money.
2. The *deed of trust or mortgage*. This is the document that gives the creditor a lien or claim against the debtor's real estate to secure the note.

Both are contracts, and the laws governing contracts apply to them.

Promissory note

A promissory note is the instrument used to evidence a debt or obligation to pay money. Three common types are used:

1. A *straight note*, calling for the periodic payment of interest, with the entire sum of the note due at the end of the term of the note—that is, on the maturity date. (See Figure 8–1.)

2. An *installment note*, calling for periodic payments on the principal plus any accumulated interest. (See Figure 8–2.)
3. An *amortized note*, shown in Figure 8–3, is an installment note in which all the payments are the same amount. The amount of the payments is calculated so it will pay off the exact amount of the entire principal plus interest during the term of the note—say, ten years. The amount of the payments is determined from a loan amortization payments booklet as described in Chapter 12. This is the most common type of note used in home financing.

Negotiability

"Negotiability" is a special and very valuable quality possessed by notes, checks, and instruments called "bills of exchange." Negotiability is the quality that allows these instruments to circulate as money does. In fact, today's paper money is descended from "bank notes" issued by banks in the early history of the United States. These notes circulated in place of silver dollars and other coins.

To understand a note better, let us compare it with a negotiable instrument we are all familiar with—a check:

Check
(Figure 8–4)

1. A check is a *three-party* instrument: The first party is the maker and signs it. The second party is the bank that is directed to pay the money. The third party is the payee to whom the check is made out.

Figure 8–1

2. A check is due and payable as soon as it is presented to the bank.

3. A check directs the bank to pay the payee.

Note
(Figure 8–1)

1. A note is a *two-party* instrument: The first party is the maker who signed it and promised to pay the money. The second is the payee to whom the money is to be paid.

2. A note is due whenever its terms state. It may be due ''on demand''; or it may be due at a future date, such as ''on December 31 of this year,'' or ''30 days after today.''

3. A note is the promise of the maker to pay the payee.

A bill of exchange is similar to a check, and the rules covering both are almost the same. You will seldom see one in the real estate business, so we won't discuss it here.

A check or a note must meet seven essential requirements to be negotiable. It must be

1. In writing.

2. Made by one person to another.

3. Signed by the maker.

4. Unconditional—that is, there must be no condition on the promise to pay or the directions to the bank to pay.

5. Payable on demand, or at a fixed future date, or at a future date that can be determined.

6. For a definite sum of money.

7. Payable to the *bearer, to the order of* some fictitious name such as *cash*, or *to the order of* a named person. When it is payable ''to the order of'' a named person, he or she may, by endorsing it, ''order'' that it be paid to someone else.

DO NOT DESTROY THIS ORIGINAL NOTE: When paid, said Original Note, together with the Deed of Trust securing same, must be surrendered to Trustee for cancellation and retention before reconveyance will be made.

NOTE SECURED BY DEED OF TRUST
(INSTALLMENT – INTEREST INCLUDED)

$ *10,000.00*   *San Francisco*   , California, *April 1, 1982*

In installments as herein stated, for value received, I promise to pay to *Robert S. Smith and Bertha B. Smith*---or order, at *Wells Fargo Bank, 4648 Mission Street, San Francisco, California* the sum of *ten thousand and no/100*--------------------------------DOLLARS, with interest from *April 1, 1982*------------------------------on unpaid principal at the rate of *fourteen (14%)*----------per cent per annum; principal and interest payable in installments of *two hundred thirty-two and no/100*-----------($232.69)-------------Dollars, or more on the -----*first (1st)*---------day of each --------------------month, beginning on the-----*first (1st)*---- day of *May*--and continuing until said principal and interest have been paid.

Each payment shall be credited first on interest then due and the remainder on principal; and interest shall thereupon cease upon the principal so credited. Should default be made in payment of any installment when due the whole sum of principal and interest shall become immediately due at the option of the holder of this note. Principal and interest payable in lawful money of the United States. If action be instituted on this note I promise to pay such sum as the Court may fix as attorneys' fees. This note is secured by a Deed of Trust. Said Deed of Trust contains the following provision:
In the event the herein described property or any part thereof, or any interest therein is sold, agreed to be sold, conveyed or alienated by trustor, or by the operation of Law or otherwise, all obligations secured by this instrument, irrespective of the maturity dates expressed therein, at the option of the holder thereof and without demand or notice shall immediately become due and payable.

-------------------------------------   -------------------------------------
            Jacob P. Trustor   *Christine Trustor*

WESTERN TITLE FORM NO. 302-AC

DO NOT DESTROY THIS NOTE

DO NOT DESTROY THIS ORIGINAL NOTE: When paid, said Original Note, together with the Deed of Trust securing same, must be surrendered to Trustee for cancellation and retention before reconveyance will be made.

NOTE SECURED BY DEED OF TRUST
(INSTALLMENT – INTEREST EXTRA)

$ *10,000.00*   *Sacramento,*   , California, *March 23, 1982*

In installments as herein stated, for value received, I promise to pay to *Jose S. Sanchez and Maria A. Sanchez*--, or order, at *88899 Folsom Boulevard, Sacramento, California*--------------------- the sum of *ten thousand and no/100*------------------------------------DOLLARS, with interest from *March 23, 1982*--------------------------------on unpaid principal at the rate of *ten (10%)*-------per cent per annum, payable *on the 23rd day of each month*--; principal payable in installments of *five hundred and no/100*---Dollars, or more on the *23rd*-------------------day of each --------------------month, beginning on the -----*23rd*--------- day of *April.*---and continuing until said principal and interest have been paid.

Should default be made in payment of any installment of principal or interest when due the whole sum of principal and interest shall become immediately due at the option of the holder of this note. Principal and interest payable in lawful money of the United States. If action be instituted on this note I promise to pay such sum as the Court may fix as attorneys' fees. This note is secured by a Deed of Trust. Said Deed of Trust contains the following provision:
In the event the herein described property or any part thereof, or any interest therein is sold, agreed to be sold, conveyed or alienated by trustor, or by the operation of Law or otherwise, all obligations secured by this instrument, irrespective of the maturity dates expressed therein, at the option of the holder thereof and without demand or notice shall immediately become due and payable.

-------------------------------------   -------------------------------------
            Henry E. Borrower   *Joyce P. Borrower*

WESTERN TITLE FORM NO. 304-AC

DO NOT DESTROY THIS NOTE

Figure 8–2   Installment Note. (This note has been typewritten. It could even be handwritten; a printed form is not required.)

NOTE

$ __5,000.00__   ___Los Angeles___ , California __March 20__ , 19 __82__

In installments as herein stated, for value received, I promise to pay to __Bill Jones Company__

X __ X __ X __ X __ X __ X __ X __ X __ X __ X __ , or order,

at ___20756 Waverly Drive, Los Angeles, California___

the sum of ___Five Thousand and No/100   X   X   X   X   X___ DOLLARS,

with interest from __today__ on unpaid principal at the

rate of __Ten X   X   X   X__ per cent per annum; principal and interest payable in installments of

__One Hundred Twenty Six and 81/100   ($126.81)   X   X   X   X   X__ Dollars

or more on the __first__ day of each _____ month, beginning

on the __first__ day of __May, 1982___

and continuing until said principal and interest have been paid.

Each payment shall be credited first on interest then due and the remainder on principal; and interest shall thereupon cease upon the principal so credited. Should interest not be so paid it shall thereafter bear like interest as the principal, but such unpaid interest so compounded shall not exceed an amount equal to simple interest on the unpaid principal at the maximum rate permitted by law. Should default be made in payment of any installment of principal or interest when due the whole sum of principal and interest shall become immediately due at the option of the holder of this note. Principal and interest payable in lawful money of the United States. If action be instituted on this note I promise to pay such sum as the Court may fix as attorney's fees.

William Brown

Figure 8-3

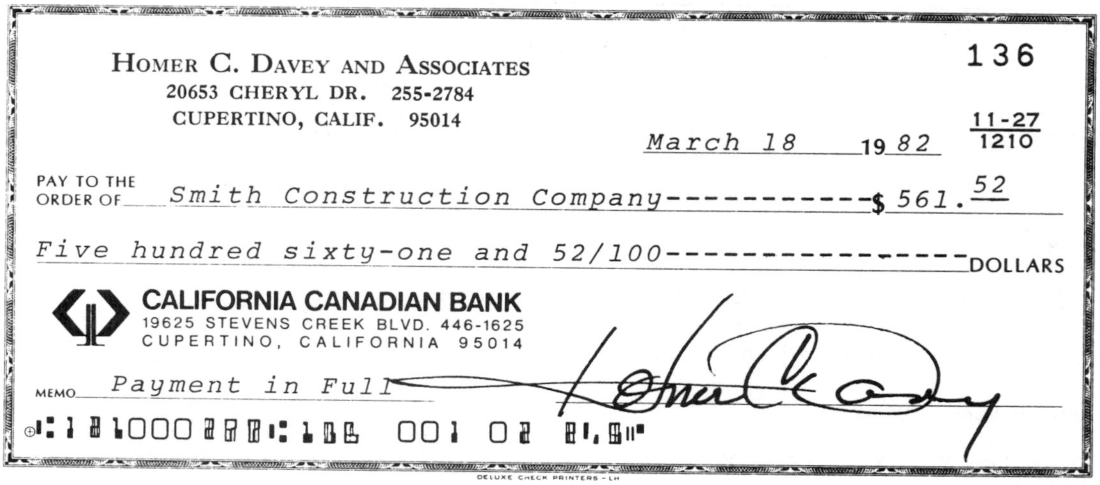

Figure 8–4

If one of the seven requirements is missing, the instrument is not negotiable. However, it may be valid between the two parties involved and may be freely transferred from one person to another. It simply lacks the benefits that come from negotiability, which are discussed below. A nonnegotiable note can be used in financing.

Advantages of negotiability

The most important advantage of negotiability arises when the holder transfers the instrument to a new holder who can qualify as a *holder in due course*. The holder in due course will enjoy a favored position under the law and may get more rights than the original holder had. He or she is defined as one who takes a *negotiable* instrument under the following conditions:

1. When the instrument was transferred to him or her, it was not overdue if it was a note; if it was a check, the bank had not previously refused to pay it.

2. He or she took it in good faith and gave valuable consideration for it.

3. When it was taken, the new holder had no notice of any defect in the title of the person who transferred it to him or her.

4. It was complete and regular on its face.

To understand the advantages the law gives the holder in due course, consider this case:

You owe Joe Allen $1,000 and give him a note for this amount due in one year. Allen accepts the note. Before the year is up, Allen borrows back $400 from you, leaving $600 as the net debt you owe him.

Allen sells the note to Sara Green before it comes due. Green has no knowledge or notice of the $400 that Allen borrowed back from you.

When the note comes due, Green demands payment of $1,000 from you. You say that you will pay only $600 because that is all you owed to Allen, and that Allen could not transfer to her greater rights than he himself had against you.

In legal terms, what you are claiming is the right of *setoff.* This is the right to set off your claims against Allen's to cancel part of the debt you owed him. Ordinarily, when an instrument or a claim is assigned, the *assignee* (the person to whom it is assigned or transferred) gets no greater rights than were possessed by the *assignor* (the person who assigned it). The law says that "The assignee stands in the shoes of the assignor."

Under the principle of setoff, Sara Green could collect only $600 from you. But if she is a holder in due course, the transfer to her cuts off your right of setoff; she may collect the full $1,000 from you.

The defenses cut off by selling a negotiable instrument to a holder in due course are called *personal defenses.* They include

1. Setoff.

2. Lack of consideration or failure of consideration. That is, you did not get the thing you gave the note for. Assume you buy a lot from Ima Swindler and give her your negotiable note as part of the purchase price. You find that Swindler never owned the lots, so her deed to you is worthless. You have her prosecuted and sent to prison. But before the note comes due, she manages to negotiate it to Hargis, a holder in due course. You must pay the note in full to Hargis.

3. A claim of previous payment or cancellation of the debt evidenced by the note. Suppose you pay off a note before it comes due, but fail to pick it up or get it marked "paid." The payee transfers the note to a holder in due course. The personal defense of previous payment is cut off, and you must pay the note a second time.

4. Fraud *in the inducement*. Suppose you know that the instrument is a note, but you are induced to sign it by false statements or some other type of fraud. Such fraud is a personal defense that is cut off.

Although the personal defenses above would not be good against a holder in due course, they would be good against the original payee.

There are other defenses called *real defenses* that are good against all persons, including a holder in due course. These include

1. Fraud *in the inception*. This type of fraud causes a person to sign an instrument thinking it is something else. For example, a man signs a note thinking he is signing a birthday card.

2. The incapacity of the parties to contract. Suppose the maker of the instrument is someone a court had adjudged to be mentally incompetent. This real defense would be good even against a holder in due course.

3. The instrument had been executed in connection with gambling or other illegal conduct.

4. Forgery, or intentional material alteration of the instrument. Suppose your name is forged on a note, or suppose Brown, the payee, materially changes the amount payable.

Negotiation

A negotiable instrument can be transferred in two ways:

1. By assignment. This is simply the transfer of ownership from one person to another. It can be done by a separate document assigning the check or note, or by a bill of sale, or in other ways. The new holder is *not* a holder in due course.

2. By negotiation. The manner of doing this is described below. A person cannot be a holder in due course unless the instrument is negotiated to him or her.

If the instrument is payable to "bearer," no signature is needed for negotiation. It may be handed from one person to another as cash is.

When the check or the note is payable to "the order of" a particular person (the *payee*), negotiation will require an endorsement on the back by the payee and all later persons to whom it is endorsed. You probably won't endorse many notes in your life, but you will certainly endorse many checks. Therefore, the types of endorsements will be of interest to you:

1. Blank endorsement. The payee simply signs his or her name on the back. An instrument so endorsed is payable to the bearer and may be negotiated by delivery without further endorsement.

2. Special endorsement. The payee writes, "Pay to the order of John Smith," and then signs his or her name. Before the instrument can be negotiated further, John Smith must endorse the instrument.

3. Restrictive endorsement. The payee writes: "Pay to the order of First National Bank of Bakersfield, for deposit only," and then signs his or her name. The words "for deposit only" restrict the instrument to one purpose. The bank must deposit the money in the payee's account. The bank may not, for instance, apply the check to a loan that the payee owes.

4. Qualified endorsement. The payee writes "without recourse" above his or her signature. The payee is actually saying that he or she will not be responsible—that is, no one can have recourse against him or her—if the check or note is not paid later.

The person who endorses a note or a check without using a qualified endorsement is making a promise to all later holders that he or she will pay if the maker or the bank won't. The last holder of the instrument may demand payment from the maker or anyone who endorsed it without qualification earlier than he or she did. An endorser who is forced to pay may, in turn, sue and collect from the maker or any other earlier unqualified endorser. However, to preserve his or her rights against an earlier endorser, he or she must notify him or her promptly when there is a default.

For example, suppose a check or a note is signed by Mark Maker and payable to the order of Paula Payee. Assume that it is then endorsed by

Paula Payee
Arnold Adams
Bill Baker
Charles Cole

If it is not paid, Cole must give prompt notice of the default; then he may proceed against Maker, Payee, Adams, and Baker. If Baker is forced to pay and had given prompt notice of the default, he may proceed against Maker, Payee, and Adams.

Incidentally, when a bank pays money out on a forged check or on a check where there is a forged endorsement, the bank, not the depositor, is the loser unless the bank can prove the depositor was negligent in allowing the forgery. The bank has no legal right to pay out the depositor's money on a forged check or endorsement, no matter how skillful the forger is.

DEEDS OF TRUST AND MORTGAGES

Trust deeds

When a person finances real estate, he or she signs a promissory note that evidences the debt and contains his or her promise to pay the money. To make the real estate security for the debt, he or she executes a second instrument, which may be either a deed of trust or a mortgage. In most states, the common security instrument is a mortgage. But in California, over 99 percent of such instruments are deeds of trust, because the California law makes them more advantageous for the lender than a mortgage (Figure 8–5).

A mortgage is so rarely used in California that most real estate people never encounter one. Nevertheless, we will discuss mortgages in many places in this chapter and the next so that you can see the advantages of a trust deed and because you may run across mortgages in other states. The California salesperson's or broker's examinations frequently contain questions on mortgages.

The laws covering trust deeds and mortgages are very similar. As we discuss trust deeds in this chapter and the next, you may assume that the same rules apply to mortgages, unless it is otherwise stated. Where they differ, it will be pointed out.

One word of caution: People in California frequently talk about a "mortgage." What they really mean is a deed of trust—in everyday language in California it is often called a "mortgage."

Differences between trust deeds and mortgages

There are two parties to a mortgage: the *mortgagor* and the *mortgagee*. The mortgagor borrows the money; the mortgagee lends it. A California mortgage gives the mortgagee a lien against the mortgaged property. Title remains in the name of the mortgagor.

A deed of trust has three parties: the *trustor*, the *beneficiary*, and the *trustee*. The trustor is the borrower; the beneficiary is the lender; and the trustee is a third party who holds legal title to the property. The borrower conveys legal title to the trustee, who holds it as security for the loan. The trustee reconveys the property to the borrower when the debt is paid. If the borrower fails in his or her obligation, the trustee sells the property at public sale and uses the money to pay the debt to the lender.

Statute of limitations   A statute of limitations is a law that sets out how long you may wait to file suit to

enforce a right. After the period set by the statute has passed, the right becomes unenforceable. Under the California statute of limitations, a note becomes unenforceable through court four years after its due date, or four years after the last payment on it, whichever is later. If the note is secured by a straight mortgage, the mortgage likewise becomes unenforceable at the same time.

But when the note is secured by a trust deed, there is no time limit on when the trustee may sell the property. He or she holds the legal title and may sell at any time and apply the money he or she receives to the debt. Therefore, even after the statute of limitations has run on the note, the lender may have the property sold. To the lender, this is a big advantage of a trust deed over a mortgage. The differences between a mortgage and a deed of trust are summarized in Table 8–1.

Choosing a trustee

People are surprised to learn that in California the trustee is seldom informed of being named as trustee until it is time to reconvey the property to the borrower, or the borrower has defaulted. Until that time, the trustee had absolutely no duties and does not need to be informed.

However, the lender should be sure that the trustee named is someone willing to act in this capacity, such as a title insurance company or an escrow company. These companies are willing to act as trustees because they can charge fees for reconveying or conducting a trustee's sale, and because acting in this capacity generates title insurance and escrow business for them. In fact, many distribute blank trust deed forms to real estate people on which their names are printed as the trustees.

The beneficiary has a right to eliminate one trustee and substitute another by recording a *Substitution of Trustee* in the county recorder's office. He or she may do this at any time without the consent of the old trustee.

Priority and recording

Trust deeds are a charge on real property, as a lien. Usually, charges and liens on the same property take priority according to the time of their creation. The first in time is first in right. But this is modified by the recording laws discussed in Chapter 3. When a later lienholder does not have notice of the earlier one, he or she may become first in right by recording first. To safeguard his or her interest, a lender should record his or her trust deed promptly.

Assignment and transfer

The assignment of a promissory note secured by a deed of trust carries the security with it. If the note is transferred, the new holder is entitled to the security. On the other hand, the assignment of a deed of trust transfers

SPACE ABOVE THIS LINE FOR RECORDER'S USE

CAT. NO. NN00618
TO 1939 CA (10—84) (OPEN END)

SHORT FORM DEED OF TRUST AND ASSIGNMENT OF RENTS (INDIVIDUAL)

PARCEL NO. LOT 7 BLOCK 3011A

This Deed of Trust, made this 15th day of JULY, 1985 , between

JOHN BUYER AND JANE BUYER , herein called Trustor,
whose address is 1050 North Gate, San Francisco, California
(number and street) (city) (state) (zip)
Ticor Title Insurance Company of California, a California corporation, herein called Trustee, and

ABC BANK, a Corporation
, herein called Beneficiary,

Witnesseth: That Trustor IRREVOCABLY GRANTS, TRANSFERS AND ASSIGNS to TRUSTEE IN TRUST, WITH POWER OF SALE, that property in the City of San Francisco, San Francisco County, California, described as: Lots 5 and 6, in Block 5, in the City of San Francisco, County of San Francisco, State of California, as per Map recorded in Book 11 Page 68 of Miscellaneous Records in the office of the County Recorder of said County.

IN THE EVENT TRUSTOR, WITHOUT THE PRIOR WRITTEN CONSENT OF THE BENEFICIARY SELLS, AGREES TO SELL, TRANSFERS OR CONVEYS ITS INTEREST IN THE REAL PROPERTY OR ANY PART THEREOF OR ANY INTEREST THEREIN, BENEFICIARY MAY AT ITS OPTION DECLARE ALL SUMS SECURED HEREBY IMMEDIATELY DUE AND PAYABLE. CONSENT TO ONE SUCH TRANSACTION SHALL NOT BE DEEMED TO BE A WAIVER OF THE RIGHT TO REQUIRE SUCH CONSENT TO FUTURE OR SUCCESSIVE TRANSACTIONS. THE TERM "TRUSTOR" AND "BENEFICIARY" INCLUDES THEIR SUCCESSORS.

TOGETHER WITH the rents, issues and profits thereof, SUBJECT, HOWEVER, to the right, power and authority given to and conferred upon Beneficiary by paragraph (10) of the provisions incorporated herein by reference to collect and apply such rents, issues and profits.
For the Purpose of Securing: 1. Performance of each agreement of Trustor incorporated by reference or contained herein. 2. Payment of the indebtedness evidenced by one promissory note of even date herewith, and any extension or renewal thereof, in the principal sum of $500,000.00 executed by Trustor in favor of Beneficiary or order. 3. Payment of such further sums as the then record owner of said property hereafter may borrow from Beneficiary, when evidenced by another note (or notes) reciting it is so secured.
To Protect the Security of This Deed of Trust, Trustor Agrees: By the execution and delivery of this Deed of Trust and the note secured hereby, that provisions (1) to (14), inclusive, of the fictitious deed of trust recorded in Santa Barbara County and Sonoma County October 18, 1961, and in all other counties October 23, 1961, in the book and at the page of Official Records in the office of the county recorder of the county where said property is located, noted below opposite the name of such county, viz:

COUNTY	BOOK	PAGE	COUNTY	BOOK	PAGE	COUNTY	BOOK	PAGE	COUNTY	BOOK	PAGE
Alameda	435	684	Kings	792	833	Placer	895	301	Sierra	29	335
Alpine	1	250	Lake	362	39	Plumas	151	5	Siskiyou	468	181
Amador	104	348	Lassen	171	471	Riverside	3005	523	Solano	1105	182
Butte	1145	1	Los Angeles	T2055	899	Sacramento	4331	62	Sonoma	1851	689
Calaveras	145	152	Madera	810	170	San Benito	271	383	Stanislaus	1715	456
Colusa	296	617	Marin	1508	339	San Bernardino	5567	61	Sutter	572	297
Contra Costa	3978	47	Mariposa	77	292	San Francisco	A332	905	Tehama	401	289
Del Norte	78	414	Mendocino	579	530	San Joaquin	2470	311	Trinity	93	366
El Dorado	568	456	Merced	1547	538	San Luis Obispo	1151	12	Tulare	2294	275
Fresno	4626	572	Modoc	184	851	San Mateo	4078	420	Tuolumne	135	47
Glenn	422	184	Mono	52	429	Santa Barbara	1878	860	Ventura	2062	386
Humboldt	657	527	Monterey	2194	538	Santa Clara	5336	341	Yolo	653	245
Imperial	1091	501	Napa	639	86	Santa Cruz	1431	494	Yuba	334	486
Inyo	147	598	Nevada	305	320	Shasta	684	528			
Kern	3427	60	Orange	5889	611	San Diego	Series 2 Book 1961, Page 183887				

(which provisions, identical in all counties, are printed on the reverse hereof) hereby are adopted and incorporated herein and made a part hereof as fully as though set forth herein at length; that he will observe and perform said provisions; and that the references to property, obligations, and parties in said provisions shall be construed to refer to the property, obligations, and parties set forth in this Deed of Trust.
The undersigned Trustor requests that a copy of any Notice of Default and of any Notice of Sale hereunder be mailed to him at his address hereinbefore set forth.

STATE OF CALIFORNIA
COUNTY OF _____ } ss.
On _____ before
me, the undersigned, a Notary Public in and for said State,
personally appeared _____

personally known to me or proved to me on the basis of satisfactory evidence to be the person __ whose name ___ subscribed to the within instrument and acknowledged that ___ executed the same.
WITNESS my hand and official seal.

Signature _____

Signature of Trustor

JOHN BUYER

JANE BUYER

(This area for official notarial seal)

Title Order No. _____   Escrow or Loan No. _____

Figure 8–5   103

To Protect the Security of This Deed of Trust, Trustor Agrees:

(1) To keep said property in good condition and repair; not to remove or demolish any building thereon; to complete or restore promptly and in good workmanlike manner any building which may be constructed, damaged or destroyed thereon and to pay when due all claims for labor performed and materials furnished therefor; to comply with all laws affecting said property or requiring any alterations or improvements to be made thereon; not to commit or permit waste thereof; not to commit, suffer or permit any act upon said property in violation of law; to cultivate, irrigate, fertilize, fumigate, prune and do all other acts which from the character or use of said property may be reasonably necessary, the specific enumerations herein not excluding the general.

(2) To provide, maintain and deliver to Beneficiary fire insurance satisfactory to and with loss payable to Beneficiary. The amount collected under any fire or other insurance policy may be applied by Beneficiary upon any indebtedness secured hereby and in such order as Beneficiary may determine, or at option of Beneficiary the entire amount so collected or any part thereof may be released to Trustor. Such application or release shall not cure or waive any default or notice of default hereunder or invalidate any act done pursuant to such notice.

(3) To appear in and defend any action or proceeding purporting to affect the security hereof or the rights or powers of Beneficiary or Trustee; and to pay all costs and expenses, including cost of evidence of title and attorney's fees in a reasonable sum, in any such action or proceeding in which Beneficiary or Trustee may appear, and in any suit brought by Beneficiary to foreclose this Deed.

(4) To pay: at least ten days before delinquency all taxes and assessments affecting said property, including assessments on appurtenant water stock; when due, all incumbrances, charges and liens, with interest, on said property or any part thereof, which appear to be prior or superior hereto; all costs, fees and expenses of this Trust.

Should Trustor fail to make any payment or to do any act as herein provided, then Beneficiary or Trustee, but without obligation so to do and without notice to or demand upon Trustor and without releasing Trustor from any obligation hereof, may: make or do the same in such manner and to such extent as either may deem necessary to protect the security hereof, Beneficiary or Trustee being authorized to enter upon said property for such purpose; appear in and defend any action or proceeding purporting to affect the security hereof or the rights or powers of Beneficiary or Trustee; pay, purchase, contest or compromise any incumbrance, charge or lien which in the judgment of either appears to be prior or superior hereto; and, in exercising any such powers, pay necessary expenses, employ counsel and pay his reasonable fees.

(5) To pay immediately and without demand all sums so expended by Beneficiary or Trustee, with interest from date of expenditure at the amount allowed by law in effect at the date hereof, and to pay for any statement provided for by law in effect at the date hereof regarding the obligation secured hereby any amount demanded by the Beneficiary not to exceed the maximum allowed by law at the time when said statement is demanded.

(6) That any award of damages in connection with any condemnation for public use of or injury to said property or any part thereof is hereby assigned and shall be paid to Beneficiary who may apply or release such moneys received by him in the same manner and with the same effect as above provided for disposition of proceeds of fire or other insurance.

(7) That by accepting payment of any sum secured hereby after its due date, Beneficiary does not waive his right either to require prompt payment when due of all other sums so secured or to declare default for failure so to pay.

(8) That at any time or from time to time, without liability therefor and without notice, upon written request of Beneficiary and presentation of this Deed and said note for endorsement, and without affecting the personal liability of any person for payment of the indebtedness secured hereby, Trustee may: reconvey any part of said property; consent to the making of any map or plat thereof; join in granting any easement thereon; or join in any extension agreement or any agreement subordinating the lien or charge hereof.

(9) That upon written request of Beneficiary stating that all sums secured hereby have been paid, and upon surrender of this Deed and said note to Trustee for cancellation and retention and upon payment of its fees, Trustee shall reconvey, without warranty, the property then held hereunder. The recitals in such reconveyance of any matters or facts shall be conclusive proof of the truthfulness thereof. The grantee in such reconveyance may be described as "the person or persons legally entitled thereto." Five years after issuance of such full reconveyance, Trustee may destroy said note and this Deed (unless directed in such request to retain them).

(10) That as additional security, Trustor hereby gives to and confers upon Beneficiary the right, power and authority, during the continuance of these Trusts, to collect the rents, issues and profits of said property, reserving unto Trustor the right, prior to any default by Trustor in payment of any indebtedness secured hereby or in performance of any agreement hereunder, to collect and retain such rents, issues and profits as they become due and payable. Upon any such default, Beneficiary may at any time without notice, either in person, by agent, or by a receiver to be appointed by a court, and without regard to the adequacy of any security for the indebtedness hereby secured, enter upon and take possession of said property or any part thereof, in his own name sue for or otherwise collect such rents, issues and profits, including those past due and unpaid, and apply the same, less costs and expenses of operation and collection, including reasonable attorney's fees, upon any indebtedness secured hereby, and in such order as Beneficiary may determine. The entering upon and taking possession of said property, the collection of such rents, issues and profits and the application thereof as aforesaid, shall not cure or waive any default or notice of default hereunder or invalidate any act done pursuant to such notice.

(11) That upon default by Trustor in payment of any indebtedness secured hereby or in performance of any agreement hereunder, Beneficiary may declare all sums secured hereby immediately due and payable by delivery to Trustee of written declaration of default and demand for sale and of written notice of default and of election to cause to be sold said property, which notice Trustee shall cause to be filed for record. Beneficiary also shall deposit with Trustee this Deed, said note and all documents evidencing expenditures secured hereby.

After the lapse of such time as may then be required by law following the recordation of said notice of default, and notice of sale having been given as then required by law, Trustee, without demand on Trustor, shall sell said property at the time and place fixed by it in said notice of sale, either as a whole or in separate parcels, and in such order as it may determine, at public auction to the highest bidder for cash in lawful money of the United States, payable at time of sale. Trustee may postpone sale of all or any portion of said property by public announcement at such time and place of sale, and from time to time thereafter may postpone such sale by public announcement at the time fixed by the preceding postponement. Trustee shall deliver to such purchaser its deed conveying the property so sold, but without any covenant or warranty, express or implied. The recitals in such deed of any matters or facts shall be conclusive proof of the truthfulness thereof. Any person, including Trustor, Trustee, or Beneficiary as hereinafter defined, may purchase at such sale.

After deducting all costs, fees and expenses of Trustee and of this Trust, including cost of evidence of title in connection with sale, Trustee shall apply the proceeds of sale to payment of: all sums expended under the terms hereof, not then repaid, with accrued interest at the amount allowed by law in effect at the date hereof; all other sums then secured hereby; and the remainder, if any, to the person or persons legally entitled thereto.

(12) Beneficiary, or any successor in ownership of any indebtedness secured hereby, may from time to time, by instrument in writing, substitute a successor or successors to any Trustee named herein or acting hereunder, which instrument, executed by the Beneficiary and duly acknowledged and recorded in the office of the recorder of the county or counties where said property is situated, shall be conclusive proof of proper substitution of such successor Trustee or Trustees, who shall, without conveyance from the Trustee predecessor, succeed to all its title, estate, rights, powers and duties. Said instrument must contain the name of the original Trustor, Trustee and Beneficiary hereunder, the book and page where this Deed is recorded and the name and address of the new Trustee.

(13) That this Deed applies to, inures to the benefit of, and binds all parties hereto, their heirs, legatees, devisees, administrators, executors, successors and assigns. The term Beneficiary shall mean the owner and holder, including pledgees, of the note secured hereby, whether or not named as Beneficiary herein. In this Deed, whenever the context so requires, the masculine gender includes the feminine and/or neuter, and the singular number includes the plural.

(14) That Trustee accepts this Trust when this Deed, duly executed and acknowledged, is made a public record as provided by law. Trustee is not obligated to notify any party hereto of pending sale under any other Deed of Trust or of any action or proceeding in which Trustor, Beneficiary or Trustee shall be a party unless brought by Trustee.

REQUEST FOR FULL RECONVEYANCE

To be used only when note bas been paid.

Dated _____

To Trustee:

The undersigned is the legal owner and holder of all indebtedness secured by the within Deed of Trust. All sums secured by said Deed of Trust have been fully paid and satisfied; and you are hereby requested and directed, on payment to you of any sums owing to you under the terms of said Deed of Trust, to cancel all evidences of indebtedness, secured by said Deed of Trust, delivered to you herewith together with said Deed of Trust, and to reconvey, without warranty, to the parties designated by the terms of said Deed of Trust, the estate now held by you under the same.

MAIL RECONVEYANCE TO:

_____   _____
_____   _____
_____   _____

Do not lose or destroy this Deed of Trust OR THE NOTE which it secures. Both must be delivered to the Trustee for cancellation before reconveyance will be made.

TICOR TITLE INSURANCE

COMPLETE STATEWIDE TITLE SERVICE WITH ONE LOCAL CALL

Ticor Title Insurance Company of California AS TRUSTEE

WITH POWER OF SALE (INDIVIDUAL)

Short Form Deed of Trust

Figure 8–5 (Continued)

Table 8-1   Mortgages and Deed of Trust

	Deeds of Trust	Mortgages
Parties	Beneficiary (borrower) Trustor (lender) Trustee (holds title)	Mortgagor (borrower) Mortgagee (lender)
Title	Passes to trustee ("bare legal title")	Borrower retains
Statute of Limitations	No effect	When run, blocks foreclosure
Foreclosure Procedure	1) Record notice of default, 2) reinstate up to 5 days before sale, 3) after ninety days publish 3 times in 20 days the notice of sale, 4) Sale and trustee's deed. Average time 4 months. Alternatively, can be foreclosed like a mortgage (judicially).	1) File lawsuit, 2) reinstate up to time of trial, 3) trial and judgment, 4) judicial sale. Average time 6–18 months. If deficiency judgment desired, 2 more steps. 1) one year equity of redemption, 2) sheriff's deed issued.
Deficiency Judgment	None (unless foreclosed like a mortgage and deficiency allowed by law.	Yes, if property sold for less than judgment and deficiency allowed by law.

no rights unless the note that is the principal obligation is also transferred.

"Assuming" versus "taking subject to"

When property covered by a trust deed is conveyed and the trust deed is to be left on the property, the new owner either may agree to "assume" the trust deed or may take the property "subject to" the trust deed. If the new owner assumes, he or she agrees to pay the trust deed and is liable on the note as though he or she were the original maker. The original maker, of course, remains secondarily liable on the note and may have to pay it if the new owner does not do so. If the original maker is forced to pay it, he or she can sue and collect from the party who assumed it.

If the new owner takes "subject to" the deed of trust without assuming it, he or she does not promise to pay and does not become liable on the note. Of course, if he or she does not pay, the lender will have the trustee sell the property to pay the debt. The maker continues to be liable on the note.

However, if the deed of trust is a *purchase-money deed of trust*, the original borrower would not have any liability. Most loans on owner-occupied residences, and all deeds of trust executed by the buyer and taken back by the seller, are purchase-money loans. (These loans are described in detail later in the chapter.) Since the borrower would not be personally liable when taking out the original loan, the borrower would not incur any liability on transfer.

Alternatively, if the borrower is truly concerned about having a secondary liability on the deed of trust, the new property owner could execute a *novation*. A novation is like an amendment to the loan. The new owner agrees to become solely liable for payment, and the lender agrees to look only to the property and the new lender in the event of default. It removes and relieves the original borrower from any liability for the loan.

Reconveyance

When the promissory note secured by a trust deed is paid, the borrower should have the lender mark the note "Paid" and have the lender execute the "Request for Reconveyance" on the back of the deed of trust. Both the note and the request for reconveyance are sent to the trustee along with a fee for executing the reconveyance, usually $25, and a recording fee of $4. The trustee executes a deed of reconveyance (Figure 8-6) conveying legal title back to the borrower and sends it to the county recorder for recording along with the $4 fee. After recording, the deed of reconveyance is mailed by the county recorder to the borrower.

Because the note must be sent to the trustee, the borrower should not destroy it when it is paid.

When a mortgage has been paid in full, the lender executes a satisfaction of mortgage, which releases the mortgage and which the borrower records.

SPECIAL CLAUSES AND RIGHTS

Partial release clause

A trust deed may contain a partial release clause, which requires that particular parts of the land must be released from the trust deed when certain conditions have been fulfilled. A partial release clause might provide that upon

RECORDING REQUESTED BY

Ticor Title Insurance Company of California
160 Pine Street
San Francisco, CA 94111

AND WHEN RECORDED MAIL TO

Name: Ted Gordon, Esq.
Gordon, McFarlan, Stewart and Blecher
Street Address: Holiday Plaza, Suite 475
1050 North Gate Drive
City & State: San Rafael, Ca 94903

SPACE ABOVE THIS LINE FOR RECORDER'S USE

TITLE ORDER NO.	TITLE OFFICER	A.P.N.

CAT. NO. NN01064
TO 20430 CA (1–83)

Full Reconveyance

Ticor Title Insurance Company of California, a corporation, formerly Title Insurance and Trust Company, as duly appointed Trustee under Deed of Trust hereinafter referred to, having received from holder of the obligations thereunder a written request to reconvey, reciting that all sums secured by said Deed of Trust have been fully paid, and said Deed of Trust and the note or notes secured thereby having been surrendered to said Trustee, for cancellation, does hereby RECONVEY, without warranty, to the person or persons legally entitled thereto, the estate now held by it thereunder. Said Deed of Trust was executed by John Buyer and Jane Buyer, his wife

Trustor, and recorded in the official records of San Francisco County, California, as follows:

REC. July 15, 1982 AS INSTR. NO. C 51862 IN BOOK/REEL C156 PAGE/IMAGE 542

DESC. Lots 5 and 6, in Block 5, in the City of San Francisco, County of San Francisco, State of California, as per Map recorded in Book 11 Page 68 of Miscellaneous Records in the office of the County Recorder of said County.

In Witness Whereof, Ticor Title Insurance Company of California, a corporation, formerly Title Insurance and Trust Company, as such Trustee, has caused its corporate name and seal to be hereto affixed by its Assistant Secretary, thereunto duly authorized on the date shown in the acknowledgement certificate shown below.

Ticor Title Insurance Company of California, a corporation, formerly Title Insurance and Trust Company, as such Trustee

By ______________________________
Assistant Secretary

STATE OF CALIFORNIA
COUNTY OF ______________________

On ______________________, before me, the undersigned, a Notary Public in and for said State, personally appeared ______________________________, personally known to me, or proved to me on the basis of satisfactory evidence to be the person who executed the within instrument as the Assistant Secretary of TICOR TITLE INSURANCE COMPANY OF CALIFORNIA, and acknowledged to me that such corporation executed the same as such Trustee. WITNESS my hand and official seal.

Signature ______________________________

(This area for official notarial seal)

Figure 8–6

payment of $10,000 by the debtor, a certain portion of the property will be released free and clear and a partial deed of reconveyance executed. In developing residential property, subdividers may put a trust deed on the whole tract and use this clause to release lots as they are sold.

Subordination clause

A trust deed may contain a subordination clause or agreement providing that the trust deed will be subordinate in priority to any existing or anticipated future lien on the property. Suppose an owner sells land to a developer and takes back a deed of trust as part of the purchase price. As part of the agreement, the deed of trust may include a subordination clause permitting the developer to obtain a construction loan and making the purchase money deed of trust subordinate to the construction loan.

Attorney's fees clause

Most notes, deeds of trust, and mortgages have a clause stating that if suit is filed on the instrument, a reasonable attorney's fee to be set by the court will be added to the judgment if the lender wins. This was covered in Chapter 5 in the discussion of contracts. Under California statute, if the lender may recover an attorney's fee when he or she wins, the borrower can also recover such fee when he or she is the winning party.

Prepayment penalties and the lock-in clause

Some notes state that the borrower has the right of prepayment—that is, the right to pay ahead of the due date. Other notes say that payment is due "on or before" a certain date or "by" a certain date, and this wording allows the borrower to pay ahead of time. But when the note does not allow prepayment, the lender may refuse to accept payment until the money is due.

Many notes provide for prepayment only upon payment of some penalty, such as six months' interest on the part prepaid. Some notes also provide for a period of time after the start of the loan during which no prepayment is allowed. This is called a *lock-in period*.

When a loan is obtained through a mortgage loan broker on a single-family, owner-occupied dwelling, the prepayment privileges and the right to prepay are greatly liberalized by statute as described in the next chapter in the section covering Mortgage Loan Brokers.

Impound accounts

To protect his or her security, a lender must know that the real estate taxes and the insurance on the property will be paid. Therefore, lenders, especially those financing the buying of a home, require the borrower to

pay an additional monthly amount to be set aside by the lender in a special account. The lender pays taxes and insurance out of this account as they come due. The moneys accumulated are called *impounds*; such an account is called an *impound account* or a *loan trust account*.

A California statute effective in 1974 relieves buyers of single-family homes they reside in from having to pay into an impound account unless one of the following conditions exists:

1. The impound account is required by state or federal regulatory authority.
2. The loan is made, guaranteed, or insured by a state or federal agency.
3. The buyer has been delinquent in paying two consecutive tax installments.
4. The loan was 90 percent or more of the purchase price or appraised value of the property.

The borrower and the lender are permitted to agree upon an impound program, provided the lender gives the buyer a writing stating (1) that the buyer does not have to agree and (2) that the buyer is paid 2-percent interest on the impound account.

Beneficiary statements

The borrower may make a written demand on the beneficiary for a statement showing the condition of the debt. This is called a beneficiary statement or offset statement, and includes the following:

1. Unpaid balance of the debt
2. Amount of any periodic payments
3. Due date of the debt in whole or in part
4. Real estate taxes and special assessments due and payable
5. Premium, term, and amount of hazard insurance in effect
6. Amount in any account maintained to pay property taxes and insurance premiums
7. The nature and amount of any additional charges, costs, or expenses paid or incurred by the lender that have become a lien on the property

The lender may charge $25 for this statement. The lender is subject to penalties for failure to deliver it within twenty-one days. Such a statement should be obtained whenever a person buys property subject to a trust deed.

Acceleration clauses

Most notes and deeds of trust contain "acceleration" clauses. An acceleration clause states that the holder of the note and trust deed has the right to declare the entire amount of the obligation due and payable at once upon the occurrence of some specified event. For example, the lender may exercise this type of option if the debtor does not pay the installments on the note as they come due, fails to pay the real estate taxes, or fails to keep the property properly insured.

One important type of acceleration clause that appears in many notes and deeds of trust provides that the entire amount becomes due and payable, at the holder's option, if the owner conveys the property. This is called a *due-on-sale clause* or an *alienation clause*, or sometimes, somewhat erroneously, it is simply called an "acceleration clause."

This clause will prevent a purchaser from buying the property with a deed of trust left on it unless the holder of the deed of trust consents. The holder has the legal right to demand something in return for giving his or her consent. For example, the holder may require that the interest rate be raised or that he or she be paid a bonus, called "points."

In California, a special statute covers a due-on-sale clause when the property contains four or fewer residential units. The statute says that the clause is invalid if executed on or after July 1, 1972, unless it appears in full in *both* the note and the trust deed. Because of federal due-on-sale legislation, it is uncertain whether the California statute is still valid. In any event, sound lending practice dictates that the clause be in both instruments.

Reasons for due-on-sale

Due-on-sale clauses allow a lender to be paid off when the property secured by the loan is sold. Most loans are for thirty years. On these loans, most of the first five years' payments are interest, with very little going for principal reduction. On thirty-year loans, the total interest is based on a thirty-year amortization period. The average home in California is sold every five to seven years.

If the lender collects most of the interest on a thirty-year loan but has the loan outstanding for only five to seven years, the lender's yield is greatly increased.

If, when the property is sold, the interest rates have decreased, the new buyer would obviously obtain a new loan. Why take over a 17-percent loan when you can obtain a new, 14-percent loan? If, as is usually the case, the current loan rates are higher than the original loan rates, the lender can call the loan due. Why would a lender allow someone to take over a 13-percent loan when current rates are 17 percent? Actually, most lenders allow a new buyer to take over the loan, but at a higher interest rate.

Early California history

Until 1974 the law of California held that a lender could call a loan due upon any sale. In 1978 the California Supreme Court decided *Wel-*

lencamp vs *Bank of America*, commonly referred to as the *Wellencamp* case. *Wellencamp* held that lenders could not accelerate and declare their loans due upon a sale unless they could demonstrate that the transfer constituted an impairment of their security. Later cases held that *federal* savings and loans were exempt from this rule and could declare their loans due upon a sale.

In summary, in the late 1970s and early 1980s, most home loans could be transferred with the property. The interest rates were rising, and buyers were very happy to take over existing low-interest loans. Lenders were finding this practice very unprofitable.

✓ Garn–St. Germain Act

In October 1982 Congress passed the *Garn–St. Germain Act*, often simply called the *Garn Act*. This federal legislation held that all state laws were bound by the federal statute, and any inconsistent state laws, such as the *Wellencamp* decision, were superseded.

The *Garn Act* basically allows all due-on-sale clauses to be enforceable.

Transition rules defined loans made or taken over during the period between *Wellencamp* and the passage of the *Garn Act* ("window-period loans"). These loans could be taken over during various grace periods, depending on the type of loan. The last grace period expired in October 1985. Since that time, all due-on-sale clauses are enforceable.

FHLBB regulations

The *Garn Act* was implemented through regulations issued by the Federal Home Loan Bank Board (FHLBB). These regulations stated that due-on-sale clauses in loans secured by owner-occupied residences cannot be accelerated when a listed type of transfer occurs. The exceptions are:

1. Transfer upon death of the borrower and transfer to certain relatives.

2. Transfers to the borrower's spouse or children who then occupy the property.

3. Transfers to surviving joint tenants on the death of a joint tenant.

4. Certain transfers to a trust, which does not affect the owner's right of occupancy or the percentage of ownership.

5. Several other listed transfers are exempt, including junior deeds of trust and leases under three years in length not having an option.

Unsettled issues

The *Garn Act* exempted certain transfers; such transfers are exempt from the lender's right to call the loan due. The FHLBB regulations limited these exceptions to owner-occupied residences. The courts have yet to rule if administrative regulations can place greater restrictions than allowed by the actual statute.

Most attorneys believe the rules will be upheld by the courts.

Also, almost all transfers allow the loan to be called due and payable. The courts have not specifically approved acceleration merely because an owner places a junior deed of trust on the property, or allows a foreclosure of a junior lien. The exact limits of the transfers allowing acceleration will have to be settled by the courts.

Yearly statements

For each calendar year, the borrower is entitled to an itemized accounting of the moneys the lender has received for interest, principal, and payment into any impound account, or that has been paid out of any impound account.

The borrower is entitled to one such statement free of charge within sixty days after the end of each year. He or she may request additional statements upon payment of a small fee.

ALTERNATIVE MORTGAGE INSTRUMENTS

In the 1970s and 1980s lenders faced new problems never before encountered. Potential homeowners could not qualify for fixed rate loans. Further, lenders needed to charge higher interest rates to offset the losses due to old, low yield loans. Finally, lenders were fearful of the uncertain future, and the potential for greatly fluctuating interest rates. To meet these needs, lenders created new mortgage instruments.

There are over one hundred types of alternative mortgage instruments. The key feature of these loans, is that the interest rate and/or monthly payment is not fixed, but fluctuates. The most commonly used alternative loans are:

1. Adjustable Rate Mortgages. Adjustable rate mortgage ("ARM") is any loan which allows the lender to adjust the rate of interest over the term of the loan. The initial interest rate is offered at a lower interest rate than available for fixed rate loans. The interest rate is tied to an index, and as the index fluctuates, so does the interest rate.

As the interest rate changes, the monthly payments could change, or more commonly, the loan payback period is merely extended to adjust to the increased amount due. If you have a $100,000, thirty-year loan, your monthly payment is $1,028 at 12 percent. If the interest rate increased to 14.5 percent, the payment would be $1,224. If, however, the monthly payment remained the same, each payment would be $196 short, which amount would be added to the loan principal and would earn interest.

After several years, you could find yourself owing more than you borrowed. This problem is called "negative amortization."

In accepting one of these loans, you should review several items about the loan. Is there a maximum limit ("cap") on the amount the interest rate can increase? How frequently can the increases occur and is there a maximum limit on each increase? What is the reference rate that is used? Can you pay off the loan without prepayment penalty whenever there is an increase? Shop around, since different lending institutions offer different ARMs.

2. Graduated Payment Mortgages. The graduated payment mortgage ("GPM") has a fixed interest rate throughout the life of the loan. The payments are lower in the early years, and increase over time.

Finally, the payments are sufficiently over market value to cover the normal payment and recover the deficiency occurring during the under-market period. These loans are ideal for people unable to initially qualify for a loan but whose future earning capacity looks good.

3. Growing Equity Mortgages. The Growing Equity Mortgage ("GEM") also has a fixed interest rate, lower initial monthly payments, and higher later payments. However, in the GEM, the increases in payments are applied directly to reduce the principal. Thus, the loan is paid off before maturity.

4. Reverse annuity mortgage. The reverse annuity mortgage loan works almost opposite to a regular loan. It is designed for people, usually elderly, who have a lot of equity in their homes and need a monthly income. The lender pays the borrower-owners a monthly payment, deducting that amount from their equity and charging interest on the monthly loan payment.

Usually, upon the death of the borrower, the sale of the secured property, or a specified time period (for example, ten years), whichever is earliest, the loan must be repaid.

Creative mortgage instruments

Creative financing is similar to and often confused with alternative mortgage instruments. However, creative financing uses existing methods of financing that are not normally available through institutional lenders. Alternative mortgage instruments are available from institutional lenders.

Wraparound deed of trust

One of the most common forms of creative financing is the wraparound loan. It is also known as an "all inclusive deed of trust." This loan usually arises by the seller carrying back a loan.

For example, instead of a seller paying off an existing

$100,000 first deed of trust, and taking back a second deed of trust for $40,000, the seller takes back a second deed of trust for $140,000. This loan includes (wraps around) the existing $100,000 first deed of trust. Wraparounds are discussed more fully in Chapter 9.

REMEDIES OF THE LENDER IN CASE OF DEFAULT

Trustee's sale versus judicial foreclosure

When the borrower defaults, the remedies under a trust deed differ from those under a mortgage. Under a trust deed, the lender always has a choice of two possible remedies:

1. *Trustee's sale.* The lender may have the trustee sell the property without court action and apply the money obtained from the sale on the debt.

2. *Judicial foreclosure.* The lender may bring a foreclosure action through court. This means he or she asks the court to render a judgment stating how much the debtor owes and ordering the property sold at a foreclosure sale through court to obtain money to apply on the debt.

Under a mortgage, the lender has only the second remedy—judicial foreclosure. He or she cannot use the first remedy—sale without foreclosure—unless the mortgage contains a "power of sale" provision allowing such a sale.

In California, the lender almost always prefers to use the power of sale instead of foreclosing through court. One advantage is that he or she can have the property sold in about one hundred and twenty-five days. A foreclosure action generally takes from five months to several years, depending on the court's backlog of cases.

A second advantage is that when the property is sold by trustee's sale, the defaulting owner cannot redeem it afterward. If it is foreclosed and a deficiency judgment results, the defaulting owner has a year after the foreclosure sale to redeem it. If the owner is occupying it, he or she may stay in possession for that year.

The main disadvantage in using a trustee's sale arises when the property does not sell for enough to pay off the debt. When there is a foreclosure through court, the lender can get a judgment for any amount left unpaid if the foreclosure sale does not bring enough money to pay the debt. This is called a *deficiency judgment*. However, no deficiency judgment can be obtained when the property is sold at a trustee's sale. As a practical matter, this disadvantage seldom arises, because California has a number of statutes, too detailed to describe here, that prevent a lender from getting a deficiency judgment in most cases.

No deficiency judgment is allowed in loans involving almost all owner-occupied residences, and loans taken back by the seller of property. Deficiency judgments are discussed later in this chapter under *purchase-money trust deeds*.

A word of caution: A foreclosure sale through court and a trustee's sale are two different procedures. Nevertheless, many people—even real estate people—erroneously call a trustee's sale a "foreclosure."

Trustee's sale

When the borrower defaults, the lender may elect to start the procedure that leads to a trustee's sale.

First, the lender or trustee notifies the borrower by recording a Notice of Default and Election to Sell in the county recorder's office. A copy is sent to the borrower. Figure 8–7 is such a notice. It tells the borrower that he or she must cure the default or the trustee will sell the property, along with giving other information required by law.

Other people with an interest in the property, such as lienholders, may want to know whenever such a notice is filed. Such a person should record a Request for Notice of Default (Figure 8–8) with the county recorder to be sure that the lender or trustee will send him or her a copy of the notice.

After the Notice of Default is recorded the borrower has up to five business days before the sale to cure the default. This time period to cure the default is not less than 105 days. During this time period he or she cannot be required to pay more than the amount needed to cure the default: this is the amount necessary to bring the loan and deed of trust current, plus a small reinstatement fee set by statute. The fees are set forth in Table 8–2.

During this reinstatement period, the lender may not accelerate the loan or demand the entire balance because of default. About 90 to 95% of all defaults are cured during this reinstatement period.

If the loan is cured, it is as if nothing ever happened. The loan is reinstated in good standing, and the borrower continues thereafter to make the normal monthly payments.

If the loan is not cured, then five business days before the sale, the lender may accelerate the loan because of the default and may demand the entire amount of the note, if he or she chooses.

Once 90 days has passed, the lender may publish a Notice of Sale, which sets a date to proceed with the sale. He or she executes a Notice of Sale, which must be published three times in twenty days, which works

AND WHEN RECORDED MAIL TO

NAME	Ticor Title Insurance Company of California
STREET ADDRESS	160 Pine Street
CITY & STATE	San Francisco, CA 94111
	ATTN: FORECLOSURE DEPT.

Trustee's Sale No. EX001

Notice of Default and Election to Sell Under Deed of Trust

IMPORTANT NOTICE

IF YOUR PROPERTY IS IN FORECLOSURE BECAUSE YOU ARE BEHIND IN YOUR PAYMENTS, IT MAY BE SOLD WITHOUT ANY COURT ACTION, and you may have legal right to bring your account in good standing by paying all of your past due payments plus permitted costs and expenses within three months from the date this notice of default was recorded. This amount is $1,624.98 Plus Estimated Fees and Expenses as of 10-11-85 (Date), and will increase until your account becomes current.

You may not have to pay the entire unpaid portion of your account, even though full payment was demanded, but you must pay the amount stated above.

However, you and your beneficiary or mortgagee may mutually agree in writing prior to the time the notice of sale is posted (which may not be earlier than the end of the three-month period stated above) to, among other things, (1) provide additional time in which to cure the default by transfer of the property or otherwise; (2) establish a schedule of payments in order to cure your default; or both (1) and (2).

After three months from the date of recordation of this document (which date of recordation appears hereon), unless the obligation being foreclosed upon or a separate written agreement between you and your creditor permits a longer period, you have only the legal right to stop the sale of your property by paying the entire amount demanded by your creditor.

To find out the amount you must pay, or to arrange for payment to stop the foreclosure, or if your property is in foreclosure for any other reason, contact:

ABC BANK
160 Pine Street
San Francisco, CA 94111
ATTN: COLLECTIONS DEPT. - Mary Smith 123-456-7899

If you have any questions, you should contact a lawyer or the government agency which may have insured the loan.

Notwithstanding the fact that your property is in foreclosure, you may offer your property for sale, provided the sale is concluded prior to the conclusion of the foreclosure.

Remember, YOU MAY LOSE LEGAL RIGHTS IF YOU DO NOT TAKE PROMPT ACTION.

NOTICE IS HEREBY GIVEN: TICOR TITLE INSURANCE COMPANY of CALIFORNIA, a corporation, formerly Title Insurance and Trust Company, is duly appointed Trustee under a Deed of Trust dated 7-15-85 executed by John Buyer and Jane Buyer as Trustor, to secure certain obligations in favor of ABC BANK, a corporation, as beneficiary, recorded 7-17-85 as instrument no. EX1234, in book 56, page 789, of Official Records in the Office of the Recorder of SAN FRANCISCO County, California, said obligations including one note for the principal sum of $ 50,000.00

that the beneficial interest under such Deed of Trust and the obligations secured thereby are presently held by the undersigned; that a breach of, and default in, the obligations for which such Deed of Trust is security has occurred in that payment has not been made of:

the installment of principal and interest which became due 8-1-85, and all subsequent installments of principal and interest, and any further breach of any term or condition contained in subject Note and Deed of Trust,

that by reason thereof, the undersigned, present beneficiary under such Deed of Trust, has executed and delivered to said duly appointed Trustee, a written Declaration of Default and Demand for Sale, and has deposited with said duly appointed Trustee, such Deed of Trust and all documents evidencing obligations secured thereby, and has declared and does hereby declare all sums secured thereby immediately due and payable and has elected and does hereby elect to cause the trust property to be sold to satisfy the obligations secured thereby.

THIS NOTICE MUST BE RECORDED BY TICOR TITLE INSURANCE COMPANY OF CALIFORNIA, FORMERLY TITLE INSURANCE AND TRUST COMPANY

ABC BANK

BY:

Dated 10-11-85

Figure 8–7

RECORDING REQUESTED BY

Ted Gordon, Esq.
Gordon, McFarlan, Stewart and Blecher
Holiday Plaza, Suite 475
1050 North Gate Drive
San Rafael, CA 94903

AND WHEN RECORDED MAIL TO

Name Ted Gordon, Esq.
Gordon, McFarlan, Stewart and Blecher
Street Address Holiday Plaza, Suite 475
1050 North Gate Drive
City & State San Rafael, CA 94903

SPACE ABOVE THIS LINE FOR RECORDER'S USE

CAT. NO. NN00608
TO 1934 CA (3-83)

Request for Notice

UNDER SECTION 2924b CIVIL CODE

ALL | PTN.

In accordance with Section 2924b, Civil Code, request is hereby made that a copy of any Notice of Default and a copy of any Notice of Sale under Deed of Trust recorded as Instrument No. C51861 on July 15, 1982, in Book/Reel C156, Page/Image 541, Official Records of San Francisco County, California, and describing land therein as Lots 5 and 6, in Block 5, in the City of San Francisco, County of San Francisco, State of California, as per Map recorded in Book 11 Page 68 of Miscellaneous Records in the office of the County Recorder of said County.

Executed by John Buyer and Jane Buyer, as Trustor, in which ABC Bank, a corporation is named as Beneficiary, and Ticor Title Insurance Company of California, as Trustee, be mailed to Stephen Bene, a single man at 160 Bush Street
Number and Street

San Francisco, CA 94109
City and State

Dated November 15, 1985

Stephen Bene

FOR CORPORATE ACKNOWLEDGEMENT

STATE OF CALIFORNIA
COUNTY OF ______ } SS.

On ______ before me, the undersigned, a Notary Public in and for said State, personally appeared ______ personally known to me or proved to me on the basis of satisfactory evidence to be the person who executed the within instrument as the ______ President, and ______ personally known to me or proved to me on the basis of satisfactory evidence to be the person who executed the within instrument as the ______ Secretary of the Corporation that executed the within instrument and acknowledged to me that such corporation executed the within instrument pursuant to its by-laws or a resolution of its board of directors.

WITNESS my hand and official seal. Signature ______

FOR INDIVIDUAL ACKNOWLEDGEMENT

STATE OF CALIFORNIA
COUNTY OF ______ } SS.

On ______ before me, the undersigned, a Notary Public in and for said State, personally appeared ______, personally known to me or proved to me on the basis of satisfactory evidence to be the person___ whose name ______ subscribed to the within instrument and acknowledged that ______ executed the same.

WITNESS my hand and official seal. Signature ______

FOR PARTNERSHIP ACKNOWLEDGEMENT

STATE OF CALIFORNIA
COUNTY OF ______ } SS.

On ______ before me, the undersigned, a Notary Public in and for said State, personally appeared ______

personally known to me or proved to me on the basis of satisfactory evidence to be the person___ who executed the within instrument as ______ of the partners of the partnership that executed the within instrument, and acknowleged to me that such partnership executed the same.

WITNESS my hand and official seal.

Signature ______

(This area for official notarial seal)

Title Order No. ______ Escrow or Loan No. ______

Figure 8–8

Table 8–2   Fees on Foreclosing Deed of Trust

Costs
—costs of recording, mailing, publishing and posting notices
—costs of trustee's sale guarantee policy from title company
—costs of postpone of a sale, at trustor's request, not to exceed $50 per postponement

Portion of Unpaid Principal Due	Trustee's Fees, or Attorney's Fees	
	Before Mailing Notice of Sale	After Mailing Notice of Sale
$50,000 or less	$200	$300
$50,001 to $150,000	1/2%	1%
$150,001 to $500,000	1/4%	1/2%
Over $500,000	1/8%	1/4%

Example
A trustee foreclosing a $180,000 deed of trust, after notice of sale, can collect attorneys' fee of $1,450, calculated as follows:

$$\$50,000 \ldots = \$\ \ 300$$
$$\$100,000 \times 1\% = \$1,000$$
$$\underline{\$30,00 \times 1/2\% = \$\ \ 150}$$

plus all actual costs incurred, reasonable in amount, for a trustee's guarantee policy, and costs of recording, mailing, publishing and posting notices.

Reference
Since the statutory fee schedule is often amended, check the latest figures in Civil Code Sections 2924c(d) and 2924d.

out to once a week for three weeks. The notice is published in a newspaper of general circulation, is posted in one public place, and is posted in a conspicuous place on the property. The notice states

1. A description of the property.
2. The reason for the sale.
3. The place of sale, which must be in the same county and city as the property.
4. The time of sale, which must be at least twenty-one days after the first publication.

The lender may postpone the sale one or more times.

At the sale, the property is sold at auction to the highest bidder. All bidders except the lender must pay cash. The lender may bid up to the amount owing to him or her on the trust deed without putting up cash and must pay any amount above this in cash.

The trustee's sale is final; the borrower has no right to redeem the property later. The trustee executes a trustee's deed to the buyer. If the borrower won't vacate, the buyer may file an unlawful detainer suit to evict him or her, with speedy remedy through the courts.

The buyer gets whatever title the borrower had when he or she gave the deed of trust. If there were prior deeds of trust or other prior liens or encumbrances on the property when the deed of trust was given, they will remain against the property. Any junior liens are extinguished, as discussed later.

Foreclosure through court action

To foreclose a deed of trust or a mortgage, the lender must file a suit in superior court against the borrower and anyone else who has an interest in the property that is junior or inferior to his or her interest. The court will enter a judgment ordering foreclosure, determining the amount due and appointing a commissioner to conduct the sale. Up to the time the court enters this judgment, the borrower may cure the default and reinstate the loan by paying only the amount required to bring the loan and deed of trust current, plus a small statutory set fee based on the amount of the loan, usually one-half of 1 percent of the unpaid balance of the loan. But once the judgment of foreclosure is entered, the lender may demand the full amount of the note if he or she wishes.

The sale is conducted according to statute. Notice of sale is given by a publishing and posting procedure similar to that in a trustee's sale. The property is sold to the highest bidder for cash, with the lender having the right to bid up to the amount due him or her without paying cash.

No deficiency judgment   If no deficiency judgment is sought, the sheriff holds the sale not less than 150 days from the date of the court judgment. During this time period the borrower continues to live in the property.

Deficiency judgment   If the lender seeks a deficiency judgment, then the buyer is subject to a very important *right of redemption.* At the sale, the sheriff issues a *certificate of sale* instead of the normal *sheriff's deed.*

Under the certificate, the buyer at the sheriff's sale takes title subject to the borrower-owner's right to redeem the property anytime within one year from the sale.

He or she may redeem at any time during this year by paying the buyer

1. The sales price.
2. Any amounts paid on senior liens.
3. Any taxes, assessments, and fire insurance premiums paid by the buyer.
4. Any reasonable sums paid by the buyer for maintenance, repairs, and upkeep of improvements.
5. Interest at 10 percent on the above sums.
6. Less any rents and profits received (or less the rental value to the purchase).

The statutes also give the debtor the right to stay in possession during the redemption period. He or she is liable to the buyer for only the rents and value of the use of the property during that period. At the end of the redemption period, the buyer is entitled to a deed to the property.

This redemption period on foreclosure is one of the reasons most trust deed holders prefer to use a trustee's sale.

Deed in lieu of foreclosure

A defaulting borrower may agree to deed the property to the lender and thus avoid the need for a trustee's sale or foreclosure. Such a step should be handled by someone knowledgeable of the subject to take care of the many technical problems involved.

JUNIOR DEEDS OF TRUST

A real estate owner can put more than one deed of trust on his or her property if he or she wishes to raise more money. The second, third, and later deeds of trust are called *junior trust deeds.* The holder of such a trust deed has a lien that is subject to and comes after any trust deeds that are senior to that trust deed.

To illustrate, suppose Adam has three trust deeds on his property: The first is for $100,000; the second is for $50,000; the third is for $20,000. Adam defaults on the first deed of trust and the holder has it sold by the trustee. If the property is sold for $160,000 above the cost of sale, the money will go to the trust deed holders or any other lienholders in the order of their priority:

$100,000 to the first trust deed holder
$50,000 to the second trust deed holder
$10,000 to the third trust deed holder

Since there was not enough money to pay the third trust deed holder in full, he or she would be the loser.

On the other hand, suppose the same property sold at the trustee's sale for $200,000 above costs. There would then be enough to pay off all trust deed holders and the excess would go to Adam. The money would be divided as follows:

$100,000 to the first trust deed holder
$50,000 to the second trust deed holder
$20,000 to the third trust deed holder
$30,000 to Adam, the owner

In the example above, one of the junior trust deed holders might not wish to have the holder of the first trust deed sell the property. He or she might be afraid that the property would not bring enough at the sale to pay off the junior trust deed holders. Therefore, he or she might pay up the amount that is delinquent on the first, and add this amount to his or her own trust deed. He or she could, of course, have his or her trustee sell the property subject to any trust deeds that are prior to his or hers.

If, as is often the case, the property sells for only the amount of the foreclosed lien, then the junior lienholders get nothing. They are wiped out, and if the loans are purchase-money loans, such lenders are unable to sue the borrower personally for their loans. Lending on junior liens can be very risky if there is not ample equity over and above the amount of the junior lien.

A junior lienholder should record a Request for Notice of Default (see Figure 8–8) with the county recorder so that he or she will be mailed a copy, should any be filed. This will give him or her time to protect himself or herself.

On its face, a junior trust deed looks like a senior trust deed. However, it is riskier, so it usually has a higher rate of interest. For example, if a first trust deed carries 8-percent interest, a second trust deed may carry 10-percent. Many lenders specialize in lending on junior deeds of trust, and many investors consider them good investments.

AGREEMENTS OF SALE

Often the buyer does not pay the entire amount in cash and the seller has to finance part of the purchase. In such a purchase the seller usually deeds the property to the buyer, and the buyer gives back a note and trust deed to the seller to cover the amount being financed. Sometimes the parties use a different procedure: The seller keeps title to the property, and the buyer executes a contract by which the buyer agrees to make payments to the seller. The seller agrees in the contract that, when the full purchase price has been paid, he or she will give a deed to the buyer. Such a contract is known by such names as *contract of sale, land contract, installment sales contract*, and *agreement of purchase and sale*, and was described in Chapter 5.

Problems In California this type of contract is a poor substitute for a deed with a note and deed of trust. Contracts of sale were once popular as a means of voiding the due-on-sale clause in a loan. However, because the current law holds that a contract of sale is a transfer for which the lender can accelerate the loan, and as the courts have removed most of the benefits of these contracts, installment sales contracts are rarely used today.

Seller's problems From a seller's point of view removing a defaulting buyer's interest in the property can prove more expensive and take longer, than foreclosing on a deed of trust. Further, in certain situations, the buyer may default and still be entitled to a refund of part of the payments made. Finally, the law is evolving in this area and it is always possible that a buyer may tie up the property in litigation for years.

Buyer's problems From a buyer's point of view, the property is less saleable under a contract of sale. Also lenders find the security less attractive, and may not loan as readily on such property. Under certain circumstances, liens against the seller could seriously affect the buyer. For that reason, buyers usually prefer deeds of trust as well.

Protection If a buyer is purchasing property under an installment land sales contract, the contract should be recorded. Once recorded it creates a cloud on title, which can only be removed by a quitclaim deed or court action. The only one place where contracts are safe and acceptable to the buyer is with Cal-Vet loans, described in the next chapter. In this situation their use is sanctioned by law, and in fact, they are the only security device allowed.

PURCHASE-MONEY TRUST DEEDS

A purchase-money deed of trust can arise in one of two ways:

1. The buyer of any type of property may not be able to pay the entire amount in cash, and the seller takes back a note and deed of trust on the property as part of the purchase price.
2. The buyer may borrow from a third party all or part of the money he or she uses to purchase a dwelling to be owner occupied and give a trust deed on the property to secure the loan.

A purchase-money trust deed has special attributes in California. The most important is that no deficiency judgment is allowed against the borrower, even though the property may be foreclosed through court. Since the borrower is not liable for a deficiency, neither is a later purchaser who assumes and agrees to pay a purchase-money deed of trust.

An agreement of sale that substitutes for a note and purchase-money deed of trust is subject to the same protection against a deficiency judgment. The deficiency-judgment protection extends to any trust deed given by the buyer to the *seller* as part of the purchase price. But when the buyer borrows money from a *third party* to use to pay the purchase price, the buyer is protected only if the property is a dwelling for four or fewer families and the buyer occupies all or part of the premises.

Assume you buy a home for $200,000, paying nothing down, by obtaining a new $160,000 loan from the bank, and having the seller carry back the additional $40,000 on a note secured by a second deed of trust on the property. Further, assume there is an earthquake that destroys the structure, so that the fair market value of the property is now only $65,000. You can walk away from the property and owe nothing. The bank and the seller, by extending purchase financing, agreed to accept the property as their sole and exclusive security for repayment of their loans.

Hard money and soft money

This is a good place to point out two terms that real estate people use: "hard money" and "soft money." "Hard money" means actual cash lent. "Soft money" is the part of the purchase price the seller finances by taking back a purchase-money deed of trust.

INTEREST

Maximum interest rates

Although in ancient times it was considered wrong to charge interest on a loan of money, the outlook has gradually changed. Today, charging interest on any type of financing is standard practice. The interest is viewed as "rent" the borrower pays for the use of the lender's money.

Each state has its own statutes regulating interest rates. When interest is implied but not stated, the legal rate of interest, 7 percent per year, will prevail.

Classification   Before November 1979, the maximum rate allowed in California was 10 percent. On that date, Californians voted to amend the constitution. The maximum rate per annum is now one of three rates, depending on the lender and the purpose of the loan. The rate is either unregulated, 10 percent, or the Federal Reserve Rate plus 5 percent.

Unregulated—any rate   Many lenders, real estate brokered loans, and seller-extended (purchase-money) loans are exempt from regulation. Such loans may bear any rate the market will allow. Any loan secured by property that is made or arranged through a real estate broker is exempt. A large variety of regulated lenders are also exempt, including banks, savings and loan associations, credit unions, industrial loan companies, and nonprofit associations. A seller who takes back a promissory note secured by a deed of trust as a part of the purchase price of real property is also exempt from the usury law. For instance, it is permissible for the Fishers to sell their home to the Smiths and as a part of the purchase price agree to take back a $10,000 promissory note secured by a second purchase-money deed of trust at 15 percent per annum interest.

10 percent limitation   Any nonexempt lender, which includes most people, is limited to 10 percent per annum if the loan is made for personal, family, or household purposes. However, if the loan is made for another purpose—such as the purchase, construction, or improvement of real property, or financing business activity—it becomes subject to the new interest rate ceiling of "Fed plus 5 percent."

Fed plus 5 percent limitation   All other loans not defined in the preceding two categories are subject to a special interest rate. The new interest rate ceiling on these nonpersonal loans will be the higher of (a) 10 percent per year or (b) the prevailing annual interest rate charged to member banks for moneys advanced by the Federal Reserve Bank of San Francisco, plus 5 percent per year. For example, in June 1979 the interest rate (discount rate) charged by the Federal Reserve Bank was 9½ percent. Thus, the allowable rate on loans made during that month would have been 14½ percent had this new measure been in effect.

Usury

If the lender charges an amount over the maximum legal limit, the loan is considered *usurious*. The lender has violated the *usury laws*. A violation of the usury laws subjects the lender to penalties, which most commonly are:

1. All unpaid interest (usurious and nonusurious) is forgiven. Thus, on a loan where no interest has yet been paid, the borrower would only need to repay the principal when the loan is due.
2. The lender could be guilty of the crime of loan-sharking, although it usually takes a blatant case of usury before the district attorney will prosecute.
3. The borrower can recover three times the excessive interest that has been charged or collected in the last twelve months.

The borrower can set off the two civil penalties against what he or she would otherwise owe the lender on the loan, or he or she can file a separate suit for them.

By statute in California, interest is defined as "the compensation allowed by law or fixed by the parties for the use, forebearance, or detention of money." Using this definition, the courts may consider any charge as interest if it is made by the lender in connection with the loan, even though it may be labeled "points," "service charge," "placement fees," or the like. Such extra charges may run up the interest to over the maximum allowable rate in one year, and this is usury, even though the rate may be less in other years.

Before the total interest and charges can be considered usury, it must be reasonably certain that they will exceed 10 percent per year. For example, it is proper for a lender to contract to be paid 9¾ percent per year interest, plus 25 percent of the future profits of a real estate project. This is not usury, because the amount of the profits are always uncertain, and in fact there may be no profits. Therefore, the total to be paid is not reasonably certain to exceed 10 percent per year.

Late charges

A late charge is an extra charge made by the lender when the borrower's payment is late, and it is not considered interest. It must be set out in the note or deed of trust.

California courts will not enforce a late charge that is too large. The courts say that the amount must be "fairly measured by the period of time the money is wrongfully withheld plus the administrative costs reasonably related to collecting and accounting for the late payment." A late charge of 2 percent of the total balance owing on the deed of trust has been held excessive. But a charge of $5 or 10 percent of the late installment would probably be held reasonable. Loans on owner-occupied residences have special restrictions on the amount of fees that can be charged.

Real estate points

A real estate point may be defined as a bonus to the lender for making a loan on real property. One real estate point is equal to 1 percent of the total loan. Thus, one real estate point on a $40,000 loan would be $400.

To illustrate: A lending institution may be making good conventional loans and securing 9 percent per year interest on these loans. Why, then, would a lender be willing to make a loan at 8½ percent? The lending institution may be willing to do so providing four points can be charged at the time the loan is made.

Points increase the yield to the lender. Lenders use a rough formula: One point collected at the time a loan is made is the economic equivalent of one eighth of 1-percent interest charged upon the loan. This formula takes into account the fact that money received now is economically more valuable than money to be received in the future.

The points are usually paid by the borrower. But sometimes the seller of real property pays points to persuade a lender to make a loan to a buyer so the sale will go through.

Some points charged by savings and loan associations, banks, and others are intended to cover the lender's costs of making the loan. They are considered a service charge rather than interest or a bonus.

On VA loans, the law will not allow the borrower to pay more than one point. All additional points must be paid by the seller. In all other contracts, points are a matter of negotiation between the parties. By custom, the buyer, usually but not always pays most of the points.

Tax treatment of interest

Interest and points are taxable as income to the person who receives them. But for tax purposes, the person who pays them may not always be able to deduct them.

The Tax Reform Act of 1986 will almost certainly be amended over the years, and you need to always check the latest edition of the tax code to be sure of the current law.

Interest is generally deductible on the taxpayer's principal residence and second home. However, on refinancing, interest can only be deducted on loans not exceeding the cost of the property plus any improvements, unless the proceeds will be used for medical or educational purposes. Interest on commercial properties is generally deductible up to the amount of the next investment income. However, the tax laws are very complex in this area, and beyond the scope of this book.

At one time points were deductible by the borrower the same as interest. The IRS is currently and emphatically taking the position that points must be amortized over the term of the loan.

A real estate investor may usually deduct the interest he or she pays as an expense. But interest paid on a home loan may be deducted only if the taxpayer itemizes deductions on his or her tax return. Nevertheless, the fact that this deduction is available is a strong incentive to many people to buy a home rather than rent.

The borrower or debtor who pays points can deduct them like interest if they are compensation to the lender for the use of money, as opposed to a service charge. But a *seller* who pays points to persuade the lender to make a loan to a buyer may not deduct them like interest. He or she may only add them to the selling expenses and use them to reduce his or her profit or gain on the sale.

Fluctuations in the interest rate

The interest rate on real estate loans varies from time to time. When money is scarce, especially when there is a real "credit crunch," the interest rate is high; it drops when money becomes plentiful. The Federal Reserve Bank, as one of its duties, decides the amount of the money supply in the United States and also, by its operations, directly influences interest rates.

TRUTH IN LENDING

The federal Truth-in-Lending Law and Regulation Z which implements it are part of the consumer protection legislation enacted by Congress. The law covers the whole field of consumer credit, but we will consider only its effects on real estate financing.

The law applies only to consumer credit—that is, to loans made and credit extended primarily for personal, family, household, or agricultural purposes. It does not cover business loans or credit to businesspeople. It protects only natural persons, not corporations.

The persons regulated are those who, as a part of their business, regularly extend credit. Therefore, a homeowner who is not in the real estate business and sells his or her home is not regulated by this act.

The major effects of the law are

1. *Disclosure.* The creditor must disclose certain details of the loan, including the true rate of interest being charged. This allows the borrower to be fully informed and to compare the rates of different lenders.

2. *Right of Recission.* The borrower has the right for three business days to cancel the transaction when it involves a lien on his or her residence.

3. *Advertising.* Advertising regarding credit is restrained so that if the advertiser states part of the credit terms he or she must state them all.

Disclosure

One of the key requirements under Truth in Lending is that the person to whom credit is given must be furnished a Disclosure Statement (Figure 8–9) before he or she binds himself or herself in the transaction. The Disclosure Statement must include the *finance charge* and the *annual percentage rate* (abbreviated APR). These must be printed more conspicuously than any other material in the statements.

The finance charge and the annual percentage rate are the two most important concepts in the legislation. They tell the customer the total dollar amount he or she is paying for credit and the relative cost of the credit in percentage terms.

In general, the finance charge is the total dollar amount of all costs imposed by the creditor paid directly or indirectly by the borrower. It includes such costs as interest for the entire life of the loan, time-price differential, discounts, service or carrying charges, loan fees, points, finder's fees, appraisal fees, credit reports (except in real property transactions), and the premiums for credit life insurance required by the creditor as a condition to granting the loan.

Some charges paid in connection with real property transactions need not be included in the finance charge if they are bona fide, reasonable in amount, and not contrary to the purpose of Truth in Lending. These include fees for title examination, title insurance, surveys, preparation of deeds, settlement statements, escrow payments to cover future taxes, insurance, utility costs, notary fees, and credit reports.

The annual percentage rate is the finance charge expressed as a yearly percentage rate. It is computed on the unpaid balance over the life of the loan, using actuarial methods, and must be accurate within one quarter of 1 percent. Regulation Z provides tables and instructions for the computation.

There is a special exception when a *first* deed of trust is used to finance the purchase or construction of a dwelling. Such obligations may run for twenty years or more. The total that must be paid on the loan, when the finance charge is added in, is so great that Congress thought it might discourage would-be borrowers. Therefore, the total amount of all payments and the total finance charge need not be disclosed in such a transaction. But it is still necessary to state the annual percentage rate and other information that is required for other financing. There is no exception made for a second trust deed, or for a loan to buy vacant land on which to build a dwelling, or for refinancing. Regulation Z applies for such trust deeds and must be complied with.

Right of rescission

The right to rescind, also called the right of recission, is the right to cancel or put an end to a transaction and cause each party to be given back what he or she contributed under the agreement. Under Truth in Lending the buyer or borrower has the right to rescind any transaction that gives the creditor a security interest or lien against his or her real property that is or is expected to be his or her principal residence. The debtor may rescind at any time up until midnight of the third business day after the consummation of the contract or delivery of the disclosure statement, whichever is later. Notice or rescission must be in writing on a special form and must be mailed, delivered, or telegraphed to the lender. Notice by phone is not allowed.

When the borrower rescinds, he is not liable for any type of charge. The creditor must return all money or property he or she received and do it within ten days after receiving the notice of recission. The borrower then must return anything he or she received from the creditor.

There is one important exception to the right of rescission: The borrower has no right to rescind when he or she gives a *first* deed of trust on real estate to finance its purchase or the construction of a residence on it, or when he or she assumes such a deed of trust.

Whenever a credit transaction is subject to the right of rescission, the creditor must give the borrower two copies of a special form of notice advising the borrower of his or her rights. Figure 8–10 shows such a notice.

Advertising

Truth in Lending regulates the advertising of residential real estate, which includes advertising by newspaper, TV, handbills, and signs. The regulations may be summarized by this principle: If you give one credit detail, except the annual percentage rate, you must give them all.

Thus, you could advertise "FHA financing available" or "low down payment," because these are not details. You may also state the "annual percentage rate" if you label it with that term.

But if you give any other detail of the credit terms, such as down payment, lack of down payment, monthly installments, or how long the loan will run, you must give all the other details, including cash price, amount of down payment, annual percentage rate, and the number and due dates of the payments.

Creative financing disclosure law

Whenever the seller carries back part of the purchase price on a one to four family residential property, the

FEDERAL REAL ESTATE LOAN DISCLOSURE STATEMENT
CALIFORNIA ASSOCIATION OF REALTORS® STANDARD FORM

Broker/Arranger of Credit:

Carl J. Broker
(name)
2345 Homestead Road, Santa Clara, CA
(address)

Creditor:

Excellent Mortgage Company
(name)
1500 The Alameda, San Jose, CA
(address)

YOUR LOAN IN THE AMOUNT OF $ 10,000.00 IS TO BE SECURED BY A DEED OF TRUST IN FAVOR OF CREDITOR ON REAL PROPERTY LOCATED AT 6789 Linda Sue Court, Cupertino, California 95014

ANNUAL PERCENTAGE RATE The cost of your credit as a yearly rate.	FINANCE CHARGE The dollar amount the credit will cost you.	AMOUNT FINANCED The amount of credit provided to you or on your behalf.	TOTAL OF PAYMENTS The amount you will have paid after you have made all payments as scheduled.
12.98 %	$ 4,388.20	$ 8,701.84	$ 13,348.20

YOUR PAYMENT SCHEDULE WILL BE:

Number of Payments	Amount of Payments	When Payments Are Due
Sixty (60)	$222.47	Monthly, beginning May 5, 1982

ITEMIZATION OF THE AMOUNT FINANCED OF $_____

Amount given to you $_____
Amount paid on your account $_____
Amount paid to others on your behalf:
1. Appraisal . . . . $ 35.00
2. Credit report . . . . $ 25.00
3. Notary . . . . $ 5.00
4. Recording . . . . $ 7.00
5. Title insurance . . . . $ 68.16
6. Document preparation . . . . $ 25.00
7. Property insurance . . . . $ 28.00
8. Other _____ (DESCRIBE) $_____
9. Other _____ (DESCRIBE) $_____

Insurance:
Property insurance may be obtained by Borrower through any person of his choice. If it is to be purchased through Broker or Creditor, you will pay $ 28.00 .
Credit life and disability insurance are not required to obtain this loan.
Late Charge: If any payment is not made within 15 days after it is due, a late charge must be paid by Borrower as follows: 10(10%) percent of the monthly payment or $22.25 .
Prepayment: If you pay off early, you ☒ MAY ☐ WILL NOT have to pay a penalty.
Acceleration: If the property securing this loan is sold or otherwise transferred, the Creditor ☒ HAS ☐ DOES NOT have the option to require immediate payment of the entire loan amount.
SEE YOUR CONTRACT DOCUMENTS FOR ANY ADDITIONAL INFORMATION ABOUT NONPAYMENT, DEFAULT, ANY REQUIRED REPAYMENT IN FULL BEFORE THE SCHEDULED DATE, AND PREPAYMENT REFUNDS AND PENALTIES.

I HAVE READ AND RECEIVED A COMPLETED COPY OF THIS STATEMENT.

Date April 10 , 19 85 .

_____
(Borrower)

_____
(Borrower)

*IMPORTANT NOTE:
Asterisk denotes an estimate.
To order, contact — California Association of Realtors®
525 South Virgil Avenue, Los Angeles, California 90020
Copyright ©1970, 1978, by California Association of Realtors®
(Revised, 1983)

FORM LD-11

Figure 8–9

Joe Realtor, Mortgage Lender
(Creditor)
123 Jones Street
(Office)
San Rafael, California 94903
(City)

NOTICE OF RIGHT TO CANCEL
CALIFORNIA ASSOCIATION OF REALTORS® STANDARD FORM

Name(s) of Customer(s) ___Joe Homebuyer and Mary Homebuyer___

Type of Loan ___Second (2nd) Deed Of Trust___

Amount of Loan ___Ten Thousand Dollars___ $___10,000.00___

Notice to Customer Required By Federal Law:

You have entered into a transaction on ___May 5,___ , 19_82_ which may result in a lien, mortgage, or other security interest on your home. You have a legal right under federal law to cancel this transaction, if you desire to do so, without any penalty or obligation within three business days from the above date or any later date on which all material disclosures required under the Truth in Lending Act have been given to you. If you so cancel the transaction, any lien, mortgage, or other security interest on your home arising from this transaction is automatically void. You are also entitled to receive a refund of any downpayment or other consideration if you cancel.

If you decide to cancel this transaction you may do so by notifying:

Joe Realtor, Mortgage Lender
(Name of Creditor)

at ___1500 The Alameda, San Rafael, California 94903___
(Address of Creditor's Place of Business)

by mail or telegram sent not later than midnight of ___May 8___ , 19_85_ .
(Date 3 business days after date
of receipt of this notice.)

You may also use any other form of written notice identifying the transaction if it is delivered to the above address not later than that time. This notice may be used for that purpose by dating and signing below.

I hereby cancel this transaction.

_____ , 19_____   _____
(Date)   (Customer's Signature)

                                    _____

ACKNOWLEDGEMENT OF RECEIPT

I hereby acknowledge receipt of TWO copies of the foregoing Notice of Right to Cancel.

___May 5___ , 19_85_   *Joe Homebuyer*
(Date)   (Customer's Signature)

                              Mary Homebuyer
                              (All joint owners must sign)

See reverse side for important information about your right of rescission.

Figure 8–10

arranger of credit must provide certain disclosures. These disclosures are made to both the buyer and the seller, unless the seller is the only arranger of credit. However, this disclosure is not required when the buyer receives disclosure under Truth in Lending or through RESPA.

The purpose is to stop the many abuses in creative financing. Buyers often lost their property not understanding short-term notes and balloon deeds of trust. Sellers frequently misunderstood the nature of anti-deficiency legislation (discussed later in this chapter), the limits of credit reports, and the protections available to them. This disclosure form was intended to help remedy the parties' confusion and risks.

FINANCING PERSONAL PROPERTY

Security agreements

In a deed of trust or a mortgage, real property is pledged as security for a debt or obligation. When *personal* property is used as security, a document called a security agreement is used. In the past, it was called a "chattel mortgage" or a "conditional sale contract," and some people still use these terms. It gives the creditor a security interest in the personal property.

The security agreement must conform to the Uniform Commercial Code and must, therefore, be in writing and signed by the debtor. The agreement must identify the personal property covered, which may be by manufacturer's model number, by serial number, or in any other reasonable way.

Financing statement

The instrument filed to give constructive notice of the *security agreement* is the *financing statement*, also known as a *UCC-1 Form*. It must be in the form set out by law and signed by both the creditor and the debtor (Figure 8–11, and it must be filed in the following places:

1. *For consumer goods.* With the county recorder in the county where the debtor resides. If the debtor does not reside in California, it must be filed with the county recorder of the county where the goods are kept.

2. *For timber to be cut, and for crops growing or to be grown.* With the county recorder of the county where the crops are growing or will be grown, or where the timber is standing. The description of the land must appear in the financing statement and gives constructive notice to any later purchase or encumbrance of the land.

3. *For all other cases.* With the secretary of state at Sacramento.

If a financing statement is not filed or if there is a mistake in the place of a filing made in good faith, the security agreement is valid between the parties but will not be valid against those who did not know of it.

For a debt that extends beyond a five-year period, the filing is effective for only five years unless a *continuation statement* is filed identifying the original statement by file number and declaring that it is still effective. For a debt that is due in less than five years, the filing will be effective for the entire period and for sixty days afterwards.

When the debt has been paid in full, a *termination statement* is filed by the creditor, releasing the claim. The debtor should make a written demand on the creditor for such a release.

REAL ESTATE SETTLEMENT PROCEDURES ACT

The Real Estate Settlement Procedures Act of 1974 is federal legislation that affects many types of real estate transactions. Its main impact is on financing, so we will discuss it in this chapter. The act also affects escrows (Chapter 13) and selling.

The act applies to trust deeds or mortgages on one- to four-family units, including condominiums and cooperatives. It requires lenders to give copies of settlement and closing costs to both buyer and seller not less than twelve days before the loan closes.

These costs include down payment, fees for loan or mortgage, origination, title insurance, surveys, legal services, credit reports, services of a real estate agent, appraisals, and interest on the loan between not less than one day before the loan closes.

The intent of the law is that each person will know precisely what costs each is expected to pay when the loan is closed. This information should eliminate the misunderstandings that now arise between buyer and seller at closing when either or both are faced with additional or unexpected costs.

The disclosure requirement may be waived if both buyer and seller agree.

The law applies to FHA and VA loans and to conventional mortgages from a lender with a federal charter or to state-chartered institutions that are members of the FDIC (Federal Deposit Insurance Corporation). The Department of Housing and Urban Development (HUD) has authority to set maximum settlement charges in connection with FHA-insured loans and VA-guaranteed loans.

One purpose of the act is to standardize mortgage procedures and paperwork, requiring lenders to provide uniform settlement forms that itemize charges imposed on both borrower and lender. Such standardization is expected to help make mortgages more salable and simplify the flow of mortgage money from one part of the

This **FINANCING STATEMENT** is presented for filing pursuant to the California Uniform Commercial Code

1. DEBTOR (LAST NAME FIRST)		1A. SOCIAL SECURITY OR FEDERAL TAX NO.
SMITH, John William		147-18-4639

1B. MAILING ADDRESS	1C. CITY, STATE	1D. ZIP CODE
151 Calderon Avenue, Apartment 275	Orange, California	92667

1E. RESIDENCE ADDRESS (IF AN INDIVIDUAL AND DIFFERENT THAN 1B)	1F. CITY, STATE	1G. ZIP CODE

2. ADDITIONAL DEBTOR (IF ANY) (LAST NAME FIRST)		2A. SOCIAL SECURITY OR FEDERAL TAX NO.
SMITH, Cecilia Jean		564-76-8574

2B. MAILING ADDRESS	2C. CITY, STATE	2D. ZIP CODE
Same as above.		

2E. RESIDENCE ADDRESS (IF AN INDIVIDUAL AND DIFFERENT THAN 2B)	2F. CITY, STATE	2G. ZIP CODE

3. DEBTOR(S) TRADE NAME OR STYLE (IF ANY)	3A. FEDERAL TAX NO.

4. ADDRESS OF DEBTOR(S) CHIEF PLACE OF BUSINESS (IF ANY)	4A. CITY, STATE	4B. ZIP CODE

5. SECURED PARTY

		5A. SOCIAL SECURITY NO., FED. TAX NO. OR BANK TRANSIT AND A.B.A. NO.
NAME JONES, Samuel Howard		
MAILING ADDRESS 775 West Stuyvesant Drive		545-19-6154
CITY Anaheim STATE California ZIP CODE 92803		

6. ASSIGNEE OF SECURED PARTY (IF ANY)

	6A. SOCIAL SECURITY NO., FED. TAX NO. OR BANK TRANSIT AND A.B.A. NO.
NAME	
MAILING ADDRESS	
CITY STATE ZIP CODE	

7. This FINANCING STATEMENT covers the following types or items of property (if crops or timber, include description of real property on which growing or to be grown.)

One living room suite at 151 Calderon Avenue, Apartment 275, Orange, California, consisting of one maroon couch, 2 walnut chairs, and 2 walnut end tables

7A. Maximum amount of indebtedness to be secured at any one time (OPTIONAL)

$ 500.00

8. Check ☒ If Applicable	A [X] Proceeds of collateral are also covered	B ☐ Products of collateral are also covered	C ☐ Proceeds of above described original collateral in which a security interest was perfected	D ☐ Collateral was brought into this State subject to security interest in another jurisdiction

9.

(Date) January 31   , 19 82

John William Smith

By: *Cecilia Jean Smith*
SIGNATURE(S) OF DEBTOR(S)   (TITLE)

Samuel Howard Jones

By:
SIGNATURE(S) OF SECURED PARTY(IES)   (TITLE)

C O D E
1
2
3
4
5
6
7
8
9

10. This Space for Use of Filing Officer
(Date, Time, File Number and Filing Officer)

11.   *Return Copy to*

NAME
ADDRESS
CITY, STATE
AND ZIP

Mr. Samuel Howard Jones
775 West Stuyvesant Drive
Anaheim, California 92803

(1) *FILING OFFICER COPY*

UNIFORM COMMERCIAL CODE—FORM UCC-1   Approved by the Secretary of State   STANDARD FORM—FILING FEE $2.00

Figure 8–11

REQUEST FOR INFORMATION OR COPIES. Present in Duplicate to Filing Officer

1. ☒ INFORMATION REQUEST. Filing officer please furnish certificate showing whether there is on file any presently effective financing statement naming the Debtor listed below and any statement of assignment thereof, and if there is, giving the date and hour
of filing of each such statement and the names and addresses of each secured party named therein.

1A DEBTOR (LAST NAME FIRST)		**1B.** SOC. SEC. OR FED. TAX NO.
1C SMITH, John William		000-00-0000
MAILING ADDRESS	**1D.** CITY, STATE	**1E.** ZIP CODE
1F. 151 Calderon Avenue, Apt. #275	Orange, California	92667

Date___January 1_____19_87___   Signature of Requesting Party_____

2. CERTIFICATE:

FILE NUMBER	DATE AND HOUR OF FILING	NAME(S) AND ADDRESS(ES) OF SECURED PARTY(IES) AND ASSIGNEE(S), IF ANY

The undersigned filing officer hereby certifies that the above listing is a record of all presently effective financing statements and
statements of assignment which name the above debtor and which are on file in my office as of _____19___ at _____ ___M.

_____19_____
(DATE)   (FILING OFFICER)

                                                By:_____

3. ☒ COPY REQUEST. Filing officer please furnish___one___copy(ies) of each page of the following statements concerning the
debtors listed below ☐ Financing Statement ☐ Amendments ☐ Statements of Assignment ☐ Continuation Statements
☐ Statement of Release ☐ Termination Statement ☒ All Statements on file.

FILE NUMBER	DATE OF FILING	NAME(S) AND MAILING ADDRESS(ES) OF DEBTOR(S)	DEBTORS SOC. SEC. OR FED. TAX NO.

Date___January 1_____19.87___   Signature of Requesting Party_____

4. CERTIFICATE:

The undersigned filing officer hereby certifies that the attached copies are true and exact copies of all statements requested above.

_____19_____
(DATE)   (FILING OFFICER)

                                                By:_____

5.   **Mail Information or Copies to**

NAME   ⌐TED H. GORDON   ⌐
MAILING   GORDON, McFARLAN, STEWART & BLECHER   USE THIS FORM TO FIND OUT IF ANY
ADDRESS   1050 Northgate Drive, Suite 475   FINANCING STATEMENTS HAVE BEEN
CITY, STATE   San Rafael, California 94903   FILED IN SACRAMENTO.
AND ZIP   ⌐   ⌐

UNIFORM COMMERCIAL CODE—FORM UCC 3

Figure 8–11   (Continued)

country to another. The major responsibility under this law falls on lenders.

Under the act, the following are prohibited: (1) charging any fees other than those paid for legitimate settlement services actually performed; (2) acceptance by anyone of a fee, kickback, or thing of value relating to a real estate settlement business referral; (3) sellers forcing buyers to purchase title insurance from a specified firm; and (4) lenders requiring home-loan borrowers to make excessive deposits in escrow account for property taxes and insurance.

The act requires the lender to provide the customer with a booklet describing the nature and cost of real estate settlement services.

If the seller has owned but lived on the property for less than two years prior to the loan application, he or she must inform the buyer in writing of the purchase date and price of the property when he or she bought it, including a description of all improvements (excluding maintenance repairs) and the costs.

CHAPTER QUESTIONS

1. Explain the principal differences between a *deed of trust* and a *mortgage*.

2. What are the essential elements of a negotiable promissory note?

3. Distinguish between taking a deed ''subject to'' and the ''assumption of'' the existing loan.

4. Explain the difference between a subordination clause and an acceleration clause.

5. Define ''real estate points.'' Why does the lender charge points?

MULTIPLE-CHOICE QUESTIONS

1. Mr. Reed purchased a home from Mr. Goodman and gave him as part of the purchase price a first trust deed on the property. Mr. Reed later needed money to send his son through school. He borrowed money from a finance company and gave a second trust deed on his home. Mr. Reed then lost his job and could not make the payments on either trust deed. Upon judicial foreclosure: (a) Mr. Goodman can get a deficiency judgment; (b) the finance company can get a deficiency judgment; (c) the finance company and Mr. Goodman can get a deficiency judgment; (d) current statutes prevent a deficiency judgment in either case.

2. A person endorses a note in such a way as to indicate that he or she is not responsible for payment in the future to the person or subsequent persons receiving the note. This endorsement is called: (a) an endorsement at will; (b) an endorsement in blank; (c) an endorsement without recourse; (d) a special endorsement; (e) a restrictive endorsement.

3. A person who is an innocent purchaser of a negotiable note for value without knowledge of any defects is called: (a) a principal; (b) an agent; (c) an assignor; (d) an endorser in blank; (e) a holder in due course.

4. On which of the following will a deficiency judgment be allowed? (a) Second deed of trust to the seller; (b) deed of trust given for the purchase of a car; (c) any deed of trust; (d) deed of trust as a part of the purchase price of a home.

5. Deeds of trust are outlawed under the statute of limitations: (a) when the note is outlawed; (b) three years after the note is due; (c) never; (d) the same as straight mortgages.

6. The instrument used to remove the lien of a deed of trust from record is called: (a) a satisfaction; (b) a release; (c) a deed of reconveyance; (d) a certificate of redemption; (e) a satisfaction of security.

7. The instrument used to secure a loan on personal property is called: (a) deed of trust; (b) a security agreement; (c) a bill of sale; (d) a bill of exchange; (e) a mortgage.

8. A property at a trustee's sale brought $10,000. The first deed of trust was for $7,000 and the second deed of trust was for $5,000. Disregarding the costs and expenses of the sale, the second trust deed holder should receive: (a) nothing, as it would all go to the holder of the first trust deed; (b) $5,000; (c) $3,000; (d) 75 percent of the entire proceeds of the sale; (e) the same amount as the holder of the first trust deed.

9. An amortized mortgage or deed of trust is one that: (a) must be paid in monthly installments of principal only; (b) must be paid in equal monthly installments, including principal and interest; (c) requires monthly payments of interest only; (d) does all of the foregoing; (e) does none of the foregoing.

10. In order to relieve himself or herself of the *primary* liability for payment of a trust deed note, a seller must find a buyer willing to: (a) sign a subordination agreement; (b) take title subject to the trust deed and note; (c) assume the trust deed and note; (d) accept a land contract of sale; (e) sign an acceleration clause.

SOURCES OF REAL ESTATE LOANS

In the previous chapter we discussed the general field of real estate finance and the laws and documents involved. In this chapter we will cover the procedures and policies of lenders and discuss the various lenders who provide money for real estate financing.

The field of finance changes constantly—even from week to week.* The real estate broker or salesperson who wants to be successful must keep up with the latest practices of lenders and the best sources of loans.

LENDERS' PROCEDURES AND POLICIES IN LOANING

There are many types of lenders. But, in a general way, all follow the same procedures and policies in making a loan.

Application

The borrower starts the loan procedure by making an application. A written application on the lender's form is required, which will be reviewed by an officer or other employee of the lender to screen out loans that could not be accepted. Usually, he or she will counsel the applicant so that the application is properly made.

If the screening officer approves the loan, the lender will proceed with an appraisal and a credit check.

Credit check

A wise lender wants to be assured that the borrower will repay the loan with no delay, trouble, or expense to the lender. The best way to do this is to look at the borrower's track record—his or her history of paying other creditors. Therefore, the borrower has a credit experience report prepared by a credit bureau or some other organization that keeps credit records and makes such reports.

Three C's of credit

In making a loan, the lender, like most creditors, considers the "three Cs of credit"—Character, Capacity, and Capital.

Does the borrower have:

Good *character* and a good credit reputation?
Enough earning *capacity* to repay the loan?
Sufficient *capital*—that is, enough assets for security and to assure that he or she will pay?

Along with the three Cs, the lender will want the borrower to meet other standards considered important by the lending institution; for example, a sound motivating reason to buy the home that is being financed. If these standards are met, the lender will usually approve the loan.

Appraisal

A wise lender, in the final analysis, looks to the property that is used as security for the loan. If the borrower fails to pay, often the only way the lender can recover his

---

*Interest rates are not quoted in this chapter. By the time you read this, they may have changed from what they are as the book goes to press. Maximum loan limits and loan periods *are* quoted in this chapter, and they too may have changed since this writing.

money is to sell the property. Without adequate security, the lender will take a loss.

Most lenders make their own appraisals, using their own employees as appraisers. But some use independent appraisers. The subject of appraisal is covered in Chapter 14. An appraisal for loan purposes is usually on the low side because lenders must be conservative to be safe.

Lenders have policies as to what percent of the appraised value they will lend. This may be 50 to 90 percent of the appraisal, depending upon the type of lending institution, the location and type of real estate, the financial ability of the borrower, government regulations, and the current situation in the money market. When there are plenty of funds available for lending, the percentage may be high. When funds are scarce, lenders are more selective and the percentage is low.

The laws and regulations governing various lending institutions usually restrict their loans to some maximum percentage of appraised value.

Loan committee

Lenders are conservative. Most lenders want substantial loans reviewed by a loan committee before they are finally approved. This committee serves as a check on the person who first approved the loan. Because the officer or employee who gives first approval knows that the committee will finally approve, the loans he or she passes are usually approved by the committee.

Period of loan

Lenders vary greatly on how long a period of time they will grant a loan for. Often the governmental body that regulates the lending institution will set the maximum period of the loan.

Most lenders want the loan to be *amortized*, that is, paid off in equal installments over the period of time the loan will run. *Straight loans*, loans that are not amortized, are uncommon in real estate and usually run for a relatively short period.

When funds for lending are plentiful, the period of the loan, like other terms, tends to be liberal. When funds are scarce, lenders shorten the loan period.

Preferred types of property

Different lenders favor different types of real estate as security, such as single-family homes or commercial property. We will discuss these preferences as we consider the various types of lenders.

Private mortgage insurance

Private mortgage insurance is insurance paid for by the buyers which protects the lender in case of a default.

Part of the loan is insured, so that should the lender be forced to foreclose and not recover sufficient money from the foreclosure sale, the insurance company will pay the difference. With this added protection, the lender will make higher loan to value ratio loans than would be made without such insurance. This private mortgage insurance is commonly called ''PMI'' by lenders.

PRIMARY MONEY MARKET

The various sources of real estate loan funds, when considered together, are called the *mortgage-money market*. In this market, the borrower shops for loan funds and the lenders may shop for good loans. Actually, there are two parts:

1. *The primary money market*—the lenders loan money directly to borrowers

2. *The secondary money market*—existing mortgages and deeds of trust are sold or used as collateral for new loans

Institutional lenders—savings and loan associations, commercial banks, and insurance companies—make up the largest group directly loaning money on real estate in the primary market.

These lenders and their residential loans are summarized on Table 9–1.

Savings and loan associations

Savings and loan associations make more home loans than any other lending institution. Some are federally chartered and governed by the Federal Home Loan Bank Board. Others are state chartered and operate under the supervision of the savings and loan commissioner of California. All federal savings and loan associations and most state associations can qualify as members of the Federal Home Loan Bank System. If they become members of this system, they are subject to its supervision and are permitted to borrow from a district home-loan bank whenever funds are needed to pay withdrawal demands or to finance additional loans.

Most associations also have their savings accounts insured by the Federal Savings and Loan Insurance Corporation, which insures each account up to $100,000.

Savings and loan associations accept deposits from depositors. Some deposits are passbook accounts, from which the depositor can ordinarily withdraw at will. Also, an association may issue certificates of deposit, which draw a higher rate of interest than passbook accounts. But they call for the depositor to leave the money on deposit for a particular period of time such as ninety days, one year, or five years. There is a substantial pen-

Table 9–1 Maximum Loans by Institutional Lenders
(for fully amortized loans on single-family, owner-occupied residences)

	Loan-to-Value Ratio	Maximum Dollar Amount	Maximum Term	Applicable Statutes & Government Regulator
Federal savings and loan associations	100% allowed by law	No limit	40 years	12 CFR §545.32(d)
	The Depositary Institutions Deregulation and Monetary Control Act of 1980 largely deregulated savings and loans, and left them to make loans within sound lending practices.			Federal Home Loan Bank Board ("FHLBB")
State savings and loan associations	The Savings and Loan Commissioner has the authority to adopt lending regulations in parity with any regulations established for federal savings and loan associations, and so far the Commissioner's regulations have exactly equalled the federal regulations. So state associations can also have 100% loan-to-value ratios, with no dollar limit, up to 40 years.			Cal. Fin. C. §8054 Department of Savings and loan (which is part of the Business and Transportation Agency)
National banks	No limit	No limit	No limit	12 USC §371(a)
	The Garn–St. Germain Depository Institutions Act of 1982 (the *Garn Act*) removed all limitations on individual loans, and left such regulation to the Comptroller of the Currency, whose regulation requires only that dictated by prudent lending practices.			Comptroller of the Currency
State banks	90% of the purchase price or the appraised value, whichever is less	No limit	30 years	Cal. Fin. C. §1227 State Banking Department
Insurance companies	80% of the purchase price or the appraised value, whichever is less	No limit	No limit	Cal. Ins. C. §1176 Department of Insurance (California) If incorporated in another state, any regulations of that state which are more restrictive than California law
Notes:	Most lenders authorized to lend up to 100%, still limit their loans to 90% to 95%, depending on the size of the loan and the borrower qualifications	Most lenders without limits still restrict their loans to the maximum amount allowed by secondary markets; e.g., Freddie Mac will not accept any loan over $133,250	Most lenders will not exceed 30 years	You should check with the governmental agency or check the appropriate codes for current changes in the laws and regulations

alty if the money is withdrawn sooner. The state or federal regulatory body sets the interest rates that associations are allowed to pay on deposits.

The funds received from depositors are lent to real-estate borrowers. Normally, the associations have tried to maintain a margin of 2 percent between the interest they pay a depositor and the interest they charge a lender. But in a competitive money market, a full 2 percent margin may not be realistic.

All federally-chartered associations are owned by their depositors. State-licensed associations, with a few exceptions, are stock companies owned by the stockholders of the corporation.

Types of Loans

Most loans made by savings and loan associations are secured by first deeds of trust upon single-family dwell-

ings. They also may make some loans on commercial property and, in a few cases, on industrial property.

The common type of loan made by savings and loan associations is what is known as a *conventional loan,* one that is not insured or guaranteed by any governmental body. It is secured by a first deed of trust on real estate, and it is amortized over some particular period of time say, thirty years.

Straight loans, FHA, and VA loans (which will be discussed later in this chapter) may also be made.

Loan Limits

The limits set by state and federal regulations for conventional loans on owner-occupied, single-family dwellings (including condominiums and cluster developments) vary according to the size of the loan, the security offered, and the nature of the lender. In discussing loans, it is important to remember the difference between what an association *can* lend, and what it *will* lend. An association *can* loan up to the maximum amount permitted by statute and regulation. However, most associations *will* only loan within the policies and guidelines followed by that individual lender.

Legal limits—federal associations Legislation passed in the 1980s basically deregulated federal savings and loan associations. Although they are still regulated by the Federal Home Loan Bank Board (FHLBB), the FHLBB regulations allow any loan on residential property which is "within sound lending practices." From a strictly legal point of view, a federal savings and loan association could make a 100 percent loan, of an almost unlimited size, which could be fully amortized in 40 years.

Legal limits—state associations After the liberal policies set for federal associations, state savings and loans began switching to federal charters to take advantage of the liberal lending practices. To stop this switch, California passed laws allowing the State Savings and Loan Commissioner to adopt and meet any lending policies permitted for federal associations. As of this date, the California savings and loan associations have the same lending limitations as federal institutions.

Actual loan policies Most institutions have three sets of loan policies for family residences. First, any government backed loans, such as FHA or VA, must follow the guidelines specified by those agencies. Secondly, any loans within the amounts specified by Fannie Mae, Freddie Mac or others in the secondary money market usually follow the guidelines set by those associations. Finally, all other loans follow the individual lender's own guidelines.

Government loans are discussed later in this Chapter. The third category of loans varies significantly between lenders, and even branches of the same lender. Usually, however, even these loans tend to roughly follow the general guidelines of the secondary market. The reason is that these policies are sound lending guidelines which lenders tend to follow on their own.

The second category of loans concerns the limits set by the secondary market. Secondary institutions are discussed later in the chapter. The two biggest secondary markets are Fannie Mae and Freddie Mac, and both of their lending policies for home loans are approximately equal.

Fannie Mae guidelines The guidelines for single family loans set by Fannie Mae, as of this time, are as follows:

1. *Loan Limits*. The loan cannot exceed $133,250.
2. *Loan-to-value ratio*. The loan on owner-occupied

principal residences cannot exceed 95 percent of the lesser of (a) the sales price, or (b) the appraised value.

3. *Loan term*. The loan must be fully amortized in not more than 30 years.

4. *Mortgage insurance*. If the loan-to-value ratio is over 80 percent, then the borrower must have private mortgage insurance (PMI). The PMI must cover that portion of the loan that is over 75 percent of the value of the property.

Other loans

Other limits govern other types of loans, such as construction loans, commercial loans, loans on unimproved land, loans for mobile homes or condominiums, special variable interest rate loans, and government insured or guaranteed loans.

The interest rate and loan fees (charges for setting up the loan) vary from time to time and from area to area. The interest a savings and loan association charges is generally higher than the rate charged by banks and insurance companies. In most cases, a prepayment penalty is charged if a loan is paid off ahead of time.

Insurance companies

Insurance companies in the 1950s to 1970s ranked second in importance in the residential-mortgage money market. Beginning in the late 1970s, insurance companies have severely restricted, if not abandoned, the home finance market.

These companies now favor large residential complexes, commercial developments, and industrial buildings. Insurance companies apparently feel the stability and profitability of the residential market is questionable.

Insurance companies are governed by the laws of the state in which they are incorporated and by the laws of the states in which they operate.

Since many large companies have their main offices on the East Coast, they operate through *loan correspondents* that are paid a fee for placing the loan. These loan correspondents may be mortgage banking companies or individuals. In many cases, the loan correspondent also services the loan on a fee basis, which is worked out between the mortgage banking institution and the insurance company. For example, the servicing fee might be two-thirds of 1 percent of the loan. When the mortgage company is servicing many of these loans, these can be profitable items on a volume basis.

Loan Limits

Insurance companies' loans are restricted to 80 percent of the appraised value of single-family residences and 66⅔ percent for all other types of property. In most cases, the terms of insurance company loans will not exceed twenty-five or thirty years, but no state restriction is imposed.

Commercial banks

Commercial banks rank second in residential mortgage loans. Like savings and loan associations, they may operate under either federal or state charter. Federal laws or statutes govern national banks, and state laws control state banks. By law, they must maintain a liquid position at all times, which means they must be able to pay out any deposits their depositors demand. Therefore, they tend to favor short-term loans.

Types of Loans

Commercial banks lend upon residential, commercial, industrial, and agricultural properties.

Loan Limits—Fixed Rate

National banks were basically deregulated in 1982. These banks no longer have any legal limitations on the dollar amount, length, or loan-to-value ratio of loans secured by single family owner-occupied residences.

State banks are limited to fully amortized loans not to exceed 30 years and not in excess of 90 percent of the value of the property. There is no dollar limit on the amount of the loan.

These are maximums allowed by government regulation. The actual policies of the bank may call for maximums that are considerably less. While the bank may loan these amounts on prime or excellent property, they will generally not loan more than two-thirds of the appraised value on agricultural property and a maximum of 50 percent on special-purpose property, industrial, or commercial property. Commercial banks also make FHA and VA loans.

Mutual savings banks

Mutual savings banks, as the name implies, are owned by the depositors of such banks. As owners, the depositors share in the earnings of the bank. These institutions are located principally in the New England states. Although their funds do flow into the mortgage money market in California, they represent only a small amount. They are more active in the secondary than in the primary mortgage money market.

Mortgage loan brokers

Only a licensed real estate broker or salesperson is allowed to negotiate ''hard money'' loans, that is, to arrange to lend clients' money on new loans secured by deeds of trust. When a broker does this, he or she is considered a *mortgage loan broker*. The types of loans negotiated vary greatly. Some are on first deeds of trust, some on second. The property may be of any type, depending upon what the borrower and the lender want. Some real estate brokers act as mortgage loan brokers full-time, others only occasionally or not at all.

Lenders' rules of thumb

There are a number of rules of thumb real estate lenders may use to give them a quick estimate of when a loan is within the proper size limits. These vary among lenders, and some conflict:

Homes. The price of a home should not exceed two and one-half times the buyer's annual income. Some lenders use a figure of three times annual income, or some other multiplier.

Housing expense ratio. The monthly payments on the loan, including taxes, insurance, principal and interest, should not exceed 28 percent of the borrower's monthly take-home pay. Some lenders require 25 percent, while others go as high as 30 percent. All lenders will increase the percent when there is sound justification.

Maximum obligations ratio. The borrower's fixed monthly expenses, such as car payments, installment loans, revolving debt, monthly housing expenses (principal, interest, taxes and insurance) should not exceed 36 percent of the borrower's take-home pay. Some lenders require 30 percent, while others go as high as 40 percent. All lenders will increase the percent when there is sound justification.

Example—Home. Assume your family's total net income is $3,000 per month. Assume car payments and monthly payments on consumer loans equals $400 per month.

Your monthly housing expenses should not exceed 28 percent of your take-home pay, or $840 per month.

Your fixed expenses should not exceed 36 percent of your take-home pay, or $1080. Since your car payments and consumer loans equal $400 per month, you only have $680 left for housing costs.

By ratio #1 you have $840 for housing costs, and only $680 by ratio #2. Lenders use the lower of the two ratios, or $680.

After substracting real estate taxes, homeowner's insurance premiums, and any homeowner's association dues from $680, you have the amount available for your mortgage loan payments.

Income property. The gross income of the property must be at least twice the mortgage payments and real estate taxes.

A mortgage loan broker is strictly regulated by the Brokers Loan Law, which is a part of the California statutes, and by the Real Estate Commissioner's regulations. If he or she does a certain volume of loan brokerage, he or she must file an annual report and submit his or her advertising to the Commissioner for advance approval.

Controls That Apply to Mortgage Loan Brokers

Fees and expenses charged to borrowers   A mortgage loan broker usually charges the borrower a fee. The statutes set a maximum on such fees:

Loans secured by a first deed of trust:

5 percent for a loan of less than three years
10 percent for a loan of three years or more

Loans secured by a second or other junior deed of trust:

5 percent for a loan of less than two years
10 percent for a loan of two years but less than three years
15 percent for a loan of three years or more

However, there is no maximum on first trust deeds of $20,000 or more or on junior trust deeds of $10,000 or more.

The statutes also set a maximum on costs and expenses, other than commissions. The total charged to the borrower may not exceed 5 percent or $195, whichever is greater. But in no event may it exceed $350 or the actual costs or expenses, or exceed the fee customarily charged for the same or comparable services in the community.

Other controls   When a loan on real estate is negotiated by a mortgage loan broker, the terms and conditions of the loan must meet certain standards. These include

1. *Interest.* The interest rate may be any amount, since interest is unregulated when made or arranged through a real estate broker.

2. *Late charges.* A late charge may not be charged on an installment payment until it is over ten days late. The maximum late charge is 10 percent of the installment due or $5, whichever is greater.

3. *Prepayment penalty.* A prepayment penalty is prohibited when the security is a single-family dwelling occupied by the owner, unless the prepayment is made within six years after making the loan. Such a penalty is allowed only on amounts in excess of 20 percent of

the unpaid balance of the loan paid within a twelve-month period. The maximum penalty is six months' interest on the excess amount.

It is possible the *Garn-St. Germain Act* superseded state law on the matter of prepayment penalties. There have been no cases as yet. If so, the seller could charge any reasonable prepayment penalty specified by the contract.

4. *Balloon payment.* A "balloon payment" is more than the usual installment payment. On a loan that has a term of six years or less, no payment may be required that is more than twice the size of the smallest installment payment.

5. *Mortgage Loan Disclosure Statement.* The broker must prepare and present to the borrower a Mortgage Loan Disclosure Statement. Figure 9–1 presents such a form and shows the information that the statement must contain. The borrower must sign this statement before he or she obligates himself or herself to complete the loan. Its purpose is to give the borrower a reasonably exact picture of the amount of money he or she will actually receive. A broker who negotiates a loan and receives no more than a 2-percent commission from the borrower may be exempt from the requirement to give this statement in certain cases. After July 1, 1976, a copy of the statement must also be furnished in the Spanish language if one of the parties requests this and if the loan agreement was negotiated primarily in Spanish, whether orally or in writing.

Note that the controls outlined cover mortgage loan brokers, not organizations or people lending their own money directly.

Mortgage banking companies

Mortgage banking companies operate under the laws of the state in which they are located. Those operating in California are licensed as mortgage loan brokers and come under any applicable statutes and regulations described in the previous section. They act primarily as loan correspondents for various lending institutions including insurance companies, savings and loan associations, commercial banks, mutual savings banks, and sometimes individual lending institutions. In many cases, they have funds of their own.

These mortgage companies perform the task of taking loan applications and shopping among the various lending institutions to find a company that will accept the loan. They receive a loan fee from the borrower for placing the loan.

The greatest asset of the mortgage banking company is its *Loan Source Book.* Ideally, the mortgage company prefers to be appointed the exclusive loan correspondent

MORTGAGE LOAN DISCLOSURE STATEMENT (BORROWER)

CALIFORNIA ASSOCIATION OF REALTORS® STANDARD FORM

Carl J. Broker
(Name of Broker/Arranger of Credit)

2345 Homestead Road, Santa Clara, California
(Business Address of Broker)

I. **SUMMARY OF LOAN TERMS**

A. PRINCIPAL AMOUNT OF LOAN . . . .$ 10,000.00

B. ESTIMATED DEDUCTIONS FROM PRINCIPAL AMOUNT

1. Costs and Expenses (See Paragraph III-A) . . . .$ 270.16

2. Commission/Loan Origination Fee (See Paragraph III-B) . . . .$ 1,000.00

3. Liens and Other Amounts to be Paid on Authorization of Borrower
(See Paragraph III-C) . . . .$ 28.00

C. ESTIMATED CASH PAYABLE TO BORROWER (A less B) . . . .$ 8,701.84

II. **GENERAL INFORMATION ABOUT LOAN**

A. If this loan is made, you will be required to pay the principal and interest at <u>twelve(12)</u>% per year, payable as

follows: <u>sixty (60)</u>   <u>monthly</u> payments of $ 222.47
    (number of payments)   (monthly/quarterly/annually)

and a FINAL/BALLOON payment of *$ -0- to pay off the loan in full.

> ***CAUTION TO BORROWER:** If you do not have the funds to pay the balloon payment when due, it may be necessary for you to obtain a new loan against your property for this purpose, in which case you may be required to again pay commissions, fees, and expenses for arranging a new loan. Keep this in mind in checking upon the amount and terms of the loan that you obtain at this time.*

B. This loan will be evidenced by a promissory note and secured by a deed of trust in favor of lender/creditor on property located at (street address or legal description):

6789 Linda Sue Court

Cupertino, California 95014

C. Liens against this property and the approximate amounts are:

Nature of Lien	Amount Owing
First Deed of Trust	$80,000.00
Street Improvement Bond	1,400.00
- -	

CAUTION TO BORROWER: Be sure that the amount of all liens is stated as accurately as possible. If you contract with the broker for this loan, but it cannot be made or arranged because you did not state these lien amounts correctly, you may be liable to pay commissions, fees, and expenses even though you did not obtain the loan.

D. If you wish to pay more than the scheduled payment at any time before it is due, you may have to pay a **PREPAYMENT PENALTY** computed as follows:

A charge equal to six months' interest on any amount prepaid in

excess of twenty (20%) percent of the unpaid balance of the loan

during any twelve (12) month period.

E. The purchase of credit life or credit disability insurance is not required of the borrower as a condition of making this loan.

F. The real property which will secure the requested loan is an "owner-occupied dwelling"* YES <u>X</u> NO ___
         (Borrower initial opposite YES or NO)

> *An "owner-occupied dwelling" means a single dwelling unit in a condominium or cooperative or a residential building of less than three separate dwelling units, one of which will be owned and occupied by a signatory to the mortgage or deed of trust for this loan within 90 days of the signing of the mortgage or deed of trust.

To order, contact—California Association of Realtors®
525 S. Virgil Avenue, Los Angeles, California 90020
(Revised 1983)

FORM MS-14

Continued on reverse side

Figure 9-1

131

III. DEDUCTIONS FROM LOAN PROCEEDS

    A. ESTIMATED MAXIMUM COSTS AND EXPENSES to be paid by borrower out of the principal amount of the loan are:

	PAYABLE TO	
	Broker	Others
1. Appraisal fee	$ 35.00	
2. Escrow fee		$ 40.00
3. Fees for policy of title insurance		68.16
4. Notary fees		5.00
5. Recording fees		7.00
6. Credit Investigation fees		25.00
7. Other Costs and Expenses:		
Termite Inspection		65.00
Document Preparation		25.00
TOTAL COSTS AND EXPENSES .... $		$ 270.16

    *B. LOAN BROKERAGE COMMISSION/LOAN ORIGINATION FEE .... $ $1,000.00

    C. LIENS AND OTHER AMOUNTS to be paid out of the principal amount of the loan on authorization of the borrower are estimated to be as follows:

	PAYABLE TO	
	Broker	Others
1. Fire or other property insurance premiums	Ø	$ 28.00
2. Credit life or disability insurance premium (see Paragraph II-E)	Ø	Ø
3. Beneficiary statement fees	Ø	Ø
4. Reconveyance and similar fees	Ø	Ø
5. Liens against property securing loan:		
	Ø	Ø
	Ø	Ø
6. Other:		
	Ø	Ø
TOTAL TO BE PAID ON AUTHORIZATION OF BORROWER $		$ 28.00

If the loan to which this disclosure statement applies is a loan secured by a first deed of trust in a principal amount of less than $20,000 or a loan secured by a junior lien in a principal amount of less than $10,000, the undersigned certifies that the loan will be made in compliance with Article 7 of Chapter 3 of the Real Estate Law.

*This loan ☐ may/☐ will/☒ will NOT (check one) be made wholly or in part from broker-controlled funds as defined in Section 10241(j) of the Business and Professions Code.

*NOTICE TO BORROWER: This disclosure statement may be used if the broker is acting as an agent in arranging the loan by a third person or if the loan will be made with funds owned or controlled by the broker. The broker must indicate in the above statement whether the loan "may" be made out of broker-controlled funds. If broker-controlled funds are then used to make this loan, the broker must notify the borrower of that fact before the close of escrow.

_____	_____
(Name of Broker)	(Name of Designated Representative)
Ø-222777-8	
(License Number)	(License Number)
OR	
(Signature of Broker)	(Signature)

NOTICE TO BORROWER

DO NOT SIGN THIS STATEMENT UNTIL YOU HAVE READ AND UNDERSTOOD ALL OF THE INFORMATION IN IT. ALL PARTS OF THE FORM MUST BE COMPLETED BEFORE YOU SIGN.

Borrower hereby acknowledges the receipt of a copy of this statement.

DATED: April 10, 1985   _____
                                    (Borrower)

                                      _____
                                      (Borrower)

Approved DRE 3/10/83

Figure 9-1 (Continued)

for several insurance companies, commercial banks, and savings and loan associations. Many of the administrative expenses incurred by lending companies can be saved by operating through mortgage banking companies, permitting the lending company to select the loans of their choice.

Mortgage Banking Loan Companies

Effective in 1974, the legislature authorized a special type of industrial loan company to make ''mortgage banking loans.'' These loans are for a minimum of $100,000 and may be made only to corporations and partnerships, not to individuals. The security is restricted to real estate, furniture, and fixtures. The maximum interest rate is 1½ percent per month, which is 18 percent per year.

The lender must hold the loan for ninety days. After that the loan may be assigned to a third person and continued with the same rate of interest. But even after assignment, the servicing of the loan must always be performed by the original lender.

Other sources of real estate financing

Individuals   Real estate brokers and salespeople may find individuals within their community who are willing to loan money on good first and second deeds of trust, particularly when the interest rates paid on these loans are high and the property is adequate security for such loans. Individuals are limited to a maximum of 10 percent per year on most loans. However, if they make the secured loan through a real estate broker, the broker may create a loan with any interest rate without concern for usury.

Individuals are particularly helpful in the secondary mortgage-money market and for short-term loans extending up to three or, on a straight loan basis, five years.

Syndications   A syndication is a group of individuals who band together to finance, develop, or purchase a piece of property, or to loan money. Syndications are described in Chapter 17.

Pension funds and union funds have recently entered the mortgage market. The State of California Retirement Fund for State Employees, for example, is now actively in the market, although it is limited to a maximum of 25 percent of its available funds.

FEDERAL AND STATE GOVERNMENT PARTICIPATION IN FINANCING

The state and federal governments are involved in numerous loan programs. The most common programs are those administered by the Federal Housing Administra-

tion and Veterans Administration at the federal level, and by the Department of California Veterans at the state level. The most popular residential programs are explained in the text and summarized in Table 9–2.

Federal Housing Administration insured loans

Prior to 1934, we were a nation of renters. Many uncertainties existed when lending institutions made a property loan. A loan was made for a maximum of only 50 to 60 percent of the appraised property value on a straight loan basis. Property owners would pay the interest periodically during the life of the loan, usually a four- or ten-year period. After that, the entire loan would become due and payable. Many were unable to pay their loans in full when they became due and faced one of two choices: having their loans refinanced by the same institutions or obtaining a new loan (a sometimes impossible task).

The Federal Housing Administration (FHA) was created under the National Housing Act of 1934. Among other things, it provided insured loans that could be amortized over a period of years. The FHA does not lend money. It merely *insures* loans made by supervised lending institutions, including banks, life insurance companies, federal savings and loan associations, state savings and loan associations, and any other institutions in which deposits are insured by the Federal Deposit Insurance Corporation or the Federal Savings and Loan Insurance Corporation. Other lenders included in this group would be approved mortgage companies and pension funds, as well as individuals.

All approved insured mortgages must be serviced in accordance with practices of prudent lending institutions. If the borrower defaults on his or her obligation, the lender may apply to the FHA, which will take over the property and pay the lender in government debentures or cash for any remaining portion of the loan. In the alternative, the individual lender may decide to hold the property and dispose of it through a trustee's sale. The latter may be a timesaving device to the individual lender.

FHA-insured loans have many advantages over other types of conventional financing. These include

1. Low interest rates, plus one-half of 1 percent mortgage premium, based on the average outstanding balance of the loan in any one year.

2. Elimination of short-term financing, second trust deeds, and mortgages.

3. Larger ratio of loan to the appraised value.

4. Protection of the lender by providing him or her with a ready secondary market through the sale of his or her loan to the Federal National Mortgage Association.

5. Improved housing standards through minimum specifications and building standards set up by the FHA.

Table 9–2 Comparison of Types of Loans
(single-family, owner-occupied residences)

	Conventional	FHA (Title II, 203b)	VA ("GI Loan")	Cal-Vet
Governmental agency	None	Federal Housing Administration	Veteran's Administration	State of California
Who is eligible	Anyone	Anyone	Any veteran discharged other than dishonorably	Honorably discharged California veterans
Source of funds	Any lending institution or private person	Approved lending institutions	Approved lending institutions	State of California, state bond issues
Maximum loan	Depends on individual lender	$90,000 ($108,000 if home uses solar energy)	None, but guarantee not to exceed 60% of loan of $27,500, whichever is less	$75,000 or 95% of appraised value, whichever is less
Down payment	Depends on type of lender	3% first $25,000 appraised value 5% balance appraised value All excess over appraised value	None, except veteran must pay any amount over VA appraisal (CRV)	5% down, plus balance over appraised value
Interest rate	Unregulated	Unregulated, plus 1/2% mortgage insurance	Set by government	Variable interest rate set by State, plus amount for life insurance
Maximum purchase price	None	None	None	None
Maximum loan period	Varies, usually up to 30 years	30 years	30 years	25-year base, but varies with variable interest rate, not to exceed 40 years
Points charged	Unregulated	Unregulated	Unregulated, but veteran cannot pay more than 1 point; seller pays balance	None
Restrictions on transfer	Usually due-on-sale clause	None	None, but borrower not released from liability without "Release of Liability" signed by new buyer	None, but increased interest rate if not qualified California veteran
Prepayment fee	Varies, usually percentage during first five years	None	None	2% of loan amount, if during the first two years, then none
Government insurance or guarantee	None	Insurance on entire loan	Guarantee, to 60% of loan or $27,500, whichever is less	State owns property
Security interest	Deed of trust	Deed of trust	Deed of trust	Contract of sale

6. Provision for one monthly payment that includes principal, interest, insurance, taxes, and so on.

The FHA has developed a system to reduce the risks in loaning money on real property by careful evaluation of the individual borrower and establishment of standards for the appraisal of the property involved.

FHA appraisals are good for six months after which the property must be reappraised.

An individual's rating includes an investigation of his or her credit characteristics, property-buying motives, ratio of effective income to total obligations owed, adequacy of other available assets, and stability of effective income. Property appraisal is based upon livability, the estimated economic life of the property, and appropriate adjustments for economic and social obsolescence.

Two types of commitments may be made by the FHA. A *firm commitment* is requested when the mortgagee desires a definite commitment on a specific piece of property with a definite borrower. When the borrower or mortgagor is not known, a *conditional loan commitment* is requested. A conditional commitment is usually good for six months and, of course, is contingent upon a mortgagor qualifying for such a loan.

A pamphlet entitled *Digest of Insurable Loans* may be obtained from the local FHA district office or from the Federal Housing Administration, Washington, D.C. 10025. This pamphlet outlines the many minimums and maximums allowable under FHA-insured loans and further outlines the many titles under which such loans are made.

Basically, the National Housing Act permits the FHA to insure loans for the purpose of (1) making improvements, repairs, or alterations to the property and (2) insuring lending institutions making loans on one- to four-family dwellings and large rental developments.

Property improvement loans Title I of the National Housing Act permits prudent lending institutions to make FHA-insured loans for improvements, alterations, and repairs to property. It also insures the building of small new structures for nonresidential use. With these individual loans FHA limits their liability to 90 percent of the loss and to 10 percent of the total of such loans made by the individual institution. Individuals must own the property or have a lease expiring not less than six months after the expiration of the loan.

Mobile-home purchase loans In addition to the above programs, the federal government through the Federal Housing Administration is interested in the mobile-home industry. Perhaps this industry will help solve the housing crisis in this country, particularly in California. Buyers who qualify may obtain loans up to $40,500 for the purchase of multisection mobile homes and up to $13,500 for the purchase of a mobile-home lot. The mobile home being purchased must be owner occupied.

Residential housing Under Title II of the National Housing Act, the FHA may insure individual mortgage loans. This is the largest and most important section of the FHA lending program. When most people speak of FHA loans, they mean loans under this title.

There are several sections under this title; however, in this textbook we will concern ourselves with Section 203(b), which deals with loans for construction or purchase of one- to four-family dwellings. The other sections in Title II are more properly considered in a course on real estate finance. The percentages, loan maximums, and interest rates change; so students are urged to consult their instructors or local lending institutions as to the current amounts. For example, the interest rates have varied over the years from 4½ percent to 16½ percent,

while the rates were government controlled and mandated. Since December 1, 1983, FHA interest rates have been unregulated and allowed to vary with the mortgage market.

FHA maximum mortgage amounts Maximum insurable loans to purchase a single-family home may be made up to $90,000 ($108,000 with solar heating) for single-family dwellings, and up to a maximum of $142,650 ($171,150 with solar heating) for four-family dwellings. However, the maximum loan may not exceed specified loan-to-value ratios.

Most FHA loans that are made on residential homes have been either FHA-approved before construction or completed over one year ago. As to these situations, the typical loan, the loan-to-value ratio is:

1. 97 percent of the first $25,000 of appraised value and closing costs;
2. 95 percent of the remainder up to the appraised value; and
3. 0 percent of any amount over the appraised value.

Actually, the percentages are based on the purchase price or the appraised value, whichever is less. Since the purchase price is rarely less than the appraised value, most people speak of the percents as a part of the appraised value.

FHA down payments The down payment required is the opposite of the preceding formulas. Therefore, the typical down payment required is:

1. 3 percent of the first $25,000 of appraised value;
2. 5 percent of the remainder up to the appraised value; and
3. 100 percent of any amount over the appraised value.

Other FHA residential loans Under section 203(b), if the home was not built pre-approved or completed over one year ago, or will not be owner occupied, or will be occupied by a veteran, the loan-to-value ratios are:

1. On dwellings not approved for insurance prior to the beginning of construction and completed within one year before the application for insurance, the FHA-insured loan may not exceed:
90 percent of the appraised value and closing cost or acquisition cost, whichever is less.
2. For a nonoccupant owner, the loan may not exceed 85 percent of the amount an owner-occupant may obtain under an FHA-insured loan.
3. For a veteran who served at least ninety days of active military service and received an honorable discharge, the loan may not exceed:
100 percent of the first $25,000 of appraised value and

closing cost; $25,000 plus prepaid expenses, less $200, whichever is less; or 95 percent of value and closing costs in the excess of $25,000.

The above are special terms for veterans. The veteran must obtain a "Request for Certificate Veterans Status" and submit it signed, with copies of his or her discharge and separation papers, to the VA. When the VA issues an eligibility certificate, it should be attached to the FHA application, which is submitted to the mortgagee for loan approval.

Mortgage loan cost   A borrower must pay a mortgage insurance premium at the time of the loan. On a 30 year loan, the premium is 3.66 percent of the loan amount. Usually, the premium is paid by the lender, and the amount added to the loan balance. FHA allows the insurance to be added to the loan, without reducing the maximum loan available to the borrower.

Other expenses charged when the loan is first made include an FHA application fee, recording fees, credit reports, a survey of title, a title insurance, and an initial service charge.

Graduated mortgage loan   The Housing Act of 1977 provided for a graduated payment mortgage. There are five different plans that permit lower monthly payments initially and increase 2½ to 7½ percent per year for 5 to 10 years, depending upon the plan chosen. At this point, the payment reaches and remains at a level higher than it would have been on the normal FHA-insured loan under Section 203(b). In these plans a larger cash down payment is required because of lower monthly payments. The program is designed for young people whose income is expected to rise as the monthly payments increase. There is no stated age limit, however.

Special FHA features   Besides the low down payments and somewhat lower interest rates due to government insurance, FHA loans offer other attractive features. An FHA loan can be prepaid at any time, without any prepayment penalty. There is no due-on-sale clause in FHA loans. Therefore, the loans can be freely taken *subject to*, without the consent of either the lender or the FHA. The lender can only charge a nominal fee to cover his or her processing costs.

Veterans Administration guaranteed loans

The Servicemen's Readjustment Act, sometimes referred to as the "GI Bill," was passed in 1944 to provide benefits, including loans, hospitalization, education, reemployment, and unemployment allowances. Many veterans went to school under the "GI bill" and took advantage of its many other benefits.

Title III of this Act authorized the Veterans Administration (VA) to guarantee loans made to veterans to purchase their own homes. The Veterans Administration does not make direct loans. Rather, it guarantees part of the loan made by approved institutional lenders. The guarantee is designed to mean less risk to the lender and, therefore, easier borrower qualifications, with more loans and lower interest rates.

Other benefits include provisions for buying farms, repairing and improving existing homes, and several other loan purposes. This book will discuss only loans made for the purchase of single-family residences and will briefly mention loans for mobile homes.

Benefits of VA loans   Veterans qualifying for the VA loan guarantee (commonly known as the "GI loan") enjoy several benefits. The most important are

1. *Lower rates of interest.* The VA sets the maximum interest rate that lenders can charge for their loans. This rate is usually below the current market rate. Lenders are willing to loan at the lower rate because of the reduced risk brought about by the guarantee and by the loan origination fee ("points") they charge.

2. *Borrower's limit on points.* The borrower, the veteran, is prohibited by law from paying more than one point for the loan. A "point" is a one-time charge of 1 percent of the loan amount. Therefore, on a $150,000 loan, one point would be $1,500 and five points would be $7,500. The seller must pay all points over the one point paid by the buyer. If the average VA loan in San Rafael costs five points, the seller must pay four points ($6,000 in the preceding example), which reduces the seller's net and explains why sellers prefer buyers who do not use VA financing.

3. *No down payment.* The VA does not require a down payment, and the veteran may purchase the home paying only specified closing costs. If the purchase price exceeds the Veterans Administration appraisal of the property (CRV), the veteran has to pay any amount over the appraised value.

4. *No prepayment penalty.* The veteran may prepay the loan at any time without any prepayment penalty.

5. *Qualified appraisal.* The Veterans Administration determines by appraisal the property's fair market value and issues a Certificate of Reasonable Value (CRV). The veteran then knows the true value of the property.

6. *Established building requirements.* The VA will not accept as collateral any home that does not meet its established building requirements. Thus, the veteran is assured of purchasing a home with established mimimum building standards.

Amount and nature of guarantee   The Veterans Administration will guarantee up to 60 percent of the loan, not to exceed $27,500. There is no limit on the amount of the loan. Thus, if the veteran obtains a $150,000 loan, the VA will guarantee the loan for $27,500, since 60 percent of the loan exceeds $27,500.

VA loans are made only to veterans who intend to be owner-occupants. No maximum limit is set on the amount the veteran may borrow. The lender, however, may set maximum limits. The loans must be amortized over a thirty-year period.

Qualified buyers may assume VA-guaranteed loans at the interest rates at which they were made; however, the borrower remains secondarily liable on the loan until it is paid. Once a VA loan has been paid, the veteran is eligible for another loan with a reduced guarantee from the Veterans Administration.

Mobile-home loans The VA also guarantees loans made by private lenders for the purchase of mobile homes. To be eligible for such a loan, the mobile home must be a minimum of forty feet long and ten feet wide, having a minimum area of at least four hundred square feet. The maximum loan amounts and terms vary, so interested purchasers should check with the lender or the Veterans Administration at the time of purchase.

Eligibility The following veterans are eligible for VA loans:

1. *World War II veterans*—any veteran who served the United States between September 16, 1940, and July 25, 1947, provided the veteran was discharged under conditions other than dishonorable after at least ninety days active service, or in less than ninety days for a service-incurred disability

2. *Korean veterans*—any veteran who served in the armed forces any place in the world between June 27, 1950, and January 31, 1955, and otherwise meets the conditions for World War II veterans

3. *Post-Korean veterans*—any veteran who served after January 31, 1955, for a period of more than 180 days and otherwise meets the conditions for World War II veterans

4. *Veterans who served allied countries in World War II*—an American citizen who served in the armed forces of a government allied with the United States in World War II and who has not received any loan guarantee benefits from the foreign government and who is a resident in this country at the time of filing for the loan

5. *Unremarried widows* whose veteran husbands died as a result of service

6. *Servicemen or servicewomen* still in service who have served at least six months in active duty status, as long as their service continues without a break

VA procedures If a veteran is planning to buy a home he or she should first obtain a Certificate of Eligibility (Figure 9–2). This certificate states that the veteran served in the armed forces and qualifies for a VA loan.

Veterans Administration
7747428

Certificate of Eligibility

FOR LOAN GUARANTY BENEFITS

NAME OF VETERAN *(First, Middle, Last)*		SERVICE SERIAL NUMBER/SOCIAL SECURITY NUMBER
John J. DOE		529 40 7780
ENTITLEMENT CODE	**BRANCH OF SERVICE**	**DATE OF BIRTH**
4	U. S. Air Force	12-8-43

IS ELIGIBLE FOR THE BENEFITS OF CHAPTER 37, TITLE 38, U.S. CODE, AND HAS THE AMOUNT OF ENTITLEMENT SHOWN AS AVAILABLE ON THE REVERSE, SUBJECT TO THE STATEMENT BELOW, IF CHECKED.

☐ Valid unless discharged or released subsequent to date of this certificate. A certification of continuous active duty as of date of note required.

ADMINISTRATOR OF VETERANS AFFAIRS

B. H. Betts
(Signature of Authorized Agent)

Anydate, 1985
(Date Issued)

Anystate VA Regional Office
(Issuing Office)

Figure 9-2

Next, the veteran must choose the home he or she desires to purchase. When the veteran makes a deposit to bind the transaction, the deposit receipt or other contract used should provide for the return of the deposit in case the veteran fails to get the loan. After such an agreement is signed, the veteran should present the contract to the lending institution from which he or she expects to secure the loan. The property is then inspected by a qualified appraiser from the Veterans Administration, who will determine the reasonable value.

VA appraisals are good for six months after which the property must be reappraised. Further, to stop the practice of VA appraisals for FHA and other loans, VA will now only issue an appraisal after the veteran has a binding contract to purchase, refinance or rehabilitate property.

A *Certificate of Reasonable Value* (CRV) is issued by the Veterans Administration and sent to the prospective lender, who will decide whether to approve or disapprove the loan. (See Figure 9–3.)

When a real estate broker or salesperson is in the course of selling a VA home, he or she should advise the veteran-owner to get a *release of liability* from the Veterans Administration; otherwise, the seller may be liable in the event of a later foreclosure loss.

Before signing the sales contract, the veteran should request a release from the VA office that guaranteed the loan. The new buyers must qualify as acceptable credit risks.

A release of liability will not restore the veteran's eligibility for another VA loan. This is possible only when the VA is no longer liable to the lender on the guarantee or under certain other limited circumstances, such as a sale to another veteran who uses his or her guarantee.

Cal-Vet loans

California has a program to assist veterans to build homes and buy homes and farms. Its full name is California Veterans Farm and Home Purchase Program, usually

Form Approved
OMB No. 2900-0045

[X] VA CERTIFICATE OF REASONABLE VALUE
[ ] HUD CONDITIONAL COMMITMENT

HUD Section of Act

1. CASE NUMBER
923633

2. PROPERTY ADDRESS *(Include ZIP Code and county)*
1953 Union Street
Anytown, Anystate 94115
Any County

3. LEGAL DESCRIPTION
Lot 15, Block 15
Angel Subdivision

4. TITLE LIMITATIONS AND RESTRICTIVE COVENANTS
those of record

1. [ ] CONDOMINIUM 2. [ ] PLANNED UNIT DEVELOPMENT

5. NAME AND ADDRESS OF FIRM OR PERSON MAKING REQUEST/APPLICATION *(Include ZIP Code)*
A B C Mortgage Company
150 State Street
Anytwon, Anystate 94105

6. LOT DIMENSIONS:
42 x 105
1. [ ] IRREGULAR: SQ/FT 2. [ ] ACRES:

7. UTILITIES (✓)	ELEC.	GAS	WATER	SAN. SEWER
1. PUBLIC	X	X	X	X
2. COMMUNITY				
3. INDIVIDUAL				

8. EQUIP.
1. [X] RANGE/OVEN 4. [ ] CLOTHES WASHER 7. [X] VENT FAN
2. [ ] REFRIG. 5. [ ] DRYER 8. [X] W/W CARPET
3. [X] DISH-WASHER 6. [X] GARBAGE DISP. 9. [ ]

9. BUILDING STATUS
1. [ ] PROPOSED
2. [ ] SUBSTANTIAL REHABILITATION
3. [ ] UNDER CONSTRUCTION
4. [X] EXISTING
5. [ ] ALTERATIONS, IMPROVEMENTS, OR REPAIRS

10. BUILDING TYPE
1. [X] DETACHED 2. [ ] SEMI-DETACHED 3. [ ] ROW 4. [ ] APT. UNIT

11. FACTORY FABRICATED?
1. [ ] YES 2. [X] NO

12A. NO. OF BUILDINGS: 1
12B. NO. OF LIVING UNITS: 1

13A. STREET ACCESS
1. [ ] PRIVATE 2. [X] PUBLIC

13B. STREET MAINT.
1. [ ] PRIVATE 2. [X] PUBLIC

14. ESTIMATED REASONABLE VALUE OF PROPERTY
$ 93,500

15. REMAINING ECONOMIC LIFE OF PROPERTY IS ESTIMATED TO BE NOT LESS THAN:
40 YEARS

16. EXPIRATION DATE
12.30.85

NOTE: This Certificate of Reasonable Value is valid only if VA Form 26-1843p showing VA General Conditions and the applicable Specific Conditions is attached.

18. ADMINISTRATOR OF VETERANS AFFAIRS, BY *(Signature of authorized agent)*, OR HUD AUTHORIZED AGENT
C. B. Roe

19. DATE ISSUED
6.30.85

20. VA OR HUD OFFICE
VA

21. PURCHASER'S NAME AND ADDRESS *(Complete mailing address. Include ZIP Code.)*
John J. Doe
4762 Star Drive
Anytwon, Anystate 94115

17. HUD COMMITMENT TERMS

A. MAXIMUM MORTGAGE AMOUNT	$
B. NO. OF MONTHS	
C. NOTICE OF REJECTION	
D. "AS IS" VALUE	$

E. MONTHLY EXPENSE ESTIMATE

FIRE INSURANCE	$
TAXES	$
CONDO. COMMUNITY EXPENSE	$
MAINTENANCE AND REPAIRS	$
HEAT AND UTILITIES	$
F. ESTIMATED CLOSING COST	$

G. [X] EXISTING [ ] PROPOSED *(See General Condition 3 on attachment.)*

H. IMPROVED LIVING AREA 1243 SQ/FT

NOTE: This Conditional Commitment is valid only if HUD Form 92800-5a is attached.

VA FORM 26-1843, NOV 1982 HUD FORM 92800-5

REQUESTER'S COPY 2

Figure 9-3

called the "Cal-Vet" Program. Some of its advantages are low interest rates, inexpensive life and disability insurance, low-cost fire and hazard insurance, and, further, the assurance that the property will be suitable as a residence for the veteran and his or her family.

The program is self-supporting and results in no cost to California taxpayers. The state issues bonds to obtain money for the loans. As the loans are repaid, the bonds can be paid off.

The plan is administered by the state Department of Veterans Affairs. The department has many offices throughout the state that will furnish information and application forms.

Because the maximum loan is small, the maximum purchase price is limited, loans are made only when the voters have allocated the sale of bonds to raise money for Cal-Vet loans, and supply of funds available for lending is always less than demand, Cal-Vet loans are not always an option for purchasing homes.

Eligibility

To be eligible, you must be a "California veteran." This means that at the time you entered into active service you must have been a "native" of California, a bona fide resident of California, or a minor who had lived in the state for the preceding six months.

You must have served ninety days in the armed forces of the United States, a part of which must have been within one of the war periods below:

World War II: December 7, 1941, to December 31, 1946
Korean Hostilities: June 27, 1950, to January 31, 1955
Vietnam Period: August 5, 1964, to September 25, 1974
Any campaign or expedition for which a medal was
    awarded by the United States, if the veteran partici-
    pated in the campaign or expedition

Also eligible are

California veterans discharged with less than ninety days
    service because of service-connected disabilities in-
    curred during one of the above periods.
Surviving spouses of California servicemen or service-
    women who died in war service.
Spouses of California servicemen or servicewomen miss-
    ing in action.

A veteran must have been released from the service under honorable conditions or still be in service. Military service solely for processing, physical examinations, or training does not qualify.

A veteran must apply for a Cal-Vet loan within twenty-five years following release from active service, or he or

she loses eligibility. There is no time limit for a veteran who was wounded, disabled, or a prisoner of war.

Veterans who were wounded or disabled as a result of their war service are given first preference for Cal-Vet loans. Those released from active duty within ten years of their application are given second preference when funds are in short supply.

Property Qualifications and Loan Limits

A veteran may obtain a loan for one of the three purposes described below, provided the property qualifies. The Department will appraise the property and loan up to a certain percentage of the appraised value. The veteran must pay the seller the difference between the sale price and the loan.

1. Purchase of a home or a mobile home   The property must be a single-family dwelling, suitably located, and adequate to meet the veteran's housing needs and the department's minimum property standards. A condominium unit or townhouse designed for single-family occupancy and a mobile home on property owned by the veteran may also qualify.

The Department will loan up to $75,000 for the purchase of a home. Under limited circumstances, secondary financing is permitted.

2. Purchase of a farm   A veteran who wants to buy a farm may borrow up to 95 percent of the department's appraised value, not to exceed $200,000. However, the Department's appraisal of a farm property is based on income from agricultural production. Therefore, its loan value may be considerably less than the sales price.

Terms of Loan Contract

A Cal-Vet loan is financed in an unusual manner. The state buys the property when the loan is finally approved and gives the veteran a long-term installment contract to purchase it. The state keeps the title until the loan is paid off.

The loan term is determined by the amount of the loan, and the age and income of each veteran applicant. Most loans are for twenty-five years. A loan may be paid in full at any time. A service charge of 2 percent of the original loan is made upon any loan prepaid during the first two years.

Interest on Cal-Vet loans is substantially below the rate for FHA or VA loans. On loans made after September 26, 1974, state law allows a variable interest rate based upon the rate the state pays on the bonds it sells to secure loan funds. Therefore, the rate may increase or decrease during the life of the loan whenever the state bonds are selling at a higher or a lower interest rate than when the loan was made. If the rate goes up, the veteran's monthly payments remain the same, but the loan term is lengthened because more of the payment is applied toward interest and less toward paying off the principal.

In the purchase of a home, a second deed of trust may not be placed on the property, but in the purchase of a farm, a second loan is allowed in some instances.

A veteran may transfer his or her loan balance to another suitable property when necessary because of property condemnation, health reasons, employment transfer, or increase or decrease in the number of dependents, or because real estate taxes have increased beyond his or her ability to pay.

Cal-Vet loans can be made on an approved mobile home up to $75,000 for fifteen years if it is located on property owned or controlled by the veteran.

Low-Cost Insurance

The Department provides mandatory low-cost insurance. There is life insurance to pay off the loan if the veteran dies, and disability insurance is available to a veteran who is working full-time. Under it, the insurance company pays the veteran's loan installment if he or she is fully disabled for three months or more.

The Department contracts for fire and hazard insurance on all Cal-Vet properties. The premium is low and is included in the loan payment. A special assessment is made to cover catastrophic hazards not ordinarily insured against, such as flood and earthquake.

Veteran Should Apply Before Buying

A veteran must apply for a Cal-Vet loan *before* acquiring an interest in the property. The only exception is when the veteran owns land on which he or she wants to build a home. When a real estate transaction is contingent—that is, conditioned—upon obtaining a Cal-Vet loan, the contract should state this so that the veteran will not be liable if the loan is not made.

SECONDARY MONEY MARKET

Lending institutions at times may find they need more money to pay depositors who are withdrawing funds or to make more loans. One way to obtain cash without having to borrow it is to sell their mortgage loans. The *secondary money market* purchases these loans at a discount.

Other lenders, especially in the eastern United States, find that the weather hinders building during a large part of the year. These lenders often want to invest their funds in mortgages but are unable to do so locally. They can buy mortgages from the secondary mortgage market.

The secondary mortgage market serves a vital need in selling seasoned mortgages and in providing funds for lenders. It stimulates and stabilizes the country's mortgage practices by offering a transcontinental market for qualified mortgages.

The secondary market is made up of three federal agencies, or federally regulated corporations. They are "Fannie Mae," "Freddie Mac," and "Ginny Mae." Qualified lenders may sell to one or more of these institutions, depending on the type of lender. While a brief discussion follows, a real estate finance course will provide a detailed analysis of their functions and practices.

For this book, the importance of the secondary money market is that these institutions will not purchase loans unless the loans meet their guidelines. Most banks and savings and loan associations are unrestricted by law as to the amount they may loan on many loans. However, to retain the financial flexibility to sell a lender's loan on the secondary market, most lenders restrict their residential loans to the limits set by the three agencies.

In 1986, Fannie Mae would not purchase a loan secured by a deed of trust on an owner-occupied residence that was not fully amortized within thirty years and under $133,250 in value.

"Fannie Mae"

The Federal National Mortgage Association is nicknamed "Fannie Mae" because of its initials, FNMA. Fannie Mae buys government-guaranteed or government-insured loans and specified conventional loans secured by first deeds of trust on one- to four-family homes, condominiums, and mobile homes. FNMA will also purchase specified second deeds of trust on such property. It purchases these seasoned loans from savings and loan associations, banks, and other approved lenders. To raise capital, FNMA sells long-term notes and debentures on the money market.

"Freddie Mac"

The Federal Home Loan Mortgage Corporation, abbreviated FHLMC and called "Freddie Mac," is a government corporation with a function similar to Fannie Mae. It buys conventional, FHA, and VA loans made by savings and loan associations, banks, and other qualified lenders. Congress allocates the funds for its operation. The funds go to the Federal Home Loan Board, which in turn makes them available to Freddie Mac.

"Ginnie Mae"

The Government National Mortgage Association, abbreviated GNMA and dubbed "Ginnie Mae," is a corporation wholly owned by the United States government within the Department of Housing and Urban Develop-

ment. It is authorized to guarantee the payment of securities that are based on or backed by a pool composed
of mortgages issued by the Federal Housing Administration or the Farmers Home Administration, or guaranteed by the Veterans Administration. FNMA operates
the special assistance functions for such federally aided
housing programs as lower-income home ownership and
urban renewal programs.

CREATIVE FINANCING

The lender's sharing in the ownership or income of the
financed property is a recent concept generally described
by the term *creative financing*. It has brought about a
basic change in the character of the industry. This method
is used for financing commercial, industrial, and apartment-house properties, but not for home financing.

These transactions now command such attention that
it is predicted that a two-rate structure will be not only
prevalent but also permanent; that is, there will be one
rate if a borrower pays only interest on his or her loan,
and there will be a lower rate if the borrower allows the
lender to participate in the ownership or income from
the property.

The inflationary spiral of past years and the fear of
future inflation are generally credited with triggering this
phenomenon. Investors are seeking means to avoid being
caught with fixed interest rates and a fixed yield, while
the purchasing power of their principal declines. At times
the decline in purchasing power has been more than the
interest they were collecting. Creative financing was devised to solve these problems and meet the competition
for funds from other types of investments with high yields.

The new approaches require infinitely more sophisti-
cation and are being applied to every type of property
except single-family homes. There are many formulas
but they can basically be divided into (1) a participation
in equity ownership and (2) a participation in income or
cash flow.

Equity participations are usually one of the following:

1. Joint venture. The joint venture is often referred to
as the "front-money deal." The lender supplies the money
and the developer supplies the land and the expertise.
The profits are usually divided equally.

2. Sale and leaseback. This is probably the oldest of
such devices, but new refinements have been added, such
as prepaid interest or "soft" money.

3. Sale and leaseback of land and mortgaging of the
leasehold. One technique involves selling only the land
under a structure. It is then leased back to the developer
and a mortgage is placed on the resulting leasehold.

4. Sale-buyback (sometimes termed an installment sales

contract). This is a refinement of the sale-leaseback with
a difference: The "lender" has an interest in the title
and can take depreciation.

Income participations have several variations of the
following:

1. Contingent interest or the variable interest rate. This
rate is stated in two parts: a fixed rate and an additional
rate based on the performance of the property—an add-
on of the percentage of the gross income or a percentage
of the net income.

2. Purchase of mortgaged land. The lender buys land
subject to an existing mortgage and leases it back for
forty or more years. Ground rents are approximately 10
percent or more per year, with additional rent if the
project's rents increase.

Some of these applications have been used for many
years; others are comparatively recent. There are many
variations, each tailored to fit a particular application.

Wrap-around contract of sale

This creative financing device goes by many names: "wrap-
around," "all-inclusive," "hold harmless," or "overriding" contract of sale. Some people praise it, but beware
of its pitfalls!

Here's how it works: Assume an owner has a piece of
property worth $100,000. It has an $80,000 deed of trust
on it that calls for 6-percent interest (a low rate). The
owner's payment on the loan, covering both principal
and interest, is $1,000 per month.

Value of property	$100,000
Balance owing on deed of trust	80,000
Owner's equity	$ 20,000

Let us assume the owner sells the property for $100,000
and gets $5,000 cash as a down payment. He or she takes
back a "wrap-around" long-term installment contract on
the property for the remaining $95,000, with $1,500
monthly payments, and the interest is set at 9 percent.
In this wrap-around contract, he or she agrees to pay the
$1,000 monthly payments to the holder of the first deed
of trust out of the $1,500 monthly payments he or she
receives. Thus, the first deed of trust with its low, 6-
percent interest stays on the property, and each month
the seller has the following financing result:

Monthly payment to seller	$1,500
Deduct seller's payment on first deed of trust	$1,000
Difference kept by seller each month	$ 500

By this device, the seller may secure a very high return on his or her money. In the example above, only $15,000 of his or her own money is invested in the wrap-around contract, yet the seller collects 9 percent on the full $95,000.

Monthly 9-percent interest on $95,000	$712.50
Deduct 6-percent interest on $80,000 paid on first trust deed	400.00
Monthly return to seller on his or her $15,000 investment	$312.50

This return would be 25 percent on $15,000, which is high indeed. Also, the seller keeps control of the payment to the first trust deed holder, and thus he or she is sure that the payments are made and his or her security preserved. Also, if the buyer defaults and the seller must take the property back, he or she still has the low-interest first deed of trust on the property.

However, the wrap-around device does have legal pitfalls. For example, if the first trust deed contained a due-on-sale clause and the holder of it felt that the transaction impaired his or her security, the holder might attempt to call the loan, that is declare it all due. Therefore a knowledgeable attorney should be consulted before using this device, and a CPA, because of the tax consequences under the new tax law.

CHAPTER QUESTIONS

1. What is meant by *primary* and *secondary* in reference to mortgage lenders or mortgage markets?

2. What advantages to the borrower do FHA loans normally have over "conventional" loans?

3. What are the chief differences between a VA loan and an FHA loan as far as the borrower is concerned?

4. Explain the respective merits of FHA, VA, and Cal-Vet loans for the purchaser of a home.

5. What do the regular monthly installment payments under an FHA loan include?

MULTIPLE-CHOICE QUESTIONS

1. FHA-insured loans are generally made by: (a) individuals; (b) the state of California; (c) institutional lenders; (d) the Federal Housing Administration; (e) the United States government.

2. When the Veterans Administration (VA) "guarantees" a loan, it does so to protect the: (a) homeowner; (b) lending institution; (c) assets of the Federal National Mortgage Association; (d) Government National Mortgage Association; (e) real estate broker.

3. If a VA loan is paid off within two years, the prepayment penalty is: (a) 1 percent; (b) 2 percent; (c) 3 percent; (d) 4 percent; (e) there is no prepayment penalty on a VA loan.

4. The purpose of the Federal National Mortgage Association is to: (a) lend money to builders; (b) make loans that a regular lender cannot make; (c) stabilize the mortgage-money market; (d) make loans on subdivisions; (e) make loans to the individual states to stabilize the building industry.

5. The interest rate for a "conventional" loan secured by a first trust deed is usually: (a) the same as that of an FHA loan; (b) more than that of a VA loan; (c) the same regardless of the source of the funds; (d) the maximum rate allowed by law; (e) less than that of FHA, VA, and Cal-Vet loans.

6. *Federally* chartered savings and loan associations doing business in California are regulated by: (a) the Federal Reserve Bank; (b) the Savings and Loan Commissioner of California; (c) the Corporation Commissioner of California; (d) the Federal Home Loan Bank Board; (e) the California Real Estate Commissioner.

7. The maximum amount guaranteed by the federal government on a VA loan is: (a) 75 percent of the value of the property; (b) 50 percent of the value of the property; (c) 60 percent or $27,500, (d) 70 percent or $25,000; (e) the full amount of the loan.

8. The California Farm and Home Purchase Act provides that the purchaser acquires possession through a: (a) land contract; (b) grant deed; (c) quitclaim deed; (d) warranty deed; (e) deed of trust.

9. A real estate broker negotiated a second deed of trust for $5,000 for three years. The maximum commission allowed by law is: (a) 5 percent; (b) 10 percent; (c) 15 percent; (d) 20 percent; (e) 2 percent.

10. The broker's loan law would apply to a first trust deed note of: (a) under $20,000; (b) $15,000; (c) $14,000; (d) less than $8,000; (e) all of the foregoing.

THE LANDLORD-TENANT RELATIONSHIP

A lease, more properly referred to as a leasehold estate, may be called a *chattel real*. The term *chattel* refers to personal property, and *real* refers to real property. A lease is a personal interest in real property and, therefore, is governed by the laws applicable to personal property.

A lease or a rental agreement is also a contract and is therefore subject to the law of contracts. If a promise in a contract, called a "covenant," is broken, this does not cause a forfeiture of the leasehold estate, but it may give rise to liability for damages for breach of contract. However, the lease may provide that certain or all covenants in the leasehold agreement are also conditions; then a breach of such a covenant, like the breach of any condition in a conditional estate in land (Chapter 3), can result in a termination or forfeiture if the landlord so desires.

Example of a covenant: Tenant herein agrees to keep lawn of the residence watered.

Example of a condition: This lease is conditioned upon the tenant paying all rent promptly when due.

A provision for a forfeiture must be clear; otherwise, the courts will not enforce it.

The person who holds the leasehold interest has exclusive right to possession of the land and is called the *tenant* or *lessee*. The *landlord* or *lessor* is the one who grants exclusive use of the property to the tenant.

The question as to whether the occupant of real property is a tenant or a licensee may be an important one, since different results may follow. The distinguishing feature between tenants and licensees is that the latter have no exclusive right to possession; therefore, they are

Use of the terms lessor, lessee, landlord, and tenant:

Lesso*r* designates the owne*r* who leases out the property.
Lesse*e* designates the person who rec*e*ives the leasehold interest.
Better practice: Use terms "landlord" and "tenant" and avoid confusion.

not governed by the laws relating to landlord and tenant. A license is defined as a personal right or privilege to perform some act on the land of another, which would otherwise be considered a trespass. Examples of a license

Leasehold	License
a. An estate in land	a. Not an estate in land
b. Exclusive right of possession Tenant liable for maintaining premises in safe condition	b. No right of possession Licensee may get right to use, such as a seat in theater Licensee not liable to maintain premises in safe condition Can be liable for own negligence, but landlord is liable for maintaining premises in a safe condition
c. Assignable—unless terms provide otherwise	c. Not assignable—unless terms or custom provide otherwise
d. Not revocable by landlord	d. Revocable at any time by landowner—unless terms or custom provide otherwise

include permission given by a landowner to hunt upon his or her land; a ticket to a stadium to see a sporting event; and a lodger who has the right to use a room (while the owner maintains the room and keeps the keys).

TYPES OF LEASEHOLD ESTATES

1. *Estate for years*. This is a misnomer, because it can be for years, months, days, or only hours. All that is required is that it be a lease for a definite period of time.

2. *Periodic tenancy*. This is a tenancy from period to period—month to month, quarter to quarter, and so on.

3. *Estate at will*. There is no fixed period of time. Section 789, California Civil Code, requires either the landlord or the tenant to give a thirty-day notice to terminate it. It is uncommon today in California.

4. *Estate at sufferance*. This is an estate in which the tenant rightfully came into possession of the land, but retains possession after the expiration of his or her term without consent of the landlord. The tenant is not a trespasser because his or her original entry was legal. But the landlord may file suit to evict him or her at any time.

ESSENTIAL ELEMENTS OF LEASES

All pertinent facts, including covenants and conditions, should be covered even in the simplest lease agreement. Let us now consider some of the more important facts in the residential lease. Other types of lease agreements will be covered later in the chapter.

Parties—landlord and tenant

All parties to the lease agreement should be named and properly described as follows:

1. The tenants.

2. The landlord. If the lease involves jointly owned property, all owners must sign. If the lease involves community property and the term is over one year, both the landlord and the spouse must sign. Either spouse, however, has authority to lease community real property for one year or less without the consent of the other.

It is the best policy to have all tenants—husband, wife, and all persons over 18 who will occupy the premises—sign the lease agreement. However, the signature of the landlord alone is sufficient provided the tenant takes possession of the premises and accepts delivery of the lease: Taking possession and paying rent is sufficient to acknowledge acceptance by the tenant. It is, of course, better practice to obtain all the tenants' signatures.

Sufficient description of the premises

The requirement that a deed contain an adequate description of the property equally applies to a lease agreement; however, a street address (and an apartment number) will normally meet the minimum requirements for a residential lease. If the lease is to be recorded, a legal description is required.

The exact legal description is of utmost importance in the case of commercial or industrial leases. For example, a street address should be avoided in the case of parking lots adjacent to a store or a restaurant. In addition, when a portion of a commercial building is being leased, its exact square footage and a legal description should be given. In the latter case, blueprints or other sketches of the premises should be attached to the lease as exhibits to show the exact spaces to be leased.

Term of the lease

Statute of frauds   An agreement to lease property for more than one year must be in writing and signed by the party to be charged (the landlord) to be enforceable. If you orally agree to lease premises for 11 months, the agreement is fully binding and enforceable. However, if you agree to orally lease premises for 13 months, the landlord cannot enforce the agreement if you refuse to move in and accept the premises.

Even if the lease is for one year or less, it will need to be in writing if the lease starts at a future date, so that its ending date is more than one year from the date the agreement is made.

Duration of lease   Certain statutory restrictions on the power to lease real property are set forth in the California Civil Code:

1. Agricultural or horticultural lands may be leased for a maximum period of fifty-one years.

2. Property belonging to a minor or an incompetent person may be leased only for a period specifically authorized by a probate court.

3. Urban property within a city or town may be leased for a maximum period of ninety-nine years.

4. Ordinarily, leases on property owned by municipalities are limited to twenty-five years in length.

If it is not specified in the lease agreement, the term of the lease is presumed to extend over the period for which the rent is collected. If the tenant remains in possession after the lease has expired and the landlord accepts rent, the lease agreement is presumed to be renewed for that period for which rent is collected. For example, it is not to exceed one month when the rent is payable monthly—this is referred to as a "holdover."

Language creating the lease

No particular form or language is required to create a leasehold as long as the intention to rent the property is apparent. Phraseology may include the words "let" or "demise," but these are not necessary to make the lease legal. Thus, the following would create a lease: "Landlord leases to Tenant and Tenant hires from Landlord. . . ." The agreement must, however, contain the names of the parties, a description of the premises, the duration of the lease, and the amount of rental payments.

Figure 10–1 is the California Association of Realtors (formerly the California Real Estate Association) standard form release agreement. Many times standard lease forms do not provide enough space for additional covenants and conditions that the parties may wish to agree to. In this case, addendums or exhibits may be attached (Figure 10–2). Each addendum or exhibit should refer to the lease agreement. Figure 10–3 is a form of credit application for a lease used by many landlords.

After July 1, 1976, a copy of a lease or rental agreement covering a dwelling or mobile home must be furnished in Spanish if (1) the agreement was negotiated primarily in Spanish, orally or in writing, and (2) one of the parties requests a Spanish-language version.

Rent

Rent is the consideration for the use of the leasehold. The method and time of payment is usually a matter of agreement. Unless otherwise specified in the agreement, rent is due at the end of the period. Thus, unless stated to the contrary, rent would be payable at the end of the week, month, quarter, or year. It is customary today for the rent to be paid in advance. Often in residential leases, for security reasons, the first and last months' rent is paid at the beginning of the lease. Most residential and commercial leases provide for the rent to be paid monthly. However, in large properties the rent may be paid quarterly, semiannually, or even annually. Some commercial and industrial leases may provide for the first and last six months' rent in advance.

Long-term commercial and industrial leases often contain variable rent clauses, which provide that the rent will increase or decrease when some index (like the cost-of-living) goes up or down. Different provisions in commercial leases, like net and gross rent provisions, percent of profits, and other rental obligations are discussed later in the chapter under Commercial Leases.

Rent should be paid by the tenant on or before the due date. But when the tenant has habitually paid the rent late and the landlord has done nothing to enforce his or her rights, a court might hold that the landlord cannot suddenly take advantage of the late payment to declare that the leasehold is at an end—at least not until he or she has given the tenant fair warning.

Security deposits

It is a common practice today for the landlord, particularly in residential dwellings, to require deposits to secure the tenant's performance of the lease or rental agreement. These deposits—in addition to advance rent paid—are usually in the form of a *security deposit* or a *cleaning deposit* or both. These deposits are required to be held by the landlord for the tenant, and the tenant's claim to such funds are prior to the claim of any other creditor of the landlord other than a trustee in bankruptcy. The landlord may retain only such sums as are necessary to remedy defaults in rent payments, to pay damages caused by the tenant's negligence, or to clean the premises upon termination of the lease or rental agreement if the deposit was made for these express purposes. The deposits, or the unused portions thereof, must be refunded to the tenant within 14 days of the tenant vacating the premises, or the landlord will be liable for specified damages. Under certain limited circumstances there are reasons for extending this time period.

Limits on amount of deposit   In residential leases, the landlord is limited to the amount of all deposits collected, no matter how they are classified. All advance payments, whether last month's rent, cleaning deposits and/or security deposits, cannot cumulatively exceed three times the amount of the normal monthly rental.

In unfurnished residential property the limit is two times the month's rent. Therefore, if the monthly rent is $300.00 a month, in a furnished residential apartment, the landlord cannot collect more than $1,200. in deposits.

Type of deposits   Common types of payments a tenant is required to make at the beginning of a lease are listed below. Of the payments below, only those that may be refundable are the true deposits.

1. *Advance Payment of Rent.* In residential leases this is usually the last month's rent. Such advance rent is taxed to the landlord in the year it is received. The landlord may apply it on any unpaid rent if the tenant vacates, and he or she must refund the excess to the tenant.

2. *Amount Expressly Agreed to Be a Bonus or Consideration for Execution of the Lease.* This is taxed to the landlord in the year it is received. It belongs to the landlord when it is received and is not refundable when the tenant vacates.

3. *Payment in Advance of Future Damages.* This is a forfeiture. The courts say, "Equity abhors a forfeiture," and will not allow the landlord to keep it, but the tenant may recover it.

RESIDENTIAL LEASE

THIS IS INTENDED TO BE A LEGALLY BINDING AGREEMENT—READ IT CAREFULLY.

CALIFORNIA ASSOCIATION OF REALTORS® STANDARD FORM

Santa Barbara _____, California _____ June 3, _____ 1985 _____

Dr. James Oscar Smith---, Landlord, and

Robert E. Jones and Betty M. Jones, his wife--------------------------; Tenant, agrees as follows:

1. Landlord leases to Tenant and Tenant hires from Landlord those premises described as: a two (2) bedroom, 1 bath furnished apartment, except for a desk, filing cabinet, and desk chair, which the tenant is given permission to move in. Apt 14, 1334 Santa Marie Way,

together with the following furniture, and appliances, if any, and fixtures: As shown in EXHIBIT "A" attached hereto and made a part hereof.---

(Insert "as shown on Exhibit A attached hereto" and attach the exhibit if the list is extensive.)

2. The term of this lease shall be for a period of ____ six (6)----------------------------months, one-half years commencing ____ July 1,----------------19 82 ____ and terminating Dcember 31,----------------19 82

3. Tenant is to pay a total rent of $ 3,000.00----------------- payable as follows: $1,000 as the first and last months' rent payable upon execution of this lease agreement, $500 shall be payable the 1st day of each month thereafter commencing August 1, 1982, through and including November 1, 1982. In the event that said rent is not received by the end of the 2d day of each month, tenant agrees to pay a $5 late charge. Al rents are payable by check only.

The rent shall be paid at 1334 Santa Marie Way, Apartment #1, Jose Romero, Resident Manager.

or at any address designated by the Landlord in writing.

4. $ 500.00----------- as security has been deposited. Landlord may use therefrom such amounts as are reasonably necessary to remedy Tenant's defaults in the payment of rent, to repair damages caused by Tenant, and to clean the premises upon termination of tenancy. If used toward rent or damages during the term of tenancy, Tenant agrees to reinstate said total security deposit upon five days written notice delivered to Tenant in person or by mailing. Balance of security deposit, if any, together with a written itemized accounting shall be mailed to Tenant's last known address within 14 days of surrender of premises.

5. Tenant agrees to pay for all utilities and services based upon occupancy of the premises and the following charges://////////// // // except _ water // which shall be paid for by Landlord.

6. Tenant has examined the premises and all furniture, furnishings and appliances if any, and fixtures contained therein, and accepts the same as being clean, in good order, condition, and repair, with the following exceptions: no exceptions. See EXHIBIT "A" attached hereto and made a part hereof.-----------------------------------

7. The premises are leased for use as a residence by the following named persons: Robert E. Jones and Betty M. Jones, his wife and their daughter, Anne Marie--

No animal, bird, or pet except ----------------------no exceptions----------------------------- shall be kept on or about the premises without Landlord's prior written consent.

8. Any holding over at the expiration of this lease shall create a month to month tenancy at a monthly rent of $ 600.00 payable in advance. All other terms and conditions herein shall remain in full force and effect.

9. Tenant shall not disturb, annoy, endanger or interfere with other Tenants of the building or neighbors, nor use the premises for any unlawful purposes, nor violate any law or ordinance, nor commit waste or nuisance upon or about the premises.

10. Tenant agrees to comply with all reasonable rules or regulations posted on the premises or delivered to Tenant by Landlord.

11. Tenant shall keep the premises and furniture, furnishings and appliances, if any, and fixtures which are leased for his exclusive use in good order and condition and pay for any repairs to the property caused by Tenant's negligence or misuse or that of Tenant's invitees. Landlord shall otherwise maintain the property. Tenant's personal property is not insured by Landlord.

12. Tenant shall not paint, wallpaper, nor make alterations to the property without Landlord's prior written consent.

13. Upon not less than 24 hours advance notice, Tenant shall make the demised premises available during normal business hours to Landlord or his authorized agent or representative, for the purpose of entering (a) to make necessary agreed repairs, decorations, alterations or improvements or to supply necessary or agreed services, and (b) to show the premises to prospective or actual purchasers, mortgagees, tenants, workmen or contractors. In an emergency, Landlord, his agent or authorized representative may enter the premises at any time without securing prior permission from Tenant for the purpose of making corrections or repairs to alleviate such emergency.

14. Tenant shall not let or sublet all or any part of the premises nor assign this lease or any interest in it without the prior written consent of Landlord.

15. If Tenant abandons or vacates the premises, Landlord may at his option terminate this lease, and regain possession in the manner prescribed by law.

16. If any legal action or proceeding be brought by either party to enforce any part of this lease, the prevailing party shall recover in addition to all other relief, reasonable attorney's fees and costs.

17. Time is of the essence. The waiver by Landlord or Tenant of any breach shall not be construed to be a continuing waiver of any subsequent breach.

18. Notice upon Tenant shall be served as provided by law. Notice upon Landlord may be served upon Manager of the demised premises Jose Romero, Resident Manager--

at Apartment #1, 1334 Santa Marie Way----------Said Manager is authorized to accept service on behalf of Landlord.

19. Within 10 days after written notice, Tenant agrees to execute and deliver a certificate as submitted by Landlord acknowledging that this agreement is unmodified and in full force and effect or in full force and effect as modified and stating the modifications. Failure to comply shall be deemed Tenant's acknowledgement that the certificate as submitted by Landlord is true and correct and may be relied upon by any lender or purchaser.

20. The undersigned Tenant acknowledges having read the foregoing prior to execution and receipt of a copy hereof.

Landlord _James Oscar Smith_____ Tenant _Robert E. Jones_____

Landlord _____ Tenant _Betty M. Jones_____

NO REPRESENTATION IS MADE AS TO THE LEGAL VALIDITY OF ANY PROVISION OR THE ADEQUACY OF ANY PROVISION IN ANY SPECIFIC TRANSACTION. A REAL ESTATE BROKER IS THE PERSON QUALIFIED TO ADVISE ON REAL ESTATE. IF YOU DESIRE LEGAL ADVICE CONSULT YOUR ATTORNEY.

To order, contact—California Association of Realtors®
525 South Virgil Avenue, Los Angeles, California 90020
Copyright © 1977, 1978 by California Association of Realtors®
(Revised, 1978)

FORM LR-14

Figure 10-1

EXHIBIT "A"

Lease Agreement between

Dr. James C. Smith, Landlord, and Robert E. Jones and Betty M. Jones, Tenants

The following inventory of personal property, not built in, is located in Apartment #14 of 1334 Santa Marie Way, Santa Barbara, California.

Kitchen

    Hotpoint refrigerator

Bedroom

    2 double-sized box springs mattresses
    2 headboards
    2 night stands
    2 table lamps

Living Room

    1 wooden rocker
    1 divan (new) 6 foot
    1 dining room table
    6 dining room chairs
    2 end tables
    2 table lamps
    4 sets of draperies

The undersigned have made a physical inspection and have taken inventory of the above furnishings and find them to be clean and free of marks except as noted above.

_____   _____
Landlord   Tenant

_____   _____
Landlord   Tenant

Figure 10-2

4. *Deposit to Secure Faithful Performance of Terms of the Lease. Example:* Security deposit or cleaning deposit. Landlord may keep such deposits *only* to the extent of actual damages suffered by him or her.

5. *Nonrefundable Cleaning Charge.* The law makes all "nonrefundable" cleaning deposits refundable. The landlord cannot keep more than required to clean the premises. Further, the landlord, by law, cannot charge for ordinary wear and tear on the premises.

Bad faith retention of deposit The deposits must normally be returned in 14 days after the tenant vacates the premises.

If the landlord, in bad faith, retains a deposit or any portion of it, he or she may be subject to an assessment of damages not to exceed $200 plus actual damages suffered by the tenant (Section 1951, California Civil Code).

Possession

The tenant is entitled to possession of the property at the beginning of the lease and has the right to retain possession until the expiration of the lease, unless the agreement states otherwise. When a building is under construction, there is an implied covenant that the building will be ready for occupancy upon the date the lease agreement is to commence. The tenant's right to possess is exclusive. He or she may bar even the landlord unless the landlord reserves the right, expressed or implied, to make a reasonable inspection of the property.

An implied covenant—that is, an implied promise—exists by the landlord that the tenant will have quiet enjoyment of the leasehold estate. This covenant, however, is against the landlord's acts and not acts of strangers. A breach of this covenant may constitute an eviction.

An *eviction* occurs when the landlord ousts the tenant or allows the tenant to be ousted by someone with superior title. A *constructive eviction* occurs when there is a substantial disturbance by the landlord of the tenant's possession, such as a threat of expulsion, an attempt to lease to others, an act rendering the premises unfit or unsuitable in whole or in substantial part for the purposes for which they were intended, or entering and making extensive and unwarranted alterations. The tenant who has suffered constructive eviction may leave the premises and be released from the obligation to pay rent.

Occasionally you may hear of the "clever" landlord who makes a tenant move without going through court by removing the front door, cutting off the utilities, or the like. Woe betide this clever person! He or she is liable for all the tenant's damages plus, in many cases, a penalty of $100 per day, possible punitive damages, and even potential criminal action by the district attorney.

The tenant is also released from the obligation to pay rent when the entire leasehold is taken under the right of eminent domain. Condemnation action should be covered in all leases, particularly long-term commercial and industrial leases.

Maintenance

Who has the duty to repair and maintain the premises? Under most commercial and industrial leases, the tenant

TENANT APPLICATION

Property Address: 1334 Santa Marie Way, Santa Barbara, CA   Apt. No. 14

Name(s) of Applicant(s): Robert E. Jones and Betty M. Jones, his wife

Other Name(s) used within last 3 years: None---

Names and Age of other Occupants: Anne Marie, three (3) years of age-----------------
----

Pets (Number & Type): None---

Present Address: 1515 Holly Dr., Apt. 6 City-State West Covina, California zip _____

How long? 5 years Reason for leaving: Advancement by employer from Assistant Bank
Manager to Bank Manager

Name and Address of Owner or Owner's Agent: ---

Previous Address (Past 3 Years): ----------------- City-State ----------------- zip -------

How long? --------- Reason for leaving: --

Name and Address of Owner or Owner's Agent: --

Previous Address (Past 3 Years): ---

How long? --------- Reason for leaving: --

Name and Address of Owner or Owner's Agent: --

Employment:

Social Security Number 4 4 4 — 1 6 — 3 3 3 3   Drivers License Number F 1 2 3 4 5 6

Birth Date (Mo.-Day-Yr.) _____ (State and Expiration Date) _____

Present Employer: Everybody's Bank---------------- How long? Five years

Address: 1345 Commercial Way, West Covina, CA   Telephone: 365-6666

Employed as: Assistant Bank Manager   Salary: $ 15,000.00 per Year.

Other Occupant:

Social Security Number 3 3 3 — 1 7 — 9 9 9 9   Drivers License Number F 6 7 8 9 3 4

Birth Date (Mo.-Day-Yr.) _____ (State and Expiration Date) _____

Present Employer West Covina High School   How long? Four years

Address: West Covina, California   Telephone: 365-0000

Employed as: a teacher   Salary: $ 14,500.00 per Year.

Other Income: $ None   Source: None

Credit References (2): California Teachers Credit Union, Sears Roebuck & Company

Credit Cards: Issuer BankAmericard Acct. No.   Issuer Mobil Oil Acct. No.
4000 5551 1100 00   888 000 999 555

Name of Bank   Branch Address
_____|_____

Automobile License No. KKK 000   State of Registry: California

Make & Model: Chevy Nova   Year: 1972   Color: Green

IN CASE OF EMERGENCY:
Name of Person to be Informed: Robert E. Jones, Sr.   Relationship: Father
1000 West Bonnie Brae Court
Address: Ontario, California   Telephone: 456-2789

AUTHORIZATION TO VERIFY INFORMATION

I Authorize Landlord or his Authorized Agents to Verify the above information, including but not limited to obtaining a Credit Report and if this application is accepted I agree to execute the residential lease or rental agreement as set forth on the reverse side hereof.

Date June 3 19 85   Applicant: *Robert E Jones*

Telephone No. 365-1234   Applicant: *Betty M Jones*

RECEIPT FOR DEPOSIT
The undersigned acknowledges receipt of $ 1,500.00 in the form of ( ) Cash. (XX) Personal Check
//bill//////////////////////payable to Dr. James Oscar Smith as deposit on the above
described property. $1,000.00 as first and last months' rent plus a security
deposit of $500. June 3, 1985   Agent *William Broker*

Date _____

CAR FORM RA-14

Figure 10-3

must repair and maintain the interior—and often the exterior as well.

But when the building is an apartment or dwelling house, the statutes put a duty on the landlord to keep the premises *tenantable*, that is, fit for human habitation. The landlord must, for example, repair broken windows, stopped-up plumbing, or a leaking roof. Exception is made when the damage was caused by the acts or negligence of the tenant.

If the landlord fails in his or her duty, the tenant should give the landlord reasonable notice to make the repairs. Thirty days' notice is presumed reasonable. Should the landlord still fail to make the repairs, the tenant of a residence has three remedies:

1. The tenant may spend up to one month's rent to make the repairs and deduct the cost from the rent he or she pays the landlord. However, this right to repair may be used only twice each twelve-month period (California Civil Code, Sec. 1942). The landlord may be restrained by court order if he or she should try to evict the tenant, raise the rent, or decrease services within 180 days after the tenant exercises this right. A provision in a lease waiving this right is void.

2. The tenant is entitled to a reduction in rent proportionate to the extent that the *habitability* of the premises has been reduced by the need for repairs and maintenance. This right to reduced rent may be claimed if the landlord sues for rent or tries to evict the tenant through court. The court will decide the percentage of reduction and give the tenant credit for this percentage. Although unlikely, it is theoretically possible for the reduction to be 100 percent of the rent.*

3. The tenant may move out. He or she is obligated to pay rent up to the date of the move, with a proportionate reduction for the reduction in habitability.

Retaliatory eviction is the name courts give a landlord's attempt to evict a tenant because the tenant has exercised some legal right. Suppose the tenant complained to the city building inspector because the landlord did not maintain the premises as required by the building code. In retaliation, the landlord might try to evict the tenant. The courts will not allow retaliatory eviction. Any attempted eviction or termination of a lease or month-to-month tenancy within 180 days of a tenant exercising a legal right is presumed to be retaliatory.

Fixtures

The tenant should receive written permission from the landlord before installing fixtures that may be considered

California State Bar Journal (July–August 1974), p. 374.

real property, if he or she wishes to remove them upon the expiration of the lease. When such fixtures are removed, the tenant must restore the property to its original condition.

Use of the premises

The tenant's right of possession is exclusive, and he or she may therefore use that possession in any legal manner he or she sees fit unless it is prohibited in the agreement. The tenant must not allow excessive waste, however, such as waste of timberland, and so on.

The parties to the lease may agree on a limited use of the property; for example, the lease may state "for residential purposes only."

Liability for injuries

The landlord may place a covenant in the lease that attempts to exempt him or her from any liability for injuries to tenant's or others while they are on the property. These clauses are referred to as *exculpatory clauses*.

In residential leases exculpatory clauses are illegal. Further, a landlord is prohibited by law from exculpating himself or herself from his or her own intentional acts and affirmative negligence.

Assignment

Nature of assignments   An assignment is a transfer of all of a tenant's rights, duties and interest in a lease to a third person, called an *assignee*.

A tenant may assign all his or her interest, rights, and duties under a lease to a third person, called the *assignee* of the lease. The assignee then pays rent directly to the landlord. The landlord may sue the assignee directly if he or she violates a term of the lease.

The original tenant no longer has any interest in the premises. But, unless the landlord has released him or her, he or she remains liable to the landlord if the assignee does not perform as the lease provides. The assignee has the same rights against the landlord as the original tenant had. If the lease contains an option to buy the property, the option passes to the assignee.

Typical clause   A typical assignment clause reads: "The Tenant shall not assign this lease or any interest in it without the prior written consent of the landlord."

Right to assign   If the lease contains no clause or no restrictions about the right to assign, the tenant may freely assign the lease. If the lease contains a typical clause, like the one above, then its effect depends on the type of lease.

1. *Commercial leases.* In commercial leases, a landlord cannot unreasonably withhold consent to an assign ment, even if the lease prohibits such assignments. The courts have held that withholding consent to an assignment merely to charge a higher rent is unreasonable.

2. *Residential leases.* In residential leases, if a lease prohibits transfers, the landlord can arbitrarily withhold consent to an assignment. Therefore, as a tenant, it would be advisable to add a phrase to the assignment clause, providing "the landlord cannot unreasonably withhold consent to an assignment."

Assignment without consent   If a tenant makes an assignment in violation of the lease, there is no effect on the lease unless the landlord timely acts. The landlord must timely declare the lease in default and sue to terminate the lease. A landlord commonly waives any right to enforce the violation of the assignment by knowingly accepting rent from the assignee.

Death of tenant   Contrary to popular belief, a lease does not terminate upon the death of the landlord or the tenant. The lease agreement continues for the entire term. Most lease agreements will carry a clause that reads: "The terms and conditions of this lease agreement shall bind the heirs, successors, and assigns of the respective parties." The word *assigns* means "assignees."

Sublease

Instead of assigning his or her lease, a tenant may sublease the premises. That is, he or she leases his or her interest in the premises to a third person. The latter is called a *subtenant* or *sublessee*. The original tenant may sublease all or a part of the premises, and for all or part of the remaining term.

The subtenant holds under the original tenant and pays rent directly to him or her. The original tenant continues to pay rent to the landlord and remains primarily liable to the landlord for the performance of the lease. If the subtenant does not perform as agreed, the original tenant may sue to evict him or her and take back the premises.

Sandwich leases are sometimes arranged in long-term commercial and industrial leases. For example, a landlord leases a commercial building for twenty-five years to Adam for 40 cents per square foot. Sometime later, Adam subleases the property to Brown for 45 cents per square foot; Brown in turn subleases the property to Cole for 55 cents per square foot. Cole is responsible to Brown for the payment of rent, Brown is responsible to Adam for the payment of rent, and Adam would remain liable to the original landlord for the fulfillment of the leasehold contract. Brown's sublease is called a sandwich lease because it is "sandwiched" between the primary lease and the operating lease.

Covenant to pay utilities

In residential lease agreements, the landlord often agrees to pay for water, electricity, and gas. But in commercial and industrial leases these charges are usually the responsibility of the tenant.

A sewage tax has been instituted by some cities. This is a special tax and is calculated on the amount of water entering the property. Thus, as the water bill goes up, so does the sewage tax. Since the sewage tax is added to the water bill, the landlord may want to protect himself or herself by making a provision in the lease agreement.

Option to renew the lease

The leasehold agreement may contain an option that allows the tenant to renew (extend) the lease for the duration of the option period. A typical option clause reads: "If the tenant is not in default of this lease, then at any time during the last six months of the lease, he may, by written notice to the landlord, elect to renew this lease for another two years, upon the same terms and conditions, except that the rent shall be increased to $900 per month."

Without an option clause, the landlord has no obligation to again rent to the tenant. If he or she does rent to the tenant, the landlord can charge whatever rent he or she wants. Tenants like to have options, since they are not obligated to exercise them, but if they do, the terms are set, and they are usually more favorable than the general market terms.

Automatic renewal or extension clause

A few residential leases provide for an automatic renewal or extension of the lease agreement (not just an option to renew) for a part or all of the original term of the lease, providing the tenant remains in possession or fails to give notice to the landlord of his or her intention not to renew before expiration of the term. This clause is *void* unless

1. It appears in the body of the lease in at least eight-point boldface type, and
2. A statement of this fact appears immediately before the space where the tenant signs in at least eight-point boldface type.

Option to purchase property

An option to purchase provides that during the term of the lease, the tenant has the right to purchase the property for a specified price or at a price derived by a formula.

A common variation of this clause is the right of first refusal. The right of first refusal provides that if the landlord receives any offers to sell his or her property, the landlord must first offer to sell it to the tenant on the same terms as those contained in the offer.

Offers to purchase and rights of first refusal are very valuable to a tenant. Besides giving the right to purchase the property, these clauses inhibit the salability of the property. Buyers do not like to submit offers knowing their price will be used as a guideline for the tenant to decide if he or she wants to purchase the property.

The consideration for the option may be the payment of rent or other acts. The option, unless personal to the tenant, may be transferred or otherwise assigned separately from the other provisions of the lease agreement.

There are many methods used to set the purchase price of the property. Sometimes it is a specified, arbitrary price. Other times the price is set by complicated formulas or appraisals. One commonly used method provides for one appraiser to be appointed by the landlord and another to be appointed by the tenant. The two appraisers then select another appraiser. Each appraiser then appraises the subject property, and the decision of any two is binding upon the parties.

Sales clause

In some cases the landlord may find that a lease agreement will restrict the salability of his property. He or she may, therefore, include in the lease agreement a cancellation clause in the event of sale. Thus, if the property sells, the lease is canceled. The tenant may want to protect himself or herself against this clause by adding a right of first refusal.

Subordination of lease to mortgage

A subordination clause usually provides for blanket subordination of the lease to any future mortgage or deed of trust. The leasehold rights of the tenant would probably not be disturbed if the future loan were placed by a lending institution, but most lenders will not loan money unless they are given a senior lien, superior to any existing leases. That way, if the lender forecloses, the new buyer has the option of evicting all tenants or reaffirming the lease, at either the same or increased rent. These options make the property far more saleable at a foreclosure sale.

The tenant, to protect himself or herself, might wish to consider the following:

1. Agree to subordination only if the mortgagee will agree that the lease will not be terminated as long as the tenant is not in default of his or her lease

2. Agree to subordination, providing future mortgages or deeds of trust are placed only with lending institutions

RECORDING THE LEASE

A lease agreement may be recorded in the county where the property is located, providing it contains a legal description of the property and the signature of the landlord is acknowledged. The recording will give constructive notice to all persons that such a lease agreement exists. It is advisable to record all long-term commercial and industrial leases. When the property is located in more than one county, the agreement should be recorded in both counties.

REMEDIES OF THE LANDLORD

The law of landlords' and tenants' rights has been changing rapidly in recent years, usually to protect tenants' rights, but also to fill in gaps in landlords' remedies. Traditional landlords' remedies found in older publications have often been wiped out or greatly reduced by court decision and legislation. These include the "baggage lien" that a landlord had on the tenant's personal property, the "writ of possession" that gave the landlord immediate possession if the tenant was insolvent, the right to attach the tenant's property and paycheck before judgment, and so on. Other changes may be expected after this book goes to press—be alert for them.

Thirty-Day Notice

A *periodic* tenancy continues from period to period *until* one party decides to give notice to the other party to end the tenancy. To end a periodic tenancy *without cause* (not because of a breach of the lease), the party uses what is commonly referred to as a "Thirty-Day Notice." The landlord does not have to give any reason for terminating the tenancy.

Actually, the notice must be given as long in advance as the tenancy period. Therefore, a week-to-week tenancy is terminated by seven days' notice, and in no event may the notice period ever be less than seven days.

Since almost all periodic tenancies are month-to-month, the usual notice period is thirty days. Figure 10–4 is such a Thirty-Day Notice.

A Thirty-Day Notice to the tenant is required when the landlord wants to end the tenancy. Likewise, the tenant must give the landlord a Thirty-Day Notice before the tenant can end the tenancy. If the tenant does not, he or she is liable for the rent for a thirty-day period after he moves.

Another type of thirty-day notice is one in which the landlord changes the terms of the tenancy. The landlord states that if the tenant stays in the property after the time stated in the notice, he or she is deemed to have

THIRTY (30) DAY NOTICE
OF TERMINATION OF TENANCY

TO: Joseph Tenant
All residents (tenants and subtenants) in possession (full name) and all others in possession

PLEASE TAKE NOTICE that your tenancy of the below-described premises is terminated, effective at the end of a thirty (30) day period after service on you of this notice.

The purpose of this notice is to terminate your tenancy of the below-described premises.

If you fail to quit and deliver possession, legal proceedings will be instituted against you to obtain possession and such proceedings could result in a judgement against you which could include costs and necessary disbursements.

The premises herein referred to are situated in the city of San Rafael

County of Marin, State of California,

designated by the number and street as 123 Jones Street

Apartment #124

DATE November 24, 1985

____
Owner/Agent

To order, contact—California Association of Realtors®
525 S. Virgil Avenue, Los Angeles, California 90020

FORM CAA-7.0

Figure 10-4

accepted the changed terms (usually, increased rent). See Figure 10–5.

The parties can agree to dispense with the Thirty-Day Notice and end the tenancy on a specified date. The tenant *surrenders* the premises, and the landlord accepts the tenancy as ended. Unless the surrender is in writing, the tenant will have a very difficult time proving no breach occurred.

Three-Day Notice

If a tenant does not pay the rent when due, the landlord is not permitted to file a suit to evict the tenant until the landlord first terminates the tenancy. Any type of lease, whether month-to-month or fixed-term (for example, ten years), can be terminated *for cause.*

The tenancy is terminated by serving a Three-Day Notice on the tenant, telling him to either pay up or vacate. Figure 10–6 is a form of Three-Day Notice to Pay Rent or Vacate. If the tenant pays up the past-due rent within the three-day period, the tenancy continues. (Of course the landlord may then serve the tenant with a Thirty-Day Notice and end the tenancy that way.) If the tenant neither pays up nor vacates, the landlord may proceed with a suit to evict him or her.

While nonpayment of rent is the most common breach of a lease, it is not the only violation that can occur. Other violations by the tenant that can be terminated by three-day notices include

1. Maintaining or committing a nuisance on the premises, or permitting the maintaining or committing of a nuisance upon the premises.

2. Using the premises for an unlawful purpose.

3. Committing waste contrary to the conditions or covenants of the lease.

4. Assigning the lease or subleasing the premises contrary to the conditions or covenants of the lease.

Unlawful detainer suit

When the time period in the Thirty-Day Notice or the Three-Day Notice expires without proper response from the tenant, he or she becomes a *tenant at sufferance,* and the landlord may file suit at once to evict him or her. Such a suit is called an *unlawful detainer action.* In it the landlord is restricted to obtaining a judgment for possession and for any rent owing up to the date of the judgment. If the landlord wants to sue for damages to the premises, he or she must file a separate suit.

The landlord may file the unlawful detainer action without an attorney. However, the authors recommend that the landlord use an attorney unless he or she plans to sue in small-claims court. Small-claims court can be beneficial in simple cases involving little money. However, small-claims court has its drawbacks:

1. If the tenant wins, the landlord cannot appeal. However, if the tenant loses, he or she can appeal.

2. Since the rules of evidence do not apply, and since the hearing is very informative, tenants tend to contest small-claims court actions more than municipal court litigation.

3. Judges tend to favor the tenant more in small-claims court than appears to be the case in municipal court, where strict rules of evidence and procedure direct what action a judge can take.

4. The landlord must give up any claim for rent over $1,500, because the small-claims court cannot give a judgment over this amount.

5. If the tenant has not vacated voluntarily by the time the landlord gets judgment, the landlord must wait an extra twenty days before he can enforce the judgment.

6. The landlord usually needs expertise to properly handle eviction matters.

Because of these and other drawbacks, the average landlord will be better off using an attorney experienced in landlord-tenant relationships. For example, let us say rent is $600 per month, which amounts to $20 per day. In other words, it will cost the landlord $20 for each day he or she delays—a convincing argument to use an experienced attorney able to file suit that same day.

The attorney will file suit in municipal court, which can give judgment for up to $15,000 rent. The order of procedure is as follows:

1. Complaint is filed and summons is issued.

2. Summons and a copy of the complaint are served on the tenant. These may be served by the sheriff's office, a professional process server, the apartment manager, or a friend of the landlord. However, the landlord may not serve them.

3. The tenant has five days to file an answer after he or she is served. If he or she does not answer—and most tenants do not—the landlord may take judgment against him by default.

4. If the tenant files an answer, the case gets priority for trial. Usually trial is held within a few days. Judgment is rendered for possession, and the rent owing, if the landlord proves his or her case.

5. As soon as he or she gets judgment, the landlord may have a Writ of Execution issued directing the sheriff to put the landlord in possession. After a day or two, a deputy sheriff goes to the premises and serves notice on the tenant either personally or by tacking it on the door. The tenant is notified that he or she must be out in five or sometimes six days. Most tenants still in possession will leave during the allowed period.

6. If the tenant stays in possession after the five or six days, a deputy sheriff goes to the premises again. Ordinarily the landlord or the landlord's agent should go,

NOTICE TO PAY RENT OR QUIT
("Three Day Notice")

To _____ Joseph Tenant _____
       All tenants and subtenants in possession (full name)
       and all others in possession

WITHIN THREE DAYS after the service on you of this notice, you are hereby required to pay to the undersigned or XXXXXXXXXXXXXXXXXXXXXXX his authorized agent, the rent of the premises hereinafter described of which you now hold possession amounting to the sum of __Nine Hundred__ dollars ($ _900.00_) enumerated as follows:

$ _300.00_____ Due From _August 1_____ 19 _85_ To _August 31_____ 19 _85_

$ _300.00_____ Due From _September 1___ 19 _85_ To _September 30_ 19 _85_

$ _300.00_____ Due From _October 1_____ 19 _85_ To _October 31_____ 19 _85_

OR QUIT AND DELIVER UP THE POSSESSION OF THE PREMISES.

The premises herein referred to are situated in the city of ___San Rafael_____ , County of ___Marin_____ , State of California, designated by the number and street as _123 Jones Street_____ , apt. _224____ .

YOU ARE FURTHER NOTIFIED THAT, the undersigned does hereby elect to declare the forfeiture of your lease or rental agreement under which you hold possession of the above-described premises and lessor will institute legal proceedings to recover rent and possession of said premises which could result in a judgment against you including costs and necessary disbursements together with treble damages as allowed by law for such unlawful detention.

Dated this ___2nd_____ day of ___October_____ , 19 _85_ .

_____   _____
              AGENT   LESSOR

To order, contact — California Association of Realtors®
525 South Virgil Avenue, Los Angeles, California 90020

California Apartment Association, revised 4/78.
Reprinted by permission.   CAA-4.0

Figure 10-5

NOTICE OF CHANGE OF TERMS OF TENANCY

To: ___Joseph Tenant_____ and to all others

in possession of the premises commonly known as _____# 224_____

___123 Jones Street_____, _____San Rafael_____,
Street Address   Apt #   City

___California_____.
State

You are hereby notified, in accordance with Civil Code Section 827, that 30 days after service upon you of this

notice, or ___11/1/85___ whichever is later, your tenancy of the above designated premises will be changed as
Date

follows:

1. The monthly rent which is payable in advance on or before the ___first___ day of each month

   will be the sum of $__350.00__, instead of $__300.00__, the current monthly rent.

2. OTHER CHANGES: None.

Except as herein provided, all other terms of your tenancy shall remain in full force and effect.

DATED:___October 1, 1985___

_____
Owner/Agent

To order, contact—California Association of Realtors®
525 S. Virgil Avenue, Los Angeles, California 90020
(Revised 1983)

California Apartment Association
Reprinted by permission.

CAA-5.0

Figure 10-6

too. The tenant is then persuaded by the deputy to leave the premises or, if necessary, is forcibly removed. The landlord may simply change the locks to the premises, or he or she may put a padlock on the door and store the furniture and belongings in the premises until they can be moved elsewhere. The tenant may get them back upon payment of reasonable storage costs. If the tenant does not do this, the statutes set out detailed instructions stating how the landlord may store and later sell them.

TERMINATION OF THE LEASE AGREEMENT

A leasehold estate may be terminated by any of the following:

1. Expiration of the lease
2. The tenant's acquisition of the fee title or a title superior to that of the landlord
3. Mutual agreement of the landlord and the tenant
4. Surrender, in which the tenant voluntarily gives up possession and the landlord accepts possession intending to end the leasehold estate
5. Destruction of the premises
6. Cancellation at the option of the aggrieved or injured party in case of a breach of any condition stated in the lease agreement
7. Abandonment by the tenant (discussed later in this chapter)

When a lease expires, there is no requirement to give notice to the landlord or the tenant that it has expired. When the tenant continues in possession fulfilling all conditions of the expired lease and the landlord continues to accept rent, and no provision is made otherwise, the lease is presumed to be renewed. But the lease period is valid only under the same conditions and for the same period of time for which rent is paid. Thus, when rent is collected on a month-to-month basis, such renewal of the lease shall not be considered to extend beyond that period.

The landlord and the tenant may mutually agree to rescind (cancel) the lease agreement if, for example, the tenant is transferred to another part of the state or the country, making it impossible for him or her to complete the lease agreement. The landlord may release the tenant from the contract, thereby rescinding it, or the landlord may hold the tenant to the contract. If the tenant is transferred often, he or she may desire to negotiate a clause in the lease allowing him to rescind.

When destruction of the premises occurs through fire or other causes, the tenant is released from the agreement and need not pay further rent; but if the tenant has paid rent in advance, he or she may not recover it unless the agreement so provides. If fire, earthquake, or the like causes minor damage, the tenant must complete his or her household agreement, providing the landlord makes immediate repairs within a reasonable length of time.

A tenant cannot have a leasehold estate longer than the estate of the landlord. *Example:* When the holder of a life estate has leased his or her estate in the property, the leasehold estate ends upon the death of the life tenant.

When the tenant or the landlord breaches a condition of the lease, the aggrieved party may cancel the lease agreement. Written notice usually must be given by the aggrieved party on such cancellation.

Abandonment of the premises

Abandonment of the premises occurs when the tenant moves out before the end of the lease period without an agreement with the landlord that he or she may do so. However, abandonment requires more than just leaving the premises unoccupied: The tenant must intend to abandon.

When the tenant abandons, the landlord may enter the premises and lease it to another party. He or she may sue the tenant and get judgment for the rent the tenant would owe to the end of the lease term, with a deduction for the amount the landlord recovers or could have recovered by leasing to a new tenant. The statutes set out a detailed formula for the amount that may be recovered.

Abandonment is a troublesome problem for a landlord. Suppose the tenant stops paying rent, disappears, but leaves some of his or her furniture in the house or apartment. Has the tenant abandoned the premises? Suppose the landlord enters, relets the property, disposes of the furniture—thinking the tenant has abandoned—and then the tenant returns and claims he or she did not intend to abandon. The tenant could sue the landlord for damages, claiming he or she was illegally evicted.

To help the landlord, the statutes (California Civil Code, Section 1951.3) provide that the premises will be considered abandoned if (1) the tenant has failed to pay rent for fourteen days; (2) the landlord reasonably believes the tenant has abandoned; (3) the lessor has mailed or handed the tenant a written notice stating his or her belief that the premises have been abandoned; and (4) the tenant does not notify the landlord that he or she does not intend to abandon within fifteen days of personal delivery of the notice, or within eighteen days after mailing it. This provision does not prevent the landlord from proving abandonment by other means.

If the tenant leaves personal belongings in the abandoned premises, the statutes provide a method by which the landlord may store and later sell them.

PREVENTIVE LAW AND PRECAUTIONS FOR THE LANDLORD AT TIME OF RENTING

Many of the following items have already been covered in the chapter. The student is advised to read the California Association of Realtors Standard Form Lease (Figure 10–1) *and* the Credit Application for Lease (Figure 10–3) included in this chapter. Precautions a landlord should take at the time of renting include:

1. Screen prospective tenants. A credit report is helpful. All prospective tenants must be treated alike, regardless of race, religion, sex, or place of national origin.

2. Get complete information that you may need later if you must collect a judgment. Use the CAR Credit Application for Lease or another form. Have it dated and signed.

3. Get the lease or rental agreement in writing and signed by the landlord and the tenant. This may avoid arguments later. Have husband, wife, and, if possible, all persons over 18 who will occupy the premises sign the agreement.

4. Incorporate many of the covenants and conditions set forth in this chapter, in case of later disagreements.

Discrimination in leasing

When renting, some landlords try to discriminate against particular groups. The most common discrimination is racial; for example, refusal to rent to minority groups, or discrimination against most physically handicapped individuals.

Federal and California statutes forbid discrimination based on race, religion, ancestry, or national origin. A person who can prove he or she has been discriminated against may recover a substantial judgment in court. Consider the newspaper article reproduced as Figure 10–7.

A real estate licensee who practices discrimination jeopardizes his or her license. The National Association of Realtors condemns discrimination by a Realtor as unethical.

Rent control

Many communities in California have adopted rent control. Most rent control ordinances restrict a landlord's ability to raise rents and to evict a tenant. Those ordinances that restrict eviction, usually prohibit eviction, even on month-to-month tenancies, except for certain situations specified in the ordinance. If property is covered by rent control, the local ordinance as well as state law will have to be followed.

SPECIAL COMMERCIAL LEASES

Net lease

Sometimes the term "net lease" confuses some people in the real estate industry. A true *net lease*, often called a "net, net, net lease" or "triple-net lease," provides a net amount to the landlord—all expenses, including taxes and insurance, are paid by the tenant. When the term "net, net, lease" is used, the tenant usually pays for everything except insurance and taxes. Another term sometimes used is *broker's net*. In this case only a portion of the major expenses are paid by the tenant. Using the term "broker's net" in a lease without further description of what is meant may result in an agreement that is not binding; there has been no agreement about what is really meant and what expenses the tenant is to pay.

Percentage lease

The *percentage lease* is one in which the amount of rental is based upon the gross sales of a business. It may also provide for a minimum rental, regardless of the percentage of gross sales. Examples of percentages that may be paid are as follows:

Auto accessory stores	8–10%
Drugstores, regular	6–10
Cleaners and dyers	10–12
Barbershops	10–15
Groceries, chain	3–5
Hardware stores	6–8
Theaters	8–10
Variety stores	6–8

These percentage figures vary throughout the country.

Oil and gas leases

Real estate brokers in many states become involved in *oil and gas leases*. An oil company may wish to lease a piece of land because it believes that oil or gas or both may be found on the property. A flat sum of money, often called a "bonus," is usually paid by the oil company for a stated period of time, often one year, giving the company the right to drill for oil and gas during this period. The lease will normally provide that in the event drilling operations are not started within one year, another flat sum of money will be paid to continue the lease from year to year for a stated number of years. If oil or gas is found, a royalty is usually paid to the lessor, often one-eighth of the oil or gas produced.

Broker's authorization to lease

Figure 10–8 is the California Association of Realtors

The Mercury

★★★ SAN JOSE, CALIF., SATURDAY MORNING, MAY 3, 1975 25

$5,000 Housing Bias Award Won by Ex-Redwood Renters

SAN FRANCISCO—A black family who said they were denied the right to rent a house in Redwood City because of their color has been awarded $5,000 plus court costs by a federal court jury here.

The award to Leo Fountila and his wife Pauletta, who now live in San Jose, is one of the largest amounts given in Northern California for a case of housing discrimination.

Fountila, a counselor at Ravenswood High School in East Palo Alto, said he called the owner in April, 1974, and asked about a house she had for rent. Fountila said he had learned of the house through a rental agency where they had paid a $25 fee.

At the end of the conversation, he said, he told the owner he was black. Fountila said she then told him she would not rent to him and there would be no point in looking at the house the next day.

Mrs. Fountila, an electronics technician at the Stanford Linear Accelerator Center in Menlo Park, said she called Robert H. Moulton Jr., associate director of SLAC, and asked for help since the firm subscribes to the fair housing services of the Mid-peninsula Citizens for Fair Housing.

The next day a white volunteer went to the house, looked at it and was told it was for rent. The Fountilas went to the house as soon as the voluneer had left, but were told it already had been rented.

They later filed suit under the Federal Civil Rights Acts and California's Unruh Act. The $5,000 award was made in San Francisco on April 1.

Figure 10–7

EXCLUSIVE AUTHORIZATION TO LEASE OR RENT
THIS IS INTENDED TO BE A LEGALLY BINDING AGREEMENT—READ IT CAREFULLY
CALIFORNIA ASSOCIATION OF REALTORS* STANDARD FORM

In consideration of the services to be rendered by ___William C. Broker and Associates___
hereinafter called agent, I hereby grant said agent the exclusive and irrevocable right to lease or rent for a period of ___sixty (60)___
days from date hereof, and ending at midnight ___May 2___, 19 ___85___, the property situated in the ___City of Orange___
County of ___Orange___ State of California, described as follows, to wit:
Lot 15, Block 10, Tract 6720 as shown on map recorded September 16, 1979 in
Book 713, page 196, Official Records of Orange County.
A 2-story, 4-bedroom, 2 1/2 bath home with approximately 2,500 square feet
of living area. Located at 50624 Saratoga Court, Orange, California.

within said time for ___Eight Hundred and No/100--___
DOLLARS ($ ___800.00___) per ___month___ payable in advance on the ___first (1st) day, each month___
and I hereby authorize said agent to accept and hold a deposit thereon.

The lease shall be for a period of not less than one year, shall allow no pets, shall
require $1,600 deposit as a first and last months' rent, a $500 refundable security deposit,
and $100 cleaning deposit, all due and payable upon execution of this Lease Agreement.

Terms of Lease:
The following deposit moneys will be required of the tenants upon execution of the
lease agreement:

$1,600.00	As the first and last month's rent.
500.00	Refundable security deposit for their faithful fulfillment of the lease agreement.
100.00	Nonrefundable cleaning deposit.
$2,200.00	TOTAL DEPOSIT REQUIRED

I hereby agree to compensate agent as follows: ___A commission of six (6%) percent of the total___
___rental price to said agent___

whether property is leased or rented through the efforts of agent, or by me, or by another agent, or through any other source. Said compensation shall be paid to agent in the event the property is transferred or conveyed or withdrawn from agent's authority during the time set forth herein.

In the event lease is extended or renewed, I agree to pay an additional compensation of ___three (3%) percent-----___
I hereby agree to pay agent the compensation stated above if property is leased or rented within ___60___ days after the termination of this authority or any extension thereof to anyone with whom agent has had negotiations prior to final termination, provided I have received notice in writing, including the names of prospective lessees before or upon termination of this agreement or any extension thereof. If action be instituted on this agreement to collect compensation or commissions, the prevailing party shall be entitled to recover reasonable attorneys fees and costs.

This property shall be offered in compliance with state and federal anti-discrimination laws.
I hereby acknowledge receipt of a copy of this exclusive authorization to lease or rent.

In consideration of the foregoing employment, the undersigned agent   DATED: ___May 2, 1985___
agrees to use diligence in procuring a lessee for said property.

OWNER: _____
Listing Agent ___William C. Broker & Associates___ ___Edgar H. & Wilma A. Landlord___

By _____
ADDRESS: ___Suite A., Orange Financial Plaza___
___Orange, CA   92668___
PHONE: ___(714) 558-4000___

NO REPRESENTATION IS MADE AS TO THE LEGAL VALIDITY OF ANY PROVISION OR THE ADEQUACY OF ANY PROVISION IN ANY SPECIFIC TRANSACTION. A REAL ESTATE BROKER IS THE PERSON QUALIFIED TO ADVISE ON REAL ESTATE. IF YOU DESIRE LEGAL ADVICE CONSULT YOUR ATTORNEY.

To order, contact—California Association of Realtors®
525 S. Virgil Avenue, Los Angeles, California 90020
Copyright© (1982), California Association of Realtors®

FORM L-11

Figure 10-8

Exclusive Authorization to Lease or Rent standard form. The agreement provides that the agent will receive his or her commission no matter who leases the property.

Property managers

Many landlords, especially those with larger buildings, employ property managers to manage their property. The property managers usually receive a percentage of the gross monthly rents for their services. Their services vary, and often include acting as a rental agent, screening tenants, accepting rents, keeping records, and physically managing the building. The law requires that any apartment more than 15 units in size have a full time, on-site manager.

Many property managers are professionals and bear the designation ''CPM'' after their name. These initials stand for Certified Property Manager.

CHAPTER QUESTIONS _____

1. Describe the four common types of leasehold estates that exist in most states.

2. Give the reason for recording a lease and its legal significance.

3. Explain assignment and subletting of leaseholds with reference to responsibility of the parties.

4. How may lease agreements be terminated and what are the remedies of the landlord in case of default in rent?

5. What is meant by ''constructive eviction''?

MULTIPLE-CHOICE QUESTIONS _____

1. The time limit on a lease on urban property is: (a) 15 years; (b) 51 years; (c) 25 years; (d) 99 years; (e) 21 years.

2. A tenant who continues in possession of a property after the expiration of a lease is said to have: (a) an estate of inheritance; (b) an estate for years; (c) an estate at sufferance; (d) a life estate; (e) an estate in fee simple.

3. The time limit on agricultural or horticultural property is: (a) 99 years; (b) 25 years; (c) 15 years; (d) 51 years; (e) 30 years.

4. Which of the following is *true* regarding the termination of a lease: (a) A lease terminates upon the death of a landlord; (b) a lease terminates upon the death of a tenant; (c) a lease terminates upon the death of a landlord or a tenant; (d) a lease does not terminate upon the death of a landlord or a tenant; (e) a lease may not be terminated under any circumstances.

5. Which of the following applies to a lease: (a) It must always be in writing; (b) it is better verbal than written; (c) it is required to be in writing if it is for a period of three years; (d) it is required to be in writing if it is for one year or less; (e) it is required to be in writing if for a period of more than one year.

6. A lease: (a) creates an interest, both real estate and personal property; (b) conveys an interest in real estate; (c) is a chattel real; (d) is all of these.

7. A landlord must, before filing an unlawful detainer action: (a) obtain judgment for possession; (b) secure a sheriff's eviction; (c) serve the tenant with a three-day notice to pay rent or quit the premises; (d) serve the tenant with a sixty-day notice; (e) do all of the foregoing.

8. In a lease agreement, assigning means: (a) subletting; (b) paying rent in advance; (c) changing managers; (d) transferring all rights to another person; (e) transferring the fee simple interest in the property.

9. Rent is best defined as: (a) the tenant's interest in real property; (b) a contract between a landlord and a tenant; (c) a month-to-month tenancy; (d) consideration for the use and possession of property.

10. The percentage lease is one in which the rental consideration is based upon: (a) the net sales of a business; (b) the gross sales of a business; (c) the gross profit of a business; (d) the net profit of a business; (e) the value of the real property.

11 DEEMS

THE DEVELOPMENT OF LAND TRANSFER

Years ago, under English common law, the transfer of property was accomplished by "livery of seisin." The seller of the land would meet the purchaser on the property and pass a clod of dirt, a small branch from a tree, a stone, or some other symbol, say, "This land belongs to you," and the transfer was accomplished. If any questions were raised in future years concerning this transfer, a witness was usually around to say, "Yes, I saw the transfer take place." Ownerships of property were common knowledge and transfers were few, usually from father to son. In the early history of California the transfer of property was somewhat like that under English common law.

The Certificate of Title that stated the location and the condition of the title to the subject property came later in the development of the transfer of property in California. There was no guarantee as to the condition of the title, however. The later development of title insurance companies, with their huge title plants (large reference libraries composed of records indicating the chain of title of county property) of individual property, gave the first guarantees of title backed by an insurance fund. Today in California a grant deed is usually employed to transfer real property.

THE GENERAL NATURE OF DEEDS

A deed is a written document transferring property from the owner, called the *grantor,* to another person, called the *grantee.* Such document must be properly executed by the grantor and delivered to and accepted by the grantee.

Essential elements of deeds

No special form is required for a deed. Most deeds are prepared by title companies as formal documents, like the deed in Figure 11–1. However, a deed would be just as valid if handwritten on a piece of binder paper.

There are seven requirements for a deed: It must be written out; it must be to a grantee capable of holding title; it must be from a grantor legally capable of conveying title; it must contain a description of the property; it must contain words of conveyance; it must be signed by the grantor; it must be delivered and accepted.

In writing   First, the statute of frauds requires that all transfers of real property be made in writing. Legal instruments may be drawn only by a person authorized by the State of California Bar Association. Form deeds, such as those shown in Figures 11–1 and 11–2, may be filled in by licensed real estate brokers, provided such forms are essential to the real estate transaction being handled by the broker. Persons filling in such form deeds are cautioned on giving legal advice as to how parties should take title. The decision as to whether title is to be taken as community property, in joint tenancy, or as tenancy in common should be left to the grantee and his or her attorney, or the broker would be giving legal and tax advice without the proper licenses.

Grantee able to hold title   Second, the grantee must be legally capable of holding title. Almost everyone except an unincorporated association can hold title. Minors, and even felons, can hold title. If a minor holds title, it is usually the result of a gift.

161

SPACE ABOVE THIS LINE FOR RECORDER'S USE

Individual Grant Deed

CAT. NO. NN00582
TO 1923 CA (2—83)
THIS FORM FURNISHED BY TICOR TITLE INSURERS

The undersigned grantor(s) declare(s):
Documentary transfer tax is $ 2,500.00 .
(X) computed on full value of property conveyed, or
(   ) computed on full value less value of liens and encumbrances remaining at time of sale.
(   ) Unincorporated area: (   ) City of _____ , and

FOR A VALUABLE CONSIDERATION, receipt of which is hereby acknowledged,

    Sam E. Seller, a single man

hereby GRANT(S) to
    John J. Buyer and Lisa P. Buyer, husband and wife as community property

the following described real property in the   City and
County of   San Francisco   , State of California:

    Lots 5 and 6, in Block 5, in the City of San Francisco, County of San Francisco,
    State of California, as per Map recorded in Book 11 Page 68 of Miscellaneous
    Records in the office of the County Recorder of said County.

Dated: November 5, 1985   _Sam E. Seller (signature)_
                                                Sam E. Seller

STATE OF CALIFORNIA
COUNTY OF _____ }SS.
On _____ before
me, the undersigned, a Notary Public in and for said State,
personally appeared _____

personally known to me or proved to me on the basis of satisfactory evidence to be the person ___ whose name_____
subscribed to the within instrument and acknowledged
that _____ executed the same.
WITNESS my hand and official seal.

Signature _____

(This area for official notarial seal)

Title Order No._____   Escrow or Loan No. _____

MAIL TAX STATEMENTS AS DIRECTED ABOVE

Figure 11–1 Individual Grant Deed

Ticor Title Insurance Company of
California

AND WHEN RECORDED MAIL TO

Name   Buyer
          1234 West Street
Street   San Francisco, CA 94111
Address

City &
State

MAIL TAX STATEMENTS TO

Name   Same as above

Street
Address

City &
State

_____ SPACE ABOVE THIS LINE FOR RECORDER'S USE _____

CAT. NO. NN00580
TO 1922 CA (2—83)

Individual Quitclaim Deed

THIS FORM FURNISHED BY TICOR TITLE INSURERS

ALL | PTN.

The undersigned grantor(s) declare(s):
Documentary transfer tax is $ 2,500.00
(x) computed on full value of property conveyed, or
(   ) computed on full value less value of liens and encumbrances remaining at time of sale.
(   ) Unincorporated area: (   ) City of _____ , and

FOR A VALUABLE CONSIDERATION, receipt of which is hereby acknowledged,

     Sam E. Seller, a single man

hereby REMISES, RELEASES AND QUITCLAIMS to

     John J. Buyer and Lisa P. Buyer, husband and wife as community property

the following described real property in the   City and
County of San Francisco   , State of California:

Lots 5 and 6, in Block 5, in the City of San Francisco, County of San Francisco,
State of California, as per Map recorded in Book 11 Page 68 of Miscellaneous
Records in the office of the County Recorder of said County.

Dated: _November 15, 1981_   _Sam E. Seller_
                                Sam E. Seller

STATE OF CALIFORNIA
COUNTY OF _____ } SS.
On _____ before
me, the undersigned, a Notary Public in and for said State,
personally appeared _____

personally known to me or proved to me on the basis of satisfactory evidence to be the person __ whose name_____
subscribed to the within instrument and acknowledged
that _____ executed the same.
WITNESS my hand and official seal.

Signature _____

(This area for official notarial seal)

Title Order No._____ Escrow or Loan No. _____

MAIL TAX STATEMENTS AS DIRECTED ABOVE

Figure 11–2 Individual Quitclaim Deed

Grantor competent to convey title   Third, the grantor must be legally competent to convey title. While minors and those under legal disability can hold title, they cannot convey the property. For minors, a guardian must be appointed to transfer title. A conservator or other court-appointed individual transfers title for legally disabled adults.

Obviously, it is important that the person who acquired title conveys title. When the grantee changes names, the deed must so reflect. To illustrate: Jane Doe, a single woman, acquires title to property under her name. She later marries and wishes to transfer the property to another individual. Jane Doe would be described in the following manner: "Jane Doe Jones, formerly Jane Doe, under which title was acquired . . ."

Description of the property   Fourth, the deed must contain a description of the property. The description is usually prepared by the escrow company and is considered a "legal description." Such descriptions are usually in lot and block, by metes and bounds, or by township and range (government survey).

However, any description from which a surveyor can ascertain the property boundaries is legally adequate. Thus, in residential property, a street address is sufficient. Even a name like "The Gordon Ranch" would be acceptable if the ranch was known. Of course, such common descriptions should be avoided if possible.

Many deeds also contain words of restriction or addition. The deed may grant the entire property except certain listed easements, water uses, or other retained rights. Deeds often add that they include all *appurtenances*, although such language is implied. *Appurtenant* means "belonging to" and includes anything that is by right used with the land for its benefit. This may be a right-of-way or another type of easement. A clause is usually added following the legal description that may read, "together with all appurtenances thereto and all rights therein."

Words of conveyance   Fifth, the deed must contain some operative words of conveyance. The law does not require specific words, only words evidencing an intent to transfer property. The most common word is *grant*, such as "Ted grants to John." Other common words are *convey* and *transfer*. Even the word *to* (such as "Ted to John") is legally adequate.

Signed by the grantor   Sixth, the deed must be signed by the grantors, the persons making the grant or conveyance of real property. It is unnecessary for the grantee to sign the deed. For the instrument to be valid, the grantors or the persons making the conveyance must sign, since this is a charge against their title. Deeds are void when the instrument is signed in blank by the grantor with the provision that it is to be filled in later by the broker.

Delivery and acceptance   Finally, there must be legal delivery and acceptance. Acceptance is almost never a problem. The grantee must accept title, which is presumed. However, delivery often poses problems. The law is concerned with *legal* delivery, not *physical* delivery.

The mere turning over of the possession of the instrument does not transfer title. The grantor must intend title to pass immediately. When Adam gives a deed to his son with instructions to record the deed upon Adam's death, the intention to pass title immediately is not present and there is no proper delivery. Also, in cases where a husband and wife each give the other deeds on their separate property with instructions to the other to record upon the death of either, no proper delivery has occurred. Such a delivery must be absolute with intention to transfer title immediately. There is a presumption at law of a valid delivery when the deed is recorded in the office of the county recorder and it is found in possession of the grantee. These presumptions, however, may be open to refutation in a court of law.

Elements not required in a deed

The preceding seven elements are all that is legally required for a deed to be valid. Generally, however, the deed contains other elements. The commonly found elements are consideration, date, acknowledgment, and recording.

Consideration   Since a deed is not a contract, no consideration is required. Indeed, property is not infrequently given as a gift, for which the only "consideration" is love and affection.

If a deed lacks consideration, certain legal situations can arise affecting that deed, all of which are beyond the scope of this book. The grantee of such a deed is not a bona fide purchaser for value and faces certain detriments in dealing with conflicting claims. Also, if the deed is given in fraud of creditors, the deed can be set aside in certain situations.

Date   Surprisingly, a date is not required for a deed to be valid. The date can be ascertained from external evidence. However, it would be foolish to leave out the date. Title companies might not insure the deed, even though it would be valid. In such a case, legal action might be necessary to verify the date.

Acknowledgment   While a deed does not have to be acknowledged to be valid, it cannot be recorded without proper acknowledgment. Acknowledgments are usually taken in the form of a notary and are discussed later in this chapter.

Recordation A deed is invalid if not recorded, but as this chapter will later show, an unrecorded deed does not provide constructive notice. As such, other deeds, liens, or other claims can take priority over the unrecorded deed. Therefore, it is always advisable to record the deed.

TYPES OF DEEDS

Grant deed

In California a grant deed is the most commonly used type of deed. The word *grant* is used as the operative word of conveyance. Thus, stating ''Ted grants to Bill'' is a grant deed.

In California all deeds are usually presumed to be grant deeds unless the words or circumstances express otherwise. Therefore, a deed merely stating ''Ted to Bill'' following a sale would be a grant deed. However, it is very rare to find a grant deed not using the word *grant*.

The grant deed contains two implied warranties not written in the deed but recognized by California law:

1. That the property has not previously been conveyed by the grantor.
2. That the property being conveyed is free from all liens and encumbrances of the grantor or any person claiming under him or her except those set forth in the transaction. These include taxes, assessments, and other such liens. Such warranties include encumbrances made during the ownership of the grantor but of no other. (See Figures 11–1 and 11–2.)

Quitclaim deed

The grantor in a quitclaim deed releases any right or claim that he or she may have in the property. The deed may convey a fee simple title or any title that the grantor may have in property. The quitclaim deed makes no warranties and guarantees nothing. It does not even guarantee that the grantor owns any interest in the property.

One of the popular uses of quitclaim deeds is to clear title of any actual or imaginary claims. For example, a husband may acquire property by gift. As such, his wife would own no interest in the property. However, in California all property acquired during marriage is presumed to be community property.

To prove to the world (especially to the title company) that the wife owns no interest, she would execute a quitclaim deed to her husband. Since she owns nothing, the wife transfers nothing. However, the deed clears title of any imaginary community property interest.

Quitclaim deeds contain the operative words of conveyance: *assign, transfer of all right, title and interest*, or *remise, release and quitclaim*. (See Figure 11–2.)

Warranty deed

The warranty deed usually specifies the interest of the grantor being conveyed and will include convenants to protect the grantee should the title not be as represented and the grantee suffer damages. In a majority of states the warranty deed is considered the best deed that can be given. In California the warranty deed is legal but rarely used because of the implied warranties in the grant deed and the widespread use of title insurance policies.

There are five common covenants found in a warranty deed. These include legal possession of seisin, quiet enjoyment, further assurance, encumbrance, and warranty of title.

The grantor in the warranty deed promises to ''insure'' and defend title. However, title insurance companies are widespread in California. Since title insurance companies a neutral party, professionally trained to search title and ready to pay off quickly as an insurer if title is defective, grantors naturally prefer their ''guarantee'' over that of the grantor. Hence, warranty deeds are unused in California.

Special deeds

There are many public and private deeds given after sales and foreclosures that are, in effect, quitclaim deeds. These deeds do not contain any warranties. The two most common such deeds are

1. A *sheriff's deed*, given after sale of property to satisfy a judgment that has been rendered by a court.
2. A *trustee's deed*, given by a trustee to the purchaser at a foreclosure sale.

ACKNOWLEDGMENT AND NOTARY

Acknowledgment

An acknowledgment is made before a duly authorized officer or person and is a formal declaration that the instrument so executed is his or hers. The acknowledger, a neutral and reliable third person, testifies that the person whose signature appears really signed the document. Almost all documents must be acknowledged to be recorded.

When may acknowledgments be taken and by whom in the state of California? Acknowledgments may be taken by a justice or a clerk of the supreme court or district court of appeals, the judge of a superior court, the clerk of a court of record, a county recorder, a county clerk, a court commissioner, a notary public, or a judge of a municipal or justice court. In the military, certain officers are authorized to take acknowledgments of persons serving in the armed forces. Of course, most acknowledgments are taken by notaries (discussed below).

An acknowledgment can be taken only by a qualified person, and then only if the officer taking it *personally knows* or has *satisfactory evidence* as to the identity of the person signing. The Civil Code specifies the exact form that acknowledgments must take. For example, the acknowledgments of individuals taken by a notary must be in substantially the following form:

State of California   )
) ss.
County of _____   )

On this ____ day of _____, in the year, 19__, before me [name of notary], a notary public in and for the State of California, personally appeared _____, personally known to me (or proved to me on the basis of satisfactory evidence) to be the person whose name is subscribed to this instrument, and acknowledged to me that he executed it.

[NOTARY SEAL]

_____
Notary's Signature

An acknowledgment is void if a person who is an interested party to the transaction—a grantee, mortgagee, trustee, and so forth—executes an acknowledgment. Employees or officers of corporations may take acknowledgments when the corporation is involved in a transaction, as long as they do not have a personal interest in it. Employees or officers may not acknowledge the document as an officer of the corporation; they must do so as a notary public. Once an instrument has been delivered, the acknowledgment may not be amended. When a proper acknowledgment has been made but is defectively certified, it may be amended by a superior-court action.

Notary

Most acknowledgments in California are taken by notary publics. Notaries are people who are licensed by the Secretary of State to take acknowledgments. The notary passes an open-book test about the law of acknowledgments, and posts a bond. A notary is liable to any person who loses property or an interest in property because of a forged signature that could have been caught by the diligence required by law.

RECORDING

Recording is a process whereby documents affecting title or possession of real estate are made part of the public records. Once a deed or other document is recorded, it gives *constructive notice* to the public of its existence. Constructive recording notice means that by law you are deemed to know about the recorded document, even if you never see it or have actual notice of its existence.

Generally, nothing can be recorded unless it is acknowledged. (There are a few, very minor, exceptions.) The document should be recorded in the county where the property lies. If the property extends into two or more counties, it should be recorded in both counties.

Priority between conflicting claims

A deed or other instrument is fully effective and valid between the parties without recording. In fact, recording adds little between the parties.

However, if other people have interests in the property, then their rights are frequently dependent on the date of recording. Usually, the first person to record a document without notice of another person's prior claim has priority over other claims.

For example, assume that Ted owns Black Acre and that he executed a deed of trust of Homer Davey in 1980, which Homer never recorded. The deed of trust is fully valid between Ted and Homer.

However, assume that Ted, in 1982, needs additional funds and executes another deed to Glenn Mercer, and that Glenn has not had notice of Homer's deed. If neither deed of trust is recorded, then Homer's 1980 deed of trust is the senior lien, and Glenn's instrument is a junior lien.

If, on other the hand, Glenn recorded his deed of trust, then his lien would be the first deed of trust. The first person to record without notice of prior claims has the senior document. The law states that Homer could have easily protected himself by recording his deed of trust. Since Homer chose not to record, he ran the risk of someone else's recording first and getting a superior position.

The rule is simple: Always record. Most transactions are completed in escrow, which automatically records the appropriate documents.

Constructive notice by occupancy

The possession of real property gives constructive notice of the rights of those in possession. Such notice is the same as if the one in possession had recorded his or her deed. The party in possession, however, would be well advised not to depend upon his or her possessory rights alone—he or she should record his or her instrument.

The purchaser of property should not rely upon recordation rights alone but should make a physical inspection of the property; when persons are found to be in possession, he or she should determine what rights such persons may have. The purchaser may find that a legal interest exists in the property. Those in possession may be there under a contract of sale; these are prior contract rights with title still remaining in the name of the seller.

DOCUMENTARY STAMP TAX

In the sale of property, county documentary stamps in the amount of 55 cents per $500 or fraction thereof must be attached to the grant deed. The number of stamps required will be based upon the difference between an existing trust deed or mortgage and the purchase price of the property. When a new purchase-money trust deed or mortgage is involved, the dollar amount of the new encumbrance may not be deducted. To illustrate:

"$100,000 sales price and a $65,000 existing first deed of trust." The county documentary stamps will be calculated on the difference—$35,000. The total amount required in stamps is $38.50.

$100,000	Sale price
65,000	Existing first deed of trust
$ 35,000	Equity upon which county stamps will be calculated 35 × $1.10 = $38.50

If the grantor fails to attach stamps to the grant deed, it does not invalidate the deed. It does, however, subject the grantor to liability for the amount of the county stamps due, plus penalties. (County documentary stamps may be purchased at any county courthouse.)

When the consideration on a conveyance of real property is $100 or less, no stamps are required; thus, a gift deed would require no stamps.

A few counties have adopted a different cost for stamps. Check with each county before recording a deed.

CHAPTER QUESTIONS

1. What are the essential elements of a deed?
2. What protection is given to a purchaser by the recording of a grant deed?
3. In the conveyance of property, what will constitute proper delivery of the deed?

4. Does a fictitious person and a fictitious name mean the same thing in taking title to property?
5. Give five types of deeds. Under what circumstances is each used?

MULTIPLE-CHOICE QUESTIONS

1. A deed can be (a) assigned; (b) transferred; (c) foreclosed; (d) signed by a mark; (e) both *b* and *d* are correct.
2. A grant deed contains (a) two expressed warranties; (b) two implied warranties; (c) one expressed and one implied warranty; (d) no warranties at all.
3. A quitclaim deed (a) conveys the interest of the grantor; (b) conveys the interest of the grantee; (c) is used to convey only an easement; (d) will not convey fee simple title.
4. State which of the following a deed must contain to be valid: (a) signature of the grantee; (b) legal description; (c) granting clause; (d) consideration; (e) both *b* and *c*.
5. A deed made and delivered but not recorded is (a) invalid as between the parties and valid as to third parties with constructive notice; (b) valid as between the parties and valid as to subsequent recorded interest; (c) valid as between the parties and invalid as to subsequent recorded interests without notice; (d) invalid as between the parties.
6. Recording a deed (a) guarantees possession; (b) insures ownership; (c) presumes delivery; (d) none of these.
7. The person who conveys property under a deed is called the (a) grantor; (b) grantee; (c) lessor; (d) lessee.
8. A grant deed warrants (a) that there are no encumbrances on the property; (b) that the property is community property if the deed is executed by married persons; (c) that there are no prescriptive easements against the property known to the grantor of which he or she has not informed the grantee; (d) none of these.
9. Seven basic elements are essential to a valid deed. State which of the following is not essential to a valid deed: (a) The grantor must be competent to convey; (b) the deed must be acknowledged; (c) the property conveyed must be adequately described; (d) there must be a granting clause.
10. The most common instrument used in connection with the conveyance of real property in California is (a) an abstract of title; (b) a certificate of title; (c) a warranty deed; (d) a quitclaim deed; (e) a grant deed.

REAL ESTATE MATHEMATICS

By law the examination given for real estate salesperson's and broker's licenses must cover the "arithmatical computations" used in the real estate field. Mathematical calculations are used in all phases of real estate, including determination of interest payments, loan amounts, commissions, percentages, property size, and prorations. This chapter will cover the basic arithmetic needed for the salesperson's and broker's examination. As an introduction, the chapter will also briefly review basic arithmetic.

EQUATIONS

The basic mathematical concept is the *equation*. Despite the complex-sounding name, an equation is nothing more than a notation meaning that two things ("values") are equal to each other. For example,

2 + 1 = 3

is an equation. Everything on the left side of the equal sign (2 + 1) is the same value as (equal to) everything on the right side of the equal sign (3).

Calculations with equations

In equations, you can do any mathematical calculation on one side of the equation, as long as you do the exact same calculation on the other side.

For example, you could multiply both sides of the above equation (2 + 1 = 3), and the equation would still be true.

Equation:	2 + 1 =	3
Multiply × 3:	×3	×3
New value:	6 + 3 =	9

Six plus three is equal to nine, so the equation remains true.

Obviously, the new value, 9, is not the same as the old value, 3. However, an equation only states that two things are equal to each other. It is not concerned with the size of those numbers, only with their equality.

It does not matter whether you add, subtract, multiply, or divide the equation, as long as you use the same process on both sides. The concept of equations involves most of real estate mathematics.

FRACTIONS

A fraction is part of a whole number. For example, ½ is part of a number. A fraction is composed of two parts. The first part is the upper number, called the *numerator*. The second part is the bottom number, called the *denominator*. Thus, a fraction would be expressed as:

$$\frac{\text{numerator}}{\text{denominator}}$$

Improper fractions and mixed numbers

The denominator is always the larger number, unless you are dealing with an *improper* fraction. An improper fraction is a number greater than 1. For example three halves, expressed ³⁄₂, is greater than 1.

A mixed number is a whole number and a fraction, such as 3½. Frequently, mixed numbers are changed to improper fractions to do calculations.

Changing to and from improper fractions

To change an improper fraction to a proper fraction, just divide the numerator by the denominator. For example, 3/2 would be:

$$2\overline{)3} \text{ which is } 1\frac{1}{2}$$

To change a mixed number to an improper fraction, (1) multiply the whole number by the denominator, and (2) add the numerator to the result. This amount is the new numerator. Keep the same denominator.

For example, to change 2⅔ to an improper fraction:

Multiply: 2 × 3, which is 6
Add numerator: 6 + 2,   which is 8

Therefore, the mixed number 2⅔ is the same as the improper fraction 8/3.

Adjustments to fractions

You can multiply or divide the numerator and the denominator by any number and the result will not change. For example, in the fraction ⅔, both 2 and 3 can be multiplied by 4:

Numerator: $2 \times 4 = \dfrac{8}{}$
Denominator: $3 \times 4 = \dfrac{}{12}$

The fraction 8/12 is exactly the same as the fraction ⅔. In fact, most fractions are reduced to the lowest common fraction. This is found by dividing the numerator and denominator by the largest number that will exactly go into both parts of the fraction. In the fraction 8/12, if you divide both 8 and 12 by 4, you get ⅔:

Numerator: 8 ÷ 4 = 2
Denominator: 12 ÷ 4 = 3

Addition and subtraction of fractions

In adding or subtracting fractions, it is desirable to find the lowest common denominator. Usually the student can determine the common denominator by inspection—simply looking at the denominators. If this method fails or is too time-consuming, then simply multiply all denominators together, to get a common denominator.

Problem: Add 3/4 + 5/6 + 7/8 = ?
4 × 6 × 8 = 192 (common denominator)

Add: 3/4 = 144/192 (192 ÷ 4) × 3 = 144
5/6 = 160/192 (192 ÷ 6) × 5 = 160
7/8 = 168/192 (192 ÷ 8) × 7 = 168
472/192 = 2 88/192 = 2 11/24 472

Note the fractions should be reduced as far as possible. In the preceeding example:

$$\frac{88 \div 8}{192 \div 8} = \frac{11}{24}$$

To subtract fractions, find the lowest common denominator, then subtract the numerators. Subtract 3/10 from 7/8 as follows:

$$\frac{7}{8} = \frac{35}{40}$$
$$\frac{3}{10} = \frac{12}{40}$$
$$\frac{35 - 12}{40} = \frac{23}{40}$$

Multiplication of fractions

When multiplying fractions, simply multiply numerator by numerator and denominator by denominator:

Problem: Multiply 3/4 × 5/6 × 7/8 × 1/4 = ?
First:
Multiply the numerators: 3 × 5 × 7 × 1 = 105
Second:
Multiply the denominators: 4 × 6 × 8 × 4 = 768
Answer: $\dfrac{105}{768} = \dfrac{35}{256}$

Numerators may also be canceled into denominators before performing the above process:

$$\overset{1}{\underset{2}{\frac{3}{4}}} \times \frac{5}{6} \times \frac{7}{8} \times \frac{1}{4} \times \frac{35}{256}$$

Division of fractions

To divide fractions, the divisor must be inverted and the fractions multiplied:

$$\frac{7}{8} \div \frac{3}{4} = ? \quad \frac{7}{8} \times \frac{4}{3} = \frac{28}{24} = 1\frac{4}{24} \text{ or } 1\frac{1}{6}$$
$$\frac{1}{2} \div \frac{1}{6} = ? \quad \frac{1}{2} \times \frac{6}{1} = \frac{6}{2} = 3$$

Sample problem

Broker Thompson sold 1/4 of Mr. Green's ranch for

$25,000, leaving Mr. Green with 90 acres of land. How many acres were there in the ranch before the sale? Answer: One-fourth of the ranch was sold, leaving Mr. Green with 3/4, or 90 acres of land (90 acres = 3/4).

$$90 \div \frac{3}{4} = \frac{\overset{30}{\cancel{90}}}{1} \times \frac{4}{\underset{1}{\cancel{3}}} = 120 \text{ acres}$$

DECIMALS AND PERCENTAGES

Fractions, especially larger ones, are cumbersome to work with. Therefore, decimals are usually used in real estate problems. Fractions can easily be converted to decimals.

Decimals and percentages are equivalent to common fractions that have 100 for a common denominator. Note the illustrations below:

$$1/2 = 50/100 = .50 = 50\%$$
$$1/4 = 25/100 = .25 = 25\%$$
$$1/5 = 20/100 = .20 = 20\%$$
$$1/10 = 10/100 = .10 = 10\%$$
$$1/20 = 5/100 = .05 = 5\%$$

It is important to remember that if a percent sign (%) follows a number, it indicates that the number has been multiplied by 100. To change a fraction to a decimal or a percent, divide the denominator into the numerator and place a decimal point in the proper location. The result may be expressed as a percentage by moving the decimal point two places to the right and adding the percent sign (%).

$$\frac{1}{4} = .25 \text{ or } 25\%$$

```
        .25
    4|1.00
      8
      20
      20
       0
```

$$\frac{2}{5} = .40 \text{ or } 40\%$$

```
        .40
    5|2.00
      20
      00
      00
       0
```

Note the importance of a decimal point:

$$2. = 200\%$$
$$.2 = 20\%$$
$$.02 = 2\%$$
$$.002 = .2\%$$

In adding or subtracting decimals it is important to align all decimal points:

Add:

```
1.246      1.246
24.1       24.100
2.13       2.130
 .7         .700
-------    -------
28.176     28.176
```

Subtract:

```
2,741.72      2,741.7200
  28.9437       28.9437
----------    ----------
2,712.7763    2,712.7763
```

In multiplication of decimals, the number of decimals in the answer must equal the sum of decimals in the *multiplicand* plus the *multiplier*:

```
746.28     2 decimals
   .167    3 decimals
--------
522396
447768
74628
--------
124.62876  5 decimal places in answer
```

In the division of decimals, move the decimal point in the dividend as many places to the right as there are decimal points in the divisor:

```
                2498.228995
    7.284|18197.100
```

```
                    .78042
    124.6|97.2,203
```

When dividing a larger number into a smaller number, it is necessary to add zeros to the *dividend*:

```
            .83 2/8 = .8333 etc.
    5/6   6|5.00
           48
           20
           18
            2
```

PERCENTAGE PROBLEMS

Many real estate problems involve percentages. Percentages are easy to calculate. A percentage is composed of three parts:

Base: This is the entire amount, 100%, the total sum.

Rate: This is the percentage used on the base or the portion.

Percentage: This is the part of the whole (base). It is sometimes called the portion, although it will be called the percentage in this book.

For example, one-fourth (25 percent) of 100 acres is 25 acres. The base would be 100, the entire acreage. The rate would be 25 percent. The percentage would be 25 acres.

Usually, only two parts of a percentage problem are known and you need to find the third part. The basic rules (equations) are stated below and could be visualized as a triangle:

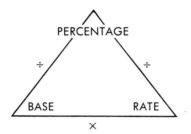

Rules

Base × Rate = Percentage
Percentage ÷ Base = Rate or percent
Percentage ÷ Rate = Base

Examples

2,500 × .20 (20%) = 500
500 ÷ .20 (20%) = 2,500
500 ÷ 2,500   = .20 or 20%

Uses in real estate

The percentage formula (*Base × Rate = Percentage*) is often used in real estate. The most common uses of the formula are for finding commissions, determining sales price on net listings, calculating profits for investments, and deriving costs and sales price.

Sometimes the formula words (*Base × Rate = Percentage*) may be changed for convenience, but the formula remains exactly the same. Calling the formula *Amount × Rate = Yield* or *Sales Price × Rate = Commission* does not change any of the calculations or procedures to use.

Commissions

Assume a broker receives 6 percent of the selling price

as a commission. If the house sold for $200,000, what is the amount of the broker's commission.

The formula is *Base × Rate = Percentage*, sometimes stated *Sales Price × Rate = Commission*. You know the base is $200,000 and the rate is 6 percent. Therefore, the broker's commission is $12,000 calculated as follows:

Base   × Rate = Percentage
$200,000 × .06   = Percentage
$12,000 =   Percentage

If a salesperson sold the above property, and had to split the commission with the brokerage firm, how much would the salesperson receive? Just divide the commission by two:

$12,000 ÷ 2 = $6,000

The problem also could be resolved using *Base × Rate = Percentage* and using .03 percent as the percentage.

Net Listing

Assume the seller wants $150,000 net from the sale. The broker receives 6 percent commission. How much will the broker have to sell the property for to receive the full commission.

The $150,000 the seller wants to receive is only part (a portion or percentage) of the whole. Therefore this amount is the percentage.

The rate is not 6 percent, since the $150,000 represents more than 6 percent of the selling price. Rather, the seller is receiving the entire purchase price *less* the broker's commission. Therefore, the rate is 100 percent less 6 percent or 94 percent.

You use the same formula, *Base × Rate = Percentage*. Since the unknown is the base, the base must be alone on one side of the equal sign of the equation. The formula, restated for convenience, is:

$$\text{Base} = \frac{\text{Percentage}}{\text{Rate}}$$
$$= \frac{\$150,000}{.94}$$
$$= \$159,574$$

Profit

Profit problems use the same *Base × Rate = Percentage* formulas, but usually you need to first determine the profit. Use the following formula:

Selling Price
− Cost
―――――――
Profit

A lot cost $6,000. It sold for $8,500. What is the percentage of the profit on the *cost* and *on the selling price*? Remember that the profit is the *percentage*, and that the formula will be:

$$\text{Rate} = \frac{\text{Percentage}}{\text{Base}}$$

Based on cost

$8,500	Selling price
−6,000	Cost (Base)
$2,500	Profit (Percentage)

$2,500 ÷ $6,000 = .41667 or 41.67% or 41 2/3%

Based on selling price

$8,500	Selling price (Base)
−6,000	Cost
$2,500	Profit (Percentage)

$2,500 ÷ $8,500 = .294118 or 29.41%

Cost and selling price

Sometimes you will know the sales price and the amount of profit and need to determine the original costs.

The selling price equals the costs plus the profit. The cost will be 100 percent, therefore the percentage will be 100 percent plus the profit. In other words, the sales price equals *more than* the cost.

The cost is the *base* which is the factor for which you are solving in the Base × Rate = Percentage equation. The formula is:

$$\text{Base} = \frac{\text{Percentage}}{\text{Rate}}$$

$$\text{Base} = \frac{\text{Sales Price}}{100\% + \text{Profit} - \%}$$

1. A house and lot cost $25,000. The property was later sold, making a profit for the owner of 20% *based on the selling price*. Find the selling price.

100%	Selling price (unknown)
−20%	Profit
80%	Cost or $25,000

$25,000 ÷ .80 = $31,250 (selling price)

Check: 20% of $31,250 = $ 6,250 Profit
+ $25,000
$31,250

2. A home sells for $45,000, making the owner a profit of 30% *based on the cost* of the house. Find the cost.

$45,000	Selling price
100%	Cost (unknown)
+ 30%	Profit based on cost
130%	Selling price of $45,000

$45,000 ÷ 1.30 = $34,615.3846 = $34,615.39

CALCULATING INTEREST

When you borrow money, you pay a fee to the lender for the money's use. This fee is called interest.

The formula for determining interest is:

Formula: Interest = Principal × Rate × Time

For simplicity, the formula is often expressed in letters representing each of the values. Thus, the formula is also expressed:

$I = P \times R \times T$

I = Interest. It is found by multiplying the principal by the rate by the time.
P = Principal. This the amount of money borrowed (or outstanding). Interest on real estate loans is calculated on the unpaid balance of the loan.
R = Rate. This is the interest rate, expressed as a decimal.
T = Time. Time is always expressed as part of a year, which, unless otherwise stated, is always calculated as 360 days. Five months would be 5/12 of a year. Months are always calculated as having exactly 30 days. Therefore, 5 months is also 5 × 30, or 150, days. Time is either expressed as a fraction (e.g., 5/12 or 150/360) or converted into a decimal (e.g., .416).

Example

What is the interest on $900 for 60 days at 5 percent?

$I = P \times R \times T$
$I = 900 \times .05 \times \frac{1}{6} = \$7.50$

Wherever any three parts of the formula are given, the other may be found easily:

$$I = PRT \quad R = \frac{I}{PT} \quad P = \frac{I}{RT} \quad T = \frac{I}{PR}$$

Example

How many days will it take $900 to earn $7.50 at 5 percent simple interest?

$$T = \frac{I}{PR} = \frac{7.50}{900 \times .05} = 1/6 \text{ of a year, or 60 days}$$

AMORTIZATION OF LOANS

Amortization is the liquidation (paying off) of a mortgage debt in installments. Generally recognized methods of amortization are (1) principal plus interest and (2) equal payments of the total of principal plus interest.

Principal plus interest

Under this plan of amortization, each time a payment is made a constant sum is paid on the principal. In addition, the borrower pays the interest up to the date of the payment. Thus, the payments on the principal remain the same, but the amount of interest decreases on each payment because there is less principal to draw interest on.

Example

Smith borrows $1,000 from Jones and agrees to repay the money in ten monthly installments with interest in addition, at 6 percent per year.

Solution   Each payment toward the principal will be $100, and interest will be based on the unpaid balance at one-half percent per month.

Equal payments— Principal including interest

The equal, or level, payments method is the usual way of setting up a home loan, and it is frequently used in other types of financing, as well. In fact, when a real estate salesperson talks about an "amortized loan," he or she means an equal payment loan.

The size of the payments remains the same over the life of the loan. The amount of payment is calculated so that the exact amount of principal plus interest is paid off over the life of the loan. At first, much of the payment may be applied upon interest, but as the principal is paid down, there is less interest, and more and more of the payment goes on the principal. Table 12–1 shows the first ten installments on a loan of $10,000, payable at $100 per month with 6 percent interest.

The simple way to compute the size of the payments is to use an amortized payment booklet that can usually be obtained from banks, title insurance companies, and savings and loan associations. Every real estate salesperson should have one. Figure 12–1 is one page from such a booklet.

Suppose you wanted to set monthly payments on a $25,000 loan for thirty years at 9 percent. From Figure 12–1 you can see that the amount would be $201.16 per month, which includes principal and interest.

The monthly payments could also be derived by using Table 12–2. From the table you determine that the payment to amortize a $1,000 loan at 9 percent for thirty years is "8.05". Since the loan is for $25,000 and not $1,000, you multiply $8.05 times 25 to obtain $201.25, the cost of a $25,000 loan.

TYPICAL LICENSE EXAMINATION PROBLEMS

Prorations

Proration simply means the division of financial responsibilities between the buyer and the seller in proportion to their time of ownership. The seller is responsible for expenses and income during his or her period of own-

Table 12–1

Unpaid Balance	Interest Amount	Principal Amount	Total Amount	Installment Number
$10,000.00	$50.00	$50.00	$100.00	1
9,950.00	49.75	50.25	100.00	2
9,899.75	49.50	50.50	100.00	3
9,849.25	49.25	50.75	100.00	4
9,798.50	48.99	51.01	100.00	5
9,747.49	48.74	51.26	100.00	6
9,696.23	48.48	51.52	100.00	7
9,644.71	48.22	51.78	100.00	8
9,592.93	47.96	52.04	100.00	9
9,540.89	47.70	52.30	100.00	10

9% MONTHLY LOAN AMORTIZATION PAYMENTS 9%

AMOUNT	5 YEARS	10 YEARS	15 YEARS	20 YEARS	25 YEARS	30 YEARS
$ 100	2.08	1.27	1.01	0.90	0.84	0.80
200	4.15	2.53	2.03	1.80	1.68	1.61
300	6.23	3.80	3.04	2.70	2.52	2.41
400	8.30	5.07	4.06	3.60	3.36	3.22
500	10.38	6.33	5.07	4.50	4.20	4.02
600	12.46	7.60	6.09	5.40	5.04	4.83
700	14.53	8.87	7.10	6.30	5.87	5.63
800	16.61	10.13	8.11	7.20	6.71	6.44
900	18.68	11.40	9.13	8.10	7.55	7.24
1 000	20.76	12.67	10.14	9.00	8.39	8.05
1 000	20.76	12.67	10.14	9.00	8.39	8.05
2 000	41.52	25.34	20.29	17.99	16.78	16.09
3 000	62.28	38.00	30.43	26.99	25.18	24.14
4 000	83.03	50.67	40.57	35.99	33.57	32.18
5 000	103.79	63.34	50.71	44.99	41.96	40.23
6 000	124.55	76.01	60.86	53.98	50.35	48.28
7 000	145.31	88.67	71.00	62.98	58.74	56.32
8 000	166.07	101.34	81.14	71.98	67.14	64.37
9 000	186.83	114.01	91.28	80.98	75.53	72.42
10 000	207.58	126.68	101.43	89.97	83.92	80.46
11 000	228.34	139.34	111.57	98.97	92.31	88.51
12 000	249.10	152.01	121.71	107.97	100.70	96.55
13 000	269.86	164.68	131.85	116.96	109.10	104.60
14 000	290.62	177.35	142.00	125.96	117.49	112.65
15 000	311.38	190.01	152.14	134.96	125.88	120.69
16 000	332.13	202.68	162.28	143.96	134.27	128.74
17 000	352.89	215.35	172.43	152.95	142.66	136.79
18 000	373.65	228.02	182.57	161.95	151.06	144.83
19 000	394.41	240.68	192.71	170.95	159.45	152.88
20 000	415.17	253.35	202.85	179.95	167.84	160.92
21 000	435.93	266.02	213.00	188.94	176.23	168.97
22 000	456.68	278.69	223.14	197.94	184.62	177.02
23 000	477.44	291.35	233.28	206.94	193.02	185.06
24 000	498.20	304.02	243.42	215.93	201.41	193.11
25 000	518.96	316.69	253.57	224.93	209.80	201.16
26 000	539.72	329.36	263.71	233.93	218.19	209.20
27 000	560.48	342.03	273.85	242.93	226.58	217.25
28 000	581.24	354.69	283.99	251.92	234.98	225.29
29 000	601.99	367.36	294.14	260.92	243.37	233.34
30 000	622.75	380.03	304.28	269.92	251.76	241.39
31 000	643.51	392.70	314.42	278.92	260.15	249.43
32 000	664.27	405.36	324.57	287.91	268.54	257.48
33 000	685.03	418.03	334.71	296.91	276.93	265.53
34 000	705.79	430.70	344.85	305.91	285.33	273.57
35 000	726.54	443.37	354.99	314.90	293.72	281.62
36 000	747.30	456.03	365.14	323.90	302.11	289.66
37 000	768.06	468.70	375.28	332.90	310.50	297.71
38 000	788.82	481.37	385.42	341.90	318.89	305.76
39 000	809.58	494.04	395.56	350.89	327.29	313.80
40 000	830.34	506.70	405.71	359.89	335.68	321.85
41 000	851.09	519.37	415.85	368.89	344.07	329.90
42 000	871.85	532.04	425.99	377.89	352.46	337.94
43 000	892.61	544.71	436.14	386.88	360.85	345.99
44 000	913.37	557.37	446.28	395.88	369.25	354.03
45 000	934.13	570.04	456.42	404.88	377.64	362.08

9% MONTHLY LOAN AMORTIZATION PAYMENTS 9%

AMOUNT	5 YEARS	10 YEARS	15 YEARS	20 YEARS	25 YEARS	30 YEARS
$46 000	954.89	582.71	466.56	413.87	386.03	370.13
47 000	975.64	595.38	476.71	422.87	394.42	378.17
48 000	996.40	608.04	486.85	431.87	402.81	386.22
49 000	1017.16	620.71	496.99	440.87	411.21	394.27
50 000	1037.92	633.38	507.13	449.86	419.60	402.31
51 000	1058.68	646.05	517.28	458.86	427.99	410.36
52 000	1079.44	658.72	527.42	467.86	436.38	418.40
53 000	1100.19	671.38	537.56	476.86	444.77	426.45
54 000	1120.95	684.05	547.70	485.85	453.17	434.50
55 000	1141.71	696.72	557.85	494.85	461.56	442.54
56 000	1162.47	709.39	567.99	503.85	469.95	450.59
57 000	1183.23	722.05	578.13	512.84	478.34	458.64
58 000	1203.99	734.72	588.28	521.84	486.73	466.68
59 000	1224.75	747.39	598.42	530.84	495.13	474.73
60 000	1245.50	760.06	608.56	539.84	503.52	482.77
61 000	1266.26	772.72	618.70	548.83	511.91	490.82
62 000	1287.02	785.39	628.85	557.83	520.30	498.87
63 000	1307.78	798.06	638.99	566.83	528.69	506.91
64 000	1328.54	810.73	649.13	575.83	537.09	514.96
65 000	1349.30	823.39	659.27	584.82	545.48	523.00
66 000	1370.05	836.06	669.42	593.82	553.87	531.05
67 000	1390.81	848.73	679.56	602.82	562.26	539.10
68 000	1411.57	861.40	689.70	611.81	570.65	547.14
69 000	1432.33	874.06	699.84	620.81	579.05	555.19
70 000	1453.09	886.73	709.99	629.81	587.44	563.24
71 000	1473.85	899.40	720.13	638.81	595.83	571.28
72 000	1494.60	912.07	730.27	647.80	604.22	579.33
73 000	1515.36	924.73	740.42	656.80	612.61	587.37
74 000	1536.12	937.40	750.56	665.80	621.01	595.42
75 000	1556.88	950.07	760.70	674.80	629.40	603.47
76 000	1577.64	962.74	770.84	683.79	637.79	611.51
77 000	1598.40	975.40	780.99	692.79	646.18	619.56
78 000	1619.15	988.07	791.13	701.79	654.57	627.61
79 000	1639.91	1000.74	801.27	710.78	662.97	635.65
80 000	1660.67	1013.41	811.41	719.78	671.36	643.70
81 000	1681.43	1026.08	821.56	728.78	679.75	651.74
82 000	1702.19	1038.74	831.70	737.78	688.14	659.79
83 000	1722.95	1051.41	841.84	746.77	696.53	667.84
84 000	1743.71	1064.08	851.98	755.77	704.93	675.88
85 000	1764.46	1076.75	862.13	764.77	713.32	683.93
86 000	1785.22	1089.41	872.27	773.76	721.71	691.98
87 000	1805.98	1102.08	882.41	782.76	730.10	700.02
88 000	1826.74	1114.75	892.56	791.76	738.49	708.07
89 000	1847.50	1127.42	902.70	800.76	746.89	716.11
90 000	1868.26	1140.08	912.84	809.75	755.28	724.16
91 000	1889.01	1152.75	922.98	818.75	763.67	732.21
92 000	1909.77	1165.42	933.13	827.75	772.06	740.25
93 000	1930.53	1178.09	943.27	836.75	780.45	748.30
94 000	1951.29	1190.75	953.41	845.74	788.85	756.35
95 000	1972.05	1203.42	963.55	854.74	797.24	764.39
96 000	1992.81	1216.09	973.70	863.74	805.63	772.44
97 000	2013.56	1228.76	983.84	872.73	814.02	780.48
98 000	2034.32	1241.42	993.98	881.73	822.41	788.53
99 000	2055.08	1254.09	1004.13	890.73	830.80	796.58
100 000	2075.84	1266.76	1014.27	899.73	839.20	804.62

Figure 12–1

ership *up to and including the date of closing.* The buyer is responsible for expenses and income *after* the closing date. Examples of expenses and income to be prorated include property taxes, interest expense on assumed mortgages, insurance premiums, and rents.

It is the usual custom to use a *statutory year* of 360 days and a *statutory month* of 30 days. Decimals should be carried out—as examples will show—to four places and not rounded off until the final answer. A few escrow agents may use three decimal places. For example, if the third decimal place is five or more, the second decimal place should be increased by one. Thus $561.1253 would appear in the final answer at $561.13.

Consider the following problem as it relates to property taxes.

Problem   Broker Smith sold a home for $63,000 and the transaction closed March 3. The property taxes for the year 1976–77 had been paid in full by the seller. The taxes were $1,260. How much of a tax refund is the seller entitled to?

Solution   Seller is entitled to a refund from March 4 (the day after closing) to and including June 30, or 3 months and 27 days. We could also say 117 days, since we use 30 days to a month.

$1,260 annual taxes ÷ 12 months = $105 taxes per month

$105 taxes per month ÷ 30 days = $3.50 taxes per day

$3.50 taxes per day × 117 days = $409.50 amount of refund on taxes due seller.

When an existing amortized loan [equal payments] is

Figure 12–2 Payments to amortize $1,000 loan

Term of years	5%	5¼%	5½%	5¾%	6%	6¼%	6½%	6.6%	6¾%	7%	7.2%	7¼%	7½%	7¾%	7.8%	8%	8.4%	8½%	9%	9½%	10%
5	18.88	18.99	19.11	19.22	19.34	19.45	19.57	19.62	19.69	19.81	19.90	19.92	20.04	20.16	20.19	20.28	20.47	20.52	20.76	21.01	21.25
6	16.11	16.23	16.34	16.46	16.58	16.70	16.81	16.86	16.93	17.05	17.15	17.17	17.30	17.42	17.44	17.54	17.73	17.78	18.03	18.28	18.53
7	14.14	14.26	14.38	14.49	14.61	14.73	14.85	14.90	14.98	15.10	15.20	15.22	15.34	15.47	15.49	15.59	15.79	15.84	16.09	16.35	16.61
8	12.66	12.78	12.90	13.03	13.15	13.27	13.39	13.44	13.51	13.64	13.74	13.76	13.89	14.01	14.04	14.14	14.35	14.40	14.66	14.92	15.18
9	11.52	11.64	11.76	11.89	12.01	12.13	12.26	12.31	12.39	12.51	12.61	12.64	12.77	12.89	12.92	13.02	13.23	13.28	13.55	13.81	14.08
10	10.61	10.73	10.86	10.98	11.11	11.23	11.36	11.41	11.49	11.62	11.72	11.75	11.88	12.01	12.03	12.14	12.35	12.40	12.67	12.94	13.22
11	9.87	9.99	10.12	10.24	10.37	10.50	10.63	10.68	10.76	10.89	10.99	11.02	11.15	11.29	11.31	11.42	11.64	11.69	11.97	12.24	12.52
12	9.25	9.38	9.51	9.63	9.76	9.89	10.02	10.08	10.16	10.29	10.40	10.42	10.56	10.69	10.72	10.83	11.05	11.11	11.39	11.67	11.96
13	8.74	8.86	8.99	9.12	9.25	9.38	9.52	9.57	9.65	9.79	9.89	9.92	10.06	10.20	10.22	10.34	10.56	10.62	10.90	11.19	11.48
14	8.29	8.42	8.55	8.68	8.82	8.95	9.09	9.14	9.22	9.36	9.47	9.50	9.64	9.78	9.80	9.92	10.15	10.20	10.49	10.79	11.09
15	7.91	8.04	8.17	8.31	8.44	8.58	8.72	8.77	8.85	8.99	9.11	9.13	9.28	9.42	9.45	9.56	9.79	9.85	10.15	10.45	10.75
16	7.58	7.71	7.85	7.98	8.12	8.26	8.40	8.45	8.54	8.67	8.79	8.82	8.96	9.11	9.14	9.25	9.49	9.55	9.85	10.15	10.46
17	7.29	7.43	7.56	7.70	7.84	7.98	8.12	8.17	8.26	8.40	8.52	8.55	8.69	8.84	8.87	8.99	9.23	9.29	9.59	9.90	10.22
18	7.04	7.17	7.31	7.45	7.59	7.73	7.87	7.93	8.01	8.16	8.28	8.31	8.45	8.60	8.63	8.75	9.00	9.06	9.37	9.68	10.00
19	6.81	6.95	7.08	7.22	7.37	7.51	7.65	7.71	7.80	7.95	8.07	8.10	8.25	8.40	8.43	8.55	8.80	8.86	9.17	9.49	9.82
20	6.60	6.74	6.88	7.03	7.17	7.31	7.46	7.52	7.61	7.76	7.88	7.91	8.06	8.21	8.25	8.37	8.62	8.68	9.00	9.33	9.66
21	6.42	6.56	6.70	6.85	6.99	7.14	7.29	7.35	7.44	7.59	7.71	7.74	7.90	8.05	8.08	8.21	8.46	8.53	8.85	9.18	9.51
22	6.26	6.40	6.54	6.69	6.84	6.98	7.13	7.19	7.29	7.44	7.56	7.59	7.75	7.90	7.94	8.07	8.32	8.39	8.72	9.05	9.38
23	6.11	6.25	6.40	6.54	6.69	6.84	7.00	7.06	7.15	7.30	7.43	7.46	7.62	7.78	7.81	7.94	8.20	8.27	8.60	8.93	9.28
24	5.97	6.12	6.27	6.41	6.56	6.72	6.87	6.93	7.03	7.18	7.31	7.34	7.50	7.66	7.70	7.83	8.09	8.16	8.49	8.83	9.18
25	5.85	6.00	6.15	6.30	6.45	6.60	6.76	6.82	6.91	7.07	7.20	7.23	7.39	7.56	7.59	7.72	7.99	8.06	8.40	8.74	9.09
26	5.74	5.89	6.04	6.19	6.34	6.50	6.65	6.72	6.81	6.97	7.10	7.14	7.30	7.46	7.50	7.63	7.90	7.96	8.31		
27	5.64	5.78	5.94	6.09	6.24	6.40	6.56	6.62	6.72	6.88	7.01	7.05	7.21	7.38	7.41	7.55	7.82	7.88	8.23		
28	5.54	5.69	5.84	6.00	6.16	6.31	6.48	6.54	6.64	6.80	6.93	6.97	7.13	7.30	7.34	7.47	7.75	7.81	8.16		
29	5.45	5.61	5.76	5.92	6.08	6.24	6.40	6.46	6.56	6.73	6.86	6.89	7.06	7.23	7.27	7.40	7.68	7.75	8.10		
30	5.37	5.53	5.68	5.84	6.00	6.16	6.33	6.39	6.49	6.66	6.79	6.83	7.00	7.17	7.20	7.34	7.62	7.69	8.05		
35	5.05	5.21	5.38	5.54	5.71	5.88	6.05	6.12	6.22	6.39	6.53	6.57	6.75	6.93	6.96	7.11	7.40	7.47	7.84		
40	4.83	4.99	5.16	5.33	5.51	5.68	5.86	5.93	6.04	6.22	6.37	6.40	6.59	6.77	6.81	6.96	7.26	7.33	7.71		

assumed by the buyer, the interest is calculated on the previous balance remaining during the preceding month. For example, when the payment on the loan was made July 1, interest was not included for that day—only the interest earned during the month of June.

Problem The buyer of a home assumes a loan with a current balance on July 1 of $25,000. The transaction closed July 18. How much interest for the month of July should be charged to the seller if the loan is at 8-percent interest?

Solution July 1 to and including July 18 = 18 days

$25,000 principal × .08 interest ÷ 360 days = $5.5555 interest per day.

18-days × $5.5555 per day = $99.9999 or $100 total interest charged to seller.

When the seller transfers to the buyer an existing fire insurance policy, the buyer should reimburse the seller for the advance premiums paid. The premiums, like other prorations, are computed the day *after* closing *to and including the policy expiration date*. Most policies are written on a basis of one or three years.

FIRST: Determine the expiration date of policy.
SECOND: Determine the closing date.
THIRD: Use thirty days to a month.

Problem A seller has a three-year fire insurance policy, effective July 5, 1975, on which she paid a premium of $162.50. Buyer agrees to take over the policy. Assume that the transaction closes January 15, 1977. What is the buyer's share of the policy?

Solution The policy expires July 5, 1978.

	6	35	
1978	7̶ (July)	5̶	Expiration date
1977	1 (Jan.)	15	Proration date
1 yr.	5 months	20 days	Unexpired portion of policy

$162.50 3-yr. premium ÷ 36 months = $4.5139 premium per month

$4.5139 ÷ 30 days = $.1505 premium per day

17 months × $4.5139 = $76.7363
20 days   × .1505 =   3.01
          Buyer's share $79.7463 or $79.75

When tenants pay rent in advance on the first of the month and title to the property is transferred on the eighteenth of the month, the buyer is entitled to receive an adjustment in his favor for two weeks' rent (using thirty days to the month). The seller is entitled to rent up to and including the eighteenth of the month and is obligated to account to the buyer for rent from the nineteenth to the first of the next month.

Problem Buyer purchases a single-family home that is rented for $350 per month, with the rent paid in advance the first day of each month. The transaction closed July 18. How much of the advance rent is the buyer entitled to?

Solution Seller is entitled to rent from July 1 *to and including July 18*.

Buyer is entitled to rent for twelve days (thirty days to a month).
$350 per month ÷ 30 days = $11.6667 rent per day
12-days × $11.6667 per day = $140.0004 or $140.00

Capitalization of income

The capitalization method of appraising real property will be discussed more in detail in Chapter 14. Under this method—capitalization of income—the market value is determined on the basis of the net income that a property will produce.

FIRST: Determine the gross annual income.
SECOND: Determine the annual expenses *exclusive* of depreciation and interest on the mortgage.
THIRD: Subtract the annual expenses from the gross annual income.
FOURTH: Divide the net annual income by the capitalization rate—the expected rate of return. The result should be the value of the property.

Problem Mr. Smith wishes to purchase a duplex and obtain an 8-percent return on his total investment. How much can he pay for the duplex and maintain an 8-percent return on his total investment if the property produces $150 per month per unit and has the following monthly expenses?

Taxes	$ 48.00
Insurance	3.50
Maintenance	24.00
Management	48.00
	$123.50

(123.50 × 12 months = $1,482)

$	300	Gross income per month
×	12	Months
$	3,600	Gross annual income
−	1,482	Annual expenses
$	2,118	Net annual income ÷ .08 capitalization rate = $26,475.00

Area problems

In computing the area in a rectangle or a triangle, the student should simplify the problem as much as possible. The formula for square footage in a rectangle is

Length × Width = Square Footage

Example

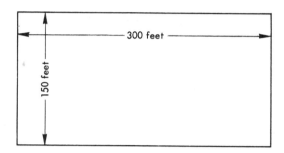

300 feet × 150 feet = 45,000 square feet.

Now let us consider a triangle. Examine the following triangle and determine the square footage within the triangle.

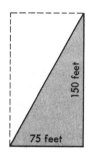

FIRST: Square out the triangle as represented by the dotted lines.
SECOND: Use the formula for determining the square footage in a rectangle.

75 feet × 150 feet = 11,250 square feet

THIRD: Divide by 2.

11,250 square feet ÷ 2 = 5,625 square feet in the triangle.

Most counties and cities have *set-back* ordinances. This type of ordinance prohibits the erection of a building or structure within a certain number of feet between the curb and the set-back line.

Problem   Jones Manufacturing Company wishes to build a 15,000 square-foot plant fronting on Industrial Way and Jones Avenue. Taking into consideration the thirty-foot set-back lines, how many lots must the firm buy?

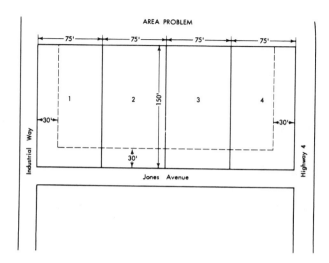

Solution

Lot 1: (75 − 30) × (150 − 30) or
    45 × 120 =   5,400 square feet
Lot 2: 75 × (150 − 30) or
    75 × 120 =   9,000 square feet

    Total, Lots 1 and 2   14,400 square feet

The firm needs 15,000 square feet; therefore, Lots 1, 2, and 3 will be needed.

CHAPTER QUESTIONS

1. A salesman sold a property for $36,000. His broker's commission was 6 percent, out of which the salesman was to receive 60 percent. How much was the salesman's commission?
2. Alice receives $150 per month on an investment. Her return is equal to 7.5 percent. How much money did she invest?
3. An apartment house cost $120,000 and returns a net income of $7,440. What percentage profit is made on the total investment?
4. An investor receives $273.75 per month interest. The interest rate is 9 percent. How much is the loan?
5. Fifteen lots remain in a subdivision and represent 16⅔ percent of the lots in the tract. How many lots were there in the subdivision?

MULTIPLE-CHOICE QUESTIONS

1. After paying a 6-percent commission, a property owner wants to receive $9,800 net. What must be the price of the home to receive this? (a) $10,425.53; (b) $1,042.55; (c) $9,800; (d) $9,990.

2. A man purchased two lots for $9,000 each and divided them into three lots, which he sold for $7,200 each. What was his percentage of profit, based on cost? (a) 10%; (b) 20%; (c) 30%; (d) 40 %.

3. A seller received $13,584 after deducting $140 escrow charges and a 6-percent commission. The property sold for (a) $12,700; (b) $14,200; (c) $14,560; (d) $14,600.

4. What would be the maximum number of 50′ × 100′ lots that can be created from an acre? (a) 2; (b) 4; (c) 5; (d) 8; (e) 9.

5. On a sale amounting to $12,300, a broker receives a 6-percent commission. The salesperson who obtained the listing receives 15 percent of the gross commission and the selling salesperson 45 percent of the gross commission. How much commission with the broker receive? (a) $642.80; (b) $442.80; (c) $295.20; (d) $259.20.

6. The depth of a 60′ lot that contains 1,080 square yards is (a) 160′; (b) 162′; (c) 70′; (d) none of these.

7. A seller is debited with $182 escrow fees and a 6 percent broker's commission. She receives a net amount of $12,280. What was the sales price of the property? (a) $13,255.11; (b) $13,257.45; (c) $13,450.11; (d) $13,455.

8. A broker secured a buyer who offered 12 percent less than the listed price of $27,750. The seller agreed, providing the broker would take a 4-percent commission. What amount of commission did the broker receive? (a) $651.70; (b) $654.20; (c) $976.80; (d) none of these.

9. Smith has a new loan in the amount of $13,000 which bears an interest of 6 percent and monthly payments of $95. What will be the amount due on the first trust deed after the first month's payment has been made? (a) $12,970; (b) $13,900; (c) $13,930; (d) none of these.

10. Broker Jacobs sold one-fifth of the Smith Ranch for $30,500, leaving Mr. Smith with 120 acres of land. How many acres were there of the land before the sale? (a) 640; (b) 160; (c) 150; (d) 320; (e) 240.

11. Peterson borrows $2,400 and agrees to repay the money in ten monthly installments with *interest in addition* at 9 percent per annum. The amount of interest on the second payment would be: (a) $162.00; (b) $18.00; (c) $180.00; (d) $16.20; (e) $14.07.

12. Broker Williams sold a home for $69,500 and the transaction closed December 2. The property taxes for the year 1975–76 had *not* been paid. The taxes for the year were $1,584. The seller's share of the taxes would be: (a) $660.00; (b) $668.80; (c) $783.20; (d) $729.00; (e) $800.80.

13. The buyer of a home assumes an 8½-percent loan with a current balance on June 1 of $34,000. The transaction closed on June 22. The interest that should be

charged to the seller is: (a) $186.61; (b) $196.61; (c) $340.00; (d) $176.61; (e) $166.61.

14. A seller has a three-year fire insurance policy effective August 7, 1980, on which she paid a premium of $189. Buyer agrees to take over the policy. Assume the transaction closes May 15, 1981. The buyer's share of the policy would be: (a) $48.65; (b) $140.35; (c) $155.35; (d) $160.00; (e) $181.42.

15. Buyer purchases a duplex (two units), and each unit is rented for $275 per month, with the rent paid in advance on the first day of each month. The transaction closes March 16. How much of the advance rent is the buyer entitled to? (a) $220.00; (b) $219.99; (c) $275.00; (d) $293.33; (e) $256.67.

16. Mr. Andrews wishes to purchase a six-unit apartment and obtain a 9-percent return on his total investment. How much can he pay for the six units and maintain a 9-percent return, if each unit rents for $200 per month and the expenses are 40 percent of the annual gross income? (a) $86,000; (b) $96,000; (c) $95,000; (d) $101,647.06; (e) $96,500.

17. A lot cost $5,000 and sold for $8,200. Based on cost, the percentage of profit is: (a) 43 percent; (b) 46 percent; (c) 54 percent; (d) 64 percent; (e) 45 percent.

18. Broker Kelley sells a home for $55,000, making the owner a profit of 25 percent based on the cost price of the home. The seller's purchase price of the home was: (a) $55,000; (b) $45,000; (c) $44,000; (d) $43,000; (e) $43,500.

19. In taking a listing on a home, Broker McCormick is told by the property owner that the monthly payments on the home are $266.01 per month, and of this amount $76.32 is interest at 8½ percent per annum as of May 1. The current balance of the loan on May 1 should be: (a) $9,574.79; (b) $11,874.59; (c) $10,774.59; (d) $12,674.59; (e) $10,674.59.

20. A lot that is 50′ wide and 150′ deep has a front setback of 20 feet and a 4-foot setback on the other three sides. How many square feet are there in the lot for building? (a) 3,912; (b) 3,800; (c) 5,292; (d) 6,292; (e) 4,292.

21. The price of a lot is $.35 per square foot. The lot contains a depth of 150 feet and 300-foot frontage. What is the price for the lot? (a) $15,750; (b) $14,750; (c) $16,750; (d) $13,750; (e) $12,750.

22. If a property has a fair market value of $60,000, is assessed at half that, and the tax rate is $5.75 per $100 of assessed valuation, what is the annual tax? (a) $3,450; (b) $1,725; (c) $34,500; (d) $17,250; (e) $2,507.50.

23. An investor bought four lots for $1,500 each. She divided these four lots into six lots and sold them for $1,400 each. What is the return rate on the *investment*?

(a) 10 percent; (b) 40 percent; (c) 12 percent; (d) 8 percent; (e) 45 percent.

24. A property purchased for $10,000 returned an annual gross income of 8 percent. The owner's only expense was 6-percent annual interest on a deed of trust of $9,000. What percent of return did the owner receive on his *equity*? (a) 8 percent; (b) 10 percent; (c) 20 percent; (d) 26 percent; (e) 32 percent.

25. An investor receives $132 income per month on an investment at a 9 percent rate of return. What is the amount of her investment? (a) $17,600; (b) $1,584; (c) $14,666.66; (d) $146.66; (e) $18,400.

ESCROW PROCEDURES AND TITLE INSURANCE

Almost all real estate sales transactions involve an escrow and title insurance. However, there is no legal requirement that an escrow be used, or even that title insurance be obtained. An escrow is used because it is for the benefit of the parties. Further, if a lender is involved, that lender will require the protection of an escrow as a condition of its loan. For almost the same reason, title insurance is obtained by the buyer.

Since the escrow agent normally orders and obtains title insurance as part of the escrow package, escrow will be discussed first. It is assumed that the parties have entered into a binding contract, since a binding contract is a condition to the creation of a valid escrow.

ESCROW PROCEDURES

The California Financial Code defines *escrow* as

> *. . . any transaction wherein one person for the purpose of effecting the sale, transfer, encumbering, or leasing of real or personal property to another person, delivers any written instrument, money, evidence of title to real or personal property or any other thing of value to a third person to be held by such third person until the happening of a specified event or the performance of a prescribed condition, when it is then to be delivered by such third person to a grantee, grantor, promissee, promissor, obligee, obligor, bailee, bailor, or any agent or employee of any of the latter.*

The California Civil Code states it in these terms:

> *A grant may be deposited by the grantor with a third person to be delivered on the performance of the con-*

dition, and, on delivery by the depository, will take effect. While in the possession of the third person, and subject to the condition, it is called an escrow.

The escrow agent, then, is a stakeholder. He or she is the agent of both parties until the escrow is closed and then becomes a trustee for documents and money until they are distributed in accordance with the instructions of the escrow.

Purpose of escrow

Assume a child wishes to trade a toy car for another child's marbles. As often happens, one child says, ''Give me the car; *then* I'll give you the marbles.'' The other child wants the marbles before parting with the car. To solve the dilemma, they go to an adult who supervises the transaction.

In effect, the preceding example defines a very simplified escrow. A neutral third person whom all parties trust agrees to carry out the instructions of the parties. Instead of trading marbles and cars, the parties are trading cash and sometimes notes for title to real estate. Further, a lender is often a party who requires certain conditions before releasing the loan funds.

The escrow, following the parties' specific instructions, accepts each party's consideration and gives it to the appropriate party only when all requirements are met. Further, and pursuant to instructions (and special training), the escrow usually also calculates prorations and obtains title insurance. The escrow also provides a clearinghouse for the payment of liens and refinancing and for computing prorations of such items as taxes and insurance.

ESSENTIAL REQUISITES FOR A VALID ESCROW

Essential requisites for a valid escrow include a binding contract between the buyer and the seller and the conditional delivery of transfer instruments to a third party. The binding agreement may be a deposit, a receipt, an agreement of sale, an exchange agreement, an option, or mutual escrow instructions of the buyer and the seller. Escrow instructions supplement the original contract, which may be any one of the accepted binding agreements, and in case of litigation, they are interpreted together whenever possible. If a conflict exists between the original contract and the escrow instructions, the latter constitute a subsequent contract and will therefore prevail over the original agreement. It is important that the original agreement be concise and contain all of the conditions binding on each of the parties, buyer and seller.

The conditional delivery of transfer instruments to a third party must be accompanied by instructions to the escrow agent to deliver the instrument, usually the grant deed, on the fulfillment or performance of the condition. The escrow agent must be neutral to the transaction. Before the delivery of the transfer instruments and the fulfillment of the conditions on the part of the grantee, the transaction is termed an "escrow."

Complete, or perfect, escrow

A complete, or perfect, escrow is one that contains all necessary instructions, instruments, and moneys, and reflects an understanding of all parties to the transaction.

Usually, to have a proper escrow, a valid and binding contract must be entered into between the buyer and the seller. Such contracts should contain an irrevocable deposit of documents or moneys or both with the escrow holder. When no such contract exists, the grantor may usually recover his or her deed from the escrow agent at any time before the condition is performed. The escrow agent exceeds his or her authority if he or she attempts to deliver instruments to the grant deed before the performance of the conditions specified.

ESCROW AGENT

No individuals may act as escrow agents in California. All escrow agencies must be licensed by the Corporation Commissioner of California. Certain exemptions to the law are made, however; these exemptions include real estate brokers, attorneys, banks, trust companies, savings and loan associations, insurance companies, and title insurance companies. Real estate brokers may escrow only the transactions in which they act as the broker, and attorneys are limited to those transactions pertaining to

fulfilling a client's account or estate. The real estate broker must maintain all escrow funds in a trust account, with the account subject to inspection by the Real Estate Commissioner.

Incorporated escrow agencies must be financially solvent. They must also furnish a surety bond in the amount of $10,000 and make an arrangement for bonding responsible employees. The amount of the latter will depend upon the volume of business conducted. All moneys deposited with the escrow agent must be deposited in a trust account. This account is exempt from attachment or execution of any personal creditors of the escrow agent. The agent must keep accurate records for the inspection of the Corporation Commissioner. The maintenance of these records must be done at the agent's own expense, and he or she must submit an independent audit annually.

The escrow agent may not pay any referral fee to anyone other than a regular employee of the company. Fees paid to real estate brokers, salespeople, or any other outsider sending business to the escrow agent is prohibited. Fees include any gifts of merchandise or anything of value.

ESCROW INSTRUCTIONS

An escrow must be confidential. Figures 13–1 and 13–2 are samples of the buyer's and the seller's escrow instructions. Only the parties to the transaction are entitled to information concerning the escrow. For example, if the seller is paying off a loan and the buyer is obtaining a new loan, the buyer is not entitled to know the terms and conditions of the seller's loan, nor is any relative of either party entitled to obtain information from the escrow agent without written permission of the party involved.

The agent is a disinterested stranger to the transaction. He or she must be impartial to the transaction and may not give legal advice. Advice on all legal matters should be referred to the attorney of the respective party. (Such advice would include information on how title to the property should be taken.)

An escrow agent may not exceed the authority granted him or her in the escrow instructions. He or she should see that unnecessary conversation is avoided; the instructions should be positive rather than negative, and they should be brief so as to afford the parties to the transaction little or no difficulty in interpreting them at a later date. Questions asked by the escrow agent should be pertinent to the instructions, and these instructions should be prepared while the parties asked by the escrow agent are present. Questions might include:

Who is the seller?
Is the seller married or single?

WESTERN TITLE INSURANCE COMPANY

SELLERS INSTRUCTIONS AND ESTIMATED CLOSING STATEMENT

ORDER NO. LA 12345 sl
DATE November 1, 1982

Herewith are the following:
☐ Deed to John M. Buyer and Louise S. Buyer
☐ Fire Insurance Policy No. 23-84-00 ☐ copy thereof
☐ Approved Copy of New Note from Buyers to Smiths
☐

☐ Tax Bills ☐ City ☐ County
☐ Request for Notices of Default
☐
☐
☐

TO BE DELIVERED ON THE FOLLOWING TERMS:

	DEBITS	CREDITS
Sale Price (includes $ -0- on *personal property)		$ 160,000.00
☐ balance of existing loan Northern California Savings & Loan	$ 79,233.27	
☐ paid direct to seller		
☐ ☐ 1st ☐ 2nd ~~1/3rd deed of trust~~ trust deed to seller***	40,000.00	
(CASH DEMAND BEING $)		
☐ Standard Policy Fee	582.00	
☐ Pay Taxes 1st Installment 1982-83	550.00	
☐ Pay Assessment		
☐ Termite repair work Pay upon receipt of Notice of Comp.	650.00	
☐ Commission 6% to Success Realty, Inc. Listing No. 1283	9,600.00	
☐ Drawing Papers $ 7.50 ☐ Notary Fee $ 4.00	11.50	
☐ Revenue Stamps Equity	89.10	
☐ Reconveyance Fee		
☐ Recording Reconveyance		
☐ Other Recordings		
☐ Prorate Fire Insurance		
☐ or return policy for further disposition if buyer furnishes policy		
☐ Prorate FHA Mortgage Insurance Premium		
☐ Balance in Loan Trust Fund		
☐ Prorate Taxes $550.00 for 1/2 year paid to 1/1/83		137.50
☐ Prorate Interest $20.358 from 11/1/82 to 12/15/82 Est.	305.37	
☐ Prorate Rent at $100 per day from date of recording.	2,500.00	
☐ ~~Pay Demand of~~ Hold for mutual instructions from		
☐ buyer and seller as to disposition.		
☐		
☐ Escrow fees	199.00	
☐		
BALANCE TO BE DISBURSED TO SELLERS ORDER	26,417.26	
Totals:	$ 160,137.50	$ 160,137.50

The subject premises are described in Report No. LA 62341 or as follows: Oak Arms Apartments, Lots 10 & 11, Tract 9016 as shown on map recorded September 26, 1978 in Book 912, page 18, Official Records of Santa Clara County, California.

***Said Deed of Trust to be subject to:

**Terms of Note: Payable $ 400.00 or more per month ☐ including ~~or~~ ☑ ~~plus~~ 12 % interest per annum with interest from ☐ Date of Closing or ☐ Estimated 12/15/82
First Payment Due January 1, 1983

*Title Co. assumes no liability as to transfer of personal property

REMARKS:

All prorating provided for in the above statement to be computed as of December 15, 1982 on the basis of a 30 day month. Fire Insurance policies, the premiums of which have been prorated, are to be transferred to the grantee in the above deed. Taxes are prorated on the basis of the latest available tax bill.

These instructions effective for 45 days, and thereafter until revoked by written demand on you by any of the undersigned. The undersigned hereby agree to pay all proper costs and fees, including any adjustments in prorating.

Received the above instructions and documents referred to on November 1, 19 82

WESTERN TITLE INSURANCE COMPANY

By ____________

X Donald B. Smith

X Sandra F. Smith
Sellers

Address 1062 California Avenue
Mountain View, CA. 95040

Figure 13–1

WESTERN TITLE INSURANCE COMPANY

BUYERS INSTRUCTIONS AND ESTIMATED CLOSING STATEMENT

ORDER NO. _LA 12345 sl_

DATE _November 1, 1982_

You are authorized to disburse the sum of $ _10,000.00_ which is handed you herewith and the sum of $ _21,837.16_ which will be handed you later in accordance with the statement below and deliver the deed of trust and note for $ _40,000.00_ also handed you herewith, when you can issue a standard form title insurance policy in the amount of $ _160,000.00_, insuring title to the property described in Report No. _LA 62341_ of //////// //

To be vested in: _John M. Buyer and Louise S. Buyer, his wife as community property._ . Subject to

1. The usual printed exceptions and stipulations contained in said policy.
2. Taxes that are not delinquent.
3. Covenants, conditions, restrictions and reservations of record.
4. Existing rights of way or easements.

5. _Approval of Preliminary_ ☒ Also herewith are the following: _Note and TD to sellers_
6. _____ Report ☐
7. _Approval of Termite_ ☐
    Inspection

	DEBITS	CREDITS
Purchase Price (includes $ _-0-_ on *personal property)	$ 160,000.00	
☒ balance of existing loan		$ 79,233.27
☒ deposit paid to _Success Realty, Inc._		10,000.00
☒ ☐ 1st ☒ 2nd ☐ 3rd new note and trust deed to seller		40,000.00
☐ Credit for Loan Proceeds from		
☐ Standard Policy Fee		
☐ ALTA Policy Fee		
☐		
☒ Recording: Deed $ _7.00_ Trust Deed (s) $ _7.00_	14.00	
☒ Drawing Papers $ _22.50_ ☒ Notary Fee $ _4.00_	26.50	
☐ Prorate FHA Mortgage Insurance Premium		
☐ Prorate Fire Insurance		
☒ New Fire Insurance Premium _First years premium_	325.00	
☐ Loan Trust Fund		
☐ Loan Charges: Lenders Fee $ Tax Res. $		
Insurance Res. $ FHA Mtg. Ins. $		
Interest $		
Assumption Fee, Northern Calif. S & L	683.00	
☐ Tax Service Fee $		
☐ Pay Taxes		
☒ Termite Inspection Fee _Bug Rite Termite Company_	75.00	
☒ Prorate Interest @ _$20.358 from 11/1 to 12/15/82_		305.57
☒ Prorate Taxes @ _$550 for 1/2 year. Pd. to 1/1/83_	137.50	
☐ Prorate Rent		
☒ _Transfer fee_	115.00	
☐		
☐		
☐ Amount Paid to Title Company		
☒ To be Received		31,837.16
TOTALS	$ 161,376.00	$ 161,376.00

*Title Co. assumes no liability as to transfer of personal property

REMARKS: _Item No. 5 of Preliminary Report being a deed of trust in favor of Northern California Savings & Loan with a loan balance of $79,233.27 with interest paid to November 1, 1982 at the rate of 9.25 percent._

You are hereby instructed to hold the sum of $2,500.00 from the seller for rent from date of record to December 10, 1982 to be released upon receipt of written instructions from buyers and sellers as to the deposition of said monies.

You are authorized to accept the statement of the seller as to the condition of rent payment and the payment of any premium of any insurance policy, which is being prorated. Fire insurance policies, the premium for which is being prorated, are hereby approved.

All prorating provided for in the above statement to be computed as of _December 15, 1982_ on the basis of a 30 day month. Taxes are prorated on the basis of the latest available tax bill.

These instructions effective for - - - 45 - - - - days, and thereafter until revoked by written demand on you by any of the undersigned. The undersigned hereby agree to pay all proper costs and fees, including any adjustments in prorating.

Received the above instructions and documents referred to on _November 1,_ , 19 _82_

WESTERN TITLE INSURANCE COMPANY

By _____

X _____

X _____
Buyers

Address _276 Bonnie Brae Court_
Cupertino, CA. 95014

Figure 13-2

Who is the buyer?

How does the buyer wish to take title?

What is the purchase price?

How will it be paid?

What moneys have been taken outside of escrow?

Will these be transferred to the escrow agent?

Have the parties agreed on how much money is to be deposited?

At the inception of escrow, will the buyer "assume" the loan or take the loan "subject to"?

Will normal prorations and adjustments (taxes, fire insurance, rent) be made?

Upon what basis will they be prorated?

Are leases involved in the transaction? If so, is the buyer familiar with the terms of the lease agreement(s)?

Will an assignment be made of such agreement(s)? Will water stock be transferred with the property?

Is personal property involved in the transaction? If so, is personal property transferred by a bill of sale rather than a conveyance?

In the case of personal property, will a chattel search be made? If so, will the escrow agent make such search? If so, how many years back?

The escrow agent will request an Offset Statement from the beneficiary, or lender, to check the terms of the loan as shown in the escrow instructions. If such statement differs from the escrow instructions given, the approval of the buyer must be obtained if there is to be a mutual assent to the contract. If a loan installment falls due during the escrow period, such payment should be made to the escrow agent so that the Offset Statement may be kept current. If the buyer is obtaining a new loan as a part of the purchase agreement, he or she should state that the closing of the escrow is contingent upon his or her obtaining a loan, and he or she should indicate the desired amount. The following statement may suffice as a part of his or her escrow instructions:

The closing of this escrow is contingent upon obtaining a loan in the amount of $20,000 on the following terms and conditions: A minimum loan in the amount of $20,000 payable at $179.95 per month including principal and interest at not more than 9 percent per annum, said loan to be for not less than 20 years. The execution of loan papers by me in connection with this escrow is my waiver of said contingency provided the loan is consummated.

The subject of a termite clearance or report should not be mentioned by an escrow officer. As a matter of practice in California, the buyer will usually request a termite report; if so, it is the responsibility of the broker to obtain it. An agreement between the parties is usually reached prior to escrow. It should be pointed out in connection with this report that it would be impossible for an escrow

officer, real estate broker, or other individual to give a termite clearance. The only way that a "clearance" could be obtained would be to tear down the entire structure piece by piece to make certain that no termites were in the building. The termite reports say, in effect, that there is no visible evidence of termites.

The escrow agent becomes trustee for each party to the transaction when all moneys and documents have been deposited in the escrow. The escrow agent is:

The buyer's agent for the deed and other items to which the buyer is entitled

The seller's agent for money and other items to which the seller is entitled

The lender's agent for the loan documents as per the lender's escrow instructions

The delivery of the deed and all other instruments must strictly comply with the escrow instructions.

TERMINATION OF ESCROW

An escrow may be terminated in one of the following ways:

1. Full performance by both parties
2. Mutual consent to cancellation
3. Revocation by one of the parties
4. Death or incapacity of one of the parties

When all parties to the escrow have fully performed and a proper distribution of money and instruments has been made, the escrow is closed.

The parties who entered into the escrow may, by mutual consent, cancel it. Certain costs and expenses will have been incurred, however, and it will be necessary for them to agree as to who will pay for these items. Third-party beneficiary rights may also be involved. For example, the real estate purchase contract and escrow instructions may have provided for a broker's commission. The escrow agent cannot ignore this fact.

One of the parties to the escrow may revoke the escrow agreement. When a valid and binding contract is in effect prior to escrow, an attempted revocation by one of the parties is ineffective. If no valid or binding contract existed prior to escrow, then the offer is revocable until its acceptance by the other party. When there is a breach of the contract by one of the parties not performing as agreed upon, the other party may withdraw and be discharged from his or her obligation. The escrow agent, however, may not legally concern himself or herself with controversies between parties to the escrow. When parties disagree and a distribution of moneys or documents cannot be made by the escrow agent, an action of *interpleader* to compel them to litigate among themselves may be obtained by the escrow agent.

If one of the parties to an escrow dies or is adjudged incompetent and a legal escrow has been established, it may not be revoked by either party during the time fixed for the performance of the escrow. When the person entitled to the benefits of the instrument performs within the time limit prescribed, he or she is entitled to receive the delivery of the deed.

When no binding contract exists prior to escrow and the grantor deposits a deed with the escrow holder with instructions to deliver it to the grantee upon payment of a specified price, no contract exists until the grantee deposits money and issues escrow instructions; thereafter, an offer exists, to be terminated only upon the death of the grantor.

After the grantor and the grantee have signed escrow instructions that result in a binding contract but the grantor has not delivered a deed to the escrow holder, then, should the grantor die, the grantee may not acquire title through the escrow. When the grantee is not in default on his or her obligations, he or she may acquire title by action of specific performance against the representatives of the grantor. If the grantee is successful, they will be required to deliver title to the property.

PRORATION OF CHARGES

Escrow customs will differ between Northern and Southern California, but in general practice, the distribution of charges will be as follows:

The seller is usually responsible for

1. Drawing instruments in favor of the purchaser, including the grant deed which passes title from seller to buyer, and any quitclaim deeds necessary to clear the title.
2. Documentary tax stamp on the deed.
3. Notary fees on instruments in favor of the purchase.
4. Title insurance policy fee; if the transaction takes place in Southern California (and in some Northern California counties), it is the custom for the seller to pay this fee.
5. Real estate broker's commission; legally, the broker has earned his or her commission when he or she has furnished a buyer ready, willing, and able to purchase property. As a matter of practice, however, real estate commissions are paid out of escrow through the seller's instructions.

The purchaser is usually responsible for

1. Drawing instruments in favor of the seller and, if financing is involved in the transaction, drawing instruments in favor of the lender. Such instruments would include a purchase-money trust deed to the seller or a trust deed to the beneficiary.
2. Recording fees in favor of himself or herself, including the recording of the grant deed giving constructive notice of the new ownership.
3. Recording fees for trust deeds in favor of the lender, or beneficiary.
4. Title insurance policy fee; if the transaction takes place in San Francisco County or San Mateo County, it is the custom for the buyer to pay this fee. (*Exception:* In the agricultural counties in the extreme northern part of the state, this fee is equally divided between the buyer and the seller.)
5. Notary fees on instruments in favor of the seller or the lender; such acknowledgments will accord the instruments the privilege of being recorded.

Buyer's normal costs on FHA or VA loans

Points (FHA)
1 percent loan fee (VA loans)
Appraisal fee (FHA: $400; VA: $350)
Credit report
Tax impounds
Insurance impounds
Interest on new-loan funding
Fire insurance premium
Tax service fee
Termite inspection fee (FHA only)
Title insurance policy
Recording grant deed and trust deed
Tax prorations

Sellers' normal costs on FHA or VA loans

Points
Transfer tax
Drawing and notary on grant deed
Termite work (also Inspection Fee on VA loans)
Disclosure statement fee (new loans)
Pay off total on any existing loans
Commissions

Checklist

After securing a written listing on a piece of property and having a client ready, willing, and able to purchase the property, the real estate broker must ascertain certain facts and make certain preparations before executing the contract of sale. They are

1. The date of the contract.
2. The name and address of the seller.

3. Is the seller a citizen of full age and competence?

4. The name of the seller's spouse,

5. The name and residence of the purchaser.

6. A full description of the property.

7. The purchase price, including the amount to be paid on signing the contract and the amount to be paid on delivery of the deed.

8. The kind of deed that is to be delivered—that is, whether separate, community, joint tenancy, or tenancy in common.

9. What agreement has been made with reference to any specific personal property on the property to be conveyed, such as gas ranges, heaters, machinery, fixtures, window shades, carpets, rugs, hangings, and TV antenna?

10. Is purchaser to assume the mortgage or trust deed, or take the property subject to it?

11. Do mortgages or trust deeds contain acceleration or restrictive provisions (alienation clause)?

12. Are there to be any exceptions or reservations in the deed?

13. Are there any special specifications or conditions to be inserted in the contract?

14. Stipulations and agreements with reference to tenancies and rights of persons in possession.

15. Stipulations and agreements with reference to any facts the survey would show, such as party wall and easements.

16. The items to be adjusted on the closing of the title.

17. The name and address of the broker who brought about the sale, and the amount of commission to be paid.

18. Agreements as to any liens, easements, assessments, taxes, covenants, restrictions, and so on, affecting the title, and who is to draw the purchase-money mortgage or trust deed and pay the expense thereof.

19. Is time to be the essence of the contract?

20. Any alterations to be made on the premises between the date of the contract and the date of the closing?

21. Name and address of escrow holder.

22. Who pays title and recording charges?

23. Is structural pest control report to be furnished, and who shall pay the cost for any recommended corrections or replacements?

24. The date of possession and adjustments of taxes, interest, and so on.

Upon the closing of title, the seller should be prepared to furnish

1. The seller's copy of the contract.

2. The latest tax, water, and receipted assessment bills.

3. The latest possible water-meter readings.

4. Receipt for last interest payment on mortgages or trust deeds, if any.

5. The fire, liability, and other insurance policies.

6. A certificate or offset statement from the holder of any mortgage or trust deed on the property showing the amount due and the date to which interest is paid.

7. Any subordination agreements that may be called for in the contract.

8. Certificate showing satisfaction of mechanic's liens, chattel mortgages, judgments, or mortgages that are to be paid at or prior to the closing of the title.

9. A list of the names of the tenants, amounts that are paid and unpaid, the dates when rents are due, and an assignment of unpaid rent.

10. An assignment of all leases affecting the property.

11. Letters to tenants to pay all subsequent rent to the purchaser and reaffirm conditions of tenancy.

12. Authority to execute the deed of the seller if acting through an agent.

13. Bill of sale of the personal property covered by the contract.

14. The seller's last deed.

15. Any unrecorded instruments affecting the title, including extension agreements.

16. Deed and other instruments that the seller is to deliver or prepare.

Purchaser should have or check

1. The purchaser's copy of the contract.

2. Certificate of title or policy of title insurance, showing title vested in the grantor.

3. Examination of the deed to see if it conforms to the contract.

4. Comparison of the description to see if it coincides with the description of the deed and a true description of the lot or property to be conveyed.

5. Examination of the deed to see if it is properly executed.

6. Sufficient cash to make payments required in accordance with the provisions of the contract.

7. Disposition of all liens that must be removed.

8. Names and details with reference to tenants and rent.

9. Assignment of unpaid rent and assignment of leases.

10. Certificate with reference to mortgages, showing the principal due and the date of the last payment.

11. Letters to tenants from seller reaffirming conditions of tenancy.

12. Authority if the seller acts through an agent.

13. Bill of sale of personal property covered by the contract.

14. The seller's deed.

15. An examination of the survey.

16. An examination to see if the policy or certificate of title shows any covenants, restrictions, or other matters affecting the title or the use of the property.

17. All bills for any unpaid tax, water, or assessments, and have interest computed up to the date of the closing.

18. The adjustments completed if called for in the contract.

19. An examination of purchase-money mortgages.

20. Any unrecorded instruments affecting the title, including extension agreements.

The professional broker's Ten Commandments for an escrow

First Read your preliminary report and consider each item. Be fully prepared to explain them to your client.

Second Read your escrow instructions word for word, and be assured they comply with the real-estate purchase contract.

Third Check all prorations, figures, and so on, never assuming your escrow officer is perfect.

Fourth Fully understand the fiscal tax year, debits, credits, impounds, and due and delinquency dates, so that this information will be easily assimilated by your client. (See Figure 13–3.)

Fifth Learn the differences in such terms as *alienation, acceleration, assume, subject to, demand* and *statement of condition.*

Sixth *Do not* deliver any buyer's closing papers to your escrow officer short of any money needed to close

unless you are willing to pay such a shortage out of your own pocket.

Seventh Check each signature for accuracy, as to middle initials and spelling, and have your client immediately correct any errors. Make sure *all* required papers are signed.

Eighth Always include clients' addresses and telephone numbers in the space provided by the escrow instructions.

Ninth Do not assure your customer that the title company or other escrow agency shall "do this or do that" without first clearing it with your escrow officer.

Tenth *Remember* that you are a "professional broker," so considered by the courts, and that the image you give the public is the image of the real estate profession.

TITLE INSURANCE

We now turn our attention to methods by which the buyer will be protected against receiving an unmarketable title. In California, title insurance companies are used exclusively for guaranteeing titles to property. In many other parts of the United States, an Abstract of Title, a Certificate of Title, or a Guarantee of Title is sometimes used.

An *abstract of title* is a summary of all pertinent documents in the chain of title to the property. To transfer title in a sale, the abstract of title is taken by the seller to an abstract company, which brings the document up to date. It is then turned over to the buyer, who takes the instrument to an attorney for examination. Upon finding no defects in the title, the attorney will give the new buyer a letter of opinion stating, in effect, that he or she will receive clear title to the property. No guarantee of title is made. If there appear to be defects, the attorney will call them to the attention of the buyer.

In some cases where the abstract company records are complete, a *certificate of title* may be given. This certificate states that the property is vested in the name of the present owner, and it will note certain encumbrances against the property. Again, no guarantee of title is made. The use of this certificate is limited today.

Title insurance policies

Under the title insurance policy used in California, the title company does more than just research and certify title to the property. It also *insures* that title to the owner. Under such an insurance policy, the title company agrees to reimburse the buyer for any losses that are suffered because of defects in the title. Such insurance also in-

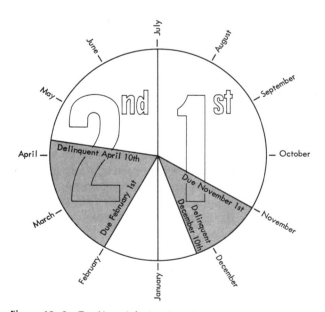

Figure 13–3 Tax Year: July 1 to June 30

cludes attorney's fees and other costs in clearing title or compensating for the loss of title.

The title insurance policy insures against defects in the title that can be ascertained from the county records. Equally important, title insurance policies also insure some risks not ascertainable from public records. The policies also insure against deeds and other documents obtained by fraud, forgery, duress, mental incompetence, minority, and other defects that can render documents invalid.

In California, there are two forms of title insurance available: CLTA standard form, and ALTA extended form. Figure 13–4 is a sample CLTA form.

CLTA standard form

The CLTA title insurance policy is the standard form obtained by buyers. It is also used by noninstitutional lenders, such as sellers insuring a deed of trust they took back as part of the purchase price.

This insurance policy is designed to cover the risks faced by most buyers. It covers forgeries and other such defects in documents. It also ensures that the interest insured (title) is fully vested in the buyer, subject only to the exceptions specifically stated in the policy. The policy protects against documents that are of public record. Thus, the policy insures against federal tax claims, easements, and other documents of record.

Exclusion   The CLTA standard form of title insurance does not insure against

1. Facts that are not of public record, such as unrecorded deeds of trust or grant deeds.
2. Facts that could be ascertained from a physical inspection of the property, such as rights of an adverse possessor or rights of a holder of an unrecorded easement by prescription.
3. Facts that are known to the insured but not disclosed in writing to the title company.
4. Governmental regulations (police power) of property, such as zoning, building-code violations, and setback line defects.

ALTA extended coverage

Institutional lenders seldom visit the property and are very concerned about mechanic's liens and other unrecorded liens having priority over their deed of trust. They feel the CLTA standard form policy does not offer enough protection. Therefore, the lenders obtain the extended coverage.

This policy covers all the items insured by the standard form policy. Additionally, it covers the first two exceptions we listed under the CLTA standard policy: facts not of public record and facts ascertainable from a physical inspection of property.

The ALTA extended policy contains two of the same exceptions found in the CTLA policy: It gives no protection against defects concerning the title known to the insured at the date the policy was issued but not communicated to the insurer; and it will not provide against governmental regulations concerning occupancy and use of the property.

TITLE SEARCH

In California, title insurance is used almost exclusively. A title search is a prepared summary of all pertinent documents that affect the title to a parcel of land. All material facts as set forth in the public record will be included. A preliminary title report, which precedes the issuance of the title insurance policy, will be given to the purchaser for examination. This report will show the current vesting of title, taxes and special assessments, deeds of trust, mortgages, easements in gross, and other liens. It will also include exceptions that the title insurance company may wish to make in the title policy.

The chain of title

The grantor conveys legal title to the property by executing a grant deed in favor of the grantee. The deed should then be recorded—providing the grantor's signature is acknowledged—in the county where the real property is located. The deed is cross-filed in the recorder's office under the names of both grantor and grantee. This system is known as the grantor-grantee system of indexing. In this way the vesting ownerships on a single parcel of land can be checked back to the earliest records kept in that county. Each deed recorded will show the legal description of the property, the acknowledgment, the date and time of recording, the easements, the restrictions, and other special covenants or conditions.

In order to simplify the system, title companies have developed a system of indexing by parcel of land. The student of real estate will recognize the difficulties that may arise from very common names like Smith and Jones. In a very large county there may well be one hundred James Smiths. When there is a question of liens that have been filed, title companies frequently use identification sheets filled in by the individual.

Purpose of the title search

A title search or examination is made to discover whether there are defects in the grantor's chain of title or whether clouds exist on the title that might prevent the grantor from granting a merchantable title to the purchaser. The

**TICOR TITLE INSURANCE**

Policy of Title Insurance

SUBJECT TO SCHEDULE B AND THE CONDITIONS AND STIPULATIONS HEREOF, TICOR TITLE INSURANCE COMPANY OF CALIFORNIA, a California corporation, herein called the Company, insures the insured, as of Date of Policy shown in Schedule A, against loss or damage, not exceeding the amount of insurance stated in Schedule A, and costs, attorneys' fees and expenses which the Company may become obligated to pay hereunder, sustained or incurred by said insured by reason of:

1. Title to the estate or interest described in Schedule A being vested other than as stated therein;

2. Any defect in or lien or encumbrance on such title;

3. Unmarketability of such title; or

4. Any lack of the ordinary right of an abutting owner for access to at least one physically open street or highway if the land, in fact, abuts upon one or more such streets or highways;

and in addition, as to an insured lender only;

5. Invalidity of the lien of the insured mortgage upon said estate or interest except to the extent that such invalidity, or claim thereof, arises out of the transaction evidenced by the insured mortgage and is based upon

    a. usury, or
    b. any consumer credit protection or truth in lending law;

6. Priority of any lien or encumbrance over the lien of the insured mortgage, said mortgage being shown in Schedule B in the order of its priority; or

7. Invalidity of any assignment of the insured mortgage, provided such assignment is shown in Schedule B.

TICOR TITLE INSURANCE COMPANY OF CALIFORNIA

By _(signature)_ President

Attest _(signature)_ Secretary

TO 1012 CA (10-84) California Land Title Association Standard Coverage Policy—1973

CAT. NO. NN00240

Figure 13–4 CLTA Title Insurance Policy

1. Taxes or assessments which are not shown as existing liens by the records of any taxing authority that levies taxes or assessments on real property or by the public records.

Proceedings by a public agency which may result in taxes or assessments, or notices of such proceedings, whether or not shown by the records of such agency or by the public records.

2. Any facts, rights, interests or claims which are not shown by the public records but which could be ascertained by an inspection of the land or by making inquiry of persons in possession thereof.

3. Easements, liens or encumbrances, or claims thereof, which are not shown by the public records.

4. Discrepancies, conflicts in boundary lines, shortage in area, encroachments, or any other facts which a correct survey would disclose, and which are not shown by the public records.

5. (a) Unpatented mining claims; (b) reservations or exceptions in patents or in Acts authorizing the issuance thereof; (c) water rights, claims or title to water.

6. Any right, title, interest, estate or easement in land beyond the lines of the area specifically described or referred to in Schedule C, or in abutting streets, roads, avenues, alleys, lanes, ways or waterways, but nothing in this paragraph shall modify or limit the extent to which the ordinary right of an abutting owner for access to a physically open street or highway is insured by this policy.

7. Any law, ordinance or governmental regulation (including but not limited to building and zoning ordinances) restricting or regulating or prohibiting the occupancy, use or enjoyment of the land, or regulating the character, dimensions or location of any improvement now or hereafter erected on the land, or prohibiting a separation in ownership or a reduction in the dimensions or area of the land, or the effect of any violation of any such law, ordinance or governmental regulation.

8. Rights of eminent domain or governmental rights of police power unless notice of the exercise of such rights appears in the public records.

9. Defects, liens, encumbrances, adverse claims, or other matters (a) created, suffered, assumed or agreed to by the insured claimant; (b) not shown by the public records and not otherwise excluded from coverage but known to the insured claimant either at Date of Policy or at the date such claimant acquired an estate or interest insured by this policy or acquired the insured mortgage and not disclosed in writing by the insured claimant to the Company prior to the date such insured claimant became an insured hereunder; (c) resulting in no loss or damage to the insured claimant; (d) attaching or created subsequent to Date of Policy; or (e) resulting in loss or damage which would not have been sustained if the insured claimant had been a purchaser or encumbrancer for value without knowledge.

10. Any facts, rights, interests or claims which are not shown by the public records but which could be ascertained by making inquiry of the lessors in the lease or leases described or referred to in Schedule A.

11. The effect of any failure to comply with the terms, covenants and conditions of the lease or leases described or referred to in Schedule A.

Conditions and Stipulations

1. Definition of Terms
The following terms when used in this policy mean:

(a) "insured": the insured named in Schedule A, and, subject to any rights or defenses the Company may have had against the named insured, those who succeed to the interest of such insured by operation of law as distinguished from purchase including, but not limited to, heirs, distributees, devisees, survivors, personal representatives, next of kin, or corporate or fiduciary successors. The term "insured" also includes (i) the owner of the indebtedness secured by the insured mortgage and each successor in ownership of such indebtedness (reserving, however, all rights and defenses as to any such successor who acquires the indebtedness by operation of law as described in the first sentence of this subparagraph (a) that the Company would have had against the successor's transferor), and further includes (ii) any governmental agency or instrumentality which is an insurer or guarantor under an insurance contract or guaranty insuring or guaranteeing said indebtedness, or any part thereof, whether named as an insured herein or not, and (iii) the parties designated in paragraph 2(a) of

these Conditions and Stipulations.

(b) "insured claimant": an insured claiming loss or damage hereunder.

(c) "insured lender": the owner of an insured mortgage.

(d) "insured mortgage": a mortgage shown in Schedule B, the owner of which is named as an insured in Schedule A.

(e) "knowledge": actual knowledge, not constructive knowledge or notice which may be imputed to an insured by reason of any public records.

(f) "land": the land described specifically or by reference in Schedule C, and improvements affixed thereto which by law constitute real property; provided, however, the term "land" does not include any area excluded by paragraph 6 of Part I of Schedule B of this Policy.

(g) "mortgage": mortgage, deed of trust, trust deed, or other security instrument.

(h) "public records": those records which by law impart constructive notice of matters relating to the land.

(Conditions and Stipulations Continued on the Inside of the Last Page of This Policy)

Figure 13–4 (Continued)

Schedule A

No. 123456	Date of Policy: July 21, 2018
Amount of Insurance: $ 195,000.00	Premium $ 787.50

1. Name of Insured

       John E. Homebuyer and Jane F. Homebuyer

2. The estate or interest referred to herein is at Date of Policy vested in

       John E. Homebuyer and Jane F . Homebuyer,
          husband and wife as joint tenants

3. The estate or interest in the land described in Schedule C and which is covered by this policy is a fee.

Figure 13—4 (Continued)

Schedule B

This policy does not insure against loss or damage, nor against costs, attorneys' fees or expenses, any or all of which arise by reason of the following:

Part I

All matters set forth in paragraphs numbered 1(one) to 11(eleven) inclusive on the inside cover sheet of this policy under the heading of Schedule B Part I.

Part II

1. General and Special County and City Taxes for the fiscal year 1985-1986, a lien not yet due or payable.

2. The lien of supplemental taxes, if any, assessed pursuant to the provisions of Chapter No. 3.5 (commencing with Section 75) of the Revenue and Taxation Code of the State of California.

3. Street Encroachment Agreement, upon the terms and provisions contained therein
    Dated: January 16, 1985
    Executed By: Sam E. Seller and Louise P. Seller, his wife
    Recorded: February 18, 1985 in Book E310 Official Records
                             Page 64, Official Records
    Instrument No.:   R61361

4. Covenants, Conditions and Restrictions as contained in Declaration thereof
    Dated: January 17, 1985
    Executed By: Homebuilder Development Company
    Recorded: January 21, 1986 in Book F286 Official Records
                             Page 126. Official Records
    Instrument No.:   T22220
    Said instrument does not contain express words of forfeiture.

5. Deed of Trust to secure an indebtedness of the amount stated herein
    Dated: July 21, 2018
    Amount: $156,000.00
    Trustor: John E. Homebuyer and Jane F. Homebuyer, his wife
    Trustee: Ticor Title Insurance Company of California,
                             a California corporation
    Beneficiary: ABC Bank, a corporation
    Recorded: July 21, 2018, in Book ZZ242 Official Records
                             Page 392
    Instrument No.:   TT21212

Figure 13-4 (Continued)

Continued

TO 1866 C (7-75) American Land Title Association Loan Policy-1970 with ALTA Endorsement Form 1 Coverage or American Land Title Association Owner's Policy Form B-1970 or California Land Title Association Standard Coverage Policy—1973

Schedule C

The land referred to herein is described as follows:

All that real property situated in the City and County of San Francisco, State of California, described as follows:

Lots 5 and 6, in Block 5, in the City of San Francisco, County of San Francisco, State of California, as per Map recorded in Book 11 of Miscellaneous Records Page 68 in the Office of the County Recorder of said County and State.

Figure 13–4 (Continued)

title search may be ordered and paid for by either the seller or the purchaser, depending upon their contract of sale and the custom in the particular area. The sales agreement will usually provide that the purchaser, at his or her option, may rescind the contract if the seller is unable to convey a merchantable title.

A title search may be ordered by a lender at the debtor's expense if a new loan is being placed on the property. The lender, in placing a new loan on property, will want to make sure that there will be no superior liens to jeopardize his or her security. Banks, for example, are only permitted to make loans secured by first mortgages and deeds of trust. The lender will want to be assured that the taxes, assessments, and water charges are current, because these are paramount liens on real property. The lender may further require that the new owner establish a loan trust fund account (impound account) to protect the loan. If the title search shows delinquencies, these can be disposed of in closing the transaction.

A title search may be made by a lender prior to the foreclosure of a mortgage or deed of trust. The same would apply to a mechanic's lien foreclosure. When inferior liens are discovered by the forecloser, he or she will be required to join these inferior lienholders in the action; otherwise the foreclosure action against the debtor will be defective. Thus, all persons having a title interest in the foreclosed property will be informed.

Lis pendens index

A *lis pendens* or *notice of action* may be filed by the plaintiff in the county recorder's office when legal action commences that may affect title to real property. The filing system or index is set up alphabetically according to plaintiffs and defendants. When the plaintiff's attorney files a lawsuit, a file number will be assigned to the case. All pertinent papers or documents, including a record of the disposition made, will be filed in the folder bearing this case number.

In addition to the names of the plaintiff and the defendant, the index will include the date of filing, a column for file numbers, and the file number of the action. Before title can pass to the grantee, the legal action must be settled, or the dismissal must be filed and the docket marked "canceled."

Mortgages and deeds of trust

The mortgage index should be checked to determine whether persons in the chain of title had a deed of trust or a mortgage on the property and whether this lien remains in force. The title examiner starts with the most recent trust deed or mortgage and works in reverse. A search may disclose a mortgage that had been paid off by a mortgagor without a proper release being recorded. Assignments may have been made by both the mortgagee and the mortgagor over a period of time. The validity of these assignments must be checked. A mortgage may still remain of record when the statute of limitations has run its course. Such an instrument is not ignored by the title insurance company.

Judgments

When an abstract of judgment is recorded, it is a lien on all the real property of the debtor within the county of recordation. The duration of the judgment lien will vary according to the statutes of each state. In California it extends over a period of ten years, and it can be renewed for an additional ten years. Thus, the title examiner must search the title back for at least ten years, because those persons who had title during this period may have had a judgment lien against the property that continued until the date of the current search. The judgments are entered alphabetically on the judgment rolls in the county clerk's office. These rolls indicate the judgment creditor, judgment debtor, time, date, entry of judgment, and file number. They will further indicate whether or not the judgment was satisfied.

Taxes—city and county

In most parts of the state it is difficult to examine the county records to determine whether the city taxes have been paid. It may not be so difficult when the city has arranged to have the county collect taxes in its behalf. The purchaser of property will sometimes require that the seller sign a statement that certifies that the city taxes have been paid in full.

Real property taxes are due and payable at a time specified in the state statute. Taxes and assessments are superior to all other liens; therefore, a search of tax records is necessary to determine whether the taxes are current or in arrears. The tax records will disclose a sale to the state and any existing penalties. These liens must be cleared before title passes; otherwise, they will carry over to the new owner. The tax rolls are usually found either in the tax assessor's office or in the county treasurer's office where the property is located. Indexing will normally be by the property description.

Probate court records

It may be necessary to examine the records of the surrogate or probate court when the searcher finds a break in the chain of title, or when an executor's or administrator's deed is found in the chain of title. Let us assume that in searching the title we find a deed with Susan Adams as the grantor but we find no deed conveying the title to Susan Adams. The probate files must be searched for the death record of a certain deceased Adams from whom Susan may have inherited the property. If no such death records are found, an invalid deed may exist and steps must be taken to perfect the title.

In those states that have an inheritance tax, it must be determined whether the tax has been paid. If there is no record of payment, an inquiry should be made of the tax department to determine whether any tax is still due or to receive a waiver from the state tax department.

Chattel mortgages and security agreements

Chattel searches are not usually a part of the title examination of real property. When the purchaser is in doubt about such liens, however, a chattel search may be in order. Often a search covering approximately the preceding six months will disclose such liens, although such liens are good for five years, unless extended.

The security agreement is used where personal property is pledged for a debt or for an obligation due. The financing statement is filed to perfect the security agreement. If the seller has purchased personal property and has attached it to the real property and a financing statement has been filed, the vendor of said goods has a lien therein that will run with the title. For example, the seller may have had stereo units, television, and intercom systems built into the real property, and the vendor may have his or her security interest protected.

Petitions in bankruptcy

Bankruptcy proceedings must be disposed of before a merchantable title to property can pass. Generally the same procedures apply as in judgments.

Preparation of title search

The searcher or title examination officer will keep notes on all conveyances or transactions that may affect the title to the subject property. When he or she has completed the examination, his or her notes will be organized into a brief history or abstract of the property, which will be concluded with a certification of the search with any exceptions set forth. This certification will contain an opinion of title whereby the searcher states that he or she has examined the title for deeds, mortgages, judgments, and so forth, and that no defects have been found except those listed in the certification.

CHAPTER QUESTIONS

1. What is the purpose of title insurance?

2. Distinguish between the *standard policy of title insurance* and the *American Land Title Association Policy of Title Insurance*.

3. Give the essential requisites for a valid escrow.

4. What does the term *prorate* mean with reference to the closing of a real estate transaction?

5. Define the *complete*, or *perfect*, escrow in the conveying of real property.

MULTIPLE-CHOICE QUESTIONS

1. The status of the escrow holder for *both parties* is that of (a) an employee; (b) an independent contractor; (c) a subagent; (d) a trustee; (e) none of these.

2. The standard policy of title insurance does not insure against (a) matters of record; (b) forgery; (c) mining claims; (d) capacity of the parties.

3. A real estate broker can handle an escrow (a) for anyone; (b) whenever he acts as the broker; (c) but must comply with all escrow laws including incorporation; (d) all of these; (e) none of these.

4. In the event of a dispute in escrow, the decision is left to (a) the escrow officer; (b) the real estate commission; (c) the city attorney; (d) a court of law.

5. Escrow companies normally base their prorations on a year of (a) 350 days; (b) 355 days; (c) 360 days; (d) 365 days; (e) 366 days because of leap year.

6. One might compare an escrow agent with (a) a mortgagee; (b) a stakeholder; (c) a mortgagor; (d) a beneficiary; (e) none of these.

7. The seller does not ordinarily pay for (a) the Documentary Transfer Tax; (b) part of the escrow charges; (c) recording the deed; (d) unpaid taxes; (e) any of the above.

8. The item that normally appears as a debit on the seller's closing statement is (a) prepaid taxes; (b) existing loan to be assumed; (c) selling price; (d) fire insurance.

9. The broker must inform the buyer and the seller in writing of the selling price of the property within (a) sixty days; (b) one month; (c) six months; (d) ten days; (e) broker may keep selling price a secret from either or both of the parties.

10. Which of the following statements is correct? Escrow cannot be completed or terminated (a) by mutual agreement of the parties to escrow; (b) when all terms of the escrow instructions have been complied with; (c) by the broker advising the escrow holder to cancel the escrow; (d) all of these are correct.

REAL ESTATE APPRAISAL AND PROPERTY OWNERSHIP

DEFINITION OF APPRAISAL

An appraisal is *an estimate or opinion of value as of a given date*. It is usually a written statement by a qualified appraiser of the market value or loan value of property, after his or her analysis of many facts. This analysis is affected by the appraiser's ability to assemble pertinent data and his or her experience and judgment. Professional appraisers have long worked together to standardize their methods and techniques.

It is not expected that real estate brokers and salespeople should qualify as expert appraisers, but they should be familiar with the theoretical concepts of value, the forces that influence value, and the methods by which values can be derived. This knowledge is essential in arriving at the highest and best use or the most profitable use of property. A prime corner location with an apartment house on it may very well be worth $250,000, but its value may be increased, for example, by as much as 50 percent if the owner puts it to the highest and best use by substituting a commercial building.

PROPERTY VALUE DEFINITIONS

Nature of value

The value of an item differs depending on the type of value sought. For example, *utility value* differs from *market value* and both terms differ from *cost*. Further, the purpose of the appraisal can determine the value placed on the property.

Utility value

The concept of utility value is a *subjective* value. It measures the value of the property to the owner-user. It includes amenities attached to the property. Amenities are extra comforts for enjoyable living, such as trees, location, view and design.

Market value

Market value is the price that a willing seller would sell for and a willing buyer would buy for, with neither being under abnormal pressure to buy or sell. Market value, as defined by the courts, is the highest price paid in terms of money that a property will bring if exposed to sale in the open market for a reasonable length of time to find a buyer ready, willing, and able to purchase the property with full knowledge of its use and capabilities. It is based on a "willing buyer" and "willing seller" concept. Market value is often referred to as *objective value* or *value in exchange*.

Cost vs market value

The cost of an item does not create value, and it should not be confused with value. Sometimes the cost may approximate value. However, frequently the cost is of historical importance only to the seller.

Cost is a measure of expenditure of labor, materials, or other sacrifices of some nature. *Price*, on the other hand, is the sum paid for something. *Value* is the combination of all factors, including present and anticipated enjoyment or profit.

Appraisal purpose

The purpose for which an appraisal report is being made will usually dictate the evaluation methods employed and will influence the estimate of value. The concept of value employed may be assessed value, condemnation value, liquidated value, mortgage-loan value, or fire insurance value. For example, the value placed on property by a fire insurance company will be based upon the replacement of the improvements alone and will not include the value of land. The assessed value, however, will include the value of both land and building. The law states that the tax assessor will assess at full cash value; in practice, however, the amount of assessment is usually significantly less than fair market value.

ESSENTIAL ELEMENTS OF VALUE

There are four essential elements of value, but none alone will create value. These elements include *utility, scarcity, demand*, and *transferability*. An item may be scarce, but if it has no use—utility—there will be no demand for it. Utility creates demand, but demand, to be effective, must be implemented by purchasing power. For example, a tract of homes in an overbuilt area may have utility, but since an oversupply of homes exists, demand will not be present.

Highest and best use

Value is based upon the principle of *highest and best use*. ''Highest and best use'' may be defined as that use which is most likely to produce the greatest net return over a given period of time. This is an important concept which appears frequently in appraisal.

The current use of the property is not always the highest and best use. Assume, for example, that a neighborhood has changed over time. If a single family residence is surrounded by commercial development, then residential use would not be the property's highest and best use.

Appraisal principles

There are four value principles that aid in understanding the nature of the appraisal theory. They are:

1. *Supply and demand*. If the number of homes (''supply'') remains the same, then the greater the demand, the more the price tends to increase.

2. *Conformity*. Properties that are similar to those in the neighborhood, tend to be worth more than those which are vastly different. A $200,000 house in a tract of $80,000 is worth much less than $200,000.

3. *Substitution*. The value of a property is by the value of similar properties. If a purchaser can buy an equally desirable house next door for $150,000, then he or she will not pay $180,00 for your house.

4. *Change*. The factors influencing value are in constant change. Yesterday's value may not be today's value.

FORCES INFLUENCING VALUES

Three principal forces influence real estate values:

1. *Social ideals and standards,* such as marriage rates, population growth and decline, birthrates, attitudes toward education, divorce

2. *Economic adjustments,* such as industrial and commercial growth or decline trends, wage levels within the community, natural resources, employment trends, wage levels, availability of credit and mortgage moneys, interest rates, price rates, and taxes

3. *Governmental regulations,* such as building codes, zoning laws, FHA and VA loans, credit controls, stock market controls, and health measures

4. *Physical factors* about the property, such as size, shape, location, soil conditions and climate.

FACTORS THAT INFLUENCE VALUE

Directional growth of the city The appraiser, real estate broker, or salesperson should be aware of the growth trends of the community. Properties located in the direction of growth will usually maintain their values or appreciate, if the growth is rapid and steady.

Location Location of property cannot be overemphasized. Factors to consider include ingress, egress, traffic patterns and counts, easements, and rights-of-way or alleys. A piece of land may have an excellent location but may not have access to the street and, therefore, would lose some of its value.

Utility The highest and best use to which the property can be put should be considered. Factors affecting the utility of the property will include zoning ordinances, building codes, and private and public deed restrictions.

Size The width and depth of property will determine to a large measure the uses to which a parcel of land can be put. Commercial property may front on an excellent boulevard, and yet the depth of the property may not be sufficient to permit its development. A fifty-foot lot may lose much of its value for a residence, since many of our home designs now require a wider frontage.

Shape A parcel of land cannot ordinarily be developed to its best advantage if it is irregular in shape. For example, a twenty-acre parcel of land measuring 660 × 1,320 feet but lacking a lot of 150 × 150 feet in one corner will lose some of its advantage to a real estate developer because it prohibits maximum yield in lots.

Thoroughfare conditions   The conditions of streets, their width, and traffic patterns will affect properties with street frontage. Value of lots in a residential subdivision, for example, will be affected by a main thoroughfare going through the subdivision. If the traffic is slowed down by curved streets, the value of the lots will normally increase.

Social atmosphere in residential districts   Many residential areas will be affected by prestige value. Lots in such desirable areas command a higher price than similar lots in other areas with less prestige.

Plottage   Plottage occurs when several parcels of land are brought under a single ownership to command a higher utility than could be found for smaller parcels. An older residential neighborhood may contain a substandard subdivision of lots twenty-five or fifty feet in width. The individual lots as they are may bring a low value, but by being brought under one ownership they will increase in value.

Conspicuousness   Conspicuousness refers to the publicity or advertising value of property. An oil company will put a service station only on a corner where it is conspicuous and accessible to traffic.

Grades   The topography of the land will affect value. Value will vary from level land, rolling hills, and hillside properties to steep mountainous land.

Obsolescence   Obsolescence may be caused by architectural design, construction, layout of rooms (in residential properties), outdated equipment, and so forth. Changes in the use of neighborhood properties may also contribute to such obsolescence.

Appreciation   Appreciation of property may be caused by city growth and increased costs of land. It may also result from rising labor costs or materials costs. In all cases it must be more rapid than physical and economical obsolescence to maintain value on the market.

Building restrictions and zoning   Restrictions and zoning may increase value or be detrimental to value. Assume that an area is zoned for R-1 (single-family residence) use, but across the street, the property is *rezoned* for light manufacturing use. This change may be detrimental to the value of residences in the R-1 zone. Property zoned R-1 may sell for $10,000 an acre, but rezoned to R-4, it may increase in value to $20,000 an acre.

APPLICATION OF VALUES

Residential property   In arriving at an estimate of the value of residential property, consideration is given to the lot and the present value of the building, allowing for depreciation, neighborhood analysis, and other factors such as assessed valuation and recent sales in the neighborhood. The value of the improvement may be estimated at the cost per square foot for replacing the building (allowing an adequate amount for depreciation). Consideration should be given to such items as the condition of the building, fixtures, workmanship, interior decorating, plumbing, heating, condition and type of the roof, lawn, shrubbery, and foundation. Raw land zoned for residential use is usually sold by the net acre.

Industrial property   Industrial property is usually sold by the square foot or by the acre. An industrial firm coming into the area will normally not want to buy more land than necessary to construct a building and provide adequate parking. In comparing industrial property sites, consideration may be given to the cost per square foot. Other factors to be considered are the topography of the land and the type of subsoil. Rock or other types of subsoil may make a site impossible to develop, or the ground may contain quicksand. Improper drainage could be an important factor. A chemical plant, for example, would give consideration to drainage in choosing a site.

Plottage value is important to the industrial developer, and consideration must be given to possible expansion. If the site is too small, it could be detrimental to future growth, but an area that is unusually large will have a lesser unit of value. The assistance of a competent engineer to plan the tract and plan layout is an advantage to the industrialist, for improper planning could cost his or her firm a considerable amount of capital.

Agricultural or farm lands   In the evaluation of agricultural or farmland properties, consideration should be given to the long-term trend of prices for crops grown or expected to be grown on the land. Factors to be considered will be the suitability of soil for crops, water supply (and the cost of producing such water), location of markets, labor supply, and climate conditions. Agricultural or farm land is usually priced per gross acre.

METHODS OF APPRAISAL

Three principal methods are used in appraising real property: (1) comparative analysis, or market data, (2) replacement cost, and (3) capitalization, or income. The skilled appraiser will consider all three methods and select the one most appropriate for purposes of the appraisal.

Comparative analysis, or market data

The comparative-analysis, or market-data, approach is particularly applicable to residential property. It is the simplest method of appraisal and the one most likely to be used by real estate brokers and salespeople. This method is based on the *principal of substitution*, which assumes that a willing buyer should pay no more for a property than the cost of acquiring a comparable substitute property. This method is an excellent check against the other two methods of appraising. A comparison is made between the subject property and similar properties as to time of sale, location, utility, and physical characteristics of the improvement.

The basic information needed will be actual sales and listings or offerings of similar or substitute properties. In each instance, consideration should be given to the date of sale, for it may be necessary for the appraiser to project an outdated price using criteria of the age, style, and size of the property. He must also give consideration to possible amenities. The conditions under which the sale was made are also important. If the sale was a depressed one, the sale price may not reflect market value, for market value is reflected by a willing buyer and a willing seller, both being informed as to market conditions and neither being under pressure to buy or sell. When the sale was financed with a very low down payment and a large second deed of trust, the sale price of the property may be inflated and adjustments may be necessary to arrive at the market value as distinguished from the market price. A further distinction should be made between listings for sale and actual sale transactions. When listings are used, they tend to reflect the upper limits of value, whereas offers to purchase tend to reflect the lower limits of value. Therefore, the appraiser should use caution in dealing with such figures.

The county assessor's office will disclose sales of property that have been recorded. Such information will include the date of recording, the legal description, and the amount of county revenue stamps placed on the grant deed. The county revenue stamps will give a hint as to the sales price. The state law decrees that documentary stamps, in the amount of 55 cents for each $500 or fraction thereof of the owner's equity, be placed on the grant deed. These stamps represent the total sale price less the amount of any existing loan that is assumed. The appraiser should use caution, however, because excess stamps may have been placed on the deed to mislead individuals as to the sale price. This practice is no longer legal. The California Association of Realtors provides an excellent form for a comparative analysis of substitute properties. See Figure 14–1.

Replacement cost method

Reproduction cost is interpreted by most authorities to mean the cost involved in reproducing an exact duplicate of the building under construction, with no changes or additions. If a building has existed for a number of years, it would be impractical to reproduce the same structure, same fixtures, and so forth. Therefore, this method might more appropriately be termed the *replacement cost method*.

The cost approach is an estimate of the sum required to replace a property in its present condition. It tends to reflect the upper limits of value, since people would not normally be willing to pay more than it would cost to reproduce the property or more than their ability to obtain an equally satisfactory property. The following four steps are involved in the cost approach to appraisal of property:

1. An estimate is made as to the value of land.
2. The replacement cost of all improvements is arrived at by one of the methods described in this section.
3. Existing depreciation subtracted.
4. The depreciated cost of the building is added to the value of the land.

Value of land An independent estimate must be made as to the value of land. This would normally be the highest and best use to which the property could be put. The value of the land should always be the current market value based upon the market-data approach.

Replacement costs The replacement cost of the improvements may be figured by one of several methods —a quantitative survey analysis, units-in-place method, segregated cost method, or square-foot cost method.

The *quantitative survey analysis* method should be used by experienced appraisers. Under this method, the building is broken down into its original materials, excavation of the site, and so forth. All materials are then priced, including the builder's overhead and profit.

Figure 14–2 shows many of the parts of a house that must be individually estimated.

Under the *units-in-place* method, the cost to erect or install a single portion of a structure is calculated. For example, the cost of a square foot of brick wall, a square foot of floor covering, a board foot of lumber, or a cubic foot of concrete in place is determined. These costs will include the costs of labor, overhead, and, usually, the builder's profit.

The *segregated cost* method provides for separate consideration to each of the major components of a building, but it does not require excessive measuring. Usually the total floor area and the linear feet of exterior walls are the only quantities required.

The *square-foot* and *cubic-foot* methods are used by

COMPETITIVE MARKET ANALYSIS
CALIFORNIA REAL ESTATE ASSOCIATION STANDARD FORM

PROPERTY AT 1979 Opportunity Street, Your City, California   DATE April 1, 1987

FOR SALE NOW	BED ROOMS	BATHS	FAMILY ROOM	1ST LOAN	LIST PRICE	DAYS ON MARKET	TERMS
2721 Hillside Avenue	3	2	yes	$102,400	$178,000	5	$ 75,600 CTL/CTNL
1850 Opportunity St.	3	2	yes	104,600	176,900	8	72,300 CTL/CTNL
1918 Wentner St.	3	2	yes	105,728	179,200	27	73,472 CTL/CTNL
2842 Hillside Avenue	3	2	yes	106,500	177,500	31	71,000 CTL/CTNL
1810 Wentner St.	4	2½	yes	109,200	210,000	114	100,800 CTL/CTNL
1416 Circle Drive	4	2½	yes	117,200	180,000	25	62,800 CTL/CTNL

SOLD PAST 12 MOS	BED ROOMS	BATHS	FAMILY ROOM	1ST LOAN	LIST PRICE	DAYS ON MARKET	DATE SOLD	SALE PRICE	TERMS
1963 Opportunity St.	3	2	yes	$110,112	$177,600	4	11/16	$177,500	CTL
2826 Hillside Avenue	3	2	yes	106,140	176,900	34	8/14	$176,000	CTNL
1239 Circle Drive	3	2	yes	107,980	177,000	28	3/21	$176,500	CTNL
1970 Opportunity St.	3	2	yes	124,270	176,100	8	10/16	$176,000	CTL
1974 Opportunity St.	3	2	yes	122,640	175,200	10	1/16	$175,200	CTL
2650 Hillside Avenue	4	2½	yes	125,200	174,850	18	2/14	$174,500	CTL

EXPIRED PAST 12 MOS	BED ROOMS	BATHS	FAMILY ROOM	1ST LOAN	LIST PRICE	DAYS ON MARKET	TERMS
1239 Circle Drive	3	2	yes	$109,200	$186,000	90	$76,800 CTL
1924 Opportunity St.	3	2	yes	107,400	190,000	120	82,600 CTL
1910 Wentner St.	3	2	yes	101,900	185,200	60	83,700 CTL/CTNL
2721 Hillside Avenue	3	2½	yes	102,600	187,000	90	84,400 CTL/CTNL
1850 Wentner Avenue	3	2	yes	103,500	192,000	120	88,500 CTL/CTNL
1960 Opportunity St.	3	2	yes	99,800	186,500	90	86,700 CTL/CTNL

F.H.A.—V.A. APPRAISALS

ADDRESS	APPRAISAL	ADDRESS	APPRAISAL
None			

BUYER APPEAL
(GRADE EACH ITEM 0 TO 20% ON THE BASIS OF DESIRABILITY OR URGENCY)

1. FINE LOCATION _Near schools and shopping_ 15 %
2. EXCITING EXTRAS _Landscaped to perfection_ 10 %
3. EXTRA SPECIAL FINANCING _No_ %
4. EXCEPTIONAL APPEAL _Neat and clean_ 5 %
5. UNDER MARKET PRICE _____ YES ____ NO 0 %
   RATING TOTAL 30 %

MARKETING POSITION

1. WHY ARE THEY SELLING _Purchased new home_ 10 %
2. HOW SOON MUST THEY SELL _60 days_ 5 %
3. WILL THEY HELP FINANCE . . . . YES 20% NO ____ %
4. WILL THEY LAST AT COMPETITIVE MARKET VALUE . . . . YES 20% NO ____ %
5. WILL THEY PAY FOR APPRAISAL . . YES 20% NO ____ %
   RATING TOTAL 75 %

ASSETS _Convenient location—beautiful landscaping_
DRAWBACKS _Backs up to shopping center parking lot - neighbors yard untidy._
AREA MARKET CONDITIONS _Active but extremely competitive. Homes offered with 3% of CMV._
RECOMMENDED TERMS _Buyers may assume, if they qualify, existing 9½% loan with approximate balance April 1, $98,200. Sellers will, depending upon buyers qualification, consider carrying back a promissory note secured by a TD in the amount of $25,000, 12% interest, for five years._

TOP COMPETITIVE MARKET VALUE . . . . $ 178,000.00
PROBABLE FINAL SALES PRICE . . . . $ 176,500.00

SELLING COSTS

BROKERAGE S.P. ($176,500.00)	$ 10,500.00
LOAN PAYOFF	$ 98,200.00
REPAYMENT PRIVILEGE	$
FHA—VA POINTS	$
TITLE AND ESCROW FEES IRS STAMPS RECONS RECORDING	$ 1,200.00
TERMITE CLEARANCE	$
MISC PAYOFFS: 2ND T.D., POOL, PATIO, WTR. SFTNR., FENCE, IMPROVEMENT BOND	$ 500.00
2nd TD from buyers	$ 25,000.00
TOTAL	$135,400.00

TOTAL $ 135,400.00

NET PROCEEDS $ 41,100.00   PLUS OR MINUS $ 500.00

For these forms address California Real Estate Association,
520 So. Grand Ave., Los Angeles 90017. All rights reserved.

FORM CM 14
REV. 9/64

Figure 14–1

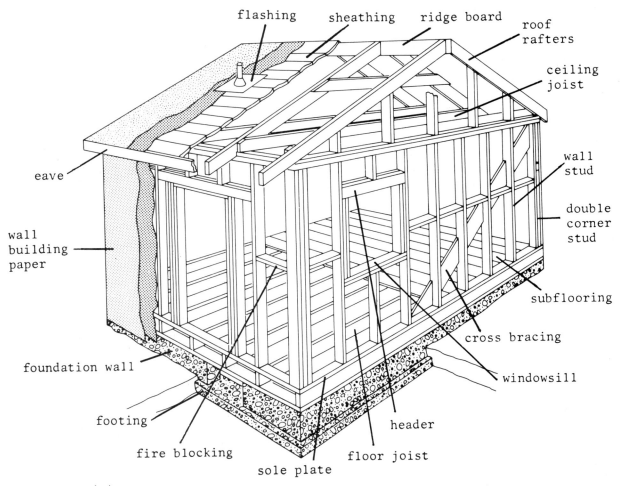

Figure 14–2 Parts of a house

most appraisers and are considered the simplest shortcut methods. In California it is customary to use the square-foot method for residences and to use the cubic-foot method for warehouses, loft buildings used for storage, and so on.

Under the square-foot method, a cost index supplied by a professional appraising firm such as Marshall and Swift (Los Angeles) is applied to the overall square footage of the improvement. It is usually graded as very good, good, fair, or poor. Actual cost figures are also obtainable from local contractors in the area; however, building costs will vary considerably from one area to another.

Depreciation The third step required in the cost approach is to determine the existing depreciation of the improvement. This amount is deducted from the replacement cost of the building to determine the present value (or book value). Difficulties are sometimes encountered in correctly estimating the depreciation on older prop-

erties. These estimates require a good deal of skill, experience, and judgment on the part of the appraiser.

The types of depreciation and methods of calculating such depreciation are discussed later in this chapter.

Combine land and building The final step is to combine the appraised value of the building to the appraised value of the land.

Example Find the appraised value of a 1700 square foot home in Sonoma County resting on a 21,000 square foot lot. Assume such homes are worth $60 per square foot new, and the home has $10,000 in accrued depreciation. Finally, land is worth $1 per square foot. The property is worth $110,000 calculated as follows:

Land (21,000 × $1) =	$ 21,000
Building	
1700 × $60	= $102,000
Depreciation	= − 10,000
Value	= $ 92,000
Appraised Value	= $113,000

Income (capitalization) method

Under the capitalization, or income, method, the market value is determined on the basis of the income that a property will produce. This method is particularly applicable to income-producing properties, such as apartment houses and commercial buildings. In determining the value of income-producing property, the progressive steps are:

1. The net annual income of the property is determined by making proper allowances for vacancies, collection losses, taxes, insurance, maintenance and management, and a reserve for replacement of equipment and furnishings prior to the end of their estimated economic life.

2. An appropriate capitalization rate or present-worth factor is selected. The rate selected will be the actual rate that investors demand to be attracted to such an investment and will also depend upon the mortgage-money market and interest rates in general.

3. The final step is to divide the net income by the capitalization rate. The following example may be helpful in understanding this process:

Example

An eight-unit apartment house, five years old. Each apartment leased for $100 per month.

$8 \times \$100 = \$800$ per month
or $\$800 \times 12 = \$9,600$ per year

10% vacancy factor $= \$960$ per year

$9600.00   Gross scheduled income
$-960.00   Proven vacancy factor
$8640.00   Effective gross income (adjusted for vacancy factor)

Annual expenses		
	Property Taxes	$1,640.00
	Maintenance	501.00
	Utilities	180.00
	Insurance	175.00
	Management	960.00
		$3,456.00

$8,640.00   Gross annual income
$- 3,456.00   Annual expenses
$5,184.00   Estimated net income

Capitalization rate: 8%

$$\frac{\$5,184.00}{.08} = \$64,800.00 \text{ Estimated value.}$$

Note   The higher the capitalization the lower the value of the property. Lower capitalization rates yield higher property values. If the estimated net income of property is $10,000, then:

Capitalization Rate	Value of the Property
8 %	$125,000
10 %	$100,000
12 %	$ 83,333

Gross multipliers

Many of our real estate transactions deal with the selling of older or middle-aged residential property. Therefore, the real estate broker or salesperson should understand the gross multiplier method of appraising, which is based upon the relationship between rental value and sale price of comparable properties. This is a "rule of thumb" method whereby we say that a certain type of property is worth 100 to 130 times its gross monthly income. (To make a valid comparison of older residential property to income property, a comparison of *like kind* must be selected on the rental market.)

Gross multipliers may also be used to compare income-producing properties. The gross multiplier in such cases is determined by dividing the gross monthly income into the actual sale price of income-producing units that have sold. The following illustration shows the value of this method:

Property	Sold at		Gross monthly income		Gross multiplier
A	$175,000	+	$1,750	=	100
B	$190,000	+	$2,000	=	95
C	$165,000	+	$1,700	=	97
D	$159,000	+	$1,390	=	114
			$6,840		406

$\frac{101.5}{4)\,406}$ = Average Gross Multiplier

The subject property of our appraisal has a gross monthly income of $1,690.

Gross monthly income $1,690 $\times$ 101.5 = $171,535.00 estimated value. This *rule of thumb* is not a substitute for a more complete appraisal.

THE APPRAISAL PROCESS

The appraisal process is divided into five steps:

1. Definition of problem
2. Preliminary survey
3. Collection of data
4. Analysis of data
5. Writing of report

Definition of problem

The real property to be appraised should be properly identified. The mailing address of the property, including the city and the state, should be given. A formal appraisal report will also include the complete legal description, whether it be a lot and block, tract, metes and bounds, or government survey description. The description will include the county where the property is located.

The purpose of the appraisal should be clearly stated. Is the property to be appraised a vacant lot? A single-family residence? A multiple-family residence? What interests are to be appraised? (In appraising property, the rights of ownership are appraised, not merely the physical land itself or the improvements.) Is a fee simple ownership being appraised with an easement across the property? Are we asked to determine the lessor's or the lessee's interest?

In identifying the property, the purpose and function of the valuation will determine the types of information needed in the appraisal process. Are we appraising a home for its market value or for mortgage-loan purposes? An appraiser may be asked to appraise property for insurance purposes or for condemnation proceedings, among other reasons. If the appraisal is being made for insurance purposes, only the improvements on the land will be considered. Thus, the insured value will be quite different from the market value, which would include both improvements and land.

Preliminary survey

The preliminary survey will include the highest and best use to which the property may be put. The appraiser should consider the present improvement on the site. Is it a proper improvement? In making a neighborhood analysis, the appraiser may discover that the highest and best use for the subject property under consideration is not single-family residential income use. If the property being appraised is a single-family unit, emphasis will be placed on the comparative-analysis, or market-data, approach. In a multiple-family unit, major emphasis will be placed upon the capitalization, or income, approach.

Collection of data

The value of property will depend upon utility, supply, and demand, together with the purchasing power of a given community. Data needed by the real estate appraiser will include population trends, income levels, and employment opportunities. General data may be obtained from various governmental publications, newspapers, and magazines. Regional data may be obtained from governmental agencies and regional commissions. Some of the larger banks publish valuable monthly reports on business conditions, such as the *Federal Reserve Bulletin.* Much community data may be obtained from local chambers of commerce, planning commissions, city councils, lending institutions, and boards of Realtors. Neighborhood data, on the other hand, may be obtained from personal inspection and from Realtors and builders active in the area. Important data will include growth trends in the community, percentage of increase in population, age and appearance of the neighborhood, planned developments, and proximity of the subject property to schools, churches, business, recreation, and the like. Data concerning substitute properties may be obtained from reports on sales and listings. These will be available to the appraiser or the Realtor from the assessor's records, the county recorder's office, property owners in the neighborhood, multiple-listing associations, and title insurance companies. The most accurate source of information will probably come from the Realtor's files and the multiple-listing association.

Analysis of data according to selected value

The data so collected are now put to use and analyzed according to the approach to value the appraiser has selected.

The appraisal report

When the appraiser arrives at his or her final opinion of value from the data collected, his or her reasons for reaching those conclusions are reported. The form of report used will depend upon the type of property and the needs or desires of the client.

Letter report This is the type of report used when the client is familiar with the area and supporting data are not needed. A letter is written giving a brief description of the property, the purpose of the appraisal, the date and estimate of value, and the signature of the appraiser.

Short form report This report is normally used by lending institutions and generally consists of a check sheet to be filled in by the appraiser. It includes pertinent data on the property and will vary from one to five pages, depending upon the client.

Narrative report This is a complete, documented appraisal report that includes all pertinent information about the property, as well as reasons and computations for value conclusions. It is written for court cases and for clients not in the area who need detailed information. The report includes maps, pictures, charts, and plot plans.

DEPRECIATION

Depreciation may be defined as the loss of value from any cause. Loss of value is brought about by physical deterioration and functional or economic obsolescence of the structure. Depreciation occurs only on the improvement. Land does not depreciate. The principal forces or influences are often grouped under three major headings:

1. *Physical deterioration,* which may result from
   a. Wear and tear from use of improvements
   b. Deferred maintenance or neglected care
   c. Dry rot, termites, or fungus
2. *Functional obsolescence,* which may result from
   a. Utility loss, which is inherent in the property itself
   b. Poor architectural design, such as high ceilings, undersized garage, inadequate number of bathrooms
   c. Inadequate number of modern facilities or lack of modern facilities
   d. Out-of-date equipment
3. *Economic or social obsolescence,* which may result from
   a. Misplacement of improvements, improper zoning, or legislative restrictions
   b. Lack of supply or demand
   c. Change of locational demand

It has been said that everything that man creates moves toward its "deterioration year" from the first day of its creation. Certain depreciation that takes place, however, may be deferred. The owner may repaint, remodel, or replace components of the building (such as the roof) and thereby defer some of the depreciation.

Accrued depreciation, the property loss in value that has already occurred, is considered in the cost approach to value. Future depreciation, the property loss in value that will occur at some time in the future, is considered in the income approach to value.

Accrued depreciation

Let us now turn to methods of estimating accrued depreciation. The first method is referred to as the *straight-line method.* This method is based on depreciation tables that have been developed to reflect age-life experience and the depreciation of improvements, assuming average care and maintenance. The age-life appraisal concept is based on tables recommended by the Internal Revenue Service. The tables are available through its office.

For example, if a building has a total economic life of forty years, it would take 2.5 percent depreciation per year to depreciate the building completely. If, to replace the building, it would cost $50,000 and the estimated economic life was forty years, or 2.5 percent per year, $1,250 would be charged for each year of actual age of the building. This is sometimes referred to as chronological age (the actual number of years that the building has been in existence). The straight-line method of depreciation has been used by the Internal Revenue Service, and it is perhaps the one most easily understood by laymen. It is by far the easiest to calculate of the various methods used.

This method does not take into account the actual physical condition of the building. Nor does it consider economic conditions affecting the property, such as zoning and legislative actions. In actual practice, as is true with an automobile, a building does not depreciate at a given percentage each year. The highest percentage of the depreciation occurs during the early life of the building.

A second method used to calculate depreciation is called the *observed condition method.* The accrued depreciation is determined by establishing the cost of making all needed repairs to correct curable physical deterioration and functional obsolescence, plus the estimated loss in value due to any curable physical deterioration and functional obsolescence. The deficiences inside and outside the structure are observed, and their cost to cure is calculated. The *cost to cure* is the actual amount of accrued depreciation that has taken place. Certain functional obsolescence, however, may not be cured, as with such items as poor room arrangements or outdated construction materials. Functional obsolescence is measured by calculating the loss in rental value due to the condition of the property. Functional obsolescence due to outdated plumbing fixtures, lighting fixtures, or kitchen equipment is determined and assigned a dollar value.

A third method for estimating accrued depreciation is called the *building residual method.* This is a technical approach used by professional appraisers. Under this approach, the land is valued separately, and its annual net return is deducted from the estimated annual net return of the property, including land and building. The balance of the income is then attributed to the building. This amount is divided by the capitalization rate. The depreciation figure is the difference between the residual value of the building and the value of a new structure of similar type.

Accrual depreciation

Accrual depreciation, also called future depreciation, is the loss of value to a building that has not yet occurred but that will occur sometime in the future. Future depreciation occurs annually over the economic life of the improvements and is a deduction from annual income.

This amount, set aside annually, must provide for the return of the value of the entire capital investment over the remaining economic life of the building. Future depreciation may be measured by three different methods.

Under the *straight-line method* of depreciation, a percentage is deducted each year over the estimated economic life of the improvement to fully replace the capital investment. This method was described earlier in the chapter.

The *sinking-fund method*, sometimes referred to as the reinvestment method, assures the recapture of the investment in the improvement by setting aside a certain amount each year and investing it in a sinking fund or in an account that accumulates compound interest. At the end of the economic life of the improvement the fund will equal the total amount of capital invested. Amortization tables are available to the appraiser to determine the amount that must be set aside each year to reach a given dollar amount at the end of any given period of time; thus, under this method, we are dealing with the present value of dollars.

The declining-balance methods—200 percent, 150 percent, and 125 percent—are also known as accelerated methods of depreciation. The methods are explained in Table 14–1. These accelerated methods allow for a greater amount of depreciation to be taken during the early years of ownership, when the investor has laid out the initial investment of capital. Salvage value must be considered under straight-line depreciation, but it is not deducted under these methods. No matter what method is used, improvements should not be depreciated below reasonable salvage value. The following is an illustration of the four methods just discussed:

Cost of improvement $100,000
Estimated economic life: 50 years
(*Economic life* may be defined as the remaining useful life of the improvement.)

DEPRECIATION AND INCOME TAX

The current income tax laws and regulations are far too complex and detailed for coverage in this text. However, a very brief notation of taxes is warranted. A professional accountant or an attorney specializing in taxation should be consulted when questions concerning tax arise.

In 1981 President Reagan signed the *Economic Recovery Tax Act* (ERTA) into law, which changed many of the tax laws affecting real estate, especially depreciation.

Then in 1986, President Reagan signed the *Tax Reform Act of 1986*. This Act is the first major redesign and comprehensive overhaul of the internal revenue code since 1954.

Depreciation before 1981

Because the pre-1981 depreciation methods are so thoroughly ingrained in many people's minds, the pre-1981 system needs review. By understanding pre-1981 methods, it is easier to see how the new laws have changed existing taxation. Also, the old laws still apply for any property acquired before 1981. The old laws also apply to property acquired by a tax-free ("IRC 1031") exchange of property held by the taxpayer before the year 1981.

All property purchased before 1981 was depreciated based on the improvement's *useful life*. The useful life was the time during which the property was estimated to be useful to the taxpayer. The time was selected by the taxpayer, usually, twenty to thirty years for wood-frame buildings and, generally, thirty to forty years for cement and steel buildings.

The useful life divided by 100 percent provided the straight-line depreciation allowed per year. Thus, a twenty-year-old building depreciated 5 percent per year.

There were four methods of accelerated depreciation

Table 14–1 A Comparison of Accelerated Methods of Depreciation

Year	Straight-line (2%)	125% (1¼ × straight-line)	150% (1½ × straight-line)	200% (2 × straight-line)
	$100,000	$100,000	$100,000	$100,000
1	2,000	2,500	3,000	4,000
	98,000	97,500	97,000	96,000
2	2,000	2,438	2,910	3,840
	96,000	95,062	94,090	92,160
3	2,000	2,377	2,823	3,686
*Book Value	$ 94,000	$ 92,685	$ 91,267	$ 88,474

Book value is an accounting term. The book value of an improvement is cost less the amount of depreciation that has been taken to date.

available, depending on the type of property: 125 percent, 150 percent, 200 percent, and sum-of-the-years-digits method.

Depending on the type of property involved, only certain accelerated percentages could be used. New residences were 200 percent; used residences with useful lives of at least twenty years was 125 percent, new nonresidential property was 150 percent, and all other real property was limited to straight-line depreciation.

If you used accelerated depreciation, then when you sold the property you faced special tax problems. All depreciation taken in excess of (over the amount allowed by) straight-line depreciation was "recaptured." That is, the excess was taxed as ordinary income.

If straight-line depreciation would have yielded 30 percent ($300,000) depreciation, but you took 40 percent ($400,000) by accelerated methods, then the extra 10 percent ($100,000) depreciation would be taxed as ordinary income. The rest of the gain on the sales price would be taxed as capital gains.

Depreciation in 1981 and after

The new laws made several drastic changes in depreciation methods. The 1981 tax laws established the Accelerated Cost Recovery System (ACRS). Under ACRS, all four methods of accelerated depreciation were eliminated and were replaced with one method, the 175 percent method. Useful life was abolished. Real property could be depreciated over eighteen, thirty-five, or forty-five years, which means almost everyone would select eighteen years.

Congress has frequently changed the depreciation laws. The past history of tax reform efforts means there will likely be many future changes in depreciation after the publication date of this book.

Since 1987 real property can no longer be depreciated on a 15, 18 or 19 year basis. All newly acquired real estate must be depreciated over 27.5 years for residential property and 31.5 years for commercial and industrial real estate, on a straight line basis. Further, the concept of long-term capital gains has been repealed, and all such gains are taxed as ordinary income.

Therefore, be sure to check the latest editions of the Internal Revenue Code to determine the laws on depreciation. (It should be noted, however, that the appraiser can use any depreciation he or she desires. However, for income tax purposes, the IRS regulations control.

Many accountants question the advantage of ever taking accelerated depreciation under the new laws.

COMMERCIAL PROPERTY

Appraising, tax aspects of real estate, and investments are complex subjects and should be studied in separate courses. Only a summary of each is proper in real estate principles.

Consider the following illustration. Assume you purchase a six-unit apartment for $100,000 and each unit rents for $200 per month.

Gross annual income	*$14,400.00*
Vacancy factor (5 percent)	*720.00*
Effective gross income	*13,680.00*
Less operating expenses	*5,040.00*
Estimated net income	*8,640.00*
Less payments on first trust deed	*8,056.80*
$80,000, 9 percent, 25 years	
(interest plus principal $671.40	
per month)	
Estimated spendable income	*$ 583.20*

For tax reporting purposes the first year:

Estimated net income		*$ 8,640.00*
Less: interest on first trust deed		
(approx.)	*$7,150*	
Depreciation (straight line)	*$4,772*	*$11,872.00*
Land $15,000		
Building $85,000		
Economic life, 18 years		
Estimated Tax Loss, first year		*$ 3,232.00*

A key factor for any successful investment is a proper accounting system so that all expenditures may be accounted for. The following is a list of various types of expenses; however, the investor should let an accountant handle his or her books if possible.

Annual Fixed Charges

Real property tax
Personal property tax
Insurance

Operating Expenses

Electric
Water
Fuel
Rubbish
Hauling
Advertising
Auditing and legal

Maintenance Expenses

Building improvements
Personal property (furniture)
Yard and ground care
Swimming pool service

Reserve for Replacement

Building components (roof)
Personal property

Management

Residential manager's apartment
Professional management
Janitor service

Sundry Expenses

Brooms
Mops
Soap
Brushes
Light bulbs, and so on

RESIDENTIAL PROPERTY

Most residential property is used for single family homes, and most homes are purchased for occupancy rather than investment. People also purchase condominiums, town houses and mobile homes as alternatives to single family residences.

Buy vs rent

Of course there are advantages and disadvantages to purchasing a home. Purchasing a home provides you with an appreciating asset, some tax write-offs, freedom in using and improving the property. Conversely, the initial costs are significant, your equity is tied up in a non-income producing asset, it can be expensive and time consuming to sell, and upkeep costs are significant and generally increasing.

Another benefit of homeownership concerns the use and postponement of capital gains. If you sell your home and buy another one within two years, and the new home is of equal or greater cost then the adjusted sales price of the old home, all capital gains tax is deferred.

If when you sell the home, you or your spouse is over age 55 and you have lived in the home for three of the last five years, you can exempt up to $125,000. in capital gains. This over age 55 exemption is only available once in your lifetime.

Renting has its own benefits and disadvantages. Renting requires minimal initial outlay, lower monthly payment and upkeep, greater mobility, and less responsibility. However, rents can be raised at the whim of the landlord in most communities, you have no guaranties of renewing your lease, you acquire no equity in the property, you receive only nominal tax relief, and your use of the property is restricted.

Assuming you can qualify for a loan, the decision about home ownership often centers around two major questions. The first is how long you plan to remain in one location. As a general rule brokers suggest you need to stay at least three to five years in a home before the property's appreciation in value exceeds the purchasing costs and the sales expenses. Secondly, you need to balance the appreciation and tax benefits of home ownership with the after tax return you could receive with your money in other investments.

Types of homes

Assuming you are purchasing a home it is important to know the type of homes available. One story homes are easier to maintain. Two story homes have lower per square foot costs, but require maintenance and the inconvenience of stairs. Split level homes that fit into hills or sloping land generally cost more to build than other residences.

Design

Consumers should know (and real estate licensees *must know*) the fundamentals of home construction and design. In keeping with the Chinese proverb that "One good picture is worth a thousand words," this section is based largely on diagrams (Figures 14–3 and 14–4). Study these until you are familiar with the terms used.

Construction

Real estate salespersons and brokers must be familiar with the basic construction of homes. Purchasers generally benefit from understanding basic home construction. Again, most of this section will be explained through pictures.

Property investigation

In selecting a home many factors need to be considered. Table 14–2 is from the Federal Housing Administration and used in evaluating homes. It can serve as a valuable guideline to assist you in planning the evaluation of a home, or to assist you in developing your own checklist.

MOBILE HOME

A mobile home is designed as a vehicle containing up to two dwelling units without a permanent foundation. As such it is not and should not be called a trailer.

Some of the advantages of mobile homes include their lower prices as compared to single family residences, transportability of such homes, and depending on the park, better protection and less yard upkeep. Further, financing is now available through most lenders. Con-

Continued on page 215

Figure 14–3   Architectural Styles

Colonial   Colonial, Early Cape Cod, and California Cape Cod are usually small homes with symmetrical windows balanced on both sides of the front door. They may be one or one and one-half stories, with little headroom upstairs. These homes have an exterior of wood siding and fairly steep gable or gambrel roofs covered with wood shingles.

New England Colonial   These homes have a square or rectangular structure with a maximum of usable space and windows balanced on both sides of the front door. They may be one, two, or two and one-half stories. They have a gable roof covered with wood shingles and an exterior wood finish that is generally painted white. There is usually an impressive front entrance with a transom fan of glass above the door.

Georgian and Southern Colonial   These styles have elaborate front entrances with plain or fluted columns and are generally constructed of brick or wood. They usually have prominent gable or hip roofs. These homes require a large lot and may be two, two and one-half, or even three stories.

Dutch Colonial   This is a moderate-sized home, generally not more than fifty feet wide. It has a symmetrical front, an entrance in the center balanced by windows, and a low-sweeping gambrel roof. The exterior is usually of stone and has dormer windows. The home may be one and one-half stories or two and one-half stories high.

Figure 14-3   Architectural Styles Continued

Early English   This style has Gothic refined lines with molded stone around windows and doors. The roof is steep-pitched and covered with slate or shingles; the windows are usually metal casement. The home is usually constructed of brick, stucco, or stone and requires a large building site.

English Half-Timber   This style has protruding timber faces with stucco between the faces. It is generally two stories high, with the lower story constructed of heavy masonry. It has a steep-pitched roof and requires a large lot.

English Tudor   This home is usually two stories and has distinguishing features such as bay windows, truncated roofs, massive chimneys, diamond-pane windows, timber in the stucco, and roofs of various heights. It may also be characterized by flattened arches, much carving, and paneling.

True Spanish   The True Spanish home has enclosed patios, red mission tiled roof, and wrought iron decorations. The walls are stucco and usually painted white.

Figure 14–3   Architectural Styles Continued

Monterey Spanish   This home has two stories, a red mission tiled roof, and a stucco finish generally painted white. The second story usually has balconies with decorative iron railings.

California Spanish   This home is stucco and has a flat composition roof with mission tile trim in front. It is one story, usually with no patio, and is suitable for small lots.

French Normandy   The French Normandy generally has turrets at the entry and a steep-pitched shingle roof. The walls are of brick or stone and unsymmetrical.

French Provincial   This home is usually a large house on a sizable lot. It has masonry exterior walls, with high roofs and large windows with long shutters. It is usually one and one-half to two and one-half stories.

Figure 14–3   Architectural Styles Continued

A-Frame   This house is usually built on a concrete slab floor and is largely used for a second home. It may be one or two stories, with windows and doors in the front and the back.

California Bungalow or Ranch House   This is a one-story, stucco and wood frame house. It is often built on a concrete slab and has a shingle or shake roof. It is low and rambling, generally with attached garage, and provides for indoor and outdoor living.

Modern and Contemporary   This home is generally one story but may be two stories and is often built on a concrete slab. There is usually a large amount of glass to give the feel of indoor-outdoor living. The roof is usually flat or low-pitched.

Figure 14—4 Types of roofs

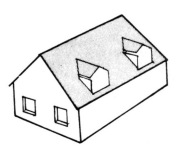

Single dormers are vertical windows set in a gable roof that project outward from the roof.

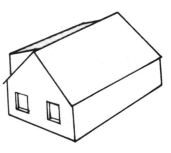

The *dust pan or shed dormer* is a large vertical projection set in a gable roof. It resembles the single dormer except it is much larger and longer and may run the entire length of the house.

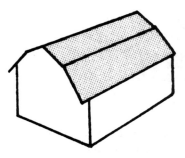

Gambrel roofs have two added ridges parallel to the center gable ridge, making steep slopes below each side of the upper flatter slopes.

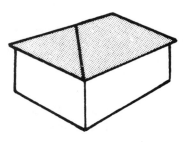

The *hip* roof has four sides sloping up from all four walls.

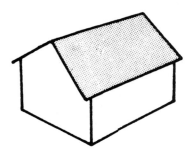

A *gable* roof has two sides sloping to a center ridge.

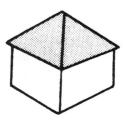

The *pyramid* roof typically has a square base and triangular sides meeting in an apex.

Figure 14—4 Types of roofs Continued

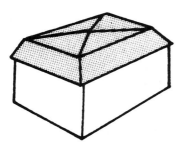

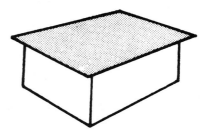

Mansard roofs have added ridges below the center one like the gambrel, but these ridges are on four sides like the hip roof.

The *flat* roof, as the name implies, is flat and usually constructed out of tar and gravel. It appears the least complicated, but it requires extra waterproofing and extra wall support for heavy ceiling joists.

Table 14—2 Housing Investigation Checklist

Building quality:

A. Low quality.
   1. Competitive low cost house which does not exceed the minimum building codes.
B. Fair quality.
   1. Plain and inexpensive finishes on both interior and exterior.
   2. Cheap quality finish hardware, lighting fixtures, and heating.
   3. Generally erected in areas of low purchasing power.
   4. Typically—stucco exterior; concrete slab floor; composition roof.
C. Average quality.
   1. Meets VA and FHA standards.
   2. Usually purchased by persons of moderate income.
   3. Medium standard of construction with some low cost refinements.
   4. Usually of stucco exterior, hardwood flooring, composition roof or shingle.
   5. Finish hardware, lighting fixtures and heating of average quality.
   6. House found in large tract developments.
D. Good quality.
   1. Good architectural design, workmanship and materials.
   2. Stucco walls with wood and masonry trim, hardwood floors, shingle roofs.
   3. Usually contains two bathrooms, forced air furnace or equal heating, good quality lighting fixtures and finish hardware.
   4. Usually has extra built-in equipment in kitchen.
E. Very good quality.
   1. Generally, custom designed by architect.
   2. Home contains many extra features.
   3. Stucco walls with extensive wood or masonry trim, hardwood flooring, shake roofs.
   4. Two or more bathrooms, forced air heating, very good quality finish hardware and lighting fixtures.
   5. Custom fireplaces.

Functional utility and layout:

A. Building
   1. Living room.
     a. Adequacy of floor and wall space for proper placement of furniture.
     b. Circulation—should not have to pass through long living room to reach other parts of the house.
     c. Fireplace should be away from the traffic flow.
     d. Wall spaces—adequate for furniture arrangements.
   2. Dining room or area.
     a. Ease of access to kitchen.
     b. Size of room or area governed by overall size of house.
     c. Best if room is nearly square.

Table 14–2   Continued

3. Bedrooms.
   a. Master bedroom should be of adequate size (minimum 10′ × 12′).
   b. Other bedrooms (minimum 9′ × 10′).
   c. Cross ventilation should be provided.
   d. Located away from family areas and kitchen for privacy.
   e. Should not have to go through one bedroom to enter another.
   f. Closet space should be adequate (minimum depth 2 feet—6 square feet).
4. Kitchen.
   a. Workspace should be ample and efficient in plan.
   b. Equipment should be centrally located to eliminate unnecessary foot travel.
   c. Walls, ceilings and floors should be of easily maintained materials.
   d. Adequate provision should be made for proper lighting and ventilation.
   e. Kitchen should be conveniently located in relation to dining areas and family room.
   f. Kitchen should have an exterior entrance.
   g. Laundry facilities should be adjacent to kitchen.
5. Bathrooms.
   a. Proper location with respect to other rooms.
   b. If only one bathroom exists, it should be located off the central hall.
   c. Bathroom should not open directly into kitchen or living room.
   d. Adequate ventilation—exterior window or automatic exhaust fan is necessary.
   e. Floors, walls, and ceilings easily cleaned and maintained.
6. Closets and storage.
   a. At least one clothes closet per bedroom.
   b. Adequate linen closet space.
   c. Storage closets should be centrally located.
   d. A storage area should be provided near the laundry equipment
   e. Exterior storage necessary if there is only a carport.

B. Site
   1. Construction should be related to the size of the building site.
   2. The house should be so located on the land that it relates to the building site or "belongs."
   3. Adequate front, rear and side yards are necessary for light and privacy. Yards may be clustered in planned unit developments.
   4. A private service yard for drying clothes and storage of refuse should be convenient to the kitchen.
   5. Entrance to the garage should be convenient and readily accessible.
   6. Proper landscaping.
   7. Recreational and garden facilities.
   8. Adequate yard improvements.

(Overall guidelines)

A. Visual appeal of property. How well will the property as a whole retain its market appeal?
   1. Exterior design of structures.
      a. Visual appeal based upon the probability of continuing market acceptance.
      b. Certain architectural styles are short-lived in their acceptance and become obsolete.
   2. Setting.
      a. Measures the property's appeal in the market because of terrain, accessory buildings, walks, landscaping.
      b. The dwelling and surroundings should present a pleasing and unified composition.
   3. Interior design of dwelling.
      a. The interior design should exhibit simplicity of treatment, harmony in proportions and refinement in design.
      b. Interior permanent features should be up-to-date and of adequate construction.
B. Livability of property. The degree of usefulness, convenience and comfort which the property affords is determined by:
   1. Size utilization.
      a. Considers all aspects of the site and its arrangements as these affect the livability of the entire property.
      b. The lot characteristics including size, shape, topography, orientation and natural advantages are considered.
   2. Dwelling space utilization.
      Consideration is given to the size and efficient distribution of space within the structure.

Table 14–2 Continued

3. Room characteristics.
   Consideration is given to the size and proportion of the rooms in relationship to the overall area of the dwelling. The following factors are considered:
   a. Room orientation.
   b. Circulation.
   c. Privacy.
   d. Closet and storage space.
   e. Kitchen efficiency.
   f. Service facilities.
   g. Insulation.
C. Natural light and ventilation. The effect of natural light and natural ventilation of the desirability, livability and healthfulness is considered.
   1. The proper amount of ratio of natural light to room area should be maintained.
   2. Ventilation of all rooms is studied to measure its effect on desirability of the dwelling.
   3. Cross ventilation desirable in all bedrooms.
D. Structural quality. The quality of structural design, materials, and workmanship is determined for the dwelling. The component elements to be considered are as follows:
   1. Foundations.
   2. Wall construction.
   3. Partitions.
   4. Floor construction.
   5. Ceiling construction.
   6. Roof construction.
E. Resistance to elements and usage. A determination is made as to the resistance of the dwelling to the effects of weather, decay, corrosion, fire, and deterioration. Consideration is given to three categories:
   1. Lot improvements.
      a. How is the soil protected from erosion?
      b. Is the land properly graded so that the structure is not damaged by water?
      c. The yard improvements such as walks and walls should be of adequate materials.
   2. The building exterior.
      Analysis is made with reference to the resistance of the exterior of the building to the effects of the elements.
   3. Building interior.
      Consideration is given to the resistance of interior surfaces and materials to determine wear and tear and deterioration.
F. Suitability of mechanical equipment. Measures the extent that the equipment contributes to the desirability and appeal of the dwelling through convenience, economy, and comfort.
   Consideration is given to:
   1. Plumbing system.
   2. Heating system.
   3. Electric system.
   4. Supplementary equipment.

versely, it is often difficult to find spaces in mobile home parks, and you are subject to some of the same disadvantages as a renter. Additionally, homes tend not to appreciate in value nearly as fast as conventional homes. Financing is also less favorable than with other residential property.

Sale by brokers

Brokers can now sell used mobile homes which are less than one year old, provided certain prerequisites have been met to transform the mobile home into real property. Basically you must have obtained a building permit, placed the mobile home on a foundation, obtained a certificate of occupancy and recorded a document that the mobile home is affixed to a foundation.

Evidence of title

If the mobile home is not affixed to the real estate, then a Department of Motor Vehicles pink slip will continue to be evidence of title to the mobile home. But once the home has been legally attached to a permanent foundation, the mobile home is treated the same as any other real property. You are then dealing with deeds and title insurance.

Pad lease

Besides the ownership of the mobile home, the owner also has a lease within a mobile home park. Termination of a tenant's lease in such a park is different from terminating a normal tenancy.

The Civil Code sets forth specific violations which permit a mobile park owner to terminate a lease. No other violation can allow for termination. The extra protections available to a mobile home owner are because of the tremendous cost involved in moving such a home. Further, the tenant must be served with a 60-day notice to terminate, and not the normal 3-day and 30-day notices.

CHAPTER QUESTIONS

1. Give the accepted definition of *appraisal*. Distinguish between *utility value* and *market value*.

2. What characteristics and principal forces influence real estate values?

3. List the three principal methods of appraising real property and briefly define each.

4. Define the word *recapture* as it relates to depreciation and your federal income tax.

5. Distinguish between *accrued depreciation* and *accrual depreciation*.

MULTIPLE-CHOICE QUESTIONS

1. All of the following are among the four essentials of value *except:* (a) utility; (b) appreciation; (c) scarcity; (d) transferability; (e) demand.

2. In an appraisal involving real property, utility value is best defined as: (a) historical value; (b) liquidation value; (c) book value; (d) use value; (e) exchange value.

3. Which of the following best describes *market value:* (a) market price; (b) cost; (c) willing-buyer, willing-seller concept; (d) directional growth; (e) assessed value.

4. An appraiser intends the estimate of market value disclosed in his or her appraisal report on a property to be valid: (a) as of the date of the appraisal only; (b) for a period of three months after the appraisal date; (c) for a period of six months after the appraisal date; (d) for a period of one year after the appraisal date; (e) for a period of ten days after the appraisal date.

5. Which of the following is not a proper charge in determining net income for capitalization purposes: (a) vacancy and collection losses; (b) mortgage interest; (c) city license fee; (d) maintenance expenses; (e) real property taxes.

6. Loss in value of real property because it is out of date or out of style is said to be caused by: (a) economic or social obsolescence; (b) functional obsolescence; (c) physical deterioration; (d) deferred maintenance.

7. The replacement cost method of appraisal is most useful in appraising: (a) income properties; (b) vacant land; (c) single-family residences; (d) public service properties such as schools and public buildings; (e) leasehold estates.

8. The term "highest and best use" can best be defined as: (a) that which produces the greatest net return on the investment over a given period; (b) that which produces the greatest gross income; (c) that which contributes to the best interests of the community; (d) that which complies with the zoning laws of the community; (e) that which provides the greatest net return for the salesperson selling the property.

9. The method that, for tax purposes, would offer the greatest amount of depreciation in the early years of a building's life is: (a) curved line; (b) straight-line; (c) accelerated; (d) recapture; (e) ACRS.

10. In appraising a fifteen-year-old, single-family, one-story home in a good residential area, that had only one owner, you would most logically use which method to determine market value? (a) replacement cost; (b) book value; (c) capitalization; (d) comparing it with selling prices of other homes in the neighborhood; (e) gross multiplier.

ZONING, ENVIRONMENTAL REPORTS, AND RESTRICTIONS

This chapter covers the various ways an owner may be restricted in the use of real property. These restrictions on use are of two kinds:

1. *Governmental restrictions*, including zoning, building codes, set-back lines, and environmental requirements.

2. *Private restrictions*, which are the restrictions set up by private parties. These are usually simply called "restrictions."

Evidence of community planning can be found in the Middle Ages, but the orderly planning of counties and cities did not start in the United States until the twentieth century. The rapid growth of our city and suburban populations has created a need for better and more efficient use of our land resources.

Rapid growth of our urban areas has created enormous problems for the federal, state, county, and city governments. These problems include air and water pollution, mass transportation, sewage, slums, and blight. We must continually strive to develop a proper balance for single and multifamily dwellings and commercial, industrial, and recreational land use.

A hundred years ago cities were dominated by industry, which sprang up in almost any location it desired. Housing, usually poorly constructed and inexpensive, developed around the factories to house the workers. The streets were often poor, the utilities were highly inadequate, and the smoke and pollution were dense and unhealthy. Some people felt that the older inner cities were nothing more than giant slum areas.

Through the police power (discussed later), and zoning governments planned to meet the needs of its citizens. Zoning defined areas for buildings, and the types of building allowed within designated zones. Traffic was funneled in the most desirable directions. Building codes ensured minimum safety standards and habitability requirements. Set-back lines and green-belt areas prevented overcrowding.

Sewer, water, electricity, other utilities, schools, and other support systems had to be adequate before the city or the county would allow additional, new development. Further, such new development had to conform to the government's long-range objectives and development plans for the community.

As cities grew closer together, it was evident that planning just within cities was inadequate. City development had to meet with the needs of the county. Further, even intercounty coordination was required for adequate development. To help in such broad planning, some states, including California, have developed regional planning organizations.

A *regional planning commission* is composed of representatives from the counties and the cities that make up a certain geographical area. An example would be the San Francisco Bay Area Region, composed of the city and county of San Francisco, and the counties of Marin, San Mateo, Santa Clara, Alameda, and Contra Costa. The purpose of a regional planning commission is to discuss common planning problems and tie together, where possible, the various master plans of the counties and cities.

AUTHORITY OF COUNTY AND CITY GOVERNMENTS TO ZONE

Police power may be defined as the sovereign power of the state—usually delegated to the city and the county—to safeguard public health, morals, and safety, and to promote the general welfare and interests of the public. Zoning laws are an important use of police power. A zoning law must be clearly arbitrary or unreasonable or have no substantial relationship to the safeguarding of public health, morals, and safety to be found unconstitutional. The zoning laws, building codes, and related regulations have far-reaching effects on almost every phase of real property.

PLANNING POLICIES

Policies are guides to decision making adopted and followed by governments in their attempts to meet the many-faceted land-use problems associated with city and county growth. Policies should provide a consistent framework for decision making both on a day-to-day basis and for the distant future. They should be statements of methods these governments will use to achieve their goals.

The agreed-upon policies will be the basis for a *master plan*. The master plan is a more detailed guide for development—an interpretation in concrete form of agreed-upon policies.

Planning legislation

During the nineteenth century and prior to the passage of the *enabling acts*, any change from a city or county plan required a special act of the state legislature. As the growth of urban centers began to accelerate in the early years of the twentieth century, the state legislatures were induced to pass *enabling* acts that authorized cities and counties to embark on comprehensive planning.

DEVELOPING THE MASTER PLAN

Under California law, every city must have a *master plan*. The Standard City Planning Enabling Act of 1928, Section 7, has this to say concerning the master plan:

> The plan shall be made with the general purpose of guiding and accomplishing a coordinated, adjusted, and harmonious development of the municipality and its environs which will, in accordance with present and future needs, best promote health, safety, morals, order, convenience, property, and general welfare, as well as efficiency and economy in the process of development; including among other things adequate provisions for traffic, the promotion of safety from fire and other dam-

> ages, adequate provision for light and air, the promotion of the healthful and convenient distribution of the population, the promotion of good civic design and arrangement, wise and efficient expenditure of public funds, and the adequate possession of public utilities and other public requirements.

The purpose, then, of the master plan is to serve as a guide for arriving at decisions—both public and private—that will, it is hoped, result in a constantly improving urban environment. A master plan can be developed only after sufficient information has been obtained through surveys to determine both present and future needs. Information should include population growth and age groups, breakdown of the labor force, economic activity, traffic on main arteries, and building trends.

A master plan does not implement itself. It is a guide to be actively carried out, but it must be flexible in order to meet the ever-changing needs of the urban environment. The plan should be reviewed at least each year, and any sections that must be updated should be changed.

PLANNING COMMISSION

Cities and counties are allowed to appoint a *planning commission* or *board* and hire a qualified staff to implement a comprehensive plan. Further, all incorporated cities or counties must have a Planning Department.

The commission or board is usually appointed by the city manager or the mayor with the approval of the city council. The county planning commission is usually appointed by the county board of supervisors. All matters relating to planning must be referred to the planning commission. The city or county planner, sometimes called the planning technician, is usually a full-time employee of the governmental unit, except in very small communities.

ZONING

A zoning ordinance sets up zones where certain uses are permitted. For example, one area may be zoned "R-1," meaning that the land there may be used for only one-family residences. Other areas may be zoned for two-family dwellings, apartment houses, commercial use, light industrial use, and the like.

The purpose of zoning is to implement the master plan. Zoning ordinances determine the type of use, intensity of use, density of living or working population, and essential facilities required, such as parking standards or ratios. Zoning protects against nuisances and physical hazards. It also protects the safety, health, morals, and welfare of the citizens.

Both cities and counties have zoning laws. The counties exercise their powers in unincorporated areas, and the cities within their jurisdictional limits. Cities and counties must work closely together for harmonious land use and development.

Zoning priorities

Generally, planning authorities take the position that the most important zoning problem for a community is ensuring safe and adequate housing. Therefore, residential uses are given the highest priority. Next is commercial use; last is industrial use.

Traditionally, "R" stood for residential zoning, "C" for commercial, and "I" for industrial. "R-1" meant that single-family housing was allowed. "R-2" allowed duplexes, and "R-3" allowed structures containing up to three housing units. "R-20" allowed apartment complexes of twenty units, and so on.

Today, many cities and counties have their own notations, and it is important to read each government's designation.

In San Francisco, for example, "RH-1(D)" allows one single-family detached dwelling. "RH-1" allows one single-family dwelling per 3,000 square feet of lot area, with a maximum of three structures per lot with conditional use approval. "RH-1(S)" allows one single-family detached dwelling, with a small second unit ("mother-in-law unit") up to 600 square feet of net floor area.

Cumulative zoning

Cumulative zoning allows the designated zoning and all lesser zoning. Thus, R-2 zoning allows R-1 and R-2. C-3 allows C-1, C-2, C-3, and all residential zoning. I-2, allows industrial 1 and 2 and all commercial and residential zoning. Years ago most zoning was cumulative.

Noncumulative zoning

Now, most zoning is noncumulative. C-2 allows only C-2 use, and not C-1 as well, unless expressly specified by statute. Often cities will mix cumulative and noncumulative zoning. R-20, for example, allows twenty-unit apartment buildings and all lesser residential uses, but C-1 will not allow residential uses.

Nonconforming use

When a new zoning ordinance is passed, any existing lawful use that does not conform to it—a *nonconforming use*—is usually permitted to remain until that use ends or the building is destroyed. This is mainly to avoid

hardship for owners or because of unusual difficulties that would otherwise result.

RELIEF FROM ZONING

As was discussed earlier, the court almost never overturns zoning ordinances. Further, it is extremely difficult to get the zoning authorities to amend a zoning ordinance for the benefit of one parcel of property. Very rarely, a zoning ordinance may be amended to exclude a parcel from the zone. Such zoning creates "islands" zoned differently from surrounding property and could even be subject to judicial attack unless grounded in reasonable purposes.

To obtain relief from oppressive zoning, a property owner applies to the zoning body for special relief. There are two types of zoning relief that allow specific property to be exempt from zoning. The exemption applies only to the exempted property and does not affect any other properties in that zone. The two exemptions are conditional use permits and variances.

Conditional use permit

Zoning ordinances may authorize the planning commission to grant a *conditional use permit*, usually called simply a "use permit," if the facts presented by the applicant justify the permit and if the permitted use seems desirable for public convenience. This allows a use forbidden by the zoning ordinances. Land zoned for industrial purposes will usually permit a limited number of commercial facilities, such as service stations, to serve the people working in the industrial area. When the commission turns down the request, the applicant may usually appeal to the city council or the county board of supervisors.

Variance, or exception

A *variance*, or *exception*, is designed to give some degree of flexibility to zoning administration dealing with hardship or exceptional circumstances. The administrative body granting the variance may attach conditions to it to conform with the purpose of the master plan. A variance, or exception, is an approved deviation from the plan.

BUILDING CODES AND SET-BACK LINES

Each state has a law setting forth certain minimum standards of construction for buildings. In addition to the state law, counties and cities may have their own local building codes to supplement and strengthen the state law. The local building inspector enforces the building code. The construction company or the owner of property must always comply with the more stringent of the two codes.

The Federal Housing Administration and Veterans Administration have indirectly influenced local building standards through their financing programs. Their requirements may, in some cases, be more restrictive than those of either the state or the local code.

Set-back lines are established by city and county ordinance and state how close to the street and the side and rear lot lines a person can build.

CONFLICT BETWEEN ZONING AND RESTRICTIONS

Sometimes zoning will permit a use that the restrictions on the property forbid, or the restrictions will permit a use that the zoning forbids.

For example, the property may be zoned R-2, which means two-family dwellings are allowed, but the restrictions may allow only single-family dwellings; or, the restrictions may allow any type of residential use, even apartments, but the zoning permits only single-family dwellings.

There is one rule you should memorize, because it covers all such situations: *Whichever is the more restrictive must be followed, whether zoning or restrictions.*

Thus, if zoning permits two-family dwellings but the restrictions permit only one-family dwellings, the restrictions are the more ''restrictive'' and they control; only one-family dwellings are permitted. In this example, the restrictions and zoning don't really conflict. When the zoning in our example allows two-family residences, it does not *require* them. It simply permits them if the owner is not prevented from building them by the restrictions.

ENVIRONMENTAL IMPACT REPORTS

Environmental impact reports are required for any project if it will have a ''substantial effect upon the environment'' and if the project is undertaken by

1. A governmental agency.
2. A private person or company, if some governmental action or permit is required, such as a building permit or approval of a subdivision. The governmental action or permit must involve the use of discretion on the part of the government, rather than a purely routine act.

Sometimes it is hard to say whether a project will have a ''substantial impact on the environment.'' The remodeling of a home will not. A large subdivision or the building of a freeway will. Between these two is a gray area not yet fully defined. When in doubt, it is best to have the report filed.

The ordinances of the city or county involved will set out the details of how the report is prepared. Ordinarily, it is prepared by the governmental agency that issues the permit or takes the action, or by someone under that agency's direction. The person seeking the permit or governmental action may contribute ideas and must pay for the preparation of the report. After it is filed, others have the right to complain or even take court action, if they think it is incomplete. The governmental body that will issue the permit or take requested action must consider the report, but it does not have to be guided by it exclusively.

COMMUNITY REDEVELOPMENT AGENCIES (CRA'S)

In Chapter 14 we discussed the three principal causes of depreciation and learned that social or economic obsolescence occurs from misplaced improvements, improper zoning or legislative restrictions, lack of supply or demand, and change of locational demand. This type of obsolescence is the most difficult to correct and will eventually require urban renewal or redevelopment of the area affected.

The primary purpose of a redevelopment agency should be to develop property, improve housing opportunities in urban renewal areas, and relocate residents displaced by this redevelopment. The agency may condemn smaller parcels of land and assemble them into one large development project. The agency might then enter into an agreement with a professional developer and restrict him or her in the amount of profit he or she can make from the project.

The Community Redevelopment Law (Health and Safety Code) authorizes the establishment of CRA's to carry out redevelopment programs at the local level. An ordinance declares a need for such an agency to function in the community and is subject to a referendum. The legislative body appoints the governing board of the CRA, which may be a separate body or the legislative body itself. City council members head most CRA's.

CRA's may acquire property through condemnation, assemble and dispose of property, borrow money, sue and be sued, and engage in a range of activities mandated by redevelopment law.

Under the current law, all plans and amendments adopted must develop, at a minimum, replacement housing on a one-to-one basis for all units destroyed or removed from the low- and moderate-income housing market because of the redevelopment project. The plan or amendment must demonstrate that at least 30 percent of all new or rehabilitated dwelling units will be for low- and moderate-income persons and at least 50 percent of these units must be for low-income persons. Community Redevelopment Agencies do not have the authority to operate rental housing projects, and they must sell or lease such developments within a reasonable time after completion.

Redevelopment projects may be funded through increased tax revenues resulting from the redevelopment to pay off debts incurred by the CRA in improving the area. Under this financing method, the assessed value of the taxable property in the area under redevelopment is frozen on the date the redevelopment plan is adopted. After this date, the taxing agencies receive only the amount of taxes they would have received if there had been no redevelopment. The difference between property taxes before the redevelopment and the increased property taxes after these new physical improvements goes to the redevelopment agency. In theory at least, the local taxing entities will enjoy increased tax revenues from the project area once the CRA has paid off its debts. These tax monies may be used by the CRA to clear these debts directly or as security for the sale of bonds.

The Property Tax Relief Act of 1972 allows subtractions from a school district's total assessed value of property on which tax revenue is paid to a redevelopment agency. This adjustment allows school districts to recover revenues directed to CRA's through a combination of tax rate limitations and additional state aid. Current legislation allows, but does not require, the CRA to compensate any local taxing entity for fiscal problems caused by redevelopment.

By selling bonds at the outset of a project, a CRA can gain early access to monies that would be received through tax increments over a long period. Construction of public facilities in California has traditionally been financed by general obligations bonds, which require approval by two-thirds of the voters. Tax allocation bonds, however —since they are not obligations of the city or any public entity other than the CRA—can be issued by a CRA without voter approval. Bondholders cannot require a levy of additional property tax to assure the payment of principal and interest for an unsuccessful project, and because of the added risk, tax allocation bonds are less attractive to investors than general obligation bonds.

A municipal bond looked on more favorably by bond investors is the lease revenue bond. These bonds are used to raise money to enable the CRA to construct certain facilities. The CRA then leases the facilities to the city, and the lease payments are used for the annual payment to the bondholders. The CRA can use tax increment funds to subsidize the city's lease payments.

COASTAL CONTROL

After a long political dispute, California enacted the 1976 California Coastal Act to protect its shoreline from improper and haphazard development. Proponents of the new law argued that local cities and counties could not resist the pressure from developers.

The Act installed the California Coastal Commission to set up guidelines controlling development of the strip of land bordering the ocean. Generally the strip extends 1,000 yards inland; in some built-up city areas it narrows to only one block, while in certain scenic or ecologically sensitive areas it reaches back for ten miles. Along the scenic Big Sur coast it widens to an average of five miles.

Within the coastal zone the commission rules on development applications and must issue a permit before most types of development are allowed. This task is being taken over by the cities and the counties once they have brought their local plans and regulations into conformity with the state guidelines. Certain improvements to existing single-family homes and some repair and maintenance work are exempt from control.

The coastal zone starts at the mean (average) high-tide line. Below this line the land belongs to the state and the public has the right to use it.

CHAPTER QUESTIONS

1. Define and give at least two illustrations of the following: (a) police power; (b) nonconforming use; (c) variances, or exceptions.

2. Briefly describe the *enabling acts.*

3. What is the purpose of the *master plan?* Does it implement itself?

4. Are the members of the city or county planning commission elected by the public, or are they appointed by a city official? Explain.

5. When there is a conflict between zoning and deed restrictions, which will usually prevail?

16 SUBDIVISIONS

No other state has experienced growth comparable to that of California in the last two decades. With a population of over 24 million, and still increasing each day, California will continue to grow until the saturation point has been reached, about the year 2025. The two most rapidly growing areas are the San Francisco peninsula and greater Los Angeles. Los Angeles, already one of the great cities of the United States, is destined to become one of the largest in the world. The continued growth of this area would result in a "megalopolis" with a coastline of 225 miles, extending from San Diego to Santa Barbara, and an inland boundary encompassing San Bernardino.

Government at the federal, state, and local levels is involved in nearly every phase of the real estate business. Not only do government units buy, own, and sell real estate, but they are also involved in other fields such as real estate finance, the regulation of real estate agents, and land subdivisions. California has set the pattern for real estate subdivisions for many other states in the nation. Regulations imposed by state legislation include those for the prevention of fraud, misrepresentation, and deceit in the sale of subdivisions. These restrictions also control building firms and their advertising media. Many physical improvements are further controlled by the cities and counties in which they are located. Without proper governmental controls, our cities would be allowed to grow haphazardly, and slum and blight would develop almost immediately in newly constructed subdivisions.

The two principal laws governing subdivisions in California are

1. The *Subdivision Map Act*, which regulates *land use*. It is enforced by local governments.

2. The *Subdivided Lands Act*, which is part of the group of statutes called the "real estate law." It regulates *land sales* in new subdivisions and is enforced by the California Department of Real Estate.

SUBDIVISION MAP ACT

To the average person interested in real estate, the Subdivision Map Act may be of more concern than the Subdivided Lands Act.

The Subdivision Map Act is regulated by the local government—the cities and the counties. It does not involve the Real Estate Commissioner. Each community enacts a subdivision ordinance, which allows local statutes to govern all procedures not mandated by state law. Therefore, each community's ordinances need to be reviewed.

The Act regulates the physical development and division of property and the improvements required before a division is allowed. It often has more impact than the Subdivided Lands Act, because it applies to *any* division of a lot or a tract of land—even a division into two parts. The Subdivided Lands Act ordinarily applies to a subdivision into *five* or more parts and applies only to the first sale of each lot in a new subdivision.

The Subdivision Map Act is concerned mainly with local regulation and control of subdivision layout, lot size, and required improvements, such as road surfacing, gutters, sidewalks, drainage, water mains, street lights, and sewage disposal facilities.

The Act covers "the division of any improved or unimproved land, shown on the latest county assessment

222

roll as a unit or as contiguous units, for the purpose of sale, lease or financing, whether immediate or future.''
It covers condominiums and community apartment projects, but the leasing of apartments, offices, stores, and the like in a building is not covered. Neither are mineral, oil, and gas leases, or cemetery lots. Condominiums are included as subdivisions, regardless of the number of units.

At one time the law was concerned only with divisions into five or more parcels. Now a parcel map is required for subdivisions of fewer than five units. For subdivisions of five or more units, both a parcel map and a final subdivision map are required.

Subdivisions into five or more parcels

The first step for this type of subdivision is the filing of a *tentative map* by the subdivider. This shows the proposed subdivision, the layout of lots, the location and type of streets, utilities, and so on.

Procedures vary, but ordinarily this map is submitted to an advisory body, such as a planning commission of the city or county involved. There it is subject to examination, and if it is found satisfactory, it is approved. The official approval may be given by the advisory body, if it has that authority, or it may be given by the local legislative body (the city council or the county board of supervisors).

Usually the body that examines the map circulates it to other interested agencies—for example, the local fire department and the city or county engineering department. After such interested parties have their say, the body to whom the tentative map was submitted usually imposes certain conditions it wants satisfied before the map will be approved. These conditions may include a variety of things. For example, the owner may be required to deed a drainage easement to the local flood control district; streets may have to be made wider or paved in a way different from that which the subdivider proposed; or the subdivider may be required to dedicate some land to the public for a park.

A subdivider who is dissatisfied with an advisory body's requirements may appeal to the local legislative body.

When the subdivider has complied with all the conditions imposed on the tentative map, he or she must file a *final map* and have it approved. Then, at last, he or she may sell lots in the subdivision as far as this Act is concerned. But, since this is a new subdivision with five or more lots, he or she must also comply with the Subdivided Lands Act.

If the project will have a significant effect on the environment, an environmental impact report (ERP) must be prepared. The government must then consider the environmental impact of the project, the nature of which is discussed in Chapter 15.

Subdivisions into four or fewer parcels

When the subdivision is into four or fewer parcels there are usually fewer requirements. Ordinarily a *parcel map* is required. Local ordinances regarding these small subdivisions are usually analogous to the requirements for larger subdivisions. Most call for filing a tentative parcel map, which may be conditionally approved, and then for the filing of a final parcel map when the conditions are met. But even with this simpler procedure, the conditions imposed may still be expensive. In some rural areas only one parcel map is needed, and the filing of a tentative parcel map may be omitted.

Penalties for noncompliance

It is a misdemeanor to sell, lease, or finance a parcel of land that has been subdivided without compliance with this Act. The government concerned may get an injunction to prevent violation. The buyer (but not the seller) may void a sale or a contract to sell an illegally divided parcel within a year after he or she discovers the violation.

The Subdivision Map Act is administered by local agencies and concerns physical improvement to the property. The Subdivided Lands Act concerns the sale of subdivided lands, and is regulated by state laws administered by the Real Estate Commissioner. It was designed primarily to prevent fraud, and it basically requires full and complete disclosure before any lots can be sold.

THE SUBDIVIDED LANDS ACT

Subdivision section

Subdividing is a process of plotting land for purposes of sale or development. Chapter 1, Section 11000, of the Business and Professions Code (last amended in 1980) defines a subdivision as follows:

> ''*Subdivided lands*'' *refers to improved or unimproved land or lands divided or proposed to be divided for the purpose of sale or lease or financing, whether immediate or future, into five or more lots or parcels. However, land or lands sold by lots or parcels of not less than 160 acres which are designated by such lot or parcel description by government surveys and appear as such on the current assessment role of the county in which such land or lands are situated shall not be deemed to be ''subdivided lands'' or ''a subdivision'' within the meaning of this section unless such lands or land are divided or propose to be divided for purposes of sale for oil and gas purposes in which case such land or lands shall be*

deemed to be "subdivided lands" or "a subdivision" within the meaning of this section. This chapter also does not apply to the leasing of apartment buildings, offices, stores, or space within an apartment building, industrial building or commercial building or mobile home park . . . except that the offering of leases for a term in excess of five years to tenants within a mobile home park as a mandatory requirement and prerequisite to tenancy within the mobile home park shall be subject to the provisions of this chapter. The leasing of apartments in community apartment project . . . and the creation of a time-share project . . . in an apartment or similar space within a commercial building or complex, as defined in Sections 11004 shall be subject to the provisions of this chapter.

A subdivision, then, refers to improved or unimproved lands divided into five or more parcels for the purpose of sale, lease, or financing, whether immediate or future. The Subdivision Map Act defines a subdivision in exactly the same manner.

The purpose of the real estate law, as it relates to subdivision, is to protect the buying public from misrepresentation, fraud, or deceit in the sale of new subdivisions. The law also covers out-of-state subdivisions.

The Real Estate Commissioner of the state of California is permitted under the law to adopt, amend, or make such rules or regulations as are reasonably required to enforce this section of the real estate law. The Commissioner is further empowered to issue orders, permits, decisions, demands, or requirements to affect this purpose.

Notice of intention to subdivide

Before land can be subdivided into lots and sold or leased in California, a Notice of Intention to Subdivide must be filed with the Real Estate Commissioner. Usually this notice is accompanied by a questionnaire supplied by the Department of Real Estate. The filing is usually done by the owner, the subdivider, or the subdivider's agent. All persons (with a few exceptions) must be licensed as real estate brokers or salespeople to sell the lots in the subdivision, including salaried employees of the owner or the subdivider. The Commissioner's Public Report must be obtained before the property is offered for sale or lease. The Notice of Intention to Subdivide should include the following information:

1. The names and the addresses of the owners
2. The name and the address of the subdivider, if different from that of the owners
3. A legal description of the lands to be subdivided
4. A certified statement of the condition of the title to the property, with particular reference to all encumbrances
5. A statement of terms and conditions under which

the owners or the developers intend to dispose of their land; this should be accompanied by copies of all contracts that will be used in the sale of the land
6. A statement of provisions as to public utilities in the proposed subdivision, including water, electricity, gas, and telephone facilities
7. A statement as to the use or uses of the proposed subdivision, such as residential housing, community apartments, or condominiums
8. A statement of restrictions as to the use and occupancy of the parcels within the subdivisions, including private restrictions
9. A statement of the amount of any liens placed on all or any part of the subdivision to pay for any subdivision or community improvements
10. A statement, or estimate, of any taxes or charges that are or will arise from any taxing agency or district for improvements to the subdivision or the community
11. The location of any existing or planned airports within two miles of the subdivision
12. A statement of any soils or geological reports obtained on the subdivision
13. A statement indicating whether any fill has been or will be used in the subdivision, and the location of the government agency having soils information on the subdivision.
14. Additional provisions or information concerning the owner, agent, or subdivider that they may want to include in the final Public Report

Questionnaire requirements

Besides the necessary and basic information included in the Notice of Intention to Subdivide, the questionnaire will require additional information and certain documents. Some of the documents include the following:

Title report This report must show record-owners and all liens and encumbrances against the property and must be issued after the final subdivision map is recorded. It may take the form of a preliminary report, a policy of title insurance, or a Certificate of Title. A preliminary title report is particularly helpful, since it will show many items that can be corrected before the recording or processing of the final map. For purposes of the Preliminary Public Report issued by the Real Estate Commissioner, a preliminary title report issued by a title insurance company may suffice. The Preliminary Public Report will enable the subdivider to take advance reservations. When this is done, the owner, the subdivider, or the subdivider's agent must agree to release the potential buyers before they sign a binding agreement stating they have read the Preliminary Public Report. This receipt must be retained by the subdivider, the owner, or the agent for three years.

Sale documents   The developers must present to the Commissioner, prior to the sale of any lots in the subdivision, all preliminary and final sale contracts proposed to be used. These will include deeds, deeds of trust, leases or option agreements, agreements of sale, and so forth. Once these documents have been presented to the Commissioner and approved by him or her, they cannot be changed without the permission of the Commissioner and the submission of the new agreements.

Covenants and conditions   A copy of all covenants, conditions, restrictions, and reservations must be presented to the Commissioner if they are proposed to be used. These will be called to the attention of the potential buyer in the Preliminary Public Report and finally in the Public Report.

Final subdivision recorded map   The developer must submit to the Real Estate Commissioner a copy of the final subdivision map, which is recorded in the office of the county recorder where the property is located. If recordation of the map is pending, a copy of the tentative subdivision map should be submitted.

Water supply provisions   All subdivisions for the sale or lease of lots must have definite provisions as to water facilities, which must meet all local health standards. The Commissioner will require a letter from the company furnishing the water, stating that an adequate supply is available and that such water will be furnished on demand without exception to all lots in the subdivision. If exceptions or reservations are made by the water company, they should be set forth in the letter. If the water supply is to come from other than a municipal or publicly owned water company, additional information will be needed. If a mutual water company is involved in supplying water to the subdivision, a permit from the State Division of Corporations will be required showing that a permit has been given to issue shares in the water company. If water is to be obtained through other private sources, the Commissioner will usually require that evidence be submitted in the form of a permit from the State Department of Public Health. If a well is to be drilled on each lot, these documents will be required:

1. A licensed well-driller's estimate of cost for drilling and casing a well to meet county health standards
2. Documents indicating the depth of the water table
3. Estimate of the cost of the pressure-pump system
4. A letter from the local health authorities stating that such wells will be permitted

Health permit   A health permit must be obtained from the appropriate health department. This permit will show the sewage disposal plans, if public sewers are not available. If septic tanks or cesspools are to be used in the tract, permission must be obtained from the appropriate health officers.

Fire protection letter   If fire protection is available, a letter should be obtained from the fire department or fire district stating that protection will be furnished. When no such protection is to be given, the subdivider, the owner, or his agent must so state.

Flood and drainage   The owner, the subdivider, or the subdivider's agent must obtain from the flood control engineers—county or city, depending upon jurisdiction—a letter stating that proper provisions have been made for flood and drainage problems. In some counties, it may be necessary for the developer to furnish these reports at his or her own expense if jurisdictional health officials are not available.

Fill report   When fill ground is involved in the subdivision, the developer must show an engineer's filled ground report. This report will contain the number of lots filled, the depth of the fill, the method of filling, the amount of compaction, and an opinion from the engineer on the ability of the fill to sustain construction loads.

Private road cost estimate   When roads are other than public-dedicated roads, the developer shall submit an estimate from an engineer showing the cost per linear foot for constructing roads to county standards and the estimated cost per linear foot for maintaining such roads. The maintenance of private roads has been the concern of some counties. The width is usually approximately thirty-two feet, and in some cases counties are requesting that these roads also be dedicated for public use. This assures the future maintenance of the roadway for prospective buyers.

Common area   The subdivider must include detailed information about any common areas, including pro forma budgets, covenants, conditions and restrictions, management association bylaws, or other management organization documents.

Fees   The subdivider must also enclose the required fees, which are set by statute and vary depending on the number of units involved.

The Real Estate Commissioner's Public Report

The real estate law requires that the Commissioner issue a Public Report concerning his or her findings in a subdivision and that a true copy of the Public Report be given by the subdivider or the subdivider's agent to any prospective purchaser of the property before he or she becomes obligated for the sale or lease thereof. Not only must the subdivider or developer furnish him or her with a copy, but also the prospective buyer must sign a receipt stating that he or she has received and read the copy of the report. Once issued, the reports are good for five years, or until there is a material change in the subdivision. Developers are required to keep copies of these reports for three years. The purpose of the report is to set forth to the buyer all facts concerning the subdivision. If the Public Report is not issued following the Commissioner's investigation of the proposed subdivision, a hearing is called to determine whether or not the subdivision should be stopped. This hearing is governed by the California Code of Civil Procedure.

The Commissioner may deny the developer the right to proceed with the subdivision and may hold up the Public Report for reasons of misrepresentation, deceit, fraud, inability of sellers to deliver a clear title to the property, inadequate financial arrangements to improve the proposed subdivision, or inability of the developer to comply with any provisions of the real estate law. In summary, then, the Public Report has a twofold purpose:

1. To supply the prospective buyer with all information that the Real Estate Commissioner has obtained in his or her investigation of the proposed tract

2. To assure the prospective purchaser that he or she will receive what the developer has represented he or she would receive

Preliminary Public Report

When an owner, a subdivider, or a subdivider's agent has not complied with all provisions required by the Commissioner but it appears to the Commissioner that he or she will be able to do so within a reasonable period of time, the Commissioner may issue a Preliminary Public Report. This will permit the subdivider, the agent, or the owner to take reservations and deposits on lots within the subdivision. The Preliminary Public Report is good for one year, or until there is a material change in the subdivision, whichever occurs first. The subdivider must agree, however, to return the deposit money to the prospective purchaser if, after receiving the Public Report, he or she does not wish to be bound to the transaction. All deposits in such cases must be deposited in a neutral escrow along with a copy of the Commissioner's Preliminary Public Report.

Financing requirements

A *blanket mortgage* or *deed of trust* covers all the lots within the subdivision. It is unlawful for the developer, the owner, or the subdivider to sell or lease lots within the subdivision unless these lots can be released free and clear from the blanket encumbrance. This may be done by an unconditional partial release clause if the mortgage or deed of trust so provides.

A partial release clause provides that a stipulated parcel within a subdivision may be released after a certain sum of money has been paid to the holder of the blanket encumbrance. When there is no partial release clause in the mortgage or deed of trust, it is unlawful for the owner, the developer, or the subdivider to sell or release lots except under certain statutorily specified conditions, designed to ensure that the buyer will ultimately receive his or her property free and clear of the blanket deed of trust.

False advertising

The Real Estate Commissioner may require that all advertising to be used in the sale of the subdivision be submitted to him or her for approval. It is unlawful for any owner, subdivider, agent, or employee of a subdivision, directly or indirectly, to use false advertising in connection with the promotion of a subdivision. Any person who falsely advertises a subdivision shall be guilty of a public offense and shall be punished by a fine not exceeding $5,000 or imprisonment in a state prison for a period not exceeding five years or in a county jail for a period not exceeding one year. The person may be subject to both fine and imprisonment. The Commissioner's Rules and Regulations set forth what shall constitute misleading or false advertising.

Subdivision sales contracts

Sales contracts relating to the purchase or sale of real property in a subdivision must set forth the legal description of the property, all liens and encumbrances outstanding at the date of the contract, and the exact terms and conditions of the sale.

When an agreement of sale (sale contract, land contract, installment sale contract) is used, the sellers are prohibited from encumbering the parcel of land beyond the amount due in the contract of sale. When a piece of property is sold under such an agreement, all moneys from the buyer must first be applied to the mortgage or trust deed to ensure that the buyer will receive a clear and marketable title. Any violations of the above are considered misdemeanors.

Penalties for not complying with the provisions of the Real Estate Law

After the Real Estate Commissioner has approved all provisions in the subdivision, the subdivider should be able to proceed with subdividing the land with minimum difficulties, and the purchaser in such subdivision should have no basis of complaint; also, there should be no cause for complaint of fraud or misrepresentation against the owner, the subdivider, or the subdivider's representatives.

Failure of the owner, the subdivider, or the agent to comply with the provisions of the Real Estate Law under the subdivision section is a public offense punishable by a maximum fine of $5,000 or up to one year imprisonment in a state prison or one year in the county jail or by fine and imprisonment. All prosecutions for such violations are carried out by the county district attorney. In addition to the above penalties, the licensee's license may be suspended or revoked. The time period prescribed by the statute of limitations for the prosecution of violators will commence with the most recent deed, lease, or other contract of sale that is placed on record with the county recorder.

If the Real Estate Commissioner determines that an owner, subdivider, agent, or other person is violating the provisions of the subdivision section of the Real Estate Law, he or she may issue a *desist* and *refrain order*. This order tells the owner, subdivider, or agent to stop all activities. When such an order is issued by the Commissioner, the respondent may file a request in writing for a hearing within thirty days after its issuance. The Commissioner is duty-bound to hold such a hearing within a fifteen-day period, or if a postponement is requested on valid grounds, within fifteen days plus the number of days that the postponement is granted. Failure to hold such a hearing within thirty days after such a request is made will result in rescission of the order of denial and the issuance of a public report.

OUT-OF-STATE SUBDIVISIONS

If subdivided property outside the state is to be sold in California, the out-of-state subdivider must comply with the sections of real estate law dealing with subdivided property. The developer from outside the state is requested to file a Notice of Intention to Subdivide and the questionnaire with the Real Estate Commissioner as an in-state developer would do. In addition, he or she must furnish the following:

1. A qualified independent appraiser's estimate as to the value of the lots or parcels proposed to be sold
2. A bond in the amount of $5,000 issued by a corporate surety insurer admitted and approved by the Commissioner, giving protection to the people of California for their use and benefit

The filing fee for an out-of-state subdivision is $50 per lot for nine or fewer lots and $500 plus $3 per lot for ten or more lots, to a maximum of $5,000. The subdivider is required to pay the costs incurred in the inspection and appraisal of the property by the Commissioner's appraiser. Out-of-state subdivisions are treated as real estate property securities, and the Real Estate Commissioner has set up certain rules and regulations pertaining to them. In addition to the filing fees, a recompense of ten cents for each mile going to and returning from the subdivided property must accompany the questionnaire. If public transportation is available, the actual round trip from the Commissioner's office in Sacramento is estimated by the Commissioner. An additional amount of $50 for each day spent in the examination of the project may also be charged.

TYPES OF SUBDIVISIONS

Subdivisions are of various types including the following:

1. *Lot and residential subdivisions*
2. *FHA-insured subdivisions.* Under an FHA-insured cooperative subdivision, an association of members is usually formed, each is issued one share of stock, and each is given the right to occupy a particular part of any improvements erected. When all moneys have been paid and the entire subdivision has been sold, a grant deed is usually delivered to the buyer of the property.
3. *Community apartment houses.* Community apartment houses are also known as cooperatives and are sometimes referred to as ''own your own'' apartments. Under such an arrangement, a board of directors is usually formed and the users of the various apartments make their payments directly to the board of directors, who in turn apply the amount so paid to one mortgage payment. The same would be true of taxes, assessments, and so forth. If an owner desires to remodel or repaint, he or she is usually required to obtain permission from the board of directors. Permission to sell must also be obtained from the board of directors.
4. *Condominiums.* Under a condominium, a prospective buyer or purchaser actually holds a fee title to his or her individual apartment unit or space. He or she further owns an undivided interest in the common areas and facilities of the building, including an undivided interest in the land. Under a condominium, the individual owner secures and pays his or her own mortgage, taxes, and so forth. For all practical purposes, he or she is the sole owner.
5. *Mineral, oil, and gas subdivisions.* The definition of an oil and gas subdivision includes parcels of any size, even those over 160 acres that are excluded from other types of subdivisions. No public report on a mineral, oil, and gas subdivision has been approved for many years. The Commissioner has specific regulations for such subdivisions when they are applied for.
6. *Resort-type subdivisions.* When resort property is subdivided, all local regulations must be observed, including those pertaining to water and sewage.
7. *Commercial subdivisions.* Commercial shopping

228 *Subdivisions*

centers in California have been growing during the last two decades. When land is subdivided for purposes of developing a commercial or store area, the subdivisions fall within the real estate law. The developers of such commercial centers must comply with all provisions of the real estate law in their subdivision of the property.

8. *Mobile-home subdivisions.* A mobile-home subdivision is a parcel of land subdivided into lots, each lot individually owned and used as the site for placement of a single mobile home and its facilities. The subdivision differs from a mobile-home park in that the former is under single ownership and has been planned and improved for the placement of mobile homes for nontransient use.

9. *Time-share project.* A time-share project is one in which the purchaser has a right to use the property for specified periods of time, established from the use or occupancy periods into which the project has been divided. For example, some resorts sell the right to exclusive use of a condominium for a week at a time for a one-time purchase cost.

ENVIRONMENTAL IMPACT REPORTS

Environmental impact reports are required in every subdivision that will have a "substantial effect upon the environment." These reports were discussed in Chapter 15.

THE PROCESS OF LAND DEVELOPMENT

The first logical step in a subdivision for the real estate developer or the owner is to make a real estate market analysis. In actual practice, this will be based on judgment and opinion rather than on a complete feasibility study. Such an analysis is necessary to determine whether a market exists for the type of subdivision under consideration. The venture's success depends largely upon the accuracy and scope of the market analysis.

The developer or the subdivider should pay close attention to the location of the subdivision. A critical analysis should be made of such things as proximity to employment and to shopping and whether the subdivision will be harmonious with others in the surrounding area and with any existing improvements.

Careful analysis must be made of all costs upon which the purchase price of the property is based. Included in these costs are interest to be paid on the encumbrance during the development of the property, real estate points, development costs, and prepayment penalties on the property. After the cost analysis is completed, a thorough investigation of the requirements of governmental bodies should be made. This will include close cooperation with such administrative offices as the city or county planning commission, city council or county board of supervisors, sanitation control, the California Department of Real Es-

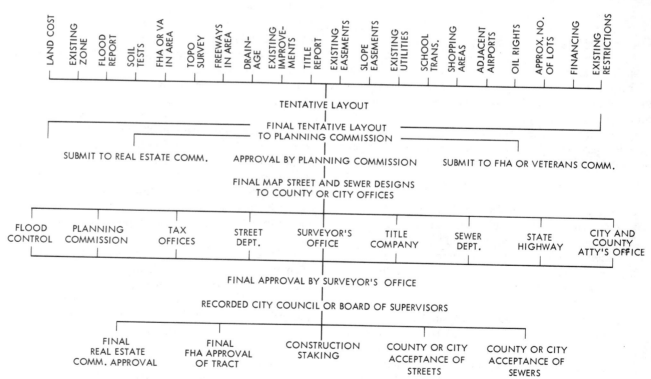

Figure 16–1 Subdivision Procedure: What the developer should know before the purchase of property.

tate, flood control engineers, the county road department, city engineers, and planning technicians (see Figure 16–1). Figure 16–2 illustrates the Commissioner's form required of developers and subdividers.

INTERSTATE LAND SALES FULL DISCLOSURE ACT

Title XIV (Interstate Land Sales Full Disclosure Act) of the Housing and Urban Development Act of 1968, which became effective April 28, 1969, is administered by the Office of Interstate Land Sales Registration (OILSR) in the Department of Housing and Urban Development.

For the purposes of the federal act, a *subdivision* is defined as any land divided or proposed to be divided into fifty or more lots, whether contiguous or not, for the purpose of sale or lease as part of a common promotional plan.

The act makes it unlawful for any developer to sell or lease lots in a subdivision as a common promotional plan in interstate commerce, or by utilization of the mails, unless a statement of record is in effect and a copy of the property report is furnished to the purchaser or lessee.

The property report is similar to the California Public Report and includes such information as the distance of nearby communities over paved or unpaved roads, recording of sales contracts, provision made for refund in case of buyer's default, existence of liens on property, conditions under which contract payments will be placed in escrow, availability of recreational facilities, present and proposed utility services and charges, number of homes currently occupied, soil and other foundation problems in construction, and title to be conveyed to buyer.

Unless the method of disposition is adopted for the purpose of evading the act, the act does not apply to

1. Properties that consist of lots of five acres or more.
2. Properties improved with a residential, commercial, or industrial building or sold under a contract obligating the seller to erect such a building thereon within two years.
3. Sale or lease pursuant to a court order.
4. Sales or evidences of indebtedness secured by a mortgage or a deed of trust.
5. Sales of securities issued by a real estate investment trust.
6. Sale or lease by any government or governing agency.
7. Sale or lease of cemetery lots.
8. Sale or lease to a person who acquires the property for the purpose of constructing a residential, commercial, or industrial building or for the purpose of resale or lease to persons engaged in such business.
9. Sale or lease of lots free and clear of liens, encumbrances, and adverse claims at the time of sale or leasing, and if each person purchasing such lot or his or her spouse has personally inspected the property prior to signing a contract to purchase.

The phrase "at the time of sale" is deemed to be the date the sales contract or lease is signed or the effective date of the conveyance if the deed is to be delivered within 120 days and initial deposits and other payments made on account of the purchase price are deposited in a trust account.

Also excluded are the following:

1. Sale or lease of lots each of which exceeds 10,000 square feet and will be sold for less than $100, including closing costs
2. Lots leased for a term of not more than five years, provided the lessee is not obligated to renew
3. The sale or lease of lots when the offering is entirely or almost entirely intrastate (regulations do not specify what is or is not "almost entirely intrastate")

A limited registration procedure is provided for California developments. In order to comply, the California developer is required to file with OILSR a copy of the subdivision questionnaire filed with the Department of Real Estate, together with all supporting documents and the appropriate filing fee.

An abbreviated statement of record is also required.

The filing is completed when a copy of the California Final Public Report (which substitutes for the federal property report) is received. When all of the material is submitted, the filing becomes effective immediately. The thirty-day waiting period applicable to filings from other states is not required.

Under the federal act the prospective purchaser must receive not only the final public report but also a document entitled "State Property Report Disclaimer." The disclaimer must include a statement that OILSR has not inspected the property or passed upon the accuracy of the report or any of the advertising material.

Contracts or agreements for the purchase or lease of a lot in a subdivision when the property report has not been given to the purchaser in advance or at the time of signing the contract are voidable at the option of the purchaser.

A purchaser may revoke the agreement or contract within forty-eight hours if he or she did not receive the report at least forty-eight hours before signing, and the contract shall so provide.

The option and revocation requirements can be avoided if the purchaser receives the property report, inspects the property in advance of signing the contract, and acknowledges in writing that he or she has done both.

DEPARTMENT OF REAL ESTATE
OF THE
STATE OF CALIFORNIA

In the matter of the application of

CALMARK PROPERTIES, INC.,
a corporation

for a final subdivision public report on

TRACT NO. 33743
"CREST VIEW"
LOS ANGELES COUNTY, CALIFORNIA

**FINAL SUBDIVISION
PUBLIC REPORT**

FILE NO. 41716

ISSUED: FEBRUARY 24, 1978

AMENDED: MARCH 14, 1978

EXPIRES: FEBRUARY 23, 1983

This Report Is Not a Recommendation or Endorsement of the Subdivision But Is Informative Only.

Buyer or Lessee Must Sign That He Has Received and Read This Report.

This Report Expires on Date Shown Above. If There Has Been a Material Change in the Offering, an Amended Public Report Must Be Obtained and Used in Lieu of This Report.

Section 35700 of the California Health and Safety Code provides that the practice of discrimination because of race, color, religion, sex, marital status, national origin or ancestry in housing accommodations is against public policy.

Under Section 125.6 of the California Business and Professions Code, California real estate licensees are subject to disciplinary action by the Real Estate Commissioner if they make any discrimination, distinction or restriction in negotiating a sale or lease of real property because of the race, color, sex, religion, ancestry or national orgin of the prospective buyer. If any prospective buyer or lessee believes that a licensee is guilty of such conduct, he or she should contact the Department of Real Estate.

Information Regarding Schools can be found on Page 3.

READ THE ENTIRE REPORT on the following pages before contracting to purchase a lot in the SUBDIVISION.

Figure 16–2

THIS DEVELOPMENT IS THE FIRST OF TWO PHASES.

LOCATION AND SIZE: This subdivision contains eighteen (18) lots on 3.6 acres and is located at Azusa Avenue and Payson Street within the city limits of Azusa.

EASEMENTS: Easements for ingress and egress, sewers, and other purposes are shown on the title report and subdivision map recorded in the Office of the Los Angeles County Recorder, Book 888, Page 55.

USES AND ZONING: Property to the north, and part of the property to the south and west is zoned C-1, Commercial.

RESTRICTIONS: This subdivision is subject to restrictions recorded in the Office of the Los Angeles County Recorder, on February 2, 1978 as Instrument No. 78-13007.

FOR INFORMATION AS TO YOUR OBLIGATIONS AND RIGHTS, YOU SHOULD READ THE RESTRICTIONS. THE SUBDIVIDER SHOULD MAKE THEM AVAILABLE TO YOU.

TAX ESTIMATES: If the subdivider is unable to give you the current tax information for your lot, you may approximate your taxes as follows:

TAKE 25% OF THE SALES PRICE, DIVIDE BY 100, AND THEN MULTIPLY BY THE TOTAL TAX RATE. THE TAX RATE FOR THE 1977 78 FISCAL YEAR IS $12,8547. THE TAX RATE AND ASSESSED VALUATION MAY CHANGE IN SUBSEQUENT YEARS. FOR EXAMPLE, ANY BONDED DEBT OR SPECIAL DISTRICT ASSESSMENT APPROVED AFTER THE ABOVE TAX RATE HAD BEEN SET COULD INCREASE THE FUTURE RATE.

INTEREST TO BE CONVEYED - CONDITIONS OF SALE: If your purchase involves financing, a form of deed of trust and note will be used. These documents contain the following provisions:

An *acceleration clause*. This means that if you sell the property, the lender may declare the entire balance due and payable.

A *late charge*. This means that if you are late in making your monthly payment, you may have to pay an additional amount as a penalty.

A *prepayment penalty*. This means that if you wish to pay off your loan in whole or in part before it is due, you may be required to pay an additional amount as a penalty in accordance with the terms of the loan.

BEFORE SIGNING, YOU SHOULD READ AND THOROUGHLY UNDERSTAND ALL LOAN DOCUMENTS.

PURCHASE MONEY HANDLING: The subdivider must impound all funds received from you in an escrow depository until legal title is delivered to you. (Ref. Section 11013, 11013.2 (a) of the Business and Professions Code).

-2- of 3 pages   FILE NO. 41716
                        Amended

Figure 16-2 (Continued)

FILLED GROUND: Some lots will contain filled ground varying to a maximum depth of 3.5 feet. These soils are to be properly compacted for the intended use under the supervision of a state licensed engineer.

SOIL CONDITIONS: An engineering report has been filed which indicates soil is expansive, and included in the report are certain recommendations. Subdivider has certified that he will comply with the recommendations of the engineer, that the purchasers' funds will be impounded in escrow, and that no escrows will close until recommendations have been completed.

PUBLIC TRANSPORTATION: Regularly scheduled local and regional R.T.D. public transportation is available on Azusa Avenue.

SCHOOLS: The Azusa Unified School District advises as follows:

Murray Elementary School, K-6, 605 East Renwick Road, Azusa, California, .4 distant.

Center Intermediate School, 7-8, 5500 North Cerritos Avenue, Azusa, California, .6 distant.

Gladstone High School, 9-12, 1340 North Enid Avenue, Covina, California, .9 distant.

School bus transportation, if required, shall be available at the District's expense in accordance with existing Board rules.

NOTE: This school information was correct as of the date of this report. Purchasers may contact the local school district for current information on school assignments, facilities and bus service.

For further information in regard to this subdivision, you may call (213) 620-2700, or examine the documents at the Department of Real Estate, 107 South Broadway, Room 7001, Los Angeles, California 90012.

IM/db   *-3- and last*   *FILE NO. 41716*
Amended

Figure 16-2 (Continued)

The act includes administrative, civil, and penal sanctions. Willful violations of any of the provisions of the act, rule, or regulation are punishable by a fine of not more than $5,000 or by imprisonment for not more than five years, or both.

CHAPTER QUESTIONS

1. What two principal laws govern subdivisions in California? How do these two laws differ?
2. Discuss the penalties for not complying with the provisions of the Subdivision Map Act.
3. What is the primary difference between the Real Estate Commissioner's *Preliminary Public Report* and the *Final Public Report?*
4. Distinguish between a *community apartment house* and a *condominium*. Are these within the definition of a subdivision under the subdivision act?
5. How does the Interstate Land Sales Full Disclosure Act define subdivision? Who administers this act?

MULTIPLE-CHOICE QUESTIONS

1. A subdivider must notify the Commissioner of any material change in the subdivision that occurs after issuance of the Commissioner's Final Public Report. Which of the following would constitute a material change? (a) A change in the ownership of the subdivision; (b) a change in the size of the lots; (c) a change in the manner by which title will be transferred; (d) a change in the sales contracts to be used; (e) all of the foregoing constitute material changes.
2. A man owned nine acres of land. He decided to sell it off in parcels of one acre, three parcels to be sold each year. He would have to: (a) abide by the California real estate law; (b) abide by the Subdivision Map Act; (c) abide by neither *a* or *b*; (d) abide by both *a* and *b*.
3. In a subdivision, the Real Estate Commissioner has primary regulatory authority over: (a) alignment of the streets; (b) drainage; (c) financial arrangements for completion of community facilities; (d) street signs; (e) none of these.
4. The Commissioner's Final Public Report expires:

(a) one year after it is issued; (b) five years after it is issued; (c) never, unless there is a "material" change; (d) if no off-site improvements are installed within two years from the date of issue; (e) three years after it is issued.
5. A broker is not permitted to accept an offer to purchase a lot in a subdivision prior to: (a) furnishing a copy of the Commissioner's Final Public Report to the customer; (b) giving the customer a chance to read the report; (c) obtaining the signature of the customer for a copy of the report; (d) doing all of the foregoing.
6. The Subdivision Map Act provides for: (a) submission of proposed sales contracts for subdivision lots to the local governing body for approval; (b) execution of an improvement contract between subdivider and city; (c) obtaining the signature of the customer for a copy of the Final Public Report; (d) all of the foregoing; (e) none of the foregoing.
7. A subdivision is defined as land that is: (a) improved; (b) mapped by a surveyor; (c) planned for residential purposes; (d) divided for purposes of sale, lease, or financing into five or more parcels; (e) mortgaged.
8. A subdivision located outside the state of California that is to be offered for sale or lease in California: (a) does not come under the jurisdiction of the Real Estate Commissioner; (b) must be filed with the Real Estate Commissioner; (c) cannot be financed by a blanket mortgage; (d) must be in parcels of not less than one acre; (e) must be in parcels of not less than ten acres.
9. Under the basic procedures set forth in the Subdivision Map Act, a tentative map is prepared and filed with: (a) the Real Estate Commissioner; (b) the state land commissioner; (c) the state of California; (d) the secretary of state; (e) the city or the county.
10. In the sale of five lots to a contractor, the original subdivider gave an option on five other lots. If the subdivider has secured his or her final public report, what additional requirements must be met? (a) The subdivider must report the sale of the five lots to the Real Estate Commissioner; (b) the subdivider need not report anything to the Real Estate Commissioner; (c) the subdivider must report the option to the Real Estate Commissioner; (d) the subdivider must report both the sale and the option to the Real Estate Commissioner.

LICENSING AND STATE LAWS REGULATING REAL ESTATE BUSINESS

California leads all states in regulating the activity of people in the real estate business. The prime purpose of this regulation is to protect the public, but it also has benefited real estate people by raising the standards of the business. Many other states watch what California does and model their own real estate laws after ours.

The special group of California statutes that *regulate* the real estate business are called the *Real Estate Law*. It should be distinguished from what is known as real estate property law, legal aspects of real estate, and the like—all the law and court decisions that *affect* real property. From time to time, changes are made in the Real Estate Law, so some of the material outlined in this chapter is subject to change.

Regulation of the real estate business is largely in the hands of (1) the Real Estate Advisory Commission, (2) the Real Estate Commissioner, and (3) the Department of Real Estate (which consists of the deputies, clerks, and other employees who work for the Commissioner). The Commission does certain advisory work and passes upon some matters, but, as we shall see, the actual enforcement of the Real Estate Law is done by the Commissioner and the Department of Real Estate under him or her.

REAL ESTATE ADVISORY COMMISSION

The Real Estate Advisory Commission consists of eight members, five of whom shall be real estate brokers and three of whom shall be public members. The members of the Advisory Commission are appointed by the Real Estate Commissioner.

The Commissioner is required to meet and consult and advise with the Advisory Commission on the functions and policies of the Department of Real Estate and make such recommendations and suggestions of policy as it deems beneficial and appropriate.

The meetings of the Advisory Commission shall be called at least four times each year, and written notice of the time and place of such meetings shall be given to the members and other persons requesting same at least ten days before such meetings. The meetings of the Advisory Commission are open to the public, and the views of both licensees and the public are solicited.

The Real Estate Commissioner is required to notify the Advisory Commission of his or her intention to adopt rules and regulations at least thirty days prior to such adoption.

THE REAL ESTATE COMMISSIONER AND THE DEPARTMENT OF REAL ESTATE

The Department of Real Estate is set up by the Real Estate Law; the Real Estate Commissioner is made its chief officer. The Commissioner is a salaried state employee, is appointed by the governor, and serves at the governor's pleasure. It is his or her duty to enforce the Real Estate Law and to issue, control, and revoke real estate licenses. To avoid conflict of interest, the law provides that the Commissioner, his or her deputies, clerks, or employees of the department must have no interest in any (1) mineral, oil, or gas business; (2) mineral, oil, or gas brokerage firm; (3) real estate company; or (4) real estate brokerage firm as director, stockholder, officer,

234

member, agent, or employee. None may act as a partner or an agent for any broker or salesperson.

The Commissioner's principal office is in Sacramento, with branch offices in San Francisco, Fresno, Santa Ana, San Diego, and Los Angeles. His or her legal adviser is the attorney general of the state, who acts as legal counsel in all actions and proceedings brought against the Commissioner under the Real Estate Law. Every three months the Commissioner publishes the *Real Estate Bulletin* containing material relating to the department and other items that he or she believes would be of importance and interest to licensees.

The Commissioner also publishes each year, through the department, the *Reference Book*. This book contains a vast amount of very useful information, and we urge you to buy one if you are going to be actively engaged in real estate. The *Reference Book* contains a complete discussion of the real estate business in California and the law and regulations covering the real estate business.

The Commissioner is empowered, after proper notice, to issue, amend, or repeal regulations to aid in the administration and enforcement of the Real Estate Law. These actions have the same force and effect as the Real Estate Law itself.

If the Commissioner believes that any provision of the Real Estate Law is violated or is about to be violated, action can be brought in any superior court to enjoin the people involved from continuing the violation; but no injunction or restraining order may be granted without at least five days' notice to the opposing party. The district attorney of the county where the action is brought represents the Commissioner in such actions.

As the chief executive officer of the Department of Real Estate, the Commissioner has many duties. One of these duties includes the issuance of Commissioner's Regulations. These regulations are part of the California Administrative Code.

The regulations do not have to be approved by the Legislature. However, they are binding on licensees, the same as other laws. The Commissioner has also approved a Code of Ethics which is binding on licensees. This code is part of the Commissioner's regulations.

REAL ESTATE LICENSING— REQUIREMENTS AND FEES

One of the main purposes of the Real Estate Law is to license and regulate people engaged in the business. Licenses issued by the Department of Real Estate include those for real estate broker; real estate salesperson; mineral, oil, and gas broker; and real estate securities dealer endorsement.

Most of the licenses issued by the Commissioner are for real estate brokers and real estate salespeople. The license authorizes a broker to engage in the occupation of real estate broker. A salesperson is authorized to work for a broker.

Real estate broker Under the Real Estate Law a person is considered a real estate broker, and must be licensed as such, if he or she negotiates to do any of the following actions for compensation or in expectation of compensation, regardless of the form or time of payment, for another person or other persons:

1. Sells or offers to sell, buys or offers to buy, solicits prospective sellers or purchasers of, solicits or obtains listings of, or negotiates the purchase, sale, or exchange of real property or a business opportunity

2. Leases or rents, or offers to lease or rent, or places for rent, or solicits listings of places for rent, or solicits for prospective tenants, or negotiates the sale, purchase, or exchange of leases on real property, or on a business opportunity, or collects rents from real property, or improvements thereon, or from business opportunities

3. Assists or offers to assist in filing an application for the purchase or lease of, or in locating or entering upon, lands owned by the state or federal government

4. Solicits borrowers or lenders for, or negotiates loans or collects payments or performs services for, borrowers or lenders or note owners in connection with loans secured directly or collaterally by liens on real property or on a business opportunity

5. Sells or offers to sell, buys or offers to buy, exchanges or offers to exchange a real-property sales contract or a promissory note secured directly or collaterally by a lien on real property or on a business opportunity, and performs services for the holders thereof

6. Engages as a principal in the business of buying from, selling to, or exchanging with the public, real estate sales contracts or promissory notes secured directly or collaterally by liens on real properties, or makes agreements with the public for the collection of payments, or for the performance of services in connection with real-property sales contracts or promissory notes secured directly or collaterally by liens on real property

7. Engages in the business of claiming, demanding, charging, receiving, collecting, or contracting for the collecting of an advance fee in connection with any employment undertaken to promote the sale or lease of real property, or of a business opportunity, by advance fee listing, advertisement, or other offerings to sell, lease, exchange, or rent property or a business opportunity, or to obtain a loan or loans thereof

8. Issues or sells or solicits prospective sellers or purchasers of, solicits or obtains listings of, or negotiates the purchase, sale, or exchange of securities (unless registered as a broker-dealer or agent of a broker-dealer licensed as such by the Commissioner of Corporations)

However, certain people can do the preceding acts without a real estate license. Those persons performing acts that ordinarily require a license and who are exempt from licensing are:

1. Anyone who is directly dealing with his or her own property.

2. Any regular corporate officer, who, as part of his or her regular duties, and without special compensation, deals with the corporate property.

3. Anyone acting under a valid power of attorney from the owner, in dealing with the owner's property.

4. Attorneys rendering services in performance of their duties as attorneys.

5. Any receiver, any trustee in bankruptcy, or any person acting under order of any court.

6. Any trustee selling under a deed of trust.

7. Anyone specifically excluded by statute from needing a license.

PENALTIES FOR BEING UNLICENSED

An unlicensed person who acts as a broker or a salesperson is subject to all the following sanctions:

1. He or she may not collect a commission or any compensation for his or her acts. In fact, when a broker sues for a commission, he or she must allege and prove that he or she was licensed when the commission was earned.

2. The Commissioner may sue to enjoin him or her from continuing his or her acts.

3. He or she may be prosecuted criminally and, upon conviction, is subject to a fine up to $1,000 or sentence of up to six months in jail, or both.

If a corporation is found guilty, it may be fined up to $10,000. A licensed broker paying a compensation to a nonlicensee for acting as a broker or a salesperson is guilty of a misdemeanor and may be fined up to $100 for each offense. In addition, a broker may have his or her license suspended or revoked.

PREREQUISITES FOR LICENSING

Real estate broker

An application for a real estate broker's license must be made in writing to the Commissioner and accompanied by an application fee of $25. The broker applicant must be at least 18 years of age.

Experience requirements An applicant must have held a real estate salesperson's license for at least two years and qualified for renewal of real estate salesperson status within the five-year period immediately prior to the date of his or her application for the broker's license. The mere fact that an applicant has held a salesperson's license for two or more years, as shown by the department's records, does not qualify him or her to take the examination. The applicant must present evidence of full-time employment (at least forty hours per week) with his or her application. The Commissioner's office furnishes forms on which the employing broker or brokers can certify the extent and scope of the person's activity as a real estate salesperson. The Commissioner may suspend without a hearing, within ninety days after issuance, the license of any real estate licensee who procured a license for himself or herself by fraud, misrepresentation, or deceit, or made any material misstatement of fact in his or her application.

An applicant may claim equivalent experience in the general field of real estate or graduation from a four-year college or university with a major in business subjects and a specialization in real estate. The equivalent educational experience requires approval of at least three members of the Real Estate Commission. If the approvals are obtained, the applicant can be issued a broker's license immediately upon passing the examination and other license requirements.

Equivalent experience must be supported by valid evidence. The evidence presented may be in letter form over the applicant's signature or by letters or statements from employers or other parties who have been in a position to note the applicant's duties or activities as they are related to the general field of real estate and who will certify them in some detail. A licensee from another state is expected to furnish sufficient evidence that his or her activities as a real estate agent were on a full-time basis. He or she is also expected to furnish an official statement from the licensing authority of that state, giving his or her complete record as a licensee.

Claims of qualification based upon education with specialization in subjects relating strictly to real estate must also be supported by transcripts of record or certificates of achievement.

The applicant who fails to qualify for the license because of inability to pass the examination or lack of experience is not entitled to a refund of the application fee. The fee will, however, remain to his or her credit for two years.

Educational requirements The Real Estate Law also requires that, in addition to having real estate salesperson's experience or equivalent work experience, the applicant must meet certain educational requirements.

The applicant must have completed all of the following courses:

1. Real estate practice
2. Legal aspects of real estate
3. Real estate appraisal
4. Real estate finance
5. Real estate economics or accounting

The applicant must also have completed any three of the following courses:

1. Advanced legal aspects of real estate
2. Advanced real estate finance
3. Advanced real estate appraisal
4. Business law
5. Escrows
6. Real estate principles
7. Property management
8. Real estate office administration

All those courses must be three semester unit courses, completed at an accredited college or university* or taken by an equivalent course of study offered by private vocational schools approved by the Real Estate Commissioner.

Attorneys are exempt from the educational requirements.

Real estate salesperson

An applicant for the real estate salesperson license must be at least 18 years of age. The applicant must not have been convicted of a felony or a crime involving moral turpitude. Application for the license examination must be in writing on a form approved by the Commissioner. The applicant must sign the application and submit it with the examination fee of $10. If successful in passing the examination, the applicant will be mailed an application for the real estate salesperson's license, which must be signed by his or her employing broker and submitted to the Commissioner along with the license fee. The license fee is $120, unless the salesperson is qualifying under a conditional license, where he or she must complete certain courses within eighteen months, in which case the fee is $145.

Educational requirements The applicant must complete a real estate principles course.

The applicant must also complete, prior to the examination or within eighteen months of obtaining his or her license, two of the following courses:

* An *accredited institution* within the meaning of the law is a college or university accredited by the Western Association of Schools and Colleges or by any other regional accrediting agency recognized by the United States Department of Health, Education and Welfare, Office of Education. It may also be a college or university that, in the judgment of the Commissioner, has a real estate curriculum equivalent in quality to that of the institutions accredited.

1. Real estate practice
2. Real estate finance
3. Real estate appraisal
4. Business law
5. Escrows
6. Legal aspects of real estate
7. Property management
8. Real estate office administration
9. Accounting
10. Real estate economics

All the preceding courses must be three semester unit courses, completed at an accredited college or university or taken by an equivalent course of study offered by private vocational schools approved by the Real Estate Commissioner. Attorneys are exempt from the educational requirements.

Conditional licenses If the salesperson obtains his or her license by meeting only the real estate principles course, the license will be suspended until he or she has completed the two additional courses required. If he or she has not passed those two courses within eighteen months, the conditional license will be revoked.

Out-of-state applicants

There is no provision in the California license law for reciprocity (other than examinations, discussed later in this chapter) with other states in the matter of licensing. Each applicant must qualify in a written examination in this state and meet all other requirements; however, residency in the state is not a requirement for licensure.

In applying for a real estate broker's examination, the applicant should obtain the following documents to support his or her application:

1. A letter or statement from the residential state's licensing agency, setting forth his or her license record.
2. Letters must be secured from at least two businessmen in the area where the applicant practiced as a licensee, testifying to the number of years the applicant was active in the business and whether his or her activity was on a full- or part-time basis.
3. Course transcripts evidencing completion of the statutorily required courses.

Fingerprints

Applicants for any real estate license must submit a set of fingerprints unless licensed by the Department of Real Estate within the past five years. Fingerprints may be taken at any of the department's district offices, or arrangements may be made to have the prints taken at most sheriff's offices or police stations.

Broker applicants should file the fingerprints with their

applications for license examination. Real estate sales-person applicants must first qualify in the examination and then submit the fingerprints when the application for license is filed.

Types of licenses

Individual broker　This is the most common type of broker license. The licensed individual may act on his or her own account in conducting a brokerage business or under a fictitious business name. When a fictitious business name is used, Sections 2730–2733 of the Regulations of the Commissioner must be complied with. The broker or corporation is required to submit to the Commissioner a certified copy of the fictitious business name filed with the county clerk in compliance with Sections 17900–17930 of the Business and Professions Code. A fictitious name is one that does not include the surname of the operator or one that implies the existence of other owners; or, if a corporation, it includes a name other than the name given in the articles of incorporation. The purpose of this section of the law is to protect the consumer by enabling him or her to find out the indentities of the persons with whom he or she is dealing.

Corporation license　The licensed broker may set up a corporation; the corporation may be licensed as a real estate broker, but at least one officer of the corporation must be a qualified real estate broker. In addition the articles of incorporation must be on file with the secretary of state. Real estate salespeople may be officers of the corporation if the chief officer primarily responsible for management and operations has a real estate broker's license to act on behalf of the corporation.

Partnership　There is no special partnership license issued by the Department of Real Estate. In a partnership, however, each partner who intends to conduct real estate business on behalf of the partnership must be licensed as a real estate broker. A salesperson may not be a general partner in a partnership, but he or she may be licensed as a salesperson under one of the individual brokers.

Broker members of a partnership formed by written agreement may conduct business from a branch office without obtaining a branch-office license if one member of the partnership is licensed at that location.

Salesperson　This license covers individuals who are employed as salespeople under the supervision and control of a licensed real estate broker. The salesperson is not an independent agent, and his or her activity in the real estate business is limited to his or her employing broker. The compensation paid to the salesperson is through his or her employing broker only.

The holder of a broker's license may, during the term of that license, request inactivation of his or her broker's license and, upon filing the appropriate application and fee, be issued a salesperson's license of the same class. Under this procedure he or she need not qualify in the salesperson's examination.

All real estate agreements prepared or signed by a salesperson that would materially affect the rights or duties of the parties to the transaction shall be reviewed and initialed by the employing broker within five working days of the execution thereof or before the close of escrow, whichever occurs first. In addition, salespeople, or brokers acting as such, must disclose principal transactions to their supervisors in writing within five days. The broker has overall responsibility and supervision, but he or she may delegate these duties

1. To any licensed real estate broker who has entered into a written agreement relating thereto with the broker.

2. When circumstances warrant, to a real estate salesperson licensed to him or her, providing such salesperson has entered into a written contract relating thereto with the broker and has accumulated at least two years full-time experience as a real estate salesperson during the preceding five-year period.

Each broker must have a written agreement with each of his or her salespeople, whether they are licensed as brokers or salespeople. This agreement must be signed by both parties and retained by them for a period of three years after termination of employment.

Restricted license　The Commissioner may issue a restricted license when a person has held a valid license in the state of California but has violated certain provisions of the Real Estate Law. A restricted license is not subject to renewal and may be suspended without a hearing. The license may be restricted by term, employment by a particular broker, or any other conditions that the Commissioner may apply. The Commissioner may further require the filing of a surety bond in such form and condition as he or she sees fit.

Branch office　A branch-office license is required for each branch office operated by a real estate broker other than the principal office. The branch-office license must be available for inspection.

License fees

License or examination fees must be sent with each application for a real estate license. All fees are deemed earned when sent to the Department of Real Estate, and no fee is refundable. The following fee schedule is subject to change.

License fees

Broker (4 years)	$165
Broker (restricted)	$165
Salesperson (3 ed. courses)	$120
Salesperson (2 courses to go)	$145
Salesperson (restricted)	$120
Real property securities dealer endorsement	$100
Late renewal (broker)	$220
Late renewal (salesperson)	$160

Examination fees

Broker's exam or reexam	$ 50
Salesperson's exam or reexam	$ 25
Change exam date (broker)	$ 15
Change exam date (salesperson)	$ 10
Second change of exam date, broker or salesperson	$ 25

Exemption from license fees

The following persons are exempt from real estate license fees in the state of California according to the Real Estate Law:

Any person in the military service of the United States who notifies the Real Estate Commissioner of this fact within two months of entry into the service shall be exempt from further license fees until discharged from the military service. Such military service includes the United States Army, Navy, Marine Corps, Merchant Marine in the time of war, Coast Guard and all Public Health Service officers detailed for duty with either the Army or Navy. Military service further includes federal service with any branch of the service as well as training or education under the supervision of the United States or induction into the military service. The terms active service or active duty include the period during which a person in military services is absent from duty on account of sickness leave or other lawful cause. The military licensee is further exempt from the responsibility of renewal of his license until the beginning of the license period which commences after he again engages in the real estate business or one year following the termination of his military service, whichever date is earlier. Where the licensee receives a dishonorable discharge from the military service, or if through his voluntary act remains in the service for six months following the termination of all wars in which the United States is engaged, he shall not be entitled to the renewal of his license.

Renewal of licenses

A licensee should renew his or her real estate license on or before the expiration date. If the license expires, it may be renewed by paying a late fee and meeting the continuing education requirements. The Real Estate Commissioner has authority to require an expired licensee to take a new examination to obtain his or her license. However, if the applicant meets the continuing education requirements and has held an unrevoked or unsuspended license in the immediate two years, such examination is almost never required.

Continuing education law for real estate licensees

In 1919, when the Real Estate Act was first adopted, the requirements for licensing were almost nonexistent. Over the years, certain requirements crept into the law, including the requirement that licensees be of good moral character. However, little was done toward requiring any formal education.

In 1966 the Real Estate Commissioner released his formulated preliminary blueprint for professionalism. That blueprint established for the first time an outline of courses that would be required to qualify for real estate licenses. Since that date, the educational requirements have increased, and they are still changing frequently.

Therefore, the educational requirements presented here may have changed by the time of your review. You should check the Department of Real Estate *Reference Book* for the latest requirements.

Courses required A real estate salesperson who renews his or her license for the first time needs to take only three hours of continuing education. He or she must take the "ethics, professional conduct, and legal aspects of real estate" course. All further renewals require the salesperson to meet the normal continuing education requirements.

All licensees, except first-time salesperson renewals, must have forty-five hours of specified continuing education courses. The forty-five hours must be broken up as follows:

Ethics, professional conduct, and legal aspects of real estate	3 hours
Consumer protection courses	21 hours
Consumer protection courses or professional competency courses	21 hours

Consumer protection courses include "real estate financing relative to serving consumers in the marketplace; land use regulation and control; pertinent consumer disclosures; agency relationships; capital formation for real estate development; fair practices in real estate; appraisal and valuation techniques; landlord-tenant relationships; energy conservation; environmental regulation and consideration; taxation as it relates to consumer decisions in real estate transactions; probate and similar disposition of real property; governmental programs such as revenue bond activities, redevelopment, and related programs; business opportunities; and mineral, oil, and gas conveyancing."

Beginning in July 1987, three units of consumer protection courses must be for a course in agency relationships.

The educational requirements to obtain a broker's license and a salesperson's license have already been discussed. Once you have a license, you will need to renew it at the end of four years. You do not need to pass an examination to renew. However, you must meet certain continuing education requirements to obtain your new license.

Course standards   The Real Estate Commissioner establishes the standards for continuing education courses. As stated in B.&P.C. 10170.4(f):

> . . . *the commissioner shall establish standards which will insure reasonable currency of knowledge as a basis for a level of real estate practice which will provide a high level of consumer protection and of competence in achieving the objectives of members of the public who engage the services of licensees.*
>
> *The standards shall permit a variety of alternatives of subject material to licensees, taking cognizance of specialized areas of practice, and alternatives in sources of programs considering availability in area and time.*
>
> *The standards shall include, where qualified, generally-accredited educational institutions, private vocational schools, correspondence institutions, educational programs, workshops, and seminars of professional societies and organizations, other organized educational programs on technical subjects, or equivalent offerings.*

The Real Estate Commissioner has detailed procedures for qualifying courses for continuing educational requirements. If you are taking a continuing education course, be sure it is currently qualified by the Commissioner.

The professional competency courses cover ''the transfer, financing, or similar objectives with respect to real property, including organizational and management techniques.'' Typical courses might include real estate office management, deposit receipts, listing agreements, and mortgage lending.

All courses require an examination, with the licensee obtaining a passing grade of 70 percent or higher. Where on-site courses are offered, the licensee must be in attendance throughout the entire course.

Certificates   Upon successfully completing a continuing education course, the licensee is issued a certificate. This document contains a thirteen-digit number identifying the course. When it is time to renew your license, you fill out a special form (RE Form 251), listing all courses you have attended.

CANCELLATION AND TRANSFER OF SALESPERSON'S LICENSE

Whenever a real estate salesperson enters the employ of a real estate broker, the broker must immediately notify the Commissioner in writing. Furthermore, notification must be given to the Commissioner by the broker when the real estate salesperson's employment is terminated or when he or she is discharged. Whenever a licensee acquires a business address different from the address shown on his or her license, the licensee must mark out the former address on the face of the license, type or write the new main-office address in ink on the reverse side, and date and initial same. Whenever a real estate salesperson enters the employ of a new real estate broker, he or she must mark out the name of his or her former broker on the face of the license, type or write the name of the new employing broker in ink on the reverse side, and date and initial same. An appropriate written statement by the transferring salesperson of the reason he or she was unable to obtain the signature of his or her former employing broker when transferring to a new broker is now required.

DISPLAY OF LICENSE AND BUSINESS TITLE

A broker licensed by the state of California is required to maintain a definite place of business to serve as his or her office for the transaction of business and for personal consultation with clients. The broker's license and the licenses of all salespeople in his or her employ must be on file at his or her principal place of business. The broker's license does not authorize him or her to do business except from the location stipulated on the license.

Although the broker must have one principal place of business, he or she may have as many branch offices as he or she desires. A broker is still responsible for proper supervision of his or her salespeople, however. Applications for branch-office licenses are obtained from the Commissioner's office, and a $4 fee is charged for each license. Licenses of all real estate salespeople must be on file in the principal place of business, regardless of the locations of the branch offices.

DISCIPLINARY ACTION

The Commissioner may, upon his or her own motion, and shall, upon receiving a verified complaint in writing from any person in the state of California, investigate the actions of any licensee in business. He or she may temporarily suspend or permanently revoke a license at any time if the licensee has been found guilty of any of the following:

1. Making any substantial misrepresentation
2. Making false promises likely to influence, persuade, or induce

3. Making false promises through real estate agents or salespeople and pursuing a continued and flagrant course of misrepresentation of property

4. Acting for more than one party to a transaction without the knowledge or consent of all parties

5. Commingling business or personal money with the property of others that is received and held by him or her in trust

6. Claiming, demanding, or receiving a fee or commission under an exclusive authorization and right-to-sell listing agreement or an exclusive agency agreement, when such an agreement does not bear a definite date of termination

7. Claiming or taking a secret profit without the knowledge of the principal

8. When a combined-listing option agreement is used by the real estate broker before exercising option to purchase, failing to reveal to the purchaser in writing the full amount of his or her profit and failing to obtain the written approval of the principal before the taking of such a profit

9. Any other conduct, whether of the same or of a different character that could constitute fraud or dishonest dealing

10. Having a prospective purchaser sign an agreement to buy, exchange, or lease a business opportunity, without first having the written authorization of the owner to accept such offer

The Real Estate Commissioner may also suspend or revoke a license of any licensee or deny the issuance of a license to an applicant for any of the following reasons:

1. When an applicant has attempted to secure a license by fraud, misrepresentation, or deceit, or has made a material misstatement of fact in the application for a license

2. When the licensee has entered a plea of guilty or has been convicted of a felony or a crime involving moral turpitude and time for appeal has lapsed or the judgment or conviction has been affirmed on appeal

3. When the licensee has knowingly authorized, directed, or aided in the publication, advertisement, distribution, or circulation of any false material concerning his or her business or any land or subdivision

4. When the licensee has willfully disregarded and violated any provisions of the Real Estate Law

5. When the licensee has improperly used the term ''Realtor''

6. When the licensee is guilty of any misconduct that has warranted the denial of his or her application for the license

7. When the licensee has demonstrated negligence or incompetence in the performance of any act where a license is required

8. When a real estate broker has failed to exercise reasonable supervision over the activities of his or her salespeople

9. When the licensee has used his or her employment in a governmental agency and has used records in such a manner as to violate the confidential nature of such records

10. When the licensee has engaged in any fraudulent or dishonest conduct

11. When the licensee has violated any term or condition of a restricted license

12. When the licensee has solicited or induced any sale, lease, or listing of residential property through mention of race, color, religion, ancestry, or national origin

13. When the licensee has violated any of the Franchise Investment Law

14. When the licensee has violated any of the Corporate Securities Law

The Commissioner may suspend, revoke, or deny the issuance of a license to an applicant who has been committed or adjudged insane, mentally ill, or incompetent by any federal court of competent jurisdiction. This may be done at any time until a subsequent adjudication of competence or restoration to capacity has been made.

When a license has been suspended or revoked, the Commissioner may require the applicant to pass a qualifying examination. A member of a corporation or a partnership may have either his or her individual broker's license or his or her corporation license suspended or revoked by the Commissioner.

Accounting records

All records, books, and accounts of licensed real estate brokers and their salespeople are subject to inspection and audit by the Commissioner or his or her designated representative at any time. All agreements, including listings, deposit receipts, exchange agreements, leases, and so forth, are required to be kept by the licensee for a minimum of three years. In addition thereto, the employing broker must initial all contracts of his or her sales personnel.

REAL PROPERTY SECURITIES DEALER

The real property securities dealer portion of the statute controls bulk transactions, deeds of trust, and other real property sale contracts. It further controls investment plans dealing with such contracts.

Only a holder of a valid real estate broker's license is entitled to seek endorsement as a real property securities dealer. A written application must be sent to the Real Estate Commissioner together with a $50 endorsement fee and a corporate surety bond in the amount of $5,000.

In lieu of the bond, the applicant may submit proper evidence of having filed with the state treasurer a cash bond for $5,000, or he or she may deposit $6,000 in bonds issued by the United States or the state of California.

A *real property securities dealer* is defined as any person acting as principal or agent in the business of

  1. Selling real property securities to the public.
  2. Offering to accept or accepting funds for continued reinvestment in real properties securities, or funds placed in an account, plan, or program in which the dealer implies that a return will be derived from a specified real property sales contract or from a promissory note secured collaterally or directly by a lien on real property which directly or indirectly implies the possibility of payments from a source other than the security.

The primary definition of a security is that ''something'' other than only the note will insure the payments or terms of the note. The most common examples are express or implied promises or agreements by the broker to do any of the following:

  1. Guarantee the note holder against any losses
  2. Guarantee that payments of principal or interest will be paid on time
  3. Guarantee a specific yield or return on the note
  4. Promise to repurchase the note at any time

A security also occurs when the broker, without any previous guarantee, in fact makes monthly payments to the note holder, while the note is in default, from funds other than those from the trustor. Finally, a security can arise in the sale of a series of subdivision notes or contracts.

Excluded from this definition as ''selling to the public'' are sales made to corporations, pension retirement or similar trust funds, leading institutions or agencies, real estate brokers, or attorneys.

When a licensee has had his or her license endorsed as a real properties securities dealer, he or she must obtain a permit from the Commissioner *before selling real property securities to the public.* This permit may enable him or her to sell securities held by a principal or a principal's dealer, or it may authorize an applicant to acquire and sell securities under a plan or program. A securities dealer's statement must also be furnished to the dealer or the purchaser of a note secured by a deed of trust. The form approved by the commission is shown in Figure 17–1.

An annual audit must be submitted to the Commissioner giving the number of sales, the dollar volume, and other pertinent data concerning the transactions of the real property securities dealer.

When advertising material is to be used by the dealer, he or she must file such material with the Commissioner at least ten days prior to its use. If the dealer is informed that such advertising is false or misleading, he or she may not use the material.

Prepaid rental listing services

Prepaid rental listing services are businesses that provide prospective tenants with listings of apartments or other residential housing for rent, by publication or otherwise. The prospective tenant pays a fee before or upon receipt of the listings, and the businesses are not otherwise involved in the negotiation of rental agreements between the prospective tenant and the landlord. Such businesses must be operated either by real estate brokers or by a person licensed in that business.

Such businesses are carefully governed by rules prescribed by the Real Estate Commissioner and by laws in the Business and Professions Code. If a broker desires to operate such a business under a license other than a real estate broker's license, he or she must satisfy the qualification standards, pay the required license fee, post the appropriate bond, and comply with all the applicable laws and regulations.

Prior to accepting any fee from a prospective tenant, the licensee must provide the prospective tenant with a written contract that includes the following:

  1. The full identity and the address of the broker
  2. Acknowledgment of receipt of the fee
  3. A description of the services to be performed by the licensee, including any significant conditions and limitations
  4. A full description of the type of rental desired by the prospective tenant
  5. The contract expiration date, which cannot be greater than ninety days
  6. A complete statement of the prospective tenant's right to a refund, using the type-size and wording specified by statute
  7. The licensee's signature
  8. A clause in boldface type outlining the small-claims court remedy available to the tenant

If within five days the prospective tenant does not receive at least three current, available rental properties meeting his or her rental criteria, the prospective tenant is entitled to a full refund. If the prospective tenant does not obtain a rental through the broker, or obtains a rental through sources other than the broker, the broker must refund any portion of the fee over $25.

Anyone using the services of an advance rental agent, or planning to go into the business, should read all the many and varied regulations governing such activities.

2977. Approved Form. The following form is approved by the Real Estate Commissioner for use as the statement required by Section 10237.4, Chapter 3, Part 1, Division 4 of the Business and Professions Code of the State of California.

REAL PROPERTY SECURITY STATEMENT

_____
(Name of Firm)

_____
(Address of Firm)

1. Property Owner:
   (a) Name and Address of Fee Owner _____
   _____

   (b) Purchaser under a Real Property Sales Contract (if any)
   _____

   (c) Credit Information relative to maker or obligor:
       (1) Employed by _____
       (2) Years employed _____
       (3) Monthly salary $_____
       (4) *Other Assets* _____

       (5) List financial obligations and amount of monthly payments:
       _____ $_____
       _____ $_____
       _____ $_____

2. Securing Property:
   (a) Street address and/or legal description _____
   _____
   _____

   (b) If improved, describe type of improvement (Indicate if none) _____

   (c) Which of the following have been installed on or adjacent to property:
       (1) ☐ Sewers   ☐ Streets   ☐ Water Mains
           ☐ Curbs and gutters ☐ Other.
       (2) If improvements have not been paid, list balance due:
           $ _____

   (d) If security is a note, complete the following:
       (1) Date of last sale of property _____
       (2) Purchase price _____
       (3) Cash down payment (if other, explain) _____

   (e) If an appraisal has been made, complete the following:
       (1) Appraised value $ _____
       (2) Date of Appraisal _____
       (3) Name of Appraiser _____
   (f) Dealer's opinion of current fair market value of property .... $_____

NOTE: IF AN APPRAISAL HAS NOT BEEN MADE, THE PURCHASER MUST COMPLETE THE FOLLOWING CERTIFICATION:
   I hereby certify that I do not wish an appraisal made by the real property securities dealer or an independent appraiser and that I will obtain my own appraisal.
   _____
   Purchaser.

3. Terms and amounts of prior assessments, including taxes and improvement bonds:
   (a) _____ $_____
   (b) _____ $_____
   (c) _____ $_____

4. Terms and conditions of all prior recorded deeds of trust and other encumbrances, other than above, which constitute liens upon the property:
   (a) _____
   Status of payments _____ Principal Balance _____ $_____
   (b) _____
   Status of payments _____ Principal Balance _____ $_____
   (c) _____
   Status of payments _____ Principal Balance _____ $_____
   PRINCIPAL BALANCE OF OUTSTANDING PRIOR
       ENCUMBRANCES_____ $_____
       OWNER'S ESTIMATED EQUITY_____ $_____

5. Terms and conditions of note or contract:
   (a) Present balance _____ $_____
   (b) Original amount _____ $_____
   (c) Date of note or contract _____ Interest rate _____
   (d) Maturity date _____
   (e) Amount of monthly payment (if other, explain) _____

   (f) Status of payments (if not current, explain) _____

   (g) Will request for notice of default be recorded _____
   (h) Terms and conditions of subordination agreement, if any _____
   _____

   (i) In both words and figures, state balance due at maturity, if any.
   (If none, so state) $_____ _____ Dollars
   The undersigned certifies that this transaction is in compliance with California Real Estate Law, that he is acting as Principal ☐ or Agent ☐, and that the information set forth herein is true and correct.

   _____   _____   _____
   (date)   (Dealer)   License No.

THE UNDERSIGNED PURCHASER ACKNOWLEDGES RECEIPT OF A COPY OF THIS STATEMENT AND CERTIFIES THAT HE HAS READ THE SAME AND HAS APPROVED THE PURCHASE OF THE CONTRACT OR NOTE AND DEED OF TRUST.

   _____   _____
   (date)   Name

Figure 17–1

REAL ESTATE EXAMINATIONS

Real estate salesperson and broker examinations are devised to separate questions that are universal in their application from those that deal with subject matter peculiar to real estate law and practice in California.

In the examination for the real estate broker's license, 50 percent of the questions in the morning session of 100 questions are multistate in character. In the salesperson's examination two-thirds of the material (100 questions from the total of the 150 constituting the current examination) are multistate in character. Multistate questions are those that are applicable anywhere in the United States.

Salesperson examinations are offered in the several cities where district offices are maintained, as well as in Sacramento. Tests are given at least once a month, or as demand warrants, but the examination facilities are not necessarily located within the offices themselves.

The broker examination is administered in Los Angeles, San Francisco, San Diego and Sacramento only and not more than once each month or every other month.

The Real Estate Law makes no distinction between broker and salesperson license examinations insofar as subject material is concerned. The two examinations are similar in format and in weighting of content. The test for the broker's license contains more difficult material. The candidate for the broker's license must score 75 percent to pass the examination; the candidate for the salesperson's license must score 70 percent. (Setting passing scores is not a matter of law, and they are subject to change.) There is no limitation on the number of re-examinations that the candidate may take for the broker's or salesperson's license. The examination fee is required for the license examination each time it is given.

The candidate for the broker's license is allowed a maximum of five hours to complete the examination—two and one-half hours in the morning session and the same time in the afternoon. The time schedule for the salesperson's license examination is three and one-quarter hours. Salesperson examinations are administered in both the morning and the afternoon. Thousands of examinations are given each year for the broker and the salesperson licenses. Due to this volume, the candidate cannot be allowed to personally inspect his or her book or answer-sheet after an examination.

The area covered in the examination is divided into five fields. The candidate for the license is expected to demonstrate

1. A reasonable understanding of the Real Estate Law and its application to real estate transactions. Both listing and deposit receipts are included. This portion of the examination is weighted 34 percent.

2. A general understanding of the impact of federal, state, and local authority in zoning, subdividing, and exercising the power of eminent domain in real estate transactions. This portion of the examination is weighted 17 percent.

3. A sufficient knowledge of the appraisal of real properties to enable the licensee to serve his or her clients and the public in carrying out his or her function in the real estate market. This portion of the examination is weighted 19 percent.

4. A general knowledge of real estate finance—including but not limited to available financial sources, procedures, practices, and government participation sufficient to assist clients in obtaining and utilizing credit in real estate transactions. This portion of the examination is weighted 20 percent.

The miscellaneous fields pertaining to real estate (weighted 10 percent) include income taxation, land development, business ethics, rentals and property management, escrows, arithmetical calculations, title insurance, and residential building, design, and construction.

The questions for both the broker and the salesperson license examinations are constantly reviewed, and new test items are developed to reflect the changing conditions in the real estate business. Similar questions to those on the examinations are given throughout this text; however, no one outside of the Department of Real Estate has the exact examination questions.

The following are some examples of multiple-choice questions on material that one might expect to find in a state examination.

Mark the answer *A, B, C, D,* or *E,* coinciding with what you believe is correct.

1. A corporation owns twenty homes in a subdivision. It hired a maintenance man who did not have a real estate license, but he showed the property and quoted prices and terms: (a) This was legal because he was an employee of the corporation; (b) he need not be a real estate licensee; (c) this was legal, since he did not write up offers or accept deposits; (d) this was a violation of the Real Estate Law.

2. A change in business address must be reported to the Real Estate Commissioner: (a) within three days; (b) within one year; (c) within two weeks; (d) immediately; (e) within thirty days.

REAL ESTATE SYNDICATIONS AND INVESTMENT TRUSTS

Recently syndication has become a popular method of financing real property. It offers many small investors an opportunity to invest in real estate transactions that otherwise would not be available to them.

Real estate syndications are called *real estate programs* by the Corporation Law, which is the law governing all syndications. It defines a syndication as "a limited partnership, joint venture, unincorporated association or similar organization other than a corporation, formed and operated for the primary purpose of investment in and the operation or gain from an interest in real property."

The sale of all syndication units, involving two investors or two thousand investors, is regulated by the Corporate Commissioner. Most small syndications (under thirty-five beneficial owners), if properly structured, are exempt from securities registration.

Larger syndications come under careful scrutiny by the Corporate Commissioner. The law prescribes maximum amounts of brokerage, organization, and other fees that can be charged and the manner in which the program must be managed and structured.

An attorney should always be consulted in creating syndications.

Syndication is a complete specialty covered in other advanced courses in real estate. Some colleges and universities offer a complete course in syndication.

An *investment trust* is an unincorporated trust or association of investors, managed by one or more trustees, that, were it not for tax exemption provisions in Public Law 86–779 effective for tax years subsequent to 1960, would be taxed as a corporation.

The investment trust provides a vehicle whereby investors who prefer real estate to security investments can receive substantially the same tax benefits as those granted to mutual funds and other investment companies. Real estate investment trusts must distribute 95 percent or more of their ordinary income to shareholders. If they do so they are taxed only on their retained earnings at corporate rates.

REAL ESTATE EDUCATION AND RESEARCH

California has long been a leader in real estate legislation. It was the first state to enact a real estate license law and later to add to it provisions for funds to advance real estate education and research at the University of California campuses, state universities, and community colleges by establishing the Real Estate Education, Research, and Recovery Fund. In 1977 the legislature made an amendment whereby private California universities can undertake certain real estate research projects.

The Real Estate Commissioner uses the Real Estate Fund to carry out the functions and duties of his or her office and to pay the salaries of deputies and other employees within the Department of Real Estate. The law provides that 20 percent of the license fees collected are allocated to the education and research account and 5 percent to the recovery account; the balance, plus 100 percent of other fees collected, is for general departmental administration. The Department can spend only that which the legislature budgets. If there is a balance, that is, monies not budgeted by the legislature, it is retained in a surplus account and earns interest in a Pooled Investment Account.

Recovery fund

That portion of the fund allocated to the recovery account is used for the purpose of reimbursing an aggrieved person who obtains a final judgment in a court of competent jurisdiction against a licensee upon grounds of fraud, misrepresentation, or deceit. Upon termination of the proceedings, including the reviews and appeals in connection with the judgment, an order is entered for the aggrieved person, directing payment out of this fund for the actual damages up to a sum of $100,000 on any unpaid judgments. The actual amount depends on when the fraud occurred, how many other claimants were defrauded, and how many claims the licensee has against him or her.

After 1980, a person can collect up to $20,000 in any one transaction. If several people have been injured in the same transaction, then they may end up sharing on a pro rata basis the $20,000 recovery fund payment. The maximum amount that can be paid out as against any one licensee during his or her lifetime is $100,000.

A copy of the verified application must be served on the Real Estate Commissioner and a certificate for affidavit of the service filed with the clerk having jurisdiction. Within thirty days after the service of the application upon the Real Estate Commissioner, the aggrieved person must show

1. That he or she is not a spouse of the debtor, or the personal representative of such spouse.

2. That he or she has complied with all the requirements of this article.

3. That he or she has obtained a judgment as set out in Section 10471, stating the amount thereof and the amount owing thereon at the date of the application.

4. That he or she has obtained issuance of an order pursuant to *Section 714 of the Code of Civil Procedure* and examined the judgment debtor under oath concerning his or her property.

5. That he or she has made all reasonable searches and inquiries to ascertain whether the judgment debtor is possessed of real or personal property or other assets liable to be sold or applied in satisfaction of the judgment.

6. That by such search he or she has discovered no personal or real property or other assets liable to be sold or applied, or that he or she has discovered certain of them, describing them, owned by the judgment debtor and liable to be so applied, and that he or she has taken all necessary action and proceedings for the realization thereof, and that the amount thereby realized was insufficient to satisfy the judgment, stating the amount so realized and the balance remaining due on the judgment after application of the amount realized.

7. That he or she has diligently pursued his or her remedies against all the judgment debtors and all other persons liable to him or her in the transaction for which he or she seeks recovery from the Real Estate Education, Research, and Recovery Fund.

8. That he or she is making said application no more than one year after the judgment becomes final.

9. That he or she has posted a bond to guarantee court costs, including reasonable attorney's fees, should his or her application be denied, in the amount of 10 percent of the recovery he or she seeks from the Real Estate Education, Research, and Recovery Fund, at least twenty days before the hearing upon his or her application.

If the money in the Real Estate Education, Research, and Recovery Fund is insufficient to pay a duly authorized claim, the Commissioner must pay the unpaid claims when money becomes available. Claims will be paid in order of priority and will bear accumulated interest at the rate of 4 percent per year. When a person files false or untrue notices, statements, or other documents to the Real Estate Commissioner constituting any willful or material misstatement of fact, such an offense is punishable by imprisonment in the county jail for a period of not more than one year, a fine of not more than $1,000, or both. The Real Estate Commissioner has the right of subrogation: Upon the payment of a sum from the Real Estate Education, Research, and Recovery Fund, when the court has so ordered, he or she may proceed against the licensee to collect such moneys. The Real Estate Commissioner also has the authority to take disciplinary action against licensee.

TRUST FUND ACCOUNT

The fiduciary responsibility of a real estate broker makes the selection and maintenance of adequate trust fund records absolutely essential. Without exception, he or she must keep a true record of all trust funds passing through his or her hands. Such records must disclose in businesslike fashion all pertinent information concerning trust-fund transactions.

Most brokers maintain trust accounts. Technically, if all funds received by a broker are given to an escrow within the time required by law, and the broker handles no other funds, a trust account need not be maintained.

Deposit to trust account

Brokers frequently receive money on behalf of their principals. A typical example is when a buyer signs and offers to purchase the seller's property, enclosing a deposit ("earnest money") with the offer.

A broker is required to deposit those funds by the next business day into an appropriate escrow, deliver the funds to the principal, or place those funds in the broker's escrow.

If the offeror (for example, a potential buyer) instructs the broker not to deposit the check until acceptance of his or her offer, and this information is relayed to the offeree (for example, the seller), the broker may hold the check uncashed. Within one business day after acceptance, the check must be deposited into escrow or the broker's trust account, or delivered to the offeree (unless the offeror instructs the broker differently).

Any deviation from the above rules may render the broker guilty of commingling.

If a broker receives funds for payment of taxes, assessment, or insurance for a one- to four-family residence, the broker may deposit said funds in approved interest-bearing accounts, with interest accruing to the benefit of the owner.

Trust account records

The regulations of the Real Estate Commissioner (Section 2831) spell out records that must be maintained for both trust funds that go into a trust account and trust funds that do not go into a trust account.

The records for funds that go into a trust account must set forth in columnar form the date funds are received, from whom received, and the amount. The records must also show the date of the deposit and the check number or the date of related disbursements. Finally, they must show the daily balance of the trust account. (See Figure 17–2.)

In addition to these records, for all transactions involving moneys deposited in the trust account, the broker must keep a separate record for each beneficiary or transaction (Figure 17–3). These records also must be in columnar form and must set forth information sufficient to identify the transaction and the parties to the transaction. Columnar information must include the date and the amount of funds deposited, and the date, the check number, and the amount of each related disbursement.

What about trust funds that do not go into the trust account? Examples would be instruments that are given to the broker for delivery to a third person, such as checks

			Received				Paid out				
19__ Date Received	From Whom Received Or To Whom Paid	Description	Amount Received	Cross Ref.	Date of Deposit	xx	Amount Paid Out	Check No.	Date of Check	xx	Daily Balance of Trust Bank Account
(1)	(2)		(3)		(4)		(5)		(5)		(7)

COLUMNAR RECORD OF ALL TRUST FUNDS RECEIVED AND PAID OUT

2831. TRUST FUND RECORDS TO BE MAINTAINED. (a) Every broker shall keep a record of all trust funds received, including uncashed checks held pursuant to instructions of his or her principal. This record, including records maintained under an automated data processing system, shall set forth the following information in columnar form:

(1) date funds received
(2) from whom received
(3) amount received
(4) with respect to funds deposited to trust bank account, date of said deposit
(5) with respect to funds previously deposited to trust bank account, check number or date of related disbursement
(6) with respect to funds not deposited in trust bank account, identity of other depository and date funds were forwarded*
(7) daily balance of trust bank account

(b) Maintenance of journals of trust account cash receipts and disbursement, or similar records, or automated data processing systems, in accordance with generally accepted accounting principles, shall constitute compliance with subdivision (a).

* For compliance with requirements (6) see form entitled, ''Use For All Trust Funds which do not go into Trust Account.''

COLUMNAR RECORD OF ALL TRUST FUNDS RECEIVED AND PAID OUT

CALIFORNIA ASSOCIATION OF REALTORS® STANDARD FORM

			Received				Paid Out				
19__ Date Received	From Whom Received Or To Whom Paid	Description	Amount Received	Cross Ref.	Date of Deposit	xx	Amount Paid Out	Check No.	Date of Check	xx	Daily Balance of Trust Bank Account
(1)	(2)		(3)		(4)		(5)		(5)		(7)
4/5/82	Paul Hill	Cash to open T/A	$ 100.00	Rept. #1	4/5/82						$ 100.00
4/8/82	Troy Marsh	Rent 4/10/82	475.00	Rept. #2	4/9/82						575.00
4/8/82	Milred Hacker	Rent 4/10/82	480.00	Rept. #3	4/9/82						1,055.00
	City Water Company	Water Bill 4/82		Acc. #k			$ 25.00	1	4/9/82		1,030.00
	Paul Hill Gen. Acc.	Coll. & Mgt. Fee					85.50	2	4/10/82		994.50
	Fridolph Gazze	Rent Proceeds					894.50	3	4/11/82		100.00
4/15/82	Donald Carlson	Dep. on Saunders Property	1,500.00	Rept. #4	4/16/82						1,600.00
	Western Title Ins. Company	Dep. on Saunders Property					1,500.00	4	4/18/82		100.00

Figure 17–2

SEPARATE RECORD FOR EACH BENEFICIARY OR TRANSACTION
CALIFORNIA ASSOCIATION OF REALTORS STANDARD FORM

John Saunders

Description	Discharge of Trust Accountability For Funds Paid Out			Trust Accountability For Funds Received		Balance of Account
	Date of Check	Check No.	Amount	Date of Deposit	Amount	
Carlson Deposit on 216 Irving				4/16/82	$1,500.00	$1,500.00
Title Escrow Corporation	4/18/82	4	$1,500.00			-0-

SEPARATE RECORD FOR EACH BENEFICIARY OR TRANSACTION
CALIFORNIA ASSOCIATION OF REALTORS STANDARD FORM

Paul Hill

Description	Discharge of Trust Accountability For Funds Paid Out			Trust Accountability For Funds Received		Balance of Account
	Date of Check	Check No.	Amount	Date of Deposit	Amount	
To open Trust Acc.				4/5/82	$ 100.00	$ 100.00
	(3)	(4)	(5)	(1)	(2)	

2831.1 SEPARATE RECORD FOR EACH BENEFICIARY OR TRANSACTION. (a) A broker shall keep a separate record for each beneficiary or transaction, accounting for all funds which have been deposited to the broker's trust bank account. This record shall include information sufficient to identify the transaction and the parties to the transaction. Each record shall set forth the following information in columnar form:

(1) date of deposit
(2) amount of deposit
(3) date of each related disbursement
(4) check number of each related disbursement
(5) Account of each related disbursement

(b) Maintenance of journals of trust account cash receipts and disbursement, or similar records, or automated data processing systems, in accordance with generally accepted accounting principals, shall constitute compliance with subdivision (a).

Figure 17–3

Reproduced courtesy of the California Association of Realtors.

RECORD OF ALL TRUST FUNDS RECEIVED—NOT PLACED IN BROKER'S TRUST ACCOUNT

TRUST FUNDS INCLUDING UNCASHED CHECKS RECEIVED			Description Property or Identification	Disposition of Uncashed Checks or Other Funds Forwarded to Escrow or Principal	Date Forwarded
Date Received	Received From	Amount			
(1)	(2)	(3)		(6)	(6)

2831. TRUST FUND RECORDS TO BE MAINTAINED. (a) Every broker shall keep a record of all trust funds received including uncashed checks held pursuant to instructions of his or her principal. This record, including records maintained under an automated data processing system, shall set forth the following information in columnar form:

(1) date funds received
(2) from whom received
(3) amount received
* (4) with respect to funds deposited to trust bank account, date of said deposit
* (5) with respect to funds previously deposited to trust bank account, check number or date of related disbursement
(6) with respect to funds not deposited in trust bank account, nature of other depository and date funds were forwarded
* (7) daily balance of trust bank account.

(b) Maintenance of journals of trust account cash receipts and disbursement, or similar records, or automated data processing systems, in accordance with generally accepted accounting principles, shall constitute compliance with subdivision (a).

* For compliance with (4), (5), and (7) see form entitled, "Use For All Trust Funds Which Go Into Trust Account."

RECORD OF ALL TRUST FUNDS RECEIVED—NOT PLACED IN BROKERS TRUST ACCOUNT

CALIFORNIA ASSOCIATION OF REALTORS STANDARD FORM

TRUST FUNDS INCLUDING UNCASHED CHECKS RECEIVED			Description Property or Identification	Disposition of Uncashed Checks or Other Funds Forwarded to Escrow or Principal	Date Forwarded
Date Received	Received From	Amount			
(1)	(2)	(3)		(6)	(6)
4/25/82	Willliam Stevenson	$2,000.00	Deposit on Dunn House-100 Joyce Ln.	Title Escrow Corporation	4/25/82
4/26/82	Walter Anderson	3,000.00	Deposit on Sharum House-250 Cheryl Dr.	Office Safe-cashed upon seller's Accep.	

Figure 17–4

Reproduced courtesy of the California Association of Realtors.

SEPARATE RECORD FOR EACH PROPERTY MANAGED

CALIFORNIA ASSOCIATION OF REALTORS® STANDARD FORM

Owner *William T. Davey & Barbara Davey*
Address *10234 California Avenue, Mt. View, CA.*
Property *Davey Arms Apartments*
Tenant's Name *Bessie Sibel #1, Lona Jones #2, Ralph Adams #3*
Units
Remarks

Deposit
Monthly Rent *$500.00*
Commission:
Leases
Collection *10% of gross rent*
Management *included*

Date	Received From or Paid To	Description	Receipt or Check No.	Amount Received	Date Deposited	Amount Disbursed	Balance
3/ 8/82	Lona Jones	March rent Apt. #2	Receipt #8	$500.00	3/ 9/82		$ 500.00
3/ 8/82	Ralph Adams	March Rent Apt. #3	Receipt #9	$500.00	3/ 9/82		$1,000.00
3/ 9/82	Bessie Sibel	March Rent Apt. #1	Receipt #10	$500.00			$1,500.00
3/10/82	Santa Clara Water Company	Water Bill February				$ 35.00	$1,465.00
3/10/82	Kelley Romero	Management Fee				150.00	$1,315.00
3/12/82	William Davey	March Rental Proceeds	Check #123			$1,315.00	-0-

For these forms, address California Association of Realtors®
505 Shatto Place, Los Angeles 90020
Copyright © 1969, 1978, California Association of Realtors® (Revised 1978) **FORM TF-11-3**

Figure 17–5

Reproduced courtesy of the California Association of Realtors.

made directly payable to a title company or escrow company, personal notes, or a check representing the sales proceeds from the title company or escrow company made payable to the seller. Such checks or notes that pass through the broker's hands and are held by him or her for any period of time for the benefit of a third person are trust funds. A record must be kept of these trust funds in columnar form showing the date, the amount, and the source of the trust funds, as well as the date and the person to whom the funds were forwarded, as illustrated by Figure 17–4.

When brokers manage property, they must keep records of the rents received on a form similar to Figure 17–5. On large properties, most of the records are computerized. However, even those records, contain similar information as required in Figure 17–5.

Special forms are included here that are especially adaptable for use in a small brokerage office. A broker may develop his or her own forms, but they must contain the basic information described.

CHAPTER QUESTIONS

1. What are the major functions of the California Real Estate Advisory Commission? Who serves as chairman of the Commission?

2. Discuss the duties of the Real Estate Commissioner. What are the qualifications for the office?

3. Define *real estate broker* within the meaning of the Real Estate Law.

4. Enumerate eleven grounds for revocation or suspension of a real estate license under the Real Estate Law.

5. Discuss the various persons exempt under the Real Estate Law from obtaining a real estate broker's or salesperson's license.

MULTIPLE-CHOICE QUESTIONS

1. A corporation owns twenty homes in a subdivision. It hired a maintenance man who did not have a real estate license but showed the property and quoted prices and financing terms: (a) This was legal because he was an employee of the corporation; (b) he need not be a real estate licensee; (c) this was legal since he did not write up offers or accept deposits; (d) this was legal since the firm was incorporated; (e) this was a violation of the Real Estate Law.

2. Regulations of the Real Estate Commissioner: (a) are contained in the Civil Code; (b) have the force and effect of the Real Estate Law; (c) originate with the state legislature; (d) regulate the employees of the Department of Real Estate; (e) are contained in the probate code.

3. The California Real Estate Advisory Commission membership (including the Real Estate Commissioner) consists of: (a) two members; (b) six members; (c) seven members; (d) nine members; (e) ten members.

4. The Real Estate Law is contained in: (a) the health and safety code; (b) the business and professions code; (c) the administrative procedures code; (d) the revenue and taxation code; (e) the governor's code.

5. The Ajax Corporation is found guilty of dealing in real estate as an agent without a license. It may be fined: (a) $1,000; (b) $2,500; (c) $4,000; (d) $5,000; (e) $500.

6. One of the following would *not* come under the real property security dealer's section of the Real Estate Law: (a) guarantee of yield; (b) guarantee of prepayment; (c) subdivider selling purchase-money second deed of trust; (d) none of these would be exempt.

7. An applicant for a real estate salesperson's license must be: (a) a citizen of the United States and a resident of California; (b) a citizen of the United States; (c) a California resident; (d) neither a citizen of the United States nor a California resident.

8. A real estate salesperson licensee is entitled to: (a) engage in real estate transactions directly for a client; (b) work through a broker regarding activities for which he or she holds a license; (c) set up a real estate corporation; (d) become a partner in a real estate firm; (e) give legal advice.

9. A change in business address must be reported to the Real Estate Commissioner: (a) within three days; (b) within two weeks; (c) within one year; (d) immediately; (e) within thirty days.

10. The duties of the Commissioner do *not* include: (a) a thorough investigation of complaints against licensees; (b) regulating the sale of subdivisions; (c) laying out subdivisions; (d) screening and qualifying applicants for licenses; (e) serving as chairman of the Real Estate Commission.

REAL ESTATE OFFICE ADMINISTRATION AND PRACTICE

The real estate office is the focal point of all activities —some of which are highly specialized—so it is of paramount importance that it be efficiently run on a businesslike basis. Furthermore, the successful operation of a business is associated with good leadership. The qualities of good leadership will be discussed later in this chapter.

The well-run real estate office will have a written guide, commonly called a *policy manual*, setting forth the philosophy, rules, and regulations under which the business is to operate. This manual should be tailored to suit each particular business and the personality and philosophy of the broker-executive of the firm. A well-developed policy manual will also aid in personnel training and planning, thus eliminating a high turnover of sales personnel and staff. *Successful Real Estate Office, Policies and Procedures*, published by the California Association of Realtors, is available from CAR and should be studied by anyone interested in this subject.

The real estate executive, his or her sales personnel, and his or her staff will create an image of the real estate office. This image—favorable or unfavorable—will make a lasting impression on the public. An unfavorable impression made by one member of the firm will reflect on all personnel and operations. A favorable image is created, in part at least, by a well-planned and well-organized office.

ORGANIZATION AND FORMS OF OWNERSHIP

The broker is the head of his or her business enterprise and must select the form of ownership under which the business will operate. The success of the business will depend upon the broker's company policies and the decisions he or she makes.

Individual proprietorship

The increased real estate market activity in recent years has convinced a large number of people that anyone can succeed in the real estate business. Perhaps because of this, approximately 90 percent of the real estate brokerage firms in the United States are individually owned. The risks common to other small businesses also pertain to the real estate business. However, single proprietorship offers several distinct advantages, not the least of which are ease of organization, independence, and financial returns commensurate with the effort the owner puts into the business.

The independent broker should have sufficient capital to carry him or her in his or her basic business operations for at least one year. With such capital, he or she does not have to seek outside financing and can operate without consulting someone else on policy matters.

This independence has a strong appeal, but the broker must remember that the demands on his or her time and energy, particularly during the formative stages of the business, will be endless. He or she must solve problems without consultation with others and is, therefore, limited to his or her own skill and knowledge. In case of failure, the broker-executive will be totally responsible for all his or her business losses. Thus, to act independently, one must be willing to accept full responsibility, work long hours, give careful attention to the operation of the office, risk his or her own efforts, knowledge, and skills, and finally wait patiently and optimistically for the results.

Partnership

A partnership is a voluntary association of two or more individuals joined together as co-owners to operate a business for profit. Real estate brokers and others planning to enter into co-ownership of a business should consult an attorney. As a general rule, a partnership may be formed by an oral agreement—unless a provision in the statute of frauds declares otherwise. But it is a poor business practice to do so, for misunderstandings may result as to the duties, responsibilities, and participation of each partner. Properly drawn articles of partnership will eliminate the majority of such disagreements and will set forth, among other things, the purpose for which the partnership is formed, the names of the partners, and the duties and responsibilities of each. The articles, when recorded, will give notice ''to the whole world'' of the existence of the partnership and of the rights and interest of each partner. The laws of each state govern the relation of partnerships to the public, and in the absence of articles of partnership will govern the rights and duties between partners.

Partnerships may be classified as *general*, *special*, and *limited*. It is the general partnership with which we are primarily concerned.

A general partnership may be formed by real estate brokers to conduct a real estate office. In certain states, such as California, a salesperson may not be a general partner. Unless otherwise agreed, all partners share equally in the management, profits, and losses of the business.

The advantages of a partnership include the pooling of capital, skill, and experience of all partners, and with the division of responsibility, more efficient management. Although the partnership as such must file an information return for the Bureau of Internal Revenue, it does not pay income tax. Each individual partner pays federal and state income taxes based upon his or her share of profits or losses, an advantage over the corporation setup.

The advantages of a partnership may easily become disadvantages. As a general rule, each partner binds the partnership when he or she acts within the scope of the business. Unless each partner is thoroughly familiar with the personality, skill, and experience of the other partners, disagreements may result. All partners are jointly and severally liable for the debts of the general partnership. If insolvency results, creditors may take action against the personal assets of each or all of the partners. Death, of course, dissolves a partnership.

A *special partnership* may be formed for a single transaction, such as the development of a subdivision or the purchase of a building. The same rules of law as for a general partnership apply.

The *limited partnership* is composed of one or more general partners and one or more limited partners. The general partners are liable jointly and severally for the partnership, whereas the limited partners are liable for their investments only. The limited partner may lose his or her status, however, if he or she enters into significant management decisions not allowed by statute for limited partners. The advantages include the raising of large sums of capital without relinquishing management for them and the relative ease of dissolution when the business venture is completed. The profits are shared in proportion to the division of duties and the amount of capital investment in the partnership. A limited partnership, like a general partnership, is taxed on individual income. This agreement should be written, and an attorney should be consulted.

Corporation

A corporation is a legal entity created by law and receives its authority from the federal and state governments. As a general rule, a state may grant to a corporation any powers it chooses except those limited or placed on it by the federal or state constitution. Like an individual, a corporation may sue or be sued and may own property in its own name. The study of corporate law is a complete field in itself.

Advantages of the corporation include limited liability of stockholders for their investment only, continuation of existence in case of death or disability of a stockholder or an officer, ease of obtaining sums of capital in the sale of stock, salability of shares of stock, and paid management with experience and know-how in the business operation.

Disadvantages include dual taxation, first on corporation earnings and second on dividends distributed to the stockholders; cost and expense of incorporating; and difficulty in obtaining credit because of limited liability status.

An attorney should be consulted in the formation of a corporation to ensure strict compliance with all laws.

PROBLEMS OF ORGANIZING AND OPENING THE REAL ESTATE OFFICE

The ideal person for opening a real estate brokerage office is the successful real estate salesperson. He or she may be motivated by the feeling that he or she has acquired sufficient knowledge of the industry and is contributing more than his or her fair share for the compensation received. Even though this successful salesperson has passed a broker's license test and has some money saved, he or she should make an investigation as to why small businesses fail.

The broker-executive must have proven business experience and a specialized knowledge of office and personnel administration. Otherwise, the decision-making process will resolve itself into a trial-and-error situation.

The basic qualifications of a successful broker, then, are twofold. He or she must have had successful experience in the real estate business, its organization and operation, and he or she must also have the ability to manage the complex problems of supervision and cost control. Successful experience as an office manager would be valuable training for the broker before opening his or her own office. Other alternatives available to the ambitious broker would be employment with a small firm where there might be an opportunity to become a partner or with a large firm that might provide the opportunity to become specialized in the field of office management. In addition, educational opportunities are available in institutions of higher learning.

Departments and areas of specialization

A specialist, preferably one with several years of experience, should be selected to head up a specialized department in the real estate office. Because of the complexity of the business, it is impossible for an individual broker to be an expert in all fields. It is for this reason that most of the small brokerage firms confine their activity to the sale of residential housing. This area alone is highly specialized, and the competition is stiff.

Specialization in many areas of the business permits the large real estate firm to provide a complete service for its clients and customers.

Selecting the office location

The selection of the proper location for the real estate office is important and will be determined largely by the type of customers and clients to be served. In a highly populated area the majority of residential listings and sales will be within a one- to two-mile radius of the office. As a general rule, the higher the density of population, the smaller the sphere of operation. Selection of the location of the office should be made with these facts in mind.

A feasibility study should be conducted to determine the type of neighborhood, customers to be served and their income levels, and potential volume of sales. Neighborhood shopping centers are especially good for residential housing operations. Firms specializing in large income properties, such as commercial and industrial, may be located in a downtown professional building. Regional shopping centers may also be desirable for de-velopers and property management firms. In some cases, the property management firm may have served as the leasing agent for the center.

The exterior of the real estate office should be well designed, should be in good architectural taste, and should reflect the personality of the broker and his or her firm. A long-term lease will give assurance to the broker that he or she can continue to operate in the chosen location.

The office location must be easily accessible to automobile and foot traffic alike. A conveniently located building will aid the broker in getting his or her share of "walk-in" business. Adequate and attractive window space for advertising the office and listings should be available. Pictures of homes sold and homes for sale have considerable drawing power.

The office sign should be easy to read both day and night to provide the best institutional advertising possible. The broker must keep his or her name before the public. A well-designed sign will do much to accomplish this goal.

Office layout

First impressions are important, and the impression made on a potential customer entering the real estate office will be good if the furnishings are of uniform type and design and are in good taste. Furnishings should be adequate and comfortable to make the customer feel at ease, and yet allow the broker or salesperson to retain the attention of the customer. Overly comfortable furnishings can be distracting.

The first impression received on entering the real estate office will usually be that of the receptionist and the reception room, although in a small business operation this person may be the broker or the salesperson on floor duty. Embarrassment may result if the customer enters the office and all eyes focus on him or her, or if everyone in the office is busy and he or she is ignored. A comfortable reception room and a friendly receptionist tend to make the customer feel at ease.

Salespeople's desks should be of uniform size and of good quality. The desk size should be adequate to allow the salesperson to spread out maps, pictures, or other pertinent data concerning a parcel of property. Approximately 125 to 150 square feet of floor space per desk should be allowed, with sufficient aisle space to speed the flow of work between the various departments. Nameplates should be on each salesperson's desk. Desks should be clean, and the salesperson should not have more than one piece of work on his or her desk at a time. The salesperson on floor duty should occupy the front desk.

The ideal office will have a conference or a closing room, or both, located near the broker's desk for careful supervision and administration. Two smaller rooms with a movable divider may serve as a sales-meeting room as well. When space does not permit a closing room, the broker's private office may be used. The broker should have his or her own private office, if possible, to discuss personnel matters with the staff. Space is usually rented on a square-foot basis, so the proper utilization of space is necessary to save the company dollar.

The office budget

Management in any business consists of those individuals who direct and control the business enterprise. In the real estate brokerage business this is the broker, and the broker-administrator must plan and control the enterprise. To plan is to set up objectives to be attained and to ensure that procedures of operations conform with the established objectives. A budget is expressed in financial terms and figures and may be called a plan for the future. It is based on past experience through which projections are made.

Budgets are normally made for a fiscal year, the usual fiscal year being January 1 to December 31. Budgets should be constantly reviewed, however, preferably quarterly or semiannually.

Poor or improper accounting records and failure to budget the company dollar have been major causes of small business failures in the United States. The broker, particularly one without experience, would be well advised to consult an accountant with regard to setting up the books and making the budget.

Selection of staff and sales personnel

The number of staff and sales positions in a real estate firm will vary according to the size of the firm. However, in the selection of all personnel, staff or sales, carefully drawn job descriptions will aid the employer. They will also aid the employee by letting him or her know what will be expected of him or her once he or she is hired. A few of the qualities to look for in the selection of personnel are described next.

Secretary-receptionist   In most real estate offices the secretary will also act as receptionist. The impression he or she makes, on the telephone or in person, may give the customer his or her first impression of the firm. The qualities affecting this impression are voice, personal appearance, posture, and poise. The secretary-receptionist must learn to control his or her voice and diction, speaking in a soft, pleasant voice with a tone of helpfulness. His or her personal appearance should be neat and attractive at all times and his or her clothing should be appropriate for a business office. His or her attitude should be one of readiness to serve.

The secretary-receptionist must like people and should appreciate the material product with which real estate people work—real property. He or she can create an atmosphere of friendliness, both to customers and to sales staff, without being familiar. He or she should never discuss the transactions of the employer with anyone, especially with members of a competitive firm.

Duties of the secretary-receptionist will include receiving customers, answering the telephone, typing, filing, relieving salespeople of as much detail work as time permits, assisting the broker-executive, and keeping the office in a tidy condition. Salespeople are usually expected to keep their own desks neat. The secretary-receptionist must not perform any duties that require a state real estate license.

Custodian   In many business offices today the janitorial service is included in the office rent, but where it is not, a contract should be made with a janitorial service firm. In most real estate firms it is not economically feasible to hire a full-time custodian, but salespeople should not be expected to act as janitors.

Sales or office manager   A sales or office manager is usually employed when the sales staff numbers from eight to ten. His or her employment allows the broker-executive more time for his or her own transactions and other administrative responsibilities.

The sales manager must not only like people, but also be able to gain their respect and confidence. He or she must be available to sales personnel at the time that he or she is needed. Particularly with new personnel, patience and understanding are very important. The manager is the friend of all personnel, but he or she must be completely impartial and resolute in enforcing the policies of the firm. In general, a person who does not like detail work will not make a good manager.

The sales manager may receive a small salary plus an override on the sales commissions of the firm. He or she usually creates his or her own sales and does not take floor time or office calls if he or she is permitted to sell. The sales manager should set an example for all sales personnel, and his or her integrity should be beyond reproach.

Sales personnel   Successful real estate salespeople —men and women alike—enjoy people and like to help them solve their real estate problems.

The selection of sales personnel has sometimes been handled in a haphazard manner. The proper use of an application form and an oral interview with both the applicant and the spouse might well solve some of the problems of turnover of sales personnel. A sample of such a form is shown in Figure 18–1. The broker-executive or the sales manager should also check with former em-

INDEPENDENT CONTRACTOR APPLICATION

CALIFORNIA ASSOCIATION OF REALTORS' STANDARD FORM

GENERAL INFORMATION

Name JIM HOWARD TRAVIS   Date 11-2-85

Address 123 Jones Street, San Rafael, CA. 94904 Own ☒ Rent ☐ Phone (415) 234-5678

Birth Date May 19, 1946   Social Security Number 000-00-000

If applicable:

Spouse's Name AGNES MARY TRAVIS   Number of Dependents 2

Spouse Employed? NO   Position _____ How Long? _____

Do you belong to local Community and Civic organizations, etc., if so please list:

_____ Rho Epsilon - Real Estate - President _____

_____ Boy Scouts - Scoutmaster _____

Vehicle: ☒ own   ☐ lease   Make CHEVROLET   Type 4-door Sedan   Year 1985

Do you carry auto liability insurance? YES   Amount? $100,000/$300,000/$25,000

Name of Carrier CALIFORNIA STATE AUTOMOBILE ASSOCIATION

If you do not carry any of the above insurance, would you be willing to secure it? _____

In Case of Accident Notify: AGNES MARY TRAVIS   Telephone(s) (415) 234-5678

          Address 123 Jones Street, San Rafael, CA. 94904

          My Doctor is: DR. RICHARD BENJAMIN   Telephone(s) (415) 234-2242

EDUCATIONAL HISTORY

High School graduate? Yes   College or University? Yes

Major? Business Administration   Years 4   Degree? B.A.

Advanced Real Estate courses? Yes   How many units? 3   R. E. Certificate? Yes

GRI courses? None   How many units? _____ Graduate? _____

Other Real Estate designations? None

State what special qualifications or training you have which you think will assist you in the Real Estate profession:
  Extrovert personality; self-motivator, desire to succeed; knowledgeable and professional.

Figure 18–1 Independent Contractor Application

REAL ESTATE HISTORY

First entered Real Estate __October 10, 1985__ Where? __San Francisco, CA.__

Type of license now held: Broker _____ Salesman ____X____ License # __1234567__

Do you intend to engage in the Real Estate profession full time __Yes__ Part-time _____

If part-time, when do you plan to become full-time? _____

Are you presently associated with a Broker? __NO__ How long? _____

Broker's name and address _____

Have you given notice that you intend to leave? __Yes__ Why do you desire a change? __Real Estate is a__ __dynamic, stiumulating profession with greater financial remuneration.__

Are you a member of a Real Estate Board? __Yes__ Name __Marin County__

Membership Classification __Salesman__

Were you referred to this Company? __No__ By Whom? _____

Why do you wish to associate with this Company? __Excellent reputation, good strong management__ __support and professional approach.__

Do you know Associates in this Company? __NO__ If so, please list their names: _____

PERSONAL REFERENCES

Please list three references:

NAME	ADDRESS	Years Known	POSITION	PHONE
John Doe	600 May Street San Francisco, CA.	10	Dean, S.F. State	888-8888
John Smith	800 North Street San Francisco, CA.	6	Broker	777-7777
Bill Graham	900 Down Avenue San Francisco, CA.	6	Broker	666-6666

When do you wish to start? __Immediately__

I hereby declare that my answers to the foregoing questions are true and correct, and that I have not knowingly withheld any fact or circumstance that would, if disclosed, effect my application unfavorably.

I authorize you to communicate with references, former employers or associates, and any others you desire to contact, including a credit information agency and agree to hold you and such persons harmless with respect to any information furnished.

Applicant _Jim Howard Travis_

DATE OF INTERVIEW __11-2-85__ NAME OF INTERVIEWER _____

Figure 18–1 (Continued)

ployers with regard to the accuracy of the information on the application form.

The salesperson should have a clear understanding of what is expected of him or her when he or she is employed and should be required to be familiar with the office procedures outlined in the firm's policy manual. After being hired, he or she should be introduced to each member of the staff. All personnel should try to establish good rapport within the organization.

OFFICE PROCEDURES AND RELATIONSHIPS

The office sales meeting

A weekly sales meeting helps both the new and the experienced salesperson in the organization. Each sales meeting should be well planned and should accomplish specific objectives. Guest speakers from outside the office may be used when appropriate. Subjects covered may include such topics as the proper use of the telephone, listing and selling techniques, showing of property, and financing.

Compensation

The real estate broker will normally receive a sales commission of 6 or 7 percent or more of the selling price of property; however, this commission may be as high as 10 percent in the sale of land and recreational properties. The salesperson usually receives one half of the commission and the broker the other half.

To encourage listings, brokers will usually pay a percentage of the commission to the listing salesperson. The listing commission may vary from 10 percent on an open listing to 50 percent on an exclusive listing. The listing commission is based upon the amount of sales commission received.

Compensation procedures should be clearly outlined in the office policies and procedures handbook.

Employer-employee relationships

A broker would not normally be classified as an employee unless he or she was employed by another broker as a salesperson. Under the labor code an ordinary employee is one who renders personal service to his or her employer. With regard to salespeople, each situation, together with the specific law involved, must be examined to determine whether the salesperson is an employee as distinguished from an independent contractor.

Under the license law, salespeople are employed by brokers who must exercise supervision over their activities. This does not mean that in specific cases the sales-

person is not performing his or her work as an independent contractor—doing his or her work in his or her own way. In the real estate category he or she may be selling his or her final achievements or results rather than his or her time, and his or her physical being is not subject to the control of another. The real estate agent differs from clerical employees, and many factors must be weighed to determine whether he or she is an independent contractor or an employee.

The distinction between employee and independent contractor becomes important in the consideration of public liability, workman's compensation, social security, and unemployment insurance, and it should be carefully examined by the prospective salesperson. It is usually described in the office procedure manual, and each company may have a different policy.

Every real estate broker must—by law—have a written agreement with each licensed real estate broker or salesperson working for the firm (see Figures 18–2 and 18–3). The agreement must be dated, must include the material aspects of the employment, and must be signed by the parties. Signed copies of the agreement must be retained by the parties for a period of three years from the date of termination of the agreement.

ACTIVITIES OF THE REAL ESTATE BROKER AND SALESPERSON

The real estate broker or salesperson negotiates between buyer and seller and brings them together to consummate the transaction.

We may divide the activities of the real estate broker and salesperson into four categories: (1) listing property for sale, (2) prospecting for buyers, (3) negotiating between the buyer and the seller, and (4) closing, which involves the transfer of title to the property.

Listings and valuation of listings

The various types of listing agreements have been covered previously in this text. Article 7, Code of Ethics of the National Association of Realtors, states:

> Article 7. *In accepting employment as an agent, the Realtor pledges himself to protect and promote the interests of the client. This obligation of absolute fidelity to the client's interest is primary, but it does not relieve the Realtor of the obligation to treat fairly all parties to the transaction.*

In this chapter, we shall concern ourselves with the day-to-day activities of the real estate broker and salesperson in the actual listing, selling, and closing process of the real estate transaction.

BROKER—SALESPERSON CONTRACT
(INDEPENDENT CONTRACTOR)
CALIFORNIA ASSOCIATION OF REALTORS® STANDARD FORM

THIS AGREEMENT, made this _____ 2nd _____ day of _____ November _____, 19 85 , by and between

_____ Homer C. Davey & Associates _____ hereinafter referred to as Broker and _____

_____ Ted H. Gordon _____, hereinafter referred to as Salesperson,

WITNESSETH:

WHEREAS, Broker is duly licensed as a real estate broker by the State of California, and

WHEREAS, Broker maintains an office, properly equipped with furnishings and other equipment necessary and incidental to the proper operation of business, and staffed suitably to serving the public as a real estate broker, and

WHEREAS, Salesperson is now engaged in business as a real estate licensee, duly licensed by the State of California.

NOW, THEREFORE, in consideration of the premises and the mutual agreements herein contained, it is understood and agreed as follows:

1. Broker agrees, at Salesperson's request, to make available to Salesperson all current listings in the office, except such as Broker may choose to place in the exclusive possession of some other Salesperson. In addition, at Salesperson's discretion and at Salesperson's request Broker may, from time to time, supply Salesperson with prospective listings; Salesperson shall have absolute discretion in deciding upon whether to handle and the method of handling any such leads suggested by Broker. Nothing herein shall be construed to require that Salesperson accept or service any particular listing or prospective listing offered by Broker; nor shall Broker have any right or authority to direct that Salesperson see or service particular parties, or restrict Salesperson's activities to particular areas. Broker shall have no right, except to the extent required by law, to direct or limit Salesperson's activities as to hours, leads, open houses, opportunity or floor time, production, prospects, reports, sales, sales meetings, schedule, services, inventory, time off, training, vacation, or other similar activities.

At Salesperson's request and at Salesperson's sole discretion Broker agrees to furnish such advice, information and full cooperation as Salesperson shall desire. Broker agrees that thereby Broker obtains no authority or right to direct or control Salesperson's actions except as specifically required by law (including Business and Professions Code Section 10177 (h)) and that Salesperson assumes and retains discretion for methods, techniques and procedures in soliciting and obtaining listings and sales, rentals, or leases of listed property.

2. Broker agrees to provide Salesperson with use, equally with other Salespersons, of all of the facilities of the office now operated by Broker in connection with the subject matter of this contract, which office is now maintained at _____ 20653 Cheryl Drive _____ _____ Cupertino, California 95014 _____.

3. Until termination hereof, Salesperson agrees to work diligently and with Salesperson's best efforts to sell, lease or rent any and all real estate listed with Broker, to solicit additional listings and customers, and otherwise promote the business of serving the public in real estate transactions to the end that each of the parties hereto may derive the greatest profit possible, provided that nothing herein shall be construed to require that Salesperson handle or solicit particular listings, or to authorize Broker to direct or require that Salesperson to do so. Salesperson assumes and agrees to perform no other activities in association with Broker, except to solicit and obtain listings and sales, rentals, or leases of property for the parties' mutual benefit, and to do so in accordance with law and with the ethical and professional standards as required in paragraph 4 below.

4. Salesperson agrees to commit no act of a type for which the Real Estate Commissioner of the State of California is authorized by Section 10176 of the California Business & Professions Code to suspend or to revoke license.

5. Broker's commissions as set forth in the attached schedule, marked "Exhibit A" and hereby incorporated by reference, shall be charged to the parties for whom services are performed except that Broker may agree in writing to other rates with such parties.

Broker will advise all Salespersons associated with Broker of any special commission rates made with respect to listings as provided in this paragraph.

When Salesperson shall have performed any work hereunder whereby any commission shall be earned and when such commission shall have been collected, Salesperson shall be entitled to a share of such commission as determined by the attached commission schedule, marked "Exhibit B" and hereby incorporated by reference, except as may otherwise be agreed in writing by Broker and Salesperson before completion of any particular transaction.

6. In the event that two or more Salespeople participate in such work, Salesperson's share of the commission shall be divided between the participating Salespersons according to agreement between them or by arbitration.

7. In compliance with Section 10138 of the California Business and Professions Code, all commissions will be received by Broker; Salesperson's share of such commissions, however, shall be payable to Salesperson immediately upon collection or as soon thereafter as practicable.

8. In no event shall Broker be personally liable to Salesperson for Salesperson's share of commissions not collected, nor shall Salesperson be entitled to any advance or payment from Broker upon future commissions, Salesperson's only renumeration being Salesperson's share of the commission paid by the party or parties for whom the service was performed. Nor shall Salesperson be personally liable to Broker for any commission not collected.

9. Broker shall not be liable to Salesperson for any expenses incurred by Salesperson or for any of his acts except as specifically required by law, nor shall Salesperson be liable to Broker for office help or expense. Salesperson shall have no authority to bind Broker by any promise or representation unless specifically authorized in writing in a particular transaction. Expenses which must by reason of some necessity be paid from the commissions, or are incurred in the collection of, or in the attempt to collect the commission, shall be paid by the parties in the same proportion as provided for herein in the division of commissions.

Salesperson agrees to provide and pay for all necessary professional licenses and dues. Broker shall not be liable to reimburse Salesperson therefor.

In the event Broker elects to advance sums with which to pay for the account of Salesperson professional fees or other items, Salesperson will repay the same to Broker on demand and Broker may deduct such advances from commissions otherwise payable to Salesperson.

To order, contact—California Association of Realtors®
525 S. Virgil Avenue, Los Angeles, California 90020   FORM I-14

Figure 18–2 Broker-Salesperson Contract

259

10. This agreement does not constitute a hiring by either party. It is the parties' intention that so far as shall be in conformity with law the Salesperson be an independent contractor and not Broker's employee, and in conformity therewith that Salesperson retain sole and absolute discretion and judgment in the manner and means of carrying out Salesperson's selling and soliciting activities. Therefore, the parties hereto are and shall remain independent contractors bound by the provisions hereof. Salesperson will not be treated as an employee with respect to the service performed by such salesperson as a real estate agent for state tax and federal tax purposes. Salesperson is under the control of Broker as to the result of Salesperson's work only and not as to the means by which such result is accomplished. This agreement shall not be construed as a partnership and Broker shall not be liable for any obligation incurred by Salesperson.

11. In accordance with law, Salesperson agrees that any and all listings of property, and all employment in connection with the real estate business shall be taken in the name of Broker. Such listings shall be filed with Broker within twenty-four hours after receipt of same by Salesperson.

Salesperson shall receive a commission in accordance with the current commission schedule set forth in the Broker's written policy based upon commissions actually collected from each firm listing solicited and obtained by Salesperson. In consideration therefore Salesperson agrees to and does hereby contribute all right and title to such listings to the Broker for the benefit and use of Broker. Salesperson and all other Salespeople associated with Broker to whom Broker may give the listing. Salesperson shall have the rights provided in paragraph 13 hereof with respect to listings procured by Salesperson prior to terminations.

12. On completion of work in process, this agreement may be terminated by Salesperson at any time. Except for cause, this agreement may not be terminated by Broker except on 30 days' notice to Salesperson. On the occurrence of any of the following causes, Broker may terminate this agreement:

    (a) Election of Broker to sell its entire business, or to cease doing business at the office specified in paragraph 2;
    (b) Any breach of this agreement by Salesperson;
    (c) Cessation of Salesperson to be licensed;
    (d) Failure of Salesperson to comply with any applicable law, or regulation of the Real Estate Commissioner;
    (e) The filing by or against Salesperson of any petition under any law for the relief of debtors; and
    (f) Conviction of Salesperson of any crime, other than minor traffic offenses.

13. When this agreement has been terminated, Salesperson's regular proportionate share of commission on any sales Salesperson has made that are not closed, shall, upon the closing of such sales, be paid to Salesperson, if collected by Broker, and except in cases of termination for cause Salesperson shall also be entitled to receive the portion of the commissions, received by Broker after termination, allocable to the listing (but not the sale) as set forth in Broker's current commissions schedule, on any listings procured by Salesperson during Salesperson's association with Broker, subject, however, to deductions as provided in paragraph 14.

14. In the event Salesperson leaves and has transactions pending that require further work normally rendered by Salesperson, Broker shall make arrangements with another Salesperson in the organization to perform the required work, and the Salesperson assigned shall be compensated for completing the details of pending transactions and such compensation shall be deducted from the terminated Salesperson's share of the commission.

15. Arbitration—In the event of disagreement or dispute between Salespersons in the office or between Broker and Salesperson arising out of or connected with this agreement which cannot be adjusted by and between the parties involved, the disputed disagreement shall be submitted to the Board of Realtors* of which Broker is a member for arbitration pursuant to the provisions of its Bylaws, said provisions being hereby incorporated by reference, and if the Bylaws of such Board include no provision for arbitration, then arbitration shall be pursuant to the rules of the American Arbitration Association, which rules are by this reference incorporated herein.

16. Salesperson shall not after the termination of this contract use to Salesperson's own advantage, or the advantage of any other person or corporation, any information gained for or from the files or business of Broker.

17. Salesperson agrees to indemnify Broker and hold Broker harmless from all claims, demands and liabilities, including costs and attorney's fees to which Broker is subjected by reason of any action by Salesperson taken or omitted pursuant to this agreement.

18. All notices hereunder shall be in writing. Notices may be delivered personally, or by mail, postage prepaid, to the respective addresses noted below. Either party may designate a new address for purposes of this agreement by notice to the other party. Notices mailed shall be deemed received as of 5:00 P.M. of the second business day following the date of mailing.

19. All prior agreements between the parties are incorporated in this agreement which constitutes the entire contract. Its terms are intended by the parties as a final expression of their agreement with respect to such terms as are included herein and may not be contradicted by evidence of any prior agreement or contemporaneous oral agreement. The parties further intend that this agreement constitutes the complete and exclusive statement of its terms and that no extrinsic evidence whatsoever may be introduced in any judicial or arbitration proceeding, if any, involving this agreement.

This agreement may not be amended, modified, altered or changed in any respect whatsoever except by a further agreement in writing duly executed by the parties hereto.

    WITNESS the signature of the parties hereto the day and year first above written. In duplicate.

WITNESS   James H. McMasters

WITNESS   Barry McMasters

BROKER
20653 Cheryl Drive, Cupertino, CA
ADDRESS

SALESPERSON as INDEPENDENT CONTRACTOR
123 Jones Street, San Rafael, CA
ADDRESS

Attach Commission Schedules "Exhibits A and B."

To order, contact—California Association of Realtors®
525 S. Virgil Ave., Los Angeles, California 90020
Copyright© 1966, 1978, 1983, 1984, California Association of Realtors® (Revised 1984)

FORM I-14

Figure 18–2 (Continued)

The listing process

The multiple-listing agreement, based on the exclusive right to sell, should be encouraged. Multiple-listing associations are conducted by groups of brokers, usually members of the local real estate board, organized to present a service to property owners. The multiple listing gives the widest exposure possible for the property owner and provides the broker with a selling tool proven many times over. The listing broker continues to maintain control over his or her listing even though he or she shares it with other subagents, the members of the multiple-listing association.

For any sales organization to exist, it must have saleable merchandise, and nothing is more basic to the real estate broker than saleable listings. The real estate practitioner who is enthusiastic, energetic, aggressive, and knowledgeable, and who is able to obtain such listings, will enjoy success and financial independence.

In addition, the public-relations policy developed by the real estate brokerage firm will directly affect the success of that firm in the industry. The firm must gain the respect and confidence of the community. The purpose of a good public-relations program is to develop the personality image of the business and to popularize this image in the community. The more personal friends and contacts a person can develop, the more listings and sales the brokerage office will have.

Sources of saleable listings

Each salesperson is a public-relations officer and comes in contact in his or her everyday activities with many potential customers. Sources of listings include:

1. *Referral and follow-up program.* The broker who has developed a good public relations program and has a record of sales will always have owners wanting to list their property. Superior business service and absolute integrity result in satisfied customers.

2. *Canvassing door-to-door.* Although this method is not considered professional by some members of the real estate industry, it has developed salespeople who have been among the highest producers in the sales field. It is an excellent method of meeting people, but it requires good manners, good grooming, patience, and an optimistic point of view.

3. *"For sale by owner" signs and ads.* When the salesperson learns of property for sale by a sign or an ad, he or she can try to persuade the property owner that the sale should be handled by a professional.

4. *Expired listings.* There is usually a reason why a listing has expired and the property remains unsold. The property may have been overpriced or not properly serviced. It is not ethical for a firm to solicit a listing before

it has expired, but after the expiration date, it is open territory. The salesperson should analyze the listing to determine why it did not sell and should approach the owner with a fresh point of view. At no time should the salesperson say anything detrimental about his competitor.

5. *Newspapers.* The local newspapers will have articles concerning business promotions and transfers, births, marriages, and so forth. These items may be clipped from the paper and sent to the individuals along with a short letter of congratulation.

6. *Telephone solicitation.* In this method good telephone manners are imperative and the broker should train his or her staff in the proper telephone techniques. The salesperson who is a consistent user of the reverse telephone directory (a directory that lists telephone numbers in numerical order with the names and addresses of those to whom the numbers belong) and makes ten to twelve calls a day will produce many fine listings for his or her office. Remember, the salesperson does not take a listing on the telephone but arranges for a personal interview. A positive mental attitude is important for this technique.

7. *Office location.* The general brokerage office will do approximately 85 percent of its business within a radius of one to two miles of the office location. It is important to keep the firm name before the public; thus an attractive office with a sign that can be easily read on a busy street will draw clients.

8. *Financial institutions, trust departments, and attorneys.* When a person wants to buy or sell his or her property, he or she will often consult financial advisers. A well-established broker who has gained the confidence of bankers, savings and loan executives, and attorneys will have a built-in source of listings.

9. *Building contractors.* The contractor of homes, whether a speculative builder or a large-tract builder, is a busy specialist who may welcome the services of an enthusiastic, energetic, and aggressive real estate firm. The aggressive brokerage office will find a lucrative source of listings by cultivating the leading building contractors.

10. *Personnel directors in industry.* Executives and other key personnel in local industry are often transferred to new company locations. The transferee will want to sell his or her home as quickly as possible and obtain the fair market value for it. The alert broker and the salesperson with a successful record can help solve this problem.

11. *"Sold" signs on property.* The owner wishing to sell wants action, and a "sold" sign in front of a property just sold by a real estate firm shows that action has resulted through the efforts of that firm. Others in the neighborhood wishing to sell will want to ride with that success.

12. *Classified advertising for properties needed.* Prospective buyers will sometimes be looking for a special type of property not presently listed by the firm. A classified ad may satisfy this need. The advertisement should be honest and not just an attempt to get another listing.

13. *Direct mail.* Direct mail may be used effectively in gaining new listings or in selling property. It must be used consistently, however, to keep the firm name before the prospect. This medium may take the form of a personalized letter, postcard, folder, or brochure. Remember that any piece of advertising media must create four things: attention, interest, desire, and action.

14. *Membership in service clubs, civic organizations, and so forth.* The more personal friends and contacts a person develops, the more listings and sales the brokerage office will have. Everyone knows something about real estate, and the salesperson who belongs to various types of organizations will have an opportunity to discuss his or her services.

15. *Garage sales and furniture ads.* Prospective sellers will often dispose of surplus items prior to putting their homes on the market; therefore, a regular check of the classified section of the newspaper may produce good listings.

16. *Supermarket bulletin boards.* A world of information is readily available for the alert salesperson who will take the time to read this important advertising medium. Usually the seller is not knowledgeable about the merchandising of his or her home and needs the professional assistance of the broker and the salesperson.

Taking the listing

The serious seller, one with a strong motive for selling, will provide the salesperson with complete information necessary for merchandising his or her property. The salesperson should take adequate time to get this information. He or she should make sure that all pertinent papers, such as the deed or a mortgage, are readily available, thus saving time for the seller, the prospective buyer, and the salesperson as well.

The salesperson can provide the professional counseling that the prospective seller needs. The seller will have many questions that should be answered in a tactful, forthright manner. The salesperson should not bluff. If he or she does not know the answer to a question, a simple "I do not have the answer to your question, but I will be happy to get the information for you" indicates both interest and honesty.

It may be necessary for the salesperson to overcome certain obstacles or objections in taking the listing. These objections, if handled properly, may be turned into selling points for the office. The salesperson should be prepared to reply to any of the following:

1. We want to sell it ourselves and save the real estate commission.

2. The valuation you quote is too low. Mrs. Jones obtained $30,000 for her home and ours is much better.

3. If I wait long enough, I will get my price.

4. I won't pay the FHA points as the seller.

5. Broker X will list my home at a higher price.

6. I don't want a sign on my property.

7. We will sleep on it.

8. We will only give a thirty-day listing.

9. We will give you an open listing.

10. Wouldn't it be better for me to rent my home while interest rates are so high?

Naturally a seller wants to receive the top price for his or her property and, in the process of selling, wants to save every dollar he or she can, but it is up to the salesperson to convince the prospective seller that he or she can do both. The salesperson is in a position to suggest realistic sales prices from a competitive market analysis of such properties.

A list of all possible objections might be very long; however, if the salesperson knows the market and is familiar with what his or her firm can do for the client, each objection can be turned into a reason why the seller should list with his or her firm.

Prospecting for buyers

Prospecting starts by making a thorough analysis of the listing agreement. In taking the listing, as mentioned earlier, the salesperson should obtain complete information concerning the property. Pertinent information includes (1) proximity to transportation and to public and parochial schools; (2) data concerning the general neighborhood of the property; (3) present zoning and possibilities of zone change; (4) physical condition of the property, such as size and any deferred maintenance; and (5) price and terms of sale.

Although prospective customers can be found among the broker's or the salesperson's daily contacts, they are more frequently obtained from neighbors, tenants (in the case of income properties), advertising in newspapers and trade magazines, signs placed on properties, direct mail, "open" houses, office files on current prospects, office drop-ins, developers and subdividers, and investors or speculators.

The selling process—negotiating between buyer and seller

The successful real estate broker is skilled in bringing about a true meeting of the minds between buyer and seller. If the seller has a strong motive for selling and the property is correctly priced in comparison with similar properties, the property should sell. A property well listed is a property half sold.

Selling begins when the prospect and the salesperson meet, whether it be through a telephone conversation or face to face. The first meeting is an important one because the prospect will tend to evaluate the office and the sales staff by the impression the salesperson makes. The primary interest of the salesperson should be to provide a service for the customer and not merely to sell.

The salesperson must know how to analyze the prospective customer's present and future needs. He or she must take sufficient time to get acquainted with those needs and to determine how much the customer can afford to pay for the property, particularly residential property. The salesperson will have to know other things, such as family size, school requirements, occupations, family hobbies, and forms of recreation enjoyed by the family. In the case of commercial and investment properties, background information must be obtained. The real needs of the customer are not always apparent at the first meeting.

Each customer has real problems and basic needs and comes to the professional real estate office or firm to obtain the solutions to those problems and to have those needs fulfilled. Basically the customer has a need for confidence, information, professional counseling, and financing. If the salesperson can fulfill those needs, the real estate commission will tend to take care of itself.

The basic needs of the customer can be fulfilled through the salesperson if he or she has the data necessary, including data to justify the price of the property and data concerning the neighborhood. In addition, the salesperson should be fully informed as to current market conditions, including the mortgage-money market, and should know when it is advisable for the customer to seek the advice of an attorney or a tax expert.

The salesperson should know not only the important selling features of the property but the possible objections as well. If the alert salesperson has recognized both prior to showing the property, he or she will be able to give the customer truthful and direct answers.

The salesperson must have a sincere interest in the needs of the customer. He or she must also be able to arouse curiosity and interest, be a good listener, and have imagination and unquestioned integrity.

The use of a *sales kit* will aid the salesperson in taking a listing and in selling the properties listed by his or her firm. It should contain current materials and it should be well organized. Items in the sales kit might include: appointment book or daily planning manual; multiple-listing book; brochures on the firm and the services it performs;

checks and promissory notes; listing agreements; sales agreements; sales contracts; office and lockbox keys; street map showing schools, churches, highways; fifty-foot steel tape; flashlight; and any other information that might be important to the area. The makeup of the sales kit will vary depending upon the area of specialization. Important—keep the sales kit up to date.

Closing the real estate transaction

The closing of a real estate transaction must involve at least two persons, the buyer and the seller. Since the real estate firm may be representing both parties, care should be taken to make sure that both fully understand the transaction to eliminate any future misunderstandings. If the salesperson has fulfilled the basic needs of both, "buyer's panic" and "seller's remorse" will be eliminated.

The sales contract or deposit receipt was discussed in Chapter 6. The student is urged to review that chapter carefully. It should be remembered that the sales contract is the first binding agreement between buyer and seller, and if either defaults, he or she may be liable for breach of contract.

The salesperson should explain the contract carefully, step by step, making sure that the customer understands each part. If legal counsel is needed, the customer should get it.

The Offer to Purchase, after being signed by the customer, is presented to the sellers for their approval. As a general rule, offers should not be made over the telephone, but rather at a planned meeting with both the husband and the wife present. Again, each provision should be gone over carefully with the sellers. Remember, a counteroffer requires the approval of both buyer and seller.

After all parties have agreed to the sales contract, they are ready to proceed to the final closing through escrow or through another qualified firm, such as a law firm or a financial institution.

A broker has earned his or her commission when he or she has furnished a buyer ready, willing, and able to purchase the listed property. A professional broker or salesperson knows that service must be provided after the sales contract has been completed. The professional will cooperate with the financial institution in closing any new real estate loan or in assuming an existing one. He or she should also cooperate with the escrow agent or the firm handling the final closing of the transaction; this may include helping to prepare instructions and, after the transaction has been closed, explaining the closing statement to the buyer and the seller.

FINANCING REAL ESTATE TRANSACTIONS

The financing of real estate is a complete subject in itself. In most transactions, however, if loans have been in existence for ten years or more, it is necessary for the broker or the salesperson to secure additional loan commitments for prospective buyers. In the sale of the single-family home, obtaining the commitment is usually a service performed by the real estate broker or salesperson.

The broker or the salesperson should be familiar with current money market conditions. He or she should know what loans are available and the terms of loans from commercial banks, savings and loan companies, and other mortgage banking institutions.

REAL ESTATE ORGANIZATIONS

All business or professional groups seek some public recognition. All would like to attain that professional status held by teachers, attorneys, doctors, ministers, engineers, and others. As a profession, each of these groups tends to supervise its own members. Professional status can be attained in the real estate business if we include competency, integrity, and superior business service in defining our goals.

There is a great body of knowledge that all members of a profession must possess if they are to qualify as "competent." The broker or the salesperson should take every opportunity to avail himself or herself of knowledge pertaining to real estate so that he or she may better serve his or her principal and customer. "Integrity" must be understood as honesty and impartiality in dealing with clients.

In groups attaining a professional status, two things have been evident—education and the support of their local, state, and national organizations.

National Association of Realtors

The National Association of Realtors (formerly the National Association of Real Estate Boards) sponsors a national convention each year featuring outstanding speakers. It further cooperates with state associations and local boards in an exchange of speakers. Its many committees include education, legislation, and publishing. Two major distinctions are the Code of Ethics, adopted by all real estate boards in the United States, and its trademarked name and insignia embroidered with the term *Realtor*.

A *Realtor* is a licensed real estate broker who is a member of a local board of Realtors or an individual member of the National Association of Realtors. The term "Realtor" was coined by Charles N. Chadbourn,

a member of the Minneapolis Real Estate Board. It was presented to NAR in 1916 and was adopted by the association.

California Association of Realtors

The California Association of Realtors was formed in Los Angeles in 1905, three years before the formation of the National Association of Realtors. The California Association of Realtors has five principal objectives, as set forth in its constitution:

1. To unite its members
2. To promote high standards
3. To safeguard the land-buying public
4. To foster legislation for the benefit and protection of the real estate industry
5. To cooperate in the economic growth and development of the state

The California Association of Realtors is composed of local real estate boards throughout the state. When no board exists in the community in which the broker has his or her office, the broker may join the association as an individual. The California Association of Realtors publishes a monthly magazine and sponsors many annual educational and sales conferences throughout the state.

Other real estate organizations

As the real estate business has become more complex and specialized, various groups have organized within the framework of the National Association of Realtors. A few of these groups include the American Institute of Real Estate Appraisers, the Institute of Farm Brokers, the Institute of Real Estate Management, the National Institute of Real Estate Brokers, the Real Estate Board Secretary's Council, the Council of State Representatives, the Society of Industrial Realtors, the Urban Land Institute, the American Society of Real Estate Counselors, and the Women's Council.

The real estate broker works with many related associations, such as the National Association of Home Builders, the Building Owners and Managers Association, and the Prefabricated Home Manufacturers Institute.

In the field of finance the real estate broker or salesperson should be conversant with the United States Savings and Loan League, the American Savings and Loan Institute, the Society of Residential Appraisers, the National Association of Mutual Savings Banks, and the Mortgage Bankers Association.

FAIR HOUSING LAWS— STATE AND FEDERAL

California fair housing laws

The *California Fair Housing Act*, also known as the Rumford Act, prohibits discrimination in the sale, rental, lease, or financing of most types of housing. It covers

1. Owner-occupied, single-family dwellings.
2. Financial institutions.
3. Publicly assisted (FHA, VA, or Cal-Vet) housing.
   a. Single-family dwellings.
   b. Apartments of three or more units.
   c. Public and redevelopment housing projects.
4. Privately financed apartments of five or more units.
5. Real estate licensees.

The Fair Employment Practices Commission handles complaints and makes investigations involving violations of the law. If the committee decides that the law has been violated, the landlord must go through with the rental or sale. If the rental unit is no longer available, the person who complained is entitled to the next vacancy of a like accommodation or the landlord must pay $1,000 in damages.

The *Unruh Civil Rights Act* states that all persons within California are free and equal, regardless of their race, color, ancestry, national origin, sex, or marital status. Each is entitled to full and equal accommodations, advantages, facilities, privileges, or services in all business establishments. The person who denies these rights, under the act, is liable for actual damages for each offense, and in addition, a fine of $250.

A real estate licensee must not discriminate. He or she may not accept a restrictive listing from a principal or publish any statement or advertisement that suggests discrimination because of race, color, religion, or national origin.

The attorney general of California has ruled that a real estate agent who informs an owner of the ethnic background or race of a prospective buyer or renter violates fair-housing laws. It matters not that such information is volunteered by the agent or furnished at the owner's request.

Federal open-housing law

The federal open-housing law is administered by the Department of Housing and Urban Development, commonly known as HUD. If a state or local fair-housing law is substantially equivalent to the federal laws, HUD must turn the case over to local enforcement officials. In such cases, the person who complains cannot sue in the federal courts.

HUD regulations specify which state and local fair-housing laws are "substantially equivalent" to the federal law.

In addition to these enforcement procedures, the attorney general can bring action in cases where there is a general pattern of discrimination or an issue of general public importance.

All those connected with residential real estate—brokers, builders, lenders, buyers, sellers, and investors—are subject to the open-housing law. The law bans discrimination in the sale, rental, or financing of a dwelling. More specifically, the law (1) bans discrimination in the sale or rental of housing insured or guaranteed by the federal government or located in a federally assisted urban renewal or slum clearance project; (2) applies to all dwelling units, no matter how financed, if they are sold or rented through a real estate broker or his or her agent; however, the owner is permitted to choose any buyer he or she wishes if he or she sells or rents the house himself or herself (the owner may lose his or her exemption if his or her advertising of the home for sale or rent has any discriminatory words or references. Two exceptions are (a) single-family homes, provided the owner is a nonoccupant and does not own more than three single-family homes at one time (he or she gets the exemption for a twenty-four-month period); (b) one-to four-family dwellings if the owner occupies one of the units.

Vacant land is covered if it is offered for sale or lease for the construction of a dwelling. This, of course, may be difficult to determine in some cases. But if the land is zoned exclusively for residential purposes, it seems clear that its sale or rental would be covered.

Generally, commercial property is not covered. But this problem arises: Suppose a building contains a store on the ground floor and a residence on the second. On its face, the law would cover such a building. "Dwelling" is defined as "any building, structure, or portion thereof which is occupied as . . . a residence by one or more families. . . ."

Subleases are covered under the law. The term *to rent* includes to lease, to sublease, to let, and otherwise to grant for a consideration the right to occupy premises not owned by the occupant.

The person who believes he or she is discriminated against may file a written complaint with HUD. HUD will then try to settle the matter by conciliation and persuasion. If the matter is not settled in this way, the person making the complaint can file suit in a federal district court unless the local law is "substantially equivalent" to the federal law, in which case it must be turned over to local enforcement officials.

Although the law does not specify a special record form, it does require builders and brokers to keep records. The law further gives the government the right to inspect the records of anyone charged with discrimination.

CHAPTER QUESTIONS _____

1. What are some of the qualities that should be considered when hiring an applicant for a real estate sales position?

2. Give the advantages and disadvantages of full-time real estate salespeople versus part-time real estate salespeople.

3. How does the broker control his or her business enterprise in terms of present and future financial needs?

4. Define *multiple listing*. Upon what type of listing contract is it based? What advantages does it offer to the principal and the agent-broker?

MULTIPLE-CHOICE QUESTIONS _____

1. A licensed real estate broker must: (a) have a written agreement with each broker in his or her office; (b) have a written agreement with each salesperson in the office; (c) retain copies of employment agreements for three years; (d) do all of the foregoing; (e) do none of the foregoing.

2. The Code of Ethics was drawn up and presented by the: (a) Real Estate Commissioner; (b) California Real Estate Association; (c) National Association of Realtors; (d) California Association of Real Estate Teachers; (e) Real Estate Certificate Institute.

3. Broker Smith agreed to cooperate with Broker Kelley under an exclusive-right-to-sell listing agreement. Under the Code of Ethics, Broker Smith: (a) may solicit the listing for himself immediately; (b) may solicit the listing for himself at expiration; (c) must wait thirty days after the expiration before soliciting the listing; (d) must wait until the listing expires and the owner calls him

without being solicited; (e) may suggest that the owner made a mistake in listing with Broker Kelley.

4. If a broker employs six salespeople on a commission basis he may have obligations under the: (a) federal Workman's Compensation Act; (b) California Unemployment Tax Act; (c) federal Unemployment Tax Act; (d) California Workman's Compensation Act; (e) federal Opportunity Act.

5. The California Fair Housing Act covers: (a) real estate licensees; (b) financial institutions; (c) privately financed apartments of five or more units; (d) owner-occupied, single-family dwellings; (e) all of the foregoing.

6. To conduct a real estate business, a general partnership in California may be formed by: (a) licensed real estate brokers and salespeople; (b) licensed real estate salespeople only; (c) licensed real estate brokers only; (d) licensed real estate brokers, salespeople, and the Real Estate Commissioner; (e) any of the foregoing.

7. Multiple-listing contracts are usually based upon the: (a) net listing agreement; (b) exclusive-right-to-sell agreement; (c) exclusive agency agreement; (d) listing-option agreement; (e) net-option agreement.

8. In the event that more than one offer is made on a specific piece of property, the Realtor should: (a) present only that offer which provides the best commission; (b) present only that offer which in the opinion of the Realtor is best; (c) refuse to present all offers; (d) consult the Real Estate Board's attorney; (e) present all formal written offers for the owner's decision.

9. The agency designated to administer the federal Open Housing Law is: (a) the Department of Housing and Urban Development; (b) the Department of Health, Education, and Welfare; (c) the federal Housing Administration; (d) the California Department of Real Estate; (e) the Department of Corrections.

10. The distinction between *employee* and *independent contractor* becomes important in the consideration of: (a) public liability; (b) workman's compensation; (c) social security; (d) unemployment insurance; (e) all of the foregoing.

PROPERTY INSURANCE

Insurance is a broad and specialized field; however, its basic concepts must be considered in real estate principles. The real estate practitioner may find it profitable to engage in the property insurance business as a sideline or to associate with an insurance broker. Whether the practitioner engages in the insurance business or not, he or she must be aware of the necessity for insurance and the types of insurance that would be most suitable for his or her client. All property owners face the possibility of loss due to fire or other hazards. The types of risk that will be discussed in this chapter can be shifted to others in the form of insurance.

INSURANCE CONTRACT DEFINED

Insurance is a contract (policy) whereby one party, called the *insurer* agrees to indemnify another, called the *insured*, upon the occurrence of a stipulated contingency or event. The consideration paid for the contract is called a *premium*.

It is almost impossible for an individual to project what his or her losses through fire might be in a given period of time, but the insurance company through its vast experience can predict the probability of such losses with a high degree of accuracy. The premiums paid by a large number of property owners will indemnify the few who will suffer the losses.

The fire insurance company will try to spread its risk. In very large policies the issuing company will allow participation by other insurance companies, but it will not place all of its insurance contracts in a single city or area because one major fire would wipe out its entire assets.

INSURABLE INTEREST

The insured in the insurance contract must have an insurable interest in the subject property; otherwise, it would be considered a gambling contract.

Any individual who has a right or an interest in the subject property that would cause him or her to suffer a monetary loss in the case of destruction or damage has an insurable interest. Thus, an insurable interest in property exists not only for the property owner but also for creditors of the owner, such as lienholders and possessory interests.

Although the insurable interest must exist at the time the loss occurs, it is generally not necessary that it exist at the time the Contract To Insure is entered into. Assume, for example, that Adam is negotiating to purchase certain real property from Brown and during the negotiations he insures the improvements with Acme Insurance Company. Adam completes his contract to purchase the property from Brown, and six months later the improvements are destroyed by fire. The insurance company refuses to indemnify Adam for his loss on the grounds that Adam had no insurable interest at the time the contract was made. Adam's claim, in most states, would prevail because his insurable interest existed at the time of loss.

267

TYPES OF INSURANCE CONTRACTS

Today it is possible to obtain from one source or another an insurance contract to cover almost every conceivable risk or loss. This chapter, however, will deal with the most common insurance contracts covering risk of loss to real property. These will include fire, extended-coverage endorsement, and liability insurance.

Fire insurance

With one or two exceptions, all states have adopted the New York standard fire insurance form (of 1943).

NEW YORK STANDARD FIRE INSURANCE FORM

(A stock insurance company, herein called "the company")

The word "fire" in this policy or endorsements attached hereto is not intended to and does not embrace nuclear reaction or nuclear radiation or radioactive contamination, all whether controlled or uncontrolled, and loss by nuclear reaction or nuclear radiation or radioactive contamination is not intended to be and is not insured against by this policy or said endorsements, whether such loss be direct or indirect, proximate or remote, or be in whole or in part caused by, contributed to, or aggravated by "fire" or any other perils insured against by this policy or said endorsements; however, subject to the foregoing and all provisions of this policy, direct loss by "fire" resulting from nuclear reaction or nuclear radiation or radioactive contamination is insured against by this policy.

Concealment, fraud. *This entire policy shall be void if, whether before or after a loss, the insured has willfully concealed or misrepresented any material fact or circumstance concerning this insurance or the subject thereof, or the interest of the insured therein, or in case of any fraud or false swearing by the insured relating thereto.*

Uninsurable and excepted property. *This policy shall not cover accounts, bills, currency, deeds, evidences of debt, money or securities; nor, unless specifically named herein in writing, bullion or manuscripts.*

Perils not included. *This company shall not be liable for loss by fire or other perils insured against in this policy caused, directly or indirectly, by: (a) enemy attack by armed forces, including action taken by military, naval or air forces in resisting an actual or an immediately impending enemy attack; (b) invasion; (c) insurrection; (d) rebellion; (e) revolution; (f) civil war; (g) usurped power; (h) order of any civil authority except acts of destruction at the time of and for the purpose of preventing the spread of fire, provided that such fire did not originate from any of the perils excluded by this policy; (i) neglect of the insured to use all reasonable means to save and preserve the property at and after a loss, or when the property is endangered by fire in neighboring premises; (j) nor shall this company be liable for loss by theft.*

Other insurance. *Other insurance may be prohibited or the amount of insurance may be limited by endorsement attached hereto.*

Conditions suspending or restricting insurance. *Unless otherwise provided in writing added hereto this company shall not be liable for loss occurring (a) while the hazard is increased by any means within the control or knowledge of the insured; or (b) while a described building, whether intended for occupancy by owner or tenant, is vacant or unoccupied beyond a period of 60 consecutive days; or (c) as a result of explosion or riot, unless fire ensue, and in that event for loss by fire only.*

Other perils or subjects. *Any other peril to be insured against or subject of insurance to be covered in this policy shall be by endorsement in writing hereon or added hereto.*

Added provisions. *The extent of the application of insurance under this policy and of the contribution to be made by this company in case of loss, and any other provision or agreement not inconsistent with the provisions of this policy, may be provided for in writing added hereto, but no provision may be waived except such as by the terms of this policy or by statute is subject to change.*

Waiver provisions. *No permission affecting this insurance shall exist, or waiver of any provision be valid, unless granted herein or expressed in writing added hereto. No provision, stipulation or forfeiture shall be held to be waived by any requirement or proceeding on the part of this company relating to appraisal or to any examination provided for herein.*

Cancellation of policy. *This policy shall be canceled at any time at the request of the insured, in which case this company shall, upon demand and surrender of this policy, refund the excess of paid premium above the customary short rates for the expired time. This policy may be canceled at any time by this company by giving to the insured a five days' written notice of cancellation with or without tender of the excess of paid premium above the pro rata premium for the expired time, which excess, if not tendered, shall be refunded on demand. Notice of cancellation shall state that said excess premium (if not tendered) will be refunded on demand.*

Mortgagee interests and obligations. *If loss hereunder is made payable in whole or in part, to a designated mortgagee not named herein as the insured, such interest in this policy may be canceled by giving to such mortgagee a 10 days' written notice of cancellation.*

If the insured fails to render proof of loss such mortgagee, upon notice, shall render proof of loss in the form herein specified within sixty (60) days thereafter and shall be subject to the provisions hereof relating to appraisal and time of payment and of bringing suit. If this company shall claim that no liability existed as to the mortgagor or owner, it shall, to the extent of payment of loss to the mortgagee, be subrogated to all the mortgagee's rights of recovery, but without impairing mortgagee's right to sue; or it may pay off the mortgage debt and require an assignment thereof and of the mortgage. Other provisions relating to the interests and obligations of such mortgagee may be added hereto by agreement in writing.

Pro rata liability. *This company shall not be liable for a greater proportion of any loss than the amount hereby insured shall bear to the whole insurance covering the property against the peril involved, whether collectible or not.*

Requirements in case loss occurs. *The insured shall give written notice to this company of any loss without unnecessary delay, protect the property from further damage, forthwith separate the damaged and undamaged personal property, put it in the best possible order, furnish a complete inventory of the destroyed, damaged and undamaged property, showing in detail quantities, costs, actual cash value and amount of loss claimed; and within 60 days after the loss, unless such time is extended in writing by this company, the insured shall render to this company a proof of loss, signed and sworn to by the insured, stating the knowledge and belief of the insured as to the following: the time and origin of the loss, the interest of the insured and of all others in the property, the actual cash value of each item thereof and the amount of loss thereto, all encumbrances thereon, all other contracts of insurance, whether valid or not, covering any of said property, any changes in the title, use, occupation, location, possession or exposures of said property since the issuing of this policy, by whom and for what purpose any building herein described and the several parts thereof were occupied at the time of loss and whether or not it then stood on leased ground, and shall furnish a copy of all the descriptions and schedules in all policies and, if required and obtainable, verified plans and specifications of any building, fixtures or machinery destroyed or damaged. The insured, as often as may be reasonably required, shall exhibit to any person designated by this company all that remains of any property herein described, and submit to examinations under oath by any persons named by this company, and subscribe the same, and, as often as may be reasonably required, shall produce for examination all books of accounts, bills, invoices and other vouchers, or certified copies thereof if originals be lost, at such reasonable time and place as may be designated by this company or its representative, and shall permit extracts and copies thereof to be made.*

Appraisal. *In case the insured and this company shall fail to agree as to the actual cash value or the amount of loss, then, on the written demand of either, each shall select a competent and disinterested appraiser and notify the other of the appraiser selected within 20 days of such demand. The appraisers shall first select a competent and disinterested umpire; and failing for 15 days to agree upon such umpire, then, on request of the insured or this company, such umpire shall be selected by a judge of a court of record in the state in which the property covered is located. The appraisers shall then appraise the loss, stating separately actual cash value and loss to each item; and, failing to agree, shall submit their differences, only, to the umpire. An award in writing, so itemized, of any two when filed with this company shall determine the amount of actual cash value and loss. Each appraiser shall be paid by the party selecting*

him and the expenses of appraisal and umpire shall be paid by the parties equally.

Company's options. *It shall be optional with this company to take all, or any part, of the property at the agreed or appraised value, and also to repair, rebuild or replace the property destroyed or damaged with other of like kind and quality within a reasonable time, on giving notice of its intention so to do within 30 days after the receipt of the proof of loss herein required.*

Abandonment. *There can be no abandonment to this company of any property.*

When loss payable. *The amount of loss for which this company may be liable shall be payable 60 days after proof of loss, as herein provided, is received by this company and ascertainment of the loss is made either by agreement between the insured and this company expressed in writing or by the filing with this company of an award as herein provided.*

Suit. *No suit or action on this policy for the recovery of any claim shall be sustainable in any court of law or equity unless all the requirements of this policy shall have been complied with, and unless commenced within 12 months next after inception of the loss.*

Subrogation. *This company may require from the insured an assignment of all right of recovery against any party for loss to the extent that payment thereof is made by this company.*

IN WITNESS WHEREOF, this Company has executed and attested these presents; but this policy shall not be valid unless countersigned by the duly authorized Agent of this Company at the agency hereinfore mentioned.

Secretary   *President*

Assumption of risk

For a loss to occur there must be a *hostile* fire, that is, one that has escaped from its proper place accidentally. The fire must also be the immediate or proximate cause of the loss that has occurred. If there is a reasonable connection between the loss sustained and the fire, the insurer is generally liable.

Those losses that are reasonably foreseeable as incidental to the fire are also covered, provided clauses within the insurance contract do not state otherwise. Thus damage caused by smoke, water (where used to extinguish the fire), theft of personal property during the fire, and explosions caused by fire are generally covered.

The standard policy lists several perils not included in the contract. These are (a) enemy attack by armed forces, including action taken by military, naval, or air forces in resisting an actual or an immediately impending enemy attack; (b) invasion; (c) insurrection; (d) rebellion; (e) revolution; (f) civil war; (g) usurped power; (h) order of any civil authority except act of destruction at the time of and for the purpose of preventing the spread of fire, provided that such fire did not originate from any of the perils excluded by this policy; (i) neglect of the insured to use all reasonable means to save and preserve the property at and after a loss, or when the property is endangered by fire in neighboring premises; and (j) loss by theft.

PROOF OF LOSS AND INSURER'S LIABILITY

The fire insurance policy will provide that proof of loss be given within a certain period of time and in a specified manner by the insured. Failure of the insured to provide such proof will generally release the insurer from liability.

The insured cannot collect more than the actual extent of his or her loss. The amount of loss is the actual cash value at the time the property was destroyed. Most insurance policies will provide that the insurer has the right either to replace or restore the property destroyed or to pay the actual cash value thereof. When property is underinsured, the company is not liable for more than the face value of the policy.

A total loss may occur and yet the property may not be destroyed. When the unconsumed portion of the property is of no value for the purposes for which it was built, a total loss has occurred.

A standard policy provides for arbitration in the event that the insured and the insurer cannot agree upon the actual amount of loss. Upon written demand of either party, each will select a competent and disinterested appraiser to act as umpire. If they fail to agree upon an umpire, then the selection will be made by the court in accordance with the contract. The amount paid to the insured is the actual cash value, and the decision of any two appraisers will be binding upon the parties. Each party pays for his or her own appraiser, and the two parties equally pay the umpire.

Most insurance companies pay a loss immediately after the amount of loss has been agreed upon. A loss must be paid within sixty days after the agreement has been reached by the parties or after if has been reached by the appraisers.

ASSIGNMENT

Insurance is a personal contract between the insured and the insurer. A personal contract cannot be assigned without the consent of the insurer unless a particular state statute so provides. This is an important point for the purchaser of property to remember.

CANCELLATION

Insurance contracts will frequently contain a cancellation clause. In the absence of such a clause, however, cancellation requires the agreement or consent of both the insurer and the insured.

Generally, if the insurer is permitted in the policy to cancel the contract, the unused premiums are refunded in full. If the policy contract is cancelled by the insured, "short rates" are applicable for the period of time the policy was in force. The short rate is slightly higher than the pro rata rate and gives the insurance company compensation for the extra work involved. It is computed from a short-rate table. Cancellation requires that actual notice be given to the insurance company. Such notice may be oral or written, but written notice is preferred.

COINSURANCE

The average, or coinsurance, clause in a contract provides that the insurance company shall not be liable for a loss greater than the proportion of insurance carried to the amount of insurance required. The rates are cheaper and encourage the property owner to insure to the full value of his or her property.

The most popular coinsurance clause is the "80 percent clause," but there are other percentage clauses also. Assume that the full value of a building is $100,000. Under the 80 percent clause, the owner agrees to keep 80 percent of its value insured, or $80,000. The formula works in this manner:

$$\frac{\text{Amount of insurance carried}}{\substack{\text{Amount of insurance that} \\ \text{should be carried}}} \times \substack{\text{Actual loss =} \\ \text{Liability of} \\ \text{insurance} \\ \text{company}}$$

$$\frac{\$80,000}{\$80,000} \times \$5,000 = \substack{\$5,000 \text{ Liability} \\ \text{of insurance company}}$$

In the above example, assume that there is a loss of $5,000 with the owner carrying the full amount of insurance required. Note that the insurance company would pay the full amount of the loss because the proper amount of insurance was carried.

Now let us assume that there is a loss of $5,000 in the same example, except that the owner only carried $60,000 in insurance. The insured is penalized because he or she failed to carry the proper amount of insurance.

$$\frac{\$60,000}{\$80,000} \times \$5,000 = \substack{\$3,750 \text{ Liability of} \\ \text{insurance company}}$$

Assume that there is the same loss as in the above examples, except that the owner has the building insured for $110,000. It would seem that the insured might profit from the loss; but as stated earlier in the chapter, this is not permitted. The insured will collect *only the amount of the loss—$5,000*.

$$\frac{\$110,000}{\$ 80,000} \times \$5,000 = \$6,875$$

The property owner should periodically review his or her insurance program to make certain that he or she is carrying the proper amount of insurance on his or her property.

Mortgagee's clause

The mortgage will carry a *loss payee* clause, which states that the mortgagor will further provide that the mortgagee will be a beneficiary to the insurance contract. Therefore, when a total loss occurs to the property, the mortgagee will be paid first with any remaining moneys going to the mortgagor.

Subrogation

After the insured has collected from the insurance company, the company may require that the insured assign his or her rights of recovery against any other party to the extent of the payment made by the insurance company. This right is used only when a third party negligently causes the loss.

Pro rata insurance liability clause

The pro rata insurance liability clause states, in effect, that the insurance company shall not be liable for a loss greater than the proportion of insurance it has to the total of all existing insurance policies, including those held with other companies. For example: Assume Brown had the following insurance policies on her office building:

Company A	$30,000
B	20,000
C	10,000
	$60,000 = Total insurance carried by Brown

Each company would be liable for a loss in the following manner: Company A, one-half; Company B, one-third; and Company C, one-sixth.

Reduction by loss

When a loss to property occurs, the policy may be reduced by the amount of the loss. If the face of the policy is $50,000 and a loss of $10,000 occurs, the policy will remain with a value of $40,000. For an additional premium, the full amount of insurance may be reinstated.

Concealment and fraud

The standard policy of fire insurance provides that the insurance contract shall be void if, before or after the loss, the insured has concealed or misrepresented material facts concerning the insurance contract.

Extended coverage endorsement

The standard policy of fire insurance provides that any peril to be insured against or subject of insurance covered in the policy shall be by endorsement in writing. This clause grants permission to extend the insurance policy to include windstorm, hail, explosion, aircraft, civil commotion, vehicles, and smoke. Extended coverage gives additional protection to the mortgagee and the property owner. Many lenders require this endorsement.

LIABILITY INSURANCE

Liability insurance is actually "third-party" insurance in that it protects the insured when injuries result to another person while he or she is on the insured's property. It does not cover loss or damage to the property of the owner, but when the owner may have been negligent in protecting the public, and the law imposes liability on the owner, liability insurance gives him or her peace of mind. For example, let us assume that a guest, while staying at your home, falls and breaks a leg on a defective step and sues you for damages. Chances are he or she may be able to obtain a judgment against you. If you have proper liability insurance, you would be protected against this loss.

Many different forms of liability insurance exist; the more important ones will be mentioned here.

Owners', landlords', and tenants' liability policy

The owners', landlords', and tenants' liability policy will cover, to the limitations outlined, liabilities that occur from the ownership of apartment houses, motels and hotels, office buildings, resorts, and so forth. It will cover the use and maintenance of the premises as outlined in the insurance contract.

The policy covers bodily injury for which the insured may become legally obligated to pay—including sickness, disease, and death resulting therefrom—and it covers injury or destruction of property, including the loss of use caused by an accident in any one of the hazards outlined in the contract.

Exclusions in the policy can be covered by the payment of an additional premium. The policy will not cover cases that fall within or are covered by workman's compensation.

Elevator liability insurance

Elevators are an exclusion under the owners', landlords', and tenants' liability policy unless an additional premium is paid. This type of insurance, therefore, covers the risk of liability that results from the use, maintenance, and ownership of elevators, hoists, shafts, and so forth. Serious accidents may result from the use of elevators and like equipment; therefore, the owner may find it desirable to carry a greater amount of insurance for this type of liability.

Water-damage and sprinkler-leakage insurance policies

The water-damage liability policy is used to protect property damaged by water from refrigeration units; plumbing systems, including hot water tanks and bathroom fixtures; air-conditioning units; and heating systems. Rain coming in a door or window and leakage from the roof would be covered. Exclusions may include the sprinkler system, floods, blocked sewers, or seepage in a basement floor or wall.

Since leakage from sprinkler systems is an exclusion in this policy, the owner should protect himself or herself with sprinkler-leakage insurance. Coverage under this policy will include leakage, accidental discharge, and accidents to the system's water tank.

Glass insurance

The glass-insurance policy will cover all damage to glass except that glass damage caused by fire that would normally be covered under the fire insurance policy. Rates will vary depending upon the type of glass used, the occupancy of the premises, and the location.

Comprehensive general liability insurance

A policy is offered to provide comprehensive coverage to the insured who may wish to have all liability covered under a single policy and not under several individual policy contracts. The insurance company, in a survey, will determine and recommend the types of coverage needed by the prospective client. These hazards are described in the policy, and the premium will be based upon the liabilities to be covered.

Boiler and machinery insurance

Basically, boiler and machinery insurance covers explosion and breakdown of steam boilers, engines, electrical motors, generators, and machinery of various types. It includes damage caused by an accident, cost of repairing, bodily injury, loss to a third person's property, and any loss that may be covered by special endorsement. Limitations and exclusions are set forth in the insurance contract.

Rent insurance

Rent insurance is a form of business-interruption insurance for the lessor or landlord. It covers loss of rental income and the loss of use or rental value of the owner-occupied portion of the building. This may be by endorsement to the fire insurance policy. The maximum loss of rent paid will be set forth in the insurance contract, but in no case will a loss be paid greater than the amount of actual loss, in the event there was no damage to the property.

Leasehold-interest insurance

Leasehold-interest insurance protects the tenant against an increase or a possible cancellation of his or her lease and may also cover sublessees, losses of advance rents paid, and those who have an investment in the improvements, such as a tenant under a ground lease.

Demolition endorsement

Demolition-endorsement insurance is an endorsement to the fire insurance policy and is designed to protect the individual against increased costs of repairing buildings damaged by fire if the increased costs are due to legal requirements like a building code. While such codes are not retroactive for existing buildings, if a building does burn down or is materially damaged by fire, such new codes will be enforced.

Workman's compensation

Statutes adopting workman's compensation now exist in all states. These statutes provide that an employee may recover damages for injuries that resulted within the scope of the employee's work and from risks involved in that work. Since the adoption of such statutes, recoveries have been widened until today almost all injuries are included.

Because of the size of recoveries allowed, and with negligence no longer being a defense, an employer must protect himself or herself with workman's compensation insurance. In some states two plans are available, a state plan and a private insurance plan. California is among those states having both plans. Rates will be based upon the type of occupation and an estimate of the employer's payroll. Such estimates are subject to audit.

The length of time the employee will receive payments will depend upon whether the injury constitutes a total or a partial disability. If death results from the injury, the benefits will go to beneficiaries of the deceased employee.

CHAPTER QUESTIONS

1. Define *insurance contract* and state how an individual has an insurable interest in the property.

2. Name the common risks covered by insurance pertaining to real property and liabilities associated with real estate.

3. Distinguish between risks that are capable of being assumed and those that are excluded from normal insurance.

4. What is meant by *short rate*? By *coinsurance*?

5. Name at least five kinds of special insurance-coverage policies and explain the use of each in the ownership of real property.

6. Define the word *risk* from the standpoint of insurance.

7. Who will carry the *loss-payee clause* on a mortgaged property?

8. How do you determine the proper amount of insurance to carry on your buildings?

9. Define *third-party insurance*.

10. Explain workman's compensation insurance. How is the expense of the policy shared? How are the benefits under this policy determined?

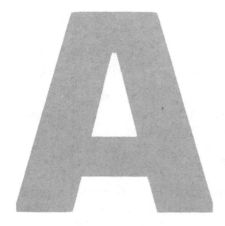

ANSWERS TO CHAPTER-END QUESTIONS

CHAPTER 2

Chapter questions

1. Real estate or real property consists of the following: (a) land; (b) anything affixed to the land; (c) that which is appurtenant to the land; and (d) that which is immovable by law. Anything that is not real property is considered personal property. Personal property is movable.

2. *Riparian rights* refer to rights of a landowner to water on, under, or adjacent to his land.

3. *Appurtenant* means "belonging to." Appurtenances include anything that is by right used with the land for its benefit.

4. (a) Metes and bounds description, which means by measurements and boundaries.

(b) U.S. government section and township system. This is a description of land by use of base lines and meridians.

(c) Lot, block, and tract description.

5. The three principal base lines and meridians in California are the Humboldt Base Line and Meridian, the Diablo Base Line and Meridian, and the San Bernardino Base Line and Meridian.

Multiple-choice questions

1. (e) Anything that is not real property is considered personal property. Personal property is movable.

2. (d) The courts have used five general tests: (a) the intention of the person affixing the personal property; (2) the method used in affixing the personal property; (3)

the adaptability of the personal property so attached for ordinary use in connection with the land; (4) the existence of an agreement between parties; and (5) the relationship between the parties involved.

3. (e) *Chattels* are items of personal property.

4. (b) See answer 3 in Chapter Questions.

5. (c)

6. (d)

7. (a)

8. (b)

9. (c) A section of land contains 640 acres, therefore one-fourth section would contain 160 acres.

10. (d) $660' \times 330' = 217,800 \div 43,560 = 5$ acres

CHAPTER 3

Chapter questions

1. California law refers to both ownership and tenancy interests in real property as estates. There are two major classes of estates: (a) freehold estates, which are not fixed or ascertained by a specified period of time, and (b) less-than-freehold estates, which extend for a fixed period of time. *Estate* denotes the ownership interest that a person has in land.

2. (a) *Will.* The three types of wills discussed were the (1) formal or witness will; (2) holographic will; and (3) statutory will.

(b) *Succession.* If a person dies intestate (without leaving a will), the law provides for the disposition of his or her property upon death. This is called *intestate succession.*

(c) *Accession.* Accession means addition to, such as the addition of fixtures.

(d) *Occupancy.*

(e) *Transfer.* The usual method used in the sale of property.

3. *Holographic will* is one written entirely in the testator's handwriting. *Formal,* or *witness will* is one made by a licensed attorney, and in California requires two witnesses. *Statutory will* is one in which you fill in the blanks on will forms established by the Civil Code.

4. (a) *Severalty* ownership is ownership by an individual. Only his or her signature is required for a transfer.

(b) *Tenancy in common* is ownership by two or more persons who hold an undivided interest, without right of survivorship. The interests need not be equal.

(c) *Joint tenancy* is ownership by two or more persons, with right of survivorship. The joint tenants all own equal interest and have equal rights in the property.

(d) *Community property* is property accumulated through joint efforts of husband and wife living together.

(e) *Tenants in partnership* is an association of two or more individuals joined together as co-owners to operate a business for a profit. Generally, all partners must join in the conveyance of property.

5. The basic purpose of the recording system is to give protection against secret conveyances of land and to provide a system whereby parties may be informed by inspection of the records as to the conditions of title. *Actual notice* consists of express information of fact. *Constructive notice* is notice through the public records.

Multiple-choice questions

1. (b)

2. (b) Intestate means that a person dies without a will. All community property goes to the surviving spouse upon the death of either. Separate property is divided as follows: (a) If there is a spouse and one child, half to the surviving spouse and half to the child; or (b) if there is a spouse and more than one child, one-third to the surviving spouse and two-thirds to the children.

3. (d) Constructive notice is notice given by the public records.

4. (d) An easement gained by prescription gives the claimant no title to the property, only a right to cross over the property.

5. (a)

6. (a) Only two witnesses are required. Often three are used out of caution.

7. (a) B's estate is measured by the life of X. The estate will continue, unless restricted, until X's death.

8. (b) A life estate is an estate measured by the life of a natural person. A life tenant can grant no greater interest than he has. When Mrs. Smith's estate ended, the estate of anyone holding under her also ended.

9. (d)

10. (b) A fee simple estate is the largest estate you can *own* in land. It gives you the entire bundle of ownership rights. Baker has a life estate, which is one type of freehold estate.

CHAPTER 4

Chapter questions

1. Encumbrances may be divided into two categories: (a) liens—encumbrances that affect title—and (b) encumbrances that restrict the use or affect the physical condition of the property.

2. The specific lien affects a specified parcel or parcels of real property, whereas the general lien affects all parcels of the debtor's property.

3. The law in California expressly provides that all persons who perform their labor or furnish materials for the improvement of real property will be paid. This is true even if the property upon which these persons worked or for which they furnished materials must be sold. It matters not if the owner of the property has paid the contractor in full; if the contractor has not paid his employees, these employees may file a lien upon the property in question. Ordinarily, the lien is valid only to the extent of labor and materials furnished for and actually used on the job. The lien must be verified before it is recorded. The student should review the statutory times for recording and the proper instruments discussed in the chapter.

4. The completion of an improvement would be any of the following: (a) the formal acceptance by the owner or his or her agent of the work of improvement; (b) the occupation of the improvement or its use by the property owner or his or her agent and cessation of labor; (c) cessation of labor for a period of thirty days or more; owner files a Notice of Cessation with the county recorder; (d) cessation of labor for a period of sixty days.

5. Private deed restrictions are placed on property by subdividers or developers for the protection of all lots in the tract. Zoning restrictions are created by governmental agencies such as cities and counties in their adoption of zoning ordinances.

Restrictions may be terminated in several ways: (a) termination of the prescribed period of restrictions; (b) agreement of the grantor and the owners of lots within the subdivision; (c) merging of ownership; and (d) operation of law.

Multiple-choice questions

1. (a)

2. (b) All involuntary liens must be verified before recordation.

3. (c)

4. (e)

5. (b)

6. (a) Once a valid Declaration of Homestead is filed it may be terminated in only two ways: (a) filing a new homestead on other property, or (b) by the claimant's filing a Declaration of Abandonment with the county recorder in the county where the property is located.

7. (c) An easement created by deed or written agreement is said to ''run with the land.'' A quitclaim deed may be used to eliminate the easement. The only easement that may be lost by non-use is one gained by prescription.

8. (c) Prescriptive easements are acquired by adverse use. The essential requirements are: (a) open and notorious use of each easement; (b) its use must be continuous and uninterrupted for a period of five years; (c) it must be hostile to the true owner's wishes; (d) the person so claiming must claim some *right* of use.

9. (a) Private deed restrictions are placed on property by subdividers or developers for the protection of all lots in the tract. Zoning restrictions are created by governmental agencies such as those of cities or counties. Deed restrictions tend to strengthen the zoning restrictions and will prevail as long as they are uniformly enforced by the lot owners.

10. (d)

CHAPTER 5

Chapter questions

1. Under the California Civil Code, a contract is defined as an agreement to do or not to do a certain thing. In an express contract, the parties declare the terms and manifest their intentions either orally or in writing. An implied contract, on the other hand, is one that is shown by the acts and conduct of the parties rather than by words.

2. An option is a contract to keep an offer open. A consideration is paid by the optionee for the right to buy the property under the terms and conditions set forth in the option agreement. The optionee is buying a right to purchase property in the future.

3. *Parol evidence rule* refers to prior written or oral agreement between the parties of the contract. If the contract is incomplete, oral evidence may be allowed to complete same. When a contract seems complete and the final expression of the parties is stated in the agreement,

parol evidence will not be allowed by a court of law to alter the agreement.

4. **(a)** He or she may sue for specific performance of the contract to compel payment and acceptance of a deed.

(b) He or she may stand upon the terms of the contract (offer to perform) and sue for damages.

(c) He or she may agree with the purchaser for mutual abandonment and rescission, in which event he or she is entitled to payments made on the contract.

(d) He or she may waive his or her security and sue for the balance of the contract.

(e) He or she may bring action to require the purchaser to pay moneys due or foreclose his or her rights.

(f) He or she may bring an action to quiet title against the purchaser, or he or she may wish to declare a forfeiture pursuant to the terms of the contract.

5. The remedy of specific performance is available only to the seller or the purchaser of property. A real estate broker as an agent *may not* sue for specific performance on a contract. The agent may, however, sue for an earned commission. Specific performance will not be allowed where a party to a contract has been induced to sign through fraud, concealment, undue influence, menace, or duress.

Multiple-choice questions

1. (c) All contracts are not required to be in writing. The statute of frauds does provide that certain contracts are not enforceable unless they are in writing. For example, a contract for the sale of real property or any interest therein *must be* in writing.

2. (d) Ordinarily, an acceptance to a contract is not effective until it is communicated to the offeror; that is, until he receives it.

3. (b)

4. (e) The usual consideration in the conveyance of real property is one of money; however, the consideration to a contract may be in any of the ways listed in the question.

5. (d) An option is a contract to make a contract in the future and is supported by a consideration. The optionee may enforce it against the optionor or his or her assigns, since he or she paid a consideration for this right.

6. (c)

7. (d) Oral agreements between *brokers* as to the division of a commission are binding and enforceable. Of course, it is best to have such agreements in written form.

8. (e) In California, a person reaches majority age the day before his or her eighteenth birthday.

9. (b)

10. (c)

CHAPTER 6

Chapter questions

1. **(a)** An open listing is one that may be given to one or more real estate agents, and the owner may sell the property himself or herself without liability to the agent for a commission. To be enforceable, it must be in writing and set forth the terms and conditions of the sale.

(b) A net listing is one in which the broker retains anything received above a certain amount set by the property owner.

(c) An exclusive agency listing is one in which the property owner appoints one agent as his or her exclusive agent to sell the property, but the owner reserves unto himself or herself the right to sell.

(d) An exclusive-right-to-sell listing gives the exclusive and irrevocable right to sell property to only the listing broker.

(e) Multiple-listing associations are conducted by a group of real estate brokers organized to present a service to property owners. These agreements are drawn up using the exclusive-right-to-sell form.

2. Multiple listing is described in answer 1e above. It differs mainly in that when submitted to the multiple-listing association, cooperating brokers become sub-agents of the listing broker. Each association may also have certain clauses added to conform to their bylaws.

3. "Time is of the essence" means that the parties will act in a timely manner (within the time periods set forth) in performing their respective duties and obligations. Failure to do so could mean a breach of contract and a suit for damages.

4. A tax-free exchange, or deferred exchange, is an exchange of real property in which a gain or loss is not at that time attributable to the taxpayer—the situation created is merely transferring the taxpayer's "cost basis" to the newly acquired property. Only the taxpayer's death will produce a truly tax-free exchange.

"Boot" is cash given in addition to the exchange of properties.

5. The broker is entitled to a commission—even though a valid listing agreement was not in effect—if signed escrow instructions provide for it in a certain dollar sum to be paid to the real estate broker. Further, when the real estate purchase contract and receipt for deposit provides for a commission and it is properly signed by the sellers, the broker may enforce a commission.

Multiple-choice questions

1. **(b)** Unless the listing agreement so provides, the agent is authorized only to find a buyer ready, willing, and able to purchase the property. The agent may, however, accept a deposit as agent for the buyer.

2. **(d)** The CAR deposit receipt names no provisions in the printed portion for discounts on loans. There are provisions, however, for those in choices a, b, c, and e.

3. **(a)** and **(b)**. A deposit receipt is valid even though the description of the property is by street address only. Title insurance companies, however, will not issue a policy of title insurance unless a correct legal description is available.

4. **(a)** The real estate law requires the broker to notify both the buyer and the seller of the amount of the sale price within one month of the closing of the transaction. The agent must disclose the amount of his compensation *prior to* or *at the time* the principal binds himself or herself to the transaction.

5. **(d)** Section 10142 of the California Real Estate Law provides that the licensee shall deliver a copy of the agreement to the person signing the agreement *at the time* the signature is obtained.

6. **(a)**

7. **(d)** All listing agreements are taken in the name of the broker or brokerage firm and therefore belong to the broker. The salesperson is an employee of the broker.

8. **(c)** The ten-day acceptance clause is binding to the seller only, since no consideration has been paid to keep the offer to purchase open.

9. **(e)** A real estate commission is a matter of agreement between the parties.

10. **(d)** If the listing agreement provides for a $1,000 minimum deposit, the broker has not fulfilled her contract.

CHAPTER 7

Chapter questions

1. An agent is defined by the California Civil Code as one who represents another (called a principal) in dealings with third persons. Real estate brokers are usually classified as agents or special agents. Salespeople are classified as employees of a broker. The real estate law requires that the broker exercise reasonable supervision over the salesperson's activities.

2. An employer-employee relationship exists when by expressed or implied agreement one person, called the employee, undertakes personal services for another, called the employer, under the employer's supervision and control. On the other hand, the independent contractor is one who is responsible to his or her employer for the *final* results of his or her work. The employer has no supervision or control in the latter relationship.

3. An agency relationship can be created in four prin-

cipal ways: (a) authorization or express appointment; (b) subsequent ratification; (c) estoppel; and (d) necessity.

4. An agency relationship may be terminated by: (a) mutual agreement; (b) expiration of the term; (c) destruction or extinction of the subject matter; (d) death of either the principal or the agent; (e) operation of law.

5. A broker has earned his or her commission when he or she has found a buyer ready, willing, and able to purchase the property at the listed price, on the *exact* terms, and within the life of the listing agreement or any extension thereof.

Multiple-choice questions

1. (a) Oral agreements as to the division of a real estate commission are binding and enforceable between licensed real estate brokers. A salesperson, however, may not obligate his or her broker for a commission split unless an ostensible agency exists. The problem, of course, is to prove that the oral agreement existed. In addition, the broker may have a complaint filed with the appropriate committee of his or her local real estate board. Most bylaws state that if the aggrieved broker sues for his or her commission, the board will leave it to the courts.

2. (b) Brokers, salespeople, and their principals or customers have a close relationship, much the same as that of the lawyer with a client. This association is termed a *fiduciary*, or *faithful, relationship*.

3. (c)

4. (d)

5. (d) An agency is created, and is called an *ostensible agency*, when the principal causes a third person to believe another to be his or her agent who is not in fact employed by him or her.

6. (b) The independent contractor is one who is responsible to his or her employer for only the final result of his or her work.

7. (b) When a person attempts to act for another without his or her expressed or implied permission, and said person's acts are approved by the principal, the principal is bound and an agency by subsequent ratification has been formed.

8. (b) All listings taken are the property of the real estate broker. The salesperson is an employee of the broker and represents the broker in finding prospects for the property listed by the brokerage firm.

9. (a) An agent is one who represents another (called a principal) in dealings with third parties.

10. (e)

CHAPTER 8

Chapter questions

1.

	Deed of Trust	Mortgage
As to parties	Trustor (borrower) Trustee Beneficiary (lender)	Mortgagor (borrower) Mortgagee (lender)
Title	Trustor (equitable) Trustee (legal)	Mortgagor has legal title, mortgage is lien
Statute of limitations	Never outlaws	Four years from due date or date of last payment
Foreclosure	Trustee's sale may also include foreclosure by court action	Foreclosure by court action only, unless it has a power of sale clause
Form of lien release	Deed of reconveyance	Satisfaction of mortgage

2. (a) There must be an unconditional promise to pay.

(b) The instrument must be in writing.

(c) The instrument must be made by one person to another.

(d) The instrument must be signed by the maker.

(e) The instrument must be payable on demand or at a fixed future date or a future date that can be determined.

(f) The payment involved must be a definite sum of money.

(g) The instrument must be payable ''to order'' or ''to bearer.''

3. If the instrument is taken ''subject to,'' the buyer cannot be held personally liable for any deficiency on the obligation. The beneficiary or the mortgagee must look directly to the original party for the obligation.

The ''assumption of'' an obligation makes the grantee primarily liable for it. He or she is responsible to the mortgagee or beneficiary. The seller remains secondarily liable—that is, he or she must pay if the grantee does not—unless he or she is released by the lender.

4. A subordination clause may be used in a prior deed of trust permitting it to be subordinated to later liens as, for example, the liens of construction loans.

An acceleration clause in a deed of trust or mortgage gives the lender the right to call all sums owing to him or her immediately due and payable upon the occurrence of a certain event.

5. A real estate point may be defined as a bonus to

the lender for making a loan on real property. One real estate point is equal to 1 percent of the total loan. Points increase the yield to the lender.

Multiple-choice questions

1. (b) When a deed of trust or a mortgage is given as a part of the purchase price in the sale of real property, or where money is loaned specifically for the purchase of specified property of four units or fewer that will be occupied by the buyer, it is a purchase-money deed of trust and no deficiency judgment will be allowed. Mr. Reed's deed of trust to Mr. Goodman, therefore, is a purchase-money deed of trust. The finance company, on the other hand, made a loan to Mr. Reed for purposes other than the purchase of the home and therefore could get a deficiency judgment.

2. (c) Certain warranties are still implied by law with this endorsement. They include: (a) that the transferor has good title to the instrument; (b) that the maker or endorsers of the instrument had the capacity to contract; (c) that the transferor had no knowledge of any defects in the instrument that would render it valueless.

3. (e) A holder in due course is one who takes a negotiable instrument under *all* of the following conditions: (a) The instrument, when negotiated, was not overdue, and no notice of previous dishonor was given; (b) the instrument was taken in good faith and for value received; (c) the instrument was taken without notice of a defect in the title by the transferor; (d) the instrument was complete and regular on its face.

4. (b) See the answer to question 1 in this section.

5. (c) Although the promissory note that acts as the principal obligation outlaws four years from the due date or four years from the due date of the last payment, the deed of trust never outlaws because title is held in the trustee (legal title) and the trustee may sell any time.

6. (c)

7. (b) The security agreement is the instrument executed by the seller and the purchaser. The financing statement is the instrument recorded or filed.

8. (c) Deeds of trust are paid in the order of their creation unless, for example, the first deed of trust contained a subordination clause. The holder of the first deed of trust would receive $7,000 and the holder of the second deed of trust would receive the remainder, which is $3,000.

9. (b)

10. (c) A purchaser, in assuming a note and deed of trust, is put in primary position so far as the obligation is concerned. The seller remains secondarily liable unless the lender releases him or her.

CHAPTER 9

Chapter questions

1. In a *primary mortgage-money market,* lenders loan money directly to borrowers. They must bear the inherent risk involved in both long- and short-term financing until the obligation is discharged. In a *secondary mortgage-money market,* existing mortgages or deeds of trust are sold or used as collateral against new loans.

2. Advantages of FHA-insured loans over conventional financing include:

(a) Usually a lower rate of interest.

(b) A larger ratio of loan to the appraised value.

(c) Elimination of short-term financing and second deeds of trust or mortgages.

(d) Protection of the lender by providing him or her with a ready secondary market through the sale to the Federal National Mortgage Association.

(e) Improved housing standards through minimum specifications and building standards set up by the Federal Housing Administration.

(f) Provision for one monthly payment that includes principal, interest, insurance, taxes, and so on.

(g) No prepayment penalty is permitted.

3. (a) FHA loans have an initial service charge of 1 percent of the loan on existing structures and 2½ percent on new construction. There is no initial charge on VA-guaranteed loans.

(b) FHA loans place maximum limitations on the amount of loan, whereas no such limitations exist with VA loans. The lender making the VA loan may require a down payment, however.

(c) VA loans may be made for purposes other than the purchase, construction, and improvement of homes.

(d) The veteran, in order to avoid default, may refinance the loan. This may be done by the mortgagee if at least 80 percent of the loan is within the maximum time period for loans in its class. FHA limits such refinancing to 75 percent of the economic life of the structure.

4. In addition to the comparison on page 280 of FHA and VA loans, the three types of loans may be compared as follows:

5. (a) Principal and interest.

(b) Payments on mutual mortgage insurance if, as is usually the case, the amount has been financed by the lender as part of the loan.

(c) Taxes, hazard insurance, and special assessments.

Multiple-choice questions

1. (c) FHA-insured loans are *generally* made by institutional lenders, but private money lenders may ad-

	FHA	VA	Cal-Vet
Interest rate	Lower than conventional	Lower than conventional	Lower than FHA or VA
Time (term)	30 years	30 years	23–25 years
Security	Note and trust deed	Note and trust deed	Conditional sales contract
Prepayment penalty	No	No	2% in the first two years
Loan limitation	$90,000 (single family)	No	$75,000 (single family)
Eligibility	Anyone	Veteral	California veteran
Mortgagee	Lending institution	Lending institution	State of California

vance such loans provided they can qualify as mortgagees. Private money lenders would include mortgage banking companies, pension funds, and individuals.

2. (b) The guarantee protects the lender. The amount of guarantee will depend upon the type of loan made. On single-family homes, 60 percent of the loan is guaranteed to a maximum of $27,500. The specified maximum that will be paid to the lender by the government is reduced proportionately as the loan is paid.

3. (e)

4. (c) In addition to stablizing the mortgage-money market, FNMA provides a secondary money market for FHA-insured loans and for VA-guaranteed loans.

5. (b) Conventional loans will usually carry a higher rate of interest than that of FHA, VA, and Cal-Vet loans. This has been one of the principal advantages of FHA, VA, and Cal-Vet loans.

6. (d) The federally chartered institutions are governed by the Federal Home Loan Bank; the state-chartered institutions operate under the supervision of the Savings and Loan Commissioner of California.

7. (c) The guarantee is set forth in the answer to question 2 in this section.

8. (a) A Cal-Vet loan is financed in an unusual manner—it is really not a loan in the true sense. The state buys the property when the loan is approved and gives the veteran a long-term installment contract also called a "land contract" or a "conditional sales contract" to purchase it. The state keeps the title until the loan is paid off.

9. (c) The commission rates on junior deeds of trust are:

   5 percent under two years
   10 percent two years but under three years
   15 percent three years or more

10. (a) It applies to all first trust deeds of less than $20,000 and all junior trust deeds of less than $10,000.

CHAPTER 10

Chapter questions

1. (a) An *estate for years* is an interest possessed by a tenant having exclusive possession of real property for a *fixed* period of time. *Example:* A lease from July 1, 1982, to June 30, 1983.

(b) An *estate from period to period* is one that runs from one period to another. *Example:* year-to-year, quarter-to-quarter, month-to-month, etc.

(c) An *estate at will* is one that may be terminated by either the tenant or the landlord at will. California and most other jurisdictions require that notice be given by either the landlord or the tenant.

(d) An *estate at sufferance* exists when the tenant has come into rightful possession of property under a lease agreement and remains after the expiration of the specified term.

2. The recording of the lease agreement will give constructive notice to all persons that the lease agreement exists. It is advisable to record all long-term commercial and industrial leases. In addition, the standard policy of title insurance does not cover those things not of public record that a physical inspection of the property will reveal.

3. An *assignment* of the leasehold interest transfers all rights and interest that the assignor had, but the assignor remains secondarily liable on the lease agreement unless he or she is specifically released by the landlord.

When the tenant *sublets* the premises or leasehold estate, he or she remains primarily liable to the landlord for payment of the rent and for upholding all covenants and conditions of the lease agreement.

4. A leasehold estate may be terminated (a) upon expiration of the lease; (b) by the lessee's acquiring the fee title or a title superior to that of the lessor; (c) by mutual agreement of the lessor and the lessee; (d) by destruction of the premises; and (e) by cancellation at the option of the aggrieved or injured party in case of a breach of any covenant or condition stated in the lease agreement.

The landlord may (a) sue for each installment as it becomes due; (b) take possession of the leased property and, upon expiration of the lease agreement, sue the tenant for the difference between what he or she was able to rent the property for and the rent stipulated in the lease; (c) serve the tenant with a three-day notice and file unlawful detainer action.

5. *Constructive eviction* occurs when there is any disturbance of the tenant's possession, such as threats of expulsion, attempts to lease to others, when the premises are rendered unfit or unsuitable in whole or in substantial part for the purposes for which they were intended, or when the landlord enters and makes extensive and unwarranted alterations. The courts have held that the tenant must surrender possession; otherwise, he or she is obligated to pay rent.

Multiple-choice questions

1. (d)

2. (c) This is an accepted definition of an estate at sufferance.

3. (d)

4. (d) Unlike certain other contracts, a lease agreement does not terminate upon the death of the landlord or the tenant unless the agreement so provides. Especially in long-term lease agreements, such termination could work a hardship on either party.

5. (e) Under the statute of frauds, leases for more than one year must be in writing. In fact, any estate exceeding one year (except for an estate at will) may be created only by written agreement. Remember, we look for the best answer. (c) is misleading because it implies that leases under three years need not be in writing.

6. (d)

7. (c) Section 791 of the California Civil Code provides that a demand for payment is necessary, and this demand is usually made a part of the three-day notice to pay or quit.

8. (d) To assign is to transfer all rights and interest that the assignor had in the property, but not necessarily the legal burdens. The assignor is still secondarily liable unless released by the owner of the property.

9. (d)

10. (b) The *percentage lease* is one in which the rental consideration is based upon the gross sales of a business. It may also provide for a guaranteed amount against a percentage of gross sales.

CHAPTER 11

Chapter questions

1. The statute of frauds requires that all transfers of real property be made in writing. The essential elements of a deed include (a) a proper writing; (b) a proper description of the parties; (c) parties capable of conveying and receiving property; (d) an adequate legal description; (e) a granting clause; (f) a signing by the parties making the grant or conveyance of real property; and (g) a proper delivery.

2. The recording of a deed protects the grantee's rights. Recording does not affect the legality of the instrument,

since it may be valid between the two parties as long as innocent third parties' rights do not intervene. Recording shows "the whole world," so to speak, the grantee's interest in the property. If the deed were not recorded, the grantor's name would remain on the public record as the owner.

3. The grantor must intend to pass title immediately to the property. There is a presumption at law of a valid delivery when the deed is recorded in the office of the county recorder and the deed is found in the hands or possession of the grantee. There is also a presumption of delivery when the deed is found in the hands of a third party, such as an escrow holder or an attorney.

4. No. A person may acquire title under an assumed name (fictitious name) or convey his or her interest therein under an assumed name. A deed to a fictitious person (nonexisting) is *void*.

5. (a) A *grant deed* is the usual deed used in California for the private transfer of real property. The deed contains two implied warranties, set forth in the chapter.

(b) A *quitclaim deed* releases any right or claim that the grantor may have. No warranties are made, either expressed or implied. Such deeds are used to remove clouds from the chain of title.

(c) A *warranty deed*, not common in California, is used to convey title to real property. It contains warranties of title and quiet possession, and the grantor thus agrees to defend the premises against the lawful claims of third persons.

(d) A *gift deed* is used to make a gift of real property to another, such as a church or an educational institution. In lieu of a gift deed, the grantor could also use a grant deed or a quitclaim deed.

(e) A *deed of reconveyance* reconveys title (legal) from the trustee to the trustor when he or she has fulfilled his or her obligation under a deed of trust.

Multiple-choice questions

1. (d) A deed may be executed by mark if the grantor is unable to write. It must have the proper witnesses and be executed properly. A deed may not, however, be assigned, transferred, or foreclosed. The exception to the rule, of course, would be the deed of trust, which is not actually a deed of trust, which is not actually a deed at all but, rather, a security instrument.

2. (b) A grant deed contains two *implied* warranties: (1) The property has not previously been conveyed to another by the grantor, and (2) the property being conveyed is free from all liens and encumbrances of the grantor or any person claiming under him or her except those set forth in the transaction.

3. (a) As little or as much interest as the grantor may have. However, there are no warranties, expressed or implied, by the grantor.

4. (e) A legal description and a granting clause are both essential to the validity of a deed. The consideration need not be given, and it is the signature of the grantor that is required.

5. (c) Recording does not affect the legality of the instrument as long as innocent third parties' rights do not intervene.

6. (c) There is a presumption at law of a valid delivery when the deed is recorded in the office of the county recorder.

7. (a) The grantor conveys the title; the grantee receives the title.

8. (c) It might appear to the student that *a* could be the correct answer; however, the implied warranty made by the grantor is that the conveyance is free from all liens and encumbrances of the grantor *except* those known to the seller or grantor and set forth in the transaction.

9. (b) Although acknowledgment of the grantor's signature is necessary for recordation of the instrument, it does not affect the validity of the instrument.

10. (e) The grant deed is generally used in a transfer sale of real property.

CHAPTER 12

Chapter questions

1. $36,000 × .06 = $2,160 × .60 = $1,296 Salesman's commission.

2. $150 × 12 = $1,800 ÷ .075 = $24,000 Money invested.

3. $7,440 ÷ $120,000 = .062 or 6.2% Return on total investment.

4. $273.75 × 12 = $3,285 ÷ .09 = $36,500 Amount of the loan.

5. 16⅔% = 15 lots
15 lots ÷ ⅙ = 15 lots × ⁶⁄₁ = 90 lots total.

Multiple-choice questions

1. (a) $9,800 divided by .94 = $10,425.53.

2. (b) 3 lots @ $7,200 each = $21,600 selling price
2 lots @ $9,000 each = 18,000 cost
Profit = $ 3,600
divided by $18,000 cost = .20 or 20%

3. (d) $13,584 + $140 = $13,724 divided by .94 = $14,600.00.

4. (d) 50 feet × 100 feet = 5,000 square feet
43,560 (square feet to an acre) divided by 5,000 square feet = 8.712 or 8 lots.

5. (c) 15% (Listing commission) plus 45% (Selling commission) = 60%

$12,300 × .06 =
$738.00 Total commission = 100%
Less: Listing and selling commission = 60%
Broker's commission = 40% ×
$738.00 = $295.20

6. (b) 1,080 square yards × 9 × 9,720 square feet divided by 60 = 162 ft. in depth.

7. (b) $12,280 Net received
182 Escrow fees
$12,462 = 94% or .94 $12,462 divided by .94 = $13,257.45 sales price.

8. (c) $27,750 Listed price × .12 = $3,330 Price
− 3,330 reduction
$24,420 Selling price × .04 = $976.80 Commission.

9. (a) $13,000 × .06 = $780 Annual interest
$780 Annual interest divided by 12 months = $65 interest first month
$95 − $65 = $30 Amount applied toward principal first month
$13,000 − $30 = $12,970 Balance of loan after first month's payment.

10. (c) ⅕ of the ranch was *sold*, leaving Smith with ⅘, or 120 acres (⅘ = 120 acres).
120 ÷ ⅘ = ¹²⁰⁄₁ × ⁵⁄₄ = 150 acres.

11. (d) The principal payment each month would be $240. Interest is calculated on the unpaid balance of the loan.

Month	Principal	Interest %	Annual interest
1	$2,400	× .09 =	$216.00 ÷ 12 months = $18.00 interest
2	2,160	× .09 =	194.40 ÷ 12 months = 16.20 interest

12. (b) Seller must pay his or her share of the taxes from July 1 *to and including* December 2.
$1,584 annual taxes ÷ 12 months = $132.00 Taxes per month
$132.00 taxes per month ÷ 30 days = $4.40 Taxes per day
5 months × $132.00 = $660.00
2 days × 4.40 = 8.80
$ 668.80 Seller's share of the taxes.

13. (d) June 1 *to and including* June 22 = 22 days.
$34,000 principal × .085 interest ÷ 360 days = $8.0278 Int. per day.
22 days × $8.0278 Int. per day = $176.61 Interest charged to seller.

14. (b) The policy expires August 7, 1983.
1983 (year) 7 (August) 37 (Days) Expiration date
1981 (year) 5 (May) 15 (Days) Proration date

2 (Years)   2 (Months)   22 (Days)   Unexpired portion of policy

$189.00 premium ÷ 36 months = $5.25 Premium per month.
5.25 ÷ 30 days = .175 Premium per day.
26 months × $5.25 = $136.50
22 days × .175 =   3.85
                     $140.35 Buyer's share of the policy.

15. (d) Seller is entitled to rent from March 1 *to and including* March 16. Buyer is entitled to rent for fourteen days (thirty days to a month).
$275 unit rent × 2 units = $550 total rent per month.
$550 per month ÷ 30 days = $18.3333 rent per day.
16 days × $18.3333 rent per day = $293.33 buyer's share of rent.

16. (b) $200 unit rent × 6 units = $1,200 per month × 12 months = $14,400
$14,400 gross annual rent × .40 expenses = $5,760 expenses
$14,400 Gross annual rent
−5,760 Annual expenses
$ 8,640 Net income ÷ .09 capitalization rate = $96,000 estimated value.

17. (d) $8,200 Selling price
  5,000 Cost
$3,200 Profit ÷ $5,000 cost = .64 or 64%

18. (c) 100% = Cost (unknown)
  +25% = Profit based on cost price
  125% = Selling price
$55,000 selling price ÷ 1.25 = $44,000 seller's purchase price.

19. (c) $76.32 Interest for month × 12 months = $915.84 ÷ .085 = $10,774.5882 *or* $10,774.59. The current balance of the loan as of May 1.

20. (c) 42 feet × 126 feet = 5,292 square feet available.

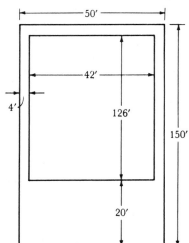

21. (a) 150 feet depth × 300 feet frontage = 45,000 total square feet.
45,000 square feet × $.35 per square foot = $15,750 purchase price.

22. (b) $60,000 divided by 2 = $30,000 assessed value.
$30,000 divided by 100 = $300 × $5.75 = $1,725 annual tax.

23. (b) 6 lots @ $1,400 each = $8,400
  4 lots @ $1,500 each = $6,000 Investment
          $2,400 divided by
          $6,000 = .40 or
          40%

24. (d) $10,000 Purchase price
  $ 9,000 × .06 = $540 annual
    9,000 Interest Note and TD
  $ 1,000 owner's equity
$800 annual return − $540 interest = $260 ÷ $1,000 = .26 or 26%

25. (a) $132 per month × 12 months = $1,584 annual return
$1,584 annual return ÷ .09 = $17,600 investment.

CHAPTER 13

Chapter questions

1. The purpose of title insurance is to protect the new owner of the property (also the lender in an ALTA policy) against risks of record and off-record hazards such as forgery, impersonation, or incapacity of the parties to transfer, and against any possibility that the deed of public record was not delivered with intent to convey title. It also protects against loss from a lien of federal or state taxes, which is effective without notice upon death, and against attorney's fees and other expenses connected with defending the title, whether or not the plaintiff prevails.

2. The American Land Title Association (ALTA) Policy of Title Insurance expands the risks insured under the standard policy of title insurance to include unrecorded liens and unrecorded easements; rights of those in physical possession of the property, including tenants or vendees; rights and claims of a correct survey or physical possession; mining claims; reservations patents; and water rights. The ALTA policy still gives no protection against defects in the title known to the insured at the date the policy was issued but not communicated to the insurer. Further, it will not provide against governmental regulations concerning occupancy and use of the property.

3. (a) A binding contract between the buyer and the seller.

(b) The conditional delivery of transfer instruments to a third party.

4. *Prorate* means to divide various expenses and income equally or proportionately between buyer and seller to time of use. Examples of expenses would include taxes, insurance, and interest. In the sale of income property the rents would be prorated according to time of ownership or another date agreed to by buyer and seller.

5. A complete, or perfect, escrow is one that contains all necessary instructions, instruments, and moneys, and reflects an understanding of parties to the transaction.

Multiple-choice questions

1. (d) The escrow agent is a stakeholder. He is the agent of *both parties* until the escrow is closed and then becomes a *trustee* for documents and money until they are distributed in accordance with the instructions of the escrow.

2. (c) The standard policy does not protect the insured against existing defects in the title up to the date of the policy and known to the buyer but not previously disclosed to the title insurance company; easements and liens not shown by the public records; any right or claim of one in physical possession of property not of public record; any rights or claims not shown of public record which could be ascertained by physical possession of the land, by inquiry of persons on the land, or by a correct survey. In addition, it does not protect against *mining claims*, reservations and patents, water rights, or zoning ordinances.

3. (b) Real estate brokers may escrow only the transaction in which they act as the broker. The broker must maintain all escrow funds in a trust account with the account subject to inspection by the real estate commissioner. The broker is exempt from the escrow law of incorporation as long as he or she escrows only those transactions in which he or she was the broker.

4. (d) The escrow officer may not legally concern himself or herself with any controversies between the parties to the escrow. When the parties to the escrow cannot agree and a distribution of moneys or documents cannot be made by the escrow holder, an action of *interpleader* to compel them to litigate among themselves may be obtained by such escrow firm.

5. (c) In most cases, the escrow holder will base his or her prorations using 360 days to a year and 30 days to each month.

6. (b) The escrow agent is a stakeholder. See the answer to question 1 in this section.

7. (c) Since the grant deed is recorded for the benefit of the grantee, or buyer, it is usually his or her responsibility to pay for this item.

8. (b) Debits on a seller's or a buyer's statement would be those items owed by either party. An existing loan is a debit or an item owed by the seller.

9. (b) The real estate law requires that the broker inform the buyer and seller in writing of the selling price within one month after the close of sale. If an escrow company handles the closing, the broker is relieved of this responsibility.

10. (c) This type of question should be read carefully by the student as it is sometimes included in the state real estate salesperson's examination. Statement *c* is a negative statement, but it is a correct statement of fact.

CHAPTER 14

Chapter questions

1. An appraisal is an estimate or opinion of value as of a given date. It is usually a written statement by a qualified appraiser of the market value or loan value of property after his or her analysis of many facts. The analysis is affected by the appraiser's ability to assemble pertinent data and from his or her experience and judgment.

Utility value, also referred to as subjective value, is the value in use to an owner-user. *Example:* A major oil firm may be willing to pay $125,000 for a corner location, but to another user the same corner may be worth only $30,000.

Market value is the price that a willing seller would sell for, a willing buyer would buy for, with neither being under abnormal pressure to buy or sell.

2. The four essential characteristics of value are *utility, scarcity, demand*, and *transferability*. These four items must be present for value to exist. The purpose for which an appraisal report is being made will usually dictate the evaluation methods employed and will influence the estimate of value.

Three principal forces influence real estate values:

(a) *Social ideals and standards*, such as marriage rates, population growth and decline, birthrates, attitudes toward education, divorce

(b) *Economic adjustments*, such as industrial and commercial growth or decline trends, wage levels within the community, natural resources, employment trends, wage levels, availability of credit and mortgage moneys, interest rates, price rates, and taxes

(c) *Governmental regulations*, such as building codes, zoning laws, FHA and VA loans, credit controls, stock market controls, and health measures

3. The three principal methods used in appraising real property are: (a) comparative analysis, or market data; (b) replacement cost; and (c) capitalization, or income.

4. *Recapture* is a term used to describe accelerated depreciation allowances that are recovered at the time of sale. The amount of recapture is either all depreciation taken for nonresidential property or only the excess depreciation taken on residential property.

5. Accrued depreciation is depreciation that has *already occurred*. Accrual or future depreciation is depreciation that *will occur* in the future.

Multiple-choice questions

1. (b) There are four essential elements of value: utility, scarcity, demand, and transferability.

2. (d) Utility value is the value in use to an owner-user. It is sometimes called subjective value and includes a valuation of amenities that attach to the property.

3. (c) Market value is the price at which a willing seller would sell and a willing buyer would buy, neither being under abnormal pressure, the property having been exposed to the market for a reasonable length of time.

4. (a) A statement of fact.

5. (b) Mortgage interest and depreciation are deductible for income-tax purposes only, and the appraiser does not use them in arriving at the net income for capitalization purposes.

6. (b) Functional obsolescence results from poor architectural design and style, lack of modern facilities, out-of-date equipment, changes in styles of construction methods and materials, and changes in utility demand.

7. (d) The replacement cost method of appraisal is most often used with new construction and "special-purpose properties," such as schools and public buildings. The comparative market analysis would be used in appraising vacant land and single-family homes. The capitalization method would be used on income properties.

8. (a)

9. (c) The straight-line method allows the same amount of depreciation to be deducted each year during the economic life of the building. The accelerated methods allow a greater amount of depreciation to be deducted during the early life of the building, but each year the amount of depreciation becomes less, and in later years it will become less than the straight-line.

10. (d)

CHAPTER 15

Chapter questions

1. (a) *Police Power* may be defined as the sovereign power of the state to safeguard public health, morals, and safety, and to promote the general welfare and interests of the public. Examples of police power would include zoning and laws and building codes.

(b) When a new zoning ordinance is passed, any existing lawful use that does not conform to it (a *nonconforming use*) is usually permitted to remain until that use ends or the building is destroyed. Examples would include an existing residential apartment house in an area newly zoned for single-family units, or a small industrial plant in an area newly zoned for single-family units.

(c) A *variance*, or *exception*, is an approved deviation from the zoning plan, usually based upon hardship or exceptional circumstances. Examples would include the following:

(1) An owner's land may consist of 19,750 square feet and the minimum lot size is 10,000 square feet. The owner desires two lots. An exception, or variance, may be granted by the appropriate governing body to allow the creation of two lots.

(2) The set-back line on a certain parcel of land may be thirty feet, yet to build the desired structure the owner desires a set-back of only twenty-eight feet. An exception, or variance, may be granted by the appropriate governing body.

2. The *enabling acts* gave cities and counties the necessary power to appoint planning boards or commissions and to hire qualified staffs to implement comprehensive plans. The powers of a planning commission may vary widely between cities and counties in the various states.

3. The purpose of the *master plan* is to serve as a guide for arriving at decisions—both public and private—that will, it is hoped, result in a constantly improving urban environment.

A master plan does not implement itself. It is a guide to be actively used and carried out, but it must be flexible enough to meet the ever-changing needs of the urban environment.

4. The commission or board is usually appointed by the city manager or the mayor with the approval of the city council. The county planning commission is usually appointed by the county board of supervisors.

5. In this question, the one rule you should memorize—because it covers all situations—is: Whichever is the more restrictive must be followed, whether zoning or restrictions.

CHAPTER 16

Chapter questions

1. These laws comprise the Subdivided Lands Act (California Real Estate Law) and the Subdivision Map Act. In general, these acts are similar, but there are some significant differences.

Planned developments of five or more lots, community apartments, condominiums, and stock cooperative projects containing two or more units are under the jurisdiction of the commissioner. The Real Estate Law is primarily concerned with the prevention of fraud, misrepresentation, and deceit in the sale of subdivisions. The Subdivision Map Act covers only community apartments and condominiums containing five or more units. It is primarily concerned with local regulation and control, and local authorities are concerned with the subdivision layout of streets, lot sizes, and improvements required, such as road surfacing, gutters, sidewalks, drainage, water mains, and sewage disposal facilities.

2. Failure of the owner, the subdivider, or the agent to comply with the provisions of the real estate law under the subdivision section is a public offense punishable by a maximum fine of $5,000 or up to five years imprisonment in the state prison, or by one year's confinement in the county jail, or by fine and imprisonment. All prosecutions for such violations are carried out by the county district attorney. In addition, the licensee's license may be suspended or revoked.

3. The Preliminary Public Report will permit the subdivider, the agent, or the owner to take reservations and deposits on lots within the subdivision. He or she must, however, agree to return the deposit money to the prospective purchaser if, after receiving the Public Report, the purchaser does not wish to follow through with the transaction. The Final Public Report sets forth the Commissioner's findings from the information submitted to him or her; it is not a recommendation.

4. In the community apartment house, a board of directors is usually formed and the residents of the various apartments make their payments directly to the board of directors, who in turn apply the amount so paid to one mortgage payment. The same would be true of taxes, assessments, and so forth.

In the condominium, the owner holds a fee simple interest in his or her apartment unit. He or she further owns an undivided interest in the common areas and facilities of the building, including an undivided interest in the land. The owner secures and pays his or her own mortgage, taxes, and so forth.

Both the community apartment house and the condominium fall within the definition of the subdivision act.

5. For the purposes of the federal act, a subdivision is defined as any land divided or proposed to be divided into fifty or more lots, whether contiguous or not, for the purpose of sale or lease, as part of a common promotional plan. The law is administered by the Office of Interstate Land Sales Registration (OILSR) in the Department of Housing and Urban Development.

Multiple-choice questions

1. (e) Section 11012 of the real estate law states: "It is unlawful for the owner, his agent, or subdivider,

of the project, after it is submitted to the Department of Real Estate, to materially change the setup of such offering without first notifying the Department of Real Estate in writing of such intended change. This section only applies to those changes of which the owner, his agent, or subdivider has knowledge or constructive knowledge."

2. (d) Both laws define a subdivision as improved or unimproved land divided for the purpose of sale, lease, or financing, whether immediate or future, into five or more parcels.

3. (e) The Real Estate Commissioner regulates aspects of the sale of subdivided property, while the city or county regulates lot design and physical improvements. The Commissioner is interested in a *full* disclosure to eliminate misrepresentation, deceit, and fraud. The Commissioner is interested in the handling of the purchaser's money (deposit money) so that the purchaser will be assured of a clear title to the property.

4. (b) A statement of fact.

5. (d) All of the answers stated in the question are requirements of the real estate law.

6. (b) The subdivider must enter into an agreement with the city or the county for the improvement of streets and easements, supported by a performance bond.

7. (d) These words are included in the definitions of both subdivision laws.

8. (b) The real estate law so provides.

9. (e) The Subdivision Map act requires that a tentative map be prepared and filed with the city or the county. After investigation, study, and recommendations by the local governing unit, a final map is prepared incorporating all the changes required by the city or the county on the tentative map. The Commissioner must receive a copy of the final map, as must the city or the county.

10. (d) Section 2801 of the Regulations of the Real Estate Commissioner defines a "material change" as follows: If the owner of any subdivision options, or sells to another, five or more parcels, such owner or original subdivider shall immediately notify the Commissioner of such options or sales.

CHAPTER 17

Chapter questions

1. The Commission is empowered to inquire into the needs of licensees, into functions of the Department of Real Estate, and into any other matters of business policy. They may make recommendations and suggest policy to the Real Estate Commissioner as they may deem necessary and proper for the welfare of the licensees and the public concerning the real estate business in California. The Real Estate Commissioner is chairman of the Commission.

2. The Commissioner's chief duties include (among many others) (a) enforcement of the Real Estate Law and (b) representation of the Department of Real Estate and the Department of Investment on the governor's council.

The Commissioner's qualifications for office include (a) five years' experience as a real estate broker actively engaged in business as such in California, or related experience; (b) execution to the people of the state of California of a bond in the penal sum of $10,000; (c) elimination of any interest that he or she may have in a brokerage firm; and (d) taking and subscribing to the constitutional oath of office and filing the same in the office of the secretary of state.

3. *Broker Defined*

10131. A real estate broker within the meaning of this part is a person who, for a compensation or in expectation of a compensation, does or negotiates to do one or more of the following acts for another or others:

(a) Sells or offers to sell, buys or offers to buy, solicits prospective sellers or purchasers of, solicits or obtains listings of, or negotiates the purchase, sale or exchange of real property or a business opportunity.

(b) Leases or rents or offers to lease or rent, or places for rent, or solicits listings of places for rent, or solicits for prospective tenants, or negotiates the sale, purchase or exchange of leases on real property, or on a business opportunity, or collects rents from real property, or improvements thereon, or from business opportunities.

(c) Assists or offers to assist in filing an application for the purchase or lease of, or in locating or entering upon, lands owned by the state or federal government.

(d) Solicits borrowers or lenders for or negotiates loans or collects payments or performs services for borrowers or lenders or note owners in connection with loans secured directly or collaterally by liens on real property or on a business opportunity.

(e) Sells or offers to sell, buys or offers to buy, or exchanges or offers to exchange a real property sales contract, or a promissory note secured directly or collaterally by a lien on real property or on a business opportunity, and performs services for the holders thereof.

4. Article 3 of the Real Estate Law sets forth the following:

Powers

10175. Upon grounds provided in this article and the other articles of this chapter, the license of any real estate licensee may be revoked or suspended in accordance with the provisions of this part relating to hearings.

Grounds for Revocation or Suspension

10176. The commissioner may, upon his own motion, and shall, upon the verified complaint in writing of any person, investigate the actions of any person engaged in the business or acting in the capacity of a real estate licensee within this state, and he may temporarily suspend or permanently revoke a real estate license at any time where the licensee, while a real estate licensee, in performing any of the acts within the scope of this chapter has been guilty of any of the following:

(a) Making any substantial misrepresentation.

(b) Making any false promises of a character likely to influence, persuade or induce.

(c) A continued and flagrant course of misrepresentation or making of false promises through real estate agents or salesmen.

(d) Acting for more than one party in a transaction without the knowledge or consent of all parties thereto.

(e) Commingling with his own money or property the money or other property of others which is received and held by him.

(f) Claiming, demanding, or receiving a fee, compensation or commission under any exclusive agreement authorizing or employing a licensee to perform any act set forth in Section 10131 for compensation or commission where such agreement does not contain a definite, specified date of final and complete termination.

(g) The claiming or taking by a licensee of any secret or undisclosed amount of compensation, commission or profit or the failure of a licensee to reveal to the employer of such licensee the full amount of such licensee's compensation, commission or profit under any agreement authorizing or employing such licensee to do any acts for which a license is required under this chapter for compensation or commission prior to or coincident with the signing of an agreement evidencing the meeting of the minds of the contracting parties, regardless of the form of such agreement, whether evidenced by documents in an escrow or by any other or different procedure.

(h) The use by a licensee of any provision allowing the licensee an option to purchase in an agreement authorizing or employing such licensee to sell, buy, or exchange real estate or a business opportunity for compensation or commission, except when such licensee prior to or coincident with election to exercise such option to purchase reveals in writing to the employer the full amount of licensee's profit and obtains the written consent of the employer approving the amount of such profit.

(i) Any other conduct, whether of the same or a different character than specified in this section, which constitutes fraud or dishonest dealing.

(j) Obtaining the signature of a prospective purchaser to an agreement which provides that such prospective purchaser shall either transact the purchasing, leasing, renting or exchanging of a business opportunity property through the broker if such property is purchased, leased, rented or exchanged without the broker first having obtained the written authorization of the owner of the property concerned to offer such property for sale, lease, exchange or rent.

Further Grounds for Disciplinary Action

10177. The commissioner may suspend or revoke the license of any real estate licensee, or may deny the issuance of a license to an applicant, who has done any of the following:

(a) Procured, or attempted to procure, a real estate license, for himself or any salesman, by fraud, misrepresentation or deceit, or by making any material misstatement of fact in an application for a real estate license.

(b) Entered a plea of guilty or nolo contendere to, or been found guilty of, or been convicted of, a felony or a crime involving moral turpitude, and the time for appeal has elapsed or the judgment of conviction has been affirmed on appeal, irrespective of an order granting probation following such conviction, suspending the imposition of sentence, or of a subsequent order under the provision of Section 1203.4 of the Penal Code allowing such licensee to withdraw his plea of guilty and to enter a plea of not guilty, or dismissing the accusation or information.

(c) Knowingly authorized, directed, connived at or aided in the publication, advertisement, distribution, or circulation of any material false statement or representation concerning his business, or any business opportunity or any land or subdivision (as defined in Chapter 1 of Part 2 of this division) offered for sale.

(d) Willfully disregarded or violated any of the provisions of the Real Estate Law (commencing with Section 10000 of this code) or of Chapter 1 (commencing with Section 11000) of Part 2 of this division or of the rules and regulations of the commissioner for the administration and enforcement of the Real Estate Law and Chapter 1 of Part 2 of this division.

(e) Willfully used the term "Realtor" or any trade name or insignia of membership in any real estate organization of which the licensee is not a member.

(f) Acted or conducted himself in a manner which would have warranted the denial of his application for a real estate license.

(g) Demonstrated negligence or incompetence in performing any act for which he is required to hold a license.

(h) As a broker licensee, failed to exercise reasonable supervision over the activities of his salesmen.

(i) Has used his employment by a governmental agency in a capacity giving access to records, other than public records, in such a manner as to violate the confidential nature of such records.

(j) Any other conduct, whether of the same or a different character than specified in this section, which constitutes fraud or dishonest dealing.

(k) Violated any of the terms, conditions, restric-

tions, and limitations contained in any order granting a restricted license.

(l) Violated Section 8616 of this code.

(m) Solicited or induced the sale, lease or the listing for sale or lease, of residential property on the ground, wholly or in part, of loss of value, increase in crime, or decline of the quality of the schools, due to the present or prospective entry into the neighborhood of a person or persons of another race, color, religion, ancestry or national origin.

5. The following are exemptions from the Real Estate Law:

Exemptions from License Requirements

10133. The definitions of a real estate broker and a real estate salesman as set forth in Sections 10131 and 10132, do not include the following:

(a) Anyone who directly performs any of the acts within the scope of this chapter with reference to his own property or, in the case of a corporation which, through its regular officers receiving no special compensation therefor, performs any of the acts with reference to the corporation's own property.

(b) Anyone holding a duly executed power of attorney from the owner.

(c) Services rendered by an attorney at law in performing his duties as such attorney at law.

(d) Any receiver, trustee in bankruptcy, or any person acting under order of any court.

(e) Any trustee selling under a deed of trust.

Exemptions from License and Other Requirements

10133.1. The provisions of subdivision (d) of Section 10131, subdivision (e) of Section 10131, Section 10131.1 and of Articles 5 (commencing with Section 10230), 6 (commencing with Section 10273), and 7 (commencing with Section 10240) of this chapter do not apply to the following:

(a) Any person or employee thereof doing business under any law of this state, any other state, or of the United States relating to banks, trust companies, savings and loan associations, industrial loan companies, pension trusts, credit unions or insurance companies.

(b) Any lender making a loan guaranteed or insured by an agency of the federal government or for which a commitment to so guarantee or insure has been made by such agency.

(c) Any nonprofit cooperative association organized under Chapter 1 (commencing with Section 5401) of Division 20 of the Agricultural Code, in loaning or advancing money in connection with any activity mentioned therein.

(d) Any corporation, association, syndicate, joint stock company or partnership engaged exclusively in the business of marketing agricultural, horticultural, viticultural, dairy, livestock, poultry or bee products on a cooperative nonprofit basis, in loaning or advancing money to the members thereof or in connection with any such business.

(e) Any corporation securing money or credit from any federal intermediate credit bank organized and existing pursuant to the provisions of an act of Congress entitled the "Agricultural Credits Act of 1923," in loaning or advancing money or credit so secured.

(f) Any person licensed to practice law in this state, not actively and principally engaged in the business of negotiating loans secured by real property, when such person renders services in the course of his practice as an attorney at law, and the disbursements of such person, whether paid by the borrower or other person, are not charges or costs and expenses regulated by or subject to the limitations of Article 7 (commencing with Section 10240) of this chapter, provided such fees and disbursements shall not be shared, directly or indirectly, with the person negotiating the loan or the lender.

(g) Any person licensed as a personal property broker when acting under the authority of such license.

(h) Any cemetery authority as defined by Section 7018 of the Health and Safety Code which is authorized to do business in this state or its authorized agent.

(i) Any person who makes collection of payments for lenders or on notes of owners in connection with loans secured directly or collaterally by liens on real property and (1) who is not actively engaged in the business of negotiating loans secured by real property or (2) who is not acting as a principal or agent in the sale or exchange of promissory notes secured directly or collaterally by liens on real property.

Other Exemptions

10133.15 The provisions of Articles 5 (commencing with Section 10230), 6 (commencing with Section 10237), and 7 (commencing with Section 10240) of this chapter do not apply to any person whose business is that of acting as an authorized representative, agent, or loan correspondent of any person or employee thereof doing business under any law of this state, any other state, or of the United States relating to banks, trust companies, savings and loan associations, industrial loan companies, pension trusts, credit unions, or insurance companies or when making loans qualified for sale to any of the foregoing insofar as such business is concerned.

Clerical Exemptions

10133.2. The provisions of Sections 10131, 10131.1, 10131.2, and 10132 do not apply to any stenographer, bookkeeper, receptionist, telephone operator, or other clerical help in carrying out their functions as such.

Multiple-choice questions

1. (e) Showing property, quoting prices, and discussing terms are all acts requiring a license; hence, the

Real Estate Law was violated even if the maintenance man performed just one of these acts once.

2. (b) The Commissioner has the authority given him or her by the legislature to supplement the law through regulations. These regulations do have the "force and effect of law."

3. (d) The Commission consists of eight members plus the Real Estate Commissioner, which makes nine.

4. (b) A statement of fact.

5. (d) A statement of fact.

6. (d) A statement of fact.

7. (d) A real estate salesperson need not be a resident or a citizen to be eligible for the license.

8. (b) A statement of fact.

9. (d) A statement of fact.

10. (c) The laying out of subdivisions is left to the subdivider, the city, or the county. The facts concerning the sale or leasing of subdivisions must be reported and a final subdivision plan must be given to the Commissioner so that he or she can include them in the Final Report to prospective purchasers.

CHAPTER 18

Chapter questions

1. The following characteristics would seem highly desirable of any sales applicant; he or she must

(a) Be an energetic person who enjoys hard work.

(b) Be a person not interested in being confined to an office all day.

(c) Be interested in studying and gaining knowledge of the community in which he or she is working.

(d) Be enthusiastic about his or her job.

(e) Have a knowledge of contracts, financing, and appraising of property value, and avail himself or herself of every opportunity to know his or her product.

(f) Be interested in the real estate business as a career and not as a hobby.

(g) Be willing to cooperate and get along with everyone.

(h) Be a consistent sales producer and have unquestioned integrity.

(i) Have the understanding and cooperation of his or her family.

(j) Be willing to support the local, state, and national trade associations.

2. This is an excellent question for class discussion, and students are encouraged to comment. Space does not permit a full discussion other than the material included in the chapter.

3. The broker-administrator must plan and control his or her enterprise. To *plan* is to set up objectives to be attained, and to *control* is to ensure that procedures of operations conform with the established objectives. A budget is expressed in financial terms and figures and may be called a plan for the future. It is based on past experience through which projections are made.

4. The multiple-listing agreement, based upon an exclusive-right-to-sell, should be encouraged. Multiple-listing associations are conducted by a group of brokers, usually the local real estate board, organized to present a service to property-owners. The multiple listing gives the widest exposure possible for the property owner and provides the broker with a selling tool proven many times over. The listing broker continues to maintain control over his or her listing even though he or she shares it with other subagents—the members of the multiple-listing association.

Multiple-choice questions

1. (d)

2. (c) The National Association of Realtors (formally National Association of Real Estate Boards) instituted the Code of Ethics; and it is adhered to by all Realtors.

3. (b) It is unethical to solicit while another exclusive listing is in force. There is no waiting period after expiration.

4. (d) The California Workman's Compensation Act considers most salespeople employees of the broker. If these salespeople were injured within the scope of their employment, the broker would be responsible for Workman's Compensation.

5. (e)

6. (c) The law does not permit licensed real estate salespeople to be general partners; however, they may work as employees for the partnership.

7. (b)

8. (e) Real estate law.

9. (a)

10. (e)

CHAPTER 19

Chapter questions

1. An insurance contract is a policy whereby one party, called the insurer, agrees to indemnify another, called the insured, upon the occurrence of a stipulated contingency or event. The consideration paid for the contract is called a premium.

Any individual who has a right or an interest in the subject property and would suffer a monetary loss in the case of destruction or damage has an insurable interest. Examples would include the owner, his or her creditors, lienholders, and any others with possessory interests.

2. (a) Fire—Under the fire insurance policy, for a loss to occur there must be a hostile fire, that is, one that has escaped from its proper place accidentally. The fire must be the immediate or proximate cause of the loss that has occurred. If there is a reasonable connection between the loss sustained and the fire, the insurer is generally liable.

(b) The extended coverage endorsement clause extends the insurance policy (standard) to include windstorm, hail, explosion, aircraft, civil commotion, vehicles, and smoke. Extended coverage gives full protection to the mortgagee and the property owner.

(c) Liability insurance is actually third-party insurance, in that it protects the insured when injuries result to another person while on the insured's property.

3. Those losses that are reasonably foreseeable as incidental to the fire are covered, provided clauses within the insurance contract do not state otherwise. Thus damage caused by smoke, water (where used to extinguish the fire), theft of personal property during the fire, and explosions caused by fire are generally covered. Exclusions would include an enemy attack by armed forces, rebellion, and insurrection.

4. If the policy contract is canceled by the insured, short rates are applicable for the period of time the policy was in force. The short rate is slightly higher than the pro rata rate and gives the insurance company a little more for the extra work involved. It is computed from a short-rate table.

The average, or coinsurance, clause in a contract provides that the insurance company shall not be liable for a loss greater than the proportion of insurance carried to the amount of insurance required. Because rates are cheaper, it encourages the property owner to insure to the full value of his or her property.

5. (a) Owners', landlords', and tenants' liability policy. It covers, to limitations outlined, liabilities that occur from the ownership of apartment houses, motels and hotels, office buildings, resorts, and so on. It will cover the use and maintenance of the premises as outlined in the contract.

(b) Elevator liability insurance—covers the risk of liability that results from the use, maintenance, and ownership of elevators, hoists, shafts, and so on.

(c) Glass insurance—covers all damage to glass except that glass damage caused by fire that would normally be covered under the fire insurance.

(d) Rent insurance—covers the loss of rental income and the loss of use or rental value of the owner-occupied portion of the building.

(e) Leasehold-interest insurance—protects the tenant against an increase or a possible cancellation of his or her lease and may also cover sublessees, losses of advance rents paid, and those who have an investment in the improvements, such as a tenant under a ground lease.

6. The word *risk* in an insurance contract (policy) whereby one party, called the insurer, agrees to indemnify another party, called the insured, upon the occurrence of a stipulated contingency or event. The chance of loss or the perils to the subject matter of insurance covered by the contract or policy.

7. The mortgagor will provide the mortgage with insurance naming the mortgage as the beneficiary to the insurance contract (loss payee clause).

8. The proper amount of insurance to carry on your building is determined by the average, or coinsurance, clause, usually 80 percent of full valuation of the property.

9. Liability insurance is actually "third-party" insurance in that it protects the insured when injuries result to another person while he or she is on the insured's property.

10. Workman's compensation insurance is required by state law to protect the employee from injuries that result within the scope of the employee's work. Rates are based on the type of occupation and an estimate of the employer's payroll. The benefits under the policy are determined by the type of injury: permanent or partial disability.

SAMPLE REAL ESTATE SALESPERSON'S EXAMINATION

DIRECTIONS

The following examination is similar to the salesperson's examination given by the California Department of Real Estate. It should be pointed out, however, that *no one has or knows the exact examination questions* of the department on any particular state examination.

You should

1. Complete the examination, allowing three hours, or approximately 1.2 minutes per question.

2. Upon completion, check your answers with the answer key at the end of the examination. A minimum passing score is 70 percent, or 105 questions correct.

3. Examine each question missed and refer to Real Estate Principles in California.

1. Which of the following best describes property? (a) Intangible; (b) bundle of rights; (c) limited rights of possession; (d) severalty.

2. The FHA loan fee that is paid by the borrower is called: (a) an accommodation fee; (b) a discount fee; (c) an acceptance fee; (d) an origination fee.

3. The use of an unlawful detainer action would be by an offended: (a) lessor; (b) trustor; (c) grantor; (d) holder of a defaulted note.

4. Mr. Smith owns an apartment house consisting of twenty-four units. Units rent for $150 per month each. Assuming 40 percent of gross for expenses, which includes management and vacancy, what would the apartment house be worth if an 8-percent capitalization rate were used? (a) $425,000; (b) $324,000; (c) $525,000; (d) $3,240,000.

5. Ron Jones builds a new four-bedroom house with only one bathroom. Before he occupies the house, it has already depreciated due to which of the following? (a) Functional obsolescence; (b) physical obsolescence; (c) economic obsolescence; (d) none of these.

6. The method which, for tax purposes, would offer the greatest amount of depreciation in the later years of a building's life is: (a) 150-percent declining balance; (b) 200-percent declining balance; (c) straight line; (d) sum of the years digits.

7. Mrs. Daws purchased a property and paid $3,000 cash, with the balance in the form of a first trust deed and note in favor of the seller. She later sold the property to Mr. Kale, subject to the first trust deed. Mr. Kale, however, failed to make the payments, and the original owner foreclosed. If the proceeds from sales were not sufficient to cover the indebtedness, the original owner could: (a) obtain a deficiency judgment against Mrs. Daws; (b) obtain a deficiency judgment against Mr. Kale; (c) not obtain a deficiency against Mrs. Daws because Mr. Kale was holding the property at the time of foreclosure; (d) not obtain a deficiency judgment against Mrs. Daws because the first trust deed was part of purchase price.

8. When an owner has paid a contractor in full for the amount agreed upon and a Notice of Completion has been filed: (a) he or she may safely assume that he or she is free from any possibility of having a mechanic's lien filed against him or her; (b) he or she can avoid the possibility of having a mechanic's lien filed by posting a Notice of Non-Responsibility at the same time he or she records the Notice of Completion; (c) he or she may be held responsible for failure of the contractor to pay subcontractors, workmen, or material suppliers, any of whom that have been unpaid may file a mechanic's lien by following the statutory provisions; (d) none of the above.

9. In order to relieve himself or herself of the primary liability for payment of a trust note, a seller must find a buyer willing to: (a) take title subject to the trust deed and note; (b) assume the trust deed and note; (c) accept a land contract of sale; (d) sign a subordination agreement.

10. In determining the value of a twenty-unit apartment property, the appraiser has established the gross income from rents. After deducting the loss for vacancies and collection losses from this gross income, he or she would have established the: (a) effective gross income; (b) gross income; (c) net income; (d) spendable income.

11. A deed made and delivered but not recorded is: (a) invalid as between the parties and valid as to third parties with constructive notice; (b) valid as between the parties and valid as to subsequent recorded interests; (c) valid as between the parties and invalid as to subsequent recorded interests without notice; (d) invalid as between the parties.

12. Which of the following is a requirement for a real estate salesperson's license? (a) California residency; (b) U. S. citizenship; (c) minimum 18 years of age; (d) all of the foregoing.

13. The four unities of title, time, interest, and possession constitute: (a) tenancy in common; (b) prescription; (c) corporate ownership; (d) joint tenancy.

14. Most buyers elect which of the following types of title insurance policies when purchasing a home? (a) ALTA; (b) ATA; (c) standard coverage; (d) extended coverage.

15. "CC&R's" as used in real estate refer to: (a) California commissioners of real estate; (b) private restrictions; (c) Department of Public Works Construction Certificates; (d) a type of certificate of value.

16. Land subject to a lien is said to be: (a) encumbered; (b) restricted; (c) appurtenant thereto; (d) alienated.

17. According to the Real Estate Law, a person must be a licensed real estate broker or salesperson to perform which of the following: (a) act on order of the court; (b) collect rents for a fee; (c) act in the capacity of an officer of a corporation selling corporate property and receive no personal remuneration for his or her services; (d) trustee selling at a foreclosure sale.

18. A corporation cannot hold title to real property in California with another as a joint tenant because: (a) it is a violation of the Securities Act; (b) of its perpetual existence; (c) it is difficult to list all stockholders in the deed; (d) a corporation cannot convey title to real property.

19. A man bought a house in a hurry and, after escrow closed, discovered that two years before a neighbor had built a fence that was three feet over the property line on his side. The broker was unaware of this. If the two neighbors were unable to reach an amicable settlement: (a) the sale would be invalid; (b) the buyer could sue the neighbor for encroachment based on trespass; (c) the neighbor had acquired title by adverse possession; (d) the buyer could sue the broker.

20. For a Conditional Sales Contract to be recorded it must: (a) contain a granting clause; (b) be signed and acknowledged by seller; (c) be signed and acknowledged by seller and buyer; (d) be signed and acknowledged by buyer.

21. Which of the following statements is always false: (a) The husband may sell personal community property for value without the consent of the wife; (b) the wife alone cannot sell community real property or community personal property; (c) a surviving spouse is entitled to onehalf of the community property, the balance may be willed to others; (d) separate property of either spouse becomes community property of the survivor upon death.

22. An owner gave an option on her property for ninety days for a cash consideration of $100. The optionee later assigned the option to another party for a valuable consideration. Before expiration of the option, the owner stated she did not want to sell the property and was taking it off the market. Which of the following is correct? (a) The option is void, since an option cannot be assigned; (b) the owner can refuse to sell, since the consideration paid by the assignee was not in cash; (c) assignee would have a good chance in civil court to compel optionor to sell to him if he exercises the option before its expiration date; (d) option is not binding on optionor because $100 is not sufficient consideration.

23. A tenant who continues in possession of a property without the permission of the landlord after the expiration of the lease is said to have: (a) an estate of inheritance; (b) an estate for years; (c) an estate at sufferance; (d) a life estate.

24. A subdivider may place deed restrictions on individual lots in a residential subdivision by: (a) zoning ordinances; (b) legislation; (c) court order; (d) covenants in the grant deeds; (e) restrictions are illegal.

25. The law that bars legal claims beyond certain time limits is known as the (a) statute of frauds; (b) statute of limitations; (c) Administrative Procedure Act; (d) Real Estate Law.

26. An administrator is appointed by the (a) court; (b) heirs; (c) decedent's will; (d) lawyer.

27. A salesperson is discharged by his or her employing broker. The broker must notify the Commissioner: (a) within ten days; (b) immediately; (c) when the license expires; (d) only if the salesperson was discharged for a violation of the Real Estate Law.

28. The initials used to designate a member of the American Institute of Real Estate Appraisers are: (a) MAI; (b) AIA; (c) NIREA; (d) NAR.

29. Under the Subdivision Map Act, control of subdivisions is the concern of: (a) the commissioner of corporations; (b) local city and county authorities; (c) the Real Estate Commissioner; (d) the state land commissioner.

30. The value of a property that earns a net income of $180 per month capitalized at 5 percent is: (a) $36,000; (b) $43,200; (c) $21,600; (d) $58,000.

31. A brother and sister own property in joint tenancy. All their other affairs are separate. The brother dies penniless, leaving many unsecured debts. The creditors could: (a) attach the property that was owned in joint tenancy; (b) place a lien against the sister's property; (c) obtain no satisfaction since the property is owned by the sister; (d) appeal to the probate court, which would be able to pay creditors out of the sale of the sister's property.

32. Mr. Jones owned two pieces of property and sold the property on the road to Mr. A, reserving in the deed an easement for access to the rear property for himself. He did not use the easement for more than five years, and Mr. A claims Mr. Jones no longer has the easement because of non-use: (a) The easement was invalid because not used for over five years; (b) the easement was still valid because non-use never terminates an easement; (c) Mr. A could sue for quiet title action on the easement and would probably be successful; (d) the easement was still valid, since it had been created by deed.

33. An investor paid $118,800 for a twelve-unit apartment house. Each apartment rents for $165 per month. It is estimated that by good management a profit of 60 percent of gross rentals could be made. What rate of return would the investor use on his or her investment? (a) 10 percent; (b) 10.5 percent; (c) 12 percent; (d) 13 percent.

34. Recording an instrument gives: (a) actual notice; (b) constructive notice; (c) implied notice; (d) right of survivorship.

35. Grantor gave a deed to a friend with instructions to return it to Grantor upon demand or, in the event of Grantor's death, to give the deed to Grantor's son. In the event of the Grantor's death, what would be the problem with giving the deed to the son? (a) Recordation; (b) acceptance; (c) delivery; (d) verification.

36. When a subdivision has been developed, the responsibility for the maintenance of the streets and curbs rests with the: (a) Real Estate Commissioner; (b) subdivider; (c) city and county departments; (d) city and Real Estate Commissioner.

37. A licensed salesperson is employed by Broker Jones. One day she decides to resign and advises the broker she is leaving. Which of the following applies to the license transfer? (a) The Real Estate Commissioner must be notified promptly; (b) application for transfer must be made on a form provided by the Department of Real Estate; (c) application must be signed by the new employing broker; (d) all of the foregoing are required by law.

38. A salesperson took an option and a listing on the same piece of property. He found a buyer and decided to exercise his option: (a) This is legal if he discloses in writing to his principal the amount of profit he will receive; (b) this is an illegal act under any circumstances and he could be disciplined; (c) real estate law prohibits taking listing and option on the same property; (d) this is legal if he splits the profit with the seller.

39. In leasing an apartment for two years beginning September 1, 1976, the owner collected the last two months' rent in advance. The prepaid rents received would be reported on her income tax: (a) as 1977 income; (b) as income for 1975 and 1976; (c) in the year collected; (d) at the end of the lease period.

40. The term "highest and best use" can best be defined as: (a) that which produces the greatest net return on the investment over a given period; (b) that which produces the greatest gross income; (c) that which contributes to the best interests of the community; (d) that which complies with the zoning laws of the community; (e) none of the foregoing.

41. No subdivision lots can be legally sold or leased prior to: (a) furnishing a copy of the Commissioner's Final Public Report to the customer; (b) giving the customer a chance to read it; (c) obtaining the signature of the customer for a copy of the report; (d) all of the foregoing.

42. Murphy built five homes on an acre of land that he owned. For the past ten years he has rented these five homes to tenants on a month-to-month basis, without securing a Subdivision Final Report from the Real Estate Commissioner. If he now wishes to sell these homes to the tenants: (a) the Real Estate Commissioner has no jurisdiction over their sale; (b) he must obtain a real estate broker's license or sell them through a licensed real estate broker; (c) the Real Estate Law has been violated; (d) he need not make a subdivision filing with the Real Estate Commissioner after the ten-year period.

43. Where would you make a search for chattel liens on claims of possible creditors of a business? (a) County Assessor's Office; (b) Board of Equalization; (c) Office of the Secretary of State; (d) both (*b*) and (*c*).

44. The document used to secure financing when personal property is sold is the: (a) financing statement; (b) agreement of sale; (c) security agreement; (d) bill of sale.

45. A subdivider hired a number of hostesses at $25

per day. They showed property, passed out brochures, and quoted prices and terms. There was a real estate licensee on the property who filled out all of the deposit receipts. The hostesses signed no documents whatsoever: (a) The broker is not in violation, since the hostesses were on a per-diem basis; (b) the broker is not in violation since the licensed salesperson filled out and signed the documents; (c) the hostesses could quote prices and terms as long as they did not fill out forms; (d) the hostesses must be real estate licensees.

46. The broker's loan law would apply to a first trust deed note of: (a) $5,000; (b) $16,000; (c) $15,000; (d) $20,000; (e) less than $20,000.

47. Broker Green obtained a deposit from Buyer Thompson. The seller did not accept the offer, however, and the broker would not return deposit. Thompson contacted the Real Estate Commissioner. The Commissioner can: (a) act only as mediator; (b) investigate as required by Real Estate Law; (c) not act on this since it involves a real estate licensee; (d) not act on this since it involves civil court action.

48. A real estate broker is using the following clause in her exclusive listing agreements: ''In consideration of the execution of this contract, the undersigned broker promises to use all possible diligence in securing buyer.'' This clause is: (a) superfluous in current contracts; (b) important in the creation of a unilateral contract; (c) important in the creation of a bilateral contract; (d) forces the broker to advertise the property.

49. *Ambulatory, Codicil,* and *devise* refer to which of the following: (a) trust deeds; (b) negotiable instruments; (c) wills; (d) attachments.

50. If a broker is sued for ''conversion,'' he or she is alleged to be: (a) commingling; (b) misappropriating client's funds; (c) misrepresenting; (d) failing to disclose material facts about the property.

51. Thomas is preparing his federal income tax return. He could claim depreciation on all of the following except: (a) a vacant duplex; (b) a house rented to a friend; (c) vacant land held for investment; (d) a rented single-family dwelling.

52. A broker had signed an agreement with an investor who was interested in a certain property. The broker determined that she could purchase this property for less than her principal was willing to pay, so she purchased the property and later sold it to the principal at a profit. This constitutes: (a) commingling; (b) conversion; (c) secret profit; (d) both (*a*) and (*c*).

53. In appraising a fifteen-year-old single-family one-story home in a good residential area which had only one owner, you would most logically use which method to determine market value? (a) Replacement cost; (b) book value; (c) capitalization; (d) comparison of selling price with prices of other homes in the neighborhood.

54. An appraiser intends that the estimate of market value disclosed in his appraisal report on a property will be valid: (a) as of the date of the appraisal only; (b) for a period of three months after the appraisal date; (c) for a period of six months after the appraisal date; (d) for a period of one year after the appraisal date.

55. Mr. and Mrs. Fisher reside in a home worth $38,000, encumbered by a first trust deed in the amount of $32,000. Mr. Fisher filed a homestead on the property without his wife's signature. Later, a mechanic's lien was filed against the property: (a) The mechanic's lien took priority over the homestead; (b) the mechanic's lien is not enforceable because it was filed subsequent to the homestead; (c) the mechanic's lien is unenforceable because there is insufficient equity over the homestead exemption; (d) the mechanic's lien is unenforceable because the wife had not signed the homestead.

56. An owner of a single-family residence sold his home with the aid of an unlicensed person. If the owner pays that person for his assistance, the one who would prosecute the unlicensed person for a violation of the Real Estate Law would be the: (a) attorney general of California; (b) Real Estate Commissioner; (c) hearing officer appointed under the provisions of the Administrative Procedure Act; (d) district attorney of the respective county.

57. The California Farm and Home Purchase Act provides that the purchaser acquires possession through: (a) land contract; (b) grant deed; (c) quitclaim deed; (d) special state deed.

58. Which one of the following concerning real estate financing is false: (a) A mortgage is a lien on real property—an execution of a mortgage does not transfer title; (b) selling a note for less than its face value is known as discounting; (c) an owner who borrows and executes a trust deed is the trustor; (d) a promissory note is the security for the trust deed.

59. A promissory note providing for payment of interest only, to be paid during its term, is: (a) a non interest-bearing note; (b) a straight note; (c) an amortized note; (d) an installment note.

60. On a conventional loan the rate of interest is generally: (a) the maximum the law will allow; (b) greater than on an FHA loan; (c) less than on an FHA loan; (d) the same as any loan source.

61. Which of the following is equivalent to an acre? (a) 43,560 square feet; (b) 1¹⁄₆₄₀th of a standard section; (c) 180 feet × 242 feet; (d) all of the above.

62. Which of the following is correct with regard to townships and ranges? (a) Ranges are numbered north and south from the base line; (b) township lines run east and west; (c) range lines run east and west; (d) townships are numbered east and west from the principal meridian.

63. Vendor sells property on a land contract. Vendee

pays $25 on same, land contract is recorded, and Vendee takes possession. Vendee pays a few months' payments and arranges to avoid seeing Vendor. Vendee moves out in the night and settles in another state: (a) Title is clouded; (b) cash purchaser would be unconcerned with Vendee; (c) title is not affected; (d) title will be marketable after one year has elapsed.

64. Which of the following is not covered by a standard policy of title insurance? (a) Mining claims; (b) unrecorded encumbrances; (c) patent exceptions; (d) all of the above.

65. Considering the comfort and habit of pedestrian shoppers, the side of the street best suited for retail business purposes is the: (a) north or east side; (b) south or east side; (c) south or west side; (d) north or west side.

66. A recorded deed of trust is removed from the records: (a) by recordation of a new trust deed; (b) when final payment has been made by trustor; (c) by posting of a surety bond; (d) when the reconveyance deed is recorded.

67. Brown and Jones had a five-year contract. After two years, they agreed to tear up this contract and replace it with a new ten-year contract. This would be called: (a) joinder action; (b) novation; (c) partition action; (d) none of these.

68. Four widowed women bought a house together and wanted to take title in such a way that upon the death of any one of them, the deceased's share would be vested equally in the remaining widows until title was finally held by the lone surviving widow. This type of holding would be: (a) community property; (b) tenancy in common; (c) tenancy in partnership; (d) joint tenancy.

69. An employer would be interested only in "results" and little else of which of the following? (a) Clerk; (b) servant; (c) employee; (d) independent contractor.

70. Which of the following best describes market value? (a) Willing buyer–willing seller concept; (b) market price; (c) cost concept; (d) directional growth.

71. The minimum age for a person who can sign a legal and binding real estate contract is (a) 18; (b) 19; (c) 20; (d) 21.

72. All of the following are among the four essentials of value *except:* (a) utility; (b) appreciation; (c) scarcity; (d) transferability.

73. A man dies intestate, leaving a wife and minor son. The community property would be distributed as follows: (a) All to the wife; (b) one-half to the son; (c) one-third to the wife and two-thirds to the son; (d) none of the above.

74. Regulations of the Real Estate Commissioner: (a) are contained in the Civil Code; (b) have the force and effect of law; (c) originate with the state attorney general; (d) regulate the employees of the Department of Real Estate.

75. Demand is one of the four elements of value. In order for demand to be effective, it must be implemented by: (a) conspicuousness; (b) objectivity; (c) purchasing power; (d) reliability.

76. The phrase "time is of the essence" would most likely be found in a: (a) listing; (b) purchase contract; (c) deed; (d) Broker's Loan Statement.

77. Certain documents must be acknowledged before they can be recorded. To acknowledge means: (a) to admit or declare that you signed a document; (b) to make an affidavit; (c) to authenticate the contents of a document; (d) none of the above.

78. An easement appurtenant is terminated by merger: (a) when the person holding the easement becomes the owner of the land subject to the easement; (b) when the owner of the easement does not use it for five years; (c) when the owner of the easement deeds it to the owner of the land; (d) in both (*a*) and (*b*).

79. An apartment owner appointed a broker to collect the rents on the apartments. All rents were due on the first of the month. On July 1, the broker had collected all the rents except from one tenant. On July 2, the owner died. The broker called on the remaining tenant on July 3, but the tenant refused to pay the rent to the broker, saying that the death of the owner had revoked the broker's right to collect. The tenant: (a) was right; (b) could not refuse, as the broker's authority continued until the appointment of an executor or administrator; (c) could not refuse, because the rent was due on July 1; (d) has to pay the rent until notified by the owner or his representative not to.

80. Which of the following is not covered by an ALTA policy? (a) Rights of parties in possession; (b) zoning regulations; (c) title report; (d) mining claims.

81. Which of the following is required for a valid contract of sale for real estate? (a) An instrument in writing; (b) an acknowledgment; (c) an insured title; (d) a recorded instrument.

82. A salesperson sold a house. Without the knowledge of the salesperson and through no fault of hers, the buyer and the seller got together and agreed to cancel the sale. Under these circumstances: (a) broker can keep entire deposit as compensation for services rendered; (b) the broker can keep half the deposit and return the other half to the buyer; (c) the salesperson's broker can keep half of the deposit and give half to the seller; (d) broker can sue seller, but must return the deposit.

83. I = PRT is a formula used mostly in connection with: (a) real estate loans; (b) proration of insurance; (c) premiums for title insurance; (d) taxes.

84. Which of the following is an example of economic obsolescence? (a) Negligence of renter; (b) termite infestation; (c) legislative regulations; (d) architectural design.

85. An appraiser, in using the market-data approach for an appraisal of a house, would use which of the following? (a) Listing price; (b) bid price; (c) sales price; (d) exchange price.

86. A subdivision located in Nevada to be offered for sale or lease in California: (a) must be parcels of not less than one-quarter acre; (b) must be filed with the California Real Estate Commissioner; (c) does not come under the jurisdiction of the California Real Estate Commissioner; (d) cannot be financed with a blanket deed of trust.

87. On a condominium, real property taxes: (a) are billed to the individual unit owner; (b) constitute a lien on the individual unit owner, but not on the individual unit; (c) are billed to the entire project and pro-rated by the project man-unit; (d) do not include value of common areas in assessment.

88. A broker's loan statement is prepared for the benefit of the: (a) trustee; (b) broker; (c) lender; (d) borrower.

89. At a trustee's sale, a property brought $88,000. The fees and costs amounted to $375. The property was encumbered with a first trust deed in the amount of $65,000 and a second trust deed of $10,000. Which is correct: (a) There would not be a surplus after the sale; (b) there would be a surplus, which would go to the trustor; (c) there would be a surplus, which could go to the trustee; (d) the beneficiary of the second trust deed could initiate court action after the sale for a deficiency judgment against the trustor.

90. Mr. Ackerman leased a property for five years to Mr. Bones. During this term, Mr. Ackerman died and Mr. Bones discovered that Mr. Ackerman's interest was a life estate. The owner of the property was correct in advocating which of the following? (a) Mr. Bones's leasehold estate is valid for the length of the lease; (b) Mr. Bones's interest was terminated upon Mr. Ackerman's demise; (c) Mr. Ackerman's heir would receive the fee title; (d) the owner has an estate in remainder.

91. The highest value of a parcel of real property expressed in terms of money is its: (a) market value; (b) insured value; (c) loan value; (d) mortgage value.

92. Which of the following furnishes an easement? (a) Utility company; (b) servient tenement; (c) dominant tenement; (d) none of these.

93. Mr. and Mrs. Grant purchased a home two years ago, financing it with a long-term first trust deed and note. They encountered some financial difficulty and were unable to make their payments for two consecutive months. As a result, the beneficiary instigated foreclosure proceedings and the Grants received a copy of the Notice of Default that had been recorded. Their best course of action at this time is to exercise their right of: (a) refinancing; (b) loan moratorium; (c) redemption; (d) reinstatement.

94. Which of the following is a requirement of valid

deed? (a) Grantee's signature; (b) acknowledgment; (c) granting clause; (d) recordation.

95. The Real Estate Commissioner's subdivision Final Public Report expires: (a) when four lots or fewer remain to be sold; (b) five years from the date of the issuance of the report; (c) never, unless a material change occurs; (d) one year from the date of the report.

96. A broker negotiated a second deed of trust for $5,050 for three years. The maximum commission allowed by law is: (a) 5 percent; (b) 8 percent; (c) 15 percent; (d) 20 percent.

97. Which of the following is not properly included in the government's power of eminent domain? The right to: (a) take private property of the owner and pay just compensation; (b) exercise police power; (c) pay the fair market value for property acquired; (d) instigate condemnation proceedings.

98. The Commissioner will permit a real estate business to operate as a partnership consisting of: (a) real estate broker and building contractor; (b) real estate broker and insurance broker; (c) three real estate brokers; (d) all of the foregoing.

99. Section 7 in a township is: (a) next to section 1 in the same township; (b) due east of section 13 in the same township; (c) an inside section of the same township; (d) part of the west boundary of the same township.

100. If A dies intestate, her heirs would receive the estate by: (a) holographic will; (b) witnessed will; (c) probate court action; (d) noncupative will.

101. The subjective value of a parcel of land is: (a) market value; (b) dollar value to the buyer; (c) utility value to the seller; (d) exchange value; (e) book value.

102. Mr. Jacobs plans to build a home and wants to borrow money in advance to pay for the various stages of construction. This type of financing is called: (a) obligatory advance; (b) release money; (c) "take-out" financing; (d) optional advance; (e) immediate financing.

103. Which of the following statements is *incorrect* regarding a condominium: (a) A condominium subdivision may be residential, industrial, or commercial; (b) the unit is the portion that is not owned in common with the other condominium owners, (c) the common areas exclude the units; (d) one disadvantage is that there are no provisions in a condominium for individual tax assessments of the units; (e) all of the foregoing statements are correct.

104. Who handles the prosecution when it becomes necessary for criminal procedures under the Real Estate Law? (a) The applicable county district attorney; (b) the attorney general of California; (c) the sheriff of the county where the act occurred; (d) the Real Estate Commissioner; (e) the secretary of state.

105. An advance fee is defined as: (a) a bonus for advancing the sale of a home; (b) advance payment of a commission; (c) advance payment for regular ads in newspapers; (d) prepayment of costs for promotional services in the form of advertising devoted to properties available for sale or lease; (e) advance payment of property taxes.

106. Which of the following statements is correct? (a) It is the duty of the escrow holder to arbitrate arguments between the buyer and the seller; (b) escrow instructions are confidential; (c) a broker may act as an escrow officer in any transaction in which he or she was not the agent; (d) a "complete" escrow takes place when an escrow agent holds a valid contract that binds the buyer and the seller; (e) the escrow officer may, when he or she feels it necessary, give legal advice.

107. The interest rate on an amortized loan is 8¾ percent. Last month the interest paid was $106.40. What is the balance on the loan? (a) $14,592; (b) $15,592; (c) $15,952; (d) $14,492; (e) not enough information is given to work the problem.

108. According to the Bulk Sales Law: (a) a publication of the notice must be put in a newspaper of general circulation; (b) a notice of sale must be advertised for five days before the sale in a newspaper of general circulation in the judicial district where the business is located; (c) a notice must be recorded in the office of the county recorder within ten days of the bulk transfer of the intention to sell a business; (d) all of the foregoing must be done; (e) none of the foregoing needs to be done.

109. In using the land residual method of appraising, you would arrive at one of the following values: (a) the land only; (b) the building only; (c) the land, buildings, and amenities only; (d) land and buildings only; (e) the book value only.

110. Mrs. Dawes purchased a second deed of trust and note for 80 percent of the $1,500 face value. The loan was scheduled to fully amortize in one year and called for payments of $131 per month including 9 percent interest. If Mrs. Dawes holds the note for one full year and the borrower pays according to the terms, what would the yield be on Mrs. Dawes's original investment? (a) 50 percent; (b) 100 percent; (c) 31 percent; (d) 48 percent; (e) 70 percent.

111. Mr. Smith is planning to build an A-frame cabin on mountain property that he owns. He paid $10,000 for the property. The downpayment was $2,000, with the balance of the purchase price carried back by the seller on a purchase-money first deed of trust securing a note for $8,000. If Mr. Smith intends to secure a construction loan for the construction of the cabin, he would include in the purchase contract: (a) a subrogation clause; (b) a subordination clause; (c) an alienation clause; (d) a release clause; (e) a "hold harmless" clause.

112. A salesperson working for a broker had been selling loan information to a company making real estate loans. When his employing broker heard of this, he im-

mediately fired the salesperson. He warned the rest of his salespeople never to do anything like this. Based on the information given, which of the following statements is *correct*? (a) The broker would not be held liable in this case, since he had no "actual knowledge" of what the salesman was doing; (b) both the broker and the salesperson were guilty; (c) the salesperson was not guilty of any wrongdoing, since every salesperson has the right to pick up a little money on the side, as long as it's in the business; (d) none of the foregoing statements is correct.

113. A twenty-unit apartment building is located in an area that is going to have a new freeway built immediately next to it. The owner estimates that her total monthly income will decrease by $200 per month from the new freeway. If you used a capitalization rate of 12 percent, the value of the property will decrease by: (a) $1,666.67; (b) $2,400.00; (c) $16,666.67; (d) $20,000.00; (e) $20,666.67.

114. Which of the following statements is *true* with respect to planning commissions? (a) All members of the planning commission are elected; (b) all members of the planning commission must have real estate or subdivision experience; (c) all members of the planning commission are authorized to give advice to the city council on subdivisions; (d) the planning commission is the final authority on all zoning matters; (e) all members of the planning commission must be licensed brokers or salespeople.

115. A real estate broker was given forty acres of land valued at $100 per acre as payment for his commission, with the knowledge and consent of the buyer and the seller. Two days after escrow closed, a stranger contacted the broker and offered him $250 per acre. If the broker accepts the offer he: (a) will be guilty of making a "secret profit"; (b) will be acting unethically; (c) will be acting in an acceptable manner; (d) must obtain written permission from the seller and the buyer; (e) must obtain written permission from the buyer only.

116. Assume a property is listed for $38,300 and the broker brings in an offer that is 12 percent less than the listed price. The owner agrees to accept the offer if the broker will reduce his 6 percent commission by 25 percent. If the broker accepts this reduced rate, his commission will be: (a) $2,298.00; (b) $1,298.50; (c) $1,516.68; (d) $2,516.58; (e) $2,298.50.

117. Every nonresident broker applicant for a California real estate license must, along with his or her application, file with the Real Estate Commissioner: (a) a statement by the applicant's home-state real estate commissioner stating that the applicant is duly licensed by his or her home state; (b) an application fee of one and one-half times the California license fee; (c) a copy of a statement filed by the applicant's county recorder showing the applicant is residing in and will operate in that county; (d) an irrevocable consent that if in any action commences against him or her in California, personal service of process upon him or her cannot be made, but must be made upon him or her by delivering the process to the secretary of state; (e) both (*a*) and (*d*).

118. Mrs. Brown purchased the entire stock of a retail store for $9,300. She sold the goods for 33⅓ percent more than what she paid for them, but *lost 15 percent* of the total *selling price* due to bad debts. The net profit on her investment was: (a) $10,540.00; (b) $3,100.00; (c) 15 percent; (d) $1,240.00; (e) 20 percent.

119. A building is insured for $24,500 at the rate of 16 cents per $100. The premium is for three years and is two and one-half times the annual rate. Based on these numbers, how much would have to be reserved each month to pay the three year premium? (a) $2.72; (b) $3.27; (c) $4.70; (d) $3.92; (e) $3.73.

120. In California, the licensed real estate salesperson's commission is paid by the: (a) buyer; (b) seller; (c) buyer and seller; (d) escrow agent; (e) real estate broker.

121. A salesperson leaves the employ of his broker. The reason is not subject to disciplinary action on the part of the Commissioner, and the broker and the salesperson part on friendly terms. According to the California Real Estate Law and the above circumstances, which of the following is most correct regarding notification of the Real Estate Commissioner? (a) It must be reported within ten days; (b) it must be reported within one month; (c) it must be reported immediately; (d) the broker does not need to notify the Commissioner in any case; (e) it must be reported within three working days.

122. Proceedings brought against a licensee *by the Real Estate Commissioner* come under: (a) the California Civil Code; (b) the Uniform Commercial Code; (c) the Law of Propriety; (d) the Probate Code; (e) the Administrative Procedure Act.

123. Mr. Perfect owned an unencumbered lot and decided to build on it. On January 1, he ordered $500 worth of lumber from the Arnold Lumber Yard and had it delivered to the property. One week later, he secured a construction loan from the Excellent Savings and Loan Association for $15,000. The loan was recorded at that time. On the following Saturday, additional lumber was delivered to the property and, subsequently, the structure was painted and completed. The lumber company and the painter were unable to collect the $1,000 owed for the lumber and the $1,200 owed for the painting. On March 12, both the painter and the materialman filed mechanic's liens for their respective amounts. If the property were sold at a foreclosure sale and the highest bid was $15,000 disregarding costs and expenses of the sale, how much would Excellent Savings and Loan Associa-

tion receive? (a) $15,000; (b) $13,800; (c) $14,000; (d) $12,800; (e) $15,800.

124. Beginning at a point located at the southwest corner of the NE ¼ of the SE ¼ of Section 27; thence to a point located 1320 feet due east; thence at a right angle 660 feet due north; thence at a right angle due west 1320 feet; thence to the point of beginning. Based on the foregoing description, how many acres would be contained in this tract of land? (a) Five acres; (b) ten acres; (c) twenty acres; (d) thirty acres; (e) forty acres.

125. Mrs. Holmes bought two lots for $9,000 and later sold them for 15 percent more than she paid. During her ownership, they had been assessed at 25 percent of the cost, with the tax rate during the four years at $8 per $100 of assessed value. Considering that she lost 5-percent interest per annum on the purchase, how much did Mrs. Holmes lose in all? (a) $1,070; (b) $2,000; (c) $2,191; (d) $1,020; (e) $2,120.

126. A $5,000 balance on a land contract of sale is payable on the principal-reduction plan at $50 per month excluding interest at 8¾ percent per annum. Based on these numbers, it would take: (a) 100 months to amortize the loan; (b) eleven years and seven months to amortize the loan; (c) twenty-five years to amortize the loan; (d) fifty-one months to amortize the loan; (e) none of the foregoing answers, because this type of loan does not amortize.

127. How many acres are there in the shaded area below? (a) 300 acres; (b) 360 acres; (c) 480 acres; (d) 640 acres; (e) 320 acres.

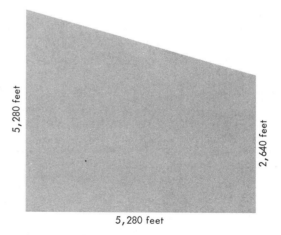

128. You are a California real estate broker. A prospect is referred to you by an out-of-state broker, and a sale is consummated by you. You want to split your commission with the cooperating broker. Under the California Real Estate Law: (a) you may divide a commission to a broker of another state; (b) you cannot divide a commission with a broker of another state; (c) you can pay a commission to a broker of another state only if he or she is also licensed in California; (d) you may pay a commission to a broker of another state if you are licensed in that state; (e) you may never pay a commission to a broker of another state without permission of the Real Estate Commissioner.

129. An owner-operator who has $20,000 invested in a business receives $7,100 annual earnings, including his salary, from the business. Allowing him $450 per month as base salary, the financial return on his investment is: (a) 5½ percent; (b) 6⅓ percent; (c) 8 percent; (d) 8½ percent; (e) 9 percent.

130. A certain promissory note has contained within the body of it a clause that accelerates the entire unpaid balance and all accrued interest due upon sale or transfer of the encumbered property in any manner. This is, of course, known as an "alienation clause." The effect of this clause on the negotiability of the note would be: (a) no effect at all; (b) the effect of making the note non-negotiable; (c) making it more desirable under the conditions of subrogation; (d) making it less desirable under the conditions of subrogation; (e) rendering it worthless.

The following questions (131–40 inclusive) refer to the *exclusive authorization and right to sell* agreement that follows this examination on page 301

131. Assume that Kelley McCormick and Associates, Inc., had shown the property to some serious customers during the term of the listing agreement, but was unable to complete the transaction. Principals knew nothing of the customers, but ten days after the listing expired, one of the serious customers purchased directly from the principals. Under the terms of the listing Broker McCormick has: (a) a valid claim for a commission from the sellers; (b) a valid claim for a commission from the buyers; (c) no valid claim for a commission from the sellers; (d) no valid claim for a commission from the buyers, in absence of misrepresentation; (e) a claim for $2,910 from the buyers and sellers.

132. On June 1, 1982, the Principals notify Broker McCormick that they are withdrawing their property from the market and order McCormick to cancel the listing agreement. Under the terms of the Exclusive Authorization and Right to Sell as shown: (a) McCormick is entitled to recover actual expenses; (b) McCormick is entitled to a full commission from the Principals; (c) Principals have a legal right to cancel the agreement at the end of sixty days; (d) McCormick is entitled to no commission; (e) McCormick is entitled to $1,000.

133. Assume that Mr. Principal, without McCormick's knowledge, owned the subject property in joint tenancy with his wife and twenty-two-year-old son. McCormick produces a buyer ready, willing, and able

to buy under the exact terms and conditions of the listing agreement, but the son refuses to sign the acceptance. McCormick claims an earned commission, but the son points out that he had never signed the Exclusive Authorization and Right to Sell: (a) McCormick would have a legal basis for bringing suit for a commission; (b) McCormick's claim for a commission is unwarranted, since he should know that all joint tenants must sign the listing agreement; (c) buyers making the offer could sue Mr. and Mrs. Principal and son for specific performance; (d) McCormick has violated the Real Estate Law; (e) the son could sue McCormick for failing to obtain his signature.

134. Mr. and Mrs. Principal inform the Real Estate Commissioner in writing that they never received a copy of the listing agreement. Under the Real Estate Law: (a) Principals' complaint is invalid because the agreement acknowledged receipt of a copy; (b) burden of proof rests entirely with the Principals to show they did not get a copy; (c) burden of proof rests entirely with McCormick to show they did in fact receive a copy; (d) Real Estate Commissioner would not be concerned with this complaint; (e) a copy of the listing can be given to the Principals at any time before expiration date.

135. Assume that McCormick assured the Principals that the Exclusive Authorization and Right to Sell which they signed was an Exclusive Agency Agreement. The Principals thereafter sold their own home and McCormick sued for a commission. Upon proof in court that McCormick had given this assurance: (a) a full commission would be awarded to McCormick; (b) McCormick's claim to a commission would be denied; (c) Principals would be obliged to pay one-half of the agreed-upon commission; (d) the matter of commission would be referred to a title insurance officer; (e) a full commission plus 2 percent of the sales price would be awarded to McCormick.

136. Assume that McCormick's salesperson finds a buyer ready, willing, and able to buy the subject property, and he prepares a Real Estate Purchase Contract and Receipt for Deposit. When the salesperson telephones the Principals of his offer, they request information on the national origin of the buyers. (a) The salesperson under the law must convey this information; (b) the salesperson should tell the Principals to quickly withdraw their property from the market; (c) if this information is given, the salesperson has violated fair-housing laws; (d) the salesperson may volunteer this information without liability; (e) the salesperson should have refused to write up the contract because he knew the sellers would object.

137. Broker McCormick presents an offer to Mr. and Mrs. Principal on the exact terms of the listing agreement with the exception of the deposit on the purchase price,

EXCLUSIVE AUTHORIZATION AND RIGHT TO SELL

THIS IS INTENDED TO BE A LEGALLY BINDING AGREEMENT—READ IT CAREFULLY.
CALIFORNIA ASSOCIATION OF REALTORS® STANDARD FORM

1. **Right to Sell.** I hereby employ and grant ___Kelley McCormick & Associates, Inc.___ hereinafter called "Agent," the exclusive and irrevocable right commencing on ___April 1___, 19__82__, and expiring at midnight on ___June 30___, 19__82__, to sell or exchange the real property situated in ___the City of Bakersfield___ County of ___Kern___, California described as follows:
___Lot 10, Block 12, Tract 12345, McCloud Estates, Recorded 1978 in Kern County___
___Records, Book 182 at Page 478. Also known as 5678 McClellan Road, Bakersfield,___
___California___

2. **Terms of Sale.** The purchase price shall be $___115,000.00___, to be paid in the following terms:
___$23,000 cash, including a cash deposit in the minimum amount of $1,000.00.___
___Buyers must obtain and qualify for an 80% loan from Kern County Savings &___
___Loan to eliminate a prepayment penalty for sellers.___

(a) The following items of personal property are to be included in the above-stated price:
___Westinghouse Refrigerator located in kitchen. Kenmore Washer and Dryer located in___
___the garage, all window furnishings, including draperies and curtains -------------------___
___--___

(b) Agent is hereby authorized to accept and hold on my behalf a deposit upon the purchase price. $1,000.00.

(c) Evidence of title to the property shall be in the form of a California Land Title Association Standard Coverage Policy of Title Insurance in the amount of the selling price to be paid for by ----------------sellers----------------------------------

(d) I warrant that I am the owner of the property or have the authority to execute this agreement. I hereby authorize a FOR SALE sign to be placed on my property by Agent. I authorize the Agent named herein to cooperate with sub-agents.

3. **Notice: The amount or rate of real estate commissions is not fixed by law. They are set by each broker individually and may be negotiable between the seller and broker.**

Compensation to Agent. I hereby agree to compensate Agent as follows:
(a) ___Six percent (6)___ % of the selling price if the property is sold during the term hereof, or any extension thereof, by Agent, on the terms herein set forth or any other price and terms I may accept, or through any other person, or by me, or ___six percent (6)___ % of the price shown in 2, if said property is withdrawn from sale, transferred, conveyed, leased without the consent of Agent, or made unmarketable by any voluntary act during the term hereof or any extension thereof.

(b) the compensation provided for in subparagraph (a) above if property is sold, conveyed or otherwise transferred within ___ninety (90)___ days after the termination of this authority or any extension thereof to anyone with whom Agent has had negotiations prior to final termination, provided I have received notice in writing, including the names of the prospective purchasers, before or upon termination of this agreement or any extension hereof. However, I shall not be obligated to pay the compensation provided for in subparagraph (a) if a valid listing agreement is entered into during the term of said protection period with another licensed real estate broker and a sale, lease or exchange of the property is made during the term of said valid listing agreement.

4. If action be instituted to enforce this agreement, the prevailing party shall receive reasonable attorney's fees and costs as fixed by the Court.

5. In the event of an exchange, permission is hereby given Agent to represent all parties and collect compensation or commissions from them, provided there is full disclosure to all principals of such agency. Agent is authorized to divide with other agents such compensation or commissions in any manner acceptable to them.

6. I agree to save and hold Agent harmless from all claims, disputes, litigation, and/or judgments arising from any incorrect information supplied by me, or from any material fact known by me concerning the property which I fail to disclose.

7. This property is offered in compliance with state and federal anti-discrimination laws.

8. Other provisions:
___Buyers must agree to use their best efforts to obtain the above-described loan.___

9. I acknowledge that I have read and understand this Agreement, and that I have received a copy hereof.
Dated ___May 31,___ 19__82___ ___Bakersfield, CA.___, California

Owner ___Joe Owner___   Address ___5678 McClellan Road___
Owner ___Harry Principal___   City, State, Phone ___Bakersfield, CA. (316) 342-1212___

10. In consideration of the above, Agent agrees to use diligence in procuring a purchaser.
Agent ___Kelly McCormick & Associates, Inc___   Address ___783 Chester Avenue___   City ___Bakersfield, CA.___
By ___VP Billy Mitchell___   Phone ___(316) 342-2424___   Date ___May 31, 1982___

NO REPRESENTATION IS MADE AS TO THE LEGAL VALIDITY OF ANY PROVISION OR THE ADEQUACY OF ANY PROVISION IN ANY SPECIFIC TRANSACTION. IF YOU DESIRE LEGAL ADVICE, CONSULT YOUR ATTORNEY.

To order contact —California Association of Realtors®
525 South Virgil Avenue, Los Angeles, California 90020
Copyright 1978 by California Association of Realtors® (Revised, 1980 Reviewed, 1984)

FORM A-11

SALESMAN'S COPY

301

which is $500. The Principals refuse to accept the offer. Broker McCormick: (a) may sue the Principals for the full commission; (b) may sue the Principals for the full commission plus his expenses; (c) is entitled to no commission since he has not fulfilled the listing contract; (d) is entitled to the $500 deposit; (e) should advise the buyers to sue for specific performance.

138. Betty Mitchell, Broker McCormick's salesperson who took the listing, decides to transfer to Broker Jose's office on May 25, 1982. The Principals insist that Betty handle the listing and that the listing be transferred to the new broker's office. The listing agreement is the property of: (a) Betty Mitchell; (b) Broker McCormick; (c) Broker Jose; (d) the Principals, and they are within their legal rights to cancel the agreement; (e) Broker McCormick and Broker Jose, jointly.

139. Broker McCormick agrees to cooperate with Broker Peterson in the sale of the Principals' home. Broker McCormick writes up an offer on the *exact* terms and conditions of the listing agreement as shown, and on the same day Broker Peterson writes up an offer for $110,000 *all cash* with a closing in thirty days. Broker McCormick should: (a) insist that the Principals accept his offer, since he is the listing broker; (b) present both offers to the Principals for their decision; (c) refuse to present Broker Peterson's offer; (d) not present either offer to the Principals; (e) call the Real Estate Commissioner and ask his or her advice.

140. On July 1, 1982, Broker McCormick's salesperson writes up an offer meeting all terms and conditions of the listing agreement. The Principals refuse to accept the offer. (a) The listing agreement, as written, protects the broker for twenty-four hours after expiration date; (b) the Principals must accept the offer, since it meets all terms and conditions of the agreement; (c) the Principals have a legal right to refuse the offer; (d) the broker has an automatic extension for ninety days after expiration of the listing agreement; (e) the broker may sue and is entitl meets all terms and conditions of the agreement; (c) the Principals have a legal right to refuse the offer; (d) the broker has an automatic extension for ninety days after expiration of the listing agreement; (e) the broker may sue and is entitled to a full real estate commission on the listed price of the property.

The following questions (141–50) refer to the Real Estate Purchase Contract and Receipt for Deposit that follows this examination on pages 303–4

141. Assume Mr. and Mrs. Buyer in signing the contract instruct Pamela Salesperson not to deposit their check until ten working days after the Sellers' acceptance. Pamela agrees to this. When Pamela presented the contract (offer) to the Sellers, she failed to inform them of this agreement. Pamela deposits the check, after ten working days as instructed by the Buyers. The bank returned the check marked "insufficient funds." Mr. and Mrs. Seller are upset and write to the Real Estate Commissioner. (a) Neither Pamela nor her broker is guilty of any wrong doing; (b) Broker Davey must take full responsibility for a material representation; Pamela takes none, since she is only a salesperson; (c) Pamela is guilty of a material misrepresentation and Broker Davey is not; (d) Broker Davey and Pamela are guilty of a material misrepresentation; (e) the Commissioner would be unconcerned since no provision of the law has been violated.

142. The real estate purchase contract provides that real property taxes, premiums on insurance acceptable to buyers, rents and interest shall be prorated as of: (a) April 15, 1980; (b) the date the Buyers take possession; (c) the close of escrow; (d) the date of recordation of deed; (e) June 4, 1980.

143. Pamela Salesperson leaves Mr. and Mrs. Buyer a copy of the real estate purchase contract when they sign it. She and the cooperating broker take her only other copy to Mr. and Mrs. Seller for their approval, and they sign it. She tells the Sellers that she will return a copy of the contract to them after she makes extra copies for the office. (a) Pamela's actions are proper in every respect; (b) Pamela has acted properly, since the Sellers acknowledged receiving a copy of the agreement; (c) leaving a copy of any agreement is unimportant to the parties, since they are on file in the broker's office; (d) Pamela has not violated any provision of the Real Estate Law as long as she returns a copy of the agreement within twenty-four-hours; (e) Pamela has violated a provision of the Real Estate Law and could have her license suspended or revoked.

144. Mr. and Mrs. Seller are notified by their lender on May 3 that there will be a prepayment penalty on their existing loan of $948. Mr. Seller is disturbed and notifies the respective brokers that the deal is off. Under these circumstances: (a) the Buyers could sue the Sellers for specific performance; (b) the Sellers have a legal right, in accordance with the contract as written, to rescind it; (c) the Sellers are entitled to retain 3 percent ($3,750) of the deposit to compensate them for their extra problems; (d) the Sellers can sue and collect from the Buyers the prepayment; (e) the brokers can be forced to pay the prepayment from their commission.

145. Homer C. Davey & Associates and Professional Real Estate Brokers, under the terms of the contract, will be paid their commission: (a) on recordation of the deed or other evidence of title; (b) upon seller's default if it prevents completion of sale; (c) upon the buyer's default if it prevents the completion of sale and only if the Sellers collect damages from the buyers, by suit or otherwise.

REAL ESTATE PURCHASE CONTRACT AND RECEIPT FOR DEPOSIT
THIS IS MORE THAN A RECEIPT FOR MONEY. IT IS INTENDED TO BE A LEGALLY BINDING CONTRACT. READ IT CAREFULLY.
CALIFORNIA ASSOCIATION OF REALTORS® STANDARD FORM

<u>San Jose</u>, California. <u>April 5,</u> 19 <u>82</u>

Received from <u>Stanley S. Buyer and Mary M. Buyer, his wife, his wife</u>—————————
herein called Buyer, the sum of <u>one thousand and no/100 dollars</u>——————————Dollars $<u>1,000.00</u>———
evidenced by cash ☑/ cashier's check ☑/ or _____ ☒, personal check ☐ payable to <u>Homer C. Davey &</u>
<u>Associates Trustee Account</u>, to be held uncashed until acceptance of this offer, as deposit on account of purchase price of
<u>One Hundred Twenty-Five Thousand Dollars</u>—————————————————————Dollars $ <u>125,000.00</u>——
for the purchase of property, situated in <u>the City of Cupertino</u>, County of <u>Santa Clara</u>, California,
described as follows: <u>Lot 4, Tract 4022, Map recorded June 1, 1963, page 72, Book 800, OR Santa Clara County</u>

1. Buyer will deposit in escrow with <u>Western Title Insurance Company</u> the balance of purchase price as follows:

<u>$120,000</u> Cash to sellers which includes a total cash deposit of $4,000 (see above
and number (2) below. This offer is contingent upon the buyers being able,
prior to April 25, 1982, to obtain and qualify for a new loan in the
minimum term of twenty-five (25) years at the prevailing interest rate
secured by a first deed of trust on the property with a maximum of two
points to be paid by the buyers on said loan. Buyers herein agree to
use their best efforts to obtain this loan. If this contingency is not
met, this agreement shall become null and void and all deposit monies shall
be returned to buyers without penalty.

<u>5,000</u> Buyers herein agree to execute a promissory note secured by a second purchase
money deed of trust on the property in favor of sellers for $5,000 payable
at $50 or more per month, including principal and interest at the rate of
ten (10%) percent per annum with the first installment payment due July 5,
1982. The entire balance of said loan shall be due and payable five (5)
years from date of said promissory note or upon sale or other transfer of
the property.

<u>$125,000</u> TOTAL PURCHASE PRICE

Property to be inspected by a licensed pest control operator. Buyers to pay for the inspection. Sellers to pay for 1) elimination of infestation and/or infection of wood destroying pests or organisms, 2) repair of damage caused by such infestation and/or infection, including fungus and wood rot, 3) correction of conditions which caused said damage, and 4)
repair of linking stall showers, in accordance with said pest control operator's report.
Except for work recommended under item (3) above, the sellers shall not be responsible for
the cost of any work for the future protection of the buildings. Funds for work to be done
at seller's expense shall be held in escrow and disbursed by escrowholder upon receipt of
proof of completion of said work or upon close of escrow, whichever occurs later. Copies of
the report to be delivered to agents of buyer and seller who are authorized to receive
same on behalf of their principals.

Set forth above any terms and conditions of a factual nature applicable to this sale, such as financing, prior sale of other property, the matter
of structural pest control inspection, repairs and personal property to be included in the sale.

2. Deposit will ☒ will not ☑ be increased by $ <u>3,000.00</u>— to $ <u>4,000.00</u>——— within <u>ten (10)</u>———— days of
acceptance of this offer.

3. Buyer does ☒ does not ☑ intend to occupy subject property as his residence.

4. The following supplements are incorporated as part of this agreement:

		Other
☐ Structural Pest Control Certification Agreement	☐ Occupancy Agreement	☐ _____
☐ Special Studies Zone Disclosure	☐ VA Amendment	☐ _____
☐ Flood Insurance Disclosure	☐ FHA Amendment	☐ _____

5. Buyer and Seller shall deliver signed instructions to the escrow holder within <u>five (5)</u> days from Seller's acceptance which
shall provide for closing within <u>sixty (60)</u> days from Seller's acceptance. Escrow fees to be paid as follows:
Fifty (50%) percent shall be paid for by the buyers.
Fifty (50%) percent shall be paid for by the sellers.

6. Buyer and Seller acknowledge receipt of a copy of this page, which constitutes Page 1 of <u>2</u> Pages.

Buyer _Stan Buyer_   Seller _Harry Seller_
Buyer _Mary Buyer_   Seller _Neal Seller_

A REAL ESTATE BROKER IS THE PERSON QUALIFIED TO ADVISE ON REAL ESTATE. IF YOU DESIRE LEGAL ADVISE CONSULT YOUR ATTORNEY.

REAL ESTATE PURCHASE CONTRACT AND RECEIPT FOR DEPOSIT

The following terms and conditions are hereby incorporated in and made a part of Buyer's Offer

7.   Title is to be free of liens, encumbrances, easements, restrictions, rights and conditions of record or known to Seller, other than the following: (a) Current property taxes, (b) covenants, conditions, restrictions, and public utility easements of record, if any, provided the same do not adversely affect the continued use of the property for the purposes for which it is presently being used, unless reasonably disapproved by Buyer in writing within _five (5)_ days of receipt of a current preliminary title report furnished at _seller's_ expense, and (c) _no other exceptions_ --

Seller shall furnish Buyer at _seller's_ expense a standard California Land Title Association policy issued by _Western Title Insurance_ Company, showing title vested in Buyer subject only to the above. If Seller is unwilling or unable to eliminate any title matter disapproved by Buyer as above, Seller may terminate this agreement. If Seller fails to deliver title as above, Buyer may terminate this agreement; in either case, the deposit shall be returned to Buyer.

8.   Property taxes, premiums on insurance acceptable to Buyer, rents, interest, // shall be pro-rated as of (a) the date of recordation of deed, or (b) //. Any bond or assessment which is a lien shall be ___paid___ (assumed) by _Seller_. Transfer taxes, if any, shall be paid by _Seller_.

9.   Possession shall be delivered to Buyer (a) on close of escrow, or (b) not later than _June 4, 1982_ days after close of escrow or (c) //

10.   Unless otherwise designated in the escrow instructions of Buyer, title shall vest as follows: _____
Stanley S. Buyer and Mary M. Buyer, his wife as Community Property

(The manner of taking title may have significant legal and tax consequences. Therefore, give this matter serious consideration.)

11.   If Broker is a participant of a Board multiple listing service ("MLS"), the Broker is authorized to report the sale, its price, terms, and financing for the information, publication, dissemination, and use of the authorized Board members.

12.   If Buyer fails to complete said purchase as herein provided by reason of any default of Buyer, Seller shall be released from his obligation to sell the property to Buyer and may proceed against Buyer upon any claim or remedy which he may have in law or equity; provided, however, that by placing their initials here Buyer: (   ) Seller: (   ) agree that Seller shall retain the deposit as his liquidated damages. If the described property is a dwelling with no more than four units, one of which the Buyer intends to occupy as his residence, Seller shall retain as liquidated damages the deposit actually paid, or an amount therefrom, not more than 3% of the purchase price and promptly return any excess to Buyer.

13.   If the only controversy or claim between the parties arises out of or relates to the disposition of the Buyer's deposit, such controversy or claim shall at the election of the parties be decided by arbitration. Such arbitration shall be determined in accordance with the Rules of the American Arbitration Association, and judgment upon the award rendered by the Arbitrator(s) may be entered in any court having jurisdiction thereof. The provisions of Code of Civil Procedure Section 1283.05 shall be applicable to such arbitration.

14.   In any action or proceeding arising out of this agreement, the prevailing party shall be entitled to reasonable attorney's fees and costs.

15.   Time is of the essence. All modification or extensions shall be in writing signed by the parties.

16.   This constitutes an offer to purchase the described property. Unless acceptance is signed by Seller and the signed copy delivered to Buyer, in person or by mail to the address below, within _two (2)_ days, this offer shall be deemed revoked and the deposit shall be returned. Buyer acknowledges receipt of a copy hereof.

Real Estate Broker _Homer C. Davey & Associates_   Buyer _Stan Buyer_

By _Homer C. Davey_   Buyer _Mary Buyer_

Address _200 State Street, Los Altos, CA. 94022_ Address _1214 Lovejoy Lane, San Jose, CA. 95129_

Telephone _(408) 253-1111_   Telephone _(415) 941-2235_

ACCEPTANCE

The undersigned Seller accepts and agrees to sell the property on the above terms and conditions. Seller has employed _Professional Real Estate Brokers, Incorporated_ --------------------------- as Broker(s) and agrees to pay for services the sum of _Seven Thousand Five Hundred and no/100_ ----------- Dollars ($ _7,500.00_ -----------), payable as follows: (a) On recordation of the deed or other evidence of title, or (b) if completion of sale is prevented by default of Seller, upon Seller's default or (c) if completion of sale is prevented by default of Buyer, only if and when Seller collects damages from Buyer, by suit or otherwise and then in an amount not less than one-half of the damages recovered, but not to exceed the above fee, after first deducting title and escrow expenses and the expenses of collection, if any. In any action between Broker and Seller arising out of this agreement, the prevailing party shall be entitled to reasonable attorney's fees and costs. The undersigned acknowledges receipt of a copy and authorizes Broker(s) to deliver a signed copy to Buyer.

Dated _April 6, 1982_ Telephone _(408) 255-0001_   Seller _Harry Seller_

Address _123 Cheryl Drive, Cupertino, CA._   Seller _Mary Seller_

Broker(s) agree to the foregoing. Broker _Homer C. Davey & Associates_ Broker _Professional Real Estate Brokers_

Dated _Apr_ By _____   Dated _Apr. 6, 1982_ By _____

Page _____ of _____ Pages

These damages must be in an amount not less than one-half of the damages recovered yet not to exceed the established commission. The broker must also deduct title and escrow expenses and expenses of collection, if any; (d) in any of the above cases; (e) in none of the above cases.

146. Mr. and Mrs. Seller invite Mr. and Mrs. Buyer to dinner at their home on April 30, and together they decide to "call the deal off." They notify neither broker of their decision. The brokers may: (a) sue Mr. and Mrs. Buyer for a full commission; (b) sue Mr. and Mrs. Seller for a full commission; (c) do nothing since brokers are never a party to a contract; (d) retain the deposit monies as liquidating damages; (e) do none of the above.

147. Mr. and Mrs. Buyer diligently try to obtain a loan in accordance with the terms of the contract; however, the best obtainable loan will be at 9¾ percent interest, three points, and $91,000. On April 23 they notify Homer C. Davey & Associates, in writing, that they cannot follow through with the contract and give them a list of the lenders contacted. Under these circumstances: (a) the brokers may sue Mr. and Mrs. Buyer for specific performance; (b) Mr. and Mrs. Seller may sue the Buyers for specific performance; (c) Mr. and Mrs. Buyer have a legal right to withdraw from the contract and demand the return of their deposit; (d) the Department of Real Estate would decide the legal rights of each party to the contract; (e) the brokers have a right to retain the deposit monies at their option.

148. Assume that Mr. and Mrs. Seller accepted the contract on April 8, 1980. Pamela notifies Mr. and Mrs. Buyer of the acceptance, and they refuse to go through with the contract. Under these circumstances: (a) Mr. and Mrs. Seller may sue the Buyers for specific performance; (b) Mr. and Mrs. Seller are entitled to 3 percent of the purchase price offered; (c) Homer C. Davey & Associates may sue the Buyers for out-of-pocket expenses; (d) there is no contract, since the offer has expired; (e) Professional Real Estate Brokers may sue the Buyers for specific performance.

149. Homer C. Davey & Associates and Professional Real Estate Brokers are members of the same multiple-listing service. On April 7, after the Sellers' acceptance, Homer C. Davey reports to the multiple-listing service the sale, its price, terms, use to the authorized board members, and financing for information, publication, and dissemination. Upon finding this out, Mr. and Mrs. Buyer contact their attorney and want to sue Davey for an invasion of their privacy. (a) Davey is in violation of the provisions of the contract; (b) Professional Real Estate Brokers are in violation of the contract provisions, not Davey; (c) Davey may give this information to authorized board members in accordance with the terms of the contract; (d) Davey has violated a provision of the Real Estate Law; (e) Under no circumstances can the above information be given to parties other than buyers and sellers.

150. Mr. and Mrs. Seller are delighted with the contract and sign it without making *any* changes. On April 7, Mr. Seller calls his friend at Ace Pest Control and orders a termite inspection. When the inspection report is delivered to all parties entitled to receive it, existing damages amount to $2,000. Mr. Seller is angry, telephones the brokers, and calls the "deal off." Under these circumstances and in accordance with the terms of the contract: (a) Sellers may terminate the contract without liability for damages; (b) brokers may sue the Buyers for a full real estate commission; (c) Buyers may sue Sellers for specific performance but would not be entitled to reasonable attorney fees and costs if they prevailed; (d) Sellers would be entitled to reasonable attorney fees, if the buyers sued, in all cases; (e) Buyers may sue Sellers for specific performance and would be entitled to reasonable attorney fees and costs in case they prevailed.

KEY TO SAMPLE REAL ESTATE
SALESPERSON'S EXAMINATION

Key to Sample Real Estate Salesperson's Examination

1. (b)	26. (a)	51. (c)	76. (b)	101. (b)	126. (e)
2. (d)	27. (b)	52. (c)	77. (a)	102. (c)	127. (c)
3. (a)	28. (a)	53. (d)	78. (d)	103. (d)	128. (a)
4. (b)	29. (b)	54. (a)	79. (a)	104. (a)	129. (e)
5. (a)	30. (b)	55. (a)	80. (b)	105. (d)	130. (a)
6. (c)	31. (c)	56. (d)	81. (a)	106. (b)	131. (c)
7. (d)	32. (d)	57. (a)	82. (d)	107. (a)	132. (b)
8. (c)	33. (c)	58. (d)	83. (a)	108. (a)	133. (a)
9. (b)	34. (b)	59. (b)	84. (c)	109. (a)	134. (c)
10. (a)	35. (c)	60. (b)	85. (c)	110. (c)	135. (b)
11. (c)	36. (c)	61. (d)	86. (b)	111. (b)	136. (c)
12. (c)	37. (d)	62. (b)	87. (a)	112. (b)	137. (c)
13. (d)	38. (a)	63. (a)	88. (d)	113. (d)	138. (b)
14. (c)	39. (c)	64. (d)	89. (b)	114. (c)	139. (b)
15. (b)	40. (a)	65. (c)	90. (b)	115. (c)	140. (c)
16. (a)	41. (d)	66. (d)	91. (a)	116. (c)	141. (d)
17. (b)	42. (c)	67. (b)	92. (b)	117. (e)	142. (d)
18. (b)	43. (c)	68. (d)	93. (d)	118. (d)	143. (e)
19. (b)	44. (c)	69. (d)	94. (c)	119. (a)	144. (a)
20. (b)	45. (d)	70. (a)	95. (b)	120. (e)	145. (d)
21. (d)	46. (e)	71. (a)	96. (c)	121. (c)	146. (b)
22. (c)	47. (b)	72. (b)	97. (b)	122. (e)	147. (c)
23. (c)	48. (c)	73. (a)	98. (d)	123. (d)	148. (d)
24. (d)	49. (c)	74. (b)	99. (d)	124. (c)	149. (c)
25. (b)	50. (b)	75. (c)	100. (c)	125. (a)	150. (e)

GLOSSARY

Abatement of nuisance   The act of ending or terminating a nuisance; a type of legal action brought to end a nuisance.

Abstract of judgment   A document containing a condensation of the essential provisions of a court judgment.

Abstract of title   A summary of the instruments affecting title to a parcel of real property as shown by the public records.

Acceleration clause   A clause in a deed of trust or mortgage giving the lender the right to call all sums owing him or her to be immediately due and payable upon the occurrence of a certain event. It is also a clause that permits a debtor to pay off a loan before the due date.

Acceptance   The act of agreeing or assenting to an offer.

Access right   The right of an owner to go into and out of his or her property.

Accretion   A gradual addition to land from natural causes; for example, from gradual action of ocean or river waters.

Accrued depreciation   (1) The difference between the cost of replacement new as of the date of the appraisal and the present appraised value. (2) The accumulated loss in value that has affected the improvements on real property.

Acknowledgment   A formal declaration before an officer duly authorized as a notary public by a person who has executed an instrument, stating that the execution is his or her act and deed.

Acoustical tile   Blocks of fiber, mineral, or metal with small holes or a rough-textured surface to absorb sound, used as covering for interior walls and ceilings.

Acquisition   The act or process by which a person procures property.

Acre   A measure of land equaling 160 square rods, 4,840 square yards, 43,560 square feet, or a tract about 208.71 feet square.

Administrator   A person appointed by the probate court to administer the estate of a deceased person. His or her duties include making an inventory of the assets, managing the property, paying the debts and expenses, filing necessary reports and tax returns, and distributing the assets as ordered by the probate court.

Ad valorem   According to value.

Adverse possession   A method of acquiring property based on open and notorious possession, under a claim of right, color or title, continuous use for five years, and the payment of taxes.

Affidavit   A statement or declaration reduced to writing, sworn to or affirmed before some officer who has authority to administer an oath or affirmation, such as a notary public or a commanding officer in the service.

Affirm   To confirm, swear, ratify, verify.

Agent   One who represents another, called a *principal*, and who has authority to act for the principal in dealing with third parties. The relationship is referred to as an *agency*.

Agreement of sale   (1) A written contract between a buyer and a seller, setting out the terms of sale. (2) An installment sales contract covering real property, especially a long-term contract.

Alienation   The transferring of property to another.

Alluvion (Alluvium)   Soil deposited by accretion on the shore of a river or body of water that increases the real property.

ALTA title policy   A title insurance policy issued by title insurance companies that expands the risks insured against under the standard type of policy to include unrecorded mechanic's liens, unrecorded physical easements, facts a physical survey would show, water and mineral rights, and rights of parties in possession (such as tenants and buyers under unrecorded instruments).

Amenities   As used in the real estate business, the features that make a piece of real property, especially a home, enjoyable.

Amortization   (1) The liquidation of a financial obligation on an installment basis, which includes both principal and interest. (2) Recovery of cost or value over a period of time.

Appraisal   An estimate and opinion of value.

Appraiser   One qualified by education, training, and experience, who is hired to estimate the value of real and personal property based on experience, judgment, facts, and use of formal appraisal processes.

Appurtenance   Something that belongs to a piece of real property so as legally to be a part of it, and which is transferred with it when the real property is conveyed, such as a building, an orchard, or an easement belonging to the land.

Assessed value   Value placed on property as a basis for taxation.

Assessment   The valuation of property for the purpose of levying a tax, or the amount of tax levied.

Assessor   The official who has the responsibility of determining assessed values.

Assignee   One to whom property is assigned or transferred.

Assignment   A transfer to another of any property or right.

Assignor   One who assigns or transfers property.

Assumption agreement   A contract by which a person agrees to pay a debt or an obligation owed by someone else.

Assumption of mortgage or deed of trust   The taking of title to property by a grantee in which he or she assumes liability for payment of an existing note secured by a mortgage or deed of trust against the property.

Attachment   Seizure of property by court order before judgment, usually done to have it available in the event a judgment is obtained in a pending lawsuit.

Attest   (1) To affirm to be true or genuine. (2) An official act establishing authenticity.

Attorney-in-fact   An agent authorized to perform certain acts for another under a power of attorney. (*See* Power of Attorney.)

Avulsion   The sudden tearing away or removal of land by the action of water flowing over or through it.

Backfill   The replacement of excavated earth in a hole or against the side of a structure.

Balloon payment   When the final payment on a note is greater than the preceding normal installments, the final installment is termed a *balloon payment.*

Base and meridian   Imaginary lines used by surveyors from which they find, measure, and describe the location of lands.

Baseboard   A board that goes around the room against the wall and next to the floor.

Base molding   Molding used at the top of the baseboard.

Base shoe   Molding used at junction of baseboard and floor, sometimes called a *carpet strip.*

Batten   Narrow strips of wood or metal used to cover joints on the interior or exterior of a building; they are also used for decorative effect.

Beam   A horizontal structural member supporting a load.

Bearing wall or partition   A wall or partition that supports any vertical load, in addition to its own weight.

Bench marks   A location indicated on a permanent marker by surveyors.

Beneficiary   (1) One entitled to benefit from a trust. (2) The lender on the security of a note and deed of trust.

Beneficiary statement   *See* Offset Statement.

Bequeath   To leave by will.

Bequest   Personal property that is given by the terms of a will.

Betterment   An improvement on real property that increases the value and is considered a capital asset.

Bill of sale   A written instrument given by the seller to the buyer to pass title to personal property.

Binder   A written statement that binds the parties to an agreement until formal contracts can be drawn; an agreement to cover a down payment as evidence of good faith.

Blacktop   Asphalt paving used in streets and driveways.

Blanket mortgage   One mortgage or deed of trust that covers more than one piece of real property.

Blighted area   An area in which real property is declining in value because of destructive economic forces.

Board foot   A unit of measurement for lumber: one foot wide, one foot long, one inch thick (114 cubic inches).

Bona fide   Good faith.

Bond   An obligation under seal. Real estate bonds are issued on the security of a mortgage or deed of trust.

Bracing   Frame lumber nailed at an angle in order to provide stability to the structure.

Breach The breaking of or failure of duty, either by an act or by an omission.

Breezeway A covered porch or passage, open on two ends, that connects the house and garage, or two parts of the house.

Bridging Wood or metal pieces used to brace floor joists.

BTU British Thermal Unit; the quantity of heat required to raise the temperature of one pound of water one degree Fahrenheit.

Building line Often called a *set-back line*, a building line is a line running a certain distance from the street, in front of which an owner cannot build. These lines are set by law.

Building paper A heavy waterproofed paper used as sheathing in exterior walls, or in roof construction as insulation and protection against moisture.

Built-ins Cabinets and other features built in as a part of the house.

Capital assets Assets of a permanent nature used in the production of income. Examples would include land, buildings, equipment, and so on.

Capitalization In appraising, a method of determining value of property by considering net income and a reasonable percentage of return on the investment.

Capitalization rate The percentage rate or rate of interest considered a reasonable return on the investment. It is used in the capitalization method of determining value based upon net return.

CAR California Association of Realtors, 505 Shatto Place, Los Angeles, California, 90020.

CARET California Association of Real Estate Teachers, a division of the California Real Estate Association.

Carpet strip *See* Base shoe.

Casement windows Windows set in frames of wood or metal that swing outward.

Caveat emptor A Latin phrase meaning ''let the buyer beware''; the legal maxim stating that the buyer must examine the goods or property and buy at his or her own risk.

Chain of title A series of conveyances, encumbrances, and other instruments affecting the title from the time the original patent was granted, or as far back as records are available.

Chattel mortgage A personal-property mortgage. (*See* Security Agreement.)

Chattel real In real estate, an estate less than a freehold estate, such as a lease.

Chattels (1) Personal property. (2) This term is sometimes used in law to describe any interest in real or personal property other than a freehold.

Circuit breaker An electrical device that automatically interrupts an electric circuit when an overload occurs. Circuit breakers can be reset and today are used instead of fuses.

Clapboard Boards used for siding that are usually thicker at one edge.

Cloud on title An instrument or condition that throws a ''cloud'' or suspicion on the title to real estate.

Collar beam A beam that connects the pairs of opposite roof rafters above the attic floor.

Collateral Property subject to a security interest; property used as security for a debt. (*See* Security agreement.)

Collateral security The transfer of property or other valuables to ensure the performance of a principal agreement; an obligation attached to a contract to guarantee its performance.

Collusion A secret agreement between two or more persons wishing to defraud another for a wrongful purpose or to obtain an object forbidden by law.

Color of title That which appears to be a good title but in fact is not; for example, a forged deed.

Combed plywood A grooved building material used primarily for interior finish.

Commercial acre A term applied to the remainder of an acre of land after the area devoted to streets, sidewalks, curbs, and so on has been deducted from the acre.

Commercial paper Negotiable instruments used in business.

Commission An agent's compensation for performing the duties of his or her agency agreement. In the real estate business, it is usually a percentage of the selling price, a percentage of the lease or rents and so on.

Commitment A pledge or a promise; a firm agreement.

Common law The body of law that grew from customs and practices developed and used in England.

Community property All property acquired by a husband and wife living together, except separate property. (*See* Separate property.)

Compaction Packing or consolidating soil. When soil is added to a lot to fill in low places or to raise the level of the lot, it is often too loose to sustain the weight of buildings. Therefore, it is necessary to compact the added soil so that it will carry the weight of the building without danger of settling or cracking.

Competent Legally qualified or capable.

Compound interest Interest paid on both the original principal and the accrued and unpaid interest that has accumulated.

Condemnation (1) The act of taking private property for public use by a political subdivision. (2) A declaration by proper governmental authorities that a structure is unfit for use.

Conditional commitment   A loan commitment for a definite amount under certain terms and conditions. It is subject to an unknown purchaser's satisfactory credit rating.

Conditional sale contract   A contract for the sale of property whereby the seller retains legal title until the conditions of the contract have been fulfilled. The buyer has an equitable interest in the property. (*See* Security agreement.)

Condominium   A system of individual ownership of units in a multifamily structure combined with joint ownership of common areas of the structure and the land.

Conduit   Usually a metal pipe in which electrical wiring is installed.

Confession of judgment   Any entry of judgment upon the debtor's voluntary admission or confession.

Confirmation of sale   A court approval of the sale of property by an executor, administrator, guardian, or conservator.

Consideration   Anything of value, or that is legally sufficient, given to induce entering into a contract.

Constructive notice   Notice given by the public records; that which is considered equivalent to actual notice even though there is no actual notice.

Consumer goods   Goods sold or purchased primarily for personal, family, or household purposes.

Contract   An agreement, either written or oral, to do or not to do certain things.

Contract of sale   (*See* Conditional sales contract.)

Conversion   The wrongful appropriation of another's goods to one's own use; to change from one character or use to another.

Conveyance   (1) The transfer of the title of real property from one to another. (2) An instrument that transfers an interest in real property from one person to another.

Corporation   A group or a body of persons recognized by law as an individual person with rights and liabilities distinct from those of the persons composing it. Since the corporation is created by law, it may continue for any length of time that the law prescribes.

Counterflashing   Flashing used on chimneys at roofline to cover shingle flashing and prevent moisture entry.

Covenant   A promise; an agreement written into deeds and other instruments promising performance or nonperformance of certain acts or stipulating certain uses or non-uses of property.

CPM   Certified Property Manager; a member of the Institute of Real Estate Property Management of the National Association of Realtors.

Crawl hole   Exterior or interior opening permitting access underneath a building, as building codes may require.

Curtail schedule   A list of the due dates and amounts by which the principal sum of an obligation will be reduced by partial payments.

Curtesy   The right that a husband has in a wife's estate at her death. Curtesy has been abolished in California.

Damages   The indemnity recoverable by a person who has sustained an injury to either his or her person, property, or rights through the act or default of another.

Debtor   (1) A party who "owns" the property that is subject to a security interest. (2) A person who owes a debt.

Deck   Usually an open porch on the roof or another part of the structure.

Dedication   An appropriation of land by its owner for some public use and accepted for such use by authorized public officials on behalf of the public.

Deed   A written instrument that conveys title, when properly executed and delivered.

Deed of trust   *See* Trust Deed.

Default   (1) Failure to fulfill a duty or promise or discharge an obligation. (2) Omission or failure to perform any act.

Defeasance clause   The clause in a mortgage or deed of trust that gives the borrower the right to redeem his or her property upon the payment of his or her obligations to the lender.

Deferred maintenance   Maintenance and accumulated repairs that have been postponed.

Deficiency judgment   A judgment given for the unpaid balance of a debt remaining after the surety is sold.

Deposit receipt   A contract used in the real estate business that includes the terms of the contract and acts as a receipt for "earnest money" to bind an offer for property by the prospective purchaser.

Depreciation   A loss in value from any cause. This loss in value to real property may be caused by age, by physical deterioration, or by functional or economic obsolescence.

Desist and refrain order   An order that the Real Estate Commissioner is empowered by law to issue, directing a person to desist and refrain from committing an act in violation of the Real Estate Law.

Deterioration   The process of gradual worsening or depreciation.

Devisee   One who receives real property under a will.

Devisor   One who leaves real property to another by will.

Directional growth   The direction in which the residential sections of a city seem destined or determined to grow.

Dominant tenement   The tenement obtaining the benefit of an easement appurtenant.

Donee   The person to whom a gift is made.

Donor The person who makes a gift.

Dower The right that a wife has in her husband's estate at his death. Dower has been abolished in California.

Duress Unlawful constraint by force or fear; to do or say something against one's will or judgment.

Earnest money A deposit of money paid by a buyer for real property as evidence of good faith.

Easement A right, privilege, or interest that one party has to use the land of another. *Example:* A right-of-way.

Eaves The lower projecting edge of a roof over the wall.

Economic life The remaining useful life of an improvement or a structure; that period during which an improvement will yield a return on the investment.

Emblements Things that grow on the land and require annual planting and cultivation.

Eminent domain The right of the government and certain others such as public utilities to acquire property for public or quasi-public use by condemnation, upon payment of just compensation to the owner.

Encroachment The projection of a structure onto the land of an adjoining owner.

Encumbrance Any claim, interest, or right in property possessed by another that may diminish the true owner's rights or value in the estate. Examples include mortgages, easements, or restrictions of any kind.

Endorsement *See* Indorsement.

Equity (1) The interest or value that an owner has in real property over and above the liens against it. (2) A part of our justice system by which courts seek to supplement the strict terms of the law to do justice between parties.

Equity of redemption The right to redeem property during the foreclosure period. In California the right of the mortgagor to redeem is within twelve months after the foreclosure sale.

Erosion The wearing away of the surface of the land by the action of wind, water, glaciers, and so on.

Escalator clause A clause in a contract that provides for the upward or downward adjustment of certain items to cover the specified contingencies set forth.

Escheat The reversion of property to the state when there are no devisees or heirs capable of inheritance.

Escrow The deposit of instruments and funds with a third neutral party with instructions to carry out the provisions of an agreement or a contract. A complete or perfect escrow is one in which everything has been deposited to enable carrying out the instructions.

Estate The degree, quantity, nature, and extent of the interest that a person has in real property.

Estate at will The occupation of real property by a tenant for an indefinite period. It may be terminated at will by one or both parties.

Estate for life *See* Life Estate.

Estate for years A lease that will expire at a definite time or date.

Estate of inheritance An estate that may go to the heirs of the deceased. All freehold estates are estates of inheritance, except life estates.

Estoppel A doctrine whereby one is forbidden to contradict or deny his or her own previous statement, act, or position.

Ethics A standard of conduct that all members of a given profession owe to the public, to clients or patrons, and to other members of that profession.

Exception *See* Reservation.

Exclusive agency listing A written agreement giving one agent the exclusive right to sell property for a specified period of time, but reserving the right of the owner to sell the property himself or herself without liability for the payment of a commission.

Exclusive-right-to-sell listing A written agreement giving one agent the exclusive right to sell property for a specified period of time. The agent may collect a commission if the property is sold by anyone, including the owner, during the term of the listing agreement.

Execute To complete, make, perform, do, or to follow out.

Executor A person named by the testator of a will to carry out its provisions as to the disposition of the estate.

Expansible house A home designed for further expansion and additions in the future.

Expansion joint A fiber strip used to separate units of concrete to prevent cracking due to expansion as a result of temperature changes.

Facade The face of a building, especially the front face.

Fee An estate of inheritance in real property.

Fee simple An estate in real property, by which the owner has the greatest possible power over the title. In modern use, it expressly establishes the title of real property with the owner without limitation or end. He or she may dispose of it by sale, trade, or will, as he or she chooses. In modern estates, the terms *fee* and *fee simple* are substantially synonymous.

Fiduciary A person in a position of trust and confidence, as between principal and broker. A fiduciary may not make a profit from his or her position without first disclosing it to the beneficiary.

Financing statement The instrument filed to perfect the security agreement and give constructive notice of the security interest, thereby protecting the interest of the secured parties. *See* Security agreement; Security interest; and Secured party.

Finish floor   The final covering on the floor, such as wood, linoleum, cork, carpet, and so on.

Fire stop   A solid, tight closure of a concealed space placed to prevent the spread of fire and smoke through the space.

Fixtures   Items that were originally personal property but have become part of the real property, usually because they are attached to the real property more or less permanently. *Examples*: Store fixtures built into the property, plumbing fixtures, and so on.

Flashing   Sheet metal or similar material used to protect a building from water seepage.

Footing   The base or bottom of a foundation wall, pier, or column.

Foreclosure   A legal proceeding to enforce a lien on such as a mortgage or deed of trust.

Forfeiture   A loss of some right, title, or interest in property because of default.

Foundation   That part of a structure or wall wholly or partly below the surface of the ground that is the base or support, including the footings.

Fraud   Deception that deprives another person of his or her rights or injures him or her.

Freehold estate   An estate in real property that is either a life estate or an estate in fee.

Front foot   Property measurement for sale or valuation purposes. The property measurement is along the street line, and each front foot extends to the depth of the lot. It is usually used in connection with commercial property.

Frostline   The depth of frost penetration in the soil.

Furring   Strips of wood or metal fastened to a wall to even it, to form air space, or to give the wall greater thickness.

Gable roof   Pitched roof with sloping sides.

Gambrel roof   A curb roof, having a steep lower slope with a flatter upper slope above.

Gift deed   A deed for which there is no material consideration.

Girder   A beam used to support other beams, joists, and partitions.

Grade   Ground level at the foundation.

Graduated lease   Usually a long-term lease that provides for adjustments in the rental rate based upon some future determination. For example, the rent may be based upon the result of appraisals to be made at predetermined times in the future.

Grant   (1) To transfer. (2) A deed. (3) When used in a deed, a technical term implying certain warranties.

Grant deed   In California, a deed that uses the word "grant" as a word of conveyance and therefore by law implies certain warranties.

Grantee   The buyer; a person to whom a grant is made.

Grantor   The seller; one who signs a deed.

Grid   A chart used in rating the borrower, property, and neighborhood.

Gross income   Total income before expenses are deducted.

Ground lease   An agreement leasing land only, without improvements, ordinarily with the understanding that improvements will be placed on the land by the tenant.

Ground rent   (1) Earnings from the ground only. (2) Earnings of improved property after an allowance is made for earnings of improvements. (3) A perpetual rent that a grantor in some states may reserve to himself or herself and his or her heirs when he or she conveys real property.

Header   A beam placed perpendicular to joists and to which joists are nailed in the framing of openings such as windows, doors, stairways, and so on.

Hereditaments   A term usually referring to real estate and all that goes with it as being incidental.

Highest and best use   An appraisal phrase that means that use of real property which is most likely to produce the greatest net return to land, buildings, or both, over a given period of time.

Hip roof   A pitched roof with sloping sides and ends.

Holder in due course   One who has taken a negotiable note, check, or bill of exchange in due course: (1) before it was past due; (2) in good faith; (3) without knowledge that it has been previously dishonored and without notice of any defect at the time it was negotiated to him; (4) for value.

Homestead   (1) A home upon which the owner or owners have recorded a Declaration of Homestead, as provided by California statutes, that protects the home against judgments up to a specified amount. (2) A *probate homestead* is a similarly protected home-property set aside by a California probate court for a widow or minor children.

Hundred percent location   A retail business location considered the best available for attracting business.

Hypothecate   To give something as security without giving up possession of it.

Incompetent   Someone incapable of managing his or her own affairs by reason of age, disease, weakness of mind, or any other cause.

Increment   Any increase; (1) A term frequently used to refer to the increased value of land because of population growth and increased wealth in the community; (2) "unearned increment" is used in this connection since the values increased without effort on the part of the owner.

Indirect lighting   A method of illumination in which the light is reflected from the ceiling or other object outside the fixture.

Indorsement (1) The act of signing one's name on the back of a check or a note, with or without further qualification. (2) The signature described above.

Injunction An order issued by a court to restrain one or more parties to a suit—proceeding from performing an act deemed inequitable or unjust in regard to the rights of some other party or parties in the suit or proceeding.

Installment note A note that provides that payments of a certain sum or amount be paid in more than one payment on the dates specified in the instrument.

Instrument A written legal document created to affect the rights of the parties.

Interest rate The percentage of a sum of money charged for its use.

Intestate Without a will.

Involuntary lien Any lien that is not voluntarily created.

Irrevocable Incapable of being recalled or revoked; unchangeable.

Irrigation districts Quasi-political districts created under special laws to provide for water services to property owners in the district.

Jalousie A screen or shutter consisting of overlapping horizontal slats that is used on the exterior to keep out sun and rain while admitting light and air.

Jamb The side post or lining of a doorway, window, or other opening.

Joint The space between the adjacent surfaces of two components joined and held together by nails, glue, cement, and so forth.

Joint note A note signed by two or more persons who have equal liability for payment.

Joint tenancy Joint ownership by two or more persons with right of survivorship. Four unities must be present: time, title, interest, and possession.

Joist One of a series of parallel beams to which the boards of floor and ceiling laths or plaster boards are nailed, and supported in turn by larger beams, girders, or bearing walls.

Judgment A court of competent jurisdiction's final determination of a matter presented to it.

Junior mortgage A mortgage second in lien to a previous mortgage.

Jurisdiction The authority of a court to hear and decide a particular type of case.

Laches Unreasonable delay in asserting one's legal rights.

Land contract A contract used in the sale of real property when the seller wishes to retain legal title until all or a certain part of the purchase price is paid by the buyer. It is also referred to as an *installment sales contract* or an *agreement of sale.*

Lands, tenements, and hereditaments Inheritable lands or interest.

Lateral support The support that the soil of an adjoining owner gives to a neighbor's land.

Lath A building material of wood, metal, gypsum, or insulating board fastened to the frame of a building to act as a plaster base.

Lease A contract between owner and tenant, setting forth conditions upon which the tenant may occupy and use the property and the term of the occupancy.

Leasehold estate The estate of a tenant under a lease. (*See* Estate for Years.)

Legal description A description recognized by law; a description by which property can be definitely located by reference to government surveys or approved recorded maps.

Lessee A tenant.

Lessor A landlord.

Lien A lien makes the debtor's property security for the payment of a debt or the discharge of an obligation.

Life estate An estate in real property that continues for the life of a particular person. The ''life'' involved may be that of the owner or that of some other person.

Limited partnership A partnership composed of some partners whose contribution and liability are limited. There must always be one or more general partners with unlimited liability and one or more limited partners with limited liability.

Lintel A horizontal board that supports the load over an opening such as a door or window.

Lis pendens A notice of pending litigation recorded to give constructive notice of a suit that has been filed.

Listing An employment contract between a broker and his or her principal (client).

Louver An opening with a series of horizontal slats set at an angle to permit ventilation without admitting rain, sunlight, or vision.

MAI Designates a person who is a member of the American Institute of Appraisers of the National Association of Realtors.

Margin of security The difference between the amount of secured loan(s) on a property and its appraised value.

Marginal land Land that barely pays the cost of working or using it.

Marketable title Title free and clear of reasonable objections and doubts; also called *merchantable title.*

Market price The price paid regardless of pressures, motives, or intelligence.

Market value (1) The price at which a willing seller would sell and a willing buyer would buy, neither being under abnormal pressure. (2) As defined by the courts, it is the highest price estimated in terms of money that a property will bring if exposed for sale in the open market, allowing a reasonable time to find a purchaser with knowledge of the property's use and capabilities for use.

Material fact   A fact that would be likely to affect a person's decision in determining whether to enter into a particular transaction.

Menace   A threat to use duress. (*See* Duress.)

Merchantable title   *See* Marketable title.

Meridians   Imaginary north-south lines that intersect base lines to form a starting point for the measurement of land.

Metes and bounds   Terms used to describe the boundary lines of land, setting forth all the boundary lines together with their terminal points and angles. *Metes* means measurements. *Bounds* means boundaries.

Minor   (1) A person under the age of majority. (2) In California all persons *under* 18 years of age—the age of majority in California.

Molding   Usually patterned strips used to provide ornamental variation of outline or contour, such as cornices, bases, window and door jambs.

Monument   A fixed object and point established by surveyors or others to establish land locations.

Moratorium   The temporary suspension, usually by statute, of the enforcement of liability for debt.

Mortgage   An instrument by which property is hypothecated to secure the payment of a debt or an obligation.

Mortgagee   One to whom a mortgagor gives a mortgage to secure a loan or performance of an obligation; the lender under a mortgage. (*See* Secured party.)

Mortgage guaranty insurance   Insurance against financial loss available to mortgage lenders from the Mortgage Guaranty Insurance Corporation, a private company organized in 1956.

Mortgagor   One who gives a mortgage on his or her property to secure a loan or assure performance of an obligation; the borrower under a mortgage. (*See* Debtor.)

Multiple listing   A listing, usually an exclusive-right-to-sell, taken by a member of an organization composed of real estate brokers with the provisions that all members will have the opportunity to find an interested client; a cooperative listing.

Mutual water company   A water company organized by or for water users in a given district, with the object of securing an ample water supply at a reasonable rate. Stock is issued to users.

NAR   National Association of Realtors.

NAREB   National Association of Real Estate Boards. This trade organization is now known as the National Association of Realtors.

Negotiable   (1) Capable of being negotiated; assignable or transferable in the ordinary course of business. (2) A special quality or attribute of certain bills, notes, and instruments that give their holders special rights.

Net listing   A listing that provides that the agent may retain as compensation for his or her services all sums received over and above a stated net price to the owner.

Note   A signed written instrument promising payment of a stated sum of money.

Notice of Non-Responsibility   A notice provided by law designed to relieve a property owner from responsibility for the cost of work done on the property or materials furnished for it when the work or materials were ordered by a person in possession.

Notice to quit   A notice to a tenant to vacate rented property.

Nuisance   Anything that is injurious to health, indecent or offensive to the senses, or an obstruction to the free use of property so as to interfere with the comfortable enjoyment of life or property, or unlawfully obstructs the free passage or use, in the customary manner, of any navigable lake or river, bay, stream, canal, or basin, or any public park, square, street, or highway.

Obligee   A promisee; a person to whom another is bound by a promise or another obligation.

Obligor   A promisor; a person who is bound by a promise or other obligation.

Obsolescence   Loss in value due to reduced desirability and usefulness of a structure because its design and construction become obsolete; loss because of becoming old-fashioned and not in keeping with modern needs.

Offeree   A person to whom an offer is made.

Offeror   A person who makes an offer.

Offset statement   Statement by owner of a deed of trust or mortgage against the property, setting forth the present status of the debt and lien. Also called a *beneficiary statement*.

Open-end mortgage or deed of trust   A mortgage containing a clause that permits the mortgagor or trustor to borrow additional money without rewriting the mortgage or deed of trust.

Open listing   An authorization given by a property owner to a real estate agent in which the agent is given the nonexclusive right to secure a purchaser. Open listings may be given to any number of agents without liability to compensate any except the one who first secures a buyer ready, willing, and able to meet the terms of the listing, or who secures the acceptance by the seller of a satisfactory offer.

Option   A right to have an act performed in the future; a right given for a consideration to purchase or lease a property upon specified terms within a specified time; a contract to keep an offer open for a particular period of time.

Oral contract   A verbal agreement, one not reduced to writing.

Orientation   Placing a house on its lot with regard to its exposure to the rays of the sun, prevailing winds, privacy from the street, and protection from outside noises.

Overhang The part of the roof extending beyond the walls that shades buildings and covers walks.

Over improvement An improvement that is not the highest and best use for the site on which it is placed, by reason of excessive size or cost.

Partition action A legal action by which co-owners seek to sever their joint ownership.

Partnership An association of two or more persons to unite their property, labor or skill, or any one or combination thereof, in prosecution of some joint business, and to share the profits in certain proportions.

Parquet floor Hardwood flooring laid in squares or patterns.

Party wall A wall erected on the line between two adjoining properties that are under different ownership for the use of both owners.

Patent Conveyance of title to government land.

Penny The term, as applied to nails, that serves as a measure of nail length and is abbreviated by the letter *d*.

Percentage lease A lease on property, the rental for which is determined by the amount of business done by the tenant, usually a percentage of gross receipts from the business with provision for a minimum rental.

Perimeter heating Baseboard heating, or any system in which the heat registers are located along the outside walls of a room, especially under the windows.

Personal property Any property that is not real property. (*See* Real property.)

Pier A column of masonry used to support other structural members.

Pitch The incline or rise of a roof.

Plate A horizontal board placed on a wall or supported on posts or studs to carry the trusses of a roof or rafters directly; a shoe or base member, as of a partition or other frame; a small flat board placed on or in a wall to support girders, rafters, and so on.

Pledge Depositing personal property by a debtor with a creditor as security for a debt or an engagement.

Pledgee One who is given a pledge as security. (*See* Security party.)

Pledgor One who gives a pledge as security. (*See* Debtor.)

Plottage increment The appreciation in unit value created by joining smaller ownerships into one large single ownership.

Plywood (1) Laminated wood made up in panels. (2) Several thicknesses of wood glued together with grains at different angles for strength.

Police power The right of the state to enact laws and regulations and its right to enforce them for the order, safety, health, morals, and general welfare of the public.

Power of attorney An instrument authorizing a person to act as the agent of the person granting it. A special power of attorney limits the agent to a particular or specific act, as a landowner may grant an agent special power of attorney to convey a single and specific parcel of property. Under a general power of attorney, the agent may do almost anything for the principal that the principal could do himself or herself.

Prefabricated house A house manufactured, and sometimes partly assembled, before delivery to the building site.

Prepayment penalty Penalty for the payment of a note before it actually becomes due.

Prescription Securing an easement by open, notorious, and uninterrupted use, adverse to the owner of the land for the period required by statute which, in California, is five years.

Presumption That which may be assumed without proof.

Prima facie (1) Presumptive on its face. (2) Assumed correct until overcome by further proof.

Principal The employer of an agent.

Priority That which comes first in point of time or right.

Privity Closeness or mutuality of a contractual relationship.

Procuring cause That event originating from another series of events that, without a break in continuity, results in an agent's producing a final buyer.

Property Anything that may be owned.

Proration of taxes To divide or prorate the taxes equally or proportionately between buyer and seller as to time of ownership.

Purchase-money mortgage or purchase-money deed of trust A mortgage or deed of trust given as part or all of the consideration for the purchase of property or given as security for a loan to obtain money for all or part of the purchase price.

Quarter round A molding whose profile resembles a quarter circle.

Quasi contract A contract implied by law.

Quiet enjoyment The right of an owner to the use of property without interference with his or her possession or use.

Quiet title A court action brought to establish title and to remove a cloud from the title.

Quitclaim deed A deed to relinquish any interest in property that the grantor may have, but implying no warranties.

Radiant heating A method of heating, usually consisting of coils or pipes placed in the floor, wall, or ceiling.

Rafter One of a series of boards of a roof designed to support roof loads.

Range A strip of land six miles wide, determined by

a government survey, running in a north-south direction.

Ratification The adoption or approval of an act performed on behalf of a person without previous authorization.

Real estate board An organization whose members consist primarily of real estate brokers and salespeople.

Real estate trust A special arrangement under federal and state law whereby investors may pool funds for investments in real estate and mortgages and yet escape corporation taxes.

Real property Land, and anything affixed, incidental, or appurtenant to it, and anything considered immovable under the law.

Realtist A real estate broker holding active membership in a real estate board affiliated with the National Association of Real Estate Brokers.

Realtor A real estate broker holding active membership in a real estate board affiliated with the National Association of Realtors.

Rebuttable presumption A presumption not conclusive that may be contradicted by evidence.

Recapture (1) The rate of interest necessary to provide for the return of an investment. (2) A provision in tax laws that reduces certain benefits from claiming depreciation.

Reconveyance A conveyance to the landowner of the legal title held by a trustee under a deed of trust.

Recordation Filing instruments for record in the office of the county recorder.

Redemption Buying back one's property after a judicial sale.

Reformation A legal action to correct a mistake in a deed or other document.

Release clause A stipulation in a deed of trust or mortgage that upon the payment of a specific sum of money to the holder of the deed of trust or mortgage, a particular lot or area shall be removed from the blanket lien on the whole area involved.

Reliction The gradual lowering of water from the usual watermark.

Remainder An estate that vests after the termination of the prior estate, such as after a life estate. *Example:* A life estate may be granted to Adams with the remainder granted to Baker.

Rescission of contract The cancelling of a contract by either mutual consent of the parties or legal action.

Reservation A right or interest retained by a grantor when conveying property; also called an *exception*.

Residue That portion of a person's estate that has not been specifically devised.

Restriction A limitation on the use of real property arising from a contract or a recorded instrument.

Reversion The right a grantor keeps when he or she

grants someone an estate that will or may end in the future. *Examples*: The interest remaining with a landlord after he or she grants a lease, or the interest an owner of land has after he or she grants someone a life estate.

Ridge The horizontal line at the junction of the top edges of two sloping roof surfaces. (The rafters at both slopes are nailed at the ridge.)

Ridge board The board placed on edge at the ridge of the roof to support the upper ends of the rafters; also called *roof tree, ridge piece, ridge plate*, or *ridgepole*.

Right of survivorship The right to acquire the interest of a deceased joint owner. It is the distinguishing feature of a joint tenancy.

Right-of-way The right to pass over a piece of real property or to have pipes, electrical lines, or the like go across it.

Riparian rights The right of a landowner with regard to a stream crossing or adjoining his or her property.

Riser (1) The upright board at the back of each step of a stairway. (2) In heating, a riser is a duct slanted upward to carry hot air from the furnace to the room above.

Sale-leaseback A situation in which the owner of a piece of property sells it and retains occupancy by leasing it from the buyer.

Sales contract A contract between buyer and seller setting out the terms of sale.

Sandwich lease A leasehold interest that lies between the primary lease and the operating lease. *Example*: A leases to B; B subleases to C; C subleases to D. C's lease is a sandwich lease.

Sash A wood or metal frame containing one or more windowpanes.

Satisfaction Discharge of a mortgage or deed of trust lien from the records, upon payment of the secured debt.

Seal An impression mark or stamp made to attest to the execution of an instrument.

Secondary financing A loan secured by a second mortgage or a second deed of trust.

Section A square mile of land, as established by government survey, containing 640 acres.

Secured party The party having the security interest in personal property. The mortgagee, conditional seller, or pledgee, is referred to as the secured party.

Security agreement An agreement between the secured party and the debtor that creates a security interest in personal property. It replaces such terms as chattel mortgage, pledge, trust receipt, chattel trust, equipment trust, conditional sale, inventory lien.

Security deposit A deposit made to assure performance of an obligation, usually by a tenant.

Security interest A term designating the interest of a

a secured creditor in the personal property of the debtor.

Seizin The possession of land under a claim of freehold.

Separate property Property owned by a husband or wife that is not community property. It is property acquired by either spouse prior to marriage or by gift or inheritance after marriage; also, in California, it is the income from separate property after marriage.

Septic tank An underground tank in which sewage from the house is reduced to liquid by bacterial action and drained off.

Servient tenement An estate burdened by an easement.

Set-back ordinance An ordinance prohibiting the erection of a building or structure between the curb and the set-back line. (*See* Building line.)

Severalty ownership Ownership by only one person; sole ownership.

Shake A hand-split shingle, usually edge-grained.

Sheathing Structural covering, such as boards, plywood, or wallboard, placed over the exterior studding or rafters of a house.

Sheriff's deed A deed given by court order in connection with the sale of property to satisfy a judgment.

Sill The board of metal forming the lower side of an opening, such as a door sill, window sill, and so on.

Sinking fund (1) A fund set aside from the income from property which, with accrued interest, will eventually pay for replacement of the improvements. (2) A similar fund set aside to pay a debt.

Soil pipe Pipe carrying waste from the house to the main sewer line.

Sole or sole plate A structural member, usually two-by-four, on which wall and partition studs rest.

Span The distance between structural supports such as walls, columns, piers, beams, girders, and so on.

Special assessment Legal charge against real estate by a public authority to pay the cost of public improvement, as distinguished from taxes levied for the general support of government.

Specific performance A legal action to compel performance of a contract, for example a contract for the sale of land.

Spouse A husband or wife.

SRA Designates a person as a member of the Society of Real Estate Appraisers.

Statute of frauds The state law that provides that certain contracts must be in writing in order to be enforceable in the courts. *Examples:* real property leased for more than one year, or an agent's authorization to sell real estate.

Straight-line depreciation An accounting procedure that sets the rate of depreciation as a fixed percentage of the amount to be depreciated, and which stays the same each year.

Straight mortgage or deed of trust A mortgage or deed of trust in which there is no reduction of the principal during the term of the instrument. Payments to interest are usually made on an annual, semiannual, or quarterly basis.

String, stringer (1) A timber or other support for cross-members. (2) In stairs, the support on which the stair treads rest.

Studs or studding Vertical supporting timbers in walls and partitions.

Subjacent support Support that the soil below the surface gives to the surface of the land.

"Subject to" mortgage or deed of trust When a grantee takes a title to real property subject to a mortgagee or deed of trust, he or she is not responsible to the holder of the promissory note for the payment of any portion of the amount due. The most that he or she can lose in the event of a foreclosure is his or her equity in the property. In neither case is the original maker of the note released from his or her responsibility. (*See also* Assumption of mortgage or deed of trust.)

Sublease A lease given by a tenant.

Subordinate To make subject or junior to.

Subordination clause Senior lien that makes it inferior to what would otherwise be a junior lien.

Subrogation The substitution of another person in place of the creditor, with regard to an obligation.

Surety One who guarantees the performance by another; a guarantor.

Survey The process by which a parcel of land is located on the ground and measured.

Tax deed Deed issued to the purchaser at a tax sale.

Tax sale Sale of property after a period of nonpayment of taxes.

Tenancy in common Ownership by two or more persons who hold an undivided interest in real property, without right of survivorship; the interests need not be equal.

Tenant One who leases real property from the owner.

Tenements All rights in real property that pass with a conveyance of it.

Tentative map The Subdivision Map Act requires subdividers initially to submit a tentative map of their tract to the local planning commission for study. The approval or disapproval of the planning commission is noted on the map. Thereafter the planning commission requests a final map of the tract embodying any changes.

Tenure in land The manner in which land is held.

Termites Antlike insects that feed on wood.

Termite shield A shield, usually of noncorrodible metal, placed on top of the foundation wall or around pipes to prevent passage of termites.

Testament   The written declaration of one's last will.

Testate   Leaving a will.

Threshold   A strip of wood or metal beveled on each edge and used above the finished floor under outside doors.

"Time is of the essence"   These words, when placed in an agreement, make it necessary that all time limitations and requirements be strictly observed.

Title   Evidence of the owner's right or interest in property.

Title insurance   Insurance written by a title company to protect a property owner against loss if title is defective or not marketable.

Topography   Nature of the surface of the land. Topography may be level, rolling, or mountainous.

Torrens title   A title included in a state-insured title system no longer used in California.

Tort   A wrongful act; a wrong, injury; violation of a legal right.

Township   A territorial subdivision six miles long, six miles wide, and containing thirty-six sections, each one mile square.

Trade fixtures   Articles of personal property annexed to real property, but which are necessary to the carrying on of a trade and are removable by the owner.

Trade-in   Method of guaranteeing an owner a minimum amount of cash on the sale of his or her present property to permit him or her to purchase another. If the property is not sold within a specified time at the listed price, the broker agrees to arrange financing to purchase the property at an agreed-upon discount.

Treads   Horizontal boards of a stairway.

Trespass   An invasion of an owner's rights in his or her property.

Trim   The finish materials in a building, such as moldings applied around openings (window trim, door trim) or at the floor and ceiling (baseboard, cornice, picture molding).

Trust   A right of property, real or personal, held by one party, called the *trustee,* for the benefit of another party, called the *beneficiary.*

Trust deed   Deed given by a borrower to a trustee to be held pending fulfillment of an obligation, which is usually repayment of a loan to a beneficiary.

Trustee   One who holds property in trust for another.

Trustor   (1) One who conveys his or her property to a trustee. (2) The borrower or debtor under a deed of trust.

Undue influence   Taking any fraudulent or unfair advantage of another's necessity or weakness of mind.

Unearned increment   An increase in value of real estate due to no effort on the part of the owner, often due to an increase in population.

Uniform Commercial Code   A group of statutes establishing a unified and comprehensive scheme for regulation of security transactions in personal property and other commercial matters, superseding the existing statutes on chattel mortgages, conditional sales, trust receipts, assignment of accounts receivable, and other similar matters.

Unlawful detainer   An action to recover possession of real property.

Urban property   City property; closely settled property.

Usury   Claiming a rate of interest greater than that permitted by law.

Valid   (1) Legally sufficient and authorized by law. (2) Having force or binding force.

Valley   The internal angle formed by the junction of two sloping sides of a roof.

Valuation   (1) Estimated worth or price. (2) The act of valuing by appraisal.

Variance   An exception or departure from the general rule.

Vendee   A buyer.

Vendor   A seller.

Veneer   Thin sheets of wood placed over another material.

Vent   A pipe installed to provide a flow of air to or from a drainage system or to provide a circulation of air within such system to protect trap seals from siphonage and back pressure.

Verification   A sworn statement before a duly qualified officer as to the correctness of the contents of an instrument.

Vested   Bestowed upon someone, such as title to property.

Void   To have no legal force or effect; that which is unenforceable.

Voidable   An instrument that appears to be valid and enforceable on its face but is, in fact, lacking some essential requirement.

Voluntary lien   Any lien placed on property with the consent of the owner or as a result of the voluntary act of the owner.

Waive   To give up a right.

Warranty deed   A deed used to convey real property that contains warranties of title and quiet possession; the grantor thus agrees to defend the premises against the lawful claims of third persons. It is commonly used in other states, but in California the grant deed has replaced it.

Waste   The destruction, or material alteration of or injury to premises by a tenant-for-life, or tenant, or tenant-for-years. *Example:* A tenant cutting down trees or mining coal.

Water table   Distance from the surface of the ground to a depth at which natural groundwater is found.

Will   A disposition of property effective upon the maker's death.

Writ   A process of the court under which property may be seized and sold.

Zone   The area set off by the proper authorities in which the real property can be used for only specific purposes.

Zoning   Act of city or county authorities specifying the type of use to which property may be put in specific areas.

INDEX

Abandonment, of premises, 156
Absolute estates, 14–15
Abstract of judgment, 36
Abstract of title, 187
Accelerated Cost Recovery System, 206
Acceleration clauses, 107–8
Acceptance, 45, 46–47, 164
Acceptance clause, 79
Accession, 17
Accord, 54
Accounting records, 241
Accretion, 17
Acknowledgment, 164, 165–66
Adaptability, 6
Administrator, 16
Ad valorem tax, 34
Adverse possession, 17
Advertising, 117
Agency, dual, 89
Agency agreements, 89–91
Agency relationship
  creation of, 89
  termination of, 93–94
Agent, 49. *See also* Brokers; Sales
      personnel
  compensation to, 60, 62
  definition of, 88
  delegation of power by, 91
  duties of, 92–93
  escrow, 181
  general, 89
  real estate, 2
  responsibility to third persons, 93
  scope of authority of, 91
  special, 88
  types of, 88–89
Agreement, 6
  agency, 89–91
  binding, 58
Agreements of sale, 115
Agreement to agree, 46
Agricultural lands, 198
Alienation clause, 108

Ambiguity, 49
American Institute of Real Estate
    Appraisers, 2
American Land Title Association (ALTA)
    policy, 77, 188
Amortization, of loans, 173
Amortized note, 96, 126
Annexation, 17
Appraisal, 2
  definition of, 196
  by depreciation method, 201
  gross multiplier method of, 202
  by income method, 202
  for loan, 125–26
  methods of, 198–99
  principles of, 197
  process of, 202–3
  qualified, 136
Appreciation, of property, 198
Appurtenances, 6, 164
Arbitration, 78
Area problems, 177
Assent, genuine, 48–50
Assessments, special, 35
Assessor, 11
Assignee, 149
Assignment, 102, 149–50
  of contracts, 51–52
  of insurance, 270
  of rights, 51–52
Attachment, 6
Attachment liens, 35–36
Attorney-in-fact, 89
Attorney's fee clause, 107
Attorney's fees, 62, 78
  provision for, 56
Authority
  of agent, 91
  customary, 91
  express, 91
  implied, 91
  incidental, 91
Avulsion, 17

Baggage lien, 151
Balloon payment, 130
Banking companies, mortgage, 130–33
Bankruptcy, 94, 195
Banks, 129
Base, 170
Base lines, 9
Beneficiary, 22, 102
Beneficiary statements, 107
Bilateral contract, 62
Bills of exchange, 96
Blanket mortgage, 226
Block description, 11
Board of directors, 22
Boiler and machinery insurance, 272
Bond
  lease revenue, 221
  tax allocation, 221
Bonus, 145
Borrowers, fees charged to, 130
Breach, anticipatory, 55
Breach of contract, 53, 54–56
Brokerage, 2, 3
Brokers, 58, 89, 235–36. *See also*
    Agents
  activities, 258–63
  authorization to lease, 157
  commissions (*see* Commission)
  controls that apply to, 130
  licensing of, 94
  listing, 92
  mortgage loan, 129
  prerequisites for licensing, 236–37
  real estate, 3
  responsibilities of in contracts, 83
  and sale of mobile homes, 215
Brokers Loan Law, 130
Broker's net, 157
Budget, office, 255
Building codes, 217, 219–20
Building contractors, 261. *See also*
    Contractor
Building requirements, established, 136

Building residual method, of accrued depreciation, 204
Bundle of rights, 13
Business and Professions Code, 223
Business entity, forms of, 21–23
Buyers, 58
  prospecting for, 262
Buying, versus renting, 207

California, 1, 3–4
California Adult Authority, 45
California Association of Realtors, 264
California Association of Realtors Structural Pest Control Certification Agreement, 72
California Civil Code, 5, 6, 78, 144
  and mechanic's liens, 26
California Coastal Act, 221
California Coastal Commission, 221
California Commercial Code, 3
California Department of Real Estate, 222
California Fair Housing Act, 265
California Land Title Association (CLTA) policy, 77, 188
California Veterans Farm and Home Purchase Program, 138–40
Cal-Vet, loans by, 138–40
Cancellation, of insurance, 270
Canvassing, 261
Capable of contracting, 91
Capacity, 125
Capital, 125
Capital gains, 207
Capitalization method, of appraisal, 202
Career, opportunities in real estate, 1–3
Certificate of Eligibility, 137
Certificate of Reasonable Value, 136, 138
Certificate of sale, 114
Certificate of title, 187
Chadbourn, Charles N., 264
Chain of title, 188
Change, 197
Character, 125
Charges, proration of, 185–87
Chattel mortgages, and security agreements, 195
Chattel real, 6, 13, 143
Chattels, 6
Choses in action, 6
Choses in possession, 6
Citizenship status, 62
Cleaning charge, 145, 147
Closing, 263
Coastal control, 221
Code of Civil Procedure, 40
Codicil, 16
Coinsurance, 270–71
Combination trusts, 23
Commercial leases, 149, 157–60
Commingled property, 21
Commingling, 93, 246
Commission, 2, 59, 79, 171
  broker's, 94
Commitment, conditional loan, 135
Common area, 225
Communication, 46
Community growth, trends of, 3
Community property, 15, 21, 144
  versus joint tenancy, 21

Community redevelopment agencies, 220–21
Community Redevelopment Law, 220
Compensation, 258
  to agent, 60, 62
Comprehensive general liability insurance, 272
Concealment, 48, 271
Concurrent ownership, 18
Conditional estates, 14–15
Conditional loan commitment, 135
Conditional promise, 51
Conditional use permit, 219
Conditions, 37, 52, 143, 225
  faulty, 53
Conditions concurrent, 52
Conditions precedent, 52
Conditions subsequent, 52, 54
Condominiums, 15, 227
Conformity, 197
Consideration, 91, 145, 164
  valid, 83
Conspicuousness, of property, 198
Constructive notice, 23–24, 166
Consumer protection legislation, 117
Contingencies, 53
Continuation statement, 121
Continuing education law, 239–40
Contracting, parties capable of, 45
Contract of sale
  facts of, 185–87
  wrap-around, 141–42
Contractor, 26, 258
Contracts, 44
  assignment of, 51–52
  bilateral, 47, 62
  breach of, 54–56
  broker responsibilities in, 83
  classification of, 44–45
  conflict between parts of, 51
  definition of, 44
  essential elements of, 45
  illusory, 50
  modifying, 52
  performance of, 52–53
  as personal property, 6
  rescinding, 49
  subdivision sales, 226
  unilateral, 47, 91
Contractual duties, discharge of, 53–54
Contractual intent, 46
Conventional loan, 127
Conveyance, 164
Convicts, 45
Cooperatives, 15, 227
Co-ownership, 18
Corporation, 22, 253
Corporation Law, 245
Cost, 172
  mortgage loan, 136
  versus market value, 196
Cost to cure, 204
Counseling, investment, 3
Counteroffer, 46
Counterperformance, 53
Covenants, 37, 52, 143, 225
  implied, 147
  to pay utilities, 150
Creative financing disclosure law, 118
Credit check, for loan, 125
Crops, 6

Cubic-foot method, 199
Custodian, 255

Damage, 49, 55
  duty to reduce, 56
  limit on special, 55–56
  liquidated, 56
  payment in advance of future, 145
Date, 164
Death, 47, 94, 150
Decedent, 16
Deceit, 48
Decimals, 170
Declaration of Homestead, 40
Deed, 7
Deed grant, 36–37
Deed in lieu of foreclosure, 114
Deed of trust, 226
  wraparound, 109–10
Deeds
  elements not required in, 164–65
  essential elements of, 161
  general nature of, 161–65
  trust, 102–5
  types of, 165
Default, remedies of lender in case of, 110–14
Defeasible estate, 14
Deficiency judgment, 110, 114
Delegation of duties, 52
Delegation of power, by agent, 91
Delivery, and acceptance, 164
Demand, 197
Demolition endorsement, 272
Denominator, 168
Department of Housing and Urban Development (HUD), 121, 265
Department of Real Estate, 234–35
Deposits, security, 145–47
Depreciation, 201, 204–5
  and income tax, 205–6
Description
  legal, 60
  methods of land, 7–11
Desist and refrain order, 227
Destruction of subject matter, 47
Deterioration, physical, 204
Development, land, 3
Direct mail, 262
Disabled persons exemption, 35
Disablement, voluntary, 55
Discharge, of contractual duties, 53–54
Disciplinary action, 240
Disclosure, 93, 117
  full, 62
Discrimination, 62, 157
Dividend, 170
Doctrine of correlative user, 5
Down payment, 83, 135, 136
Drainage, 225
Drugged persons, 45
Drunken persons, 45
Due-on-sale clause, 108
Duress, 50
Duties
  delegation of, 52
  discharge of contractual, 53–54
Dwelling house, 41

Easement by necessity, 37
Easement by prescription, 37
Easements, 18, 36–37
  creation of, 36
  implied, 37
  termination of, 37
Easements appurtenant, 36
Easements in gross, 36
Easton v. Strassburger, 68, 93
Economic adjustments, 197
Economic Recovery Tax Act, 205
Education, real estate, 1, 245
80 percent clause, 270
Election to Sell, 110
Elevator liability insurance, 272
Emblement, 6
Employer-employee relationships, 258
  definition of, 88
Encroachments, 38–40
Encumbrance, 25, 36–37, 39
Environmental impact reports, 220, 228
Equal Dignities Rule, 51, 91
Equations, 168
Equity, participation in, 141
Equity trusts, 23
Escrow, 58, 72
  essential requisites of, 181
  procedures of, 180
  termination of, 184–85
Escrow instructions, 181–84
Estate at sufferance, 144
Estate at will, 144
Estate for years, 14, 144
Estates, 13, 16
  absolute, 14–15
  conditional, 14–15
  freehold, 13–14
  less-than-freehold, 14
  on condition precedent, 14
  on condition subsequent, 14–15
Estate taxes, federal, 30
Estimate of value, 196
Eviction, 14, 147, 149
Evidence of title, to mobile home, 215
Examination, sample salesperson's, 292–305
Examinations, real estate, 244
Exception, 219
Exchange agreement, 83
Exclusive agency listing, 59
Exclusive authorization, analysis of, 60–62
Exclusive right-to-sell listing, 59–60
Exculpatory clause, 49, 149
Excuse of conditions, 53
Executor, 16
Expiration of term, 93
Express appointment, 89
Extended coverage endorsement, 271
Extension clause, 150
Extinct, 94

Fair Employment Practices Commission, 265
False advertising, 226
False promises, 93
Falsity, knowledge of, 48
Family unit, 40
Fannie Mae, 140
  guidelines for, 128
Federal associations, and legal limits,

Federal Deposit Insurance Corporation (FDIC), 121
Federal Home Loan Bank Board, 108, 126
Federal Home Loan Mortgage Corporation (*See* Freddie Mac)
Federal Housing Administration (FHA), 128, 220
  buyer's normal costs on, 185
  down payments, 135
  loans insured by, 133–36
  maximum mortgage amounts, 135
  other residential loans, 135
  seller's normal costs on, 185
  special features of, 136
Federal National Mortgage Association (*See* Fannie Mae)
Federal open-housing law, 265
Federal Reserve Bulletin, 203
Federal Savings and Loan Insurance Corporation, 126
Federal Trade Commission, 92
Fed plus 5 percent limitation, 116
Fees, 225
  attorney's, 62
  charged to borrowers, 130
Fee simple, 13
Fee simple defeasible, 14
Filing contract, 30
Fill report, 225
Final map, 223
Financing. *See also* Loans
  creative, 141–42
  government participation in, 133–40
  of a home, 83–84
  other sources of real estate, 133
  of real estate transactions, 264
Financing statement, 121
Fingerprints, 237
Fire protection, 225
Firm commitment, 134
Fixtures, 5, 6, 149
Flood control, 225
Floodwaters, 6
Foreclosure, through court action, 113–14
Fractions, 168–70
Fraud, 48, 271
  remedies for, 49
Fraud in the execution, 49
Fraud in the inception, 49
Fraud in the inducement, 49
Freddie Mac, 140
Freehold estates, 13–14
Full cash value, 34
Full disclosure rule, 48. *See also* Disclosure

Garn-St. Germain Act, 108
Genuine assent, 48–50
GI Bill, 136
Gift tax, 30, 34
Ginnie Mae, 140–41
Glass insurance, 272
Gonsalves-Deukmejian-Petris Senior Citizens Property Tax Assistance Law, 35
Goods, sale of, 6
Government
  authority to zone, 218
  local, 222
  ownership of land, 4
  and participation in financing, 133–40

Government National Mortgage Association (*See* Ginnie Mae)
Government regulations, 197
Government section, U.S., 9
Grade, of property, 198
Grant, 164, 165
Grant deed, 165
Grantee, 15, 161
Grantor, 15, 38, 161
Gross multiplier method, of appraisal, 202
Guarantee, amount and nature of, 136–37
Guidelines, for Fannie Mae, 128

Hard money, 115
Highest and best use, 197
Hold harmless clause, 62
Holdover, 144
Homeowner's exemption, 35
Homes
  financing of, 83–84
  mobile, 207, 215–16
  selecting, 84–86
  types of, 207, 208–11
Homesteads, 40–41
Housing Act of 1977, 136
Housing expense ratio, 129

Illusory contract, 50
Impossibility, of duties, 54
Impound accounts, 107
Income, capitalization of, 176
Income method, of appraisal, 202
Income tax
  and depreciation, 205–6
  federal, 30
  state, 34
Independent contractor, definition of, 88
Individual proprietorship, 252
Individuals, as source of financing, 133
Inheritance tax, 34
Injuries, liability for, 149
Insanity, 47
Installment note, 96
Instruments, types of, 96–102
Insurance. *See also* Property insurance
  fire, 268–69
  liability, 271–73
  private mortgage, 126
  title, 187–88
Insurance companies, 128
Insurance contract, 267
  types of, 268–70
Insurance premium, mortgage, 136
Insured, 267
Insurer, 267
Intent, 6
Interest, 83, 115–17, 130
  calculating, 172
  deductible, 117
  insurable, 267
  maximum rates, 115–16
  rates of, 136
  tax treatment of, 117
  unity of, 19
Interests, future, 15
Interim Occupancy Agreement, 72
Internal Revenue Code, 30, 62
Interpleader, 185
Interstate Land Sales Full Disclosure Act, 229

Intestate, 16
Investment counseling, 3
Investment trusts, 244–45

Joint ownership, 18
Joint tenancy, 18–19, 21
Joint venture, 22, 141
Judgment liens, 36
Judgments, 194
Judicial foreclosure, 101–4
Junior trust deeds, 114

Land, 5
  development of, 3, 228–29 (*See also*
    Subdivisions)
Landlord, 143, 156
  as party to lease, 144
  precautions for at time of renting, 157
  remedies of, 151–56
Land sales, 222
Land transfer, development of, 161. *See*
    also Deeds
Land use, 222
Lapse of time, 47
Late charges, 116, 130
Lawful object, 50, 91
Law of succession, 15
Laws
  preventive, 157
  tax, 7
Lease agreement, termination of, 156
Leasehold estates, 14, 144. *See also*
    Leases
Leasehold-interest insurance, 272
Lease/option agreement, 79
Lease revenue bond, 221
Leases, 143
  broker's authorization and, 157
  commercial, 149
  duration of, 144
  essential elements of, 144–51
  language creating, 145
  option to renew, 150
  recording, 151
  residential, 150
  special commercial, 157–60
  subordination to mortgage, 151
  term of, 144
Legally sufficient consideration, 50–51
Lenders
  policies and procedures for, 125–26
  remedies of in case of default, 110–14
Lending, mortgage, 3
Lessee, 143
Lessor, 143
Liability, 21, 270
  for injuries, 149
Liability insurance, 27–173
License
  cancellation of salesperson's, 240
  display of, 240
  fees for, 238–39
  suspending and revoking, 240, 241
  types of, 238
Licensing
  penalties, 236
  prerequisites for, 236–40
  requirements and fees for real estate,
    235–36

Liens, 25–36
  attachment, 35–36
  baggage, 151
  federal tax, 30, 34
  judgment, 36
  mechanic's, 25–30
  state tax, 34
  time limit to file, 26
  voluntary, 39
Life estate, 13–14
Limited liability, 22
Limited partnerships, 22
Liquidated damages, 56
Liquidated Damages Law, 69, 78
Lis pendens index, 194
Listing agreements, 59–60
  special auxiliary forms used with, 62, 68
Listing Information Disclosure Statement,
    68
Listings, 258–61
  sources of, 261–62
Loan committee, 126
Loan correspondents, 128
Loan officers, 3
Loans. *See also* Financing
  amortization of, 173
  application for, 125
  by Cal-Vet, 138–40
  comparison of types of, 134
  credit check for, 125
  graduated mortgage, 136
  insured by FHA, 133–36
  interest on (*see* Interest)
  length of, 83
  limits on, 127–28
  for mobile-home purchase, 135
  mobile-home, 137
  other FHA residential, 135
  period of, 126
  points (*see* Points)
  property improvement, 135
  sources of (*see* Lenders)
  types of, 127
  Veterans Administration, 136–38
Loan Source Book, 130
Loan-to-value ratio, 135
Loan trust account, 107. *See also* Impound
    accounts
Location, of property, 197
Lock-in clause, 107
Loss payee clause, 271
Lot description, 11

Maintenance, 147–49
Management, property, 2
Map
  final, 223
  final subdivision recorded, 225
  parcel, 223
  tentative, 223
Market data, 199
Market value, 196
Master plan, 218
Maximum obligations ratio, 129
Medians, 9
Menace, 50
Mental incompetents, 45
Metes and bounds, 9
Mexico, 4
Minerals, 5
Minors, 45

Misrepresentation, 48, 93
Mistake, 49
Mobile-homes
  loans for, 137
  subdivisions for, 228
Money market
  primary, 126–33
  secondary, 140–41
Mortgage banking companies, 130–33
Mortgagee, 102
Mortgagee's clause, 271
Mortgage instruments, alternative, 109–10
Mortgage lending, 3
Mortgage loan brokers, 129
  controls that apply to, 130
Mortgage Loan Disclosure Statement, 130
Mortgages, 102–5
  adjustable rate, 109
  blanket, 226
  cost of loan, 136
  and deed of trust, 194
  graduated payment, 109
  growing equity, 109
  reverse annuity, 109
  subordination of lease to, 151
Mortgage trusts, 23
Mortgagor, 102
Multiple listings, 60
Multiple-listing service, 92
Multiplicand, 170
Multiplier, 170
Municipal court, 153
Mutual agreement, 93
Mutual assent, 45–47, 91
Mutuality of obligation, 50–51
Mutual right, 38

National Association of Realtors, 264
National Housing Act of 1934, 133, 135
Necessaries, 45
Necessity, 89
Negligence, 48
Negotiability, 96–97
Neighborhood, choosing, 84
Net lease, 157
Net listing, 59, 171
New York Standard Fire Insurance Form,
    268–69
Noncompliance, penalties for, 223
Nonresidential property, 69, 78
Notary, 166
Note, promissory, 96
Notice of action, 194
Notice of completion, 26
Notice of Default, 110
Notice of non-responsibility, 30
Notice of Sale, 110
Novation, 105
Nuisance, 38
Numerator, 168

Observed condition method, of accrued
    depreciation, 204
Obsolescence, 204
Occupancy, 17–18
Occupancy Agreement, 72
Offer, 45, 46, 47–48
Offeree, 46
Offeror, 46
Offer to purchase, 58, 263

Office, 254
Office manager, 255. *See also* Real estate office
Offset statement, 107, 184
Oil lease, 157
Open listing, 59
Opportunities, business, 3
Option, 48, 79, 150
Option agreement, 79–83
Ostensible acts, 89
Ownership, forms of, 252–53
Ownership interests, types of, 13
Owners', landlords' and tenants' liability policy, 271–72

Parcel map, 223
Parcel number, assessor's, 11
Parol evidence rule, 51
Partial release clause, 105
Partners, general, 22
Partnership, 22, 253
    limited, 22
Payments, 83
    balloon, 130
    progress, 30
Peace Treaty of Guadalupe, 4
Penalties
    for noncompliance, 223
    prepayment, 130, 136
Pension funds, 133
Percentage formula, 171
Percentage lease, 157
Percentages, 170–72
Performance, 53
    of contracts, 52–53
Periodic tenancy, 14, 144, 151
Personal belongings, abandoned, 156
Personal property, financing, 121
Personnel, selection of, 255
Physical factors, 197
Planned development project, 15. *See also* Subdivisions
Planning commission, 38, 218
    regional, 217
Planning policies, 218
Plottage, of property, 198
Points, 117, 136
Policies, loan, 128
Policy manual, 252
Possession, 147
Power of attorney, 89
Preliminary Title Report, 23
Premises, sufficient description of, 144
Premium, 267
Prepayment penalties, 107, 130, 136
Prescription, 18
Principal
    definition of, 88
    duties of, 92–93
Principal of substitution, 199
Priority, 102, 166
Private deed restrictions, 37
Private road, cost estimate for, 225
Probate court records, 194–95
Probating the estate, 17
Procedures, office, 258
Profit, 171–72
Progress payments, 30
Promissory note, 96
Proof of loss, 270

Property. *See also* Commingled property; Community property; Personal property; Real property; Residential property
    commercial, 206–7, 265
    community, 15, 21, 144
    description of, 164
    income, 129
    industrial, 198
    methods of acquiring real, 15–18
    methods of owning, 19
    nonresidential, 69, 78
    option to purchase, 150–51
    personal, 3, 6–7
    preferred types, 126
    real, 1, 5–6
    residential, 69, 78, 198, 207
    selling and leasing of, 2
    taking possession of, 77
Property disclosure statement, 68
Property improvement, loans for, 135
Property management, 2
Property managers, 160
Property taxes, 34
Property Tax Relief Act of 1972, 221
Property value, definitions of, 196–97
Proposition XIII, 87
Pro rata insurance liability clause, 271
Prorations, 173–76
    of charges, 185–87
Public Report, of Real Estate Commissioner, 225–26
Purchase-money deed of trust, 105, 115

Qualified fee, 14
Quantitative survey analysis, 199
Quitclaim deed, 165

Range lines, 9
Range of townships, 9
Rate, 170
Real estate
    areas of specialization in, 2
    career opportunities in, 1–3
    other sources of financing, 133
    residential, 265
Real Estate Advisory Commission, 234
Real Estate Bulletin, 235
Real Estate Commissioner, 225–26, 234–35
Real Estate Investment Trust, 23
Real Estate Law, 59, 234. *See also* Licensing
    penalties for noncompliance, 226–27
Real estate licensing, requirements and fees, 235–36
Real estate office, 253–58
Real estate organizations, 264
Real estate points. *See* Points
Real estate programs, 245
Real estate purchase contract, 58, 68–79
Real estate sales contract, breach of, 55
Real Estate Settlement Procedures Act, 121, 124
Real estate taxes. *See* Property taxes; Taxes
Real estate transactions, financing of, 264
Real property, 1
    classified as to title, 18–21

Real property securities dealer, 241–43
Realtor, 85, 264
Reasonable investigation, 93
Receipt for deposit, analysis of, 68–79
Receipt of copy, 62
Reconveyance, 105
Recordation, 165
Recorded tract, 9
Recording, 23–24, 102, 166–67
    of lease, 151
Recording bond, 30
Recovery fund, 245–46
Reduction by loss, 271
Reference Book, 235
Referral, 261
Regulation Z, 117
Reinvestment method, of accrued depreciation, 205
Rejection of offer, 46, 47
Relationship, 6, 89
Release, 54
Reliance, 48–49
Reliction, 17
Remainder, 15
Remedies, 149
    for fraud, 49
    of landlord, 151–56
Renewal clause, automatic, 150
Rent, 145
Rental listing services, 242
Rent control, 157
Renting, versus buying, 207
Rent insurance, 272
Replacement cost method, 199
Request for Notice of Default, 110
Rescission, 49, 54, 56
Research, 3
Reservation, 36–37
Residential housing, 135
Residential Lease Agreement After Sale, 72
Residential leases, 150
Residential property, 69, 78
Residential purchase contracts, 56
Restrictions, 37–38
    conflict with zoning, 220
    general plan, 38
    governmental, 217
    private, 217
    single plan, 38
    termination of deed, 38
Reversion, 15
Revocation by offeror, 47
Right of the grantor, 38
Right of recission, 117
Right of redemption, 114
Right of survivorship, 18
Rights, 105–9
    bundle of, 13
Right-to-sell listing, analysis of, 60–62
Riparian rights, 6
Risk, assumption of, 269
Rumford Act, 265

Sale and leaseback, 141
Sale-buyback, 141
Sale documents, 225
Sales clause, 150
Sales kit, 263
Sales meeting, 258

Salesperson
  activities of, 258–63
  cancellation of license, 240
  prerequisites for licensing, 237
Sales personnel, 255. *See also* Agent
  commission (*see* Commission)
  examinations (*see* Examinations)
Sales tax, 35
Sandwich leases, 150
Satisfaction, 54
Satisfaction of mortgage, 105
Savings and loan associations, 126–28
Savings bank, mutual, 129
Scarcity, 197
Secretary-receptionist, 255
Secret profits, 93
Security, 242
Security agreements, 121
Security deposits, 145–47
Segregated cost method, 199
Seller, 58
Seller's affidavit of nonforeign status, 62
Selling price, 172
Selling process, 262–63
Senior citizen exemptions, 35
Senior Citizens Property Tax Postponement
  Law, 35
Servicemen's Readjustment Act, 136
Set-back lines, 219–20
Severalty ownership, 18
Shape, of property, 197
Shareholders, 22
Sheriff's deed, 114, 165
Simons Brick Co. v. Hetzel, 26
Sinking-fund method, of accrued
  depreciation, 205
Size, of property, 197
Small-claims court, 153
Social ideals, 197
Soft money, 115
Sole proprietorship, 22
Special clauses, 105–9
Special damages, limit on, 55–56
Specific performance, 56
Sprinkler-leakage insurance, 272
Square-foot method, 199
Stamp tax, documentary, 167
Standard City Planning Enabling Act
  of 1928, 218
State Board of Equalization, 35
Statements, yearly, 109
State of mind, 48
Statute of frauds, 51, 144
Statute of limitations, 54, 102
Stockholders, 22
Stop notice, 30
Straight-line method, of accrued
  depreciation, 204
Subagent, 92
Subagent cooperation, 62
Subdivide, notice of intention to, 224
Subdivided Lands Act, 222, 223–27
Subdivision Map Act, 222–23
Subdivisions, 223, 224
  out-of-state, 227
  types of, 227–28
Subdivision sales contracts, 226
Sublease, 150, 265

Sublessee, 150
Subordination, of lease to mortgage, 151
Subordination clause, 107
Subrogation, 271
Subsequent ratification, 89
Substitution, 197
Substitution of Trustee, 102
Subtenant, 150
Succession, 15–17
Successor in interest, 34
Sue for damages, 49
Supply and demand, 197
Syndications, 22, 133, 244–45

Tax allocation bonds, 221
Taxes, 194
  ad valorem, 34
  property (*see* Property taxes)
Tax laws, 7
Tax Reform Act of 1976, 30
Tax Reform Act of 1986, 205
Telephone solicitation, 261
Temporary incapacity, 45
Tenancy at sufferanace, 14, 151
Tenancy at will, 14
Tenancy in common, 18
Tenant, 143, 156
  death of, 150
  as party to lease, 144
  and right to purchase property, 150
Tenantable, 149
Tender, 53
Tenement, 36
10 percent limitation, 116
Tentative map, 223
Termination
  definite date of, 60
  of offer, 47–48
Termination statement, 121
Terms, definite, 46
Terms of sale, 60
Testament, 16
Testate, 16
Testator, 16
Three-day notice, 153
Third persons
  agent's responsibility to, 93
  duties of, 93
Thirty-day notice, 151
Tier of townships, 9
Time, unity of, 19
Title, real property classified as to, 18–21
Title insurance, 59, 187–88
Title insurance company, 59
Title report, 224
Title search, 188–95
  preparation of, 195
  purpose of, 188
Torts, 88, 92
Township lines, 9
Tract, recorded, 9
Tract description, 11
Trade fixtures, 6
Transfer, 102, 164
  property acquired by, 15
Transferability, 197
Trespass, 38

Trust deeds, 102–5
Trustee, 22, 102
Trustee's deed, 165
Trustee's sale, 110–13
Trust fund account, 246–51
Trustor, 22, 102
Trusts, 22–23
Truth in lending, 117

UCC-1 Form, 121
Undue influence, 50
Unemployment tax, 30, 34
Uniform Commercial Code, 121
Union funds, 133
Units-in-place method, 199
Unlawful detainer, 14, 153
Unruh Civil Rights Act, 265
Use, in prescription, 18
Useful life, of property, 205
Use tax, 35
Usury, 116
Utilities, covenant to pay, 150
Utility, 197

Value. *See also* Appraisal
  essential elements of, 197
  factors that influence, 197–98
Value in exchange, 196
Values
  application of, 198
  forces influencing, 197
Variance, 219
Veterans, 137
Veterans Administration, 128, 220
  buyer's normal cost on, 185
  loans by, 136–38
  procedures of, 137–38
  seller's normal costs on, 185
Veterans Administration amendments, 72
Veterans Administration loans, benefits of,
  136
Veteran's exemption, 35
Void, 44
Voidable, 44

Waiver of condition, 53
Warranty deed, 165
Water, 5–6
Water damage insurance, 272
Water supply, provisions for, 225
Wellencamp vs. Bank of America, 108
Wills, 15–17
Worker's compensation law, 35
Workman's compensation, 272–73
Writ of Execution, 153
Writ of possession, 151

Zoning, 38, 217, 218–19
  authority of governments in, 218
  conflict with restrictions, 220
  of property, 198
  relief from, 219
  trends of, 3
Zoning restrictions, 37